THE RAY SOCIETY

INSTITUTED 1844

This volume is 171 of the series.

LONDON

2008

Rifle-Green by Nature:

A Regency Naturalist and his Family, William Elford Leach

Keith Harrison & Eric Smith

We are the music makers,
And we are the dreamers of dreams,
Wandering by lone sea-breakers,
And sitting by desolate streams:—
World-losers and world-forsakers,
On whom the pale moon gleams:

Yet we are the movers and shakers
Of the world for ever, it seems.

Arthur O'Shaughnessy

THE RAY SOCIETY
2008
Volume 171

ISBN   978 0 9 03874 35 9

Published 2008
by
The Ray Society
c/o The Natural History Museum
Cromwell Road
London
SW7 5BD
UK

Designed and typeset by the author
Printed for The Ray Society by Biddles Ltd, King's Lynn, Norfolk PE30 4LS

Set in Times New Roman 11/12.5

Preface

The opening years of the nineteenth century are one of the most stimulating, productive and dangerous periods in British history. The country drifted in war from dread of invasion to jubilation at peace, and back to dread as it tottered on the brink of revolution.

Familiar names walked the Earth: Napoleon, Wellington, Nelson, Wordsworth, Byron, Shelley, Keats, Jane Austen, Beethoven, Schubert and Rossini.

There were the first steam locomotives, steam ships and steam-powered horseless carriages, and the first Luddites. *Frankenstein* first chilled its readers.

In the midst of this cultural mælstrom a young English naturalist from Plymouth stood poised between the God-given order of the Enlightenment and the coming upheaval of Charles Darwin.

William Elford Leach was the first to describe many of the animal species living around the coasts of Britain. In his own life-time he was one of the world's leading zoologists; his influence recognised from Russia in the east to America in the west. He was the friend of Lamarck and of Cuvier. Virtually single-handed he modernised the zoology of a fortress Britain, isolated by twenty years of European war. He taught the man who taught Darwin and he prepared the way to make Britain the birthplace of *natural selection*, then he sank silently from view, all but forgotten for two hundred years.

Elford Leach was a child of war. While he worked the British invaded the United States and burned Washington. They went to war with Denmark and with Sweden, took the Cape of Good Hope from the Dutch, attacked Buenos Aires, and fought their way through India, but their greatest enemy was Napoleon. A young British General called Arthur Wellesley was given the task of evicting the French from Portugal and Spain. With him went Elford Leach's brother, Captain Jonathan Leach. By the time Napoleon was defeated Wellesley would be the Duke of Wellington, and Jonathan Leach would be a Lieutenant-Colonel in one of the finest infantry regiments Britain has ever sent into combat, the 95th Rifles. Their proud boast *First into the field and last out* was not misplaced. They were the first infantry to see action in most engagements and in their camouflage green were the forerunners of modern armies everywhere.

While Jonathan Leach struggled to free Europe from the chains of Napoleon, and Elford struggled to free British zoology from the chains of the eighteenth century, their brother George fought to free British politics from the repression of an authoritarian ruling class.

The Leaches of Plymouth are a microcosm of Britain during one of its most dynamic and turbulent periods: writhing in social, political and industrial revolutions and poised on the verge of armed revolt. This book is their, and ultimately our, story.

To Zoë

Contents

Author's introduction

In the mid-1980s I was fortunate enough to spend several years working in the Zoology Department of the British Museum (Natural History), now renamed The Natural History Museum, London. Time and again the work involved animal species first made known to science by a shadowy figure from the early years of the 19th century, William Elford Leach. Leach had worked in the forerunner of The Natural History Museum, the Natural History department of the British Museum, but no-one seemed to know very much about him. Several purported biographies had been published but each was little more than one page and each clearly included errors. As many of Leach's manuscripts were in the archives of the museum, and as its various libraries contained other documents relating to him, I decided to investigate.

It was a conversation with Wyn Wheeler, then head of the Fish Section at the museum and an established historian of early British zoology, that led to the discovery Leach was also being researched by Sir Eric Smith, former chairman of the museum's trustees[1]. Leach was originally from Plymouth in Devon and Eric had been Director of the Marine Biological Association's laboratory in Plymouth until his retirement in 1974. From his home in Saltash just across the river he had an enviable access to Plymouth's West Devon Record Office and the ability to trace long lost Leach family connections.

As always, Eric welcomed a newcomer and for a number of years we collaborated, but sadly advancing years brought his involvement to an untimely end and he died in 1990 at the age of 81. Fortunately through the kindness of his family most of his notes have been made available and it is clear from these his intention was to analyse the early days of science and social networking in Devon, and the lives of the Leach family in particular, in great detail. It is a considerable loss that he was unable to contribute that accumulated expertise to the text now presented. I have concentrated more on providing an outline of Elford Leach's life which future writers can 'flesh out' with greater detail as their personal interests dictate. In particular I have made no attempt to analyse Leach's work. This is a vast undertaking and his wide interests within natural history would make it a daunting task for any individual.

In telling Elford Leach's story I think it is important that we see him in context. Too many biographies present their subjects as cardboard silhouettes drifting across a blank canvas. I have tried to avoid this. Leach lived and worked in one of the most dynamic periods of European history and was personally acquainted with many naturalists whose names are known to us today. I have tried to give a flavour of these contacts and their significance, also of his living and working conditions and of the overwhelming concerns of the people he passed on the streets.

[1] Sir (James) Eric Smith *CBE*, ScD, FRS (1909-1990). ['JES' in the notes that follow]. Born in Hull. Lecturer in zoology at Manchester, Sheffield and Cambridge Universities. Professor of Zoology, Queen Mary College, University of London, 1950-65. Vice-Principal, Queen Mary College, 1963-65. Director of the Plymouth Marine Laboratory, 1965-74. Fellow of the Royal Society 1958. Honorary D.Sc. Exeter University, 1968. Among many other positions: Member of the Science Research Council 1965-7; Vice-President of the Linnean Society of London, 1954-5; Vice- President of the Zoological Society of London, 1959-61; Vice-President of the Royal Society, 1973-4; Chairman of Trustees of the British Museum (Natural History), 1969-74; Member of the Advisory Board for the Research Councils, 1974-7; President, International Council of Scientific Unions, 1972. *CBE* 1972. Knighted 1977. Married Thelma Audrey Cornish (d. 1989) in 1938.

Jonathan Leach

While researching Elford Leach it became clear his brother Jonathan was already well known to military historians. As Jonathan's story illustrates the Britain at war in which his brother worked, I have given his life equal weight here.

Jonathan served as an officer in the 95th (Rifles) Regiment throughout the war against Napoleon's troops in the Iberian Peninsula and at the Battle of Waterloo. His memoirs, *Rough Sketches of the Life of an Old Soldier*, were published in 1831 and, unless otherwise stated, Jonathan's words in the story that follows are quoted from that work.

Several officers and men of the 95th have left us their memoirs but military historian Colonel Willoughby Verner[2] thought, "Without doubt the man who kept the most accurate records of the deeds of the 95th Rifles in the Peninsula and at Waterloo is Colonel Jonathan Leach C.B.[3]" This view was supported by Oxford Professor Charles Oman[4] who considered *Rough Sketches* "A first-rate authority[5]" for historians.

One of the reasons Jonathan's accounts are so accurate is that he kept a field diary throughout the Peninsula campaigns and wrote of events within hours or days of their occurrence. As commander of a company it was also his job, more than that of the other chroniclers from his regiment, to know what was happening. When each diary was full he posted it back to England and began another. Fifteen years later, when writing *Rough Sketches*, he drew extensively on these journals and, unlike some of his contemporaries, was not tempted to embellish or modify his account based on books that had been published in the meantime.

Sadly these journals no longer exist. While in storage some years ago the storage facility was flooded and the wrappings intended to exclude insect pests instead trapped the water. By the time the diaries were rescued their pages had dissolved into an irretrievable pulp.

Fortunately, when Willoughby Verner wrote his two volume history of the Rifle Brigade at the beginning of the last century he had access to Jonathan's journals and published several extracts. These give considerable insight into the difference between the measured prose of the 47 year old author of *Rough Sketches*, and the raw candour of the 25 year old infantry Captain. An example will serve to illustrate this. In 1809 Jonathan's brigade, the Light Brigade of infantry, had just been issued with new standing orders by their commanding officer, Brigadier General Robert Craufurd ('Crawford' to many authors, including Jonathan Leach). In 1831 Jonathan wrote:

"General Crawford at this period issued a long string of standing orders and regulations to his brigade: many of them were undoubtedly excellent, and well calculated to insure regularity, on the march, in camp, and in quarters; but they were so exceedingly numerous, and some so very minute and tedious, that a man must have been blessed with a better memory than falls to the general lot of mortals to have recollected one half of them."

[2] William Willoughby Cole Verner (1852-1922). Was Professor of Military Topography at the Royal Military College, Sandhurst 1896-1899.
[3] Verner, 1919: 503.
[4] Charles William Chadwick Oman (1860-1946). Was Professor of history at Oxford University. Wrote a classic multi-volume history of the Peninsula War. Knighted 1920.
[5] Oman, 1986: 24fn.

Captain Jonathan Leach
later
Lieutenant-Colonel Jonathan Leach *C.B.*

Painted by John Opie (1761-1807) probably in the Spring of 1806,
at the time he exchanged from the 70th (Surry) Regiment to the 95th (Rifles).
In this portrait he is wearing a red jacket which may be his 70th Regiment uniform.

What he actually wrote in his journal in 1809 is rather more revealing:

"Brigadier Robert Crawford (damn him) issued this day to the Light Brigade an immensity of the most *tyrannical* and *oppressive standing orders* that were ever compiled by a British officer."

Verner says this is one of his milder comments. We must curse the flood that deprived us of the rest.

We shall hear later from the other chroniclers of the 95th, but it is worth noting Jonathan Leach was the most senior among these and virtually all the others served under him at one time or another: riflemen Benjamin Harris and Edward Costello both served in his company; Harry Smith was one of his Lieutenants; John Kincaid finished the battle of Waterloo as his Adjutant; William Surtees was Quartermaster in the regiment's 1st battalion after the war when Jonathan Leach was its Major; and George Simmons also appears to have been a Lieutenant in the 1st battalion at that time.

Jonathan's seniority and the different perspective it brought may have contributed to the more considered writing style of his memoirs compared to those of the others. For this reason he has tended to be overshadowed by his contemporaries, who wrote more lively, personal tales. In fact, away from the battles his style is more relaxed and his views more readily expressed. As we are interested particularly in Jonathan Leach as a man and as an example of his family, not just as a soldier, the following narrative includes his asides as well as his military considerations, and focuses as much on the activities away from the battlefield, as on the fighting itself. Hopefully this gives a flavour of the world in which Jonathan Leach spent more than twenty years of his life, and of his priorities during that time.

As a man, Jonathan Leach was very much a soldier and saw the world through soldier's eyes. Another officer in the British army at this time, Lieutenant Moyle Sherer of the 34th Regiment, has contrasted the way most officers saw their surroundings and the way he, Sherer, saw them. After a visit to Lisbon he observed:

"Where I had been struck by the fine appearance of some public building, or private place, they had only seen the heaps of dirt lying near the portals;— where I had gazed, with pleasure, on some diversified groups of market peasantry, in their national costume, they had discovered a squalid beggar mingling in the crowd;—while I had seen some expressive face, leaning over a balcony, on one side of the street, and had inhaled the perfume of some rich and powerful exotics, they, on the other, had encountered a fishwoman frying Sardinias at her stall, or been saluted by some unfortunate puff of air, impregnated with garlic:—with such different eyes do men look upon the same scenes.[6]"

[6] Sherer, 1996: 15-16.

Moyle Sherer was clearly a writer soldiering, but Jonathan Leach was a soldier writing: he saw the dirt and smelled the Sardinias. He patrolled a boulder-strewn land of 'rascally priest-ridden villages', living on a diet of acorns and 'villainously bad wine' and flirting with the 'inmates' at the local convents. He was not alone.

Format

From our 21st century perspective it is important to recognise the different world that existed 200 years ago ("The past is a foreign country; they do things differently there[7]"). I have therefore tried to tell this story through imagery as much as words and have clothed the actions of the characters with descriptions of their immediate surroundings. For this I have drawn on some excellent contemporary reporting and have not hesitated to reproduce original accounts.

It is not fashionable today to use extensive quotes when telling other people's stories, but this is an attitude I cannot support. The eye-witness's observation, told in their own words, is always preferable to a watered-down (or pumped-up) story told by someone who was not there, was born in a different age with different attitudes, and who may have misunderstood the expressions or emphasis of the original. The objective in the following story is to let those who were there speak for themselves. This is especially true of the chapters dealing with Jonathan's military exploits where my contribution has been little more than adding linking paragraphs and background detail.

For the quotes: if the text of the original author is unchanged I have used quotation marks (" "); if some of the author's text has been omitted, or punctuation or spelling changed for ease of reading, I have used inverted commas (' ') and indicated missing text with an ellipsis (...).

Britain did not use metric measurements in the nineteenth century and distances are frequently given by the original authors in miles and yards[8]. I have provided convertions from miles to kilometres but as the distances are invariably only rough estimates by the observers, it is acceptable, unless otherwise stated, to substitute 'metres' for 'yards' without significantly altering the meaning.

For an international readership I have not assumed a knowledge of exclusively British references (for example obscure or archaic English words, allusions to English literature, English pronunciations) but have tried to explain these in the notes. I hope British readers will show patience.

The notes are intended to supplement the text, not be an integral part of it. They are extensive but you are invited to read the narrative in the first instance without reference to the notes unless a point interests or puzzles you.

Many individuals mentioned have been identified in the notes, but in a work such as this it is not possible to include everyone with whom the Leaches, Elford Leach in particular, had contact. This degree of detail would clog the flow of the story. I have included a selection of the better known individuals;

[7] Leslie Poles Hartley (1895-1972). From his 1953 book *The go-between*
[8] 1 mile = 1.609344 km.
   1 yard = 0.9144 m.

the remainder can be found in the original letters and other manuscripts that have been consulted[9]. The known letters and manuscripts relating to Elford Leach have been assembled and the plan is to issue these, publishers permitting, as a separate volume in the near future (although the optimistic folly of declaring this is fully appreciated).

The present volume has been twenty three years in the making. Putting pen to paper was eventually prompted by an encounter with some advice once given by Winston Churchill.

> *Aim for the Third Best –*
> *The First Best is never achieved;*
> *The Second Best comes too late;*
> *So aim for the Third Best –*
> *Something good that comes in time to be useful.*

Whether what follows is good I am not the person to say, but I hope you will find it useful and interesting.

Keith Harrison
25th February 2008

[9] Many manuscripts have been consulted in the archives of the Linnean Society of London. These manuscripts are cited in the notes throughout this book. If any readers wish to contact the Society to pursue their own lines of research they should cite the appropriate manuscript reference number. The reference number for the *MacLeay Correspondence* is Ms 237; the reference for the *James Edward Smith Correspondence* is Ms 301.

Historical Background

1789	French Revolution begins.
14th July	The storming of the Bastille.
1792	French Revolution reaches its height.
7th February	Austria and Prussia ally against France.
20th April	France declares war on Austria.
July	War between France and Kingdom of Sardinia.
21st September	French monarchy abolished. France declared a republic.
1793 16th January	Louis XVI condemned to death and executed five days later.
1st February	France declares war on Britain.
—	Reign of Terror begins and will last until late 1794.
16th October	Execution of Marie Antoinette.
1793-1799	Rise of Napoleon Buonaparte/Bonaparte[1].
1799	Royal Institution of Great Britain founded.
9th November	Coup d'état in France. Napoleon becomes First Consul.
1800	Royal College of Surgeons, London, founded. Widespread food riots in England, Scotland and Wales.
1801	American Robert Fulton[2] tests his submarine, the *Nautilus*, on the River Seine.
2nd April	Nelson destroys the Danish fleet at the naval Battle of Copenhagen.
1st October	Truce between Britain and France.
24th December	Cornishman Richard Trevithick[3] pioneers a high-pressure steam engine and publicly demonstrates a steam-driven horseless carriage for road travel[4].
1802	*West India Docks* built in London.
27th March	Treaty of Amiens between Britain, France, Spain and the Batavian Republic (The Netherlands).
April-August	Riots in Wiltshire against introduction of gig-mills (machines used in textile production).
22nd June	*Health and Morals of Apprentices Act* regulates child labour in Britain. No child can work in the cotton mills until they are 9 years old, and they cannot work at night or for more than 12 hours each day.
1803 March	Riots in Bristol against Royal Navy press-gangs.
April to May	Riots in London against Royal Navy press-gangs.
30th April	United States purchases western Louisiana from France for 80 million Francs.
12th May	War recommences between Britain and France.

[1] Napoleon Bonaparte (1769-1821). 'Buonaparte' was the original Corsican spelling but from 1796 Napoleon adopted the French style 'Bonaparte'. Many official European documents continued to use 'Buonaparte' for the remainder of his life.

[2] Robert Fulton (1765-1815). Former painter. Lived in London from 1786 working as an engineer and inventor. From 1797 lived in Paris. Experimented with steamboats on the Seine in 1803. Returned to America in 1806. Invented the torpedo. Launched an effective steamboat in 1807 and patented the design.

[3] Richard ('Captain Dick') Trevithick (1771-1833).

[4] In America at about the same time Oliver Evans (1755-1819) was engaged in similar attempts to produce high-pressure engines and road vehicles.

— 1 —

Beginnings

London, February 1814

William Elford Leach is a young man in a hurry. Barely six months have passed since he first learnt of this opportunity and already here he is, at the threshold of his career, catapulted into one of the most senior appointments in his field.

He is a lean wiry figure, even in his heavy winter coat as he strides across a bitterly cold Great Russell Street on this icy February day. The war with the United States is in its second year; the war with France in its twenty-second. His unusually dark eyes look out from a lean twenty-three year old face. He cannot remember a Britain at peace.

Passing the armed sentries and walking through the arch in the forbidding fortress frontage, he enters the courtyard of Montagu House,

that incongruous French mansion on the northern outskirts of the English capital that houses the treasures of the nation: the British Museum. He visited the Museum years ago while a young medical student at Saint Bartholomew's Hospital, a short walk away. When not engrossed in his studies he had been preparing a work of scholarship on a subject even closer to his heart and the Museum's naturalist Dr George Shaw had arranged a private examination of the national collections. After the Archbishop of Canterbury, the Lord Chancellor, the Speaker of the House of Commons and the rest of the Museum's 43 distinguished trustees had solemnly given him permission to examine their dead beetles, he had gained admission to the inner sanctum. He will need no permission today; this is now his sanctum. Dr William Elford Leach is the British Museum's new zoologist.

In his original researches Elford Leach will make an impact not just in Britain, but throughout Europe and beyond. His interests will embrace mammals, birds, reptiles, fish, insects, crustaceans, molluscs, and much

much more. He will introduce to science animal species found in Britain, Europe, Africa, America, south-east Asia and Australia. He will drag a stagnating British zoology into the brave new 19th century and he will tutor the man who will teach Charles Darwin. All this he will achieve in just seven short years.

But who is Elford Leach[1], and what brings him to the front steps of Montagu House during *The Great Frost* of 1814? His story really begins more than 50 years earlier, 200 miles[2] and an age away in the English county of Devon.

Family

William Elford Leach was the youngest of four children born to George Leach[3], a Plymouth lawyer, and his wife Jenny[4], daughter of Lancelot Elford[5] and sister of William Elford[6], after whom the youngest Leach was obviously named.

The Leach family traced its West Country roots at least to the early sixteenth century[7]. The Elfords were in this part of England even earlier. Devon and Cornwall still show their links with the Elfords in placenames like Helford and Yelverton (a corruption of Elford Town).

It seems these two ancient families first met in the early 18th century when the 22 year old Lancelot Elford and an equally young George Leach[8] (Elford Leach's grandfather) were both founder members of a Plymouth gentlemen's bathing and dining association called The Otter Club[9]. The twelve members of the club would meet in the early morning to bathe in the sea below Plymouth Hoe[10], and once a fortnight they would dine at the Pope's

West Country

Head inn in Looe Street[11]. The club was based on the classical Greek ideals of 'a healthy mind in a healthy body', and in addition to the bracing sea-bathing the members met primarily for literary, artistic and scientific discussion. Joshua Reynolds the portrait painter and first president of The Royal Academy of Arts[12] – born just outside Plymouth in 1723 – was one of the club's guests, and Dr Samuel Johnson[13], author of one of the earliest English dictionaries and a great friend of Reynolds, accompanied him to the club during a trip to Plymouth in 1762.

[1] Although his family called him William, he called himself Elford.
[2] Approximately 320 km.
[3] George Leach (6th April 1742–26th October 1823).
[4] Jenny Elford (17th August 1745–14th May 1822). Born at Bickham but christened 20th June 1756 at Kingsbridge.
[5] Lancelot Elford (1718-1782). Married Grace Wills from Kingsbridge. The records for the births of their children seem to give two dates [*fide* the *International Genealogical Index*]. We have chosen the most likely options based on other records (e.g. where only one of the recorded dates for birth pre-dates the sole date for the christening). Lancelot and Grace apparently did not christen their children until years after their birth.
[6] William ('Will') Elford (30th November 1742–1837). Born Bickham. Christened at Kingsbridge 31st October 1749.
[7] See Appendix 2.
[8] George Leach (dates not known. Born ca 1715-1720, died ca ?1790)
[9] Founded February 1740.
[10] An area of grass between the town of Plymouth and the top of the coastal cliffs.
[11] Gill, 1979: 95.
[12] Joshua Reynolds (1723-1792). Knighted 1769.
[13] Samuel Johnson (1709-1784).

Lancelot Elford must have been a boisterous youth, as his father – who died when Lancelot was 14 – left instructions with his guardian that he should be, "bred to the Ministry, if he behaves soberly, but if he misbehave let him be placed to some trade or profession.[14]" Lancelot presumably behaved soberly as after studying at Exeter College, Oxford, he did become the Reverend Lancelot Elford. He lived on the family's estate at Bickham about 11 km north of Plymouth.

His friend George Leach was a Plymouth solicitor, or 'attorney' as solicitors were then known. Since the Middle-Ages Devon had been famous for its lawyers, and the nature of English legal practice provided attorneys with opportunities to acquire real-estate and the wealth this could generate[15]. There are numerous documents in the Devon Record Office in Exeter[16] and the West Devon Record Office in Plymouth[17] showing that George Leach and the next two Leach generations bought, let and sold various plots of land in the Plymouth area; took rent as landlords; and made loans to local gentry. The Leaches were a financially secure legal family.

Class

These were very class-conscious times, and as Lancelot and George were friends within the same social class – Gentlemen and small-scale local landowners, of lower rank than the aristocracy but higher than tradesmen – it was inevitable their children would mix socially. So it was that on the 8th of August 1777 George's son George (by now, like his father, a Plymouth attorney) married Lancelot's daughter Jenny at Buckland Monachorum Church, the parish church for Bickham. To make the event even more memorable for the families, the vicar allowed Lancelot Elford to conduct the ceremony.

We do not know where George and Jenny lived when they were first married, but in 1780 their first child was born. A girl, she was named Jenny after her mother. Like all George and Jenny's children, baby Jenny was baptised at St Andrew's Church in Plymouth[18]. Two years later, while the Leaches were expecting their second child, Lancelot died. Whether Jenny's presumed inheritance or some factor related to the impending birth triggered a move is unclear, but on the 22nd of June 1782 George Jnr bought a farm called Elford and a house known as Elford Town[19], about 13 km north of Plymouth[20].

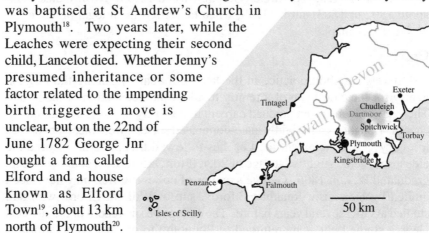

14 Will of John Elford (1680-1732) dated 22nd March 1731 (Loc: Devon Record Office, Exeter, in book of copies in Local History Section). Reported in Elford (1976: 32-33).

15 Hoskins, 1954: 250.

16 DRO refs. 48/13/6/4/29; 48/13/6/6/9; 178B/M/T81; 178B/M/T99; 50/20/3/5; 51/29/1; 365/1/12

17 WDRO refs. 32/6; 178/139; 178/140; W/522; 523/1; 524; 566/2; 645/4; 710/168; 710/128; 710/129

18 On the 15th November 1780. Later in life baby Jenny referred to herself as Jane. 'Jenny' is a familiar form of Jane as well as a name in its own right.

19 This curious use of 'Town' in Devon and Cornwall names derives from the Old English word 'tun', meaning 'farm' (Hoskins, 1971: 96).

20 From John Bulteel Esq. for the sum of £1575 (West Devon Record Office. Ref: WDR 645/4).

Elford Town house exists today as part of the community of Yelverton. There is no indication George ever farmed but Elford Town became the family home. Their second child, a boy named George after his father (in the custom of the day, as we have seen) was born around this time, possibly just before the purchase[21].

Less than two years later Jenny was expecting her third child and George was having a new wing added to the house[22], doubtless to accommodate their rapidly expanding family. A second son, Jonathan, was born in March 1784, presumably at Elford Town[23].

The Leaches lived in this house for several more years but their third son and final child, William Elford Leach, was born at Hoegate in Plymouth[24] on the 2nd of February 1791[25] and was baptised at St Andrew's Church on the 11th of August. His father George owned Elford Town House until about 1802 or 1803, but by 1799, when he retired from legal practice[26], it was let to tenants[27].

Order

It was common practice in the late 18th century among the English gentry for the eldest son of a family to adopt the occupation of his father. The younger sons often pursued careers in the army or navy, or entered the church. Daughters, in a rigidly male-dominated society, were merely expected to marry. To some extent the Leaches followed this pattern. George the eldest son, at the slightly late age of 20, left for Oxford University where he graduated B.A. in 1806. George's choice of college, Oriel, may have been guided by his cousin Jonathan Elford[28], son of William Elford, who had studied at Oriel several years before. The college has no record of the subjects George studied but as he returned to Plymouth to practise as an attorney,

[21] Baptised 5th July 1782.
[22] *pers. comm.* Colonel R.C. Spencer, owner Elford Town House, 1987.
[23] Baptised 12th May 1784.
[24] Bate & Westwood (1863: 12). Bate appears to have been told this by Jenny and George Leach in the 1850s. Why Elford was born at Hoegate is not known.
[25] Not 1790 as often cited.
[26] *Reports of the Devonshire Association*, **18**: 119 (1886) *or* **29**: 119 (1897) [JES Mss]
[27] From records of Land Tax Assessments for Buckland Monachorum 1780-1832. We have seen no records between 1786, when George Leach was the occupier, and 1799, when the resident was John Snook.
[28] Jonathan Elford (1776-1823). Banker.

St Andrew's Church

law may well have played a part. However he would have received a broader liberal arts education than this suggests. Oxford's Professor of Poetry (and a Fellow of Oriel) set out the principles of an Oxford education when he explained, "The best works in political economy, as well as in the elements of law and politics, are in the hands of many students with the full approbation of those who regulate their studies; although it is never forgotten that to lay a foundation of liberal literature, ancient and modern, before any particular pursuit absorbs the mind is our main business.[29]"

While George had been preparing to enter university, his teenage brother Jonathan had been attracted by a military life. In August 1801, at the age of 17, he purchased a commission[30] as an Ensign – the lowest rank of infantry officer, later renamed Second-Lieutenant – in the *70th (Surry) Regiment of Foot*[31]. The purchase of commissions and of promotions up to the rank of Lieutenant-Colonel was commonplace at this time and was regulated by the state, which had a scale of 'recommended retail prices'[32]. As an indication of the seriousness of these prices, by the year 1808 a commission as an Ensign cost £400; a Lieutenancy £550; and a Captaincy (giving command of a company of up to one hundred men) £1500[33]. By comparison, an Ensign's annual pay was only

[29] Copleston, 1810. [Edward Copleston (1776-1849). Provost of Oriel from 1814. Bishop of Llandaff from 1828].
[30] Presumably, at 17 years of age, his family purchased the commission for him.
[31] We do not know why he chose the 70th Regiment.
[32] Above Lieutenant-Colonel full promotions (as opposed to promotions by brevet – see later) were on seniority (i.e. length of time at that rank). If the army wished to promote someone who was not the longest-serving officer of their rank, they also had to promote all those who had been at that rank longer.
[33] Ashton, 1906: 430.

Hoegate, Plymouth.

£73. 5*s*. 10*d* [34], meaning the commission cost five and a half times the annual salary. However, it was well recognised that none but the most junior officers could live on their army pay alone, and officers tended to be drawn from the monied classes[35].

Jonathan obviously had access to money, whether from trust funds or family support. By October 1801 he had already purchased a promotion[36] and Lieutenant Leach sailed to join his regiment in Jersey, where he would spend the first eleven months of his service career. He tells us[37], "I felt that delight which I fancy is experienced by most youngsters, on making an escape from school, putting on a scarlet coat, epaulet, cocked hat, and a tremendously long feather, to say nothing of the false queue[38] affixed to a head of hair plastered with pomatum[39] and well powdered (the custom of those days[40])".

As the new century dawned and his older brothers embarked on their chosen paths, young William Elford Leach was still at school[41]. He was educated first at Plympton Grammar School[42] just to the east of Plymouth, but was later moved to the boarding school at Chudleigh[43], about 50 km away on the main road to Exeter, which at that time was held locally in very high regard.

Although he was not a lazy student, it was noticeable even at this early age that he had a strong tendency to take just as much interest in the world around him as he did in his schoolbooks. In particular he had a fondness for collecting any natural objects that sparked his curiosity, and his school friends provided many willing helpers for this extra-curricular activity. He was particularly drawn to animals and had a facility for handling even venomous snakes without harm to handler or handled.

We do not know exactly what prompted this early fascination with nature[44]. His uncle Will Elford had some interest in natural history[45]; he conducted experiments on yeast, published on 'the propagation and dispersion of animals and vegetables'; and planned, but never produced, a book on British birds. For these studies he had been elected a Fellow of the Royal Society in 1790. In addition, all the men in Elford Leach's family would have been keen field-sportsmen, as were virtually all men of their class at that time. They would have shot game and fished and engaged in hare-coursing and fox-hunting.

[34] Harvey, 1978: 21 (= £73.29p).
[35] Harvey, 1978: 21.
[36] Philippart, 1820.
[37] In *Rough Sketches of the Life of an Old Soldier* (1831) at p. 2.
[38] pigtail.
[39] A perfumed ointment or oil used to smooth hair.
[40] Pigtails and powdered hair were not abolished in the British army until 1808 (Oman, 1986: 293). Outside the military powdered hair was still in vogue as the new century began. To capitalise on this and help pay for the war with France, in 1801 the British government introduced a hair powder tax of one guinea (£1. 1*s*.) per year for all who used it (Cholmondeley, 1950: 137).
[41] For this early period of his life see *The English Cyclopædia*.
[42] Founded 1658.
[43] Founded 1668.
[44] Some authors have said his father had a strong interest in natural history. There is no evidence for this. Authors have confused his father, George Leach, with his brother, George Leach. The only reference to the father in a natural history context is in an article by W.E. Leach in 1818 on flies (*Memoirs of the Wernerian Society*, **2**: 561) when he states his father captured a specimen in south Devon. No date is given and he may have collected this insect for his son.

Field-sports. A successful hare-coursing.

Today's exclusive town-life, spent isolated from the countryside, did not exist 200 years ago; no-one was ever more than a short walk from woods or open fields.

Elford Leach was not the only brother to take more than a passing interest in nature. George would later own an extensive collection of British mammals[46], and Jonathan was a passionate field-sportsman.

Kingdom

With his particular interests Elford Leach could not have been born in a more fortuitous location. On the southwest peninsula of England, bathed by the warm current of the Atlantic Gulf Stream, Devon has one of the mildest climates in Britain, and among the richest wildlife. Mediterranean marine species, and even Caribbean flotsam, occasionally make their way to the south coast shores, and exotic feathered visitors are not unusual.

Around Plymouth the land was a rolling country chequered with enclosures, and dotted with cottages and Gentlemen's houses set against dark stands of pine. These grand houses varied in style but the cottages were typically built partly from stone and partly from rammed-earth, with a thatched roof of long straw.

Behind the beaches, cliffs and inlets of the south coast (much loved by the numerous smugglers actively dodging the Excise Men[47]), the heart of

Devon was the raised granite uplands of Dartmoor, which at this time was virtually an unvisited wilderness even to those families which, like the Leaches, had lived alongside it for centuries. On the southern coast to the east rose the great Old Red Sandstone cliffs that gave the name to a geological epoch: The Devonian. If a young mind craved stimulation, the environment of Devon would provide it.

But it was not just nature that Devon had to offer, especially to a professional family. As the war with France moved into its second decade, Plymouth, for many centuries one of Britain's great Royal Navy anchorages, was growing fast. It was really three separate communities known locally as 'The Three Towns' deep within the broad protective inlet of Plymouth Sound: *Plymouth* proper, in the harbour of Sutton Pool; *Stonehouse* about a mile to the west on the promontory between Mill Bay and Mill Lake; and beyond Mill Lake, *Plymouth Dock*, clustered around the naval dockyard and depending mainly on the Royal

[45] The following from Elford (1976) Part II: 5.

[46] Bellamy, 1839: 194-195, 454 (George may simply have acquired Elford's collection rather than building a collection of his own).

[47] Smuggling was commonplace around Plymouth in the period 1804-1815 (Gill, 1979: 102).

A West Country thatched cottage.

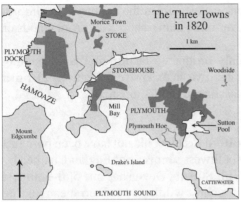

Navy for its prosperity. By 1801 Plymouth Dock, or 'Dock' as it was known locally, had outstripped its parent to become the most populated town in Devon and one of the largest in the south of England with nearly 24,000 inhabitants. Plymouth had a population of just over 16,000 and Stonehouse almost 4000[48]. When the younger George Leach returned from Oxford it was to prospering Plymouth Dock that he turned to begin his life as a lawyer.

In keeping with its rising importance and commercial activity Dock's first bank had been founded in 1773 by a group of local gentry, including the 24 year old Will Elford, Elford Leach's uncle. Will took a very active role in Plymouth public life. By 1796 he was MP for Plymouth[49], becoming a friend of the Prime Minister, William Pitt the younger[50]. In 1797 he was Mayor, and from 1798 he was town Recorder[51]. In 1800 it was his duty as Recorder to present the freedom of Plymouth[52] to one of England's greatest living heroes, Admiral Lord Nelson[53], and on the 29th of November that year William Elford *Esquire* became *Sir* William Elford *Baronet*.

In addition to his political life and scientific interests Will Elford regularly exhibited landscape paintings at the Royal Academy in London, and presented one of his works to the Prince of Wales[54]. In literary circles he is known for his regular correspondence with Mary Russell Mitford, author of the popular book *Our Village*[55].

[48] To the outside world 'Plymouth' was used for this collection of urban centres and outlying suburban villages such as Stoke and Morice Town. These figures do not include thousands of French prisoners of war (2500 by 1803) held at Mill Prison (Ashton, 1906: 100).

[49] MP for Plymouth 1796-1806; represented Westbury for some time; and was MP for Rye from 1807-8.

[50] William Pitt (1759-1806). Prime Minister 1783-1801, 1804-1806.

[51] Recorder for Plymouth from 1798-1833 and Recorder for Totnes from 1833-1836. The Recorder was the person responsible in a town for recording the business of the town council. The Recorder was a magistrate (Justice of the Peace) for the town and in the absence of the mayor would chair the Quarter Sessions (court hearings held every three months). The Recorder usually had some legal knowledge.

[52] Giving the 'Freedom of the Town/City' to someone is an honour bestowed by many British towns and cities. In practice it has few consequences.

[53] Rear-Admiral Horatio Nelson, Baron Nelson of the Nile (1758-1805). He had destroyed the French fleet at the Battle of the Nile in August 1798. Later Vice-Admiral and Viscount.

[54] The work, known as *Landscape with a distant country house*, was donated in August 1819 and is now at Windsor Castle.

[55] Mary Russell Mitford (1787-1855). *Our Village* published from 1824.

Fore Street, Plymouth Dock looking towards the dock gates.

[56] Captain 1792; Major 1795; Lieutenant-Colonel 1798; resigned 1807. Militia officers had to hold property in the regimental home region. The Rank and File were volunteers but if not enough men volunteered names were drawn by ballot. Someone whose name was drawn but did not wish to serve could pay £10 to provide a substitute; otherwise they would train for 28 days and serve for 3 years. Service covered Protestants 18-45 years of age and at least 5'4" (1.63m) in height. Many militiamen later joined the regular army.
[57] Charles, 1st Marquess Cornwallis (1738-1805). Commanded British forces in the American War of Independence (although he opposed taxation of the colonists) and was defeated at Yorktown (1781). Was Governor-General of India (1786-1793, 1804-1805) where he was noted for his concerns for Indian welfare.
[58] The Union Flag had been created after the uniting of the thrones of Scotland and England in 1603 when James VI of Scotland (1566-1625) also became James I of England following the death of Queen Elizabeth I (1533-1603) without heirs. The flag was created by combining the flag of St George (patron saint of England) with the flag of St Andrew (patron saint of Scotland). This Union Flag was formally adopted as the national flag of Great (i.e. greater, larger) Britain in 1707 at the Act of Union between the two countries. The Act of Union of 1801 created the new nation of 'The United Kingdom of Great Britain and Ireland'.
[59] This flag was flown from the jack-staff of Royal Navy vessels and hence became known as the 'Jack'. This led to its modern nick-name, the 'Union Jack'.

Will Elford was also an officer in the South Devon Regiment of Militia[56]. The militia were full-time soldiers, but were not in the numbered *Regiments of the Line* which formed the standing British army, and did not serve overseas. Nevertheless, in 1798 he saw militia service in Ireland when rebellion broke out – fuelled in August by the landing of a force of 1200 French troops at Killala Bay in the north-west. Revolutionary France found many sympathisers in Ireland, another predominantly Roman Catholic country. For their part the Irish were moved to sympathise with England's enemy more by their opposition to English policies towards Ireland, and anger at English exclusion of Roman Catholics from many public offices, than by heartfelt support for French objectives—*The enemy of my enemy is my friend*.

While the British government moved regular army regiments north to deal with the threat, militia units were sent from England to take over routine policing duties. Lieutenant-Colonel Elford and the South Devon Militia patrolled Waterford in the south-east, a relatively quiet area. They served for some months but by September British forces in the north under Lord Cornwallis[57], the Lord-Lieutenant of Ireland, had forced the French invaders to surrender.

This French-backed Irish rebellion scared the British parliament, which was determined to increase its security in the west. In 1800 an Act of Union between Great Britain and Ireland was passed in London which abolished the separate Irish parliament and replaced it with Irish MPs at Westminster. The Act came into force on the 1st of January 1801 and as a public display of its effect the British national flag was changed for the first time in nearly 200 years[58] to incorporate the red cross of St Patrick (patron saint of Ireland), creating the modern Union Flag[59].

Environment

The Leaches and Elfords lived out their lives against this backdrop of war and civil unease in a time of rapid social and technological change.

Although the British Isles was a union of nations, there was little united about the society. The social distinction between the few fabulously wealthy landed families and the vast labouring class was extreme. This was a society rooted in an 18th century view of divine order, where everyone should know their place, and where the privileged (at least) believed it was God's will that some were born to hold responsibility for government and land while others were born to work that land. However, at the end of the century, in the primarily rural economy, an

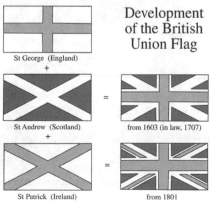

Development of the British Union Flag

St George (England)
+
St Andrew (Scotland)
=
from 1603 (in law, 1707)
+
St Patrick (Ireland)
=
from 1801

industrial revolution had begun with the introduction of mechanisation on the farms and the appearance of 'manufactories' near the urban centres. There was a mass migration of labour away from the feudal estates and towards the growing towns. For the first time in history large numbers of labourers were coming together in the new centres of employment, where they were reaching a critical mass – and these masses were *very* critical. It was becoming apparent to working people that there were more of them than there were of the ruling élite. The lessons of the recent French Revolution were not lost on them (or on the landowners) and they began to voice their protests. The coming decades were to be characterised by increasing civil unrest in Britain as the working class discovered it had a voice and the ruling class honed its fear of 'the mob[60]'. Between these two groups, and allied to neither, was a growing middle class of professionals and manufacturers, developing its own political agenda and trying to elbow some space in a society unprepared for it.

The uniting workers were not just vocal in their demands. In the Spring of 1801, after several bad harvests, food riots erupted in England and Wales. Magistrates called out the local Volunteers (part-time soldiers) to quell the disturbances but the Volunteers were also workers, and had mixed sympathies. In Devon so many refused to oppose the rioters that whole corps were disbanded. At Kingsbridge, about 30 km south-east of Plymouth, 33 of the 51 Privates in the Kingsbridge Volunteers were dismissed[61].

Nature

As the British flag changed and the Devon riots began, Sir William's young nephew and namesake, William Elford Leach, passed his tenth birthday, but even at this tender age it had become clear his interest in natural history

[60] 'mob', from the Latin term *mobile vulgus*, the 'moveable public' but usually used in the sense of intellectually moveable, 'the fickle hoards'.

[61] Harvey, 1978: 31. [The part-time 'Volunteers' who could be called out for local service should not be confused with 'volunteers' found in regular Regiments of the Line at this time. The latter type of volunteer was usually a young 'gentleman' attached to a regular army regiment in an unofficial and unpaid capacity in the hope that after proving himself in the field he might ultimately be awarded a commission in the regiment without having to purchase one. These probationer officers fought with the rank and file but dined with the commissioned officers. Battalions often had one or two such volunteers in their ranks (Oman, 1993: 196)].

Entrance to Sutton Pool, Plymouth.

was going to be more than just a childhood hobby. As the only way to acquire education in this subject was through a study of medicine – with its broader facets of herbal botany and comparative anatomy (a study of the differing anatomy of species with different body forms and life-styles) – the family decided to arrange a medical apprenticeship at the Devon and Exeter Hospital, in Exeter. The groundwork for this was rather shrewdly laid in November 1802 when his father and Sir William obtained positions as Governors of the hospital. The number of students at any one time was determined by the Governors' Court, and George and Sir William would therefore have had some influence[62]. Accordingly, in 1803[63] Elford Leach began his five year apprenticeship. At Exeter he would study under the professors of the day, Pepin, Luscombe and Sheldon. He also attended additional lectures on anatomy by Sheldon and lectures on chemistry by a Mr White. It is said he distinguished himself at Exeter by the skill with which he performed the minor operations in surgery[64] and, "for the general gaiety of his disposition and the energy and determination of purpose he evinced in whatever he undertook.[65]"

Leechcraft

The doctrines that constituted medical orthodoxy when Elford Leach was training can be gauged by following the treatment of an infantry officer shot during the Battle of Waterloo in 1815. Before becoming a soldier ten years earlier he had been apprenticed to a surgeon and had some medical knowledge himself. Like many at that time he had great faith in the practice of deliberately bleeding the patient as an aid to recovery, even following severe physical injuries which generated more than enough bleeding of their own. His story begins during a French attack when a musket ball entered his back, just missing his spine, and smashed through two ribs. He tells us the ball perforated his liver and passed forward to lodge against the inside of his rib cage. After lying on the battlefield for some time he was eventually noticed and carried to a temporary field hospital just behind the front line. It was there his treatment began[66]:

"The surgeon cut into my breast and dislodged the ball, which, being flat and terribly jagged, required some time. I was suffocating with the injury my lungs had sustained. He took a quart of blood from my arm. I now began to feel my miseries."

The extraction of the mangled ball would have been undertaken without anaesthetic; there were no pain-killers at this time. Cannon balls began to riddle the field hospital so he was put on a horse to ride the 19 km to a place of greater safety. He said "the motion of the horse made the blood pump out, and the bones cut the flesh to a jelly." On arrival at the new billet, "I had everything possible got for me, a surgeon sent for, a quart of blood taken from me, wrapped up in poultices, and a most excellent nurse. In four days I had six quarts of blood taken from me, the inflammation ran so high in my lungs."

[62] They were Governors until 1808 after which they did not renew their subscriptions (of 2 guineas each per year).
[63] *The English Cyclopædia* says 1807 but Elford Leach, writing in 1812, says he served five years before leaving Exeter, and the dates of the governorships would support this.
[64] This presumably means [?animal] dissections. An apprentice would not have been performing operations on patients.
[65] *The English Cyclopædia.*
[66] Quoted from his letter to his parents written several weeks later (Verner, 1986: 365-374)

He cannot mean a quart in the modern sense of a quarter of a gallon (2 pints or just over 1.1 litres). An adult man only contains about 4.4 quarts of blood (5 litres) in total. He probably means a quartern, a term used at the beginning of the 19th century for a quarter of a pint (142 mls).

Fifteen days after being shot he was, "attacked with convulsions, and at night with vomiting. Afterwards I lay in a state of insensibility until the morning, when a violent inflammation had taken place in my body. I was bled three times, which gave me temporary ease. In this way I went on for seven days, bled regularly two or three times a day. I felt better, but continued in a stupor for four days, when the inflammation recommenced with far more violence than ever. The lancet was the only thing to save me, so I was bled again very largely. My liver now was much swollen, and consequently my body was a good deal enlarged. I had always an intolerable burning pain in the liver. I never slept—often in dread of suffocation. Bleeding was the only remedy for it. In this way I went on for seven days more, when one evening, the pain being very violent, I sent for my surgeon to bleed me. He took two large basins from my arm. The pain abated much. I requested a little more might be taken, but I suddenly fainted. It was about half an hour before I could be brought to life. This alarmed my friend so much that he did not like to try bleeding again. He went and brought an eminent physician to see me, who recommended leeches. I had thirty immediately provided and applied to my sides. The next day, I had twenty-five more on the same spot, and the day after, twenty-five more. The last application of them was horrible. My side was inflamed and nearly raw from the biting of the others. I got fresh leeches every time; they bit directly. I was in the greatest state of debility when the last were put on the raw part; all taking hold at once made me entirely mad with anguish. I kicked, roared, and swore, and tried to drag them off, but my hands were held. Such torture I never experienced. As soon as they came off I ordered my servant to kill them, as well as about fifty more I had in the house."

This officer eventually recovered and spent another thirty years in the army, although the injury to his back required the permanent support of a corset (whether he had a Frenchman or a horse to thank for that is not clear). We might also note the surgeon's dirty knife probably contributed many of his symptoms. The need for hygiene was little understood in the early years of the 19th century.

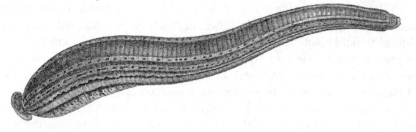

The medicinal leech

Hirudo medicinalis Linnæus

Illustration from *Supplement to the Encyclopædia Britannica*, Volume 1, Part 2 (1816), Plate XXVI of the entry ANNULOSA by William Elford Leach.

— 2 —

Redcoat to Green Jacket

We must not look to all who have fought our battles
in the vain hope of meeting heroes; we shall find
but men.

Moyle Sherer[1]

While Elford Leach pursued his Exeter apprenticeship and learned of the value of bleeding and of leeches, his brother George stayed in Plymouth Dock and built up his attorney's practice. Jenny continued her life with their parents. We can now leave these three to settle into their domestic routines, and instead follow Jonathan through the early years of his eventful army career.

In the winter of 1805 he returned to Plymouth for the first time since leaving for the Channel Islands. After Jersey he had been stationed in Kent and during the threat of French invasion in the summer of 1803 his regiment, and others, had camped on the cliffs overlooking the English Channel. From this vantage point the tents of Napoleon's invasion force could clearly be seen on the French coast. The attack never came and as the threat of invasion faded towards the end of the year, the 70th Regiment was posted to Antigua, where the proximity of French-occupied islands meant garrisons had to be maintained on their British-held neighbours. For Europeans in the Caribbean disease was the greatest enemy and the death toll among new arrivals was severe.

In April 1804, having served in the army for nearly three years, Jonathan purchased a promotion to Captain and took command of his own company. No sooner had he done so than the regiment was hit by an epidemic of Yellow Fever. During the course of the summer two-thirds of the officers died, including six Captains, and men were being buried at the rate of eight or ten a day. Jonathan did not escape but luckily recovered (a fact he attributed to having drunk a full jug of hot Madeira wine as soon as the illness struck). After this he would suffer bouts of fever at intervals throughout his army career, the first of which arrived in the autumn of 1805 with such debilitating

[1] Sherer, 1996: 50-51

severity that he was granted six months sick leave and a temporary medical transfer to Europe.

After docking at Dublin he made his way to Plymouth to spend the winter with his family, whom he had not seen for four years, and while there he did some hard thinking about his future in the army. He decided he had two choices, "either to rejoin my regiment, and spend some of the best years of my life in a sugar island, where cold punch, sangaree, cigar-smoking, musquito bites, and every now and then a friend swept off by yellow fever, were the only varieties I had to calculate on; or to exchange into one of the regiments in England or Ireland, whereby I should stand a fair chance of participating in any service going on in Europe or elsewhere, as the fates might decree." A young adventurous officer, he chose the latter.

Red to Green

While picketing the cliffs in Kent Jonathan had served alongside a relatively new infantry regiment, the 95th (Rifles) Regiment of Foot ('the Rifles'). Jonathan Leach was not the first person in the army to have admired the dashing look of the 95th's dark green uniform and black leather strapping, contrasting with the usual scarlet jacket and pipe-clayed white webbing of other regiments of the line. Since that time he had harboured an envious wish to wear the green jacket himself. This decided, during his remaining leave he sounded out the Captains of the 95th and found one who was prepared to exchange with him: they would transfer to the 70th and sail to Antigua; he would take their place in the Rifles. So, in the spring of 1806 with the paperwork completed and the necessary notices published[1], he left Devon not for the West Indies, but for Brabourne Lees Barracks in Kent to join the 2nd battalion[2] of the 95th Regiment in the uniform he would wear for the next 15 years.

Despite his wish for action, Jonathan's first year in the Rifles was spent in Kent, no doubt replacing his musketry skills with the drills required for the recently introduced Baker rifle, a weapon of quite different characteristics and potential. He would also have found the company system worked rather differently in the Rifles compared to other regiments. Captains in the Rifles were given more independent control of their companies than was usually the custom in the British infantry. When faced by the enemy they were expected to use their own initiative to support other companies and to further the general object of the action, while in times of peace they were encouraged to carry out their duties as company commanders without waiting for orders on every minute detail[3].

In the summer of 1807 Jonathan's first active duty finally arrived. His battalion sailed from Kent for Copenhagen as part of a force charged with seizing the Danish fleet. Although Denmark was neutral in the European conflict between France and her enemies, Britain was concerned the Danish fleet would fall into French hands. Following earlier concerns this fleet had

[1] Then, as now, it was necessary to publicise commissions, promotions, transfers etc. in *The London Gazette*, the official organ of the British Government.

[2] A battalion was composed of about 1000 men led by a Lieutenant-Colonel, with assistance from a Major. It was further divided into Companies of about 100 men, each led by a Captain (These numbers are ideals. Battalions were seldom at full strength, especially during the war).

[3] Verner, 1912: 51.

The Rifles

In the mid-18th century, during the wars between European colonists in North America, the formal manoeuvring of heavily laden infantry columns in brightly coloured uniforms did not serve the British well. In 1755, after they were defeated by a force of French and native Americans, a new infantry regiment was recruited from loyal Americans: the 60th (Royal American) Regiment of Foot[1]. These men dressed in buckskin and green or brown fabrics, with non-reflective horn buttons replacing the usual polished silver. Equipment was light and portable. Emphasis was put on the ability to fight from dense cover and to use initiative and independence – the opposite of the usual military stress on simply obeying orders. Success in the field proved the value of this approach.

In 1797 the regiment's 5th Battalion (5/60th) became the first unit of the British Army to carry rifles, wear green jackets with dark leather webbing[2], and use the bugle-horn and whistle, not the drum, to direct movements in the field.

To expand this capability, in 1800 fifteen British infantry regiments were plundered for promising soldiers to form an Experimental Corps of Riflemen. Training was based on that of the 5/60th and was far ahead of its time. Discipline was firm but avoided strong emphasis on precision drilling or spit-and-polish. The marching style was relaxed and economical. Field orders were explained where possible. Men were trained for the realities of war, not for blind, albeit courageous, obedience. In a sense the riflemen were the first modern British infantry, relying on irregular dispersal in the field, camouflage and concealment, accurate marksmanship, and thoughtful selection of targets. In battle riflemen would be scattered in front of the geometric formations of regular 'redcoats' to skirmish with the enemy's front line, out of range of their muskets[3]. Just as modern warfare depends upon striking the enemy's command and communications systems, so the riflemen were trained to target the enemy's officers[4] (command) and drummers/buglers (communications) leaving the enemy's formal deployments of trained-to-be-unimaginative infantrymen orderless, uncoordinated and open to assault from traditional regiments. In 1802 this Rifle Corps was elevated to a full regiment as the 95th (Rifles) Regiment of Foot and a camp was formed for it at Shorncliffe in Kent.

In 1803 three regiments were brought together as a Light Brigade of infantry: the 95th; the 43rd (Monmouthshire) Regiment, which was redesignated the 43rd Light Infantry; and the 52nd (Oxfordshire) Regiment, redesignated the 52nd Light Infantry. The brigade was coached by General Sir John Moore, still regarded as one of the finest trainers of British infantry. Light Infantry regiments did not carry rifles, but did use a lighter musket than other regiments and were trained as skirmishers[5]. The Light Brigade was the first British infantry unit trained for reconnaissance and to act as an advanced or rearguard for the army, roles usually given to cavalry. It also provided pickets (outlying guards) for the army at rest. It was the 95th's proud boast that they never lost a picket. In addition to this brigade, in the Peninsula War the Duke of Wellington attached at least one company of the 5/60th to each of his seven 'heavy' infantry brigades.

[1] Originally formed as the 62nd Foot, but later redesignated.

[2] Riflemen were known colloquially as 'sweeps' by other regiments because their uniforms were so dark. The French sometimes called them 'grasshoppers'.

[3] The enemy also used skirmishers.

[4] In an official despatch during the Napoleonic wars French commander Marshal Soult attributed his disproportionate loss of officers in combat directly to the actions of riflemen. He complained, 'whenever a superior officer goes to the front, he is usually hit.'

[5] Oman, 1986: 76, 302.

The Baker Rifle

The standard long-barrelled firearm issued to British infantry at this time was the smooth-bore flintlock India Pattern musket known as a 'common musket' or 'Brown Bess'[1]. This was not a precision weapon. Despite its 99cm barrel it was accurate only at a range of 90m or less. It was designed to be fired in volleys by bodies of men against assembled formations of the enemy. The principle was similar to firing a shotgun into a dense flock of birds. A bird may fall, but not necessarily the one intended. In 1814 an army officer felt able to write, 'A soldier's musket, if not exceedingly ill-bored (as many are), will strike the figure of a man at 80 yards; it may even at a hundred; but a soldier must be very unfortunate indeed who shall be wounded by a common musket at 150 yards, provided his antagonist aims at him; and as to firing at a man at 200 yards with a common musket, you may as well fire at the moon[2]'.

The small number of riflemen in the British army after 1800 carried the Baker Rifle. Designed by London gunsmith Ezekiel Baker, this was not an innovative firearm. It used the best of established European engineering to make it robust and soldier-proof under field conditions. The barrel was brown to prevent reflected sunlight giving away the position of a concealed man (at least until he pulled the trigger, releasing the cloud of smoke characteristic of black-powder firearms). As the name suggests, the barrel was rifled, but not so much as to make muzzle-loading difficult[3]. On the battlefield a man with average skill could reload and fire every 30 seconds. The rifling imparted a spin to the ball around the direction of travel which increased its stability through the air and hence range and accuracy.

Unlike the musket, the rifle was a precision weapon for use by individuals against individuals. Despite its shorter 76cm barrel, it was generally accurate at targets the size of a man to 275m. A first class marksman could get good results at 400m. William Surtees, an officer of the 95th Rifles, reported calculations that in the field of battle only one shot out of 200 fired from muskets 'took effect'[4], while rifles averaged one in 20[5].

In hand-to-hand combat with bayonets fitted, the shorter barrel of the rifle left riflemen at a disadvantage closing with an enemy armed with muskets. To overcome this riflemen were issued with 'sword-bayonets' with a brass sword handle and a 61cm (24") blade[6]. A sensible precaution, in reality these saw more action chopping wood; pinning down the edges of bivouacs; and tethering officers' horses.

[1] Haythornthwaite, 1979: 21. Cavalrymen carried a shorter barrelled smooth-bore carbine to allow them to fight dismounted if required.
[2] Colonel George Hanger (Haythornthwaite, 1979: 19).
[3] Seven grooves were scored on the inside of the barrel, rotating by a quarter turn.
[4] Surtees may have read Hanger, who claimed this figure (Haythornthwaite, 1979: 19).
[5] Surtees, 1973: 290.
[6] Rifle regiments in the British army still use the term 'sword' in place of 'bayonet'.

[4] Arthur Wellesley (1769-1852). Born Arthur Wesley but the family reverted to an older spelling in 1798. Born Dangan Castle, Ireland. Educated Chelsea, Eton, Brussels and a military school at Angers, France. Joined the army 1787. MP in the Irish Parliament. Served with the army in India from 1797. Returned to UK 1805. Knighted (KB). MP for Rye in Sussex. Married the Honourable Catherine Pakenham ('Kitty') in 1806. Secretary for Ireland in 1807 when the Duke of Richmond became Lord-Lieutenant.

[5] Invented by William Congreve (1772-1828). First used in 1805. Effectively huge, iron-cased versions of the firework rocket with a pole 7m or more in length. In 1807, 40,000 were fired into Copenhagen (Haythornthwaite, 1979: 88-89). Wellesley disliked them (as did many in the army). They were disliked also by those on the receiving end and could be useful for disconcerting the enemy.

[6] A respected German force forming part of the British Army (George III of Britain was also Elector of Hanover, part of modern Germany, not yet a united nation).

[7] The Danish army was on the mainland, at the border with Holstein.

[8] He had commanded several actions during earlier service in India.

already been destroyed once by Nelson at the Battle of Copenhagen in 1801, but now restored it was again deemed a tempting prize for Napoleon, still lacking sea-power following his losses at Trafalgar in 1805. In July 1807 the British government demanded Denmark temporarily hand over control of its fleet and dockyard arsenals at Copenhagen to the Royal Navy. Not surprisingly the Danes refused and by the end of the month a military expedition of 30,000 men had sailed from Britain with orders to persuade them. Five companies of the 1st battalion 95th (1/95th) and 5 companies of the 2nd battalion (2/95th) – one led by Captain Jonathan Leach – formed part of a Division led by Major-General Sir Arthur Wellesley[4]. This was the first, but not the last, time riflemen of the 95th would be under the command of the man who would later become Field Marshal the Duke of Wellington, the Iron Duke.

To War

The Rifles were landed in the ships' boats as an advanced party – their usual role – on the 16th of August and pushed forward through the pine woods towards Copenhagen. The rest of the army was landed during the following days while the British warships cannonaded the town, and bombarded it with the new Congreve Rockets[5]. On the 24th of August, just after 2 a.m., the army advanced into the western suburbs and the Rifles were engaged in fierce skirmishing in the gardens and shrubberies. After six years of wartime military life Jonathan Leach finally saw action. He would not be short of it again.

Two days after the assault on the outskirts of Copenhagen – a town under siege – intelligence was received that a force of Danes was planning to attack the besieging forces from the west. Wellesley's Division (now divided into two Brigades, the first under Wellesley including the 1/95th, the second under General von Linsengen of the King's German Legion[6] including the 2/95th) was ordered to intercept and engage them. Wellesley sent the second Brigade south to cut off the Danes' line of retreat while his Brigade made a frontal attack, but this plan failed, the Danes falling back towards the town of Køge. On the 29th Wellesley did attack but much of the fighting was over before von Linsengen's Brigade was engaged. The action did not last long. The Danes, mainly militiamen[7] and no match for career soldiers, had no intense argument with Britain (which was stealing from them, not invading) and 1500 were taken prisoner. The action at Køge had been Wellesley's first battle command in Europe[8].

With the immediate infantry threat reduced the British concentrated on cannonading Copenhagen from land and sea. The Rifles were ordered back to give supporting small-arms fire, including rifleman Benjamin Harris[9], in Jonathan Leach's company:

"we advanced and got as near under the walls of the place as we could without being endangered by the fire from our own shipping. We now received orders to commence firing. I shall not easily forget the rattling of the guns. I felt so exhilarated that I could hardly keep back. I was checked by Captain Leach, the commander of my company, who called to me by name to keep my place.[10]"

Within five minutes of the bombardment commencing fires had broken out and by the time the governor surrendered three days later more than a third of the city had been destroyed. The British had obtained control of the Danish fleet[11], the dockyards and the dockyard stores.

For the following month and a half the Rifles policed the area to the south of Copenhagen, traversing the countryside to guard against local resistance and to watch for any counter-attack from the Danish mainland or adjoining islands. The 2nd battalion was based at Næstved, with outposts at Lundby, Vordingborg and Præstø, and was billeted for part of the time on local families. Wellesley, who always expressed abhorrence of any abuse of local populations by his troops, exercised the strictest discipline, and relations with the Danish people were as civil as could be expected. Jonathan obtained leave to enter Copenhagen and with a party of fellow officers spent five days at "a capital hotel". However, what he saw in the town left a sombre impression:

"Callous and insensible must he have been who could have walked through the streets and witnessed the horrors occasioned by the bombardment, and the misery inflicted on thousands of the unoffending inhabitants, without bitterly regretting that our government should have considered it necessary to adopt such rigorous measures."

For one British chronicler the success of the Copenhagen raid proved only that might had prevailed over right. It would be 32 years before Britain compensated the Danes for 'this infamous attack'[12].

Despite the aggressive nature of the expedition, all those who have left published records speak with respect of the Danish people. Jonathan felt, 'We had every reason to be satisfied, during our stay in Denmark, with the conduct of the inhabitants, who, although they did not attempt to conceal their displeasure at our having landed, burnt their capital, and taken possession of their fleet, behaved uniformly with civility towards us... I am well inclined to respect the Danes as a brave, honourable, and manly people.' His friend Lieutenant William Cox[13] later wrote in his journal, "On the whole, we found this a most pleasing expedition. We lived on good terms with the natives of the country, had frequent balls, to which all the best families came and the

[9] Benjamin Randell Harris (1781-1858). Born Portsea, Hampshire to parents from Stalbridge, Dorset.

[10] Hathaway, 1996: 28.

[11] 18 ships of the line (main warships); 16 frigates; 9 gun-brigs; and 25 gunboats. With prize ships, transports and merchantmen the total seizure amounted to "nearly five hundred sail" according to Jonathan Leach, "the largest, perhaps, ever assembled in the Baltic or elsewhere." By the 1st of January 1808 Britain had captured from other nations – and was using in the Royal Navy – 68 ships of the line and 164 other armed vessels (*Annual Register*, 19th August 1808).

[12] Tucker (1846: 35-36). The British Parliament eventually voted £75,000 to settle claims from Danish citizens.

[13] William Cox (1751-1857) a Lieutenant in Jonathan Leach's company and his lifelong friend.

women are very fair and very handsome, the living being good and cheap and very good Rhinish wine and excellent Hoc to be had everywhere we would willingly have prolonged our stay.[14]'

It was not only the officers, with their social gatherings, who felt this way. William Surtees[15], at that time the Quartermaster-Sergeant of the 2nd battalion, found the Danes, 'kind-hearted, hospitable, and inoffensive in the highest degree... I have seldom experienced more kindness and attention than was shown me by them whenever circumstances rendered such kindness and attention suitable.[16]'

The 2nd battalion left Denmark for Kent on *The Princess Caroline*, a two-decker Danish prize vessel of 74 guns[17], on the 21st of October 1807. The previous day Napoleon had declared war on Portugal for refusing to close her ports to British shipping, refusing to sequestrate British property, and refusing to wage war against Britain[18], one of her oldest allies[19].

Home and Away Again

After overwintering in Kent, in June 1808 four companies of the 2/95th, including Jonathan Leach's[20], sailed from Dover to the Cove of Cork in southern Ireland with a fleet holding 10,000 men. They knew they were bound for overseas duty and had laid in stores for a long sea-voyage, but their destination was a closely guarded secret. South America was the talk, where the previous year's actions against the Spanish at Buenos Aires and Montevideo had already involved other companies of the 95th[21].

The troop ships and transports were anchored at Cork for more than a month and the only units allowed ashore were the four companies of riflemen, who were drilled and skirmished across the countryside to the sound of their bugle-horns until dusk, when they returned to their ships. Officers, including Jonathan, took the opportunity to arrange picturesque boating trips up the river (for themselves, not for their men) and made frequent trips into the town.

In July the fleet finally left Cork and sailed not to South America but to Portugal. France had occupied Lisbon on the 30th of November 1807 then in the spring of 1808, having obtained permission from its ally Spain to march 40,000 troops across that country to garrison Portugal, Napoleon sent 80,000 and overran Spain too. On the 2nd of May the citizens of Madrid rose against the French and put many hundreds to death, but the rebellion was crushed, the Spanish royal family was forced to abdicate, and Napoleon put his brother Joseph Bonaparte[22] on the Spanish throne.

---

[14] Verner, 1912: 128.
[15] William Surtees (1781-1830). Born Corbridge, Northumberland. A book of his memoirs *Twenty-Five Years in the Rifle Brigade* was published in 1833, edited by 'J. Surtees'; presumably his brother John (christened 5th February 1785 and twin to Hannah, named after their mother).
[16] Surtees, 1973: 70.
[17] *The Princess Caroline* accompanied the British 64-gun *HMS Agamemnon*, a veteran of Trafalgar, on which the 1/95th sailed home. Each Danish prize ship was attached to a Royal Navy vessel (Teague & Teague, 1975: 11).
[18] The weakness of the French fleet making an invasion across the Channel impossible, Napoleon hoped instead to reduce British effectiveness, especially as a sea-power, by economic warfare. By his 'Berlin Decrees' of 1806 (restated at the end of 1807) he had declared Britain to be in a state of blockade and had forbidden international trade with her.
[19] England and Portugal had been allied since at least the Treaty of Windsor, AD 1386.
[20] Verner (1912: 145-146) says Leach's company was Nº 3 company of the 2/95th in August 1808. Benjamin Harris, who was in Leach's company, tells us it was Nº 4 company in February 1809 (Hathaway, 1996: 132).
[21] Spain had declared war on Britain in 1804 and the land conflict had been fought in the Spanish colonies of South America. The actions did not go well for the British, who surrendered and withdrew in late 1807.

By now the various provinces of Spain were in open revolt against the occupation. The Spanish fought fiercely and caused the dispersed French forces some serious setbacks but in the long-term the decentralised Spanish armies were never going to be a match for Napoleon's seasoned troops.

In the summer of 1808 both Portugal and Spain appealed to Britain for military assistance. British consideration of these requests presumably accounted for the delay of the troop ships at Cork, before they sailed for the Iberian Peninsula where they would launch what was to become the Peninsula War.

To War Again

With the French occupying Lisbon, a force of 400 British marines was landed 160 km to the north, at Mondego Bay, to garrison the fort at Figueira and create a safe British landfall. This was the destination of the troops from Cork, who would be led in the Peninsula by a newly promoted Lieutenant-General Sir Arthur Wellesley[23]. On the 1st of August the four companies of Rifles disembarked as part of a light infantry brigade

[Readers may wish to bookmark this map for later reference]

[22] Joseph Bonaparte (1768-1844). Napoleon made him ruler of The Two Sicilies in 1805 then King of Spain in 1808.

[23] The rank of Lieutenant-General is higher than that of Major-General because historically Major-General is an abbreviated form of Sergeant-Major General.

commanded by Brigadier-General John Fane[24], including riflemen from the 5th battalion of the 60th (Royal American) Regiment of Foot[25] and the musketeers of the 45th (Nottinghamshire) Regiment. The British were welcomed by the local populace as liberators, as Jonathan recalled:

"Whilst we were drawing up our men near the landing-place, and waiting for further orders, we were beset with a host of padres, friars, and monks, of all ages, each carrying a huge umbrella of the most gaudy colour imaginable; intended, no doubt, to protect their complexions, which vied with those of chimney sweeps. These gentry welcomed us with *vivas*, and protested that, with our assistance, every Frenchman in Portugal should speedily be annihilated. Our visitors were not confined to the male sex; for some olive beauties, with sparkling eyes and jet black hair, were induced to take a peep at us; and, before we parted, some of the more favoured of us were pressed with flowers and fruit from the hands of these damsels."

More than a week was spent landing various units and consolidating ashore. New arrivals from Britain boosted Wellesley's force to about 14,500 men, and they were joined by 5000 Portuguese troops. This allied army headed south towards Lisbon[26], then occupied by General Junot[27] with the bulk of the French army. In their path lay another French force of 4000-6000 men under General Laborde[28] which had been detached far to the north of the capital but was now falling back as the allies advanced. Jonathan Leach's brigade formed the vanguard of this advance with some squadrons of cavalry[29], and as they approached the town of Obidos they encountered a small force of horsemen and infantry from the tail of Laborde's rearguard. Without hesitation four companies of riflemen instantly attacked.

Finding the French withdrawing, enthusiasm overtook the allies in this first Peninsula encounter and pursuing the French with vigour the leading company, under the command of Wellesley's brother in law, Captain the Honourable Hercules Pakenham[30], pushed forward onto the French rearguard proper, which had turned to assist. Heavily outnumbered, the company was rescued by a rush forward of reinforcements, including Jonathan Leach with his men, but not before Pakenham was wounded and Lieutenant Ralph Bunbury and three riflemen were killed, the first British troops to die in the Peninsula War. Wellesley said the next day his soldiers had behaved, "remarkably well, but not with great prudence.[31]"

William Cox's brother John[32], a Lieutenant in Pakenham's company, described what happened from his perspective. "On approaching the place, the enemy opened a fire of musketry from a windmill on rising ground adjoining the place, and a few shots came from the town. However, a rapid advance of the Riflemen drew the French from all points of their posts, but being rather too elevated[33] with this our first collision with the foe, we dashed along the plain after them like young soldiers. We were soon brought up by a body of French cavalry advancing from the main force. A retrograde movement was now imperative, in which we lost an officer and a few men[34]."

[24] Brigadier-General John Fane, Lord Burghersh (1784-1859). 11th Earl of Westmoreland from 1841.

[25] Jonathan Leach says these were German riflemen. Even six years later there were still 300 Germans to 400 British riflemen in the 5/60th.

[26] As a Captain Jonathan Leach would almost certainly have been on horseback. Of the officers, only Lieutenants marched on foot with the men (unless undertaking duties as an Adjutant or particularly wealthy).

[27] Général Jean Andoche Junot, Duc d'Abrantes (1771-1813). He later committed suicide by throwing himself out of a window (Stanhope, 1888: 248).

[28] Général Henri François, Comte de Laborde ['La Borde' and 'Delaborde' of authors] (1764-1833).

[29] From the 20th Light Dragoons.

[30] Son of Lord Longford and brother of Kitty Pakenham.

[31] Letter: Wellesley to the Duke of Richmond, 16th August 1808 (*Wellington's Supplementary Dispatches*, 6: 115).

[32] John Cox (1790-1863).

[33] excited.

[34] Verner, 1912: 145.

In Jonathan's company Benjamin Harris was quickly on the scene: "Their skirmishers immediately commenced operations by raining a shower of balls upon us as we advanced, which we returned without delay. The first man hit was Lieutenant Bunbury. He was pierced through the head with a musket-ball and died almost immediately. I had never heard such a tremendous noise as the firing made on this occasion, and I occasionally observed that the men on both sides of me were falling fast. Being overmatched, we retired to a rising ground, or hillock, in our rear, and formed there all round its summit, standing three deep, the front rank kneeling[35]. In this position we remained all night, expecting every moment that the whole host would be upon us.[36]"

In fact there was no further activity that night. The French withdrew to a position a few kilometres to the south on some hills near the town of Roliça.

The Battle of Roliça

Wellesley was aware Laborde was expecting his corps to be reinforced by General Loison[37] with an additional 5000 troops, and determined to attack Laborde before the reinforcements arrived. After a day spent at Obidos after their skirmish the allies moved off on the 17th of August, with the Rifles forming the infantry advance guard, and a march of 2-3 hours brought them to the French positions. Harris reports, "On the 17th, still in front, we again came up with the French. I remember observing the pleasing effect afforded by the sun's rays glancing upon their arms as they formed in order of battle to receive us. Moving on in extended order, under whatever cover the nature of the ground afforded, we – together with some companies of the 60th – began a sharp fire upon them. Thus commenced the battle of Roliça."

Jonathan Leach takes up the story in a letter written after the battle: "the 60th and ourselves attacked the enemy's right and threw in so destructive a fire upon their columns – such as we could get within shot of – as to make them retreat in great disorder. You cannot conceive, nor can anyone who was not present on that day, the situation of ourselves and the 60th. We had to ascend first one mountain so covered with brushwood that our legs were ready to sink under us[38], the enemy on the top of it lying down in the heath keeping up a hot and constant fire in our face and the men dropping all around us. Before we could gain the summit the French had retreated to the next hill when they again lay concealed and kept up a running galling fire on us as we ascended. Having beaten them off the second hill and taken possession of it, the enemy retreated to a wood, there being a valley between us and it and recommenced a most tremendous fire, having received a reinforcement. The action now became very severe[39]"..."Neither before nor since do I remember to have felt more intense and suffocating heat than we experienced in climbing the mountains to the attack; every mouthful of air was such as is inhaled when looking into an oven[40]."

[35] This was the standard drill for infantry when forming a square defence against cavalry. Sword bayonets would have been fixed, forming a wall of points, in three rows, 2m high, through which horses would seldom venture.
[36] Hathaway, 1996: 39-40.
[37] Général Louis Henri Loison, Comte (1771-1816).
[38] He was apparently not on horse-back during this combat.
[39] Verner, 1912: 151.
[40] *Rough Sketches*, p. 47.

Although Wellesley had more than 15,000 men at Roliça, from the difficulty of the terrain no more than 4000 could actually be engaged, fewer troops than the French had in the field.

Hart's Annual Army List (1848) records Jonathan Leach as having 'suffered a contusion' at Roliça. This would normally indicate a wound but Jonathan diffidently explains.

"An egotist being a character for which I never had a predilection, this trifling anecdote should not have found a place in my memoranda of occurrences, if its narration tended to place a feather in my cap; but as it was within an ace of lowering me five feet seven inches, I have ventured to note it in my log book." What had happened was[41]...

"Having driven the enemy from one of the highest mountains, and in the act of collecting our men on its summit to renew the attack on a second position,"..."I had a most providential escape. I was almost faint with anxiety to get the men properly placed and with the immense heat and fatigue. In short I was like most of the others, completely fagged and would have given a guinea for one mouthful of water, when one of our officers asked me if I would take a mouthful of wine. He held his canteen to my mouth and it was not there a second when a shot went"..."through his hand, and through the canteen, which latter it split, splashed my face thoroughly with wine, spoiled my draught, gave me a sharp blow, which cut my mouth, and spun me round like a top. For a few moments I concluded that I was wounded; but the mystery was soon explained by seeing my friend on the ground, bleeding profusely, and the broken canteen at his side."

"I left a soldier with him and proceeded with my company, pitying the Officer who was wounded but fully convinced that the ball was better through his hand than my head which has proved to be the case as he is quite recovered. The action lasted till about five or six in the evening in which time I am sorry to say we lost many a gallant officer and soldier as Sir A. Wellesley's Dispatches will show. My servant whom I have had ever since I came to the Regiment was killed, poor fellow. We had three officers wounded."

The officer shot in the hand was Lieutenant Thomas Cochrane[42]. In one of life's bizarre twists, Benjamin Harris tells us of a curiously similar occurrence in Jonathan's company that day. "Joseph Cockayne was by my side loading and firing very industriously. Thirsting with heat and action, he lifted his canteen to his mouth. "Here's to you, old boy," he said. As he took a pull at its contents, a bullet went through the canteen and, perforating his brain, killed him in a moment."

The French were eventually beaten but 17 riflemen of the 95th died and another 33 were wounded. Wellesley thought, "Roliça was one of our most important affairs; it was terrible hard work to drive off the French. When we had got possession of the heights, they attacked us, and I had only three battalions to stand firm against them. Our men fought monstrous well.[43]"

[41] This account is taken partly from *Rough Sketches* and partly from a letter written by Jonathan about a week after the battle and quoted by Verner (1912: 151).

[42] Cochrane went on to fight at Waterloo and eventually died at Kinsale, in County Cork, Ireland in 1823.

[43] Stanhope, 1888: 40.

After the battle

An army on campaign in Napoleonic times could have a large entourage of civilians moving with it. In particular a certain number of wives were allowed to travel with the men; officially, four to six, chosen by ballot, with each company[44]. When campaigns could last years this was some mitigation for the hardships placed on marriages, although the journey could be harsh, especially for women who conceived and gave birth on the march. These wives have been described as, 'the most unmanageable portion of every regimental train, being little amenable to military discipline... They were tough, expert foragers, furious partisans of the prestige of their own battalion, and often fought one another. Many of them were widows twice or thrice over—for when the husband was killed, his wife, if capable and desirable, was likely to receive numerous proposals as soon as her husband was buried.[45]' Soldiers could also form liaisons with local women who then joined the camp followers. Local tradesmen, bakers, grocers and others, would also follow the army through their region to benefit from the business.

Harris recounts from Roliça the grimmer side of wives following their husbands to war: "After the battle, when the roll was called, some of the females came along the front of the line to inquire of the survivors whether they knew anything about their husbands. Amongst other names, I heard that of Cockayne called in a female voice. It was not replied to. The name struck me, and I observed the poor woman who had called it. She stood sobbing before us, apparently afraid to make further inquiries about her husband. No man had answered to his name, or had any account to give of his fate. I had observed him fall whilst drinking from his canteen, but as I looked at the poor sobbing creature before me, I felt unable to tell her of his death. At length Captain Leach observed her, and called out to the company: "Does any man here know what has happened to Cockayne? If so, let him speak out at once." Upon this order I immediately related what I had seen, and told the manner of his death. Mrs Cockayne appeared anxious to seek the spot where her husband fell, and asked me to accompany her over the field. Notwithstanding what I had told her, she trusted she might find him alive. "Do you think you could find the place?" said Captain Leach, upon being referred to. I told him I was sure I could, as I had remarked many objects whilst looking for cover during the skirmishing. "Go then," said the captain, "and show the poor woman the spot, as she seems so desirous of finding the body." I accordingly made my way over the ground we had fought on. She followed sobbing. We soon reached the spot where her husband's body lay and I pointed it out to her. She now discovered that all her hopes were in vain. She embraced a stiffened corpse, then rose and contemplated his disfigured face for some minutes. She took a prayer-book from her pocket, and with hands clasped and tears streaming down her cheeks, she knelt down and repeated the service for the dead over the body. When she had finished she appeared a good deal comforted, and I took the

[44] The British army did not encourage marriage for the rank and file. Only six wives per company were officially recognised and permitted to live in barracks. Other men did marry, but their wives had no formal status with the army. On campaign four to six of the recognised wives per company were chosen to accompany their husbands (Haythornthwaite, 1996a: 10). The army at Roliça was more than 15,000 fighting men strong (?150-200 companies).
[45] Liddell Hart, 1994: 101.

[46] Each regiment included a number of men termed pioneers (from the Spanish 'peone', 'labourer'). As well as firearms they carried large axes and acted as the regiment's engineers. Only pioneers were allowed to wear full beards.

[47] picket/picquet – outlying sentries. Single men or light infantry or cavalry forces.

[48] The following version is taken partly from a letter Jonathan wrote soon after the battle (Verner, 1912: 160-161) and partly from *Rough Sketches* pp. 50-52. We have interleaved the two.

[49] These columns – dressed not in the usual dark blue of France but in thin khaki smocks as a concession to the heat (Verner, 1912:159) – were each 30 men wide and 52 deep (1560 men). Using massive columns was a popular French technique intended to induce terror in the enemy. The British deployed infantry in lines abreast only two or three deep ('the thin red line'). Wellesley favoured two. The advantage of this technique was the ability to bring all muskets to bear simultaneously on the solid French column. Only the first two or three French ranks (less than 100 men), and the flanks, could fire; the rest were unsighted, although they were also shielded from fire. On arriving in front of the enemy the French had to deploy to bring their arms to bear. Enemies were seldom statuesque during such deployments. Both sides also sent out swarms of skirmishers.

[50] 'Field Officers' – officers of the rank of Major up to Brigadier-General, who commanded in the field.

[51] The Queen's Germans, or Minorca Regiment, which had been redesignated the 97th in 1803.

opportunity of beckoning to a pioneer[46] I saw near with some other men. Together we dug a hole, and quickly buried the body. Mrs Cockayne returned with me to the company to which her husband had been attached, and laid herself down upon the heath near us, amongst other females, who were in the same distressing circumstances. The sky was her canopy, and a turf her pillow, for we had no tents with us. Poor woman. I pitied her much, but if she had been a duchess she would have fared the same."

The French, having been pushed back onto the plains beyond the mountains, held their lines until sunset then headed south. The Allies marched the following day – south-west towards Vimeiro to cover the arrival by sea on the 19th of August of an extra 4000 troops from England, including two companies of the 1/95th and battalions from two regiments whose history was to become inextricably linked to that of the Rifles: the 43rd (Monmouthshire) Light Infantry; and the 52nd (Oxfordshire) Light Infantry. While the allies were landing these reinforcements, Laborde had taken his French force to unite with those of Junot from Lisbon and of General Loison. This united French army now decided to surprise the allies at Vimeiro.

The Battle of Vimeiro

On the night of the 20th of August, Jonathan Leach's company provided part of a picket[47] of 200 riflemen in a large pine forest on the right and to the front of his brigade. Their shift was disturbed by the French advance. "Nothing occurred during the night," said Jonathan, "but about seven in the morning the enemy began to appear on some hills in our front, and shortly, some of their cavalry advanced towards the left of our army." He thought this might be a feint, but soon after[48], 'several immense columns made their appearance[49] towards the right and centre to take our guns which were in the first line. The pickets being only a handful of men by way of a look-out to prevent surprise, were ordered to check the French columns by a running fire as much as possible and to retreat firing. We remained in the wood until several men were killed and the shots flew like hail, when the Field Officer[50] of the pickets ordered us to retreat precipitately as our Artillery dared not fire a shot at the French columns (which were pressing hastily on) till we fell back. We retreated down a vineyard and up another hill before we could gain the British lines, the whole time exposed to the fire of a battalion of infantry. In the retreat the Field Officer of the picket received two wounds of which I believe he is since dead. I received a blow, how I cannot conceive, unless a stone was knocked up by the shot against my thigh, which gave me great pain for some days and made me lame. When we reached the lines, the artillery opened with most wonderful effect.

As soon as we had got clear of the front of the 97th[51], and passed round its right flank, that regiment poured in such a well-directed fire, that it staggered the resolution of the hostile column, which declined to close and measure its strength with them. About the same time the 2d battalion of the

52d, advancing through the wood, took the French in flank, and drove them before them in confusion... I gathered the few of my scattered picket which I could get together and found our companies with the 50th Regiment[52] in the thickest of it... on the left of the 97th. Here the business was beginning to assume a serious aspect... The regiments which we could see engaged were the 97th, 50th, 43d, 52d and 60th, the other part of the Army being on our left at a good distance. We had something else to do than to look for them.'

Benjamin Harris too had his eyes on the enemy[53]: 'The French came down upon us in a column. The Riflemen immediately commenced a sharp fire upon them from whatever cover they could get shelter behind, whilst our cannon played upon them from our rear... we were soon all hard at work. I saw regular lanes torn through the French ranks as they advanced. They were immediately closed up again as they marched steadily on[54]. Whenever we saw a round shot go through the mass, we raised a shout of delight. I myself was very soon hotly engaged. Loading and firing away I became enveloped in the smoke I created. Such was the cloud which hung about me from the continual fire of my comrades – the white vapour clinging to my very clothes – that for a few minutes I could see nothing but the red flash of my own piece. It is a great drawback of our present system of fighting that whilst in such a state, and unless some friendly breeze clears the space around, a soldier can know no more of his position, what is about to happen in his front, or what has happened – even amongst his own companions – than the dead lying around.

Our feeling towards the enemy on that occasion was the north side of friendly for, greatly outnumbering our skirmishers, they had been firing upon us Rifles very sharply, as though inclined to drive us off the face of the earth. That day was the first I particularly remarked the French lights[55] and grenadiers[56] who were, I think, the 70th. Our men seemed to know the grenadiers well. They were fine-looking young men with tremendous moustaches, and were wearing red shoulder-knots. As they came swarming up, they rained upon us a perfect shower of balls, which we returned quite as sharply. Whenever one of them was knocked over, our men called out: "There goes another of Boney's Invincibles!"

As usual the Rifles were pretty busy in this battle. The French, in great numbers, came steadily down upon us, and we pelted upon them a shower of leaden hail. Under any cover we could find we lay, firing one moment, and jumping up and running for it the next. When we could see before us, and we observed the cannon-balls making a lane through the enemy's columns as they advanced, we cheered and shouted like madmen. During the heat of the day, having advanced too near their force, we were rather hotly pressed by the enemy. Give and take is all fair enough, but we were getting more kicks than halfpence, as the saying is. Their balls stung us so sharply that the officer gave the word to 'fire and retire'. Doubtless,

[52] 50th (West Kent) Regt.
[53] Harris relates two stories about the beginning of the battle: one in which he is mending Jonathan's boots when the French start a cannonade, and another in which Jonathan calls him back from an attack on a windmill in case he - as the company's leatherworker - is killed and leaves no-one to repair their shoes. Both events may have occurred but they do not fit easily with the other accounts of the positions of Jonathan Leach and his company at the beginning of this battle. Harris's memoirs are notorious for their disjointed chronology (Oman, 1986: 23; Hathaway, 1996: 11-12) and it is not certain these events occured at this time. They are omitted here.
[54] Leach commented, "It is but justice to our opponents to admit, that no troops could have advanced with greater determination and valour to the attack, or have sustained with greater courage the deadly fire to which they were exposed."
[55] Light infantry (In the British army light infantrymen could be so designated from being members of light infantry regiments – such as the 43rd or 52nd – or from being a member of a light company formed within a standard regiment).
[56] Heavy infantry (In the British army each standard regiment had one light company and one heavy company of so-called 'grenadiers', usually the regiment's largest men. The remaining companies were simply called 'battalion companies').

many got a leaden messenger as they did so, thus saving them the unpleasant necessity of retracing their ground... In the main body, immediately to our rear, were the 52nd (second battalion), the 50th, the 43rd (second battalion), and a German corps, whose number I do not remember[57], besides several other regiments, and the whole line seemed annoyed and angered at seeing the Rifles outnumbered by the Invincibles. As we fell back 'firing and retiring' – galling them handsomely as we did so – our men cried out, as if with one voice, to charge. "Damn them!" they roared. "Charge! Charge!" But General Fane restrained their impetuosity. He desired them to stand fast, and keep their ground. "Don't be too eager, men," he said, as coolly as if we were on a drill-parade in Old England, "I don't want you to advance just yet"... The next minute he gave the word to charge, and down came the whole line through a tremendous fire of cannon and musketry. As they came up with us, we sprang to our feet, gave one hearty cheer, and charged along with them, treading over our own dead and wounded, who lay in the front. Dreadful was the slaughter as we rushed onwards."

Jonathan Leach was impressed by this charge when it finally came[58]: 'Some masses of infantry, preceded by a swarm of light troops, were advancing with great resolution, and with loud cries of "Vive l'Empereur!" "En avant!" &c. against the hill on which our brigade was posted. In spite of the deadly fire which several hundred riflemen kept up on them, they continued to press forward with great determination, until the old 50th regiment received them with a destructive volley, following it instantly with a most brilliant and decisive charge with the bayonet, which broke and sent back, in utter dismay and confusion, this column, which a short time before was all confidence and exultation... The road by which this column moved on to the attack was choked with killed and wounded, the greater part of whom lay in a small compass.'

In the French lines one infantry company had suffered badly at the hands of the Rifles. The Captain had been ordered to advance and, "skirmish against some of these in green. Grasshoppers I call them; you call them Riflemen. They were behind every bush and stone and soon made sad havoc among my men, killing all the officers of my company, and wounding myself without being able to do them any injury. This drove me to distraction. In a little time the British line advanced. I was knocked down, bayoneted, and should have been put to death upon the spot if an English officer had not saved me.[59]"

The battle was over by noon with the French withdrawing south towards the passes that guarded the route to Lisbon. During the fighting the British had been joined by Lieutenant-General Sir Harry Burrard[60], a General with seniority over Wellesley, who had been sent from England to take command of the allied force. He allowed Wellesley to command until the French retreat then, much to Wellesley's disgust (the allies still had 9000 fresh troops in reserve), he emphatically forbade any pursuit.

[57] Hathaway (1996: 178) reports this as the King's German Legion 2nd Light Battalion, although the 97th seems a probable candidate.
[58] *Rough Sketches* pp. 51-52.
[59] Quoted in Verner (1986: 102) from a story told to Second-Lieutenant George Simmons of the 95th by the English wife of an English merchant in Lisbon who knew the French officer. He died from his wounds a few days after giving the above account.
[60] Harry Burrard (1755-1813).

After the battle

All the Rifles' casualties at Vimeiro (37 killed; 47 wounded) were from the four companies of the 2nd battalion. In total the allies lost 135 men killed and 534 wounded. The French lost 1800 men and Jonathan Leach noted barely half the allied troops had been engaged, but all the French.

As Benjamin Harris and the rest of the survivors of Jonathan's company lay on the battlefield where they had ended the morning, they saw Major Robert Travers – the Field Officer commanding the four companies of the 2nd battalion and Jonathan Leach's direct superior – galloping back and forth across the field.

"He was a tight hand," said Harris of Travers many years later, "but a soldier prefers that to a slovenly officer. During the day I had observed him more than once, apparently in the highest spirits, spurring here and there keeping the men well up. He could not have enjoyed himself more if he had been at a horse-race, or following a good pack of hounds. And now, just as busy as before the firing had ceased, here he was plunging along, riding hither and thither, digging the spurs into his horse's flanks and avoiding, with some little difficulty, the dead and dying which were strewed about. The major was never a very good-looking man, being hard-featured and thin – a hatchet-faced man as we used to say – but he was a regular good 'un, a real English soldier, and that's better than if he had been the handsomest ladies' man in the army. But now he disclosed what I believe none of us knew before, namely that his head was bald as a coot's, and that up to the present time he had covered the nakedness of his nob with a flowing Caxon[61] which, during the heat of the action, had somehow been dislodged and was lost. "A guinea," he kept crying as he rode, "to any man who will find my wig!" Notwithstanding the sight of the wounded and dead around them, the men burst into shouts of laughter, and 'a guinea to any man who will find my wig', was the saying amongst us long after the affair."

A truce

After less than a week of fighting, Junot proposed a truce to discuss terms with the allies, now commanded by Lieutenant-General Sir Hew Dalrymple[62] who had arrived to supersede Burrard the day after Burrard had superseded Wellesley. This 'musical chairs' in the British command did not reflect any lack of confidence in Wellesley; it was part of a ploy to prevent Lieutenant-General Sir John Moore[63] taking command in the Peninsula. Moore was currently out of favour with the British government, being a sometimes difficult personality unsympathetic to the government's politics. At this time he was about to arrive in Portugal after an abortive mission to support Sweden. Moore had greater seniority than Wellesley – having been a Lieutenant-General for longer – and would have become

[61] A slang expression for a wig (usually used of an old weather-beaten wig but apparently not here or the men would have noticed before this).
[62] Sir Hew Whiteford ('Dowager') Dalrymple (1750-1830).
[63] Lieutenant-General Sir John Moore (1761-1809).

allied commander on his arrival. To prevent this the British government despatched the even more senior Lieutenant-Generals Burrard, from Britain, and Dalrymple, Lieutenant-Governor of Gibraltar. This had serious consequences for the ensuing negotiations. Dalrymple had never commanded war operations in Europe and had no stomach for a fight. Wellesley thought both Burrard and Dalrymple were 'old women[64]' and Moore later wrote in his diary, "Sir Hew Dalrymple was confused and incapable beyond any man I ever saw head an army[65]"!

After a week of negotiations it was agreed the French would leave Portugal, with all arms and property, and be transported from Lisbon to Bordeaux in British ships. This treaty, the 'Convention of Cintra' [Sintra], was ratified on the 31st of August 1808 and was greeted with incredulity and outrage in Britain. The offending articles were:

II. The French Troops shall evacuate Portugal with their arms and baggage; they shall not be considered as prisoners of war, and, on their arrival in France, they shall be at liberty to serve.
III. The English Government shall furnish the means of conveyance for the French Army, which shall be disembarked in any of the ports of France between Rochfort, and l'Orient, inclusively.
IV. The French Army shall carry with it, all its artillery of French calibre, with the horses belonging to it, and the tumbrils[66] supplied with sixty rounds per gun...
V.   The French Army shall carry with it all its equipments, and all that is comprehended under the name of property of the army; that is to say, its military chest[67], and carriages attached to the Field Commissariat, and Field Hospitals, or shall be allowed to dispose of such part of the same, on its account, as the Commander-in-chief may judge it unnecessary to embark. In like manner, all individuals of the army shall be at liberty to dispose of their private property, of every description, with full security, hereafter, for the purchasers.

These terms, allowing the French to keep any booty plundered in Portugal, or to sell their ill-gotten gains; allowing them to return to fight British troops again in the Peninsula (as indeed appears to have happened); allowing the British tax-payer to pay their transport costs; and depriving the British soldiers who had won the victories of any financial gain; pleased only the French. Dalrymple, Burrard and Wellesley were recalled to London to face a Court of Enquiry. Command in the Peninsula passed to Moore who, despite the British government's reticence, was a competent field commander who a few years before had laid the foundation of British light infantry training. In London the Court conveyed to Dalrymple the King's displeasure both at the armistice and at the Convention. Although the Court ultimately approved the terms (by a majority verdict) public opinion still

[64] Bamford & Wellington (1950) **1**: 233.
[65] 2nd October 1808 (see Maurice, 1904).
[66] Tumbril / Tumbrel – a small covered cart for carrying ammunition, tools etc.
[67] i.e. its money.

ran high. Dalrymple was eventually removed from his position as Lieutenant-Governor of Gibraltar, and Burrard never again held an active command. The junior General, Wellesley, who admitted signing the treaty but said he did so without taking any responsibility for the contents, effectively escaped without censure. Although attacked in some quarters, the public saw him as a soldier just trying to do his duty, as shown by the lyrics of a popular ditty of the time[68]:

> *Sir Arthur and Sir Harry, Sir Harry and Sir Hew*
> *Sir Arthur was a fighting cock*
> *But for the other two:*
> *Sing! Doodle, Doodle, Doodle, and Cock-a-Doodle Do!*

Back in August 1808, when the ink was still wet at Sintra, the French army withdrew into Lisbon to await embarkation while the allied army moved slowly towards the capital, arriving on the outskirts on the 10th of September. With other troops the four companies of the 2/95th camped in a pleasure park, the Campo Grande, in the Lisbon suburbs. The French troops were camped in the main square in the heart of the city.

This arrangement probably benefited the allies. A description of Lisbon published several years earlier did not paint a particularly wholesome picture:

'It is built on seven steep hills; the streets are ill paved, and so filthy, that strangers are almost poisoned with the bad smells: every thing is thrown into the street, the refuse of the kitchens, and even dead animals, are left to rot there... The houses are generally two or three stories high, with no other chimney but that of the kitchin: they are built of a kind of coarse marble, with iron balconies, and wooden lattices, painted green, reaching to the ground floor... The great square is surrounded by most of the public buildings; in its centre stands a fine statue of the late king on horseback. The dirt and darkness of the old Moorish part of the town are more intolerable than any place I have ever seen. The houses project at top, and almost exclude the light. Besides the nastiness of the streets, the crowds of loathsome beggars render walking quite disagreeable.[69]'

Lisbon

Benjamin Harris was lying in his tent several days after their arrival when, "Captain Leach and Lieutenant Cox[70] entered and desired me to rise and follow them. We went towards the town and wandered about the streets for some time. There were no other Englishmen in the town that I could see, and I believe we were the first men to enter Lisbon after the arrival of our army without its walls.

Both officers were good-looking men, and cut a dash in the streets of Lisbon in their Rifle uniform, with the pelisse[71] hanging from one shoulder, and with the hessian-boots[72] that were then worn. I thought we caused quite a sensation: there were glances from the windows from black-eyed lasses as we passed, and sulky scowls from the French sentinels.

[68] Verner, 1912: 170.
[69] Represented in Wakefield (1802: 352-353). For a more sympathetic view of Lisbon at this time see Sherer (1996: 2-24).
[70] William Cox.
[71] A very short fur-trimmed jacket worn by officers in bad weather. Was often worn open, slung over the left shoulder like a short cloak.
[72] High leather boots with a tassel at the top (Hessian = pertaining to Hesse).

A Rifles' officer in dress uniform, ca 1811 (Dark green with a scarlet waist sash and black Hessian boots).

We spent some little time looking about us, then the officers spied an hotel which we entered. They went upstairs, while I went into a sort of taproom below. There I found myself in the midst of a large assemblage of French soldiers. Many were wounded; some had their arms hanging in scarfs, and others were bandaged about the head and face. In short, half of them appeared to carry tokens of our bullets of a few days before[73].

Although my appearance caused rather a sensation, they were inclined to be civil to me. Three of four rose from their seats, and with all the swagger of Frenchmen, strutted up and offered to drink with me. I was young then and full of the natural animosity against the enemy so prevalent with John Bull[74]. I hated the French with a deadly hatred and I refused to drink with them. Showing by my discourteous manner the feelings I entertained, they turned off, with a '*Sacré!*' and '*Bah!*'. Re-seating themselves, they all commenced talking at an amazing rate, no man listening to his fellow.

I could not comprehend a word of the language they uttered, but I could make out that I was the subject of the noise around me. I had offended them, and they seemed to be working themselves up into a violent rage. There was one fellow in particular. He had an immense pair of mustachios, and his coat was loosely thrown over his shoulders, his arm being wounded and in a sling. He rose up, and attempted to harangue the company. He pointed to the pouch at my waist, which contained my bullets, then to my rifle, and then to his own wounded arm, and I began to suspect that unless I speedily removed myself from the house, I should get more than I had bargained for on entering it.

[73] Actually 3 weeks before.
[74] For the non-British reader: 'John Bull' is an imaginary character representing the English people – the English equivalent of the American 'Uncle Sam'.

Luckily, Lieutenant Cox and Captain Leach entered in search of me. At a glance they saw the state of affairs and instantly ordered me to quit the room, covering my retreat themselves. "Take care not to get amongst such a party as that again, Harris," said the captain. "You do not understand their language, but I do. They meant mischief."

We progressed through various streets, buying leather and implements for mending our shoes, when the two officers again desired me to await them in the street while they entered a shop close at hand. The day was hot and there was a wine-house directly opposite me. After waiting some time, I crossed over and went in. I called for a cup of wine and again found myself in the midst of a large group of French soldiers. Once more, I was an object of curiosity and dislike. Regardless of the clamour my intrusions had again called forth, I paid for my wine and drank it.

The host seemed to understand his guests better than I did. He anticipated mischief and tried in vain to make me understand him. Suddenly, he jumped from behind his bar, seized me by the shoulder, and without ceremony thrust me into the street. There I found the two officers who, uneasy at my disappearance, had been looking anxiously for me. I excused myself by pleading the heat of the day, and an anxiety to taste the good wines of Lisbon. Together, and with our purchases, we left the town and reached the camp.[75]"

William Cox wrote in his journal, 'On 13 September I entered Lisbon for the first time. The French Army was still in the Square... they appeared much annoyed at their recent discomfiture.[76]'

As the two armies rested in Lisbon while the transport ships were prepared, more allied troops entered the city and increasing contact between the two sides softened attitudes. Jonathan was able to write later that, "The best possible understanding existed between the soldiers of the two armies, who were to be seen drinking, carousing, shaking hands, and walking arm in arm about Lisbon."

In accordance with the infamous Convention the French duly left, to the disgust of many, "with bands playing, colours flying, and bayonets fixed, with all the honours of war" as rifleman Bill Green of the 1st battalion described it[77]. Of the attitudes of the local population to the departure of the French, Jonathan tells us, "when the embarkation was completed, and the national flag of Portugal once again waved on the citadel and forts in place of the tri-coloured, there was such a combination of *vivas*, sky-rockets, ringing of bells, singing, dancing, screeching, crying, laughing, old and young embracing in the streets, added to the curses and execrations uttered by the populace against their late masters, as must render every attempt at description hopeless."

With the French gone, the Rifles marched out of Lisbon on the 15th of October as part of an allied force headed for northern Spain to challenge Marshal Soult[78], who had an army of 17,000 near Sahagún, but they marched without Jonathan Leach who was ill again. He reported that while at Lisbon:

[75] Hathaway, 1996: 72-74.
[76] Verner, 1912: 173.
[77] Teague & Teague, 1975: 12 [William ('Bill') Green, from Lutterworth (1784-1881). Later wrote his memoirs. His manuscript was entitled *A brief Outline of the Travels and Adventures of William Green (late Rifle Brigade) during a Period of ten Years in the British Service.*].
[78] Maréchal 'Nicolas' Jean de Dieu Soult, Duc de Dalmatie (1769-1851).

Rifleman (1810) and Captain (1811) of the 95th Rifles. Officers' uniforms were based on an official pattern but the actual appearance varied with the whims of the individual and his tailor. Officers' jackets in particular could be more or less ornate, with braid patterning on the surface. As with other Light Infantry, Rifles' officers wore a scarlet waist sash. The tall caps are a 'shako' pattern and the peak on that of officers could be folded up (as here). The Captain illustrated (Captain E. Kent) is in campaign clothing with more durable trousers than the skin-tight leggings of the dress uniform. The uniforms here appear new and the rifleman's seems to be a good fit. Uniforms for the rank and file were not tailored and were so dark they were almost black, but as the dye was not fast they soon faded to a lighter green. Campaigning quickly destroyed the men's pristine appearance. Clothes became shredded and heavily patched with any cloth available, although pride was taken in keeping the jacket as close to the original colour as possible. The shako could become grotesquely misshapen and some men wore forage caps unless otherwise required. Despite attention from the company's leatherworkers, shoes eventually fell to pieces.

"The army began to feel the effects to which all troops are liable at the close of a burning summer's campaign, in a climate to which they are not seasoned. Fevers and agues were extremely prevalent, and I was one of the many so attacked, which confined me to my bed many weeks, and reduced me to a mere skeleton; so that it was more than probable I should find my grave in Lisbon. The intolerable stench of the small fish called Sardinias, frying in villanously bad oil under the windows of the hotel where I lingered some weeks in a sad plight, called forth maledictions on the miscreants so employed which need not be committed to paper, but which will be fully understood by those whose olfactory nerves have been put to a similar test, by inhaling that detestable odour whilst on the bed of sickness."

Jonathan may have been seriously ill, but that illness saved him from the fate of his company, which, unbeknown to them, was about to be drawn into the disastrous, albeit successful, 'Retreat to Corunna'. Moore marched the allies to Sahagún – sometimes covering more than 60 km in a day – where they were joined by another 10,000 men, bringing their strength up to about 25,000. However, it was discovered Napoleon had entered Spain with more than 250,000 troops and was leading 80,000 himself to intercept them. The allied force began a rapid retreat west to the Spanish ports of Coruña and Vigo for evacuation, marching more than 300 km through the harsh winter weather with Napoleon and Soult in pursuit. The companies of the 2/95th were in the infantry rearguard for the force retreating to Vigo; the companies of the 1st battalion performed the same function for the flight to Coruña. After bitter fighting on the 16th of January at Coruña, in which the French were blocked and Moore was killed, the evacuations were successful, but the forced march was a bitter trial for the troops, many of whom fell along the way.

Plymouth received some of the evacuated men but after their ordeal disease gripped the survivors; 1000 soldiers and 3000 townspeople were killed by a virulent fever[79].

The 2/95th had disembarked at Portsmouth and made their way to Kent for the winter. The 1st battalion went to Colchester. On their arrival back in England Jonathan's company, which had originally paraded nearly 100 rank and file[80], now paraded 3, the rest were missing in action or were too sick to attend roll-call. Few companies paraded more than 10 or 12 men. The 900 riflemen of the 2nd battalion had been reduced to 300 sickly invalids; 44 men were still unaccounted for.

[79] Gill, 1979: 97.
[80] i.e. soldiers other than non-commissioned officers (NCOs) and commissioned officers.

— 3 —

Back to war

Nobody can tell the difficulties I had to encounter in Spain.
Every one was raw—I had to teach them all their business,
down to the most trifling details, and they sent me out such
people sometimes.

Arthur Wellesley[1]

[1] Wellington, 1956: 19.
Wellesley was discussing his
senior officers [We have
changed Chad's careless
punctuation]
[2] And all the names of the
men missing in Spain were
initially added to the roll of
the 3rd battalion in case they
later made their way back to
England.
[3] Lieutenant Dudley St
Ledger Hill (1770-1851).
[4] Captain John B. Hart, the
new company Captain for Nº
4 Company, 2/95th.
[5] Reading between the lines:
it is possible Jonathan Leach
appreciated the usefulness of
Harris as a leatherworker and
had supported him within
the company. Harris would
rather transfer with his
patron than lose any benefits.
It could also be this same
usefulness that led Hill to
suggest the 2nd battalion
keep him.

In the Spring of 1809, following the losses of the retreats to Coruña and Vigo, the Rifles held a recruiting drive among the militia regiments. The reputation of the 95th was already so elevated that 1100 volunteers were obtained in three days and a swift order was issued by the Commander-in-Chief to stop recruiting. The success led to the formation of a new 3rd battalion. In parallel with the recruitment the regiment was reorganised. The shortfall of men in the 1st battalion was made up by transfers from the 2nd and 3rd[2]. There were also several transfers of officers and Jonathan Leach, now convalesced and back from Lisbon, was promoted – in status but not rank, he remained a Captain – to a position in the 1st battalion commanding Nº 2 Company. Lieutenant William Cox, with whom he had entered Lisbon, was also transferred to the 1st battalion, but not rifleman Benjamin Harris, although he did try:

"I felt too the loss of my old captain, whom I loved and respected, and who had just left the second battalion to be promoted in the first. When I heard of this, I stepped from the ranks and offered to exchange too, but Lieutenant Hill[3], who was present, hinted to Captain Hart[4], my new commanding officer, that if he let me go he might repent of it. My character had been so good in the former campaign that Captain Hart was persuaded to keep me, and I accordingly remained in the second battalion[5]".

Providence was smiling on Jonathan Leach. Having just missed the retreat to Corunna (albeit from a sick-bed), his transfer saved him from the disastrous Walcheren campaign to the Netherlands on which five companies of the 2nd battalion, including his, were now despatched. Within four weeks of landing one quarter of the 44,000 men of this 'Grand Expedition' (as the press called it) was stricken by disease and the campaign had to be abandoned. In all, 4000 men were to die and 12,000 were to be incapacitated. The illness had begun within days of coming ashore and at one time sickness was spreading through the troops at the rate of 1500 new cases each day. In the 2/95th alone 20 riflemen a day were succumbing and by the end of the first month 700 out of the 1000 men who left Kent were in hospital or otherwise unfit for duty[6]. The recurring *Walcheren Fever*, now believed to be malaria (compounded at the time with dysentery, typhus and typhoid in the overcrowded conditions of barracks, hospitals and ships), would cause serious health problems for the British army for years to come.

Return to Lisbon

Leaving the 2nd battalion to their miserable fate, on 25th of May 1809 the 1st battalion with Jonathan Leach left Dover for Portugal in three transport ships[7], escorted by the sloop-of-war *Kangaroo* and the frigate *La Nymphe*. This time the women, except one[8], stayed in England. In the Peninsula Sir Arthur Wellesley was expelling the final French units from northern Portugal and was planning to move against French forces occupying Spain. The 1/95th, and other regiments, were to reinforce the troops already there – if they could find their way out of the English Channel.

Leach: "In consequence of adverse winds, we were detained between St Helen's, Spithead, Ryde, Cowes, and Yarmouth in the Isle of Wight, until the 18th of June, during which we contrived to kill time by various excursions to Portsmouth, Ryde, Newport, Carisbrook Castle, Yarmouth, and Leamington. [N.B. We all agreed that the women of the Isle of Wight were particularly handsome.]

On the 18th of June we passed the Needles[9] with a fresh breeze; and the order of the day on board our transport was, to bombard the sea-fowl which swarm at this season on the rocks[10]. Rifles and fowling pieces, with ball, slugs, and swan-shot[11], were brought into full play on this occasion.

On the 19th, we were abundantly supplied with fish by the Torbay fishermen; and, moreover, opened another heavy and destructive fire on such unfortunate gulls and other sea-birds as ventured within reach."

They sailed south and reached Lisbon on the 28th of June where it was decided to send the men upriver in boats for the first 55 km, then march them to Santarém. The officers' animals would travel overland. At this time Jonathan had with him two horses, a mule and a donkey[12].

"About midnight on the 2d of July, the tide serving to take us up the river, we were put into flat-bottomed boats and launches, and the tedious operation of towing us against the current commenced. After twenty-four hours spent in this bewitching manner, every man's legs terribly cramped by being crammed so tight into the boat, we reached Vallada, near which place we bivouacked on the bank of the river. I never entertained the smallest doubt that all the frogs in the Peninsula had assembled, by common consent on this occasion, to welcome us to Portugal; for such an eternal croaking I never heard before or since."

[6] Kincaid, 1981: 192-193.

[7] The *Malabar, Fortune* and *Laurel.*

[8] The reason for the sole exception was not clear, even then. Lieutenant John Kincaid of the 95th (see below) said, "By what particular virtues she had attained such a dignified position among them, I never clearly made out, further than she had arrived at years of discretion, was what is commonly called a useful woman, and had seen some service." (Hathaway, 1997: 27).

[9] The *Needles*: a line of free-standing pillars of rock emerging from the sea at the west end of the Isle of Wight, southern England.

[10] Target practice from a moving ship against moving targets was useful marksmanship experience.

[11] Ball, slugs and swan-shot are decreasing sizes of projectile.

[12] *Rough Sketches*, p. 99. As an officer he would presumably have had a groom to look after the animals and a servant (a rifleman) to attend to his personal needs. The rifleman would have to be available for other military duties – especially combat – but any groom may have been recruited locally as was common (Oman, 1986: 269-272).

The Light Brigade

The troops that landed at Valada were the Peninsula War's famed Light Brigade of infantry, comprising the 1/95th[13], the 43rd Light Infantry and the 1st battalion of the 52nd Light Infantry.

The officers of these regiments allegedly conformed to their own regimental character. Captain J.H. Cooke of the 43rd reported: "The 43rd were a gay set—the dandies of the Army; the great encouragers of dramatic performances, dinner parties and balls of which their headquarters was the pivot. The 52nd were highly gentlemanly men of a steady aspect; they mixed little with other corps, but attended the theatricals of the 43rd with circumspect good humour, and now and then relaxed, but were soon again the 52nd. The Rifle Corps were skirmishers in every sense of the word; a sort of wild sportsmen, and up to every description of fun and good humour. Nothing came amiss: the very trees responded to their merriment, and scraps of their sarcastic rhymes passed current through all the camps and bivouacs.[14]"

The Light Brigade's commander was Brigadier-General Robert 'Black Bob' Craufurd[15], an experienced, if sometimes harsh, commander of riflemen ('Black' was said to refer to his moods). During the Corunna Campaign he had commanded the troops withdrawing through Vigo. It is reported that when he returned to the Peninsula to command the Light Brigade again he told them, "When I commanded you before, I knew full well that you disliked me, for you thought me severe. This time I am glad to find there is a change in yourselves[16]." As we saw in the Introduction, Jonathan Leach was not always appreciative of Craufurd. Wellesley too found him "a dissatisfied, troublesome man" who indulged in petty intrigues and tried to undermine Wellesley's authority with his senior officers[17].

Harris, on the other hand said, "I shall never forget Craufurd if I live to be a hundred years. He was in everything a soldier." Perhaps the person who comes closest to a fair assessment is Lieutenant John Kincaid of the 95th[18] when he says of Craufurd, "He had neither judgment, temper, nor discretion to fit him for a chief, and as a subordinate he required to be held with a tight rein, but his talents as a general of division were nevertheless of the first order. He received the three British regiments under his command, finished by the hands of a master in the art, Sir John Moore, and, as regiments, they were faultless; but to Craufurd belonged the chief merit of making them the war brigade which they became, alike the admiration of their friends and foes.[19]"

Jonathan Leach certainly admired this Light Brigade. After the previous year's action it contained few novices. He observed proudly in 1831, "unprejudiced persons, and those neither directly nor indirectly connected with it, have pronounced it the finest and most splendid brigade that ever took the field[20]. I will venture to go so far as to assert, that if it has been *equalled*, it has never been *surpassed*, in any army, whether the materials

[13] 1100 men; 10 companies.
[14] Verner, 1919: 102-103.
[15] Robert Craufurd (1764-1812). 'Crawford' of some authors, including Jonathan. Brother of Sir Charles Gregan Craufurd MP who had married the Dowager Duchess of Newcastle.
[16] Reported by Benjamin Harris, who must have heard this from someone else.
[17] Pool, 1967: 96-97.
[18] John Kincaid (1787-1862). Born Dalbeath, Falkirk, Scotland in January 1787 (Dalton, 1971: 200 note 15). Joined the Rifles in 1809 from the militia. Kincaid says he left school under the influence of one of his guardians, an uncle, his father having died young (1981: 178-179). He was apparently the son of John Kincaid (ca 1761-1794) and Margaret Kincaid (née Gaff) (ca 1759-1844) and would have had an elder brother Thomas (ca 1785-1848), younger brothers Alexander (ca 1788-1806) and Charles (1793-1866), and a sister Margaret (1792-1863). The guardian could have been one of his father's brothers, Alexander (1764-1854) or Thomas (born 1766), or a brother of his mother (*This Kincaid family information is from the world-wide website of Tom Paterson, listing the ancestors of Dave Kincaid*).
[19] Kincaid, 1981: 193.
[20] Presumably he means infantry brigade. It would be unkind to include cavalry in this remark, thereby not comparing like with like.

of which it was composed, its fine appointments and arms, its *esprit du corps*, its style of marching and manœuvring, and, in short, every requisite for a light brigade, be considered. Each regiment was nearly eleven hundred strong; there were many hundreds in each battalion to whom the smell of *gunpowder in earnest* was no novelty; for they had served with Nelson at Copenhagen[21], with Auchmuty[22] at Monte Video[23], with Whitelock[24] in the ill-fated and bloody business at Buenos Ayres[25], with Sir A. Wellesley at Roleia[26] and Vimeira, and with the ever-to-be-lamented Sir John Moore at Corunna[27]. If, therefore, they were not veterans in age, they had at least some claim to the appellation from their services."

Robert Craufurd

Having landed at Valada, the Light Brigade marched upriver to Santarém to await the arrival of their baggage. Jonathan, like any young man in uniform with time on his hands – he was now 25 – sought out Santarém's distractions.

"Like all towns of any size in Portugal, it is full of churches and convents. With the fair inmates of the latter we had a deal of chit-chat, although the close iron gratings which separated us from our inamoratas obscured them in great measure from view. That they were all blessed with sparkling black eyes, I am ready to swear; the rest was left to the imagination. By means of the *whirligig* concern in which various matters find their way out of and into the convent, these fair ladies presented us with preserved fruits, nose-gays, and all sorts of fine things; in return for which, certain little notes or love-letters, written in villanously bad Portuguese, were transmitted by the same mode of conveyance to them. They appeared much interested as to the result of the campaign in which we were about to take a part; and two of them, who were heartily tired of their unnatural prison, declared to myself and a brother officer, that they were ready and willing to make their escape, with our assistance, and to share our fortunes in the "tented field." When one considers that by so doing they would have brought down on them the vengeance of monks, friars, padres, and mother-abbesses, and that these black-eyed damsels must have calculated on being buried alive, or broiled on a gridiron, had they been detected in such an adventure, we must admit that they were heroines of the first class."

To Spain

After collecting their baggage at Santarém the Light Brigade set off to rendezvous with the main force under Wellesley, which was at Talavera de la Reina. The Spanish army of General Cuesta[28], co-ordinating with Wellesley, was tracking a French army, but trouble was brewing. Wellesley was convinced the French were planning a major engagement.

Craufurd decided the Light Brigade should march into the interior as regiments, not one column. Marching mainly by night to avoid the burning sun of the Spanish summer, they left Santarém at midnight on the 7th of July. Each night-march lasted at least 8 hours and the men rested in their bivouacs during the day. Jonathan was not suited to a nocturnal lifestyle:

[21] 2nd April 1801.
[22] Sir Samuel Auchmuty (1756-1822). Commanded British troops in South America.
[23] 9th February 1807. Montevideo was captured by a night assault.
[24] Lieutenant-General John Whitelocke (1757-1833). Replaced Auchmuty as commander of British forces in South America.
[25] In July 1807. A British attack on Buenos Aires was a humiliating failure. Whitelocke was made the scapegoat, court-martialled and cashiered. It is said Craufurd argued forcefully to have him shot.
[26] Roliça.
[27] 16th January 1808.
[28] General Gregorio Garcia de la Cuesta (1740-1812). He retired on 12 August 1809 following a stroke.

"I was, unfortunately, one of those restless beings who, after a night spent in marching, could not sleep in the bivouac during the day; and many a time have I envied the happy fellows who lay down like dogs, under a cork-tree, and slept most soundly, until the rations of tough beef (perhaps killed only a few hours before), boiled into an *omnium gatherum*, with an onion or two, some rice, and a mouldy ship biscuit, were pronounced in a fit state for the table; the said dinner-table being neither more nor less than the turf at the foot of a tree, with a soldier's knapsack by way of camp-chair; a japanned half-pint tin cup[29] stood for wine glass, which, with a pocket-knife, fork, and spoon, and a tin plate, constituted the whole of our dinner service. It being utterly impracticable to have a regimental mess whilst in the field, the officers of each company formed a little mess of their own. Candlesticks not being the fashion of the day, we substituted an empty bottle in their place; and a most bandit-like appearance the interior of our tents presented after dark, filled generally with such clouds of smoke from our cigars, that I have often since wondered we were not smothered in our sleep from such an atmosphere, in which we reposed rolled up in our cloaks."

The battalion was halted just outside Abrantes for a day and it was here Craufurd issued a legion of 'Standing Orders' for the regulating of marches, and earned himself Jonathan's covert damnation in that day's journal entry.

"10 July. Halted at Abrantes. Bathed in Tagus. A soldier of the 95th Regt. was drowned when bathing this morning. Brigadier General Robert Crawford (damn him) issued this day to the Light Brigade an immensity of the most *tyrannical* and *oppressive standing orders* that were ever compiled by a British officer.[30]"

John Kincaid has left us a glimpse of some of these orders when he tells us no-one on a march was permitted to leave the line of march to cross a stream via a plank if the stream could be forded in a straight line (even if the water was waist-deep), nor was anyone to stop to drink at a stream without orders to do so – imbibers risked a flogging. Troops filtering around boggy or marshy ground similarly faced harsh retribution. The Brigade was to march to its objective, it was not to meander. Speaking zoologically, Kincaid says Craufurd, "borrowed a leaf from the history of the land crabs, and suffered neither mire nor water to disturb the order of his march with impunity.[31]"

It was these minutiæ (and many more on: duties of officers and men in camp; duties of officers and men in quarters; conduct of foraging parties; conduct of fatigue parties; methods of inspection; regulations for the issue of rations; how to make reports; etc. etc. etc.) that clogged the tolerance of company commanders like Jonathan Leach, and the subsequent rigour with which Craufurd enforced these orders made him deeply unpopular within the Brigade. However, to be fair, at the time Craufurd penned these

[29] The troops called these cups 'black jacks.'
[30] Quoted in Verner (1919: 69) [Verner's 'Craufurd' has been amended to the more probable 'Crawford' used by Jonathan Leach in his published work]
[31] Kincaid, 1981: 194-195.

instructions there were few written directions governing the regulation of light troops on a march. As the Light Brigade became familiar with Craufurd's practices, they began to see the value of his philosophy, and after the first campaign the grumbling, and the need for punishments, ceased. Later, Craufurd's Standing Orders would acquire a world-wide reputation, become the model for many armies, and be translated into several languages.

Kincaid felt the problem was that Craufurd enforced his orders with unnecessary severity at the outset and it was a long time before anyone could shake off the resultant feeling of oppression. However, once in place the regime ran "like clockwork", helped by the recognition that Craufurd was a commander who was prepared to involve himself personally in the pursuit of his men's welfare[32].

On the night of the 10th of July, with the value of the new orders not yet appreciated, and with Craufurd's notoriety unmitigated, the Brigade marched from Abrantes to Castelo Branco where they halted for another two days to allow the 43rd and 52nd to join them. Castelo Branco was, "a place of considerable size, but, like the generality of Portuguese towns, extremely dirty, with narrow streets, where tens of millions of flies were amusing themselves", according to Jonathan, who added, "We tried in vain, during our short sojourn there, to get a peep at the nuns; but, as we afterwards learnt that they were old and ugly, it ceased to be a disappointment."

The reunited Brigade now pressed on and entered Spain on the 20th of July. The following day, in a wood where they camped, Jonathan shot "a beautiful bird, the name of which I am ignorant of, never having seen one of the kind before or since. It was of the crow genus, but much smaller, and the plumage variegated. On the 23d we halted at Coria. We made a fruitless effort to see and converse with the nuns in one of the convents, who, we were assured, were young and handsome. We undoubtedly had to thank the lady-abbess for their non-appearance at their prison gates." After the halt at Coria the brigade made four gruelling day marches, reaching Navalmoral on the 27th.

Battle of Talavera

"On the evening of the 27th, vague rumours reached us at Naval Moral relative to the hostile armies. We knew nothing certain further than that Sir Arthur Wellesley and the Spanish General Cuesta had united their forces in the plains some leagues in our front; and as the French under Marshal Victor, the Duke of Belluno[33], were known to be not far distant from the allied army, a general action might be expected daily.

28th.— Before day dawned we were off again, and ere long, something like a distant cannonade was heard. Our suspense and anxiety can easily be imagined, aware as we were of the proximity of the hostile armies to each other. We arrived at Orapeza at mid-day, where General Crawford considered a short halt indispensably necessary. He then directed the commanding officers of regiments to select and leave at Orapeza such men

[32] A widely reported story was the case where he threatened to throw a Commissary in the guard-house if his troops were not supplied with their ration of bread at the allotted time. The Commissary, unable to meet Craufurd's demand, took his problem to Wellesley, who told him simply, "I would recommend you to find the bread, for if he said so, he'll do it!" (Kincaid, 1981: 194)

[33] Maréchal Claude Victor-Perrin Victor, Duc de Belluno (1764-1841). From his sunny, open manner his nickname was 'Beau-Soleil'. When being considered for a title in 1808 one of Napolean's sisters joked that he should be called 'Belle-Lune'. He was accordingly created Duc de Belluno (a province of modern Italy).

as were thought incapable of enduring the forced march which he determined to make, and not to halt until he reached the British army, which was known to be engaged in our front, as the distant but unceasing cannonade plainly announced. Having rested his brigade in this burning plain, where water was not to be procured[34], General Crawford put it in motion towards Talavera de la Reina. It may well be conceived it was a march productive of the highest degree of feverish anxiety and excitement. The one only feeling was to push forward, to throw our mite into the scale, and to lend a helping hand to our brothers in arms.

We soon met *wounded* Spanish soldiers, and Spanish soldiers *not wounded*, bending their course in a direction from the field of battle. I wish I could assert with equal truth that this retrogression was confined to our Spanish allies; but the truth must be told; and I regret to say, that stragglers from the ranks of the British army, some without a wound, were also taking a similar direction to the rear. As they passed our column they circulated all sorts and kinds of reports of a most disheartening nature: "The British army was utterly defeated, and in full retreat;" "Sir Arthur Wellesley was wounded;" and, by others, "he was killed." In short, all was suspense and uncertainty. One thing was, nevertheless, certain — that the cannonade continued without cessation.

We pressed forward until ten o'clock at night, when, having reached a pool of stagnant water near the road, in which cattle had been watered during the summer, and where they had constantly wallowed, a halt was ordered for an hour or two. Those who have never been in similar situations may be inclined to doubt my veracity when I state, that the whole brigade, officers and soldiers, rushed into this muddy water, and drank with an eagerness and avidity impossible to describe. The use of such an execrable beverage, except on extreme occasions, like the one in question, where we had been the whole day without water, under a sun as oppressive as can be experienced in Europe, might indeed be deemed extraordinary; but excessive thirst knows no law.

After a short repose on the banks of this horse-pond, we again got under weigh, and without another halt joined the British army in its position at Talavera. Here we learnt that a most sanguinary contest had taken place the day before, wherein the British army gained immortal glory, the particulars of which are generally known; and as the light brigade arrived too late to take a share in the fight, I shall not be expected to describe them."

We shall: the Battle of Talavera began on the 27th of July. Wellesley with just under 20,000 men and Cuesta with nearly 35,000 had pursued the French to their position at the town of Talavera de la Reina, on the north bank of the River Tagus[35] 100 km southwest of Madrid. A short delay in the allied advance allowed the French to fall back from Talavera on the 24th of July to unite with a French corps led by Sebastiani[36] at Torrijos to the east. Sending Cuesta after the French, Wellesley had halted most of the

[34] Clear criticism here.
[35] In Portuguese *R. Tejo*; in Spanish *R. Tajo*.
[36] Général Horace François Bastien de la Porta Sebastiani, Comte (1772-1851).

British at Talavera, sending forward only two divisions of infantry and a brigade of cavalry to keep open his communications with the Spanish. The French, now with a united force of more than 40,000 men[37], took the offensive and attacked Cuesta on the 26th. Wellesley deployed his divisions at Talavera to receive the French advance and Cuesta's army fell back and joined him on the morning of the 27th.

Wellesley deployed the Spanish in rugged entrenchments between the British to their left and the town to their right. The left of the British line rested on a small hill, 'The Medellin'. The whole allied line extended more than 3 km. When the attack came, just after dark, it was against the Medellin. The French rushed up the hill and over the top, meeting the allies rushing up the other side. In the dark the British thought the French were Spaniards and ran straight through them. By the time the fighting started the combatants were completely mixed and a furious hand-to-hand mêlée ensued. Wellesley was very nearly captured and had to leap to safety as the allied troops gave way[38]. It took a fierce counter-attack to repulse the French.

After an uneasy night with some localised actions and a good deal of 'friendly fire' on both sides in the darkness, the next French attack came at 5 a.m. The battle, later described by Wellesley as one of the most bitter conflicts he ever experienced, raged all day[39] as the French primarily assaulted the centre-left of the British line, where the ground was favourable. In late afternoon the firing and explosion of shells started a grass-fire in the tinder-dry vegetation between the armies. Many of the wounded, who could not be rescued through the hail of small arms and cannon fire, burned to death where they lay. In the evening, unable to break the allied line, the French withdrew east towards Toledo, leaving a strong rearguard on the River Alberche, just upstream from Talavera. The French had lost more than 7000 men killed and wounded, the British had lost nearly 5500, a quarter of their strength, and the Spanish 1250.

The Light Brigade reached the field early in the morning of the 29th "just soon enough to be too late" according to Second-Lieutenant George Simmons[40] of Captain Peter O'Hare's company, who described the scene they found: "The horrid sights were beyond anything I could have imagined. Thousands dead and dying in every direction, horses, men, French and English, in whole lines who had cut each other down, and, I am sorry to say, the Spaniards butchering the wounded Frenchmen at every opportunity, and stripping them naked, which gave admission to the attacks of myriads of pernicious flies and the heat of a burning sun. You may be sure everything was done on our part and the commanding officer's to put a stop to such horrid brutality and give assistance, but the ground being covered for at least five miles[41] with dead and dying, and we expecting another attack, the army was drawn up in line ready to receive the enemy.[42]"

The Light Brigade was sent forward to watch the French rearguard[43]. "Our orders," reports rifleman Bill Green, "were to take the advance post

[37] The French overall commander was Joseph Bonaparte. Under him were Victor, Sebastiani, and his Chief of Staff, Maréchal Jean-Baptiste Jourdan (1762-1833).

[38] Wilson (1927) 1: 74.

[39] Apart from a lull in the French assault in late morning when it is reported both armies ate a quick lunch on the battlefield and some French and British troops met at a stream dividing their front lines and exchanged pleasantries. Some French and British soldiers also helped each other remove the wounded during this quiet spell, which was broken by a French attack along the whole front at noon (Tucker, 1846: 90).

[40] George Simmons (1785-1858). From Beverley, Yorkshire. Originally apprenticed to a surgeon. In 1805 joined Royal South Lincolnshire Militia as an assistant surgeon. In 1809 joined the 1/95th during the recruiting drive after Corunna. He induced so many of his fellow militiamen to join the regiment that he became entitled to a commission (a widely recognised right during recruiting).

[41] 8 km.

[42] Simmons in a letter to his parents, September 1809 (Verner, 1986: 32).

[43] On its arrival the Light Brigade was attached to the British 3rd Division, which was put under Craufurd's command (Oman, 1986: 345).

amongst some olive trees near the river, on the other side of it, from the place of battle! The French artillery were all formed in parks; the infantry and cavalry covering their guns.[44]" Jonathan's company was soon engaged in heavy skirmishing[45].

To arrive at Talavera the Brigade had marched more than 70 km in 24 hours, with the aid of Sir John Moore's quick-march of three steps at the march then three steps at the run[46]. Jonathan Leach considered this: "as extraordinary a march, perhaps, as is to be found on record; particularly when it is remembered that each soldier carried from sixty to eighty rounds of ammunition, a musket or rifle, a great coat, and (if I recollect rightly) a blanket, a knapsack complete, with shoes, shirts &c. &c.; a canteen and haversack, bayonet, belts, &c. &c. Such a load, carried so great a distance, would be considered a hard day's work for a horse. The heat was intense, as every soldier who has served in the Peninsula well knows is the case in the month of July, in the heart of Spain, on its sun-burnt, arid plains. Water was scarcely to be had, and of such quality that the quadrupeds doomed to drink it need not have been envied, much less the bipeds."...

"It is not my intention to question the propriety or necessity of the light brigade having been halted two days at Santarem, one day at Abrantes, two days at Castello Branco, and one day at Coria, on its march to Talavera; certain, however, it is, that one day's rest at Santarem instead of two, and one day's rest at Castello Branco instead of two, would have brought a reinforcement of more than three thousand light troops to Sir Arthur Wellesley, before the bloody battle of the 28th; and that such an addition to his force would have been highly acceptable, particularly as he was deficient in the number of his light troops. Could General Crawford have foreseen that by those halts his brigade would have arrived a *few hours too late* at Talavera, I feel thoroughly convinced that he would have pushed on, *pêle-mêle*, without a single halt between Santarem and the field of battle."

After the Battle

After Talavera Sir Arthur Wellesley – who had escaped death twice when musket balls passed through his clothing – was elevated to the peerage as Viscount Wellington of Talavera. However, the French were on the offensive again: three new French corps were converging from the north commanded by Mortier[47], Soult and Ney[48]. Mortier entered Plasencia to the west, effectively cutting off the allies' communication with Portugal north of the Tagus. Meanwhile Wellington had Victor's corps of more than 25,000 men to his east, and the combined corps of Soult and Ney to the west. It was not safe to take his army north-east to Madrid and he could not stay where he was. There was also a questionmark over Cuesta's commitment to integrated actions. Discretion being the better part of valour, a withdrawal seemed in order to restore communication lines with the Portuguese ports. Wellington had to go south across the Tagus, but Soult and Ney controlled the road west to the crossing at Almaraz, near Plasencia.

[44] Teague & Teague, 1975: 22.
[45] Smith, 1999: 19.
[46] Teague & Teague, 1975: 21 endnote.
[47] Maréchal Adolphe Edouard Casimir Joseph Mortier, Duc de Trévise (1768-1835). His mother was English.
[48] Maréchal Michel Ney, Duc d'Elchingen (1769-1815).

In the few days after the battle while this was unfolding, the troops on the ground had problems of their own. They had not received supplies and the food for sale in Talavera was soon exhausted, despite exorbitant prices. The money in the hungry soldiers' pockets was valueless when there was nothing left to buy.

Leach: "The feelings which constant hunger produces were, however, in some degree counteracted two days after the battle, by the insufferable stench arising from the hundreds of dead bodies of men and horses still unburied. The Spaniards at length were ordered to collect the bodies in heaps and burn them; and even to the present moment I am undecided whether the horrid smell arising from those funeral piles was not more trying than that which we had previously experienced.

The 31st of July proved an ill-fated day to me. I lent my saddle-horse to a brother officer, to ride from the camp into Talavera, to purchase whatever he could lay his hands on; and, to my utter horror and dismay, I saw my friend return to the bivouac late in the afternoon, *not* on horse-back, but on foot, and with a face longer than my arm. I was soon put out of suspense by learning that a rascally Portuguese or Spanish boy, to whose care he had intrusted my charger in the town whilst he went into a shop, had disappeared with him. No Peninsula soldier need be told that this was a serious mishap. The *prad*[49] was a capital one; and the saddle, bridle, the cloak affixed to the saddle, the *valise*, containing all the articles of the toilet, a blanket under the saddle, and the various *et ceteras*, which in those days constituted the sole comfort of campaigners, were not to be replaced for love nor money on the plains of Talavera. Instead, therefore, of having a chestnut quadruped to carry me on the retreat from Talavera to the frontiers of Portugal, and having the benefit of a cloak and blanket at night in the bivouac, (our tent was thrown away, by the by, in consequence of death, by starvation and fatigue, of my baggage mule) I had the felicity to tramp it on foot from the Tagus to the Guadiana, no trifling distance either[50], and to stretch myself at the foot of a tree every night, with no covering but the sky and a green jacket."

Leaving Cuesta at Talavera to protect the wounded and deter Victor, Wellington marched his army west, hoping to push back Soult's force and cross the river at Almaraz, or force Soult to give battle. Then he learned Soult had 30,000 men, not the 18,000 he anticipated; that they were not as far to the west as he had thought; that Victor was advancing from the east; and that Cuesta had abandoned Talavera and was making his own way across the river. Wellington had to take his army over the Tagus immediately and headed for the bridge at Arzobispo, just to his south. The whole army crossed on the 5th August, with the 1/95th and some cavalry forming the rearguard. Cuesta took his Spanish army over the river that night.

To the credit of the French, when they entered Talavera they treated the wounded allies left there with the utmost compassion. Marshal Victor had the French and British wounded lodged in the same houses and ensured

[49] Slang (at that time) for a horse.
[50] He would be on foot for more than a month, covering at least 320 km, not allowing for vertical changes of terrain or weeks spent patrolling areas when camped en route.

Harry Smith

[51] Tucker (1846: 109) says Victor ordered the Spanish families on whom the wounded were billeted to serve the British wounded first.

[52] Letter: Wellington to Earl Bathurst, 11th June 1815 regarding repayment of 120 Napoleons advanced by Mortier to Dr Higgins, Deputy Inspector of Hospitals, at Talavera.

[53] With the 5/60th; the 45th; and the 88th Regiment (The Connaught Rangers).

[54] Verner, 1986: 24.

[55] Romangordo.

[56] Henry George Wakelyn Smith (28th June 1787-1860). Born Whittlesea, Cambridgeshire.

[57] Jonathan Layton. Had been a Lieutenant since the 3rd of June (Dalton, 1971: 197).

[58] Smith, 1999: 20.

[59] 'Dog days'. The hottest days of the year. The Romans called the hottest summer weeks *caniculares dies* believing the heat was caused by the Dog-Star, Sirius, rising with, and adding its heat to, the Sun.

they received the best of care[51]. Marshal Mortier even lent money to the British doctors to fund their treatment[52].

South of the Tagus Wellington's army was now vulnerable if Soult crossed the river at Almaraz while the allies were in motion, so Wellington sent an infantry Division, including the Light Brigade[53], across treacherous country to secure the south side of the bridge at Almaraz. Not knowing whether they – about 6000 infantrymen – would come face to face with Soult's army of 30,000, they scrambled over the mountain tracks. Many hundreds of men, half-starved for days, collapsed with fatigue and were left to make their own way to the crossing. After two days of 15 hour forced marches they arrived on the 6th of August to find two Spanish battalions were already watching the bridge, one arch of which was now destroyed, with no sign of the French. The British took up positions for what would be two weeks of rather unpleasant guard duty. George Simmons noted later in his journal, "This was a nasty damp place, and the exhalations from the vegetable matter which was corrupting from the heat of the sun, and the half-dried swamps that were swarming with vermin, laid the foundation of disease amongst our men.[54]"

Most of the Division was camped at a nearby village[55], but the 1/95th was kept in advance, spending their days in an olive-grove on a hill, with sentries by the bridge, and at night moving down to the bridge to sleep by their rifles among the pickets. Although English newspapers now reached the battalion from the main army at Deleitosa about 15 km to the south, sufficient food did not, primarily because the main army was starving too. Supplies were not getting through. At the bridge the men of the 95th took to gathering ears of corn from the surrounding fields and grinding them between rocks to make a kind of dough. From this practice the hill on which they spent their days became known as Dough Boy Hill. Simmons thought Starvation Hill would be more appropriate. The men found some wild honey in the neighbourhood but, in the absence of substantial support, this did nothing to help their diarrhoea.

Lieutenant Harry Smith[56], of Jonathan's company, remembers that time well, "My mess — Leach's Company (Leach, Smith, Layton[57] and Bob Beckwith) — were not as badly off as our neighbours. We had a few dollars, and as I could speak Spanish, I rode into the lines of the Spanish troops, where I could always purchase some loaves of bread at a most exorbitant price. With this and some horrid starved goats we lived tolerably for soldiers in hard times.[58]" Obviously what was tolerable to Smith was less so for Jonathan who offers the following, somewhat bitter, advice:

"if any corpulent person despairs of reducing his weight by the means usually adopted, I strongly recommend a few weeks' change of air and scene at Almaraz; taking especial good care to observe the same rules and regulations for diet; and to roast himself throughout the day at the foot of a shadeless olive-tree, in the dog days[59]. If that fails to have the desired effect, I give him up, and can prescribe nothing further."

After nearly a week at the bridge a French infantry picket appeared on the far bank and was posted overlooking the crossing. The Spanish troops immediately began an exchange of fire with the new arrivals, much to the disgust of the British officers who viewed this "popping at sentries" as most ungentlemanly. During the eight days the French and British faced each other no shots were exchanged and the officers of both sides frequently doffed their caps and saluted each other.

The British and French well understood the advantages of this relaxed arrangement, and advanced posts would typically warn each other if a forward movement was in earnest, not an exercise. Wellington himself considered the killing of a picket or capture of an advanced post to be of so little consequence that when attacking in force he often sent formal warnings to the French look-outs to get out of the way[60]. Jonathan bemoaned the fact that during the whole of the Peninsula War the Spanish never quite understood this chivalrous system and never missed an opportunity to shoot a sentry if they could. He did, however, acknowledge the Spanish grievance was greater than the British; neither the British nor the French were fighting on their own soil.

Retreat to Portugal

On the 20th of August, leaving the Spanish battalions at the crossing, the whole British Division withdrew and began a long march back to Portugal as the rearguard for the allied army. On the journey baggage animals died at the rate of dozens every day and Jonathan was left only with his donkey.

On the 27th Craufurd paraded the Light Division for a lecture on discipline and to make examples of some of his men. It again earned him Jonathan's opprobrium in his journal:

"The Division paraded at six this evening when we got volleys of *abusive* and *blasphemous* language from Brigadier-General Robert Crawford, who after flogging half a dozen men for some very *frivolous offences* committed on our late harassing marches, we were dismissed.[61]"

Jonathan Leach was not the only officer vilifying Craufurd behind his back. Despite Craufurd's excellent ideas for the management of light troops in the field, at this time his arrogance, temper, bullying, and – as above – his draconian disciplining of the men, was earning him nothing but hatred[62].

By the end of the month the Division was back over the border and on the 29th, at Castelo de Vide, were finally able to gorge themselves on food and wine. There are numerous eye-witness accounts that there was not a sober person in the Division that night after what Jonathan described as their "jollification amongst the chestnut groves." With the French far to the east he could also relax for the first time in several months.

"On the 1st of September I considered it a point of duty to keep up the good old custom of waging war against the partridges, and started for the purpose at daybreak, with one lazy old Spanish pointer, whose average

[60] Pool, 1967: 120.
[61] Quoted by Verner (1919: 80). Verner's 'Craufurd' has been changed.
[62] Verner, 1919: 80.

pace was about three miles an hour[63]. Between red-legged partridges, hares, and quails, the day's sport was not despicable. On this occasion I was very nearly minus a friend, and the king a good officer; for I made a double shot, killing my partridge, and throwing several grains of shot into my friend's regimental cap, which, for want of a more sportsmanlike head-dress, he wore on the occasion.

We moved from Castello de Vide on the 7th, and reached Portalegre the same evening, where we halted two days. It is amongst the best towns in Portugal; and we saw some tolerably fair specimens of Portuguese beauty in the convents." George Simmons must have reconnoitred different convents; he "did not find the nuns either beautiful or great devotees; they seemed to like a good joke and nonsense as well as most folks.[64]"

The army turned back towards the border and dispersed to camps along the River Guadiana. Jonathan's Division was based at Campo Maior where they stayed for three months and he was able to replace his stolen saddle-horse. At this time of year the River Guadiana became sluggish and in places shrank to stagnant pools in the deeper reaches of its floor. The people of distant provinces dreaded the area in this season, knowing it to be desperately unhealthy. The concentration of tens of thousands of weakened soldiers now exacerbated the problem. Fevers and dysentery rampaged through the army until one third were on the sick list and deaths were commonplace. Some officers, Jonathan and Harry Smith among them, indulged their passion for field-sports and attributed to this their continuing good health.

Leach: 'Except when a field-day occurred to prevent it, I was amongst the number of those who lived in the open air with gun or greyhound; and to the constant exercise I attribute having enjoyed good health, at a time when hundreds of our division were suffering from agues and fevers, and very many taken to their long homes[65]. Doctors differed as to the mode of living most likely to retain health and to prevent sickness.

The water-beverage system found but very few supporters in our corps; and, as far as my own experience enables me to speak, I should recommend, *per diem*, under similar circumstances, and on the same spot, a fair allowance of generous wine, several cigars (to prevent infectious disease), the persecution of red-legged partridges, quails, &c. &c., or a gallop with the wire-haired greyhounds of the country across the plains after the hares, which occasionally give rare sport. To put in practice the

[63] Just under 5 kph.
[64] Verner, 1986: 27.
[65] to their coffins.

Red-Legged Partridge
Alectoris rufa (Linnæus)

latter part of the prescription was found exceedingly difficult, in consequence of the starved state of our Rosinantes[66] rendering even a canter next to impossible. With some good English pointers and greyhounds, in few countries could better sport be had than in this neighbourhood. There are abundance of partridges, quails, hares, rabbits, (woodcocks and snipes in winter,) bustards on the plains, and florikins also in large flocks, plovers of various sorts; also a bird of the grouse kind, which the natives call *tarambola*; ducks, teal, and other wild fowl in the Guadiana and the Caya.

In the forest of Albuquerque, a few leagues distant, are red deer, wild boars, wolves, and foxes. To that forest we made several excursions, taking with us some of our best marksmen, and sleeping the night before in the small walled town of Ouguila[67], which is on the borders of the forest. Several fine red deer were killed, one of which, a very large stag, I was so fortunate as to bring down with a ball. Although neither wolves nor wild boars were brought to bag, we nevertheless had some shots at them. I look back on those excursions as amongst the happiest days of my life.

General Crawford directed that the regiments of his division should frequently be marched to the river Caya, about four miles[68] distant, to bathe... Whether the intention of General Crawford was, that the regiments should march to the river to bathe as fully armed and accoutred as if they were about to mount guard in some stiff-starched garrison, I cannot say; but I know that every corps did harness and march forth to the river in that form, except our own. Colonel Beckwith[69], on the contrary, always ordered our men, on these occasions, to take with them neither arms, accoutrements, knapsacks, nor any one thing except their light fatigue dress, foraging-caps, and a stick, for a purpose which shall immediately be explained. The officers were desired to take with them their fowling-pieces and greyhounds; and, in this light, easy attire, we marched to the river. As soon as we were clear of the walls of Campo Maior, the whole battalion was extended in one long line in skirmishing order, bringing rather forward the wings, and proceeding in this manner straight across the great plain to the river. Hares, rabbits, and partridges were soon started at all points; when such shooting, coursing, and knocking down with sticks and stones, and such *mobbing* of quadrupeds and birds commenced, that a game-preserving John Bull would undoubtedly have stigmatised us as a most nefarious corps of poachers...

As I am inclined to believe my most bitter enemies will acknowledge that adulation and flattery are not amongst my besetting sins, I may declare, without any apprehension of being taxed with the appellation of *toad-eater*[70], that I have ever considered Lieutenant-Colonel Sidney Beckwith to have been better calculated for the command of a regiment of light troops than most men who are to be found. In the common acceptation of the word, "*a capital commanding officer of a regiment,*" too often implies a good barrack-square drill—a man whose military ideas soar but little beyond the orderly room, the exact fit of the soldier's coat, and the proper allowance of

[66] 'Rosinante' was *Don Quixote*'s scraggy old horse in the book by Cervantes.
[67] Ouguela.
[68] Just over 6 km.
[69] Lieutenant-Colonel Thomas Sidney Beckwith (1772-1831). Commanding Officer of the 1/95th. Later Sir Sidney Beckwith. His nephew John Charles ('Charley') Beckwith (1772-1862) was a Captain in the 95th.
[70] 'Toad-eater'. The full form of the modern 'toady'. A sycophant. According to Brewer (1988: 1233) it comes from the Spanish 'todita' meaning 'factotum', a servant who looks after all his master's business.

pipe-clay wherewith to plaster his belts twice every twenty-four hours. Such a man does not discover, until the moment he actually finds himself in the field in good earnest, with his regiment placed in the teeth of an enterprising and experienced enemy at the out-posts, and constantly liable to be attacked, that he is little better than a novice in his profession (the practical part of it at least), and that commanding a battalion at Dublin or Portsmouth is one thing, and in the field another. It is also no less true, that the sentiments which I have ventured to express on this subject, many men of a certain school would be perfectly horror-struck at, as sapping the foundation of what they deem the essentials of the service[71]. Be it so: Doctors differ. I speak not at hap-hazard, but from some little experience in those matters; and must confess that the marching and counter-marching in a barrack yard have but few charms for me.'

In December 1809 a strong French corps was reported to be massing at Salamanca, far to the north, and threatening the Spanish fortress of Ciudad Rodrigo. The walled towns of Ciudad Rodrigo and Almeida – on the Spanish and Portuguese sides of the border respectively – dominated the main northern route between the two countries and their control was seen as vital to keep open lines of communication between any British army operating in northern Spain, and its Portuguese supply depots.

In response to the threat the British army broke camp and forces were sent north. The 95th marched through the winter for almost a month, with few distractions other than two passing crocodiles which caught George Simmons' eye. "At Coimbra, an exceedingly good town, and possessed of several rich convents, with a beautiful church and museum of curiosities, two stuffed crocodiles attracted my notice much, being 30 feet[72] long, also tigers and a variety of different beasts of prey in a high state of preservation."

By early January the Light Brigade approached the border between the two key fortresses; a wild frontier of rivers and rocks they were going to make their own.

[71] The British Commander-in-Chief in 1809 was General Sir David Dundas (1735-1820). Author of many standard texts on drill, he was known behind his back as 'Old Pivot'.
[72] 9 m.

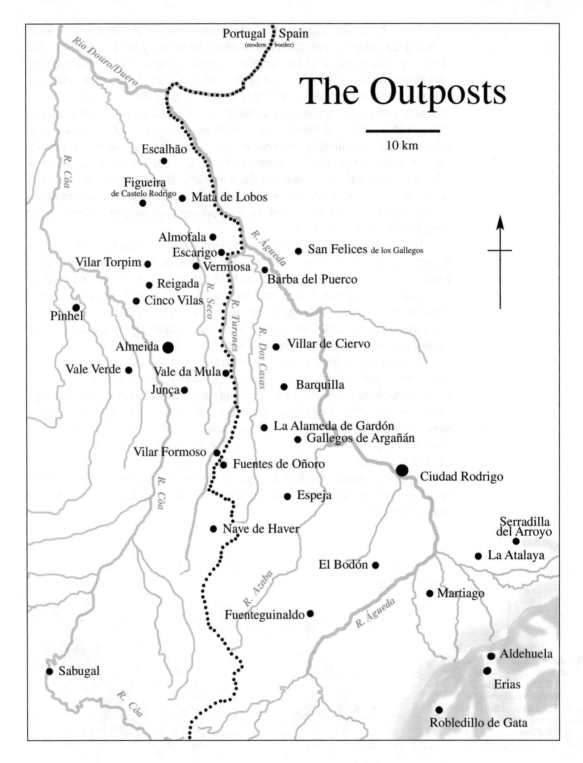

The Outposts

10 km

Portugal | Spain
(modern | border)

Río Douro/Duero

R. Côa

Escalhão

Figueira
de Castelo Rodrigo ● Mata de Lobos

Almofala ●
Escarigo ●● ● San Felices de los Gallegos
Vilar Torpim ● ● Vermiosa

R. Águeda

Reigada ● Barba del Puerco
Cinco Vilas ●

R. Seco

R. Turones

R. Dos Casas

Pinhel ●

Almeida ● ● Villar de Ciervo

Vale Verde ● Vale da Mula ●
Junça ● ● Barquilla

La Alameda de Gardón ●
● Gallegos de Argañán
Vilar Formoso ●
● Fuentes de Oñoro ● Ciudad Rodrigo

R. Côa

● Espeja

Serradilla
del Arroyo ●

● Nave de Haver
● La Atalaya

El Bodón ●
R. Azaba
● Martiago

Fuenteguinaldo ●
R. Águeda

● Aldehuela
Sabugal ● ●
Erias

R. Côa
● Robledillo de Gata

— 4 —

The Outposts

> Jealousy is a demon which rears its head in all communities and
> societies, and, I fear, is to be found in military as well as in civil
> life. Amongst a certain number (I hope a few only) of malecontents
> in the army, the very name of the 'Light Division,' or the
> 'outposts,' was sufficient to turn their ration wine into vinegar.
>
> Jonathan Leach

To face the French threat at Ciudad Rodrigo, the Light Brigade's infantry division was restructured, and the Brigade became free-standing with its own cavalry from the 1st Hussars of the King's German Legion, specialists in long-range reconnaissance as well as close-quarter fighting. This enlarged Light Brigade was now thrown forward and dispersed in outposts along the border west of Ciudad Rodrigo, with the River Côa to its back and the River Águeda to its front, where it patrolled and picketed the fords as an advanced guard and reconnaissance force. With the rest of the army in camp to the west, the Brigade would spend the winter as the allies' detached front line, watching and waiting for any sign of a possible French advance and screening the army's deployment from prying French eyes. This was a vital and onerous duty and one which Craufurd organised meticulously. Signal beacons were placed on prominent peaks and watched day and night. Every morning reports were made of the height of the river at every ford[1]. Relaxation would be difficult.

Leach: "Crossing the Côa on the 6th January 1810, our regiment marched to Villar Torpim, Regada, and Cinco Villas, three poor villages; and we were frequently moved during the months of January, February and March, (in consequence of various rumours and reports of intended attempts on the part of the French to surprise the outposts,) to other villages, lying between the two rivers, well known to old light division men of that day, viz. Figuera, Mata de Lobos, Escallion, Escarigo, &c. &c. Deep snow fell just after we had taken up our new quarters, which rendered the otherwise miserable desolate villages still more forlorn."

[1] Oman, 1986: 142-144. There were 15 fords along the Águeda.

George Simmons found this rugged impoverished region something of a culture-shock. Writing from Vilar Torpim he admitted, "Our present quarters are truly miserable; on all sides stupendous mountains; the people wretched in the extreme, clothes hardly sufficient to cover themselves, and positively not a degree above savages—I mean as to their method of living. Of a morning they will turn out of their wretched cabins and are to be seen sitting in rows upon the ground in the sun picking lice off themselves and out of each other's heads; they do not mind, or endeavour to hide themselves from your view. At first it disgusted me, but from habit I stand by and joke them about the number they have killed, which they take in great good-humour, and tell you, so many that they could not keep account!²"

When not on duty the officers' own culture was all too familiar to Jonathan: "Coursing and shooting were our chief employments by day, and at night we either whiffed away cigars over some Douro wine, and speculated on the campaign which was soon expected to commence, or danced boleros, fandangos, and waltzes, with the good-looking daughters of an Israelite, in whose house I was billeted, in Villar Torpim."

Evening dances were common and widespread throughout Spain and Portugal. An earlier visitor had noted, 'the young people of every village amuse themselves with dancing the fandango and the seguidilla to the sound of a guitar. No description can convey a just idea of the animation of the fandango, or the pleasure it appears to give them who are used to it. On the first tinkling of the guitar all feet are in motion, striking the ground quickly with their heels and toes then wheeling about with surprising rapidity. High and low are equally fond of this diversion, even the muleteers are qualified to join in these national dances.³'

The Rifles' officers adopted these ways with gusto, but even Jonathan's enthusiasm waned in the endless parade of long dark evenings.

'To detail the manner in which we killed time every day during the dreary winter months, some weeks of which we were nearly snowed up in our hovels, and in the poorest villages in the Peninsula, would be nearly a repetition of what I have just stated. Until, therefore, we began to feel for the enemy in the month of March, towards Barba del Puerco, my tale is quickly told.

It is not my intention to enter minutely into the history of Padre Joan's pigeon-house near Mata de Lobos! There are but few, very few, of the good fellows now living who understand this inuendo. Stewed pigeons and pigeon-pies were esteemed great delicacies, and a most useful accompaniment to tough, lean, ration beef, at the outposts; but the less said the better as to the mode by which we procured them.

In the said village of Mata de Lobos I passed many happy but bandit-like days in February, sitting at night over a brass pan of charcoal, and, with my three jolly subalterns, reposing in the same diminutive den, rolled up in our cloaks, on some straw. Amongst our other amusements, whilst thus detached far in front of the army, we frequently got up foot-races (our horses

² Letter to his parents, February 1810 (Verner, 1986: 49-50).
³ Wakefield, 1802: 301-302.

being in but poor trim for such feats), played matches at foot-ball, and rackets against the tower of the church, had duck-hunting with dogs in a piece of water, and sometimes turned a pig loose, with his tail greased, when he was pursued by the soldiers, and became the lawful prize of the man who could catch and hold him, which was no easy matter. Our gallant commander, Colonel Beckwith, was ever amongst the first to encourage those meetings, considering, no doubt, and very justly, that to divert and to amuse his men, and to allow them every possible indulgence compatible with the discipline of the battalion, whilst an interval of quiet permitted it, was the surest way to make the soldiers follow him cheerfully through fire and water, when the day of trial came...

If any are inclined to accuse us, whilst thus isolated in those wild regions, in the depth of a dreary winter, of having passed our time in irrational and fruitless pursuits, let me remind them at once, and without beating about the bush, that although Malta, Gibraltar, Halifax, Quebec, Portsmouth, Plymouth, and various other garrisons, at home and abroad, can boast of excellent libraries, billiard-tables, whist clubs, and dinner clubs, independent of garrison balls and garrison concerts, &c. &c., the rascally villages between the Coa and Agueda, growing out, as it were, from amongst the huge blocks of granite, and peopled by the most wretched, dirty, idle, ignorant, priest-ridden peasantry any where to be found, afforded none of these resources.'

To arms

In late February the French force at Salamanca placed its advanced guard at the Portuguese border, on the eastern banks of the Águeda, facing the Light Brigade's positions.

Leach: "On the 27th of February the first company of the battalion for detachment (Captain Creagh's) was ordered to march from Escarigo, to reconnoitre the village of Barba del Puerco, in which he found a strong detachment of French cavalry and infantry, with whom he had a skirmish, and fell back, agreeable to his orders, to Escarigo, where I joined him with my company; and a third company was pushed forward from Villar Torpim to Vermiosa, to support us.

The following day I was ordered to reconnoitre Barba del Puerco again, which, finding that the French had vacated, I occupied as a picket-post, sending a small party to the bridge at the foot of the pass; opposite to which was a picket of infantry and cavalry, detached from the French force at St. Felices[4].

By information collected at Barba del Puerco, from the padre of the village (who afterwards proved himself a vile traitor to his country), the French force at St. Felices consisted of 3000 men, infantry, cavalry, and artillery, under the command of Baron Ferez[5], a German in the French service, and a general of brigade belonging to General Loison's division. Our whole battalion was about this time ordered to close up to the Agueda, and, in conjunction with the 1st German Hussars, we held Villa de Ciervo,

[4] San Felices de los Gallegos, 6-7 km away.
[5] Général Baron de Férey.

65

with four companies; Barba del Puerco, with four companies; Almofala and Escalhao, each with one;— thus watching all the fords on the river, from Villa de Ciervo on the right, to beyond Escalhao on the left, at the junction of the Agueda and Douro;— a long line of country for so small a force, and at such a distance from support.

With a view to keeping us on the *qui vive*[6], and of enabling every officer in the battalion to make himself acquainted, in the event of being driven back, with the lines of the river, the roads leading from it towards the Coa, and the general features of the district entrusted to our charge, our companies frequently exchanged posts.

Being stationed at Almofala early in March, I witnessed a disgusting and cruel sight. Having gone with another officer to the mountainous bank which overhangs the river not far from the village, to visit the picket, we perceived a French soldier, *unarmed*, running down the mountain on the opposite side of the river, no doubt with the intention of trying to cross over and desert to us. Three Spanish shepherds who were tending their sheep on the same side of the river, intercepted him, and beat him to death with their clubs in less time than it has taken me to write an account of the sickening sight. We called out, and made signals to them to desist, and to spare him, but in vain. We fired several shots over their heads to intimidate them, but it had no effect, and the butchery went on without our being able to interfere, or to interrupt those savages in what they considered, no doubt, a most patriotic and meritorious exploit. A deluge of rain had so swollen the river, which roared at the foot of the mountain, that to pass it was impossible; and, indeed, could we have effected it, the blood-thirsty shepherds would have escaped, before we could by possibility have reached them. To have inflicted the summary punishment on them with a rifle ball, which we all felt well inclined to do, would have been only an act of justice; but it was a step, nevertheless, which the higher authorities would have visited with a heavy punishment."

In April, following intelligence that the French at San Felices had been reinforced, the Light Brigade was augmented by the addition of two new Portuguese light infantry battalions, the 1st and 3rd Caçadores[8], and redesignated the *Light Division*[9], the name it bore for the remainder of the war[10]. Squadrons of the 14th and 16th Light Dragoons were deployed to support this division (joining the existing Hussars of the King's German Legion) and a troop of light horse-artillery[11]. These gunners were the renowned 'Chestnut Troop', Royal Horse Artillery, under Captain Hew Ross[12] with their battery of six 6-pounder guns[13]. The ten companies of the 1/95th having dwindled from 1100 to 800 men – primarily from the effects of the Guadiana fever – the battalion was reorganised as eight companies and a number of officers returned to England to recruit for the regiment[14]. Jonathan Leach was not among them. With the rest of the Light Division, now containing 4000 infantrymen, he remained at the outposts.

[6] On the alert. "Qui vive?", is the French sentry's challenge; the equivalent of "Who goes there?"
[7] Simmons also witnessed this event and was apparently the other officer mentioned. He says the shepherds stoned the man to death.
[8] Caçadores – 'hunters' (the Portuguese name for riflemen)
[9] Being removed from the 3rd Division, where it was replaced by the transfer of a brigade from the 4th Division and the addition of the 9th & 21st Portuguese regiments (Oman, 1986: 348).
[10] Technically this came into existence on the 22nd of February 1810 while the Brigade was at the outposts (Oman, 1986: 168, 348) but Jonathan Leach says the 1st & 3rd Caçadores joined the Brigade "Towards the end of April" and the term Light Division was used "from that period" (*Rough Sketches*, p. 131).
[11] This must have been a colourful Division. The 43rd wore scarlet jackets with white facings; the 52nd, scarlet jackets with buff facings; the 95th dark green with black facings; 1st Caçadores mid-brown with blue facings; 3rd Caçadores mid-brown with yellow facings; the Cavalry and Horse-Artillery wore blue.
[12] Hew Dalrymple Ross, later Field-Marshal Sir Hew Ross *GCB* (1779-1868). Cousin and Godson of Sir Hew Whitefoord Dalrymple.
[13] Guns firing ball shot of 6 pounds (2.7 kg) weight (or packets of smaller projectiles)
[14] Presumably recruitment was needed so soon after the successful recruitment of the previous year because of the ravages of the Walcheren fever in the 2nd battalion.

In contrast to Britain and much of Europe, on the borders of Spain and Portugal it had been raining incessantly for months. In mid-May Jonathan wrote in his journal, "Nothing going on owing to the damnable rain" and on the 26th, "I must make a remark amongst some others on this rascally country that for the last four months with the exception of *a few days* we have had nothing but tremendous rain." Even when it was not raining the distractions were few. Several weeks earlier he had noted, "Rambled in the woods, shot an whoopo and a cucko, desperate sport!"[15]

Finally, towards the end of May, the French began to stir. This change galvanised the Light Division where Jonathan and his men were so close to the French outposts they now slept fully clothed and equipped, with their vigilance constantly tested by units of the increasingly mobile French cavalry. This renewed activity was not a bluff; a storm was beginning to gather.

The Leopards Retreat

Determined to invade Portugal and expel the British, on the far bank of the river the French were assembling a formidable assault force under the command of one of Napoleon's most able Generals, Marshal Masséna[16]. Masséna issued a proclamation to the Portuguese nation declaring he came not to invade Portugal, but to rescue it from the British and to plant the imperial eagles on the citadel of Lisbon. He would lead his 110,000 Frenchmen into the country and drive the frightened English leopard[17] into the sea. Resistance was futile.

For a month Masséna nudged army divisions to the southern end of his line around Ciudad Rodrigo, which was garrisoned by the Spanish. The British, faced with overwhelming force[18], were powerless onlookers, only the daring daily raids by Spanish guerrilla forces under their remarkably successful commander, Don Julian Sanchez[19], and other cavalry units from the fortress, caused the French any pain. When sufficient men had been assembled and artillery batteries built the French began four days and four nights of continuous bombardment of the town walls with nearly 50 pieces of heavy ordnance. After a breach 25 metres in length had been hammered in the wall the governor was called upon to surrender. He refused and the horrific bombardment rained onto the town for another twelve days.

While the cannonading continued the Light Division was positioned about 12 km to the west, between the rivers Azaba and Dos Casas, on some heights by the village of Gallegos de Argañán, from which position they could see "every shot fired by both parties most distinctly with the naked eye.[20]" On the 4th of July Masséna ordered Junot across the Azaba with 15,000 troops to assess the allies' forward strength.

Leach: "Being under arms, as usual, an hour before day-break[21], on the heights, some shots were heard from our cavalry pickets at Marialva, who shortly afterwards retired slowly and in excellent order, keeping up a

[15] Verner, 1919: 113.
[16] Maréchal André Masséna, Duc de Rivoli, Prince d'Essling (1758-1817). Napoleon nicknamed him 'l'enfant chéri de la Victoire.' (Victory's cherished child).
[17] The French called the English 'leopards' because French heralds described the lion of the Royal Arms of England as a 'lion leopardé'.
[18] Much of Wellington's army at this time was composed of newly-trained, and untested Portuguese, units.
[19] Sanchez had been the son of a farmer until his parents and sister were killed by the French. Swearing vengeance, he took it.
[20] Jonathan Leach's Journal entry for 26th June (Verner, 1919: 114).
[21] In the army at that time 'day-break' was quaintly defined as, 'when you can see a grey horse a mile away.'

continued skirmish. Captain Kraukenberg, of the 1st German Hussars, an officer of the highest merit, distinguished himself on this occasion. Forming his squadron on some eligible ground near a small narrow bridge over a rivulet which runs through Gallegos, he waited until as many of the French dragoons had crossed as he thought proper to permit, when he instantly charged and put them into confusion, killing and wounding many of them, and bringing some prisoners with him to the heights, where General Crawford had drawn out the Light Division in line. The horse artillery opened with effect on the head of Junot's troops, who advanced with caution; but General Crawford having ascertained their great superiority of numbers, decided on retiring across the Duas Casas. This movement was covered by some cavalry and our battalion, who skirmished with the French until we had passed the river, which was effected with very trifling loss on our part. Two hundred riflemen and some cavalry were left on the heights of Fort Conception[22] as a picket, the remainder being placed in a position near the Portuguese village of Val de la Mula[23], behind the rivulet called the Turon[24], which is here the boundary of the two countries."

In this action, which became known as the 'Affair at Gallegos', Craufurd showed his supreme competence as a commander of light troops under fire. The Division withdrew more than 15 km across open country, constantly outflanked by French cavalry, and suffered only five men wounded. His tactics in this withdrawal were subsequently enshrined in military textbooks as a model for future generations. Of course, that did not stop Jonathan Leach questioning whether the allies should have been where they were in the first place, but it may explain the apparent French ineffectiveness.

"It has ever been a matter of surprise to those amongst us who have given it a thought, that a general of so rash and ardent a temper as Junot has been represented, should have displayed so much caution on this occasion. Had he been aware that the only force in his front was about four thousand infantry, a troop of light artillery, and some squadrons of cavalry, and that it had no support within many leagues, it is to be presumed he would have pushed us with much more vigour in our retrograde movement to the heights of Fort Conception; and had he done so, he might have made General Crawford fully sensible that he had delayed his retreat across the Duas Casas too long, whereby the safety of his division was in some measure endangered, and for no possible purpose."

Craufurd's next decision also perplexed the ever-critical Leach. Three days later, in their new positions, he ordered two companies of each Regiment to carry out target practice. Jonathan noted in his journal that it "appears an *odd whim* to expend ammunition at *a Target* when we are only a league distant from *eighty four thousand* Frenchmen.[25]" It seems Craufurd did not like inactivity. After another three days he determined to make a foray against the French outposts.

[22] Presumably near the village of Castillejo de Dos Casas.
[23] Vale da Mula.
[24] River Turones.
[25] Quoted in Verner (1919: 116).

Leach again: "On the night of the 10th of July, General Crawford marched from Val de la Mula with seven companies of our battalion, two of the 52d, two pieces of artillery, the 14th Light Dragoons, and a part or the whole of the 1st German Hussars, to surprise a post consisting of about two hundred French infantry and a troop of cavalry, at the Spanish village of Barkela[26]. Before daybreak we reached our ground unperceived by the French. The two field-pieces and the nine companies of infantry were drawn up on some rising ground about half a mile[27], or thereabout, from the village. As soon as day broke and shewed us the enemy, in search of whom we had been marching the whole night, General Crawford ordered a charge to be made on them, as they were seen moving out of Barkela towards the French camp, on the other side of the Agueda. Their troop of cavalry was soon sabred or made prisoners; but with their infantry it was otherwise. Instantly forming a small square, they retired, rapidly and in good order, in the direction of the ford. Colonel Talbot, at the head of the 14th Light Dragoons, rode gallantly at and charged the little phalanx with great impetuosity, but without being able to break it.

No troops on earth could have conducted themselves with greater gallantry than the old and often-tried 14th Light Dragoons; and in so determined a manner did this distinguished corps make their charge, that Colonel Talbot, whose body I saw a few minutes after he was killed, bore the marks not only of bullets but of bayonets: and it is equally true, that he and many of his brave followers who actually reached the square, met their death by the bayonets of this invincible little body of Frenchmen, who steadily resisted their charges, and, without leaving in our hands one of their brave band, succeeded in making good their retreat over the plain. Some hundreds of the finest cavalry of which the British army could boast continued hovering about, ready to pounce on and break them, if the least disorder should be detected.

It was impossible not to respect and admire the exemplary conduct of the French infantry; and this affair may tend to open the eyes of many men who talk with great composure of riding down and sabring infantry on a plain with cavalry, as if it was the most simple and feasible operation imaginable. But it must be confessed that such opinions are generally advanced by theoretical, not practical, soldiers. If the simple little fact in question be not considered conclusive, I must refer all sceptics on the subject to encounters of a more recent date; and they will find that at Waterloo not one British square was broken by cavalry on that bloody day.

It will be naturally asked, where were General Crawford's nine companies of infantry and his two pieces of artillery all this time? It may be answered, that they were standing without orders on a hill about half a mile distant; but *why* they were not ordered to advance, is more than I can explain. It is to be presumed that, had the field pieces been ordered to advance at a brisk pace, with the cavalry, a few discharges of grape-shot[28]

[26] Barquilla.

[27] 800 m.

[28] Correctly 'case shot' or 'canister' (a thin-walled tin container filled with lead balls (40-80 per canister depending on their size). The tin disintegrated on firing and the cannon became a huge shotgun). 'Grapeshot' was larger diameter shot (perhaps 16 balls per load) used mainly in Royal Navy operations, but in the army the term 'grapeshot' was used loosely for canister/case and we use 'grapeshot' today for all these options (Haythornthwaite, 1979: 59-61)

would either have annihilated the square in ten minutes, or caused it to surrender; and it is no great presumption on the part of any individual belonging to the nine companies of British infantry present to pronounce, that they would have proved rather an overmatch for two companies of Frenchmen. Our loss on this occasion was, Lieut.-Colonel Talbot and a quarter-master of the 14th Dragoons killed, and about twenty-five men and horses killed and wounded."

Simmons too was exasperated, noting in his journal, "Our *wise* General had the 14th, 16th, and German Hussars all to assist, also Horse Artillery and seven companies of infantry, but let this small party of Frenchmen slip through our fingers so shamefully.[29]"

Following this action complaints were made which eventually came before Wellington[30], but he chose to dismiss them, saying Craufurd's foray failed through accident, and these happen in war. He also expressed his conviction – repeated elsewhere in his dispatches[31] – that battles should be fought, not written about. His view on the failure of the Barquilla encounter was, "All this would not much signify if our Staff and other officers would mind their business instead of writing news and keeping coffee houses. But as soon as an accident happens, every one who can write, and who has a friend who can read, sits down to write his account of what he does not know and his comments on what he does not understand.[32]"

On the day Craufurd took his detachment to attack the French outpost (for reasons that remain, despite the foregoing, as obscure to posterity as they were to Jonathan Leach) Ciudad Rodrigo surrendered and the garrison became prisoners of war. On the same day in the west, French cavalry appeared at Almeida, behind Craufurd's main position at Vale da Mula. Wellington's headquarters were well to the west of Almeida at Alverca da Beira, but just as he could not support Ciudad Rodrigo, he could not support Almeida. Jonathan Leach's Division was now the only allied unit east of the Côa. Craufurd moved his infantry about 5 km south, to Junça, leaving his cavalry as pickets, and for more than a week the French advanced posts and the Light Division virtually overlapped along the frontier. On the 21st of July Masséna ordered an advance to besiege Almeida, and a force under Ney crossed the Dos Casas. Craufurd destroyed Fort Conception with mines and began to fall back on Almeida in the face of Ney's overwhelming numbers, leaving only cavalry pickets out on the plain to their front.

Action at the Côa

Harry Smith summarises what happened next: "In the early morning of the 24th of July (I was on picquet with Leach and my Company that night) the enemy moved forward with 40,000 men. Our force, one Brigade of Horse Artillery, three Regiments of cavalry, five of infantry, were ordered by the Duke to remain as long as possible on the right bank of the Coa[33], where there was a bridge over the river on the road from Almeida into Portugal to Celerico and Pinhel, posting ourselves between the fortress and

[29] Verner, 1986: 74.
[30] Although numerous eye-witnesses were deeply critical of Craufurd's handling of this affair, it was complaints about the actions of the cavalry that brought the matter to Wellington (Verner, 1919: 117-118).
[31] Letter: Wellington to ——— Esq. from Paris, 8th August 1815 (Wellington's Dispatches). Cotton (1895: 229) says this letter was to Walter Scott the novelist and poet. Chandler (1980: 10) says it was to John Croker, 1st Secretary of the Admiralty. Neither gives authority for their identification of the recipient.
[32] Verner, 1919: 118.
[33] Smith – never a shrinking violet – is prone to hyperbole. There were probably fewer than 20,000 French troops (although Jonathan Leach thought more); they were squadrons of allied cavalry, and battalions of allied infantry, not entire regiments; and at this time Wellington was a Viscount not a Duke (and he certainly never gave that order). Otherwise the account is accurate.

the bridge[34], so as to pass over so soon as the enemy advanced in force. In place of doing this, Craufurd took up a position to our right of Almeida, and but for Colonel Beckwith our whole force would have been sacrificed. Fortunately a heavy rain had fallen[35], which made the Coa impassable except by the bridge, which was in our possession, and the enemy concentrated his force in one rush for the bridge".

At the beginning of the French advance Simmons saw, "The whole plain in our front was covered with horse and foot advancing towards us. The enemy's infantry formed line and, with an innumerable multitude of skirmishers, attacked us fiercely".

Jonathan Leach, with his company commander's eye, takes up the story: "General Crawford placed his infantry in line amongst some rocky ground and stone walls, his left being within seven or eight hundred yards of the walls of Almeida, and his right thrown back in a convex form towards the Coa. Our cavalry posts in the plain were soon forced back on the infantry, and a brisk cannonade commenced. The advance of the French cavalry were brought to bay by our infantry in the intersected ground; but Marshal Ney having more than twenty thousand infantry at his back, was not long to be delayed in this manner. Although the left of our line was under the protection of the guns of the fortress, the French assailed it with great impetuosity; and the right and centre also soon found itself beset with a swarm of light troops, supported by heavy columns constantly advancing, and aided by their artillery, which cannonaded us warmly.

It is not improbable that at this moment our brigadier began to think it would have been more prudent, and equally beneficial to the cause for which the British army was contending in the Peninsula, had he implicitly obeyed the positive orders of the Commander-in-Chief, to withdraw his corps of observation behind the Coa, on the fall of Ciudad Rodrigo, or on the first symptom of Massena's advance on Almeida, and by no means to risk an action against the superior numbers with which the French would undoubtedly advance towards that fortress. I never heard it yet doubted or denied that such were the orders transmitted to General Crawford from head-quarters, long before the 24th of July[36].

The baggage, artillery, cavalry, and the two Portuguese light battalions[37], were directed to retire instantly to the bridge over the Coa, and to gain the opposite bank without delay. Those who have seen and know this narrow and difficult defile, need not be informed, that to keep at bay as many thousand infantry as Marshal Ney might think proper to send forward, whilst the road was choked with troops, baggage, and artillery, which it was absolutely necessary should be covered and protected, during a retreat of a mile or more, and until they had crossed the bridge in safety, was no easy matter.

The troops destined to cover the retreat consisted of our own battalion, and a considerable part, or the whole, of the 43d and 52d regiments. No further description of this rocky defile is necessary, than that the road is

[34] The distance from Almeida to the Côa is about 3 km.
[35] Jonathan Leach said, "A more tremendous night of thunder, lightning, and rain, I never remember before or since, from which our only shelter was the lee side of the rocks."
[36] This is true. See later.
[37] "battalions" rather than regiments because each Portuguese regiment, like many regiments at this time, had only one battalion and for them, unlike the 95th, the terms were interchangeable.

very narrow, and as bad as the generality of mountain-roads in the Peninsula are; and moreover, that it is overhung by huge rocks in many places, from which, had our pursuers been permitted to possess themselves of them, they might have annihilated the troops underneath, without their being able to retaliate; and thus, the only option left them would have been a walk to Verdun as prisoners of war, or an instantaneous passage across the Styx instead of the Coa."

The rearguard with Jonathan Leach was to the right of the allied line to cover the second road to the bridge coming up the defile from Junça to the south, but the infantry on the left of the line had to retreat through dense vineyards intersected by deep trenches and walls up to two metres in height. This was slow work, not helped by the torrential rain which started to fall about mid-day and continued throughout the afternoon. Craufurd had hoped the walls would aid the withdrawal by hindering the French cavalry, but during the earlier downpour of the previous night British soldiers had dismantled some sections to build shelters. The gaps let the cavalry through.

Jonathan continues, "from the commencement of the action at the edge of the plain until we reached the river, every inch of ground admitting of defence was obstinately contested by the rear-guard, which was followed by fresh troops every instant arriving to support their comrades. The French artillery failed not to help us along, whenever they had an opportunity, with a nine-pound[38] shot.

As the rear-guard approached the Coa, we perceived that a part only of our cavalry, infantry, and artillery, had yet crossed the bridge; it became, therefore, indispensably requisite for us to keep possession of a small hill looking down on, and perfectly commanding the bridge, until every thing had passed over, cost what it might."

Unfortunately Craufurd ordered the Rifles to vacate this commanding position with its strong stone wall too soon, with near disastrous consequences. Reversing this mistake and driving the French off this hill became a matter of some urgency. The task was taken by a mixed contingent from the 43rd and 95th, including Jonathan Leach with part of his company[39]. Harry Smith later said that in the whole Peninsula War there was never a more severe contest. In an onslaught of furious musketry many of the officers, leading from the front, were to fall, as George Simmons discovered to his cost:

"General Craufurd ordered a number of Rifle Men who had occupied a place that prevented the French from stopping our retreat over the bridge to evacuate it before half the 52nd, who were on the right, had filed over. The enemy directly brought up their infantry to this hill, which commanded the bridge, and kept up a terrible fire. Colonel Beckwith, a most gallant and clever soldier, saw this frightful mistake and ordered us to retake the wall and hill instantly, which we did in good style, but suffered severely in men and officers. Lieutenant Harry Smith, Lieutenant Thomas Smith[40], and Lieutenant Pratt were wounded[41], and I was shot through the thigh close

[38] 4 kg.

[39] Verner, 1919: 125. Verner says there were about 50 men from each regiment, but he may be basing this on Jonathan Leach's lower estimate (see later).

[40] Thomas Lawrence Smith (1792-1877). Harry Smith's brother 'Tom' who was also a Lieutenant in Jonathan Leach's company.

[41] Tom and Harry Smith both later recovered. Pratt had been shot in the throat and died a week later when his carotid artery burst.

to the wall, which caused me to fall with great force. Being wounded in this way was quite a new thing to me. For a few moments I could not recollect my ideas, and was feeling about my arms and body for a wound, until my eye caught the stream of blood rushing through the hole in my trousers, and my leg and thigh appeared so heavy that I could not move it. Captain Napier[42] took off his neckerchief and gave it to a sergeant, who put it round my thigh and twisted it tight with a ramrod, to stop the bleeding. The firing was so severe that the sergeant, on finishing the job for me, fell with a shot through the head. Captain Napier was also about the same time wounded in the side.[43]" Jonathan Leach was luckier by a few millimetres; on his charge up the hill a musket ball grazed the left side of his head and buried itself in the earth.

The officer commanding this dangerous counter-attack was Major Charles MacLeod[44] of the 43rd. Many eye witnesses remember his leadership, including Jonathan: "If any are now living of those who defended the little hill above the bridge, they cannot fail to remember the gallantry displayed by Major McLeod, of the 43d, who was the senior officer on the spot. How either he or his horse escaped being blown to atoms, when, in the most daring manner, he charged on horseback, at the head of a hundred or two skirmishers of the 43d and of our regiment mixed together, and headed them in making a dash at a wall lined with French infantry, which we soon dislodged, I am at a loss to imagine. It was one of those extraordinary escapes tending strongly to implant in the mind some faith in the doctrine of fatality."

Harry Smith had particular reason to remember MacLeod. Smith had taken a musket ball in the ankle and "Major MacLeod, a noble fellow, afterwards killed at Badajos, put me on his horse, or I should have been taken."

That was the end of the battle for Smith, but not for Jonathan Leach: "Both my subalterns, who were brothers, were severely wounded in the defence of this hill; and we had but barely time to send them, with other wounded officers and men, across the river, ere we were obliged to retire, and to make a push in double-quick time to reach the bridge; the whole time exposed to such a fire from the hill which we had just abandoned, as might have satisfied the most determined fire-eater in existence.[45]"... "we dashed over the hills skilter-Devil-take-the-hindmost. The French in a second occupied the hill which we left, blazed into us and made damnable work among us. On the bridge stood two Artillery cars. An officer of Artillery cried out 'Don't let me lose my tumbrils. Stand by me Riflemen.' Our boys lined the battlements of the bridge keeping up a constant fire whilst he got his horses harnessed and got clear off. Then away we went and ascended the heights on the other side.[46]"

"The whole of General Crawford's corps"..."was strongly posted near the bridge behind walls, rocks, and broken ground. The torrents of rain which fell the night before had so swollen the river, that all the fords were

---

[42] William Francis Patrick Napier (1785-1860). 43rd Light Infantry. Later General Sir William Napier. Famous now for writing the epic *History of the War in the Peninsula and in the South of France 1807-1814.* (5 vols) Published 1827-1840. His brothers were [Lieutenant-General Sir] Charles James Napier (1782-1853) and [General Sir] George Thomas Napier (1784-1855). King George III had been attracted to their mother Lady Sarah Napier (d. 1826) in her youth (Cholmondeley, 1950: 236).
[43] Simmons quoted in Verner, 1986: 78-79.
[44] Major (later Lieutenant-Colonel) Charles MacLeod (1784-1812).
[45] *Rough Sketches.*
[46] Jonathan Leach Ms quoted in Verner (1919: 125).

at that moment impassable; a fortunate circumstance, as the only way by which we could now be attacked was over the narrow bridge, on which we could bring a destructive fire; and we likewise commanded the approach to it from the opposite side with musketry. An incessant fire was kept up across the river by both parties, and after it had continued some time, the French sent a party of grenadiers to storm the bridge, with the vain hope of driving us from our new position. They advanced most resolutely in double-quick time, and charged along the bridge; but few, if any, went back alive, and most of those who reached our side of it unhurt were killed afterwards.[47]"..."The officer who headed the party crossed unhurt followed by four others who attempted to ascend the heights, he was shot on this side and most of his men. I fired at him myself with my little rifle (which still stands my friend) and cursed my stupidity for missing him, but a running person is not easily hit.[48]"

After the failure of this charge by the French grenadiers, Ney ordered a unit of his chasseurs[49] to take the bridge at all costs. Under the rifles of the entrenched marksmen of the Light Division this was suicide. In less than ten minutes, 90 men were dead and nearly 150 wounded. The bridge was choked with bodies as high as the parapets. Not convinced, Ney ordered his 66th Regiment forward for another attempt. This too met a predictable fate.[50]

Leach: "The French officer who directed those attacks on the bridge, might have known, before he caused the experiment to be made, that a few hundred French grenadiers, advancing to the tune of "Vive l'Empereur!" "En avant, mes enfans!" and so forth, were not likely to succeed in scaring away three British and two Portuguese regiments supported by artillery. It was a piece of unpardonable and unjustifiable butchery on the part of the man who ordered those brave grenadiers to be thus wantonly sacrificed, without the most remote prospect of success. They deserved a better fate, for no men could have behaved with more intrepidity."

"About five o'clock in the evening the firing ceased on each side, as if by mutual consent; partly because, having been engaged since six o'clock in the morning, both parties found themselves pretty much exhausted, to say nothing, perhaps, of the hopeless case which our antagonists found it to drive us from our tenable position.[51]"..."we broke our fast and never were poor devils more completely knocked up.[52]"

"We permitted a party of the enemy, unarmed, to come on the bridge, and on our side of it, to bring away their wounded. Two officers of grenadiers of their 66th regiment lay dead at the head of the bridge, which, as well as the ground on each side of it, was covered with killed and wounded. The loss of our regiment in this action was two officers killed, and eight wounded, three of whom died a few days afterwards. We lost several sergeants, bugle-boys, and about one hundred and twenty rank and file. The total loss of the Light Division was from three to four hundred men. Thus ended the affair of the Coa"

[47] *Rough Sketches.*
[48] Jonathan Leach MS quoted in Verner (1919:126).
[49] 'Chasseur' – 'hunter'. A soldier trained and equipped for rapid action.
[50] 80% of all French casualties for this day were incurred at this bridge. This and other details from Verner (1919: 126-127).
[51] *Rough Sketches.*
[52] Jonathan Leach Ms quoted in Verner (1919: 129).

"Soon after dark, General Crawford retired with his whole force from the Coa to a wild rocky country, near the village of Valverde, where we bivouacked late that night amongst some granite rocks, drenched to the skin with the rains of the preceding day and night. We had here time to reflect on the events which the last twenty-four hours had produced, and were extremely puzzled to conjecture why General Crawford, if he was determined to give battle with the Light Division, consisting of four thousand men, to Marshal Ney's whole corps of twenty-five thousand, did not cross the Coa, without waiting to be forcibly driven over, and having taken up a position on the left bank, then and there challenge his opponent. The investment of Almeida was not retarded five minutes by our waiting under its walls for the approach of the besieging army."

This was Jonathan's measured opinion more than twenty years after the event, but in a letter written home at the time he was altogether more forthright: "You will have heard how universally General Crawford was hated and detested in the retreat from Corunna. If possible he is still more abhorred now and has been ever since we landed in Portugal. He is a damned tyrant and has proved himself totally unfit to command a company much less a division. I understand he has just got into a scrape with Lord Wellington for pitching on ground for his position which the most uninstructed boy of one month's standing would have known better than to have taken up. If ever we meet I will tell you more about him.[53]"

The "scrape with Lord Wellington" was apparent from the high praise his Lordship heaped on the officers and men "of these excellent Regiments" for their conduct at the Côa, without once mentioning their Brigadier. In a letter written to his brother a week after the action, Wellington's annoyance is still obvious, but he had decided not to pursue the matter: 'Although I shall be hanged for them, you may be very certain that not only I have had nothing to do with, but had positively forbidden, the foolish affairs in which Craufurd involved his outposts. Of the first, indeed, in which Talbot was killed, I knew nothing before it happened. In respect to the last, that of the 24th, I had positively desired him not to engage in any affair on the other side of the Coa... You may say, if this be the case, why not accuse Craufurd? I answer, because, if I am to be hanged for it, I cannot accuse a man who I think has meant well, and whose error is one of judgement, and not of intention.[54]'

Advance of the French

The Light Division spent the next few weeks patrolling the new front line west of the Côa, living in bivouacs, and augmenting the limited rations of beef with impromptu sporting excursions[55].

Leach: "On the 26th, 27th, and 28th of August, the rains fell almost without intermission, accompanied by lightning and thunder. As we were at this time vegetating under some huts made of the branches of trees, which

[53] Quoted in Verner (1919: 129-130). Verner writes 'Craufurd' and 'Coruña'. Presumably Jonathan's original Ms had his usual spellings as found in *Rough Sketches*.

[54] Letter: Wellington to his elder brother, William Wellesley Pole, dated 31st July 1810. *Wellington's Supplementary Despatches*, **6**: 563-564 (Quoted in Verner, 1919: 132).

[55] On the 4th of August the Division was formed into two Brigades, with four companies of the 1/95th in each (Oman, 1986: 349).

kept out about as much rain as a large sieve would have done, we had the full benefit of this shower-bath.

The French batteries opened on Almeida about this period; and a few hours after the bombardment commenced, most unfortunately a shell exploded in the great magazine, blew half the town about the ears of the garrison, and so injured the works, that the governor was under the necessity of capitulating[56]. This was a most unexpected misfortune, as Massena was now able to prosecute his march on Lisbon some weeks earlier than Lord Wellington had calculated on."

Indeed, Masséna was now joined by Reynier[57] with an extra 17,000 men, and the French advanced swiftly in three spearheads, under Junot, Ney and Reynier. Wellington pulled the allied army westwards across 125 km of country towards Coimbra, hotly pursued[58]. By late September the Light Division – the rearguard of the allied retreat – was being pressed hard by a very effective French vanguard of light cavalry, light infantry and flying artillery. There was little they could do but fall back swiftly on the main allied force, now deployed on the mountain-side of the Sierra de Buçaco, a 13 km ridge just north of Coimbra, 40 km from the Atlantic. Wellington had chosen his ground.

The French army rolled onto the brow of the opposing ridge, and the intervening valley filled with pickets from both sides. Masséna reconnoitred the position on the 26th of September and was advised the allies would fight. "I cannot persuade myself that Lord Wellington will risk the loss of his reputation;" said Masséna, "but if he does—I have him. Tomorrow we shall effect the conquest of Portugal, and in a few days I shall drown the leopard[59]."

Early in the morning of the 26th, Jonathan Leach's company with three others was in front of the rest of the Light Division[60], on the forward face of the mountainside in the village of Sula, when they were cannonaded by the French who then sent a "cloud of light infantry" to engage the pickets along the whole front while the French general officers surveyed the allied lines and instituted some psychological warfare.

Leach: "Massena, during the morning, closed up from his rear all his troops, cavalry, infantry, and artillery, and placed them in one vast solid mass opposite to us; no doubt with the hope of intimidating the allies at the mere sight of such legions. Their numbers I do not pretend to determine[61]; but his whole army was now in view, except the garrisons left in Ciudad Rodrigo and Almeida, and perhaps some posts of communication with the frontier."

On the reverse slope of the allied ridge, out of view of the French and unable to see what was happening, an officer of the 34th (Cumberland) Regiment[62], Lieutenant Moyle Sherer[63], chose this moment to reconnoitre:

"I walked to the verge of the mountain on which we lay, in the hope that I might discover something of the enemy. Little, however, was I prepared for the magnificent scene which burst on my astonished sight. Far as the

[56] The bombardment commenced on the morning of Sunday 26th August and the town surrendered on Monday night, the explosion having destroyed half the town's artillery, most of its ammunition, and having killed many defenders.

[57] Général Jean Louis Ebénézer Reynier ('Regnier' of authors) (1771-1814).

[58] Jonathan notes in his journal for 9th September that he had been sleeping in his clothes for three months (Verner, 1919: 136)

[59] Tucker, 1846: 153.

[60] The Division was in an advanced position left of centre in the allied line.

[61] Masséna had about 66,000 men, Wellington just over 51,000.

[62] In which George Simmons' brother Maud was a Lieutenant. Only the 2nd battalion of the 34th was in the Peninsula.

[63] Joseph Moyle Sherer (1789-1869). Promoted Captain 26th March 1811. Captured by the French in 1813. Promoted Major 22nd July 1830. Retired on half-pay 1832. Author of: *Sketches of India* (1821); *Recollections of the Peninsula* (1824); *Scenes and Impressions in Egypt and Italy* (1824); *Story of a Life* (1825) and a number of novels.

eye could stretch, the glittering of steel, and clouds of dust raised by cavalry and artillery, proclaimed the march of a countless army; while, immediately below me, at the feet of those precipitous heights, on which I stood, their picquets were already posted: thousands of them were already halted in their bivouacks, and column too after column, arriving in quick succession, reposed upon the ground allotted to them, and swelled the black and enormous masses. The numbers of the enemy were, at the lowest calculation, seventy-five thousand, and this host formed in three distinct and heavy columns; while to the rear of their left, at a more considerable distance, you might see a large encampment of their cavalry, and the whole country behind them seemed covered with their train, their ambulance, and their commissariat. This, then, was a French army[64]".

On the forward slope, up close and personal, Jonathan Leach had no time to admire the view: "The fire of the light troops throughout the 26th having been kept up without intermission, we relieved our companies at this duty every hour or two. The situation of a light bob[65], or a rifleman, was found to be no sinecure. The blaze of musketry with which the mountains and valleys had rung for twelve hours, ceased with night; and every thing was as quiet as if the two armies had been in their own countries in profound peace."

The Battle of Buçaco[66]

"*27th.*— Day had scarcely made its appearance when Massena inundated the valley with light troops, with whom we were soon warmly engaged; and, as their columns of attack moved forward to their support, we were driven gradually up the face of the mountain on our reserves. A considerable portion of the infantry of Marshal Ney's corps advanced steadily and in excellent order by the road leading to the crest of that part of the position where the Light Division was drawn out in line"..."We must give the French their due and say that no men could come up in a more resolute manner.

The 43d and 52d were formed on the summit of the heights and by most excellent management of Lord Wellington were kept rather behind the brow of the hill so that the French in their advance to the attack could see nothing but our green jackets peeping out from among the rough and broken ground and making every shot tell amongst them without their being able to do us any material injury."

"General Loison's division, which led the attack, was allowed by General Crawford to reach nearly the summit of the ridge, when he ordered a volley from his division, and a charge with the bayonet. The effect was instantaneous and most decisive; and it is impossible to describe the confusion and carnage which instantly ensued in the enemy's ranks[67]."

"All the prisoners who were taken agreed in the report that even the General who led on the attack did not conceive that the hill was defended by anything more than a few skirmishers and they were therefore not

[64] Sherer, 1996: 107-108.
[65] 'Light bob'. A slang term for a light infantryman.
[66] Also found in records as: Buzaco; Bussaco; or Busaco. Jonathan Leach's account of the battle presented here alternates between *Rough Sketches*, with which it begins, and the text of one of his letters written shortly after the event and quoted at length by Verner (1919: 148-150). Verner notes that with the possible exception of the identity of one of the French regiments (the 6th), Jonathan Leach's account is "absolutely borne out" by detailed archive researches made a century later.
[67] In this battle the Light Division suffered only 177 casualties while inflicting more than 1200 on the French facing them (Oman, 1986: 145).

agreeably surprised on their reaching the summit to be saluted with a volley and charge of bayonets from the 43d and 52d who were formed in line and ready to receive them. In an instant the irresistible three cheers and the cold steel sent the whole column to the right about and you may then fancy the confusion and destruction amongst them. Our Artillery and Riflemen and two Light Battalions firing into a whole Division racing down almost a precipice."

"It can be readily conceived, that so large a column, wedged close in a road of no great width, being once broken and forced back, those pressing on from the rear to support it were literally borne back down the mountain by the tide of fugitives, in spite of any exertions of theirs to retrieve matters.

The instant the attacking parties were turned back, they were exposed to the fire of our whole division; whilst our battalion and some caçadores were ordered to pursue, and to give them a flanking fire, and the horse artillery continued to pour on them a murderous fire of grape, as they were struggling through the narrow streets of Sula and trampling each other to death in their great haste to escape. Men, muskets, knapsacks, and bayonets, rolled down the side of the mountain in such a confused mass, as it is impossible to convey a just idea of"..."You could see them tumbling headlong over each other even those who were not hit.[68]"

"Whilst we were thus employed, General Regnier[69] made an attack equally desperate on Generals Picton[70], Leith[71] and Pack[72], far to our right. Those troops served Regnier's corps with much the same description of sauce which the Light Division had administered to Marshal Ney's. We were at too great a distance to distinguish what passed between the troops of Picton, Leith, and Regnier; but we were near enough to witness the gallant manner in which General Pack's Portuguese brigade charged and drove back with the bayonet a formidable attack made on it by the enemy, covering the ground with their dead."

"General Pack's Portuguese brigade formed line and charged in a most regular and spirited manner under a cannonade of round-shot from the enemy's batteries. I was quite hoarse with cheering and halloing. Whenever we saw the Portuguese about to charge, who were nearly a mile[73] distant, we all set up a howl which undoubtedly spirited them on and they behaved uncommonly well, much better than the most sanguine could have expected."

"This was the first trial made of the new Portuguese levies, organised by British officers, and it proved most satisfactory.

The 32d and 70th French regiments, both of high renown, were stated to have been nearly destroyed by Picton's division. The French General Simon, whose brigade was at the head of the column which attacked the Light Division, was wounded and made prisoner, with three hundred of his men, near the summit of the Sierra. No further attack was made by Massena after these failures, except by his light troops, who, like swarms of bees, filled the valley, and kept us constantly employed until towards evening, when the firing ceased on both sides, and a flag of truce came in, bringing

[68] One French soldier said he rolled from the top to the bottom of the mountain without knowing how he escaped (Tucker, 1846: 154-5).
[69] Reynier.
[70] Major-General Thomas Picton (1758-1815). He Commanded the 3rd Division. Former Governor of Trinidad but resigned in 1801 after accusations over the torture of a woman (Oman, 1986: 130-1). Smith said in the Peninsula Picton caused unnecessary loss of life by attacking when he should not, and he "was ever ready to find fault with the Light" [Division]. Made Lieutenant-General and knighted 1813.
[71] Major-General James Leith (1763-1816). Lieutenant-General and knighted 1813. British Commander-in-Chief in the West Indies and Governor of the Leeward Isles 1814.
[72] Denis Pack (1775-1823) Colonel in the army but assigned to a Portuguese brigade with local rank. Was a Brigadier-General by January 1812; Major-General 1813; knighted 1815. Was made Lieutenant-Governor of Plymouth in 1819.
[73] 1.6 km.

General Simon's baggage, and with it a pretty little Spanish woman, part of his establishment. The fair one was in tears, and appeared much agitated. During this cessation of hostilities, unarmed parties of both armies were employed in bringing away their wounded."

"During this cessation we went down amongst them for the sake of curiosity and as you may imagine it was a sad carnage. By Heaven! one little village was full of killed and wounded"..."I went down into the village of Sula[74], and had some conversation with several French officers and soldiers[75]. They acknowledged their loss to have been very severe; and one man assured me[76], that his company, which numbered one hundred men in the morning, could only muster twenty-two effective men after their repulse. Amongst the dead in the immediate front of the Light Division, I found men belonging to the following French regiments, and I cut some buttons off their coats:— the 6th, 26th, 66th, and 82d, the Legion du Midi, and a regiment of Germans"..."The French 82d and Legion du Midi are old Vimeiro friends."

"The time agreed on for the cessation of hostilities having expired, and the French evincing a disposition to hold the village of Sula with a few men, Lord Wellington, who was with our division at the moment, ordered a company of the 95th to drive them from it, which was speedily accomplished, and we established strong pickets in it for the night.

Thus ended the battle of Buzaco, a day in which the Marshal Prince of Esling was completely foiled in all his attempts, and was defeated with severe loss."

"Our Regiment lost more men than the 43d and 52d together and were in short engaged with the French light troops constantly, more or less for three days, and were much harassed. You will naturally wonder to see by the returns that our regiment lost no officers. I will account for it in two ways. In the first place we lost so many officers at the Coa which have not yet joined in consequence of their wounds (and three of whom are since dead) that we had a great scarcity, scarcely enough to do the duty. In the second place the hills occupied by the Light Division were extremely high and the approach to them near the summit full of craggy rocks. Amongst these and some fir trees our Companies lay scattered and had such excellent cover that I am puzzled to conceive how we contrived to lose forty-one men. Not an officer was hit."

"28th.— The next morning we were in expectation of another attack, as several deserters, who had come over to us in the night, agreed in the report that General Junot, whose corps had not been engaged the day before[77], had volunteered to storm, with fifteen thousand grenadiers, that point of the position where the Light Division stood.

No general attack, however, was made on the 28th; but Massena let slip swarms of light troops, as heretofore, and kept us eternally at work with them until night put an end to the contest. The French erected a half-moon battery on a hill immediately fronting us, and our artillery endeavoured

[74] The "little village".
[75] Sherer says, "In the course of the day, our men went down to a small brook, which flowed between the opposing armies, for water; and French and English soldiers might be seen drinking out of the same narrow stream, and even leaning over to shake hands with each other. One private, of my own regiment, actually exchanged forage-caps with a soldier of the enemy, as a token of regard and good-will. Such courtesies, if they do not disguise, at least soften the horrid features of war; and it is thus we learn to reconcile our minds to scenes of blood and carnage." (1996: 110-111).
[76] In the letter Leach notes this was a deserter from the Hanoverian Legion.
[77] This was the French VIII Corps which Masséna had held in reserve.

to throw shells on their working parties, but the distance was rather too long. Being on picket with my company in Sula, seven deserters came in during different periods of the night, all agreeing in the same story, that the French army had broken up, and was marching away to turn our left.

When day dawned on the 29th, we found that the reports of the deserters were correct, and that the whole allied army, except the Light Division and a small force of light cavalry, which were left on the position as a rear-guard, was already retiring on Coimbra. About nine o'clock in the morning we followed the main body, and bivouacked at night in a wood some miles from Buzaco."

In the Battle of Buçaco the allies' casualties were approximately 100 dead, 1050 wounded and 50 captured. The French lost approximately 900 dead, 3600 wounded and one general, three colonels, 33 other officers and 150 rank and file taken prisoner.

The French wounded, left on the field, were at the mercy of vengeful Portuguese locals as the allied army withdrew and Craufurd placed as many as he could in the convent on the ridge behind his position as the Light Division retired. The allied army now withdrew south towards Lisbon while the French army took up the pursuit. The Battle of Buçaco had achieved nothing militarily other than providing a morale boost to a retreating army and proving the worth of the newly trained Portuguese forces – to themselves as much as to their British allies.

The Lines

In September's autumn rains the march south continued with occasional skirmishes between the Light Division's cavalry and the French vanguard. On the 5th of October the Division reached Batalha where even the proximity of the French did not stop the Rifles getting up to mischief, including Jonathan:

'In the cathedral were buried many of the royal family of Braganza, and amongst the number a King John, in whose reign, I think, the cathedral was built. I know not who the culprits were, nor to what division of the army they belonged; but in going into the cathedral, I saw the coffin of the said King John open, and the body, which was of course embalmed, exposed to view, wrapped in rich robes of crimson velvet and gold. By way of a relic, I cut off a button and some gold fringe from his majesty's robes; whilst others, more ambitious, could be satisfied with nothing less than a royal finger[78]...

On the 6th, 7th, and 8th, we continued the retreat in unceasing rains, and halted one night in an uninhabited cottage with only half a roof on it, in which four of us, besides our servants, horses, mules, and donkeys, were huddled together. In endeavouring, by dint of a fire, to dry our clothes, which were fairly rusted on us by constant exposure to the weather by day and night, the remnant of the cottage, as the devil would have it, caught fire; and with great difficulty we succeeded in dragging forth from the flames

[78] This desecration occurred at the Monastery of Batalha, a Dominican abbey and one of the world's greatest examples of Christian Gothic architecture. It was founded in 1388 during the reign (1385-1433) of King João I. Verner suggests the body was that of João IV (1604-1656). Kincaid confirms the amputation was the work of a rifleman (Kincaid, 1981: 10)

and smoke our miserable quadrupeds and the baggage, and depositing them in the street, under as tremendous a torrent of rain as would have satisfied old Noah himself[79]. With the assistance of the soldiers, aided also by the continued rain, the flames were got under, and we re-entered our hut, where we passed the night, and started the following morning, in another delicious day of rain, to Alemquer.'

As the army withdrew towards Lisbon an edict went out to the inhabitants of the countryside through which it passed to abandon their homes and withdraw towards the capital, taking with them or destroying anything that might assist the advancing French force. The Portuguese bundled together what possessions they could, and the retreating allies were soon surrounded by a cloud of refugees. In attempting to describe the scenes Sherer despaired:

"My pen altogether fails me,—I feel that no powers of description can convey to the mind of my reader, the afflicting scenes, the cheerless desolation, we daily witnessed on our march from the Mondego to the lines. Wherever we moved, the mandate, which enjoined the wretched inhabitants to forsake their homes, and to remove or destroy their little property, had gone before us. The villages were deserted; the churches, retreats so often, yet so vainly confided in, were empty; the mountain cottages stood open and untenanted; the mills in the valley, but yesterday so busy, were motionless and silent."

Wellington was leading his army past the town of Santarém to *The Lines of Torres Vedras* just north of Lisbon. The Lines were a formidable array of fortifications along the range of hills running from the Atlantic coast in the west, near the town of Torres Vedras, to the River Tagus in the east, at this point a substantial and impassable waterway. Wellington had ordered the reinforcing of this natural barrier during the winter of 1809-1810. For this massive enterprise British army Royal Engineers had enlisted the help of 10,000 local labourers[80]. A front of 42 km was now defended by

[79] A reference to a story from the Bible in which God sent rains to flood the world and destroy all animal life, which had become corrupt. Before the rains came God warned Noah (a good man) and told him to build a ship, – an Ark – and put into it his family and just one male and one female of all animal species. When the flood came, only those aboard Noah's Ark survived to repopulate the world when the waters subsided (*Genesis*, Chapters 6-9).

[80] Testament to the quality of the work was the fact that the defences were still in excellent condition after a century of neglect when Verner visited them in 1913.

150 fortified emplacements mounting 447 heavy ship's guns, more powerful than any mobile field artillery. Arranged in three lines one behind the other, the fortifications were manned by 12,000 Portuguese troops and militia units and 8000 Spaniards, additional to the allies' incoming army of more than 50,000. Wellington could also draw on 25,000 irregulars of the Portuguese Ordenança. The ground around the lines was mined; the new arrivals dug yet more trenches and ramparts. Craufurd had the Light Division lay two lines of advance defences across a broad valley by digging up and laying out entire oak and chestnut trees, roots and all, with the interlocking crowns pointing towards the French. This *abatis* was overlooked by new stone walls nearly two metres high and one and a half thick. British warships patrolled the river to the east; and the garrison could be resupplied by the Royal Navy. The French had no idea the Lines were there. Masséna's surprise was total and his army came to a grinding halt in front of this crafted fortress; but the fortress was also a prison. The Leopard was in a cage and in October 1810 it sat with its tail flicking angrily in the sea.

— 5 —

London

Myself when young did eagerly frequent
Doctor and Saint, and heard great argument

Edward Fitzgerald[1]

[1] Edward Fitzgerald (1809-1883). English poet and scholar.
[2] Edward Donovan (1768-1837). Naturalist and author. Fellow of the Linnean Society. Originally wealthy. Built a huge natural history collection which he opened freely to the public for several years from 1807 as the London Museum and Institute of Natural History. From 1792 published a multi-volume work entitled *The Natural History of British Insects* issued in monthly parts.
[3] George Montagu (1753-1815). Born at Lackham in Wiltshire. Ornithologist and pioneer marine biologist. 'Montagu's Harrier' (*Circus pygargus* Daudin) and a number of fishes are named after him. In later life he was seen as a genial man who had a good word for everybody. See biographies by Bruce Cummings and especially Ron Cleevely which provided much of the information extracted here.

Elford Leach did not devote all his time in the five years to 1808 to his medical studies. He was also immersing himself in the literature of natural history. Even as a teenager he was showing an acute grasp of entomology, which in those days encompassed not just insects, but also spiders, centipedes, crustaceans and more. Making collecting forays into the gardens around Exeter, he found a species of centipede he did not recognise from his reading. Realising it must be new to science he gave it the name *Scolopendra hortensis* ('hortensis' meaning 'from a garden'), and sent it to the zoologist Edward Donovan[2] in London, then well known as the author of a monthly magazine on British insects. Donovan agreed with his identification and described the species as new in his publication, giving it Elford's new name. Still in his mid-teens, Elford had made his first contact with the scientific establishment outside Devon. He was also forging contacts inside Devon, and soon made the acquaintance of one of Britain's established field naturalists and a pioneer of marine zoology, George Montagu of Kingsbridge.

George Montagu[3]

George Montagu was a British ornithologist who first made his name in natural history circles with his *Ornithological Dictionary* of 1801. Born in Wiltshire, at the age of 17 he was commissioned as an officer in the 15th Regiment of Foot and spent the next five years serving in the north of England and in Ireland. In 1775, when the American colonies began fighting for recognition of their grievances, the regiment was ordered to North Carolina, arriving in May 1776, the year of the Declaration of Independence. Montagu served as a Captain during the generally successful actions against George Washington's forces during the rest of that year (when Washington

Historical Note

1804
February

In Vienna Beethoven[1] writes his 3rd symphony (*Eroica*). Richard Trevithick demonstrates the world's first steam railway locomotive on a circular track at the Penydarn ironworks in south Wales. It pulls a 10 ton load, a train of five waggons and 70 men for nine miles (14.5 km) at a speed of 5 miles per hour (just over 2 metres per second). The railway age is born.

18th May
Napoleon crowns himself Emperor of France.

12th December
Spain declares war on Britain.

1805

Jane Taylor[2] publishes her poem *Star* ("Twinkle twinkle little star, How I wonder what you are"...)

21st October
Nelson dies defeating the joint French-Spanish fleet at the Battle of Trafalgar.

1806

Building begins on the new Princetown Prison, Dartmoor ('Dartmoor Prison') to house French prisoners of war and replace the overcrowded facilities at Mill Bay.

January
6000 British troops capture the Cape of Good Hope from the Dutch.

November
Napoleon issues his *Berlin Decrees* outlawing trade with Britain for all French controlled territories. This trade ban is known as *The Continental System*.

11th November
Britain issues an Order in Council blockading all those Continental ports closed to British shipping. Neutral ships can trade at these ports, but only if they call at British ports first and pay duty on their cargo.

1807
—

Foundation of the Geological Society of London.
London acquires its first gas street-lighting.

25th March
Britain abolishes trading in slaves throughout its territories.

1808

The Times introduces the first war correspondent, Henry Crabb Robinson[3], to report from the Peninsula.

20th September
Covent Garden Theatre, London, destroyed by fire.

1809

Napoleon annexes the Papal States. In reply the Pope excommunicates him and is arrested and imprisoned.

24th February
Theatre Royal, Drury Lane, London, destroyed by fire.

September
Disturbances in Wales after the enclosure of formerly common land.

September-October
O.P. ('Old Price') riots at new Covent Garden Theatre when theatre-goers object to increased prices and the lack of public access to boxes.

25th October
Jubilee celebrations for George III, king for 50 years.

[1] Ludwig van Beethoven (1770-1827). Composer.
[2] Jane Taylor (1783-1824). English poet. Published in the work *Original Poems for Infant Minds* produced with her sister Ann (1782-1866).
[3] Henry Crabb Robinson (1775-1867). A lawyer and diarist. Later (1828) one of the founders of London University.

was forced out of Long Island and New York) and throughout most of 1777. He fought in the Danbury Raid in April 1777; at the Battle of the Brandywine in September (where the 15th Foot ran low on musket balls and all but the best shots finished the action firing blanks rather than let the Americans know); and at Germantown in October when Washington launched an unsuccessful attack against the British lines.

At the end of 1777, after just over seven years service, Montagu left the army and returned to Wiltshire where he later obtained a commission in the Wiltshire Regiment of militia. Although nominally a county force, the Wiltshire Regiment also served further afield and it was in Wales in 1791 that Montagu became the regiment's Lieutenant-Colonel, hence his common identification today as Colonel George Montagu.

He had married Anne Courtenay in 1773, and they now had six children, but it seems to have been an earthly rather than a heavenly match. In about 1795 he met Mrs Elizabeth ('Eliza') Dorville[4] and, leaving his wife, he and Eliza formed an attachment which would last for the rest of his life. She accompanied him on his military duties, which for the next two years were in the West Country, and bore him at least one child.

Montagu had been interested in ornithology since his youth and while in North America had been captivated by the colourful and exotic birds, which he shot. With an eye honed by country sports and a genuine interest in nature, the richness of the Devon wildlife was not lost on him. In 1798 he and Eliza (who he referred to in correspondence either as 'Mrs Dorville' or 'my friend') rented Knowle House, just outside Kingsbridge.

Needless to say, given the high moral stance of English 'Society' at this time[5], Montagu's separation from his wife to live openly with his friend did not endear him to his fellow officers in the regiment or (as his biographer Ron Cleevely notes) to their wives. His elder brother James also effectively cut George out of his Will as a result of the co-habitation then promptly died, which initiated a socially embarrassing and personally costly legal challenge that was to run for years. This was all too much for the militia.

In 1799 Montagu was court-martialled in Plymouth, ostensibly for actions prejudicial to junior officers and the resulting breakdown of regimental discipline – but no-one was really fooled. Montagu himself said in evidence, 'Should this Honourable Court... determine to hear a long history of wives and mistresses... it would be highly improper for me as a Prisoner to question its decision'. It did so determine and after a hearing lasting 15 days concluded his conduct

[4] née Elizabeth Woolf (died 1844).
[5] In Regency Society moral standards were so high, a single standard was frequently not enough.

Montagu's Harrier

was derogatory to his situation as Field Commanding Officer of the regiment, and not consistent with the need for good order and harmony within the corps. He was compelled to resign his commission.

Despite this his military competence was never called into question. The Commander-in-Chief of the Wiltshire Militia expressed the highest opinion of his military capability in a letter to the Judge-Advocate, and in 1803, when France threatened to invade, Montagu was persuaded to accept command of the South Devon Corps of Guides. Other than this however, his military life was over.

After his retirement from the militia he and Mrs Dorville turned their minds to natural history full-time and his *Ornithological Dictionary* was published two years later. This brought him to the attention not only of naturalists, but of sportsmen – Sir William Elford certainly corresponded with him on ornithological matters – but Montagu was more than an ornithologist. He was interested in all animals, whatever their size and whatever their habitat. Even the coastline near his home attracted his attention at a time when few naturalists took much interest in the marine animals of the shore, and he began to collect with the assistance of his servant Mr J. Gibbs[6].

Field naturalists should not cast their net too widely. This was Montagu's view. If they restrict their focus to one small geographical area, and attempt to understand as much of what they see as possible, they will shed more light than if they try to understand one type of animal over vast geographical ranges. He practised what he preached and had to invest in a microscope to do so; many of the marine species he described are only a few millimetres in length. He also expressed it as his aim, 'to have drawings taken of all the most... new and interesting subjects... while alive, ... the only possible mode of ascertaining the form of the softer Mollusca animals'. Not for him a study of shrivelled and pickled carcasses. These drawings and those of the birds would be made by Eliza Dorville as she slowly taught herself the skills with pen and watercolours.

Knowle House

[6] Mr J. Gibbs. We do not know his first name, but his toils must have been of considerable assistance, as the rather stout Montagu suffered intermittently from gout. Gibbs also had responsibility for stuffing some of Montagu's birds (Cleevely, 1978: 478 notes 62 and 64). Montagu also had birds stuffed by Nicholas Luscombe, a Kingsbridge lawyer (D'Urban & Mathew, 1892: lxxxv).

Montagu's environmental focus and his stress on examining live animals showed him to be a true naturalist, not merely an assembler of trophies. He was also willing to undertake long-term studies, as evidenced by his approach to ornithology. To ascertain whether similar birds with differing plumage were different sexes or developmental stages of the same species, he would often hand-rear clutches of birds taken from the same nest to observe how each developed. This lent Knowle House the air of a menagerie as well as a museum and it was described by a neighbour as having, "live birds all over the grounds, and ducks, gulls and all sorts of swimming birds on the pond." A wildly eccentric and exciting house like this must have been a magnet to other local naturalists.

One of these was Charles Prideaux. He was a member of an ancient Devon family, primarily of attorneys, who had lived in the Plymouth and Kingsbridge area for generations. Charles' branch of the Prideauxs had been members of the Society of Friends (Quakers) since his grand-father had joined the Society in the previous century. Natural history interests ran in the family and Charles' cousin, John Prideaux, a druggist and keen geologist, was later professor of chemistry at the Cornish Mining School[7]. Charles was more interested in zoology, especially the molluscs, and was later described as "decidedly our best British conchologist[8] as far as relates to the knowledge of the species.[9]" Charles Prideaux was also Elford Leach's cousin[10] and it was probably Charles or Sir William Elford who brought the youngest Leach into contact with Montagu. This contact appears to have opened Elford's eyes to a whole new environment. Although he would never desert entomology, he would now increasingly take an interest in the diverse animals of the coast and inshore waters.

Onwards and Upwards

The years passed and finally Elford's Exeter apprenticeship drew to a close. Although not intending to practise medicine it was still his aim to obtain a medical qualification, at that time the most credible qualification for a naturalist. However, to progress in his medical education he needed to move from Exeter, a provincial town, to a national centre of medical learning where he would encounter a greater range and depth of subject matter, and teachers of greater experience and renown. In his day the two recognised medical centres in Britain were Edinburgh – where the university had, as now, a very high medical reputation – and the London teaching hospitals. He chose London, as did eight or nine hundred other would-be doctors each year. Although not at that time a university town, London had strong traditions in medical training at its large, busy hospitals and there were opportunities elsewhere in the city to subscribe to private lectures on a wide range of subjects. The English capital was also the home of many of the national scientific societies.

So it was that in late summer, 1808, a 17 year old Elford Leach left Devon and took the coach east[11].

[7] Charles Prideaux (1782-1869). Born Kingsbridge and later a magistrate (Justice of the Peace – 'J.P.') for the town. Son of George Prideaux (1744-1819) and Anna (née Cookworthy) (1751-1774). Charles had many brothers and sisters including William (1778-1843) and Walter (1779-1832) a banker. Their grandfather George Prideaux (1707-1773) was the first to join the Society of Friends. John Prideaux (1787-1859) was the grandson of George senior through his 3rd wife Jane Morris (1753-1779). John was professor of the mining school at Camborne from 1839-1841 (Prideaux, 1989: 236-240, 251).
[8] Someone who studies sea-shells and snail shells.
[9] Letter: W.E. Leach to Alexander MacLeay, 20th October 1816 (Loc: Linnean Society of London, MacLeay Correspondence).
[10] Correctly he was Elford's second-cousin. Charles' grandmother (the 2nd wife of George Prideaux senior) was Dorothy, the daughter of Kingsbridge surgeon Alexander Wills (Prideaux, 1989: 236-241, 250-251). Dorothy's sister Grace Wills married Lancelot Elford and was Elford Leach's maternal grandmother.
[11] If the arrangement was the same as in the late 1820s, he would have been deposited in London in Piccadilly at one of the two London termini for West Country coaches: Hatchett's White Horse Cellar or the Gloucester Coffee House. Stage coaches to the West Country also started here, as did the Royal Mail coaches, which loaded mail in Piccadilly rather than at the General Post Office (Jackson, 1987: [105]).

St Paul's Cathedral from the River Thames

London

In the Autumn, as London fumed at the Convention of Cintra, Elford settled into lodgings at N° 20 Southampton Buildings, a street just off Chancery Lane in the city's legal heartland[12]. This would be his home for the next two years. Southampton Buildings survives today but has changed beyond recognition. In Elford's day it was a street of tenements containing leased apartments, the occupants of some of which additionally let their spare rooms. For a brief period during his residence, from March to the end of May 1809, brother and sister Charles and Mary Lamb[13] – authors of the ever-popular *Lambs' Tales from Shakespeare* – lived at N° 34, and in March 1811, after Elford had left, their friend the poet Coleridge[14] would live in the street while lecturing on Shakespeare. In Elford's day N° 21, at the Chancery Lane end of the street, was a coffee-house[15] which would later be frequented by another friend of the Lambs, the essayist and critic William Hazlitt[16], when he lived at N° 9.

While Elford was in London, the capital was visited by tourist Louis Simond – French by birth but now living in America with his English wife[17]. In his journals he has left us an impression of the London Elford knew[18]. They may even have passed on the street.

'Foot-passengers walk on with ease and security along the smooth flag-stones of the side pavement. Their eyes, mine at least, are irresistibly attracted by the allurements of the shops, particularly print-shops; not that they always exhibit those specimens of the art so justly admired all over Europe, but oftener caricatures of all sorts... Some shops exhibit instruments of mathematics, of optics, of chemistry, beautifully arranged; the admirable polish, and learned simplicity of the instruments, suggest the idea of justness

[12] Did a lawyer friend of the family help him find accommodation?

[13] Mary Lamb (1765-1847) and Charles Lamb (1775-1834).

[14] Samuel Taylor Coleridge (1772-1834). A Devonian, born at Ottery St Mary. Author of *The Rime of the Ancient Mariner* and numerous other works; lecturer on politics, religion and literature.

[15] This was later (ca 1820?) called the *Southampton Coffee House*, but in 1811 the only coffee-house listed for Southampton Buildings was the *Staples & Lincoln's Inn Coffee-house* which is probably the same establishment (Anon., 1811: 394).

[16] William Hazlitt (1778-1830).

[17] Louis Simond (1767-1831). A French national who emigrated to the United States just before the French Revolution. A ship owner, he had married his English wife Frances (née Wilkes), a niece of English politician John Wilkes (1727-1797), in New York in July 1791. They visited Britain as tourists in 1810-1811.

[18] Simond (1817) **1**: 26-37; **2**: 151-152.

Southampton Buildings in the 19th Century from its junction with Chancery Lane

and of perfection—recalling to your mind all you know of their uses, and inspiring a wish to know more. Jewellers' shops, glittering with costly trinkets, give me another sort of pleasure—that of feeling no sort of desire for any thing they contain. Finally, pastry-cook shops, which, about the middle of the day, and of the long interval between breakfast and dinner, are full of decent persons of both sexes, mostly men, taking a slight repast of tarts, buns, &c. with a glass of whey; it costs 6d. or 8d. sterling. A young and pretty woman generally presides behind the counter, as in the coffee-houses of Paris...

Prepossessed with a high opinion of English corpulency, I expected to see everywhere the original of *Jacques Roast-beef*. No such thing; the human race is here rather of mean stature—less so, perhaps, than the true Parisian race; but there is really no great difference... The size of London draught-horses makes up for that of men; those which draw brewers' carts and coal-waggons are gigantic—perfect elephants! On the other hand, I have observed dwarf horses passing swiftly along the streets, mounted by boys, who appeared employed in carrying letters or messages. No armed watch, *guet*, or *marechaussée*, is ever met patroling the streets, or the highways; no appearance of police, and yet no apparent want of police; nothing disorderly.'

In the genteel areas west of the City[19] the mornings are calm, 'not a mouse stirring before ten o'clock; the shops then begin to open. Milk-women, with their pails perfectly neat, suspended at the two extremities of a yoke, carefully shaped to fit the shoulders, and surrounded with small tin measures of cream, ring at every door, with reiterated pulls, to hasten the maid-servants, who come half asleep to receive a measure as big as an egg, being the allowance of a family...

[19] 'The City' is the historical heart of London, within its ancient walls. It is now the main financial centre and is also known as 'The Square Mile'. The more affluent residential areas were built to the west of The City, the labouring classes tended to live to the east (Partly because the prevailing wind in Britain is from the south-west. The rich chose to live up-wind of the smoke from the countless coal fires).

Not a single carriage—not a cart are seen passing. The first considerable stir is the drum and military music of the Guards, marching from their barracks to Hyde Park, having at their head three or four negro giants, striking, high, gracefully, and strong, the resounding cymbal. About three or four o'clock the fashionable world gives some signs of life, issuing forth to pay visits, or rather leave cards at the doors of friends, never seen but in the crowd of assemblies; to go to shops, see sights, or lounge in Bond Street—an ugly, inconvenient street, the attractions of which it is difficult to understand. At five or six they return home to dress for dinner. The streets are then lighted from one end to the other, or rather edged on either side with two long lines of little brightish dots, indicative of light, but yielding in fact very little—these are the lamps. They are not suspended in the middle of the streets as at Paris, but fixed on irons eight or nine feet high, ranged along the houses. The want of reflectors is probably the cause of their giving so little light[20]. From six to eight the *noise* of wheels increases; it is the dinner hour. A multitude of carriages, with two eyes of flame staring in the dark before each of them, shake the pavement and the very houses, following and crossing each other at full speed...

For two hours, or nearly, there is a pause; at ten a *redoublément* comes on. This is the great crisis of dress, of noise, and of rapidity—a universal hubbub; a sort of uniform grinding and shaking, like that experienced in a great mill with fifty pair of stones; and, if I was not afraid of appearing to exaggerate, I should say that it came upon the ear like the fall of Niagara, heard at two miles distance! This crisis continues undiminished till twelve or one o'clock; then less and less during the rest of the night—till, at the approach of day, a single carriage is heard now and then at a great distance.'

To the east of these upper-class residential areas, 'all is motion and activity in the city, as early as ten o'clock in the morning. The crowd, the carriages, and the mud increase rapidly as you advance from west to east, during the forenoon; and an hour of steady walking will take you from one extreme to the other...

London does not strike with admiration; it is regular, clean, convenient, (I am speaking of the best part) but the site is flat; the plan monotonous; the predominant colour of objects dingy and poor. It is altogether without great faults and without great beauties. Suppose yourself in one of the best streets, it extends *à perte de vue* before you, in an undeviating strait line; the side walks wide and smooth; every door with its stone steps, its iron railing, and its lamp; one house differing from its neighbour in no one thing but the number on the door and the name of the occupant. Turn the next corner and you have another street as long, as wide, and as strait, and so on from street to street... This palpable immensity has something in it very heavy and stupifying.'

The immensity extended to the population. By far the largest city in Britain, London now contained almost one million inhabitants and was expanding fast. Then, as now, size had its disadvantages. Simond advised the visitor who wanted courtesy from the English to look for it in the countryside, for "London is not their home; it is an encampment for business and pleasure, where every body thinks of himself. You might as well look for humanity in a field of battle[21]".

To the east of the City of London the docks absorbed the produce of home and empire. Coals from Newcastle, sugar from the West Indies and spices from India. With the Royal Navy dominating the high seas, a Britain at war was not a Britain under siege.

[20] In 1814 Russian officer Berend-Johann ('Boris') Uxkull (1793-1870) said of Paris, "This capital is enhanced by being seen and contemplated at night, from afar or from a height, when thousands of street-lamps light up its shadows. That is when it gives the impression of being a real fairyland." (Uexküll, 1966: 182). For London, Mark Lemon noted that in the 16th Century the street lighting in London "only served to make darkness visible" (Lemon, 1867: 76-77) The first street lights powered by coal gas had been introduced in London in the year before Elford arrived but few streets were yet supplied. (Lemon presumably took the phrase "darkness visible" from Milton's *Paradise Lost*: "on all sides round as one great furnace flam'd; yet from those flames no light, but rather darkness visible serv'd only to discover sights of woe" John Milton (1608-1674) English poet born in London).

[21] Simond (1817) **2**: 288-289. Two centuries have changed only the extent of the battlefield.

St Katharine's Dock,
next to the Tower of London.

To the west the moneyed classes played. This was the time of the Gentlemen's gambling clubs and of the dandies, king among whom was the incomparable George 'Beau' Brummell[22] who dedicated his life to perfecting the art of male dress, although he was admired as much for his taste in furniture, books and horses, as for his clothes, which were immaculate but muted. Brummell was not the lacey fop often portrayed. He scorned frills, gaudy fabrics or scent (he was fastidiously clean) and was the first man to wear simple black evening dress. Once being told of a Gentleman who was so well dressed that everyone turned to stare at him Brummell replied simply, "Then he is not well-dressed.[23]"

Elford Leach, doubtless less concerned with the meticulous precision of his cravats, had chosen to enrol as a student at the ancient[24] and bustling[25] St Bartholomew's Hospital (known popularly as 'Barts'). Just a few hundred metres from St Paul's Cathedral, St Bartholomew's had been a medical teaching institution for centuries (William Harvey, who discovered the circulation of the blood, had taught there from 1609 to 1643[26]) but the medical school proper had been founded only in 1791 by the activities of a teacher who would play a part in Elford's life long after he had ceased to be a student, John Abernethy.

John Abernethy[27]

In a similar manner to Elford's apprenticeship at the Devon and Exeter Hospital, John Abernethy had been apprenticed, at the age of fifteen, to Charles Blicke[28], then an assistant surgeon at St Bartholomew's. In 1787, when Blicke was appointed to a surgeoncy at St Bartholomew's, Abernethy obtained the vacant assistant surgeoncy.

Assistant surgeons at that time received no salary and their hospital role was routinely only observational. They had no hospital patients except

[22] George Bryan Brummell (1778-1840). Educated at Eton and (briefly) Oxford. Served for four years as an officer in the 10th Light Dragoons. A great favourite of the equally fashion-obsessed Prince of Wales, until they quarrelled in 1813. Brummell's gambling debts drove him from England to Calais in 1815 where he lived until he died, penniless and insane.

[23] Priestley, 1971: 48.

[24] Founded 1102 by Rahere, minstrel to King Henry I.

[25] In 1809 the hospital received 3849 in-patients and 4540 out-patients (Anon., 1811: 253).

[26] William Harvey (1578-1657).

[27] John Abernethy FRS (1764-1831). Most of the following is drawn from Macilwain (1856) who was a student of Abernethy from 1816.

[28] Sir Charles Blicke (1745-1815).

with the permission of their principals, or in their absence, and a man could be an assistant surgeon for decades. Without fee-paying hospital patients, and with the fees paid by the medical students going directly to the surgeons-in-chief[29], it was necessary for assistant surgeons to find alternative sources of income. Other than taking private patients one obvious fee-earner was giving subscription lectures. Various medical professionals lectured in this way, usually from their homes, with medical students being attracted to the better-regarded teachers and paying to attend their classes.

Despite his inherent shyness Abernethy began lecturing, not from his home but in a room at Bartholomew's Close, near the hospital[30]. He approached the art of lecturing with considerable application and careful practice and soon developed a reputation within the city. His private classes on anatomy, surgery, pathology and physiology were attracting students from all the London hospitals and within a short time the facilities at Bartholomew's Close were no longer large enough to hold his audiences. In 1791 the governors of St Bartholomew's rectified this by building the hospital's first lecture theatre. Abernethy, almost inadvertently, had founded the medical school that survives today.

Abernethy was much more than a medical practitioner. He was interested in all aspects of the study of life. He was one of the first to stress the importance to medical study of comparative anatomy (comparing the structure of humans with other species); he was a competent chemist; he analysed plants treated with acids; he grew plants on cloth soaked with distilled water to see if they would grow as well as in soil, then he fed these plants to rabbits to see if they contained the necessary nutritional requirements. He conducted experiments on animal tissues, such as the muscles from killed frogs, but had an abhorrence of vivisection or experiments involving animal suffering. Although a religious man his objections were as much a questioning of the scientific validity of such experiments as an expression of moral outrage. In his lectures he avoided religious considerations, merely taking the standpoint 'do as you would be done by'.

Of Abernethy's lecturing style, there are many appreciative eye witness reports. He apparently did not convey as much information as some of the

[29] This was the case until 1815. Before this the three full surgeons – for 500-600 patients – shared the annual income from student fees of £2000-£3000.

[30] Abernethy lived in St Mary Axe, or in Mildred's Court in the Poultry (Macilwain, 1856: 38).

[31] *fide* former student Sir Benjamin Collins Brodie *Bt* (1783-1862) (*Dictionary of National Biography*: 'Abernethy').

[32] George Macilwain (1797-1882).

[33] A subtle, student-oriented distinction that thoughtful teachers may recognise.

[34] John Butter (1791-1877). Born Exeter. Surgeon to the South Devon Militia, Plymouth in 1817. M.D. Edinburgh 1820. Co-founder in 1821 of the Plymouth Eye Dispensary (now the Royal Eye Infirmary, Plymouth). Author of *Ophthalmic Diseases* (1821) and *Dockyard Diseases, or Irritable Fever* (1825). Lost an eye in the early 1850s and later became totally blind. Was Abernethy's student according to Macilwain (1856: 9fn).

St Bartholomew's Hospital.

The enclosed well in the centre of the quadrangle was installed in about 1810. The hospital's apothecary, Thomas Wheeler, later sent Elford Leach invertebrate animals he had found in the water taken from it (*Edinburgh Encyclopaedia*, **7**(2): 402-403).

other lecturers, but what he did convey he conveyed well, and once heard it was not forgotten[31]. His biographer and former student George Macilwain[32] says he seemed to lecture, not so much as if he was telling the students what he knew, as telling them something they did *not* know[33]:

"His position was always easy and natural—sometimes homely, perhaps. In the Anatomical Lecture, he always stood, and either leant against the wall, with his hands folded before him, or resting one hand on the table, with the other perhaps in his pocket. In his Surgical Lecture, he usually sat, and very generally with one leg resting on the other.

He was particularly happy in a kind of coziness, or friendliness of manner, which seemed to identify him with his audience; as if we were all about to investigate something interesting *together*, and not as if we were going to be 'lectured at' at all. He spoke as if addressing each individual, and his discourse, like a happy portrait, always seemed to be looking you in the face."

This was the gifted and inspirational teacher at St Bartholomew's in 1808 who would guide the young Elford Leach on his arrival from Devon – and perhaps not just Elford Leach; another young Devonian was to study under Abernethy, John Butter[34]. Butter was born in January 1791, making him the same age as Elford, and both had studied at the Devon and Exeter Hospital, probably together. They may have moved to London at the same time[35].

As well as studying anatomy under Abernethy and William Lawrence[36], a former student of Abernethy's, Elford also received lectures on comparative anatomy from James Macartney[37], another of Abernethy's students, and lectures on *Materia Medica*[38] (the modern Pharmacy and Pharmacology) and *Practice of Physic*. Macartney was an outstanding

[35] They knew each other by 1821 when Elford supported Butter's election as Fellow of the Royal Society.
[36] Sir William Lawrence (1783-1876). From 1816 Professor of Comparative Anatomy at the Royal College of Surgeons. Abernethy was the Professor of Anatomy & Surgery from 1814.
[37] James Macartney (1770-1843). Born Armagh. Studied medicine at Dublin and the Hunterian (or 'Great Windmill Street') School of Medicine, London, with additional study at St Thomas' Hospital and Guy's Hospital. He also studied under Abernethy who had him appointed demonstrator in anatomy at St Bartholomew's. Lectured in Comparative Anatomy & Surgery at St Bartholomew's 1800-1811. His future at St Bartholomew's was limited as he had not been apprenticed there. FRS February 1811. MD St Andrews May 1813. Professor of Anatomy & Surgery, Dublin, from 1813.
[38] *Materia Medica*: drug use (including plants) in the treatment of disease.

anatomist and has been described as a philosophical biologist far in advance of his time[39]. He edited the publications of the great French anatomist, Georges Cuvier[40] – his work on morphology in some senses surpassing Cuvier's – and completed an excellent study of the vascular system of birds. His analysis of vertebrate systems would not have been wasted on the enthusiastic Elford Leach. Outside the hospital Elford attended winter lectures on comparative anatomy given by Everard Home[41], a surgeon at St George's Hospital[42].

While Elford studied at St Bartholomew's, these were not the only gifted lecturers he encountered. He also attended public lectures in chemistry at The Royal Institution, where their celebrated professor, Humphry Davy[43] was lecturing to record crowds.

Humphry Davy

Humphry Davy was a lifelong amateur poet and professional chemist, originally from Penzance in Cornwall. As a young man he spent several years apprenticed to a local apothecary and surgeon but in 1798 (after a meeting with Gregory Watt, the son of steam-engine pioneer James Watt[44]) he found employment at Dr Thomas Beddoes' Pneumatic Institution at Bristol[45] where research was being conducted into the medical potential of recently discovered gases. In the three years Davy was at Bristol he purified various gaseous substances and tested their effects by inhaling them himself. His sensitive health in later life may have been the result of this experimentation, but he eventually discovered the anaesthetic (and somewhat pleasurable) effects of inhaling nitrous oxide, or 'laughing gas'. This later became an established anaesthetic, especially for dentistry, at a time when most surgery was conducted without pain suppression. It is still used today.

Davy generously allowed his friends to share his laughing gas experiences, including at this time the poets Coleridge[46] and Southey[47], whom he had befriended at Bristol. Southey thought Davy a miraculous young man, and Coleridge said, "living thoughts spring up like turf under his feet.[48]" Others agreed and in 1801 the 23 year old Davy was appointed to the recently

formed[49] Royal Institution of Great Britain in London to arrange the chemical experiments used in their public lectures. The following year, when the incumbent lecturer died, Davy was made professor of chemistry[50], giving the lectures himself, but it was his original research in the Royal Institution's laboratory that was to make him a household name.

In 1800 news had reached Britain that Alessandro Volta[51] had arranged a series of copper and zinc plates in a chemical solution and this 'pile' had generated an electric current.

[39] *Dictionary of National Biography*: Macartney.
[40] Léopold Chrétien Frédéric Dagobert Cuvier (1769-1832). French comparative anatomist and administrator. Adopted the name 'Georges' (His elder brother Georges Charles Henri Cuvier (1765-1769) died in the year of his birth. Confusingly, a younger brother (b.1773) was named Frédéric Georges Cuvier, see later). 'Georges' educated (not primarily in natural history) at Stuttgart. In 1802 became Professor of Comparative Anatomy at the Muséum d'Histoire Naturelle, Paris, and Professor at the Collège de France. Made a knight (chevalier) then baron. Held many government posts in the administration of education and as a state councillor. The finest comparative anatomist of the day. Prominent in successive Revolutionary, Napoleonic and Monarchist governments.
[41] Sir Everard Home *Bt* (1756-1832). [His name was possibly pronounced 'Hewm' as is common with this name today] Professor of Anatomy & Surgery at the Royal College of Surgeons. See also page 281 note 60.
[42] Near Hyde Park Corner.
[43] Humphry Davy (1778-1829). Son of wood-carver. Developed an improved miner's safety lamp in 1815. Knight 1812; Baronet 1818.
[44] James Watt (1735-1819). Improver and manufacturer of the steam engine and inventor of the concept 'horse-power.' The unit of power, the Watt, is named after him.
[45] Thomas Beddoes (1760-1808). Educated at Oxford, then medicine at London and Edinburgh. MD Oxford University then from 1788 Reader in Chemistry at Oxford With views sympathetic to the French Revolution he resigned in

Penzance, Cornwall

1792 and moved to Clifton in Bristol where he established his 'Pneumatic Institution' for researching disease treatment by inhalation. The Wedgwood pottery family provided £1000 and James Watt designed his apparatus. Beddoes recruited Humphry Davy and married Anna Edgeworth, whom Davy described as, "The best and most amiable woman in the world." When Davy left for London the institute closed, but Beddoes remained popular as a local physician. On his death Southey (see below) said, "From Beddoes I hoped for more good to the human race than any other individual. Coleridge thought Beddoes' death took more out of his own life than any former event.

[46] Samuel Taylor Coleridge. Already noted. He was supported by an annuity of £150 from the Wedgwoods. By 1800 he was already addicted to opium.

[47] Robert Southey (1774-1843). A native of Bristol who had known Coleridge since their student days. Their wives were sisters. Poet Laureate from 1813.

[48] Priestley, 1971: 147.

[49] Founded 1799.

[50] 'Professor' at this time was applied to any teacher at an institution or university. This meaning has generally been retained in the USA but in Britain the term has since been reserved only for senior posts within a university.

[51] Alessandro Giuseppe Antonio Anastasio Volta, Count (1745-1827). Professor of Physics at Pavia University, Lombardy. The 'Volt' is named after him.

[52] By 1811 Davy was lecturing three times a week to packed houses (Anon., 1811: 236).

[53] Simond (1817) 1: 43.

He had invented the battery. Davy, like many researchers across Europe, immediately set to work exploring the potential of this device. In 1807 in the basement of the Royal Institution he linked three piles with a total of 600 double plates and passed the resulting current through molten potash. When small spheres of metallic material appeared at the negative pole Davy literally danced around the laboratory in excitement. He had discovered a new element, which he called Potassium. The same year he repeated the experiment with molten caustic soda and discovered Sodium. As a singular mark of respect, the Institute of France awarded Davy a prize – instituted by Napoleon when first Consul – of 3000 Francs 'for the best experiment using galvanic fluid' (an old name for electricity). France had been at war with Britain since 1793.

In 1808, when Elford arrived in London, Davy was at his productive height. He had just built the world's largest Voltaic pile with 2000 double plates and used it to isolate Calcium, Magnesium, Barium and Strontium. The 900-seat auditorium at the Royal Institution was crowded for his public presentations[52]. Here in these cramped rows, elbow to elbow with his neighbours in the rapt congregation, Elford Leach shared the excitement of these new wonders.

Royal Institution lectures were designed to be spectacular and entertaining as well as educational, and Davy made full use of the violently reactive nature of his new Potassium to startle and delight the audience crowded around and above him in the steeply raked amphitheatre. "A small bit of potassium thrown in a glass of water, or upon a piece of ice, never fails to excite a gentle murmur of applause." reported Louis Simond[53], who also attended the lectures. "More than one half of the audience is female, and it is the most attentive portion. I often observe these fair disciples of science taking notes timidly, and as by stealth, on small bits of paper".

Women were particularly attracted to the handsome and naturally bashful Davy, with his soft Cornish accent.

'The voice and manner of Mr Davy are rather gentle,' thought Simond[54], 'he knows what nature has given him, and what it has withheld, and husbands his means accordingly. You may always foresee by a certain tuning or pitching of the organ of speech to a graver key, thrusting his chin into his neck, and even pulling out his cravat, when Mr Davy is going to be eloquent,—for he rarely yields to the inspiration till he is duly prepared... The elocution of this celebrated chemist is very different from the usual tone of men of science in England; his lectures are frequently figurative and poetical; and he is occasionally carried away by the natural tendency of his subject, and of his genius, into the depths of moral philosophy and of religion... I have heard the moral digressions of the illustrious naturalist, and his solemn appeals to the Supreme Wisdom, severely criticised; but the greatest part of his audience hears them with delight and applause... I must say, however, that I think the satisfaction of Mr Davy's audience is sometimes expressed with more zeal than delicacy. Where clapping is allowed, hissing may follow.[55]'

Several streets away from the Royal Institution hissing had already started, but this was hissing of an altogether different kind. The mechanical hiss of escaping steam. In 1808 fellow Cornishman Richard Trevithick, flushed with the success of his horseless railway locomotive trials in Wales had brought an example to Gower Street in London (near the British Museum) where he had set up a circular track and was charging a shilling to anyone seduced by the racy advertising to ride behind this 'Portable Steam Engine'.

Catch me who can

'Catch me who can' read the posters. 'Mechanical Power Subduing Animal Speed' (The type of animal was not specified). This triumph of engineering was seen by observers as little more than a novel fair-ground attraction and its reception was lukewarm. In reality Trevithick was too far ahead of his time. It would be another 17 years before the first commercial railway was opened between Stockton and Darlington in the north-east of England, transporting coal and other freight, and running both trains pulled by steam and trains pulled by horses. It was 1830 before the first true passenger railway was opened, running between Liverpool and Manchester.

Natural history

In London, although Elford was busy with his studies and attending extra-curricular lectures, he was, as ever, making time for his beloved zoology. He seems to have made contact with London entomologists as soon as he arrived, and at the beginning of November 1808 one of these, George Milne[56], started taking him as a guest to the Linnean Society of London[57], at that time

[54] Simond (1817) **2**: 196-8.
[55] Wellington shared Simond's general concern, saying, "I hate to hear that cheering. If once you allow soldiers to express an opinion, they may on some other occasion hiss instead of cheer." (Howarth, 1968: 42).
[56] George Milne of Surrey Place, near Margate, Kent.
[57] Founded 1788 by James (later Sir James) Edward Smith (1759-1828) after he purchased Linnaeus' collections and brought them to London in 1783. Smith was the Society's President from its foundation to his death.
[58] This was formerly the Turk's Head tavern.
[59] Thomas Marsham (died 1819) (Founder Secretary 1788-98; Treasurer 1798-1816). Entomologist. Amiable and respected, but for the last decade of his life was in severe financial difficulties and 'borrowed' from the Society, which forced his resignation as treasurer and led to talk of legal action – vetoed by J.E. Smith (Walker, 1997).
[60] Alexander MacLeay (1767-1848). (Secretary 1798-1825). Entomologist. Lived at Queen's Square, Westminster. Secretary of the Transport Board 1806-1818 then pensioned. Colonial secretary to New South Wales 1825-1837; first President of the Australian Museum, 1836; first Speaker of the New South Wales Legislative Council 1843. Retired 1846.
[61] James ('Jamie') Sowerby (1757-1822). Artist, naturalist and publisher. Produced *English Botany* (36 volumes, 1790-1814) with James Edward Smith (who wrote most of the text); and *Coloured Figures of English Fungi* (1797-1815); *British Mineralogy* (1804-1817); *The Mineral Conchology of Great Britain* (1812–)(continued by his son James de Carle Sowerby to

1846); and other finely illustrated works.

[62] Charles Robert Darwin (12th February 1809-1882). Born the same day as Abraham Lincoln. His joint presentation to the Linnean Society with Alfred Russel Wallace (1823-1913) – read from the podium on 1st July 1858 with both men absent – was the first announcement of Natural Selection.

[63] Henry Ellis (1777-1869). Later Sir Henry Ellis *KH*. 1796 Under Librarian at the Bodleian Library, Oxford. 1797 Law Fellow, St John's College, Oxford. 1801 British Museum extra-Assistant Librarian, Dept of Printed Books; 1805 Assistant Librarian; 1806 Keeper of Printed Books; 1812-1828 Keeper of Manuscripts; 1814-1828 Museum Secretary; 1828-1856 Principal-Librarian (i.e. Museum Director).

[64] e.g. 7th February 1809. Linnean Society of London, *General Minute Book*.

[65] George Shaw MD (1751-1813). Born Buckinghamshire. Educated Oxford (BA 1769; MA 1772) Ordained deacon 1774 and practised as a minister, but had had a passion for natural history since infancy. Abandoned the church to study medicine at Edinburgh for 3 years (without taking a degree) then appointed deputy botanical lecturer at Oxford. MD Oxford 1787. Helped found Linnean Society 1788. FRS 1789. Curator of the Leverian Museum, London, ca 1790. Assistant Keeper of Natural History at British Museum from 1791; Keeper from 1806.

[66] Karl Dietrich Eberhard König (1774-1851).

[67] His Ms of this talk, in the Linnean Society archives, is dated June 19 1809, not 1810 as was published in the *Transactions*.

[68] *Transactions of the Linnean Society*, 11(2): 245.

housed in Soho at N° 9 Gerrard Street[58]. After less than two months Elford was proposed for Fellowship by Milne, Thomas Marsham (the Treasurer of the Linnean and author of a work on British insects, *Entomologia Britannica*)[59], Alexander MacLeay (the Society's Secretary and another entomologist)[60] and James Sowerby, the natural history illustrator and publisher[61].

After the usual period of probation – during which the Certificate of Recommendation was prominently displayed in the Society's rooms – Elford Leach was elected to Fellowship on the 7th of March 1809, oblivious to the fact that three weeks earlier, in Shrewsbury, a child had been born who 50 years later would change the face of natural history forever with a scientific paper read at a meeting of that same Society: Charles Darwin[62]. Elected with Elford was Henry Ellis[63], the Keeper of the Department of Printed Books at the British Museum. Other Museum officers who were already Fellows, and attended the same meetings as Elford[64], were zoologist George Shaw[65] (the Keeper of Natural History) and his assistant Charles König[66].

Four weeks after his election Elford applied to Shaw for permission to examine the Museum's collection of oil-beetles of the genus *Meloe* – so called from the oily secretion they exude when handled. The irritant nature of this secretion also gives them their other name, 'blister beetles'. Elford had been collecting these curious insects since he was 14 years old and by early 1809 his collection contained all the known British species. With this advantage he had noticed considerable confusion in the published literature and to remedy this he was preparing his first scientific monograph. Shaw had to obtain the permission of the Museum's Trustees before allowing the examination, but this was duly granted and Elford read the results of his investigations to the Linnean Society on the 19th of June when he was still only 18[67]. In the resulting publication – which in common with many scientific articles at that time took four years to appear in print – he reported observations made by George Milne and Thomas Marsham, two of his proposers for Fellowship. It is possible these three came together because they shared an interest in this genus.

Meloe variegatus Donovan

Meloe may have attracted the young Elford because of the comically clumsy way this group of beetles move and the fact they have unusually small wing cases, but with his medical background he later drew attention to the pharmaceutical reputation of one species, *Meloe variegatus* Donovan, as a drug for the treatment of rabies. "For this purpose" he tells us, "it is taken by slipping a hair round its neck, and suspending it until it be dry; by which means the oily secretion they throw out when first taken is preserved, in which its chief virtue is supposed to exist.[68]" Frederick the Great of

Prussia[69] had paid a great deal of money to purchase the formula for the prescription, but happily this is available to us *gratis*:

'Twenty-five of these animals that have been preserved in honey, are with two drachms of powdered black ebony, one drachm of Virginia snake-root, one ditto of lead filings, and twenty grains of fungus Sorbi, to be reduced to a very fine substance; the whole, with two ounces of theriaca of Venice (and if necessary, with a little elder-root) to be formed into an electuary [A powdered medicine mixed with honey or a similar sweetener][70]'.

It is most unlikely this nostrum was ever an effective anti-viral agent and we would not recommend it as an alternative to urgent medical assistance. In addition, the beetles themselves are not without their dangers. Their blood contains the very toxic substance cantharidin (0.03 grams can kill a man), although from ancient times one species in this family, the 'Spanish Fly'[71], has been widely employed as an aphrodisiac.

Summer 1809

By the end of July Elford's first year of London medical studies had ended but instead of returning to Devon, he had decided to spend the vacation travelling to the four corners of Britain in pursuit of his natural history interests.

As the summer began he left London and headed west to the south coast of Wales. Here he spent three days at the beginning of July in the area around Swansea walking and collecting insects with the naturalist Lewis Dillwyn[72]. Elford seems to have travelled from London with Dillwyn's friend Joseph Woods[73], who he presumably met at the Linnean Society. Dillwyn and Woods were both Friends (Quakers) who had lived in Dover during the 1790s and may have known each other since then[74]. From Swansea the three crossed to Ireland where Elford wrote to George Brettingham Sowerby[75],

[69] Frederick II (1712-1786).
[70] From Hunneman, in Leach, *Transactions of the Linnean Society*, **11**(2): 245. (1815). John Hunneman (1750?-1839) Seller of books and dried plants of 9 Queen's Square, Soho, London. Had many overseas contacts and agents.
[71] *Lytta vesicatoria* (L.)
[72] Lewis Weston Dillwyn (1777-1855) of Burroughs Lodge and Sketty Hall, near Swansea. Initially a botanist; later studied shells and beetles. From 1803 head of the Cambrian Pottery, Swansea, which his father bought in 1802. In 1805 published, with Dawson Turner of Yarmouth (1775-1858), the *Botanist's Guide Through England and Wales*. Originally a Quaker but left the Society on marriage to Mary Llewelyn (1807) who was not a Friend. Later a magistrate; Deputy-Lieutenant for Glamorganshire; High-Sheriff of Glamorganshire 1818; MP for Glamorganshire 1832. After 1835 alderman and mayor of Swansea.
[73] Joseph Woods (1776-1864). Architect, geologist and botanist. Published the *Tourists' Flora* in 1850 (Flowering plants and ferns from the British islands and European mainland).
[74] They collected together in 1801 (Hall, 1953: 20).
[75] George Brettingham Sowerby (1788-1854). Naturalist and artist. Contributed much text for his father's *Mineral Conchology*. When his father died in 1822 he continued his work and was a natural history dealer at King Street, Covent Garden, London, then Regent Street, then Great Russell Street. Is mentioned in Elford's *Meloe* paper and they presumably met at the Linnean Society.

The Mumbles rocks near Swansea

[76] The letter says 'Dellwy'. Presumably Elford did not see this Welsh name written.

[77] Letter: W.E. Leach to G.B. Sowerby, 28th July 1809 (Loc: General Library (Sowerby Archive), Natural History Museum, London). For Wood's journal from this trip see the *North Munster Antiquarian Journal*, **27**: 15-61 (1985). For Dillŵyn's journal see *Journal of the Kerry Archaeological Historical Society*, **15/16**: 83-111 (1982-3), and *Journal of the Cork Historical Archaeological Society*, **91**: 85-104 (1986). This information was kindly supplied by Anne Jarvis of Cambridge, *in litt.* (2001). KH has not seen these sources. Anne Jarvis notes Woods separated from Dillŵyn and Elford Leach part way through the trip.

[78] Ellen Hutchins (1785-1815). Born in Ireland on St Patrick's Day. Father Thomas; mother Elinor. See references in Leach, 1852.

[79] Dillŵyn, undated list of insects taken (Loc: Zoology Library (J.F. Stephens' Correspondence), The Natural History Museum, London).

[80] In his Notonectides paper (1818) he says he collected insects here but this may have been in 1810.

[81] 447 km.

[82] Simond (1817) **1**: 440-441. Although Simond did see poverty in Britain he was obviously reluctant to do so.

[83] Letter: W.E. Leach to J.E. Smith, 5th November 1810 (Loc: Linnean Society of London , Smith Mss).

[84] He called himself 'Fellow of the Royal College of Surgeons', but the College archivist, Claire Jackson, observes *in litt.* (1999) Fellowship was only instigated in 1843 when the college became the Royal College of Surgeons of England. This discrepancy is curious.

James Sowerby's son: 'My dear Sowerby, You will undoubtedly be surprised at receiving a letter from me in the land of Potatoes.— I am here on an entomologising excursion with M[r] [Dillŵyn][76] and Woods who are come here to examine the mosses &c[77]'.

Elford is being too modest. He was doing far more than just 'entomologising', he was collecting a wide range of animals. In his later publications there are numerous references to this important field trip. He obtained freshwater species from the lakes of southwest Ireland, including the "Lake of Killarney" (presumably Lough Leane); and intertidal coastal species at Bantry Bay and Clonakilty (just west of Cork where his brother Jonathan had spent more than a month the previous summer *en route* to Portugal). On the shore he collected fish, sponges (later sent to Montagu), molluscs, crustaceans and a new species of rock-boring sea-urchin. He also made contact at Bantry Bay with a local resident, Miss Ellen Hutchins[78]. She was interested primarily in seaweeds, but was also knowledgeable about the animals of the shore and gave Elford many molluscs from the area. He later honoured her by giving the name *Persephona hutchinsiana* to one of the new species she gave him.

At the end of July he returned to Swansea and spent several more days with Dillŵyn[79]. Here he added to his collection of insects and marine fish before making his way north to the Lake District to catch aquatic insects in Derwent Water[80]. The far north-west of England was not the rural hinterland we might assume today. When Louis Simond visited Lake Windermere with his family in 1810 he concluded: "There are no retired places in England, no place where you see only the country and countrymen; you meet, on the contrary, everywhere town-people elegantly dressed and lodged, having a number of servants, and exchanging invitations. England, in short, seems to be the country-house of London; cultivated for amusement only, and where all is subservient to picturesque luxury and ostentation. Here we are, in a remote corner of the country, among mountains, 278 miles[81] from the capital— a place without commerce or manufactures, not on any high road; yet everything is much the same as in the neighbourhood of London. Land, half-rock, is bought up at any price, merely on account of the beauty of the spot. The complaints about scarcity of servants and labourers, and their consequent high prices, are general. It is plain there are too few poor for the rich.[82]" (As the wars dragged on, many of the men from the poor and labouring classes were serving with the armed forces).

From the Lake District Elford moved on through Carlisle[83] and entered Scotland. There is no record of his itinerary here or an indication when he returned to London, but he was certainly back by November (as he would have to be to continue his medical course) and had by then acquired another novelty: a diploma of the Royal College of Surgeons[84].

On the 7th of November Elford read an essay at the Linnean Society about his Irish rock-boring sea-urchin. The narrative of this presentation is in the Society's archives:

"Description of a new Echinus found on the coast of Ireland,
by Wᵐ Elford Leach
Fellow of the Royal College of Surgeons and FLS

I beg leave to lay before the Society a drawing and description of a new Echinus which I discovered this summer on the coasts of Bantry Bay Ireland, in Pools left among the rocks at low water. It is the most beautiful species which has hitherto been discovered in Britain and more particularly deserves our attention from its peculiar property of boring holes in the rocks, to which it firmly adheres by white tentaculæ, in which respect it differs from every species with which we are at present acquainted. The rocks just below high water mark are covered with them and produce a very beautiful appearance. They served as food to *Actinia Equestris* Brit. Micel. and *Actinia crassicornis*. Linn.[85] both of which grow to an enormous size in the same pools which devour them voraciously notwithstanding ther spines. There is a specimen of this Echinus in the British Museum, of a superior size to any which I found, but Dʳ Shaw told me he did not know from what part of the World it was brought. I have examined the different works on this branch of natural history but can find no description of it, I have therefore ventured to name it from its mode of corroding the rocks Echinus Lithophagus".

He then gave a Latin description, which we shall not repeat here, saying specimens had been given to the British Museum, Donovan, Montagu and Sowerby (presumably James), and he had kept others.

Elford had undoubtedly discovered the species which Lamarck[86] described as new in August 1816[87], when he named it *Echinus lividus* (now *Paracentrotus lividus*). The Linnean Society did not publish Elford's paper, but the name *Echinus lithophagus* was published in Alexander Tilloch's *Philosophical Magazine* in 1812[88].

[85] Both sea-anemones.
[86] Jean Baptiste Pierre Antoine de Monet, Chevalier de Lamarck (1744-1829). Originally a botanist and keeper of the royal garden in Paris ('Jardin du Roi', which Revolutionary France renamed the 'Jardin des Plantes') which included a natural history museum. He was later Professor of invertebrate zoology. He challenged the notion that species were immutable and sought to explain what he perceived as evolution ('transformism'). He was worried by the increasing fragmentation of science and strongly promoted the new term 'biology', a term that united all life science disciplines. Personally was said to be eccentric and lacking in social graces. Was poverty-stricken all his life.
[87] *Histoire Naturelle des Animaux sans Vertèbres*, **3**: 50
[88] *The Philosophical Magazine*, **39**: 151, reporting the Wernerian Society meeting, 30th November 1811, states, "At the same meeting, also, Mr. Leach gave a description of a new British species of *Echinus*, which he had observed in plenty at Bantry Bay in Ireland, and which he proposed to call *E. lithophagus*, from the circumstance of its forming a small hollow for itself in the substance of the submarine rocks." [Actually, his paper had been read by the Secretary at that meeting – see later]. *See* Bell, 1893: 157 for a species synonymy. Alexander Tilloch (1759-1825) produced vols 1 (June 1798) – 42 (July 1813) of *The Philosophical Magazine*.

Somerset House, The Strand.

The Royal Society met in rooms on the left-hand side of the gateway every Thursday evening (8-9 pm) from November to July inclusive.

[89] Sir Joseph Banks *Bt* PC KB (1743-1820). Independently wealthy. Educated at Harrow, Eton and Oxford. Became interested in botany while a student. FRS 1766. Collected in Newfoundland 1766-7. Accompanied Captain Cook on the *Endeavour* 1768-1771 to Cape Horn, the South Pacific, New Zealand and Australia. Visited Iceland 1772. Elected President of the Royal Society in 1778 and held the Presidency – rather autocratically – until his death. In 1779 married Dorothea Weston-Hugessen. Baronet 1781, Knight of the Bath 1795 and Privy Councillor 1797.

[90] James Cook (1728-1779). Global navigator and explorer.

[91] Anon., 1811: 244-245.

[92] Elford dedicated a publication in 1812 (see 'George Low' later) to Joseph Banks "whose generous patronage of science has extended even to the obscure labours of the author". Presumably this patronage was extended during his time at St Bartholomew's.

[93] Previous proprietors allegedly included the brother of naturalist Joshua Brookes (1761-1833). Joshua is said to have benefited by the access this gave him to rare species for dissection when animals died (Dictionary of National Biography) but Wheeler (1997: 120) notes this connection has been disputed.

Exeter 'Change, The Strand.

The viewer of Somerset House (opposite) would have their back to Exeter 'Change, which would be about 100 m to their rear.

Elford's second year at St Bartholomew's leaves no record of anything noteworthy in his medical studies, but he was increasingly active in his zoological pursuits. It seems probable that by now, through his contacts at the Linnean Society, he had been introduced to the President of the Royal Society, Sir Joseph Banks[89].

Banks had accompanied Captain James Cook[90] on his first world voyage (1768-1771) to pursue his interests in travel and botany (Botany Bay in Australia had been named on that trip when Banks and the other botanists found the shore was covered with plant species they could not identify). Banks had been President of the Royal Society since 1778 and although he was not an active researcher he was an extremely active promoter and correspondent and came to personify British science, advising both king and government, especially in the application of new discoveries.

Every Sunday evening Banks opened his town house in Soho Square, London, to the city's most active scientific individuals and their guests[91], when they would hold informal discussions of a philosophical and scientific nature. He also made his extensive library available to eager enthusiasts, one of whom was obviously Elford Leach[92].

The Linnean Society and Sir Joseph Banks' library were probably not the only sources of natural history interest for Elford at this time. He must also have been aware of a rather unique establishment in London, the menagerie of exotic animals housed at Exeter 'Change.

Exeter 'Change

At the beginning of 1810 this was correctly called *Pidcock's Menagerie*[93] but it was known generally in natural history circles as *Exeter 'Change* as it

(rather surprisingly) occupied the upper floors of part of a building, Exeter 'Change[94], on the north side of The Strand in the heart of London.

The ground floor of Exeter 'Change contained unrelated businesses, at times including a bazaar and the registered offices for one of the Sunday newspapers, *The Phœnix*, but there was an entrance to the menagerie at street level, replete with a doorman dressed as a 'beefeater[95]' (a cheeky allusion to the much older Royal Menagerie at the Tower of London).

Pidcock must have decided to move on, as in March 1810 he held a major auction of his collection. Whether Elford attended we do not know, but according to the report in the *Morning Post*[96] of the 22nd of March the auction seems to have been a mixed success:

"The sale at Pidcock's, Exeter 'Change, has been well attended. The skeleton of the famous elephant was put up at 20 guineas, and knocked down[97] at 55. The skeleton of the spermaceti whale, sixty-six feet long, which formerly appeared in Rackstraw's Museum, sold for nine guineas. Many scarce and beautiful birds sold at low prices, and the whole collection, consisting of 205 lots, produced about £140."

Pidcock appears to have auctioned only his preserved animals, selling the menagerie as a going concern. By 1811 it was owned by Mr Polito and was called *Polito's Living Museum*. A contemporary tourists' guide[98] to London gives a flavour of this urban jungle:

"This collection is the property of Mr. Polito, and among many others of minor interest, contains in the apartments on the first floor —

1.   Three African lions, and two lionesses.
2.   A lion from South America.
3.   The male Nylghau, or white-footed Antelope, with short horns projecting a little forward, and sometimes called the horned horse.
4.   Male and female leopard from the East Indies.
5.   A spotted male hyæna.
6.   A black wolf from Canada, and the only one of that colour ever brought to England. There is in the same room a grey one from the Alps.
7.   A royal tiger from Bengal.
8.   The large baboon, or papio. This animal is, when standing erect, about five feet high.
      The two apartments on the second floor contain —
10.   Two ostriches, one of which has lately laid two eggs.
11.   Two emus, a small blackbird from New South Wales.
12.   A male and female beaver.
13.   Five kanguroos.
14.   The tapir, an amphibious animal from the province of Buenos Ayres, South America.
15.   The condor, an immense South American bird.
16.   The skeleton of an elephant; and also that of a whale[99].

[94] Exeter 'Change was built in 1670 on the site of Exeter House, the mansion of the Earls of Exeter (near the current Exeter Street) beside Covent Garden market. The name 'Change', short for Exchange, presumably referred to the later trading use of the site (as in the usages Corn Exchange; Stock Exchange). The ground floor was originally a grand arcade of shops facing the street with shopkeepers' lodgings above, but later the arcade was converted to two rows of business premises (milliners, hosiers, cutlers, toy shops etc.) separated by a narrow paved passage. The menagerie occupied the 1st and 2nd floors of the tower at the eastern end of the building. The whole was removed in the 1820s to widen the street.

[95] Slang term for a member of the King's Body-guard of the Yeoman of the Guard.

[96] The Morning Post was described by an author, with a strong liberal bias, thus (Anon., 1811: 334-335): "*The Morning Post*, Strand, long bore the distinction of being the Ladies' Maids and Milliners' Diary; but since it has been retained in the Wellesley interest, it has become the organ of a violent ministerial or tory party." It seems the Tories had purchased the favour of this newspaper – a common practice at the time. 'Wellesley' was Marquess Wellesley, the Foreign Secretary, who was Sir Arthur Wellesley's elder brother, Richard Colley Wellesley (1760-1842).

[97] sold.

[98] Anon., 1811: 307-308.

[99] It sounds as though Polito purchased these at the auction, unless the printed guide was out of date.

The price of seeing the two latter apartments is two shillings, or the three may be seen for half-a-crown.

Besides the above Mr. Polito has also a great number of smaller animals, and a variety of curious birds from the different countries of the world."

It is clear from Elford Leach's correspondence that at the end of 1810 there was also a live rhinoceros at Exeter 'Change. By November 1813, when the poet Byron[100] paid a visit, there was also a live elephant, a hippopotamus and a camel, as his diary reveals:

'Two nights ago I saw the tigers sup at Exeter Change. Except Veli Pacha's lion in the Morea,—who followed the Arab keeper like a dog,—the fondness of the hyæna for her keeper amused me most. Such a conversazione!—There was a "hippopotamus," like Lord L[iverpool][101] in the face; and the "Ursine Sloth" hath the very voice and manner of my valet—but the tiger talked too much. The elephant took and gave me my money again—took off my hat—opened a door—*trunked* a whip—and behaved so well, that I wish he was my butler. The handsomest animal on earth is one of the panthers; but the poor antelopes were dead. I should hate to see one *here*:—the sight of the *camel* made me pine again for Asia Minor.[102]'

The animals were housed in narrow cages around the walls of the rooms, but the elephant was displayed by its keeper and made to perform tricks. Another visitor recalled, "It was the grand joy of a boy's holiday to go there and see the elephant stamp the mangel-wurzel[103] to pieces, and take a halfpenny out of an iron box.[104]"

Within a few years this indoor zoo-cum-circus would be in the hands of Edward Cross, 'Dealer in Foreign Birds & Beasts'.

Malacostraca Britanniæ

Polito's animals were rather larger than those that generally interested Elford Leach at this time, but he had his own plans for introducing the public to unusual and seldom seen species. He was going to prepare a book, to be issued in parts, on the larger British crustaceans – the crabs, lobsters, crawfish, crayfish, shrimps and prawns. This was not to be a dry academic text. This was to be a coffee-table book. The illustrations would be life-size and hand-painted in full colour; the text would be kept to a minimum and only used to explain the images. When the parts had built to one volume they would form a full-colour identification manual.

To achieve this he came to a business agreement with James Sowerby. Elford would provide the specimens and the text; Sowerby would provide the drawings and engravings, would have them coloured, and would publish the book. Sowerby's workshop would have to put a significant effort into such a substantial work but it was agreed Elford would pay for the production of the engravings and Sowerby would keep the profits from the sales. The

[100] George Gordon Noel Byron (1788-1824). English poet. Succeeded to the title Lord Byron, from his late father's uncle, when he was 10 years old.

[101] Robert Banks Jenkinson, 2nd Earl of Liverpool (1770-1828). Prime Minister 1812-1827.

[102] 14th November 1813 (Marchand, 1974).

[103] A large root vegetable; a variety of the beet *Beta vulgaris* Linnæus.

[104] Lemon, 1867: 256-258. 'Halfpenny' pronounced 'haypnee'.

Walking dress, 1810

work was to be published in a cheaper un-coloured form as well as the hand-painted version and Sowerby insisted upon one further condition. Elford had to give plain copies to individuals; he was only permitted to give coloured copies to public institutions[105] (Knowing Elford's ability to make contacts, and his generosity, Sowerby probably feared the work involved in colouring vast numbers of copies every few months). The working title for the book was *Malacostraca Britanniæ*, which roughly translates as 'The Thin-shelled [Shellfish][106] of Britain' or 'British Crustacea'. Sowerby set to work on the illustrations.

With the arrival of the summer break in 1810 Elford set out across the parched countryside – suffering under an extended drought[107] – and again headed north via Carlisle[108], presumably to spend the summer in Scotland. Whether his visits to Scotland had endeared that country to him or whether he had firm career reasons, he decided to leave St Bartholomew's at the end of the year and complete his medical education in Edinburgh. However, before he exchanged the English capital for the Scottish there was one last thing he decided to do. William Elford Leach was about to make the biggest mistake of his life.

[105]Letters: W.E. Leach to Academy of Natural Sciences of Philadelphia, 15 June 1818 (Loc: Haverford College, Pennsylvania, in the Quaker Collection); and Leach to de Blainville, 31 March 1815 (Loc: Bibliothèque Centrale, Muséum National d'Histoire Naturelle, Paris. Ref: item 104).

[106] As opposed to the thick-shelled shellfish – molluscs (oysters, whelks etc.)

[107] Simond (1817) **1**: 307. In contrast to the rain in the Peninsula, the spring had been unusually dry for much of Europe and America. It finally rained in England in mid-July. The harvest of 1810 was very poor.

[108] Mentioned in his letter to J.E. Smith of 5th November 1810 (see above).

Historical note

1810	Walter Scott[1] publishes *The Lady of the Lake*, set around Loch Katrine in Scotland.
—	The first Indian restaurant in the UK, *The Hindoostane Coffee House*, is opened in George Street, Portman Sq., London by Sake Dean Mahomed[2]. It will trade until 1812.
April	Disturbances in London after arrest of Sir Francis Burdett[3] (a liberal MP who supported freedom of speech, Roman Catholic emancipation, prison reform and parliamentary reform). He had published a letter saying the imprisonment of a Radical orator was illegal. A warrant was issued for his arrest and he barricaded himself in his house. After two days the house was entered and he was taken to the Tower of London.
July	Food riot at Wolverhampton market.
Summer	The British harvest fails and famine is anticipated. Napoleon saves the day by allowing large scale imports of French grain into Britain (he needs British gold and hopes to strain the British economy).
September	Prison riot at Dartmouth, Devon.
September	Renewal of Old Price riots at Covent Garden Theatre.
October	Prison riot at Portchester Castle near Portsmouth.
October	Disturbances among soldiers at Wakefield.
November	Theatre riot at Plymouth.
17th November	Sweden declares war on Britain

[1] Walter Scott (1771-1832). Edinburgh lawyer, poet and novelist. Later refused to become Poet Laureate. Created Baronet 1820. In late 1811 his brother Tom was offered the paymastership of the 70th (Surry) Regiment, Jonathan Leach's former regiment (Cholmondeley, 1950: 242).

[2] Sake Dean Mahomed (1759-1851). Born Patna, died Brighton.

[3] Sir Francis Burdett *Bt* (1770-1844).

— 6 —

A very indecorous act

We do hate all impostures and lies, insomuch as we have
severally forbidden it to all our fellows, under pain of
ignominy or fines, that they do not show any natural work
or thing adorned or swelling, but only pure as it is, without
affectation of showing marvels

Francis Bacon
New Atlantis (1626)

W ith Jonathan Leach besieged in the Lines of Torres Vedras, back
in London Elford's passion for scientific integrity had been
affronted. William Bullock had been proposed for Fellowship of
the Linnean Society and Elford was not happy about it; he was going to have
it stopped.

William Bullock[1]

Will Bullock was a showman and entrepreneur with a passion for
collecting, and for business. In 1810 he owned a museum at N° 22 Piccadilly,
London, containing almost 10,000 items.

Bullock's mother had been the proprietor of a waxworks museum, but
his own interest was in natural, artificial, artistic and historical curiosities.
He had first opened his collection to the public in Sheffield in 1795, when he
displayed just over 300 items[2], but at that time this was a side-line. When he
moved to Liverpool in 1801 and opened a museum in Church Street he
still practised his main trade as a jeweller and silversmith. However, by
1809 he had become a full-time museum proprietor and moved his *Liverpool
Museum*, now with more than 4000 items, to London. He was a shrewd
businessman and his collection, and his income, grew quickly. He had
bought much of the Leverian Museum[3] at auction in 1806 (including many
specimens brought to Britain by Captain Cook)[4]. He also acquired the
Litchfield Museum[5] and other purchases, and received gifts from influential
donors including members of the royal family, Sir Joseph Banks[6], and
James Edward Smith, founder and President for life of the Linnean Society[7].
Smith had commissioned furniture from William's brother George Bullock,

[1] William Bullock (*fl.* 1795-
1843). Brother of George
Bullock (d. 1818) a well
known Regency furniture
maker and sculptor. For
a good short review of
the Bullocks see John
Edmondson (1988).
[2] Bather, 1931: 276-277.
[3] The collection of Sir
John Ashton Lever (1729-
1788) which had been moved
from Manchester to London
in 1774.
[4] William Clift (see later) *in*
House of Commons (1836:
para. 622).
[5] Shepperson, 1961: 145.
[6] Edwards (1870: 508) notes
Banks was a benefactor of
Bullock's Museum, as do
Henry Ellis (House of
Commons, 1835: para. 1605)
and William Clift (House of
Commons, 1836: para. 622).
[7] James Edward Smith
founded the Linnean
Society with (among others)
Thomas Marsham and
Samuel Goodenough (1743-
1827) who, from 1808, was
Bishop of Carlisle.

Egyptian Hall.
Bullock's Museum in
Piccadilly from 1812

an artist and cabinet-maker, as early as 1803 after a visit to Liverpool, and George had sculpted a bust of Smith at about the same time. This connection may have led to Smith's patronage of Will Bullock's collections. By 1811 Bullock would have more than 10,000 curiosities and in 1812 would build his own museum in Piccadilly – the *London Museum and Pantherion* – with an outlandish frontage in the style of an Egyptian temple, later known as *Egyptian Hall*[8].

The main departments of Bullock's *Liverpool Museum* in 1810 were: *South-sea Curiosities* (including various ethnological specimens of clothing, implements etc. many of which were brought to Britain by Captain Cook and would have been well known to Sir Joseph Banks); *Curiosities from North and South America*; *African Curiosities*; *Works of Art*; *Natural History*; *Birds*; *Amphibious Animals*; *Ichthyology*; *Entomology*; *Marine Productions* (with, "upwards of a hundred specimens of rare shells and corals, on a tripod, supported by crabs"); *Minerals*; *Miscellaneous Articles* (mainly mummified remains and natural history oddments – horns, skins, bones); and *The Armory* (armour, weapons etc.).

The zoological exhibits ranged in size from whale bones and stuffed elephants to cases of humming birds and insects. Some were arranged scientifically (many correctly identified by authorities in their fields) and his collection included items new to science and otherwise rare, but Bullock had his eye on the tastes of the fee-paying public. He set his exhibits in life-like stances, surrounding them with vegetation and rocks to give the appearance of nature[9]. A contemporary reviewer reported, "the astonished visitor is in an instant transported from the crowded streets of the metropolis to the centre of a tropical forest" but Bullock sometimes took this to extremes. Animals were fixed in dramatic, gothic poses, like the deer locked in the grip of an enormous boa constrictor.

[8] The architect of this building was P.F. Robinson.
[9] A *diorama*.

106

Louis Simond saw this display in 1811 and reported: "The boa constrictor is a gigantic snake, which makes the story of Laocoon[10] quite probable. This one crushes a deer in its ample folds, and tears it to pieces with its teeth; it is about 35 feet in length[11], and as large as a man's thigh. The giraffe is another prodigious animal. A quadruped 16 feet high[12], with a very pretty head like a horse, and mild innocent look, at the top of an immensely long, yet graceful, crane neck. This animal is singularly gifted to discover all approaching danger from his tower of observation, and to fly from it with his seven league boots. A moderate-sized elephant near him, looked quite small.[13]"

The boa constrictor and its victim must have been a great success. Later it would be joined by a boa tussling with a more spectacular tiger – the tiger's claws raking the air, head back, tongue lolling pathetically as the snake's jaws clamped like a vice on its exposed throat[14]. To Bullock this was: "one of those dreadful combats which sometimes take place betwixt this powerful and sanguinary destroyer of the human species, and the immense serpent of India, called the Boa Constrictor, in whose enormous folds its unavailing strength is nearly exhausted, and its bones crushed and broken by the strength and weight of its tremendous adversary.[15]"

Duck's feet and quackery

When Bullock sold his collection in 1819 he gave the assurance, "there is not a specimen that has been assisted by art except the head of the Boa Constricta which being part destroyed (which is the case in all the largest specimens[16]) has been modelled from life in wood and has always been described as such"; and of his birds he declared, "I pledge myself not a Feachure in my whole ornithological collection will be found spurious[17]".

It has to be said this was a courageous claim. The boa constrictor was as enormous as it was because it was actually two skins stitched together. The sale of 1819 contained many pieces of manufacture and one of Bullock's birds of paradise was found to be a composite of several species[18]. A petrel – which sold at a good price as it possessed unusual feet for that group of birds – was found to have acquired its unusual feet when they arrived on the end of the duck's legs with which it had been furnished! It seems George was not the only creative member of the Bullock family.

In November 1810 Bullock's business had recently arrived in the capital and he was advertising vigorously. His museum was open to the public every day except Sundays at an entrance fee of one shilling, with half-a-crown[19] for the catalogue. Elford had obviously paid his shilling and, whatever he felt about the museum, did not feel it qualified Bullock for fellowship of an august society like the Linnean.

In fact, this was not the first time Will Bullock had applied for fellowship. He was first proposed at the Society's meeting on the 18th of April 1809. Curiously, at the following meeting on the 2nd of May his sponsors were allowed to withdraw their recommendation[20]. The story

---

[10] A character in Greek mythology who was killed by a sea-serpent.

[11] 10-11m.

[12] 5m.

[13] Simond (1817) **2**: 252.

[14] This exhibit is now in the Rossendale Museum, Lancashire and is figured by Edmondson (1988).

[15] Edmondson, 1988: 21-22.

[16] Presumably the result of self-preservation on the part of collectors.

[17] Letter: Bullock to Robert Jameson, 9th February 1819 (Loc: Edinburgh University Library, Special Collections. Ref: 1801/1 Bullock N⁰ 2).

[18] Letter: Walter Adam to Robert Jameson, 12th June 1819 (Loc: Edinburgh University Library, Special Collections. Ref: 1801/1 Bullock N⁰ 20).

[19] 2 shillings and 6 pence (2s 6d or 2/6) [with 12 pence to one shilling, 5 shillings to one crown, and 4 crowns to one pound sterling]

[20] Linnean Society of London *General Minute Book*, volume 1.

Public Natural History Attractions in London

(i) *The British Museum*
This is covered later. The Museum was a collection of art, manuscripts, printed books and natural history open for public viewing on Mondays, Wednesdays and Fridays from 10 a.m. until 4 p.m. (last entry by 2 p.m.) except during August and September, when the establishment was closed to the public. More than 29,000 visitors viewed the collections in the year 1810-1811.

(ii) *Bullock's Liverpool Museum*
This is covered in the main text. By 1818 Bullock had changed the name from *The Liverpoool Museum* to *The London Museum of Natural History*[1].

(iii) *London Museum and Institute of Natural History*
This was the collection formed by Edward Donovan at a cost of many thousands of pounds from his personal fortune. He opened this collection to the public free of charge in 1807 and it remained open for a number of years in Catherine Street, just off The Strand by Covent Garden.

(iv) *Exeter 'Change*
A menagerie of live animals in The Strand. This was covered in Chapter 5.

(v) *The Royal Menagerie*
This was another collection of live animals, housed at this time in the Tower of London. It was described in a guide-book of 1811[2]:

"*The Lions, and other Wild Beasts and Birds*, Are kept in a yard on the right hand, at the west entrance. A figure of a lion is over the door, and there is a bell at the side to call the keeper. The visitor pays *one shilling* here, for which the keeper shews him all the wild beasts, &c. explaining their several histories. The care taken by the keepers to prevent injury to the visitors, is very great; and the wholesome cleanly condition of the dens deserves praise. The dens are very commodious. They are about twelve feet[3] in their whole height, being divided into an upper and a lower apartment; in the former they live in the day, and are shewn, and in the latter sleep at night. Iron gratings inclose the front of the dens, most of which have been recently rebuilt, with every precaution to prevent accidents. These animals are in general very healthy. It is remarkable that those which have been whelped[4] in the Tower are more fierce than such as are taken wild; strangers should be cautious not to approach too near the dens, and avoid every attempt to play with them."

Tourist Louis Simond, who visited the Tower in May 1811, saw it through rather different eyes: "our last station was the menagerie, which is small, ill-contrived, and dirty. The animals look sick and melancholy. The most curious of them was a white tiger, lately brought from India by Sir Edward Pellew, and so tame, that the sailors used to pare his claws regularly during the voyage, and on his landing, he was led through some of the streets of London, or rather followed like a dog.[5]"

[1] So designated in Bullock, 1818.
[2] Anon., 1811: 168-169.
[3] 3.6 m.
[4] which have been born.
[5] Simond (1817) **2**: 207.

behind this abortive application is lost to us, but in April 1810 he was put forward again, his proposers[21] "knowing him to be a great promoter of the Study of natural History". It was this application that was due to be balloted at the beginning of November.

Elford Leach returned from Scotland with several last minute objections. He did not want the Society associating itself with someone who filled the daily newspapers with his overblown advertisements, and he was already sufficiently versed in natural history to know a faked specimen when he saw one. An impetuous teenager, engrossed in his passion for his subject, not so much politically naive as politically oblivious, Elford decided to have Bullock black-balled[22].

Black-balling in the early years of the nineteenth century had been elevated to something of a blood-sport in several of the select gentlemen's clubs of London[23], and Elford would probably have been aware of this from the newspapers. However, this game had not spread to the scientific societies and Elford – only a Fellow himself since the previous year – is unlikely to have realised the enormity of what he was proposing. Consequently, propose it he did.

He needed to act swiftly. Bullock's election was scheduled for the meeting on the evening of Tuesday the 6th of November. On Friday the 2nd Elford sent letters to all the Fellows of the Linnean Society with London addresses urging them to attend the meeting and vote against Bullock. The following example survives in the Society's archives[24]:

'George Anderson Esq'.
Tooley Street.

[21] Including Elford Leach's friend William Jackson Hooker (see later).
[22] This is a reference to the anonymous method of election used at that time. A bag was circulated among the voters who inserted a white ball for 'yes' and a black ball for 'no'. The balls were counted by the chairman of the meeting and the decision announced.
[23] *White's* and later *The Athenæum* suffered badly. At *White's* the epidemic lasted for 20 years until a special committee was formed to solve the problem (Darwin, 1943: 22, 24).
[24] Linnean Society of London (Miscellaneous Correspondence) [Some spelling has been corrected].

Conceiving that the election of Mr Bullock (Proprietor of the Liverpool Museum) into the Linnæan Society; (should it take place,) would prove highly detrimental to the interests of that hitherto respected body; has induced me to address a few lines to the Members who reside in London, to entreat those who are friends to Science, and enemies to imposition and quackery, to attend the Meeting of the Society on Tuesday November 6th for the purpose of blackballing him. The objections are first that he is likely to bring the Society into disrepute by the puffs with which he daily fills the Newspapers, and it is not to be conceived that he will after his election cease to act in the same manner; secondly his Museum is unscientific and contains a considerable number of made up subjects,

I remain a well wisher to
the Society
Wm Elford Leach

20. Southampton Buildings. November 2nd 1810'.

Writing to all the Fellows in London was a substantial task but as we saw with his natural history collecting at school Elford had a facility for enlisting help, and he used it here. Also in the archives of the Linnean

Society is a second letter of that day, along much the same lines, to Dr Sims[25] of 60 Upper Guildford Street. This second letter is not in Elford Leach's hand. The writing is unknown to us and it would be interesting to know who else sat in that busy scriptorium at 20 Southampton Buildings on that autumnal Friday.

Both letters are stamped by the Post Office with the ominous 'Unpaid'. Louis Simond explains some arrangements for postage at that time when he says, 'Nobody thinks of writing to a friend without a frank[26], and letters are received with a perceivable expression of surprise, at least, when there is postage to pay. You may pay the postage of your own letters; and I had availed myself of the expedient, as infinitely preferable to that of begging a frank, but I found it was considered as a great impropriety.[27]' In fact it had been considered discourteous to prepay your own letters since at least the seventeenth century[28]. However, by not having his letters franked Elford obliged the recipients to pay, which cannot have helped their humour.

The fact these two letters found their way to the Society suggests George Anderson and John Sims at least were not sympathetic. Generally reaction was swift. Bullock had letters that were drawn to his attention copied and the copies sent post-haste to James Edward Smith's home at Norwich[29]. Smith wrote immediately to Elford, who received his response on the Monday morning and replied by return of post, enclosing a gift of a native plant he had collected during the summer near Carlisle. He clearly knew he was in trouble but was still prepared to fight his corner:

'Dear Sir,

I received your letter this morning and as Mr B. has sent you copies of the letters I shall say nothing on the subject; except that I was not mistaken in my Ideas respecting the horn of the Rhinocerus, as there is now a living specimen in the Exeter Change, larger than that of Mr. B., in which the horn is considerably shorter even than I could have Imagined, therefore the horn on his if it belongs to the same species... is much too large for an animal of that size, this when combined with other circumstances seems to coroborate what I advanced[30]'.

The Society's meeting the following day was a stormy affair. Bullock was elected, but more than a dozen members opposed him. John Sims persuaded the assembly to have Elford's call to arms read aloud, after which the meeting took a vote and resolved: "that the said Letter is highly disrespectful to this Society and that Mr Leach, having thus assumed an authority which neither he nor any other Member of the Society can possibly possess, be reprimanded from the chair[31]".

One of the Society's Vice-Presidents, William Maton[32], being in the chair at the time, accordingly donned the ceremonial tricorn hat[33] and promptly administered a solemn, and painfully public, official rebuke to the hapless Leach.

[25] John Sims (1748-1831) Physician and botanist. Editor of Curtis's *Botanical Magazine*. A founder of the Linnean Society.

[26] A 'frank' – a postage exemption. For example, MPs, peers and government officials could send letters free of postage. For MPs the daily allowance was up to 10 letters and packets of not more than 2 ounces (57g) each, or printed matter (including newspapers) in open wrappers. This privilege was allowed while parliament was in session and for 40 days before and after. Letters were franked by signing the cover (Cholmondeley, 1950: 21). Those entitled to franks frequently made unused allocations available to friends and contacts.

[27] Simond (1817) **2**: 200.

[28] Oswald, 1989: 173.

[29] It is clear from what follows that other letters included details not found in the two we have.

[30] Letter: W.E. Leach to Smith, 5th November 1810 (Loc: Linnean Society of London, Smith Mss, vol. 23)

[31] Linnean Society *General Minute Book*.

[32] William George Maton MD (1774-1835). Was a Physician, botanist and historian. Physician to the royal family from 1816, treating Queen Charlotte, wife of George III, and the infant [Queen] Victoria.

[33] Still used today when admitting Fellows.

Piccadilly, London (during sewer-laying) looking from the junction with Old Bond Street towards the modern Piccadilly Circus. Bullock's Museum is on the far right. On the opposite side of the street, about 50m ahead, is the low brick colonnade that separated Burlington House from the pavement. The range of buildings that later replaced this much reviled colonnade now houses the Linnean Society of London to the west of the gate and the Geological Society of London to the east.

It was probably just as well the time had come for Elford to leave for Edinburgh[34]; his removal from London doubtless helped diffuse the tension although he still left high emotions in his wake.

Maton briefed Smith two weeks later, apparently unaware of his earlier involvement:

"We have had some uncomfortable business lately at the Linnean meetings, in consequence of a circular letter sent by Mr Leach to the Fellows, with a view to prevent the election of Mr Bullock, having been consider'd by many respectable members as a very indecorous act. At the first meeting of the session (when Mr Bullock was elected, though with 13 black balls), a vote pass'd for reprimanding Mr L. from the Chair. At the last meeting, notice was given of a motion to be made in December for rescinding that vote, and I expect that there will be a good deal of unpleasant altercation on the occasion. Having been in the chair at each of the meetings alluded to, I have had a difficult task to execute, but I flatter myself that I have not Err'd in my conduct on the score of *impartiality*; and, if it should be my lot to preside at the next meeting, I am resolved to maintain as strict order as my office will authorize, for the interference of the chair seems likely to be call'd for.[35]"

By the end of the month, from his bolt-hole in Scotland, Elford had realised a little more overt humility was needed if he was to survive this social crisis. This was probably advised by the Society's long-time Secretary, Alexander MacLeay, who appears to have spoken on his behalf. From Edinburgh Elford wrote an altogether more conciliatory letter to Smith:

[34] The academic year in Scottish universities began in November and ran until Easter (about 22 weeks).

[35] Letter: Maton to Smith, 21st November 1810 (Loc: Linnean Society of London, Smith Papers).

'Dear Sir,

I am happy to find from your letter, that you are satisfied as to the purity of my motives, I must nevertheless acknowledge that I have acted with great imprudence and that I am extremely sorry that I should have given offence to the Society, you also know that I was actuated by no personal Enmity towards Mr Bullock, but merely by a zeal for what I considered the welfare of the Society, and under these circumstances I trust the Society will look with some indulgence on the improper manner to which this Zeal has inadvertently led me, and rescind the Vote of Censure, with a wish for the welfare of the Society and respect for yourself

I remain

yours very truly

Wm Elford Leach[36]'

At the December meeting this letter was read from the chair and the vote was indeed rescinded. Elford was able to thank MacLeay, "for your kind exertions in my favour at the Linnæan Society, of which Mr Milne has given me a long account. I was much pleased to find it carried by so respectable a majority.[37]"

In theory that closed the case of *Leach v. Bullock* but Elford had harmed himself; the affair would return to haunt him.

[36] Letter: W.E. Leach to Smith, 30th November 1810 (Loc: Linnean Society of London, Miscellaneous Correspondence).
[37] Letter: W.E. Leach to MacLeay, 22nd December 1810 (Loc: Linnean Society of London, Miscellaneous Correspondence).

— 7 —

Edinburgh

Taken altogether, I do not know any town
where it would be pleasanter to live. It is,
in a great degree, the Geneva of Britain.

Louis Simond (1811)[1]

Edinburgh was, and is, a capital city very unlike London. London
sprawled out from the banks of the Thames; its streets flat, and its
buildings generally low. Edinburgh – a tenth of the size at just under
100,000 inhabitants[2] – was a city of stone tenements clinging to the hillside
below its formidable castle. Like Elford, Louis Simond had moved north,
and certainly preferred the Scottish capital's appearance to that of the
English:

"The best houses in Edinburgh are very inferior certainly to those of the
same rank in London, yet the difference of the materials, a bright crystallised
stone, instead of dingy bricks, gives them a look of superior consequence
and cheerfulness; the variety of views also, and the proximity to the country,
without the fag-end of suburbs, are invaluable advantages.[3]"

[1] Simond (1817) **2**: 65.
[2] Simond (1817) **1**: 349.
[3] Simond (1817) **2**: 152.

A somewhat romanticised
interpretation of Edinburgh
from the north, as it appeared
in 1693.

Fleshmarket Close in the Old Town.

Many Edinburgh streets were narrow and steep; natural canyons between the towering walls of the habitations. Until the late 18th century this "dark, dull and dirty assemblage[4]" of 'the old town' looked out over the small North Loch[5] to the scrub and farmland beyond, but in the late 1760s a new development of fine Georgian terraces was started on the far side of the water. Broad streets and squares appeared in a regular grid of classical styling and became *the* place to live. There followed a radical social upheaval as the finest and most titled families of Edinburgh uprooted and moved to this New Town, as it had been christened. This freed their ancestral homes in the old town for families of lower rank, and over the next few years every social level moved up a rung in their standard of accommodation. Edinburgh publisher Robert Chambers[6] expressed it as, "a flooding in of the humbler trading classes where gentles once had been; the houses of these classes, again, filled with the vile and miserable."

No doubt the vile and miserable were grateful for the improvement but this transition occurred to the express regret of some of the inhabitants. Provost Creech shook his head in 1783 and bemoaned the fact that Lord Justice-Clerk Tinwald's house was now owned by a French teacher; Lord President Craigie's house by a second-hand furniture dealer; and the house where the Duke of Douglas had lived was, "possessed by a wheelwright!" Larger properties were often divided to house several families and the availability of rented accommodation (always a thriving business in Edinburgh) greatly benefited.

By the early years of the nineteenth century this new social map was well established. The New Town was fully integrated into the life of the city and the

[4] Simond (1817) **1**: 349.
[5] An artificial lake filling the depression where the railway station now stands.
[6] Robert Chambers (1802-1871). Anonymous author in 1844 of *Vestiges of the Natural History of Creation*. Wrote many works from 1822. Founded the publishers W. & R. Chambers Ltd. with his brother William (1800-1883). Quote taken from *Traditions of Edinburgh* (1869: 19).

Advocates' Close in the Old Town.

George Street in the New
Town

North Loch was all but drained, just a few shallow pools remaining to provide
local children with good skating in the coldest depths of winter – and winter
was just beginning in 1810 as Elford Leach fled north to start his life as a
university student.

Lodgings

Unlike the two English universities, it had never been the policy of the
Scottish foundations[7] to provide accommodation for their students. Students
made their own arrangements at local lodging-houses. Despite the availability
of accommodation alongside the university buildings in the old town, it was
in the modern airy terraces of the New Town that Elford made his home, at
Nº 51 Merry's Lodgings, Prince's Street[8], facing the imposing vista of the
old stone town and its brooding castle.

This choice may have been guided in part by sanitary sensibilities. The
old town (or Ancient Royalty of Edinburgh) was wedded to its medieval
habit of granting domestic waste of all descriptions the freedom of the city.
Simond observed, "Passing through the narrow streets, morning and evening,
you scarcely know where to tread.[9]" Until recently it had been the practice
every evening to eject the effluvia of bodily necessity from the upper storeys,
to the accompaniment of the timely warning, "*gardy loo*[10]", but with a recent
drive for cleaner streets this would now result in a fine of five shillings.
However, it was only the throwing that was the crime, and the timing. Now
any 'nuisances' had to be 'laid' on the street, and then only first thing in the
morning[11] so they could be removed by 'the tacksman of the dung' on his
daily rounds.

Commercial properties were not exempt from this drive for urban pride.
Shopkeepers had to sweep out their shops before, not after, the passing of

[7] At this time there were
four Scottish universities:
St Andrews (founded 1411);
Glasgow (1451); Aberdeen
(1494); and Edinburgh
(1583).
[8] Prince's Street is now
Edinburgh's main shopping
thoroughfare but was then
described as one of the
finest residential terraces in
Europe. In 1810 Simond
noted the convenience of
furnished lodgings in the New
Town. "Two large sitting
rooms, and three bed-rooms,
all on the first floor, decently
furnished, may be had for
four guineas a week. The
people of the house go to
market and cook for you.
The table costs about a
guinea a-day; a man-servant,
three guineas and a half a
month." (1817, **1**: 476).
[9] Simond (1817) **2**: 51.
[10] Allegedly a corruption of
the French 'gardez l'eau'
(beware the water).
[11] Not at all on Sundays.
[12] Anon., 1806: 280-285.

Princes Street looking east. The tower on Calton Hill (a monument to Lord Nelson) was built between 1806 and 1816. The Old Town is across the North Bridge to the right (see opposite)

the dung cart, and dunghills from stables had to be carried away at least once a week or they would be confiscated.

To ensure the authorities were kept apprised of any derelictions on the part of the inhabitants, informants received half of any fines imposed.

Across the remnants of the North Loch in the pristine terraces of the New Town matters were much more civilised. There the servants had to tip the filth straight into the dung cart. It was not allowed to touch the ground at all, even in a bucket, as the Regulations made quite clear to any lawyer who cared to read them:

'When the cart comes opposite to any house the servant or servants... shall instantly carry the filth out of the house and put it, or cause it to be put, into the cart, and shall never, on any pretence whatever, lay it, or any part of it, down upon the streets or lanes, or in buckets, or other vessels, upon any of the said streets or lanes, foot pavements, or passages thereof.[12]'

In fact they were not even allowed to leave the empty, soiled bucket on the ground afterwards. If they did, it was liable to be seized by the police.

Company

It seems Elford did not move into the New Town alone; he had recently acquired a live-in companion. He had acquired a pet wolf! This appears to have been a gift from Jonathan who procured it the previous March when, during the monotony of outpost duty, the minds of the soldiers strayed briefly to natural history:

"Near Villa de Ciervo our officers discovered some good specimens of crystal, which, when afterwards sent to England, polished, and set, made seals much resembling white cornelian. Soon after this discovery, another of the natural productions of the country came into my hands, in the shape of a young wolf, which I purchased from a peasant, but which could never,

[13] *Rough Sketches*, pp. 130-131.

[14] *English Cyclopædia*. That Elford owned a wolf is mentioned only in the *English Cyclopædia* where the dates of ownership are not given. There is no documentary evidence that the wolf sent to England by Jonathan was the wolf owned by Elford, however Elford's is described as 'of very vicious temper' and it would be a strange coincidence if they were not the same animal.

[15] James Gregory MD (1753-1821) Professor of Practice of Medicine 1790-1821. Described as a captivating lecturer who distrusted any premature theorising.

[16] Alexander Monro MD (1773-1859). In 1800 he was appointed conjoint Professor of Medicine, Surgery and Anatomy with his father Alexander Monro MD (1733-1817). From 1808 until his father's death the son delivered the course, although John Barclay (see following) also lectured in anatomy.

[17] John Barclay MD (1758-1826) Born Perthshire, Scotland. Studied at St Andrews University for the church and became a minister. Later became assistant to anatomist John Bell at Edinburgh and became MD in 1796. Lectured in anatomy at Edinburgh from 1797-1825.

The North Bridge crossing the remnanants of the North Loch and linking Princes Street on the left to the University building up the hill to the right of the picture.

[18] Professor Sir Richard Owen *KCB* (1804-1892). One of the best comparative anatomists of the 19th century. Born Lancaster and apprenticed to a surgeon. Studied at Edinburgh under John Barclay, James Home, Andrew Duncan Jnr and Robert Jameson. Did not take an MD, but moved to St Bartholomew's in London where Abernethy made him prosecutor for his surgical lectures. From 1827 he held the post of assistant conservator at the Hunterian Museum of the College of Surgeons under William Clift (see later), and was simultaneously lecturer in comparative anatomy at St Bartholomew's from 1829. FRS 1834. In 1835 married Clift's daughter Caroline. From 1836 was Professor of Comparative Anatomy at the College of Surgeons and was joint conservator with Clift from 1842. In 1842 (in an article resulting from a presentation he gave at the annual meeting of the British Association for the Advancement of Science in Plymouth in 1841) he created a new sub-order of fossil reptiles which he named the *Dinosauria* ('terrible lizards') In 1856 was appointed to the new post of Superintendent of Natural History at the British Museum. He argued for the creation of a separate Natural History Museum and was its first Director when it opened in 1881. Knighted 1884.

whilst he remained in my possession, be made to receive the same fine polish of which the crystals were susceptible; for he was such a savage and untameable brute at six months old, and, moreover, so ravenous, that I found it no easy matter to satisfy his appetite, and that of my greyhound puppy likewise, which was his foster-brother. I made a present of him, after being tormented five months with his society in camp, bivouac, or quarters; and he found his way to England, in the autumn of the year of which I am now treating, under the especial protection of a noble lord, at the time one of Lord Wellington's aides-du-camp.[13]"

Elford, in his usual way with animals, did not find him quite so unmanageable as his brother had, and this wolf followed him in his walks about town, and behaved towards him "with the fidelity of a common dog[14]".

For the winter session of his first academic year Elford registered for classes in *Practice of Medicine*, taught by Dr James Gregory[15], and *Anatomy*, taught by Dr Alexander Monro[16] with assistance from Dr John Barclay[17]. Elford, it seems, could not study too much anatomy. Anatomy and additional anatomy at Exeter; anatomy, comparative anatomy and extra comparative anatomy in London; now more anatomy at Edinburgh! Monro reputedly did little more than deliver the lectures of his father (who was joint-Professor) without much novel content, but Barclay had a reputation as a lucid lecturer with an enthusiastic interest in comparative anatomy. In 1803 he had published an influential article, *A New Anatomical Nomenclature*, with relevance far beyond the medical sciences, and he would later have a significant influence on the young Richard Owen[18] (the man who would coin the word *dinosaur*) when he too studied medicine at Edinburgh in the early 1820s. Barclay was always keen to dissect exotic animals to expand his knowledge, although his interest in animals was not always post-mortem; he was also a devoted early promoter of veterinary medicine.

Old Town from
Princes Street (1814).

Lectures at Edinburgh were open to anyone interested (and solvent) and at the beginning of 1811 Louis Simond joined one of Elford's classes and leaves us a rare insight into his medical education:

'Dr Gregory lectures in a manner peculiar to himself. Seated in the centre of a vast amphitheatre, covered with 500 heads, his hat on, and playing with the case of his spectacles, he speaks without any notes, and in a tone of conversation. The only time I was present, the subject was the disorders of the liver, occasioned, he said, almost, exclusively, by the heat of southern climates, and by intemperance. He reproved, in strong terms, the vulgar expression of keeping the liver afloat, that is to say, continuing to drink as a cure for what is the effect of drinking. To illustrate this, he told us a story

The Regency
January 1811

An Act to Provide for the Administration of the Royal Authority, and for the Care of the Royal Person during the Continuance of His Majesty's illness, and for the Resumption of the Exercise of the Royal Authority

At the end of 1810 George III lapsed into mental confusion, a condition he had suffered briefly in 1788 and 1801. This Act of Parliament gave limited powers to George, Prince of Wales, to rule as Prince Regent[19]. The king, 72 years old and nearly blind, never recovered. He remained at Windsor Castle for the next nine years in the care of the Queen, where he was occasionally glimpsed by visitors, a frail figure talking loudly to himself as he walked with his attendants. He is now believed to have suffered from the hereditary condition *Porphyria* in which particular chemicals are produced excessively in the body leading to sensitivity to sunlight, skin pigmentation, abdominal pain, and mental confusion.

[19] George, Prince of Wales (1762-1830). Prince Regent 1811-1820. King George IV from 1820. (See Priestley, 1971).

Castle from
Princes Street (1814).

of certain British officers who had fallen into the hands of Tippoo Saib[20], and were detained three years in irons, because they refused to enter his service... None of them hoped to live long; yet they not only lived, but the liver-complaints, under which several of them laboured, disappeared by degrees... This medical anecdote is possibly very well known, but it was new to me, and to a great number of students, who evidently listened to it with great interest, as well as to some others, which Dr G. introduced very naturally, and with great effect. He has certainly the art of commanding the attention of his pupils. They manifested their interest from time to time, by a little murmur of applause, which the professor checked by a motion of the hand, and went on.[21]'

The learn'd is happy nature to explore — Pope

Elford had barely settled into his studies before he was explaining to Alexander MacLeay in London that he had been out collecting "crustaceous insects" (meaning crustaceans, which at this time were classified by most naturalists as a group of insects) and he was assembling gifts of his finds for Alexander MacLeay, Marsham, Milne and the Reverend William Kirby, one of Britain's leading entomologists[22]. He was also forwarding letters to Kirby, and was working on an arrangement of insects which would be finished by the beginning of February. As usual his medical studies were not going to interfere with his natural history.

[20] Tippoo Sahib or Tipú Sultán (1749-1799) Sultan of Mysore, India. He fought hard to end the British occupation. The Duke of Wellington (then Colonel Wellesley) fought against him and was present at his death during the storming of Seringapatam.

[21] Simond (1817) **1**: 499-500.

[22] The Reverend William Kirby (1759-1850). A botanist and entomologist. BA Cambridge 1781; Holy orders 1782; FRS 1818. Co-author with William Spence (see later) of *Introduction to Entomology* (1815-1826). Lived at Barham in his home county of Suffolk.

The Rev. William Kirby

The winter of 1810-1811 was harsh, although in January the south of England suffered more than Edinburgh, which was late receiving its snow. Despite the temperatures, at the beginning of February the streets of the Scottish capital almost acquired a tropical air.

Simond: "*Feb.* 1.—There has been a snow storm in the night, and it blows a hurricane; tiles fly across the streets, and tops of chimneys fall on the pavement, to the great annoyance of passengers, and danger of their lives. The house we inhabit, built of stone, is sensibly shaken by the wind. There is at the end of our street, on the mound, an itinerant menagerie built of boards; if it should be blown down, the people of Edinburgh might see at large in their streets two lions, two royal tigers, a panther, and an elephant, besides monkies, and other underlings of the savage tribe.[23]"

Presumably Elford did not miss the opportunity to visit these alien creatures at the end of his street. In March he joined *The Wernerian Society*, founded three years earlier by Robert Jameson[24], the Professor of Natural History at Edinburgh who in 1812 would also found the university's natural history museum. At the Wernerian Elford would come into contact with many active naturalists from Edinburgh and elsewhere in Scotland. Jameson was the Society's President and John Barclay was one of the founder Vice-Presidents. Another founder and Vice-President was Edinburgh physician and naturalist, William Wright[25]. After a lifetime of travelling as surgeon and physician to the armed forces, the elderly Wright, now 76, had amassed one of the largest private natural history collections in Britain. He was a long-time correspondent of Sir Joseph Banks and an influential member of Edinburgh's natural history community.

Insecta
Eproboscidea
Genus *Oxypterum* Leach
Oxypterum kirbyanum Leach

(natural size 5-6 mm)

It was Wright who chaired the Wernerian Society meeting on the 6th of April when Elford reported the results of his insect arrangements, which seem to have taken longer to prepare than he anticipated. The wording of the Society's minute for the day is revealing:

"Mr W.E. Leach read an account of the natural tribe of diptera called Eproboscidea by Latreille, with descriptions of the species, which he illustrated by drawings and specimens.[26]"

The key word here is *natural* tribe. Elford had been studying a group of blood-feeding flies that attack

[23] Simond (1817) **2**: 47.
[24] Robert Jameson (1774-1854). 'Bob' to his friends (e.g. Charles Bell *in* University of Edinburgh Library, Special Collections. Ref: Gen. 1996/15-17). Professor of Natural History at Edinburgh 1804-54. He taught Darwin in the mid 1820s while he was (briefly) an Edinburgh medical student.
[25] William Wright (1735-1819). Scottish physician and botanist. Studied medicine at Edinburgh. Surgeon on a whaler to Greenland 1757. Royal Navy surgeon from 1758 in Europe, W. Africa and Caribbean. Graduated MD from St Andrew's University in the 1760s, never having studied there. Lived repeatedly in the Caribbean over many years. Served as Honorary Surgeon-General of Jamaica; Surgeon to the Jamaica Regiment; and Physician-General for Jamaica. Lived in Barbados 1796-98 then returned to Edinburgh where he only treated the poor or his friends. President of the Royal College of Physicians of Edinburgh 1801. Until 1811 undertook an annual tour in the N.W. highlands.
[26] Wernerian Society Minutes, 1811 (not 1810 as published). Elford told MacLeay on 16th September 1811 that he had no foreign species (Loc: Linnean Society of London, MacLeay Correspondence), but when his paper was published in 1818 it included many foreign and other specimens from the collections of Alexandre Brongniart (1770-1847), Savigny, Latreille, Francillon, Samouelle, Stephens, British Museum and Linnæus. Between 1811 and 1818 he added much information and greatly expanded this work. There is no indication he had access to these collections in 1811.

Werner and the Wernerian Society

The Wernerian Society of Edinburgh was a natural history society founded by Professor Robert Jameson and six colleagues in 1808. It was named in honour of Abraham Gotlob Werner (1749-1817), Instructor in Mineralogy and Inspector of Mining at the Mining Academy at Freiberg, Saxony.

In the late 18th century, as scientists struggled to understand the structure of the Earth, Werner argued that the planet's surface was composed entirely of rocks which had precipitated from a common aqueous 'chaotic fluid'. He saw the cooking of rock in volcanoes as a later process. Anciently, he said, there were no volcanoes.

Werner's view was in opposition to that of the Edinburgh geologist James Hutton (1726-1797), whose theory of *Uniformity* held that the surface of the Earth was formed in the past by the relentless action of the same processes we see around us today.

Around the turn of the 19th century scientists had polarised around these two views, with the factions termed *Neptunists* and *Vulcanists* (or *Plutonists*) respectively – although these eventually became terms of reproach in a dispute that increasingly generated more heat than light. The emotional fervour was not helped by the fact that religious individuals steeped in the traditions of Noah's flood saw in Werner a scientific support for their beliefs, thus "by a singular co-incidence, neptunism and orthodoxy were now associated in the same creed; and the tide of prejudice ran so strong, that the majority were carried far away into the chaotic fluid, and other cosmological inventions of Werner.[1]"

Uniformity – with the vast timescale it requires – is now accepted, but at that time Werner's views were taken very seriously. An Edinburgh guide book of 1806, discussing the public museum run by W. & G. Burrell states, "the petrifactions to be seen in this museum will convince any reasonable man that the most solid substances in nature have at some remote period been in a state of fluidity, affording a proof that the Neptunian is much more credible than the Huttonian theory of the earth.[2]"

However, concentrating on Werner's *neptunism* obscures his positive influence on geology. His popularity as a teacher greatly enhanced the reputation of Freiberg which became a major European centre. He emphasised there was more to minerals than just their appearance and composition. He drew attention to the position of minerals in the surrounding rocks and their relations with neighbouring rocks; their geographical distributions; and the importance of all this to the practical requirements of mining. He termed this holistic approach 'geognosy.' He taught his students about the economic importance of minerals; their applications in medicine; the relationship between rock composition and local soils, and hence agriculture; the constraints on architectural styles imposed by the types of rock available; and the interplay between geology and the social structure of overlying cultures (for example, an environment of shifting sands produces a requirement for a nomadic life-style).

Robert Jameson, primarily a mineralogist, studied under Werner at Freiberg from 1800 to 1802 and was one of his most devoted followers, although in later life he admitted he had been converted to Hutton's views. Jameson was instrumental in introducing Werner's ideas to Britain and throughout his life he kept the British natural history community informed of developments in German science.

[1] Sir Charles Lyell (1797-1875) in his classic work (which Charles Darwin read aboard *HMS Beagle*) *Principles of Geology* (1830-1833).

[2] Anon., 1806: 199.

mammals and birds. As a reference text he had used Frenchman Pierre Latreille's[27] influential *Genera Crustaceorum et Insectorum*[28], borrowed from the Linnean Society. Latreille, with other researchers at Paris, was striving for a 'natural' classification of living organisms as an improvement over the artificial but well established classification of Linnæus[29].

Classification

> Species are the alphabet of Natural History;
> but what is the value of an alphabet unless
> you go farther than obtaining knowledge of
> the letters?
>
> Edward Newman[30]

Today when we seek a 'natural classification' for a group of animals we attempt to produce a family tree by grouping together species that have evolved from a common ancestor and hence share a large proportion of their genetic coding. This definition of 'natural classification' cannot be applied to the pre-Darwinian and pre-genetics world in which Elford Leach worked. Western naturalists at the beginning of the nineteenth century were generally still trying to understand and appreciate the mind of God by discerning the patterns in the thousands of known species, each of which (they felt) He had uniquely and independently summoned into existence. When the new *Zoological Journal* was launched in Britain in 1824 the editors declared, "The contemplation of the works of the creation, necessarily leads the mind to that of the Creator himself—and the more intimate our acquaintance with the former, the deeper and more devoted will be our adoration of the great author of all things![31]"

The modern classification of living organisms can be traced to the Swedish naturalist Carl Linné ('Linnæus') in the mid 1700s. Linnæus set himself the task of cataloguing the entire living world. Of course he failed – as we still continue to fail, the task is too great – but the system of investigation he developed laid the foundations for all today's life sciences. One of his innovations was to separate the description of a species from the name given to that species. In the past the scientific description, in Latin, had also been the scientific name, and these could be rambling and unwieldy. Linnæus kept the description but added a convenient label, which he decided should consist of only two words, the first identifying the group to which the species belonged, the second the species itself (for example the name he gave to his own species, *Homo sapiens*). The model for this was everywhere: *Linné Carl*; *Leach Elford*; *Leach Jonathan*. This binominal (or binomial) system soon replaced the verbose labelling of previous generations and is now officially recognised as marking a new beginning in the naming of species. Linnæus's publication on botanical classification, *Species Plantarum*, 'Plant Species' (1753), is taken as the starting point for the scientific naming of all plants. Any scientific name used for a plant

[27] Pierre André Latreille (1762-1833). 'The Father of Modern Entomology.' A modest unassuming man whose health was frail throughout his life. He was the natural son of Général J-B.J. Damazit de Sahuguet, Baron d'Espagnac. Latreille was left destitute in 1778 and was adopted by the mineralogist Abbé René-Just Haüy (1743-1822). Although interested in natural history Latreille studied theology and was ordained a Roman Catholic priest in 1786, for which he was arrested and sent for transportation in 1792 during the French Revolution. He was freed at Bordeaux by naturalist Jean Baptiste Geneviève Marcellin, Baron Bory de Saint-Vincent (1778-1846) who he met after a fellow prisoner, a physician, had obtained a rare beetle, *Necrobia ruficollis* (Linnæus). He was arrested again in 1797 and was again saved by influential friends. In 1798 he became the organiser of the entomological collections of the Muséum d'Histoire Naturelle in Paris under Lamarck. In 1805 he began demonstrating on Lamarck's course in invertebrate zoology and replaced Lamarck when he became blind. When Lamarck died Latreille was nominated Professor of Entomology. Was created Chevalier de la Légion d'Honneur in 1821.

[28] '*Crustacean and insect genera*'. 4 volumes published 1806-1809.

[29] Carl Linné (1707-1778). From 1757 Carl von Linné. Better known in the latinised form Carolus Linnæus. A Swedish physician and naturalist who first attempted to produce an ordered classification of all living organisms.

[30] *The Zoologist*, **15**: viii (1857).

Stamen   Stigma

before that is not recognised as the official name. For the names of animal species the tenth edition of Linnæus's, *Systema Naturæ*, 'The System of Nature' (1758), performs the same role.

Linnæus's main contribution, however, was to provide classifications of the natural world which were relatively comprehensive in their time and comparatively easy to use and understand. He divided the animals into six *classes*: mammals, birds, amphibians, fish, insects and worms. Each of these he divided into *orders*, and each order into genera (e.g. *Homo*) and species (*Homo sapiens*). He divided plants into one class for the non-flowering plants (ferns, mosses etc.) and 23 classes of flowering plants based on the number of stamens in the flower. Each class of flowering plants was divided into orders based on the number of stigmas.

Linnæus chose characters which could be seen by an observer without complex equipment, but he did not analyse the reason for their effectiveness. If the character was widespread in the living world and it varied between species, it was used (for example the way an animal's body was supported – did it have internal bones, a hard jointed outer skeleton like a suit of armour, or no skeleton at all?) In reality Linnæus produced a field identification guide, not a logically rooted family tree. A small number of characters was used to split the animal and plant kingdoms into manageable groups of species to allow students to appreciate nature's diversity and to identify the animals or plants Linnæus had seen. Like most identification guides, the first separations produced groupings containing species with little in common other than the one or two characters used to create those separations (Linnæus had called all animals encased in external jointed skeletons 'Insects', but a lobster does not look like, or live like, a bee). In attempting to make sense of nature's apparent chaos, over-simplification was the price Linnæus had to pay. His system did not reflect nature's subtle detail, and the groups it produced were artificial. However, as a workable rationale for study, Linnæus's system was a revelation. It had an enormous impact in natural history and its use rapidly became widespread.

Linnæus himself understood perfectly well the limitations and artificiality of his approach. Before his works naturalists had been trying to classify species using a much greater range of characters, which produced groupings with a more obvious coherence. This earlier approach had been pioneered in Britain by seventeenth century workers such as John Ray[32] and his pupil Francis Willughby[33]. The difficulties in their time were the lack of both an underlying methodology and a grand overview. It was these Linnæus provided, but with them came his artificial method which pushed the more comprehensive approach into the background.

As soon as Linnæus's system was established, his own students, including the Danish zoologist Johann Fabricius[34], began to explore ways of integrating the earlier approach, using suites of characters chosen from less visually obvious aspects of the animal's form and life (Fabricius

[31] *Zoological Journal*, **1**: vii. The editors were: Thomas Bell, John George Children, James de Carle Sowerby and George Brettingham Sowerby (see later).
[32] John Ray (1627-1705).
[33] Francis Willughby (1635-1672).
[34] Johann Christian Fabricius (1745-1808). An entomologist.

classified insects using characters from their mouthparts, which needed the use of a microscope). This began to generate more groupings, splitting Linnæus's sweeping generalisations.

This modernising work was soon dominated by the research professors at the natural history museum in Paris, with the botanists taking the lead and the zoologists following. From this French activity, the movement became known as *the French School*. Instead of looking for workable characters to *separate* the species, naturalists now began to look for characters, and suites of characters, shared by some species but not others. They also broadened the definition of 'character' to include more than just the external appearance of the animal. For example they used internal anatomy and whether the animal underwent a metamorphosis during its life (caterpillar to butterfly; tadpole to frog).

As more, and different, characters were employed, species appeared to fall into natural groupings – groupings in which the contained species looked like and lived like one another. Giving these groupings their own names and referring to them as 'natural genera', naturalists speculated that species of similar form shared these characters because of an underlying close relationship. But... if each species is uniquely created, why should groups of species show relationships?

As devout Christians, steeped in a literal reading of the Bible, early naturalists saw these relationships as indicative of the plan of the 'Great Creator, Author of all Things' and of His approach to the Creation. Natural genera, and larger natural groups, were held to indicate God's preference for small variations between species, rather than radical distinctiveness. In 1826 William Kirby noted different insects had different types of mouthparts: some species had mouths that chewed; some were adapted for cutting into plants or flesh; some had tubes for sucking nectar; and some had mouthparts that absorbed liquids like a sponge:

'Consider the number of the organs, the varying forms of each in the different tribes, adjusted for nice variations in their uses... and you will see and acknowledge in all the hand of an almighty and all-bountiful CREATOR, and glorify his wisdom, power, and goodness, so conspicuously manifested in the structure of the meanest of his creatures. You will see also, that all things are created after a pre-conceived plan; in which there is a regular and measured transition from one form to another, not only with respect to beings themselves, but also to their organs—no new organ being produced without a gradual approach to it; so that scarcely any change takes place that is violent and unexpected, and for which the way is not prepared by intermediate gradations.[35]'

Despite their commitment to the concept of Special Creation, even the most pious accepted that although God had created species, variants had subsequently developed within those species by change over time, or at least change during the life of individuals. Kirby again: "A *species* is a natural object whose differences from those most nearly related to it had

[35] Kirby & Spence (1826) **3**: 474.

their origin when it came from the hands of its CREATOR; while those that characterize a *variety*, have been produced since that event. As we do not know the value and weight of the momenta by which climate, food, and other supposed fortuitous circumstances operate upon animal forms, we cannot point out any certain diagnostic by which in all cases a species may be distinguished from a variety;—for those characters that in some are constant, in others vary. [36]"

Having recognised the existence of species and having decided they were created by God, naturalists were faced with the problem of explaining why. They concluded every species was designed for a designated role in the overall 'Economy of Nature'. Elford Leach makes several references to this. For example, of spiders he said, 'The principal use of the [spider[37]] in the economy of nature seems to be that of preventing the too great increase of insects'; and of the humble garden worm, 'This is the common earthworm, whose use in the economy of nature seems to be that of rendering the earth more porous by its innumerable holes, and thus facilitating the growth of vegetables which it manures by the leaves &c. that it draws into its haunts.[38]' The idea that earthworms exist to facilitate the growth of vegetables is a long way from Darwin's "great battle of life."

This then was the mind of the naturalist at the dawn of the nineteenth century. God had created all things and all things had purpose. The world was in harmony. Since their creation some slight variation may have formed within species, but recognising these varieties merely allowed naturalists to exclude them from any significant role in a classification. Linnæus had sifted the confusion of previous generations, extracted the gems, and designed practical tools for the study of the Creator's work. Now new techniques being developed were allowing increasing light to be thrown on that great plan. God preferred small differences and had created groups of similar species. These groups were 'natural genera', they were God's own genera, and Linnæus's genera had to step aside to make way for this clearer view. Unfortunately, not everyone saw it like that.

Linnean Britain

> It is the most curious thing to see the
> force of a well-grown conventionalism
> George Macilwain[39]

To many naturalists Linnæus was more than an inspired organiser, he was a prophet and his classification was sacrosanct; to see it was to look into the eyes of God. Linnæus's scientific names were more than just familiar old friends, they were the only names needed, and disruptive modernist tinkering was a heresy perpetrated by anarchists. Sadly this view was all too prevalent in Britain. George Shaw, at the British Museum, expressed the opinion that species not in Linnæus's works ought not to exist, and he threatened to put his heel on any shell not in *Systema Naturæ*[40].

[36] Kirby & Spence (1826) **4**: 396-397. In 1737 Linnæus had expressed a similar view in his *Critica Botanica*, saying, 'today there are two kinds of difference between plants: one a true difference, the diversity produced by the all-wise hand of the Almighty, but the other, variation in the outside shell, the work of nature in a sportive mood.' (quoted in Gardiner, 2001: 24).
[37] He writes " Aranëideæ".
[38] Entry ANNULOSA, *Encyclopædia Britannica* Supplement (1816: 436 & 451).
[39] Macilwain, 1856: 83.
[40] Gunther, 1980b: 36.

British botanists were gradually acknowledging the advantages of the new approach but for the zoologists Linnæus was still unchallenged and his methods were the established convention. However, if there was one thing Elford Leach never was, it was convention's poodle. It has been said that if George Shaw was the arch priest of the Linnean System, Elford Leach was the arch heretic[41]. He once described Linnæus as "the immortal author of the misnamed Systema Naturæ.[42]"

That he had already begun to think along the lines of natural classifications, at the age of 20, in Linnean Britain, is of crucial importance for his influence on British zoology. He would later explain his views saying:

'I am a warm advocate for generic divisions founded on the consideration of every character, being fully satisfied that such exist in nature and, when distinguished with judgement, tend materially to the advancement of science. Those entomologists of the Linnean school who (by dilating the characters either of their genera or species so as to make them admit of almost any thing) bend Nature to the artificial system of their master, would do well to consider whether they do not show a greater veneration for it than for Nature[43]'.

When considering the classification of clams he similarly railed against non-natural groupings in which dissimilar species had been bundled together, obscuring Nature's pattern:

"The Linnean genus *Mya* affords an excellent example of the evil resulting from artificial arrangement: under this head we find several genera with distinct animals and shells, having no affinity with each other; some not even agreeing with the almost unlimited characters laid down, many inhabiting the sea, others fresh water, confusedly mixed together[44]".

Back in Edinburgh in 1811 his growing commitment to natural classifications would be fuelled by his contacts at the Wernerian Society, including botanist John Yule[45] who spoke the following year on 'the Natural Method in Botany.'

[41] Gunther, 1980b: 50.
[42] Leach, 1852: 250. *Systema Naturæ* can be read loosely as 'the natural system' as well as 'the system of nature'.
[43] Zoological Miscellany, **3**: 96. Sadly Elford's view is clearer than his English. The punctuation has been changed to assist the reader.
[44] Zoological Miscellany, **1**: 119.
[45] John Yule *MD, FRS, FRSE*. He contributed to the *Edinburgh Encyclopædia*.

— 8 —

Qualification

All medicine is mine, all light of art or nature

Shelley

Despite the enormity of applying the new ideas of natural classification to his studies, Elford was not satiated by his existing work. By now he had already made contact with Count Hoffmannsegg[1] in Berlin regarding the insect group Neuroptera (the lace-wings and their allies, although in 1811 the group also contained many other types of insect including the may-flies, in which Elford seems to have developed a particular interest) and Hoffmannsegg had sent specimens to London for him. He was also working on the classification of marine fish – building on collections he had made in Wales and Ireland in 1809 – and had described for the Wernerian Society a swordfish caught in the Firth of Forth[2] near Edinburgh.

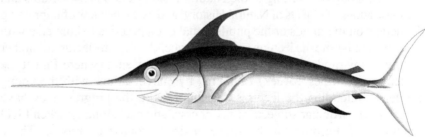

Elford's first two courses finished at Easter 1811 after which he began the summer session of this academic year. He had enrolled for two courses: *Botany*, taught by Daniel Rutherford[3], the Professor of Botany and Keeper of the Royal Botanic Gardens at Edinburgh; and *Natural History* taught by Robert Jameson. Both courses would have involved field studies and we know something of Jameson's approach to teaching from the evidence he gave before the Royal Commissioners during their routine visitation of the university in 1826 (about the time Charles Darwin, a medical student at Edinburgh from 1825, was taking Jameson's class). Jameson may have

[1] Johan Centurius, Graf von Hoffmannsegg (1766-1849). A Berlin botanist and zoologist. Elford may have been put in contact with Hoffmannsegg through his colleague and travelling companion Heinrich Friedrich Link (1767-1851) who was in London in 1809.
[2] The modern word 'Firth' (a wide inlet of the sea) was at that time written 'Frith'.
[3] Daniel Rutherford (1749-1819). Physician and botanist. MD 1772. Professor and Keeper of the Botanic Garden from 1786. William Wright had also been nominated for the Chair of Botany in 1786 but had refused to stand against Rutherford.

The swordfish
Xiphias rondeletii Leach from the Firth of Forth.
(Illustration taken from the *Zoological Miscellany*, June 1814).

Edinburgh University
building looking towards
North Bridge.

Although the foundation
stone had been laid in 1789,
in Elford Leach's day the
buildings were only half-
finished. They would not be
completed until 1834.

changed the details of his course between 1811 and 1826 but his account
still reveals much about his general attitude to natural history education. He
told the Commissioners:

"In the Museum I converse with every one, and in a short time we
become perfectly acquainted. A friendly intercourse is established; and in
time there is no hesitation in them to put any question to me; and by that
system of conversation probably more is elicited than by more formal
examination."

"The mode of teaching in the Natural History class is by lectures and
demonstrations of objects of Natural History; and, with the view of impressing
the details on the minds of the pupils, I make it a practice to converse with
them an hour before the lecture, and very frequently after the lecture. Another
feature of my mode of teaching is, that in the Museum (where I meet the
students three times a week) I attempt, by conversations with the young
gentlemen attending the lectures, to inquire as to the progress they have
made in the particular subjects of my course, and occasionally, when I feel
convinced of the progress they have made, I propose exercises. Those
exercises consist in writing descriptions of objects of Natural History with
which they were previously unacquainted; I require them to describe fully
those objects, and afterwards examine the descriptions and correct them; by
these exercises they speedily acquire correct modes of describing objects of
Natural History, which is a principal object in this study. There is another
plan of instruction which I consider a very useful one, namely, explaining to
my students in the field the mode of carrying on investigations in Natural
History; I make excursions into the neighbouring country, and sometimes go
to the Western Isles with my class. During these excursions I explain to

[4] Great Britain, 1837: 141-
142, 146.
[5] David Brewster (see later)
writing to Charles Babbage
(1792-1871), 12th February
1830, thought, "owing to the
fact that in Scotland the
professors are paid by the *fees*
of their pupils, their sole
object is to fill their classes
and to become scientific
showmen." (Thackray &
Morrell, 1984: 24).
[6] Louis Simond felt "The
professors are soldiers of
fortune, who live by their
sword,—that is to say, by
their talents and reputation."
(1817, **1**: 497-498).
[7] Jameson spent a large
proportion of his income
during his life to enhance the
collections of Edinburgh
University's museum, and
with no pension was obliged
to continue teaching up to his
death at the age of 80. In the
late 1820s Darwin found his
lectures boring and later
referred to him as, "that old
brown dry stick". (Allen,
1985: 7).
[8] University of Edinburgh,
Index to Matriculations,
General & Medical, vol. 6
(1810 – 1811): Natural
History Class List (Loc:
Edinburgh University
Library, Special Collections).

Edinburgh University
quadrangle after
completion.

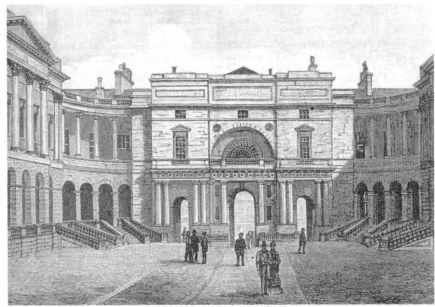

[9] Simond implies this was
the standard fee for all
Edinburgh University
courses at this time (Simond
(1817) **1**: 498).
[10] Robert Edmond Grant
(1793-1874). MD 1814.
After training he went to
Europe from 1815-1820
studying medicine and
natural history. Returned
to Edinburgh in 1820
and specialised in studies
of marine invertebrates,
especially sponges (the
sponge *Grantia* Fleming was
named after him in 1828). In
1824 he gave lectures on
comparative anatomy for his
friend John Barclay. He was
'above middle height' and
Darwin described him as
"dry and formal in manner,
with much enthusiasm
beneath this outer crust." In
1827 he was made Professor
of Comparative Zoology
and Anatomy at the new
University of London but his
Lamarckian views brought
him criticism. He fell into
financial difficulties and
his work output declined.
Later the death of a brother
eased his finances. He was
later a warm advocate of
Darwin's views on natural
selection.

them the mode of examining appearances in the mineral kingdom. When an interesting animal occurs, I point it out to their attention, and I am careful to direct their attention to the various atmospheric phenomena that occur during our walks. I also explain to them the nature of such springs, lakes, &c. as occur during our walks.[4]"

Here we see echoes of Werner's holistic approach to teaching, coupled with a calculated informality.

As teachers at Scottish universities relied solely for their income on fees paid to them by any students they could attract, it was an advantage for lecturers to have an appealing style of delivery[5] and a high academic reputation[6]. Jameson had at least the latter[7] and his summer course contained 59 students[8], each paying the standard course fee of £3. 6*s*. 0*d*[9]. One name in that class that hindsight highlights for us is a young Robert Grant of Edinburgh[10]. Fifteen years later Grant would become Charles Darwin's first mentor during his time at the university. Grant and Darwin worked closely in a study of marine invertebrates (collecting along the shore in the Firth of Forth where Elford Leach had collected 15 years earlier), and Grant taught Darwin the use of the microscope. He also presented Darwin's first original scientific paper – to the Wernerian Society in 1827 – showing that the small black bodies found inside oyster shells were the eggs of leeches. Grant surprised Darwin by questioning the orthodox view that each species was uniquely and directly created, and from the 1830s onwards he taught openly that there was evolution, which did not endear him to the scientific establishment of his day. Unfortunately the relationship between Darwin and Grant cooled at Edinburgh when Grant warned Darwin not to encroach on his research interest (the larval development of marine animals). Back in

1811, although Grant and Elford Leach were classmates we have no evidence they actually knew each other.

One person in Jameson's class who Elford clearly did know was Richard Rawlins from St Kitts in the Caribbean[11]. Rawlins, like Elford, had just studied *Practice of Medicine*, but it seems he was not destined to remain at Edinburgh for the following academic year. He travelled to London after the summer's fieldwork and by February 1812 had moved to Dawlish, in

[11] Edinburgh University, *Index to Matriculations, General & Medical*, volume 6. A John Rawlins of St Kitts is in the *Materia Medica* class list, 1808-1809 but is not in the matriculation lists. Is this Richard's brother, or were they the same person?

Historical note

1811	Jane Austen's *Sense and Sensibility* published anonymously "By a Lady" (It had first been drafted under the title *Elinor and Marianne* in about 1795).
—	The poet Shelley[1] is expelled from Oxford after producing a pamphlet, *The Necessity of Atheism*. He elopes with a 15 year-old schoolgirl, Harriet Westbrook[2], and they flee to Edinburgh and marry.
—	With the reversion of land in St Mary-le-Bone, London, to the crown, the Prince Regent has the architect John Nash[3] design a grand new Georgian street, Regent Street, to join his home at Carlton House[4] to a new park in north London, Regent's Park (work will commence in 1813).
—	The painter J.M.W. Turner[5], who has a gallery in Harley Street, London, begins lecturing at the Royal Academy as Professor of Perspective, and tours the West Country making sketches of the scenery, published between 1814 and 1826 as *Picturesque Views of the southern Coast of England*.
March	Beginning of 'Luddite' disturbances in Nottinghamshire. (Protesters fearing job losses at the introduction of mechanical looms, smash the machinery. This spreads to Yorkshire and Lancashire and frame-breaking continues until 1816. The protesters call themselves 'Ludds' – allegedly after Ned Ludd, a Leicestershire[6] man known for destroying stocking frames in about 1782).
March	A comet is discovered low in the southern sky which will rise and brighten as the year progresses to become *The Great Comet of 1811*.
August	Theatre disturbances at Peterborough.
October	*The Great Comet* is seen at its spectacular best as it reaches its closest point to the Earth. It is clearly visible in Britain and to the troops in the Peninsula, with a tail length of 160 million kilometres.
December	Theatre riots at Liverpool.

[1] Percy Bysshe Shelley (1792-1822). British poet.
[2] Harriet Westbrook (ca 1796-1816).
[3] John Nash (1752-1835). Also designed the Brighton Pavilion for the Prince Regent.
[4] Demolished 1829. Carlton House Terrace, on the same site, now includes the rooms of the Royal Society. The columns that formerly lined the front of Carlton House now line the front of the National Gallery in Trafalgar Square, London.
[5] Joseph Mallord William Turner (1775-1851).
[6] Pronounced 'Lestershuh'.

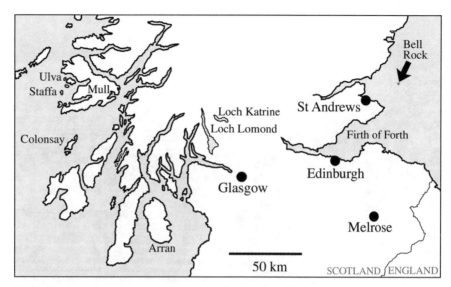

[12] James Wilson (1795-1856). Zoologist. He began studying law in 1811 but abandoned this for health reasons [the *Dictionary of National Biography* does not explain this]. In 1816 visited Holland, Germany, Switzerland and Paris, where he examined the bird collection at the museum. Later he returned to Paris on behalf of Edinburgh University and in 1819 visited Sweden. After developing a pulmonary disease he lived in Italy 1820-1821. He returned to Edinburgh and published entomology and general zoology works in the 1830s. From 1841 he made many excursions around the Scottish coast at the request of the fisheries board. Also made fishing excursions inland. His brother John alias 'Christopher North' (1785-1854) was Professor of Moral Philosophy at Edinburgh.

[13] The swordfish mentioned earlier was caught in June and Elford's paper to the Wernerian was read on 27th July by the Secretary, Patrick Neill (1776-1851), presumably during his absence on fieldwork.

[14] Elford says he collected in these lochs (*Transactions of the Linnean Society*, **12**: 15). He does not state the year but they are located on the route from Edinburgh to the Western Isles and were probably visited in 1811.

[15] In a later undated letter to Montagu (WM1812. Loc: Linnean Society, Ref: Ms 206) Elford enclosed a sponge he had collected at "Colunsa one of the Hebrides" (probably Colonsay). The sponge was presumably collected on this tour to the southern islands of the Inner Hebrides.

[16] *Zoological Miscellany*, **3**: 9 (1817).

Elford's home county of Devon. Sadly, he died shortly after arriving. Rawlins and Elford had collected millipedes together in and around Edinburgh and when he died Elford named one of the new species *Craspedosoma raulinsii*.

Another recognisable name in the class-list is James Wilson[12] from Paisley (just west of Glasgow). As a zoologist Wilson later made intensive studies of the Scottish herring fishery and was invited to become Professor of Natural History at Edinburgh when Jameson eventually died in 1854 (an invitation he declined). In 1811 Wilson was preparing to study law but, like Elford, had had a great love of natural history since childhood and had enrolled for a summer with Jameson. Elford and Wilson obviously struck up a friendship and Elford later proposed him for membership of the Wernerian Society.

Round many western islands have I been — Keats

As Jameson noted in his evidence to the Commissioners, in some years he took his class to the Western Isles. The dismal summer of 1811 was one of those years – so wet that the British harvest failed (hard on the heels of the previous year's drought-driven crop failure) pushing up food prices. In the rain Elford, Rawlins and friends toured the west of Scotland and crossed to the Isles of Arran; Colonsay; Mull; Staffa; and Ulva[13]. They also appear to have visited Loch Lomond and Loch Katrine[14]. Elford collected extensively on this trip, bringing back a range of animals including insects, crustaceans, snakes, amphibians, fish, and sponges[15]. On Arran he took a particular interest in the amphibians and in one evening he and Richard Hanson from Bristol collected nearly 600 toads around the inlet of Loch Ranza to measure the variation in this species[16]. When the group moved on to the other islands Elford left collecting apparatus on Arran with a local

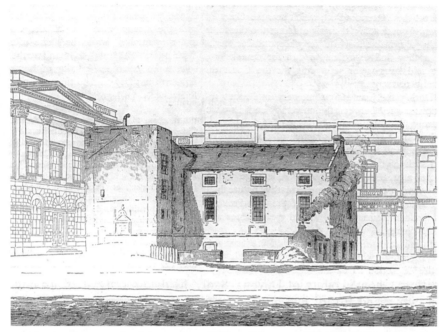

resident who promised to make additional insect collections for him. At Colonsay the group was confined to quarters for three days by the unseasonal storms but when the weather lifted Elford rowed along the coast of Mull collecting live animals from the Atlantic waters by scooping them out – with some difficulty – using a large shrimp net borrowed from one of the local fishermen[17].

The wanderers were back in Edinburgh by mid-September and Richard Rawlins headed south, carrying with him: a letter from Elford to MacLeay; some specimens Elford had borrowed; and gifts from the new collections for MacLeay, Marsham and Milne. Elford had heard from his friend Simon Wilkin in Norfolk[18] that MacLeay was thinking about selling his duplicate insects. Without waiting for confirmation he jumped at the chance:

"I understand from my friend Mr Wilkin of Norwich that all your duplicates are to be sold, if so I should be much obliged if you will put all the Neuroptera together that I may be enabled to get them, as you are well acquainted with my intentions respecting that order.— If you would let me purchase them privately you need only name your price and I will instantly

accept it, if you will do this I shall feel eternally obliged. I trust that my requesting this will cause no offence, if it should I humbly beg your pardon."

We do not know MacLeay's response[19], but Elford could not wait to hear it. He was off on more field-

The old university library, still standing in the unfinished quadrangle in Elford Leach's day.

[17] Leach, 1852: 366. He says the trip was to the Orkneys but he means Hebrides. He never visited the Orkneys.
[18] Simon Wilkin (1790-1862). Entomologist of Costessey near Norwich. His artist was John Curtis (1791-1862) who illustrated volumes 1 & 2 of Kirby & Spence's *Introduction to Entomology* (1815 & 1817).
[19] MacLeay did not sell his duplicates until 1814.
[20] This trip was probably another with Jameson.
[21] Not mathematics, as Sweet suggested (1970: 41).
[22] James Home (1758-1842) Professor of *Materia Medica* 1798-1821, having succeeded his father Francis (1719-1813). James was very successful, raising class numbers from 50 to 310 (in the winter of 1811 there were 180). Was Professor of Physic from 1821-1842, at which he was not a success.
[23] Andrew Duncan (1744-1828) Professor 1789-1819. Visited China in 1768. Renowned for his good nature and a generous attitude to students, but was a steady rather than inspired lecturer. President, Royal Medical Society six times; President, Edinburgh College of Physicians 1790. In the 1770s he founded a public dispensary which became the Royal Public Dispensary. In 1792 proposed a lunatic asylum which was begun in 1807. In 1809 founded the Caledonian Horticulture Society. Later promoted idea of a a public experimental garden. Senior physician in Scotland to the Prince of Wales for 30 years.

One of the toads collected at Loch Ranza by Elford Leach and Richard Hanson (From *The Zoological Miscellany*)

George Square, Edinburgh. Old Town suburbs. Robert Jameson lived at Nº 45 (the site now covered by the University Library).

24　　Joseph Collier Cookworthy (1792-1869). After qualifying practiced as a physician in Higher Broad Street, Plymouth. By 1822 was in Frankfort Place and by 1830 was at 26 George Street (when John Butter practised at Nº 28). Mayor of Plymouth 1839-1841 and an Alderman from 1850.
25 William Snow Harris (1791-1867). Practised as a physician in Plymouth after qualifying. Also interested in electricity. In 1820 he invented a new lightning conductor for ships. Also an improved mariner's compass. Married in 1824 then abandoned medicine for electricity. In 1826 Sir Humphry Davy invited him to report to the Royal Society on the electrical conductivity of various metals. FRS 1831. Knighted 1847. Advised government on all electrical matters from 1860 and oversaw the fitting of lightning conductors to the Houses of Parliament; Royal Palaces; gunpowder magazines &c. Played the harp and piano and was a renowned conversationalist.
26 Rowe (1871) *Proceedings of the Plymouth Institution* p. 156 says "J. Collier Cookworthy" not "Joseph C. Cookworthy".
27 Gill (1979: 114) says Cookworthy was William Cookworthy's son but Jewers (*Trans. Plymouth Institution*, **9**: 112) says he was the eldest son of Joseph Cookworthy by his 2nd wife, Mary Robins.
28 Stephen Love Hammick (1777-1867). Surgeon Extraordinary to George IV and William IV. In 1829 moved to London. Created Baronet 1834.

work, this time, "to examine geognostically the Elden hills near Melrose, on my return I shall again work at zoology.[20]"

Although it does not appear to have loomed large in Elford's mind, on his return he would also have to work at medicine. As the winter session of the new academic year began he registered for four courses: *Materia Medica*[21] taught by Dr James Home[22] (who started his lectures at 8 a.m. in the winter months); *Institutes of Medicine* (i.e. Physiology), with Dr Andrew Duncan Snr[23]; *Clinical Medicine*, taught both by Home and Duncan; and (again) Jameson's *Natural History* course.

Although he had lost his friend Rawlins, in this academic year Elford was joined in some of his classes by three medical students from Plymouth who may already have been known to him: Joseph Collier Cookworthy[24], William Snow Harris[25] and Frederick Love Hammick. Collier Cookworthy[26] was the great-nephew of William Cookworthy (1705-1780)[27] a Kingsbridge-born chemist who had discovered the means of making porcelain from West Country clays ('china clays'). William founded the British porcelain industry, which was fleetingly based at Plymouth in the 1760s but later relocated to Bristol then Worcester. William and his brother had also started a successful druggists' business in Plymouth which was still trading in 1811. William Snow Harris was the son of a Plymouth attorney and his family would certainly have known Elford's. Frederick Love Hammick was presumably related to Stephen Love Hammick[28], surgeon at the Royal Naval Hospital in Plymouth, and may have been his younger brother.

Also in Edinburgh from the West Country was Cornishman John Davy. Davy and Elford were in the same *Materia* class and clearly got to know each other as Elford presented a paper by Davy on the bones of 'the Orkney animal' (a carcass washed up on the Orkney coast several years earlier) to the Wernerian Society. Davy was the younger brother of Humphry Davy[29] and like his famous brother was a very keen angler.

Despite registering for twice as many courses as the previous winter, Elford's extra-curricular activities also escalated. At the Wernerian he proposed Simon Wilkin, Richard Rawlins, James Wilson and a J. Needham Esq. of Leicester[30] for membership. A paper on the new rock-boring sea-urchin, and a design for a new craniometer; were presented to the society by the Secretary. Elford himself read descriptions of two species of shark; and communicated John Davy's paper. He was also updating his work on oil-beetles for publication by the Linnean Society, and packing a box of specimens to send to James Sowerby[31] and to Rawlins (who was still in London). This box also contained gifts of British insects for Latreille in Paris, which Elford asked MacLeay to forward for him. Already in contact with Germany, despite the war he was now making direct contact with the progressive French school.

In addition to this, and his ongoing preparations for *Malacostraca Britanniæ*, he had acquired a job from the Edinburgh publishers. He was preparing medical and natural history entries for the *Edinburgh Encyclopædia*, edited by David Brewster[32], which had been published in parts since 1808. Presumably he obtained this commission through his links with the Edinburgh natural history community, perhaps from Robert Jameson. One of his entries, *Crustaceology*, was to be the culmination of

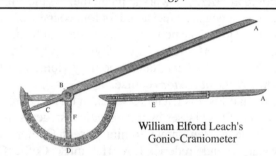

William Elford Leach's
Gonio-Craniometer

A craniometer for measuring the superior basi-facial angle of Dr Barclay

"AA represent two rods of brass, one turning on a pivot B. The skull is placed in the instrument, the teeth and alveolar processes being received into the notch F, by which contrivance an imaginary line is carried through the alveolar processes parallel with the palatine plate: (This notch may be closed by the slider E.) When the skull is in this situation, the rod AC is made to rest on the bones of the nose and forehead, (or on the junction of the nasal and superior maxillary bones); the end C showing the degrees of the angle on the semicircle D, without farther trouble."

William Elford Leach
Entry CRANIOMETRY. *Edinburgh Encyclopædia*, **7**(1): 320 (1813)

[29] John Davy (1790-1868). Physiologist and anatomist. MD 1814. Became an army surgeon. Travelled in Ceylon, W. Indies & E. Mediterranean. Edited *Memoirs of Sir Humphry Davy* 1836. Was Inspector General of Army Hospitals from about 1862.

[30] An entomologist friend at Edinburgh. Elford mentions him in a letter to MacLeay, 18th February 1812. Is proposed as non-resident member and presumably leaves Edinburgh in early 1812.

[31] Elford says "Mr Sowerby". Elsewhere this clearly means James Sowerby.

[32] David Brewster (1781-1868). Born Jedburgh. Researched magnetism and the polarisation of light. FRS 1815. In 1816 invented the kaleidoscope. Leading founder of the British Association for the Advancement of Science 1831. Knighted 1831.

[33] Some authors describe this as a translation of the French works. This is nonsense; it contained 50 new genera and 48 new species.

[34] George Paton (1721-1807). Made his library and expertise freely available to enthusiasts, including Thomas Pennant (see below).

[35] George Low (1746-1795). Naturalist. Born Edzal, Forfarshire. Studied at Aberdeen and St Andrews then tutored the Graham family in Stromness, Orkney. Accompanied Banks, Daniel Solander (1736-1782) and James Lind (1736-1812) on their visit to Orkney and Shetland 1772. Introduced to Paton and Thomas Pennant (below) by Banks. Ordained Minister of Birsay & Harray December 1774. In 1775 married Helen, daughter of James Tyrie, Minister of Stromness & Sandwick. She died in childbirth 1776. Low turned seriously to natural history. Pennant suggested he produce a Fauna and a Flora Orcadensis and funded a tour

Edinburgh Castle from the Old Town.

of the South Orkneys and Shetlands. He toured North Orkneys 1778. From 1781 tried in vain to publish his works and became bitter at Pennant's and others' increasing coldness.

36 Thomas Pennant (1726-1798). Traveller and naturalist. Born Flintshire. Educated Oxford (took no degree). Toured Iceland 1754. Corresponded with Linnæus from 1755. Began publishing *British Zoology* 1761. Visited Europe from 1765. Knew Buffon (Georges Louis Leclerc, comte de Buffon, 1707-1788). Met Voltaire (François Marie Arouet, 1694-1778) and noted his mastery of English swear-words. At the Hague befriended Peter Simon Pallas (1741-1811). FRS 1767. Published his journals from British tours. His *Arctic Zoology* (1784) included data from George Low.

37 A.M. Lysaght (1970) *J. Soc. Bibliog. Nat. Hist.*, **5**: 329-31, claimed Pennant merely, "skimmed the cream off Low's observations, published them in his *Arctic Zoology* and even used some of his illustrations" then "returned the manuscript to Low, saying that no bookseller was interested in it." (see also Dawson, 1958: 897-898 letter 23 as 'Law').

38 The *Dictionary of National Biography* wrongly says he graduated at Edinburgh.

39 It is also possible Edinburgh did not confer MDs on minors in 1812. This was the case in 1826 (Great Britain, 1837: 195). Also by 1826, and possibly earlier, Edinburgh required an examination and dissertation, both in Latin (*op. cit.* p. 84). In 1802 and probably later Edinburgh only conferred MDs in June and September (Cholmondeley, 1950: 182). This would also have hindered Elford's ambition.

his work on the Crustacea, begun with Montagu all those years ago and continued ever since during his extensive collecting and his study of the French scientific literature[33].

Not satisfied with his own work, Elford was also repaying his debts to Alexander MacLeay by visiting auctions and specialist dealers in Edinburgh to buy gems and rare coins on his behalf. The interest in coins at this time may relate to the sale of the collections of the Edinburgh antiquary George Paton[34]. Paton had died in 1807 but his manuscripts, prints, coins and antiquities were not disposed of until 1811. Elford also made purchases for himself, including an unpublished manuscript on the zoology of the Orkney and Shetland Islands (off the northern tip of Scotland) written by George Low, an Orkney minister and naturalist[35]. Low had written this in the late 1700s at the suggestion of the Scottish naturalist Thomas Pennant[36], who had seen and annotated the manuscript[37]. On Low's death in 1795 this work, together with Low's natural history collection and other manuscripts, passed to Paton who had been lending Low books to help his studies. It was now bought by Elford Leach together with some of Low's original specimens.

Medicinæ Doctor

Elford's zoological work was increasing in pace and after more than eight years, he decided it was time to bring his medical studies to an end, but this timing appears to be more than accidental.

William Elford Leach was born in 1791. The 2nd of February 1812 would be his 21st birthday, when he reached the 'age of majority' and in law passed from being a minor to being an adult; a socially and legally significant rite of passage. It is clear from his actions now that it was his ambition to be *Dr* Leach before he was 21, but that was impossible at Edinburgh[38]. Before it would award the degree of Doctor of Medicine the university required more study at Edinburgh than Elford had yet undertaken.[39]

William Wright, Vice-President of the Wernerian Society, had obtained his M.D. from Scotland's oldest university, the University of St Andrews, without ever having studied there. It may have been Wright who suggested this route to Elford, but Elford probably also spoke to Dr Robert Briggs, Professor of Anatomy at St Andrews, who was both a member of the Wernerian Society and a member of the University of St Andrews Senatus (the university's governing council).

This sounds an unlikely route to a qualification, but there were various ways to obtain the degree of M.D. in the early years of the nineteenth century[40]: *ad eundem gradum* (the award of a degree by one university, equivalent to a degree already held from another); by examination; or in recognition of existing experience. Edinburgh University had a restrictive policy and required all medical classes to have been taken at the university. They felt university attendance followed by examination would maintain quality control and lead to a better regulated profession. St Andrews University supported a more flexible approach which recognised experience wherever and however it had been gained[41].

An application for the degree of M.D. from St Andrews under the heading of existing experience had to be supported by a testimonial signed by two physicians of credit known to the university. Elford applied to Dr Briggs on the 9th of January with a supporting certificate from William Wright and John Barclay (who had studied at St Andrews for the church). The rush to meet his self-imposed deadline is clear in his letter, which survives in the University of St Andrews' archives:

"Sir,

I take the liberty of transmitting the inclosed certificate signed by D[rs] Wright and Baclay, at the same time however, I consider it proper to state my pretentions to a degree from your highly honorable College. I served an apprenticeship of five years in Exeter, during which time I attended the Devonshire and Exeter Hospital, under Mess[rs] Pepin, Luscombe and Sheldon, also the lectures of the latter on Anatomy, and M[r] White on chemistry. With the expirariton of the term of my apprenticeship I studied in London at the anatomical School in St Batsc Hospital under Mess[rs] Abernethy and Laurance, attending at the same time Lectures on Materia, & Practice of Physic and M[r] Davy's Chemical Lectures at the Royal Institution, also on Comparitive Anatomy by James M[c]partney and Everard Home during three winters. Since then I have attended the lectures of all the Medical professors in the Edinburgh University, and have the honor of being a member of the Royal College of Surgeons and Linnæan Society of London. These are the grounds on which I presume to request the honor of Doctors degree and should your college consider me as worthy that honor I should esteem it an additional favour if they would transmit the diploma to some one in Edinburgh, letting me have a short notice by letter of its being sent and the money shall be paid on delivery; if it can conveniently be sent, (should the honor be conferred) before the twenty fourth of the month[42] I shall esteem it an aditional favor conferred on your most obe[t] Ser[t]

W[m] Elford Leach."

The accompanying testimonial reads:

"We certify, that M[r] William Elford Leach is of a respectable character; That he has received a liberal Education; That he has attended a complete

[40] The following information was kindly provided by Robert N. Smart, Keeper of the Muniments at the University of St Andrews (*in litt.* to KH March 1986).
[41] Institutions that took this view were under increasing pressure. St Andrews introduced examinations in 1826 and in 1858 the *Medical Act* standardised many aspects of medical administration in Britain, introducing a nationwide system of registration for doctors and creating a General Medical Council (Smart *in litt.*).
[42] The 24th was a Friday. Elford's birthday was nine days later on the Sunday. He was apparently giving himself one week of safety.

Course of Lectures on all the branches of Medecine And being disireous of Obtaining the degree of Doctor of Physick, We do, from our personal knowlege, deem him highly deserving of that Honour

Willm Wright M D
Physician to H',M, Forces
John Barclay M.D."

The Senatus of the University was remarkably sympathetic to Elford's unseemly rush. Having received the application in time for their meeting on Monday the 13th they set the matter down for consideration at their Ordinary Meeting the following Saturday, when they agreed to confer the degree. Elford had achieved his ambition, or at least part of it. The following day he wrote to Alexander MacLeay and closed his letter, "Dr Wright is going to London, he intends to do me the honor of proposing me a member of the Royal Society, may I request your name if you think me worthy.[43]"

In his characteristic style Elford presses ahead with this plan without waiting for a reply and in a second letter written six days later tells MacLeay he is enclosing, "the certificate drawn out by Dr Wright for myself which I shall request you to honor with your name and endeavour at the next Linnean meeting to get the names of Dr Maton and any other gentlemen who may be there who know me. If you will do this I shall consider myself under great obligations; I should add, after you have done so be good enough to [*page torn*] under the cover in which I sent it and [*page torn*] to Dr Wm Wright at Dr Garthshores St Martins Lane, as he has promised to present it to Sir Joseph Banks.[44]"

Elford's ambitions regarding the Royal Society evidently caused consternation in London; eye-brows (and ghosts) rose. We do not have the response to his letters but from later reference to it[45] it is clear MacLeay replied gently but very firmly that perhaps it would be better to wait until 'the business of Bullock' was more of a distant memory, at which time he and Dr Maton would be in a better position to assist. Elford had no choice but to concur and did so graciously:

"With respect to the Royal Society I most thoroughly agree with yourself and Dr Maton, and return you many thanks for the candid manner in which you have stated your objections; will you present my most grateful thanks also to Dr Maton for his kindness, which I shall ever remember with gratitude.[46]" He would have to be satisfied with his M.D.[47]

With his medical training completed, Elford stayed in Edinburgh for several months, apparently working on Low's manuscript which he had decided to edit for publication. At the Wernerian in March he gave a presentation on the breed of pig found in the Orkneys and Shetlands. Low had described Orkney pigs in his manuscript as a variety of the common pig, but "of a very small size, and variable colour, the back full of very large and long bristles, the ears erect and sharp pointed, the nose surprisingly strong: in a word, their appearance is altogether different from those brought

[43] Letter: Leach to MacLeay, 19th of January 1812 (Loc: Linnean Society of London, Miscellaneous Correspondence).

[44] Letter: Leach to MacLeay, 25th of January 1812 (Loc: Linnean Society of London, Miscellaneous Correspondence).

[45] Letter: Leach to MacLeay, 20th of March 1815 (Loc: Linnean Society of London, Miscellaneous Correspondence).

[46] Letter: Leach to MacLeay, 18th of February 1812 (Loc: Linnean Society of London, Miscellaneous Correspondence).

[47] At this time the degree of 'M.D.' was the qualification awarded to any physician graduating from university. This system has been retained in the USA but in the UK the M.D. degree has since been elevated to the status of a higher doctorate and is now awarded only as an honorary degree to public figures or to eminent practitioners. In the UK today a physician will usually receive instead two bachelors degrees: Bachelor of Medicine, *M.B.* or *B.M.*, and Bachelor of Surgery, *Ch.B.* or *B.Ch.* or *B.Chir.* (abbrieviated from the Latin *Baccalaureus Chirurgiæ*) or *B.S.* (from the English) However, the title 'Doctor' is still used for any qualified British physician despite the fact that British physicians are no longer awarded a doctorate.

from the south, as their size is remarkably less". Elford obviously felt these differences were sufficient to warrant the separation of the Orkney pigs as a new species, although he may have changed his mind later as he never published this opinion.

He seems to have edited the manuscript quickly. An advertisement[47] included in the preface is dated *'Edinburgh, May* 14, 1812' and writing it was probably the last thing he did before leaving the city. On the 16th some of his observations on the class Insecta were communicated to the Wernerian by the Secretary, and Elford may already have left – leaving his collections in Scotland for the time-being.

County and culture

As Napoleon took his first steps east on the road that would lead to Moscow, and as the United States, after years of grievance, finally declared war on Britain, Elford Leach took the coach west to Devon[48]. This is the first record of his being in the West Country since he left for London at the end of 1808[49] and the first record of the house, *Woodland*, where his parents now lived. His father had bought part of the barton of Butshed from Sir Harry Trelawney, including the manor-house, about 5 km north of Plymouth[50].

Elford's interest in science extended to its wider promotion, and in June, probably on his way home, he approached the Mayor of Exeter, Devonshire's county town, to propose the formation of a county museum and library[51]. The idea was received warmly and fundraising began almost immediately. A similar plan was being instigated locally in Plymouth by that most active of Plymouth public figures, Henry Woollcombe[52]. Woollcombe was tireless in his efforts to improve the urban planning and

Exeter Guildhall.

[47] This was reported in the *Gentleman's Magazine*, April 1813: 337-340.

[48] He would have travelled via London but any time spent there is not obviously documented.

[49] The record is not continuous for these years and he may have visited Devon, but his summers were occupied with fieldwork and the short winter breaks would not have made the long journey from Edinburgh to Plymouth probable. He visited Cheltenham in the summer of 1809 and may have seen some of his family there. Cheltenham, a spa town, was a social focus for genteel Society at that time, who came in the summer to take the waters.

[50] Lysons & Lysons (1822: 88). Presumably George Leach replaced Elford Town with a house closer to Plymouth. It is not clear when he did this and he may have been at Woodland for a number of years by 1812. He may have moved in 1799 when he allegedly retired. Woodland must have been near the modern Woodland Wood, just east of Budshead Wood.

[51] To be housed in Exeter.

[52] Henry Woollcombe (1777-1846). A lawyer of an old Devon family; a leader in the fight for electoral reform and, "the founder of almost every institution in Plymouth at that time" (quoted in Gill, 1979: 110). His autograph journal covering the periods 1797-1819 and 1821-28 is in the West Devon Record Office, Plymouth (Ref: Catalogue 701). Extracts were supplied to JES by Mr C.A. ('Ben') Lewis of Clearbrook who has conducted valuable research into this diary and whose assistance is greatly appreciated.

53 Whitfeld, 1900.
54 After London, Manchester, Liverpool, Birmingham, Bristol. For Plymouth figures see Gill (1979: 103-4).
55 George William Soltau (d. 1859 - local Liberal political leader and mayor of Plymouth 1838 & 1841); Francis Fox; and Henry Gandy.
56 Edmund Lockyer MD (d. 1816). Mayor of Plymouth 1803, 1810-1812. A Woollcombe supporter.
57 William Eastlake (b. 1779). Attorney.
58 George Eastlake jnr (fl.1812-1820) Attorney and Deputy Judge Advocate. Mayor of Plymouth 1819.
59 Ambrose Bowden Johns (1776-1858). Painter. Friend of J.M.W. Turner (1775-1851) until some of his works were mistaken for Turner's. Also knew painters James Northcote (1746-1831) and Benjamin Robert Haydon (1786-1846).
60 Charles Lock Eastlake (1793-1865). Painter/Arts administrator. Son of George Eastlake Snr (Attorney to the Admiralty and Judge Advocate General). Eastlake and Elford both studied at Plympton Grammar School but Eastlake was two years younger. Moved in 1808-9 to Charterhouse, London, then Royal Academy (Does not appear to have known Elford well as he referred to him in 1826 only as Miss Leach's brother – see later). President of the Royal Academy and knighted 1850. A courteous man and meticulous worker but with 'constitutional timidity'. Disliked publicity. Was slightly lacking in self-confidence. Did not always do what needed doing for fear of making mistakes.

1 Jacob Ludwig Carl Grimm (1785-1863) and Wilhelm Carl Grimm (1786-1859).
2 (1762-1812).
3 Harvey, 1978: 328.

cultural opportunities in the Plymouth area. A man "of easy address and polished bearing, mild cheerfulness and gentle sympathy, with a touch of the old school in his carriage[53]", he was Mayor of Plymouth in 1813 and Recorder from 1833-1837, succeeding Sir William Elford.

As Britain's war with France became entrenched, and a South American war with Spain erupted in 1804, and a naval dispute with the United States began to simmer from 1807, and as Sweden declared war in 1810, and as supply lines were laid to the Peninsula – *The Three Towns* with their Royal Navy base, prospered. By 1811 the population of Plymouth Dock had grown to 30,000, of Plymouth to just over 21,000 and of Stonehouse to just over 5000. Greater Plymouth was now the sixth largest population centre in England[54], having for centuries been ranked about twentieth.

Devon's distance from London was such that its intellectual society formed independently and in 1810 Woollcombe and a small group of like-minded individuals[55] planned the formation of a modern *Athenæum,* a new scientific and philosophical society for this rapidly expanding community. In 1812 this became a reality with the foundation of *The Plymouth Institution.* The inaugural meeting was held in Woollcombe's house on the 3rd of October and present as founder members were: Henry Woollcombe; Dr Edmund Lockyer[56]; Dr Elford Leach; William Prideaux; William Eastlake[57]; George Eastlake jnr[58]; William Prance; Ambrose Bowden Johns[59]; and George Ogg. Within a short time William and George Eastlake would be joined as members by their brother, Charles Lock Eastlake, an artist destined to cross the path of Napoleon Bonaparte and later to become President of the Royal Academy and Director of the National Gallery[60]. In October 1812 Charles was in London, where, like Elford, he had moved in 1808.

1812	Beethoven writes his 7th and 8th symphonies (1811-1812).
—	The brothers Grimm[1] publish the first part of their collected fairy-tales, *Kinder- und Haus-märchen.*
—	Byron rises to prominence with his poem *Childe Harold.*
—	Luddite disturbances in Yorkshire.
March to April	Machine-breaking in Lancashire and Cheshire.
April onwards	Widespread food riots in industrial areas.
April	Riots in Manchester trading Exchange.
11th May	Prime Minister, Spencer Perceval[2], shot dead in the House of Commons by bankrupt Liverpool broker John Bellingham.
May	Demonstrations in Nottingham celebrating the assassination
June	Napoleon invades Russia.
19th June	USA declares war on Britain for denying America maritime freedoms. France also rejects American claims. From 1807-1812 Britain seized 917 American ships; France seized 741; Denmark 70; and the Kingdom of Naples 47[3]. War is declared just as France and Britain lift restrictions.
18th July	Peace between Sweden and Britain.

The new Plymouth Institution (or 'Plymouth Institute' as it was initially called) met every two weeks during the winter to hold lectures on science and the arts. The first four meetings were held in members' houses then moved to the Plymouth Dispensary[61].

Elford Leach had not forgotten London. Just as he had proved himself a vigorous recruiter for the Wernerian Society, he was now recruiting in Devon for the Linnean. In a letter to MacLeay[62] he mentions he has just recruited his uncle Sir William Elford and John Harris of Exeter "who wrote on two new species of Didelphis from Australasia[63]". He also recruited Sir William's son Jonathan.

In this same letter he adds in passing, "I hope Hooker will pay me a visit this summer." This is the first mention of a friend he had made at the Linnean Society[64], William Jackson Hooker[65]. Six years older than Elford, Hooker's first interest in natural history had been entomology, through which he had become a close friend of MacLeay, William Kirby and William Spence[66]. He lived at Halesworth in Suffolk but may have been travelling to visit relatives in the summer of 1812 as his father Joseph was originally from Exeter. It was probably Joseph's passion for cultivating rare plants that encouraged his son to become increasingly interested in botany. By 1810 William Hooker had already made botanical excursions to Scotland and to Iceland[67]. This change of interest was a boon to Elford because Hooker now made him a gift of his entire collection of British crustaceans[68]. In gratitude Elford named one of the new species it contained, *Sphaeroma hookeri*.

Another person who augmented Elford's crustacean collection during 1812[69] was Robert Stevenson of Edinburgh[70]. Stevenson was the civil engineer to the Scottish Lighthouse Board and was just completing an innovative new lighthouse on the Bell Rock, a particularly dangerous reef situated in the main shipping lanes off the Firth of Tay and within striking distance (literally) of the Firth of Forth. This reef was submerged by several metres at high tides and had wreaked considerable havoc with shipping.

Stevenson had started work on the lighthouse in 1807 and discovered any wooden structures placed in the sea for any length of time during construction were destroyed by small crustaceans which burrowed into them just below the water's surface. He was a member of the Wernerian

William Spence

[61] Rowe, J.B. (1871) *Proc. Plymouth Institution* : 155-6. Membership was limited to 30 with 4 Presidents: Woollcombe, Cookworthy, Lockyer and William Prance

[62] Letter: W.E. Leach to MacLeay, 2 July 1812 (Loc: Linnean Society of London, Misc. Correspondence)

[63] John Harris (FLS 1814) His family lived at Radford House near Plymouth. He was proposed in January 1813 by Elford, Montagu and Charles Mackenzie MD (Edin.), as were Edmund Lockyer and Jonathan Elford, who lived at Pound.

[64] They attended the same meetings by December 1809 (*General Minute Book* 1.)

[65] William Jackson Hooker (1785-1865) Born Norwich FLS 1806. FRS 1812. In 1814 travelled to France, Switzerland and N. Italy. Married Maria Turner of Yarmouth 1815. In 1820, on Banks' advice, accepted the chair of Botany at Glasgow University. Knighted 1836. Director, Kew Gardens, London 1841. *The Dictionary of National Biography* says mistakenly he was a founder of the Wernerian Society.

[66] William Spence (1783-1860) Born Hull. Studied economics. In 1805 became interested in entomology. In 1808 agreed to write an *Introduction to Entomology* with William Kirby. Spent 4-5 months in the summer of 1812 researching in London, especially in Banks' library. In late 1815 spent 4 months in Europe. Lived in Exmouth, Devon, 1818-1826. Travelled in Italy and Switzerland 1826-1830 then lived in London.

[67] Scotland 1806; Iceland 1809 (when the ship containing his collections was burned during civil unrest). Published *Recollections of Iceland* (1811; reprint 1813)

William Hooker in 1812.

68 Cuvier, 1818: 346. The species are described only in the Appendix to Elford's *Crustaceology* article in the *Edinburgh Encyclopædia* (written late summer 1812) not in the main text which was probably drafted towards the end of 1811.

69 Again the specimens are noted only in the Appendix to the *Crustaceology* article.

70 Robert Stevenson (1772-1850). Engineer to the Scottish Lighthouse Board for 50 years. Also designed bridges and suggested the form of rail used in railways. An originator of the Royal Observatory, Edinburgh. Also promoted fisheries. Sir Walter Scott, who travelled around Scotland with him in 1814, called him "a most gentlemanlike and modest man." Leach (1852: 336) says it was "John Stephenson Esq." who built the lighthouse and sent him specimens. This seems to be an error. He wrote only "Mr Stevenson" in the *Edinburgh Encyclopædia* (1814: 433).

71 Admitted 13th May 1809.

72 Belonging to a new genus.

73 *Ocotea rodiaei* (Schomb.) Mez.

74 Robert Lewis Balfour Stevenson (1850-1894). Was called Lewis by the family. Son of Robert Stevenson's youngest son Thomas (1818-1887- an engineer and meteorologist). Trained as a lawyer. Dropped the name Balfour and changed Lewis to the French spelling Louis.

75 The Class Myriapoda.

76 By 1815 he had correctly removed *Oniscus* from this group (*Trans. Linn. Soc.*, **11**: 306-400). *Oniscus* is a woodlouse (a crustacean); *Scolopendra* a centipede; *Julus* a millipede.

77 Letter: W.E. Leach to MacLeay, 12th December 1812 (Loc: Linnean Society of London, Miscellaneous Correspondence.)

Society[71] and sent examples of damaged logs containing the animals to Elford Leach who recognised these destructive creatures as a new species[72] which he named *Limnoria terebrans* (Greek for 'wood borer'). We now know this species as 'the gribble'. Robert Stevenson conducted experiments to find woods resistant to its attack, and to that of other marine borers, and his findings led to the universal adoption of South American *Greenheart*[73] for any marine structures. The Bell Rock lighthouse became operational in 1812 and Stevenson went on to become the grand-father of the novelist Robert Louis Stevenson[74], author of *Treasure Island, Kidnapped* and *Dr Jekyll and Mr Hyde*.

© V & A Picture Library

Elford spent the summer of 1812 – as Britain and Sweden declared peace – at Woodland engrossed in the higher classification of the crustaceans, insects, arachnids, centipedes and millipedes. Previous workers had grouped the centipedes and millipedes with the spiders, but Elford was convinced they deserved to be placed on equal footing in their own class and was painstakingly assembling his arguments. By December he was explaining to MacLeay, "My whole attention has been devoted this Summer to investigating the Crustacea and Arachnides of Latreille, and I have found it necessary to form a new Class[75], including the genera Oniscus, Scolopendra, and Julus of Linnè[76], which differ so essentially from the Arachnides and Crustacea that it appears to be perfectly warrented; I formerly mentioned to you the probability of these animals forming a distinct Class which I have now, I think established on a firm basis.[77]"

Most of Elford's collections were still in Edinburgh where he had left them in the spring and he decided it was time to retrieve them. At the beginning of January he travelled to London, where he stayed just long enough to attend the first meeting of the Linnean Society for 1813. He then headed north to Hull to see William Spence, who was working on his planned *Introduction to Entomology* with William Kirby. Although Elford and Spence had been in correspondence and Spence had sent him insect specimens for the museum of the

A myriapod

Myriapoda
Order: Syngnatha
Scolopendra Linnæus
Scolopendra alternans Leach

(Illustration from the *Zoological Miscellany*)

141

Wernerian Society[78], they had never met. Hull is mid-way between London and Edinburgh, so the visit would also be a useful break in the journey. Several weeks in Edinburgh were sufficient to pack his collections before he travelled south to spend the spring in London[79].

By late June he was back at Woodland, his collections had arrived safely, and he was busily describing crustaceans and reading background literature for his work on the British species. Despite this industry, he was not ignoring his broader promotion of science and had been in contact again with the Mayor of Exeter[80] about the proposed County Museum and Library. To MacLeay he enthuses, "The library will be the grand object, the museum the second, and if lectures can be established in Exeter, which I think may be brought about, people may be induced to spend part of their time in persuing some branch or other of Literature of Science.[81]" With friends he had already raised £1300 since the previous year and a public launch of the plan was arranged for Assize Week (when the Circuit Judges would arrive to try Exeter's serious criminal cases. Historically Assize Week in British towns was treated as a major social occasion, with Assize Balls and other events arranged to coincide with the rather more solemn business of the courts). The launch was obviously a success and by the early 1820s it could be reported, "a Devon and Exeter institution for the promotion of science, literature, and the arts, was established at Exeter, in 1813, by some gentlemen of the city and its neighbourhood. A handsome building has been fitted up for the purpose, with two spacious libraries, galleries for a museum, and reading rooms. The collection of books is already extensive and valuable: the museum is at present confined chiefly to the collection of British natural history, and is becoming rich in several departments.[82]"

Elford's programme for the creation of an Exeter institution was obviously going to exceed his expectations, but his personal plans in the summer of 1813 are less clear. He was still pursuing his entomological interests and had received another box of insects from Hoffmannsegg. He was preparing a second article on oil-beetles and was simultaneously writing several major publications on British crustaceans. While some of these may have provided sales income, others, very time consuming, clearly would not[83]. It seems he was not concerned about finances and never had been, but how he was supported is not clear. The family received rent from their holdings of land[84], but we do not know how these rents were apportioned.

However he was funded, Elford repeatedly tells others money is no object, as when he offered to purchase Alexander MacLeay's duplicates: "If you would let me purchase them privately you need only name your price". This is a common approach of his which will be repeated.

Socially, he invites MacLeay and his family to visit Devon, and hopes Spence and Milne will visit soon. James Sowerby may also have stayed with the Leaches this summer[85]. It appears that in July 1813 Elford was settling into an active life of self-funded natural history based, initially, in his parents' home. Before the month was over all that would have changed.

78 In the spring of 1812, see Wernerian Society *Minutes*, 16th May 1812 (Loc: Edinburgh University Library, Special Collections).

79 We have no proof Elford made this trip as described but he outlined this as his plan in a letter to MacLeay of the 12th of December.

80 As before he probably spoke to the Mayor during his journey from London to Plymouth.

81 Letter: W.E. Leach to [MacLeay], 24th July 1813 (Loc: Linnean Society of London, Miscellaneous Correspondence).

82 Lysons & Lysons, 1822: 234.

83 An analysis of the Classes Insecta, Crustacea, Arachnides and Myriapoda he was writing for the *Transactions of the Linnean Society* would not have earned him money and he would receive no profit from *Malacostraca Britanniæ*. Only his encyclopædia entries would have generated income.

84 This is clear from their Wills.

85 James Sowerby once stayed at Elford's father's house 'near Plymouth'. No date is known but 1813 is possible. Sowerby and Elford may have discussed their proposed work *Malacostraca Britanniæ* (Letter: George Leach Snr to G.B. Sowerby THE ELDER, 21st November 1822. Loc: Welsh Folk Museum, National Museum of Wales, Cardiff. Ref: Ms No. 75).

— 9 —

Empty dogs and empty houses

I have known of not less than 380,000 men of the French
army in Spain at one moment, and yet with no authority beyond
the spot where they stood, and their time passed and their
force exhausted by the mere effort of obtaining subsistence.

Wellington[1]

Behind the Lines of Torres Vedras in the early winter of 1810 the
plight of the displaced population was desperate. Jonathan
was moved by their suffering: "Thousands of the unfortunate
inhabitants of the provinces through which our army had recently retreated,
had abandoned their homes, and were endeavouring to exist between Lisbon
and the lines. There was, therefore, an immense population hemmed up in a
small space of country, hundreds of them without a house to cover them, or
food to eat, except what was afforded by the bounty of the rich at Lisbon,
and by the liberal subscriptions raised for them in England.

In the course of the winter, the number of Portuguese who actually died
of want was quite dreadful. It was not unusual to see hordes of those poor
wretches, old and young, male and female, in rags, the very pictures of death,
seated in despair on the wet ground, round a miserable fire, on which was
placed an earthen vessel, full of such herbs as could be gathered in the fields
and hedges. Thousands contrived to drag on a miserable existence on this
vile sustenance. Their death-like, emaciated faces were sufficient to have
touched the heart of the most callous and unfeeling. The British soldiers
assisted them by every means in their power; and in the Light Division (as
well as, I conclude, in every other) soup was made from the heads and offal
of the cattle killed for the troops, and distributed amongst the starving
inhabitants."

Among the residents of Lisbon a curious social fervour developed to
counterpoint the suffering of the dispossessed immigrants. After the first
alarm, according to Sherer, Lisbon "became as it were intoxicated by a
strong feeling of security: there never was a period when this city was more
crowded with objects of misery, or when provisions were more extravagantly

[1] Wellington, 1956: 2.

dear; yet at no time had their theatres been better filled, their societies more gay and brilliant, than when seventy thousand vindictive enemies lay within sixteen miles[2] of the city, panting for the plunder of it. It is but justice to add, that every thing which prudence and humanity could suggest was done by the inhabitants of Lisbon, to alleviate the public misfortune. The port was open to all vessels laden with provisions, the magazines were filled with them, charitable institutions were set on foot, and food was daily distributed to such of the fugitives as were necessitous and helpless, while labour was provided for the others.[3]"

In the Lines themselves the Light Division was placed in a tented encampment where they daily expected a major French assault[4]. Depending on the weather the troops spent the day in the deserted town of Arruda dos Vinhos nearby, returning at night to their camp in the hills. The officers used these trips to render their tents more habitable by the transfer of furniture from the town, although Kincaid was amused to observe "the different notions of individual comfort, in the selection of furniture, which officers transferred from their *town house* to their *no house* on the heights. A sofa, or a matress, one would have thought most likely to be put in requisition; but it was not unusual to see a full-length looking glass preferred to either.[5]"

Despite their home comforts the tents were no match for the incessant rains, which sought out every point of weakness in the canvas. The French were trying the same with the defences and there was constant skirmishing between the pickets, with Craufurd again showing his mastery of close encounter by denying Masséna any opportunity to ascertain allied strength in the field without launching a full assault. This he was not prepared to do, and while he probed, his *Army of Portugal* – not being supplied with food for men or forage for animals – soon picked its already spartan surroundings bare, watched by Jonathan Leach: "A wide open valley, which divided the pickets of the two armies, in the immediate front of the Light Division, the French frequently made foraging parties into; but after the first week, I do not believe as much provision could have been found for man or horse, in the whole valley, as would have rationed half a squadron of Lilliputian[6] cuirassiers[7] for twenty-four hours."

"Thus between constantly strengthening our position; endeavouring to keep off agues by dint of cigars, and of such fluids as were sometimes attainable from the sutlers[8] who paid us a visit from Lisbon; reconnoitering our French neighbours with telescopes; trying to keep our horses, mules, and donkeys alive during the inclement weather, with chopped straw, or what little herbage the hills afforded, with, now and then, a very diminutive allowance of barley or Indian corn; and the occasional arrival of letters and newspapers from England.— we passed some five or six weeks, wondering whether Massena would attack us, or walk away from our front."

The answer came on the 15th of November: "I happened to be on picket in front of Arruda on the night of the 14th; and looking, as usual,

[2] 26 km.
[3] Sherer, 1996: 124-125.
[4] Both Sherer and Kincaid express the view that if Masséna had assailed the Lines in the first few days after the allies' arrival, before they had learned the plan of the defences and arranged effective communications, his attack may well have succeeded. As it was, he waited for the arrival and deployment of his artillery, and the moment was lost.
[5] Kincaid. 1981: 14.
[6] A literary allusion to *Gulliver's Travels* by Jonathan Swift (1726). 'Lilliputian' = extremely small.
[7] 'Cuirassier' – a type of French cavalry. From 'cuirass' armour covering the chest and back.
[8] 'Sutler' – a merchant accompanying an army.

with all our eyes, in the twilight of the following morning, towards our opponents, the French sentries, we thought, could be discovered as heretofore: but when day broke thoroughly, we found that the cunning rogues had played us an old trick of theirs, by placing figures of straw upright, with a soldier's cap on each, and a pole by their side to represent a musket. Their whole army had retired, during the night, in the direction of Santarem; and we were sent in pursuit some hours afterwards."

Masséna's army had been suffering increasingly from disease, deprivation and desertion. He was expecting reinforcement by a force under Soult but this was currently too far distant and he could no longer wait where he was. He pulled his army back towards the fortified town of Santarém on its hill on the west bank of the Tagus, 40 km north of the Lines.

Leach: "On the 16th, the Light Division made a move to the right, which brought it close to the Tagus. We pushed on through Villa Nova[9] and Azimbuja; and although we could not reach their rear-guard, we took many prisoners, who, from sickness, fatigue, or in search of plunder, had straggled from their ranks. The road from Alemquer to Azimbuja was covered with horses, mules, and asses, belonging to the French, which had died from want of forage. We passed many French soldiers lying dead by the road-side, whose appearance indicated that disease and want of food had carried them off. Every house in every town or village which lay in their line of retreat was thoroughly ransacked. Desolation and devastation marked their track."

On the morning of the 17th the Light Division's vanguard of cavalry approached the town of Cartaxo and found six squadrons of French cavalry and three battalions of infantry drawn up on rising scrubland ahead of them. Craufurd arrived with the Light Division's infantry at mid-day and instantly determined to attack. However, before he deployed his men he made an address which Jonathan recorded in his journal the next day:

"The following speech was made by General Crawford yesterday to the Light Brigade *a few* minutes before we were to have attacked the French lines, *as was then intended but did not take place.*

"If I ever have occasion to observe *any man* of the Brigade pick his road on the march and go *round* a pool of water instead of marching *through* it I am fully *determined* to bring the officer commanding the Company to which that man belongs to a *Court Martial.* Should the Court *acquit* the *officer* it shall not *deter me* from repeating the same ceremony on any other officer *again* and *again.* Every *halting* day (if necessary) I will bring an officer to a *Court Martial* who shall *presume* to *allow* the men of *his Company* to go out of the way of a pool of water. I will insist on every *soldier* marching *through water* and I will *flog any man* attempting to *avoid* it."

[9] Vila Nova da Rainha.

145

This, with some other blackguard language was the substance of his *harangue*. A speech well calculated *no doubt* to make *men and officers* adore their leader and follow him enthusiastically up the French heights.[10]"

As noted, there was no requirement on this occasion to follow the leader, enthusiastically or otherwise, up the French heights. The assault was forestalled by Wellington who, having been informed what was afoot, arrived just in time to stop Craufurd attacking the 21,000 Frenchmen massed out of sight beyond the occupied rise.

The French continued their withdrawal north to the town of Santarém. Santarém was protected to the east by the Tagus and to the south by the marshy floodplain of the River Asseca (at that time called the Rio Maior) passable only by a long bridge and raised causeway. As it flowed under the causeway the Asseca turned south and ran parallel to the Tagus, separated from it by another marshy plain.

The French crossed the bridge then turned and took the Asseca as their front line, posting sentries at their end of the causeway. The Light Division arrived at the other end of the bridge on the 18th and, after a brief exchange of fire between the Rifles and the French defences, the 52nd Light Infantry took over the picket duty. That night, in the dark and the rain, Craufurd visited his sentries.

Leach: "General Crawford (among his other unaccountable actions) rode down to the advanced picquets on the bridge at midnight and without saying a syllable to the Field Officer of the Picquet, he went up to our advanced sentry took his musket out of his hand and moved towards the advanced sentry of the enemy at whom he *fired* which of *course* was returned and in an instant the whole French picquet opened a fire on the bridge and blazed away for some minutes on our picquet but fortunately no one was hurt.[11]"

Such an alarm was raised by this that one of Reynier's divisions also opened fire and shot at anything that appeared to be moving. By this Craufurd ascertained the French were not slipping away under cover of darkness. Daylight showed they had strengthened their position behind the river and around the town.

Santarém

Santarém, on its steep hill alongside the Tagus, was more habitable and defensible than Masséna's position in front of the Lines, and closer to any supply via Spain. With the natural defences of the surrounding rivers and hills reinforced by various engineering works the French held this position, with the allies in constant attendance, for the next four months, during which the Light Division picketed the bridge and causeway. At Santarém the French received their expected reinforcements of about 15,000 men and were resupplied, but the extra mouths merely added to the burdens of provision, and the greatly extended supply route – through country occupied by the

10 Verner, 1919: 172-173.
11 Verner, 1919: 174.

guerrillas of a vengeful and aggrieved population – failed to relieve the privations of the troops.

Wellington was well aware of the French problems of supply. It was part of his strategy to hold the French army stationary in the Peninsula while they starved for want of food and fodder[12]. Napoleon's armies had been designed for rapid deployment and sudden attack – an early use of *blitzkrieg* ('lightning war'). They were expected to obtain their food and animal fodder from the countryside they were in, but to maintain a constant supply these armies, like swarms of locusts, had to keep moving. Santarém quickly became no more hospitable than the camp in front of the Lines. One Portuguese resident managed to get a plaintive letter to Wellington complaining of his uninvited guests, "I had a cat, and Heaven forgive me if I do them injustice, but I do believe the miscreants have eat him!" and in a postscript, "I find that they *have* eat him![13]"

By contrast to the French, the allies' rations were adequate, albeit not lavish. "The Maior," recalled John Kincaid, "as far as the bridge of Vallé[14], was navigable for the small craft from Lisbon, so that our table, while we remained there, cut as respectable a figure, as regular supplies of rice, salt fish, and potatoes could make it; not to mention that our pigskin was, at all times, at least three parts full of a common red wine, which used to be dignified by the name of *blackstrap*. We had the utmost difficulty, however, in keeping up appearances in the way of dress. The jacket, in spite of shreds and patches, always maintained something of the original about it; but woe befell the regimental small-clothes[15], and they could only be replaced by very extraordinary apologies[16], of which I remember that I had two pair at this period, *one* of a common brown Portuguese cloth, and the *other*, or Sunday's pair, of black velvet. We had no women with the regiment; and the ceremony of washing a shirt amounted to my servant's taking it by the collar, and giving it a couple of shakes in the water, and then hanging it up to dry.[17]"

Sartorial elegance and laundry excepted, the officers of the Rifles made themselves as comfortable as they could and it was not long before their sedentary lifestyle prompted the usual diversions, despite the proximity of the enemy.

"The sportsmen in our division" declared Jonathan, clearly including himself in their number, "constantly had recourse to gun, pointer, and greyhound; and in the marshy plain between the Rio Maior and the Tagus we contrived to amuse ourselves very well, and often with success; hares, quails, snipes, and golden plovers, being abundant. In these pastimes the French cavalry pickets, posted on the marsh, never interferred with us, nor interrupted our sport, although we frequently coursed hares, and shot quails, within half range of their carbines. On the contrary, their conduct was courteous, and, if I may use the expression, gentlemanly to a degree. One anecdote in particular deserves being mentioned. It was customary for our cavalry pickets to patrole every morning before daybreak, to ascertain if

[12] Wellington later said of the war against Napoleon in the Peninsula, "We starved him out. We showed him that we wouldn't let him fight a battle at first, except under disadvantages. If you do fight, we shall destroy you; if you do *not* fight, we shall in time destroy you still." (Stanhope, 1888: 102).
[13] Stanhope, 1888: 77 [our italics].
[14] Vale de Santarém. A village just short of the allied side of the causeway.
[15] 'Small-clothes' were close-fitting knee breeches.
[16] i.e. unusual substitutes.
[17] Kincaid, 1981: 17-18.

any change or movement had taken place in the French chain of cavalry posts. One morning, in a thick fog, a small patrole of ours suddenly found themselves close to a superior force of French cavalry, and instantly retired; but, in a hurry, one of our dragoons dropped his cloak. Our patrole had ridden but a short distance to the rear, when it was called to by the French, one of whom, riding up to within a short distance, dropped the captured cloak on the ground and rode away, making signals to the English dragoon who had lost it, to pick it up. This was carrying on the war as it should be; and it is but justice to add, that we rarely found them deficient on this point." On another occasion the greyhounds of an officer pursued a hare into the French lines and were politely returned[18].

"In addition to shooting and coursing, the sporting characters at the outposts went through the formal process of racing, near Vallé; and I can never forget the first essay of the kind, where six or eight half-starved devils, whose diet had for some months consisted principally of chopped straw and winter-grass, started, with *gentlemen riders*, for a sweepstakes. Before they had gone one hundred yards, the horse which was ridden by my friend T. of the 43d regiment, came down heels over head, from sheer debility; and those in his wake, according to the nautical phrase, ran foul of him and his racer, who lay floundering on the earth. A greater burlesque on horse-racing never was witnessed: were I certain of seeing so amusing an exhibition at Newmarket, Epsom, or Doncaster[19], I verily believe I should seldom fail to attend their meetings.

Flags of truce frequently passed between the two armies, which afforded us many opportunities of conversing with the French officers who came with them to the bridge. One of Massena's aides-du-camp talked very big of the gaieties which were going on at Santarem, and of the theatre which the French officers had established there. It was intimated to this loquacious gentleman by the field-officer of our pickets, that the arrival at the French head-quarters of a large drove of cattle, some waggon-loads of flour or bread, and a few other necessaries of the sort, might, by possibility, be as acceptable, and rather more useful to them than all their dramatic works.

If, however, the French could get up theatrical performances, we, on the other side of the causeway, were determined not to be outdone in that respect. Accordingly, the soldiers of a certain company in our battalion did make the attempt, having converted an old house, in which olive oil had formerly been made, into a theatre: the blankets and great-coats of the soldiers made capital side-scenes; and had not too much wine and grog found their way behind them, no doubt the piece would have gone off with great éclat. But, as the truth must be told, they all forgot their parts; and it was a toss-up whether our attempt at horse-racing or play-acting was the most perfectly ludicrous."

Moyle Sherer also heard of the French theatrical diversions, and in a similar way. "About the middle of February, as I was one day walking by the river side with three or four companions, we observed an unusual crowd

[18] Kincaid, 1981: 18.
[19] English towns with race-courses for horse-racing.

on the opposite bank, and several French officers. They saluted us, with a "Bon jour, Messieurs;" and we soon fell into conversation. They were exceedingly courteous. They spoke in the highest terms of Romana[20], who had lately died, calling him "Le seul général Espagnol digne de son grade[21]." They asked after Lord Wellington; saying he had done wonders with the Portuguese, and praising him greatly for his conduct of the campaign. They next enquired, if our king was not dead[22]; and on our replying that he was not, one of them spoke, but inaudibly; another, in a louder voice, repeated "Le général dit, que tout le monde aime votre Roi George, qu'il a été bon père de famille, et bon père de son peuple[23]." We were thus, at once, let into the rank of one of their party, and not a little delighted at the manner in which they had spoken of our excellent and unfortunate sovereign. A great deal of good humour prevailed; we quizzed each other freely. They asked us how we liked bacallâo and azete, instead of English roast beef? and we, what they did at Santarem without the restaurateurs, cafés, and salles de spectacle of their dear Paris? They replied, laughing, that they had a theatre; and asked us to come over, and witness the performance of that evening, which would be, "L'Entrée des François dans Lisbon[24]." A friend of mine most readily replied, that he recommended to them "La repétition d'une nouvelle pièce, 'La Fuite des François[25].'" They burst into a long, loud, and general laugh:– the joke was too good, too home. Their general, however, did not think it wise to remain longer; but he pulled off his hat, and wishing us good day with perfect good humour, went up the hill, and the group immediately dispersed.[26]"

The rank and file of the 95th frequently met their French counterparts while bathing in the Asseca. Here the two sides challenged each other to swimming competitions, which the British usually won due to the emaciated condition of their opponents. Such was the pity generated in the Rifles, some even shared their rations of ships-biscuits. Rifleman Ned Costello voiced a widely held sympathy for the plight of their opposite numbers, noting: "All national hostility was buried in our anxiety to assist and relieve them. Tobacco was in great request. We used to carry some of ours to them, while they in return would bring us brandy[27]."

During this period of vigilant calm Jonathan obtained leave of absence for five days, "to go to Lisbon with a brother-officer, merely for the sake of a frolic. We lost no time on the road, and found ourselves at Latour's hotel[28] in as short a time as our horses could conveniently carry us thither. It is not less strange than true, that on our return from the opera, when I got into a regular-built bed, I could no more sleep than I could have taken wing and flown across the Tagus. Ever since the month of February 1810 (exactly one year), we had been constantly so near the enemy at the advanced posts, sleeping in our clothes, in bivouac, or in some hovel of a picket-house, rolled up in our cloaks on the ground, that I felt quite like a fish out of water, and was not reconciled to a bed. We spent our five days' leave of absence in Lisbon in the manner which may be supposed, after having been

[20] General Pedro Caro y Sureda, Marquis of La Romana (1761-1811). The Spanish General who commanded the Spanish army fighting alongside Wellington in 1810.
[21] 'The only Spanish General worthy of his rank'. Wellington disagreed, saying of Romana, "Oh, he was the worst of all – a good man –a very good excellent man, but no general... I never in my whole life saw a man who had acted at all with troops under-stand so little about them." (Stanhope, 1888: 10, 23).
[22] George III had just succumbed to his mental illness.
[23] 'The General says the whole world loves your King George, who has been a good father to his family and a good father to his people.'
[24] 'The French entry into Lisbon.'
[25] 'The rehearsal of a new play, Flight of the French.'
[26] Sherer, 1996: 136-138.
[27] Hathaway, 1997: 85.
[28] George Simmons also mentions staying at Latour's Hotel in December 1810 (when he was ill). It was obviously a hotel favoured by the officers.

so long estranged from civilised life. In truth we made the most of our time, and lost no opportunity of amusing ourselves in the ways best suited to our taste. When we returned to our old post at the causeway, we found everything *in statu quo*."

On his return Jonathan succumbed yet again to 'a sharp attack of fever and ague, which ... reduced me to a skeleton' and was sent to the rear to recuperate, leaving Harry Smith in command of his company. He does not appear to have rejoined his men until at least April[29], but on the 5th of March the strain on the French of maintaining their position became too great and they broke from Santarém heading north. The following day the allied army gave chase. Craufurd, however, was not with them. He had taken leave of absence and had returned to England in early February. For two months from the 9th of March[30] his place at the head of the Light Division was taken by Major-General Sir William Erskine[31], a cavalry officer who did not endear himself to the infantrymen of the Division. Quickly acquiring a reputation for rashness he was referred to by the men as 'Ass-skin'[32]. He was no more trusted among the officers. Wellington even suspected his sanity[33].

To weep for the horrors of war

As the 95th passed through the evacuated Santarém Kincaid said it "looked like a city of the plague, represented by empty dogs and empty houses". Others in the army were more explicit. One officer declared, "Such a scene of horror, misery, and desolation, scarce ever saluted the eye of man. Smoking ruins, the accumulated filth of months, horses and human bodies putrefied to suffocation, nearly caused to many a vomiting. The houses had scarcely a vestige of wood – doors, windows, ceilings, roofs, burnt; and where the sick had expired, there left to decay! The number thus left was great. Every church demolished, the tombs opened for searching after hidden plate, every altar-piece universally destroyed, and the effluvia so offensive so to defy describing[34]."

As the French retreated they repaid the allies' autumn policy of *scorched earth* in kind and with a vengeance, plundering and burning every town or village through which they passed.

Kincaid: "We halted for the night near Pyrnes[35]. This little town, and the few wretched inhabitants who had been induced to remain in it under the faithless promises of the French generals, showed fearful signs of a late visit from a barbarous and merciless foe. Young women were lying in their houses brutally violated,— the streets were strewed with broken furniture, intermixed with the putrid carcasses of murdered peasants, mules, and donkeys, and every description of filth, that filled the air with pestilential nausea. The few starved male inhabitants who were stalking amid the wreck of their friends and property, looked like so many skeletons who had been permitted to leave their graves for the purpose of taking vengeance on their oppressors, and the mangled body of every Frenchman who was unfortunate or imprudent

[29] This is clear from Harry Smith's account (Smith, 1999: 43-45). By the time he returned Smith had been seconded as Brigade-Major to the 2nd Light Brigade (a post he held from late March 1811 until March 1814) and Lieutenant Jonathan Layton had taken temporary command of the company.

[30] Verner, 1919: 221.

[31] Major-General Sir William Erskine *Bt* (1769-1813). He was sustained in the army less by his abilities than by political influence in England.

[32] Verner, 1919: 258.

[33] Oman, 1986: 151 [Correctly as it transpired. In 1812 Erskine was declared insane and cashiered from the army. He committed suicide the following year].

[34] Journal of an unidentified army officer quoted by Tucker (1846: 172-173). 'Plate' - silver-plated ware.

[35] Presumably Pernes.

enough to stray from his column, showed how religiously they performed their mission.[36]"

The unidentified officer who had described Santarém wrote, "to see the country, is to weep for the horrors of war. Such horrid excess I never saw before. Every town, village, or cottage destroyed. The growing nursery and the wild grove, each havocked for destruction's sake. The pot that refined the oil, broken; the wine-press burnt, for burning's sake; the grape vines destroyed as noxious weeds; the furniture unburnt thrown from the windows, and with carriages, &c. made a bonfire of; the large libraries strewed over the land in remnants of paper; the noble convent in ashes, and the poor, unhappy, aged inhabitants, unable to flee, hung around as ornamenting the walls, ten or twelve in a place! To bear the semblance of a female was to be tortured; to be an infant, to be a sacrifice.[37]"

On the heels of this carnage was the Light Division, harrying the French rearguard. The 11th of March saw Jonathan's battalion involved in heavy skirmishing on the approach to Pombal and in a hard-fought action driving a strong French contingent from Pombal Castle. Day after day the 95th engaged the retreating French. Portuguese militia and irregular troops had taken possession of Coimbra on Masséna's route, forcing a diversion east, and on the 14th Ney, commanding the rearguard, chose a defensive position in some difficult terrain around the village of Casal Novo and prepared to stall the pursuers.

"Lord Wellington" reports Jonathan, relying on accounts given to him later by fellow officers, "attacked Marshal Ney in front with the Light Division[38], whilst with other divisions he turned his flanks; and, after a long and extremely hard day's work, throughout the whole of which the Light Division was sharply engaged in driving the enemy from one stronghold to another, Marshal Ney fell back to Miranda de Corvo, which town, like Pombal, Condeixa, and others, was in flames.

It would be a useless repetition to detail the pitiable state of every town and village which lay in Masséna's line of retreat. Flames, ruin, murder, and devastation, marked their track. If any man is to be found bold enough to defend their conduct in this retreat, he is a fit subject to have been incorporated with that army, which disgraced the name of Europeans."

Wellington thought the retreat was "marked by a barbarity seldom equalled and never surpassed.[39]" He was so appreciative of the actions of the Light Division at this period he began his General Army Orders of the 16th of March:

"No. I. The Commander of the Forces returns his thanks to the General and Staff Officers and Troops for their excellent conduct in the operations in the last ten days against the enemy. He requests the Commanding officers of the 43rd, 52nd and 95th Regiments to name a Sergeant in each Regiment to be recommended for a promotion to an Ensigncy, as a testimony of the particular approbation of the Commander of the Forces of these three Regiments.[40]"

[36] Kincaid, 1981: 20.
[37] Tucker, 1846: 173.
[38] It was Wellington's intention to use the Light Division only to threaten the French front line while other divisions turned their flanks, but, in thick fog, Erskine pushed the 95th right up to 11 French battalions and an artillery battery. As the fog lifted and the danger became apparent, Erskine sent the 52nd forward in support, then Wellington ordered in part of the 43rd. Soon the whole Division was engaged (Verner, 1919: 231).
[39] Tucker, 1846: 174.
[40] Wellington's Supplementary Despatches, 7: 82 (Quoted in Verner, 1919: 242).

Two more weeks of skirmishing and more intense encounters for the Light Division saw the French army reach the River Côa, near the Spanish border, back where it had been eight months before. Jonathan notes, somewhat bitterly, that these engagements – the staple fare of the advance guard – were designated *affairs* and thereby received neither the public reporting nor recognition of a *battle*, notwithstanding the fact that "the numerous engagements of this description, which rarely find their way into the Gazette, except under the head of affairs of posts, are not so very trifling in their nature as some persons may be inclined to fancy".

Just such an *affair* was the heavy action at Sabugal on the 3rd of April – another rainy foggy day. Again Erskine handled the Division badly, but fortunately those under him did not and Verner notes, "Luckily the mist prevented him from seeing how his orders were ignored.[41]" This fighting saw the French pushed back from the Côa and 48 hours later they were over the border into Spain and in a new – or correctly, their old – position east of the River Águeda, leaving only a garrison occupying the important town of Almeida, a foot left in Portugal's door. "Thus" says Jonathan, "did Massena's invasion of Portugal terminate; and in this manner was his threat fulfilled of 'driving the English into the sea.' " In Lisbon there was great rejoicing and the city was illuminated for several nights.

EVICTION OF THE FRENCH FROM PORTUGAL
Louis Simond
London, 28th April 1811

"The English have had, for some weeks past, an overflowing of good news from their army in the Peninsula. The house of the Portuguese ambassador, has been magnificently illuminated during several nights. These successes are very important in more respects than one,—they establish the reputation of the army, heretofore doubtful, and put an invasion of these islands out of the question. The Spanish cause is highly popular in this country,—it is a cause to which every generous feeling is associated,—and it has excited a great degree of enthusiasm."

Battle of Fuentes de Oñoro

Jonathan seems to have rejoined his company by late April. The Light Division now occupied the same outpost villages between the Côa and the Águeda they had patrolled the previous summer. The 95th spent the next few weeks patrolling, skirmishing with French pickets, and sending men to Almeida to shoot the cattle turned out to graze under the fortress walls by the beleaguered garrison. This last activity seemed to annoy the owners, who invariably replied with cannon.

At the beginning of May Masséna determined to lift the blockade of the fortress, and on the 2nd the French crossed the Águeda in force, obliging the

[41] Verner, 1919: 258.

Light Division to fall back across the Dos Casas at Fuentes de Oñoro and take up a position with other units on the heights behind the village. Five regular divisions were already in place. The cavalry was mainly to the right of the allied position, where the ground was favourable to their operation, and the Light Division was placed near the centre as a 'flying corps', to be sent wherever the need was greatest.

After a brisk assault by the French on the evening of the 3rd of May, which was repulsed, the 4th was quiet while Masséna reconnoitred in preparation for his main attack the following day. As if anticipating the action, Craufurd returned from England and resumed his command. In the Division, most attitudes towards him had now warmed (although not Jonathan's), partly because his battlefield skills had been sorely missed during the engagements of the previous few weeks, and partly because the rank and file had realised his Orders for Marches actually made their lives easier.

Leach: "*May 5th.*— The moment daylight appeared Massena sent a powerful body of cavalry, supported by heavy masses of infantry, with artillery, under the command of General Junot, to attack our extreme right. The Light Division was instantly ordered to occupy a wood in front of and to the right of the 1st Division. The vast superiority in numbers of the French cavalry obliged the 7th Division to fall back from near Navis d'Avair[42]".

In the 7th Division, the right wing had recoiled before the first massive wave of French cavalry. Outnumbered by more than twenty to one, the British cavalry units on their ill-fed horses were powerless and although the initial French charge was halted by infantry fire, French numbers were too great for serious resistance. A withdrawal was ordered to new positions closer to the allied centre and the Light Division was sent forward to cover the 7th's crossing of the Turon River. In the 7th Division Private Bill Wheeler of the 51st Light Infantry[43] recalled this withdrawal. He had almost been recruited into the 95th, but had chosen to follow most of his friends into the 51st instead. The difference in the styles of the two regiments was marked. In contrast to the 95th's irregular 'fire and retire', the withdrawal of the 51st was conducted – terrain permitting – at a parade-ground march.

Wheeler: 'The enemy had formed again and was ready for another attack, our force was not sufficient to repel such a mass, so the order was given to retire independently by regiments. We retired through the broken ground in our rear, crossed the wall, and was pretty safe from their cavalry, but they had brought up their guns to the brow and was serving out the shot with a liberal hand. We continued retiring and soon came to a narrow rapid streem, this we waded up to our armpits and from the steepness of the opposite bank we found much difficulty in getting out. This caused some delay so the Regiment waited until all had crossed, then formed line and continued our retreat in quick time; it was now the division was suffering much from the enemy's fire...

[42] Nave de Haver. At this time the 7th Division was the weakest of all the allied divisions in manpower and experience (Verner, 1919: 269).

[43] 51st (2nd Yorkshire West Riding) Light Infantry.

153

Thanks to Colonel Mainwaring we came off safe, altho the shot was flying pretty thick, yet his superior skill baffled all the efforts of the enemy, he took advantage of the ground and led us out of a scrape without loss. I shall never forget him, he dismounted off his horse, faced us and frequently called the time 'right, left' as he was accostomed to when drilling the regiment. His eccentricity did not leave him, he would now and then call out "That fellow is out of step, keep step and they cannot hurt us." Another time he would observe such a one, calling him by name, "——— cannot march, mark him for drill Serjeant Major." "I tell you again they cannot hurt us if you are steady, if you get out of time, you will be knocked down." He was leading his horse and a shot passed under the horses belley which made him rear up. "You are a coward" he said "I will stop your corn three days." [44]

As the French turned the allies' right flank [45], Jonathan Leach and the Light Division now found themselves dangerously isolated.

"The 7th Division was now taking up a new alignment, with its right thrown back towards the heights near Villa Formosa, and communicating by its left with the 1st Division. Whilst this was in progress, the French attacked, with many battalions of infantry, the wood into which the Light Division had been ordered, and a sharp fire was kept up for some time on both sides. The British right being turned at Navis d'Avair, the mass of French cavalry, with artillery, continued to advance along the plain, threatening to cut off the Light Division from the position on the heights. We were, therefore, directed to retire from the wood, to form squares of battalions, and to fall back over the plain on the 1st Division. The steadiness and regularity with which the troops performed this movement, the whole time exposed to a cannonade, and followed across a plain by a numerous cavalry, ready to pounce on the squares if the least disorder should be detected, has been acknowledged by hundreds of unprejudiced persons (unconnected with the Light Division), who witnessed it from the heights, to have been a masterpiece of military evolutions. We sustained a very trifling loss from the cannonade, and reached our station in the position near the 1st Division [46].

Massena now halted Junot's corps pretty well out of range of our artillery; and contented himself by keeping up a heavy cannonade, and sending out swarms of light troops to amuse us".

In Fuentes de Oñoro itself the fighting was intense. Again and again the French overran and tried to hold the village, only to be ejected at the point of the bayonet by the 1st and 3rd Divisions with great loss. As evening fell the French held part of the village, the allies the rest, and with the fighting dying down part of the Light Division, including Jonathan and his company, relieved the defenders and provided a garrison and pickets for the night.

"We had been but a short time at Fuentes d'Onoro, when a flag of truce came in, requesting permission to send into the village unarmed parties to

[44] Liddell Hart, 1994: 55-56.
[45] In the French army one foreign infantry unit, the Hanoverian Legion, were unusual in wearing scarlet jackets. At Buçaco the Legion had several men shot by their own side when the French mistook them for the British. To avoid this at Fuentes de Oñoro the Legion had asked to fight in their greatcoats but this was refused. As a result they were again attacked by their own side and lost about 100 men. To prevent greater bloodshed their commander led them back through the French lines where the appearance of these 'redcoats' threw the French rear into confusion (Haythornthwaite, 1979: 126).
[46] The Light Division's 5 squares had retreated more than 3 km while harried by artillery and 5 brigades of French cavalry. They lost only one man killed and 34 wounded (Oman, 1986: 100, 145-146).

bring away their wounded, who filled the streets and houses. During this truce, several French officers came down to the little bridge over the Duas Casas, at the foot of the village, on which happened to be posted a file of men of my own company, whilst two French grenadiers were on sentry at the other end of it. On the centre of the bridge three French officers met and conversed a considerable time with the officers of my company, and were politeness itself. After offering us a pinch of snuff, by way of prelude, the events which had taken place during the day were discussed. They paid many compliments to the gallant conduct of our army, and declared that to-morrow would be a great and decisive day, and full of glory for one of the two armies.

The captain of the 9th Light Infantry was a remarkably smart, talkative, Frenchman-like, little fellow. He had two musket-shots through his cap, one of which had grazed his head, and the blood was trickling down his face at the moment. He treated it very lightly, saying it was a mere nothing—the fortune of war!

Our attention was just then called, by our little friend of the 9th Light Infantry, to a flashy young man, dressed in a gay hussar uniform, who came galloping along near the bridge: "Do you see that boy?" said he: "he is about twenty years of age only; has just arrived from France to commence his career in Spain, and commands one of our hussar regiments. But," added our friend (with a shrug of his shoulders), "he is the nephew of the war minister, which accounts for it."

It was now nearly dark, and the greater part of their wounded were carried into their own lines; so, having made profound bows to our new acquaintance on the bridge, we commenced preparations for the defence of the village from a night attack."

There was no night attack, nor was there an attack the following day. In fact, for two days the armies stood where they had ended the battle; sentries so close they could have held a normal conversation. Meanwhile Masséna instructed the garrison at Almeida to mine the defences and prepare to make a dash for the French lines. Through British ineptitude the plan worked; the mines were exploded and the garrison of 1400 escaped with a loss of only 360 killed and captured, much to Wellington's annoyance. The bridge over the river at Barba del Puerco had been unguarded because Wellington's orders that it should be occupied by a battalion of the 4th Regiment[47] were given to Erskine, who put them in his pocket and forgot about them. The commanding officer of the 4th Regiment, Colonel Bevan, was so distressed by the censure he received from Wellington for letting the French escape, he shot himself[48].

At Fuentes de Oñoro the French began a general withdrawal on the night of the 7th and crossed back over the Águeda, restoring the status quo. Masséna – having been ejected from Portugal – left for France to be replaced in Spain by Marshal Marmont[49], sixteen years his junior.

[47] 4th (The King's Own) Regiment of Foot
[48] Verner, 1986: 173-174. Stanhope, 1888: 89.
[49] Maréchal Auguste Frederic Louis Viesse de Marmont, Duc de Raguse (1774-1852).

While the bulk of the allied army had been engaging the French on the northern route between Spain and Portugal, Wellington had dispatched Marshal Beresford[50] and an allied force to besiege the French in the fortified town of Badajoz[51] to the south (The Spanish town of Badajoz and its Portuguese counterpart Elvas dominated the southern route between the two countries, just as the Spanish Ciudad Rodrigo and the Portuguese Almeida controlled the northern). On the 16th of May Marshal Soult, marching to relieve Badajoz with just over 24,000 men, engaged Beresford's force of 35,000[52] at Albuera. In one of the bloodiest contests of the Peninsula War, which saw 6000 British, Portuguese and Spanish casualties, and 8000 French, Soult's relief of the town was blocked. One of the British officers killed leading his men into action was Captain Frederick Montagu of the 23rd Regiment (Royal Welch Fusiliers), the favourite son of naturalist George Montagu of Kingsbridge.

After Albuera Marmont started to send forces south to reinforce Soult, for a renewed attempt to lift the siege at Badajoz. Wellington countered by sending allied divisions to reinforce Beresford and in early June the Light Division received its orders to march, with inconvenient timing for Jonathan.

'On the 4th, whilst we were celebrating the birth-day of George the Third, in the village of Espeja, with wine, cigars, and a dance with the Spanish fair ones, an order reached us to march before break of day. I will be sworn that our fair partners would have been fully as well pleased, as we should also, if the order had arrived some twelve hours later, for it broke up a merry party, and obliged us to retire to our hovels, to order our baggage-mules to be saddled, and to march without a wink of sleep; no, not even enough to give us a chance of dreaming of our black-eyed signoras...

On the 7th, the Light Division bivouacked near Sabugal; and as the day was favourable for fishing, I ardently longed for the necessary apparatus to wage war on the trout, which are remarkably fine in this part of the Coa; but I had neither rod, lines, nor flies.'

Marching through the heat of the Spanish summer, at night when possible, on the 23rd of June the Division joined part of the allied army on the bank of the River Caia, about 20 km north-west of Badajoz. Marmont and Soult had united their forces east of the town and Wellington, unable to resist their combined army of 80,000 troops, had been forced temporarily to lift the siege, although to the north he was now planning to besiege the garrison in Ciudad Rodrigo. The Caia, a tributary of the dreaded Guadiana, was not a healthy place to be.

Leach: "If our ranks were not thinned by the sword at this moment, they were most terribly so by fevers, agues, and dysenteries, so prevalent and destructive in Alemtejo, particularly in the hot months. In no part of the world have I experienced a more constant, sickening, deadly heat, than in the encampment on the Caya. I never enjoyed better health, nor ever exposed myself more to the sun, with gun and greyhound; and I bathed twice a day in

[50] Major-General Sir William Carr Beresford (1764-1854). Served in the Mediterranean, India and South Africa. In 1806 commanded the capture of Buenos Aires but had to surrender. Was appointed Governor of Madeira and learnt Portuguese. In the Peninsula served in the Coruña campaign, then charged with training a Portuguese army, in which he was appointed Marshal. After the war he was made a Viscount. He had lost an eye in 1786 in a shooting accident in Nova Scotia.
[51] Pronounced 'baþahoth'.
[52] 10,400 British; 10,200 Portuguese; and a Spanish army of 14,600 which had arrived the evening before.

the stagnant waters of the Caya, which abounded with water-snakes, leeches, and all manner of devils."

After a month in this unhealthy spot – the French having resupplied Badajoz and shown no interest in giving battle – the Light Division marched north again. On this march Craufurd issued what Jonathan described as, "an immense string of the most frivolous orders evidently compiled for no other reason than that of annoying the officers of his Division[53]."

By mid-August his Division was back on the Águeda, this time around Martiago, mid-way between Ciudad Rodrigo and the high peaks of the Sierra de Gata to the south. Here they were reinforced by the arrival of: three companies of the 3/95th from southern Spain where they had been serving in an allied force around Cadiz; a company of the 3rd battalion which had been commandeered by Sir Brent Spencer[54] the previous year when on its way to join the Light Division; and Jonathan's old company of the 2/95th[55], under Captain John Hart, newly arrived from England[56].

After several weeks during which Wellington[57] kept a watchful eye on the now blockaded Ciudad Rodrigo, Jonathan was ordered to patrol the narrow passes coming over the high peaks to the south, partly in case the French probed those routes and partly to obtain information about enemy movements on the other side of the mountains.

"On the 9th September I was detached with my own company, and one of Portuguese Caçadores, across the Sierra de Gata to Las Herrias and Aldea Juella[58], two villages of the worst possible description, buried in the heart of mountains, as awfully grand and terrific as I ever beheld in Spain, Switzerland, or elsewhere. The inhabitants of those wretched hovels, which I have dignified with the name of villages, were all dressed in the skins of goats, sheep, and wolves, looking more like demons than any thing human. Although no Patagonian in height, I was obliged to stoop double, in order to go in and out of the shed, which, as commandant, I took care should not be the worst in the colony. Some dried fern in a dark corner, which looked as if the devil should have been its inmate, where myriads of fleas had established themselves as "lords and masters," was my bed, and my pillow a knapsack."

[53] Verner, 1919: 290.
[54] General Sir Brent Spencer (1760-1828).
[55] Two companies of the 2nd battalion 95th were already in the Light Division, having been sent to the Peninsula after Walcheren.
[56] Rifleman Benjamin Harris was not with the company, having been an invalid since Walcheren.
[57] Wellington had been promoted to the local rank of full General in Spain and Portugal on the 31st of July.
[58] Erias and Aldehuela.

The Flea

William Elford Leach

"Notwithstanding the inconveniences attending this little insect, there is something pleasing in the appearance of the flea. Its motions are elegant, and all its postures indicate agility. The shell with which it is enveloped is in a state of perpetual cleanliness, while the muscular power which it is capable of exerting is so extraordinary, as to excite our wonder, at so much strength confined and concentrated within so small a space; this species being able to spring, on the most moderate computation, to the distance of at least 200 times its own length. It is remarkable that Socrates was ridiculed for his pretended experiments on this subject by Aristophanes."

Edinburgh Encyclopædia, **9**(1): 126 [Figure from Kirby & Spence (1818) Volume 2]

After a fortnight the patrols were recalled (much to their relief). Marmont had crossed the mountains further east and his army was advancing to raise the blockade by forcing through a supply of provisions. The allies were in no position to resist Marmont's army of 50,000 and Wellington pulled his own force west without offering battle. However, with Ciudad Rodrigo resupplied, the French continued their advance and there was a serious clash on the 24th of September involving allied cavalry and parts of the 1st, 3rd and 4th Divisions. An allied force of 15,000 had a narrow escape and was left in an exposed position at Fuenteguinaldo, south-west of Rodrigo[59]. Wellington assumed command of this force and sent word to his 1st and 7th Divisions, then 16 km away, to close in. He also sent orders to the Light Division, in an advanced position on the River Vadillo (a tributary of the Águeda rising in the sierras to the south), to join him.

In the Light Division, more than one person was beginning to feel uneasy about their somewhat isolated state.

Simmons: "About twelve o'clock at noon on the 25th the enemy, in terrible force, attacked General Picton's Division at El Bodon, which place being immediately to our left rear, and also over the Agueda, we began to think ourselves placed most curiously, though every one felt the greatest security in Lord Wellington's out-manœuvring *Johnny*[60], and bringing off the Division in safety[61]"

However, it was Craufurd, not Wellington, who had to do the manoeuvring and despite the urgency of the situation and Marmont's obvious belligerence Craufurd was surprisingly resistant to the idea of motion. Kincaid notes that while Wellington drew in his forces:

'Our division, in the meantime, remained on the banks of the Vadillo, and had nearly been cut off, through the obstinacy of General Craufurd, who did not choose to obey an order he received to retire the day before... The situation was more than ticklish with an enemy on three sides and an almost impassable mountain on the fourth... but we, nevertheless, succeeded in joining the army, by a circuitous route, on the afternoon of the 26th[62]'.

Craufurd had marched his men only five or six kilometres on the evening of the 25th before halting. They marched again the following morning but did not reach Fuenteguinaldo until the afternoon, to be met by Wellington's sarcastic, "I am glad to see you safe, Craufurd".

"Oh!" exclaimed an insensitive Craufurd, "I was in no danger I assure you." "But I was from your conduct" snapped Wellington. Craufurd allegedly muttered, "He is damned crusty today.[63]"

Fortunately for the ill-prepared allies, despite having deployed 40,000 troops in battle-order in front of the town, Marmont chose not to attack that day and during the night the allies slipped westward across the Portuguese border. There followed a week of sporadic skirmishing along the junction of the armies, but having achieved his objective, and having had to deplete his army of occupation in the east to ensure success, Marmont pulled his forces

[59] See earlier map of *The Outposts*, p. 62.
[60] *Johnny*: a slang term in the army for any enemy. Also sometimes given (for amusement or deliberate affectation) as *Jonathan*. For the French Kincaid also uses the term 'Johnny Petit', an application of pidgin French meaning 'Little Johnny'. Kincaid may have used this to distinguish the French from himself; his name was Johnny and he was more than 6 feet (1.83m) tall.
[61] Letter: George Simmons to his brother (presumably Maud in the 34th Regt), 1st October 1811 (Verner, 1986: 199).
[62] Kincaid, 1981: 46, 269.
[63] Verner, 1919: 295.

back and restored them to their positions around Salamanca and Plasencia. The allies meanwhile returned to the villages they had occupied before the French advance. Here, as autumn advanced and winter weather loomed, a campaign of serious engagements seemed unlikely. With their duties reduced to surveillance of the garrison in Ciudad Rodrigo, Jonathan and the other officers were able to relax and indulge their favourite pastimes.

Boleros, Fandangos and Snowballs

'On the 10th of October a large coursing party went out on the plains near Guinaldo, to set at rest a point long at issue amongst our sporting characters, as to the comparative merits of English and Spanish greyhounds. A capital hare was found, and she went away for a mile or two[64] over as fine a country for coursing as is anywhere to be found, before two English greyhounds, which had lately been sent out to the 43d regiment, and a Spanish greyhound, considered excellent. The hare was killed by the English dogs, which were so exhausted by the heat of the day and the severity of the course, that one of them died immediately, and the other was saved with great difficulty by bleeding. The Spanish dog came up very contentedly a long while after the hare and greyhound were dead. The heat had not affected him, because he was accustomed to the climate; and, moreover, he took particular care not to distress himself by an over-display of zeal...

When the weather permitted, we amused ourselves as usual with coursing and shooting, and at night either collected the village fair ones, and, aided by some musicians of the band, danced the night half through, or sat round a brass pan of charcoal, whiffing away care with our cigars, and speculating on what the next campaign might produce. When the winter rains confined us to our wretched hovels, and prevented us from following our usual avocations in the field, it must be allowed that we were sometimes brought to a nonplus, and sadly troubled to kill time during the day.

It should be remembered that Spanish villages do not afford the same resources as are to be found in every insignificant place in England. Books were quite out of the question. Some few individuals of a corps might possibly possess a small pocket volume or two; but when it is considered that the first and most necessary point, and that which occupied our chief attention,

[64] 1.5 to 3 km.

Greyhounds

was to procure, by some means or other, forage for our horses and mules, that the baggage which contained our few comforts and necessaries might be carried with us from place to place, it will readily be comprehended that a portable library was deemed less essential for our existence than a portmanteau containing a few changes of linen, boots, &c. &c., to say nothing of tea, sugar, chocolate, rice, bread, meat, a pig's-skin of wine, a keg of spirits, cigars, spare horse-shoes and nails, &c. &c.,—that is to say, when any of these good things could be procured for love or money, which very frequently was not the case.

Our half-starved animals had more than enough to do in scrambling along with such matters on their backs[65], without the additional weight of libraries, even had it been possible to have procured books. A good telescope and correct maps of the country were indispensable; next to which may be mentioned cigars, without which there was no getting on.

To be able to fully appreciate their utility and comfort, it is necessary that a man should sleep in a camp or bivouac in a dreary night of rain or snow,—that he should know what a night march is, and be initiated into every sort and kind of vicissitude which campaigning brings in its train. If a man in England, after having eaten an alderman's dinner[66], and lounged on a sofa, with a Turkey carpet under his feet, a blazing fire before him, and a cigar in his mouth, fancies that he really knows the comfort of tobacco in that shape, he is very much mistaken; as is in like manner the equestrian or pedestrian dandy, with unshorn lip, who whiffs his cigar all over London, and through the Park, on a fine, bright, butterfly morning. He must rise, wet to the skin and numbed with cold, from the lee side of a tree or hedge, where he has been shivering all night under a flood of rain,—then let him light his cigar, and the warmth and comfort which it imparts is incredible. Or, let him march, night after night, until he is so overpowered with sleepiness as to tumble off his horse during his momentary doze, (sleeping as he rides along, and falling in amongst the column of soldiers, who are in a similar plight); or if he is marching on foot, rolling about in the ranks in a state between sleeping and waking,—let him then apply his cigar, and he is awake again...

On the 8th of November a large party of us set out to shoot wild deer in the mountains near Serradilia[67]. We soon roused three fine ones; but our party were very noisy, and, as is invariably the case when all are talkers and no hearers, a regular plan was not adopted, as should have been the case, to out-manœuvre the game, by which means they were shot at too soon, and in too great a hurry; and one of the marksmen was much nearer killing a brother-officer than either of the deer...

On the 11th of December, having heard of a flight of woodcocks, I went, with two of my brother-officers, to a solitary farm-house in the mountains beyond the Vadillo, where we slept. We took with us our servants, a mule laden with provisions, portmanteaus, &c. &c., and the Irish piper belonging to the band. In the evening we danced boleros, fandangos, and

[65] See page 486 below for a photograph of Jonathan Leach's campaign chest, used for transporting his personal possessions. We do not know whether he had this chest in the Peninsula or acquired it later in his army career.
[66] i.e. a large sumptuous meal (similar to 'a Lord Mayor's banquet').
[67] Serradilla del Arroyo or the neighbouring Serradilla del Llano.

Irish jigs, with the farmers' daughters, and early the next morning attacked the woodcocks, which I never remember to have seen more numerous. We had capital sport, and returned late at night to our quarters at Atalaia[68]. One of our party, who was a better performer at the dance than with a gun, fired thirty shots, at least, without killing a single bird; and towards evening, by way of putting a finishing stroke to the day's work, he let fly at an enormous wild cat, which was perched on a tree above his head, not twenty yards distant, and the animal escaped unhurt. This was a standing joke against him ever after.'

1812

'New-year's day of 1812 brought with it snow and frost in abundance, which induced a party of us to obtain a few day' leave of absence, and, with gun in hand, to make an excursion, on the 3d of January, to Robadillia[69], a large village in one of the deepest and most secluded valleys of the Sierra de Gata, where a Spanish family resided with whom we had become acquainted on the other side of the mountains in the previous autumn[70]. We sent on two servants with mules, on which we carried a change of clothes, tea, sugar, cigars, meat, &c. &c.; for, be it known, that in Spain, if you wish to fare moderately well whilst travelling, nothing of this kind should be left to chance.'

Nothing was left to chance indeed, as John Kincaid, one of this merry band, explains: "Half a dozen of us immediately resolved ourselves into a committee of ways and means. We had six months' pay due to us; so that the fandango might have been danced in either of our pockets without the smallest risk; but we had this consolation for our poverty, that there was nothing to be bought, even if we had the means. Our only resource, therefore, was to lighten the cares of such of our brother-officers as were fortunate enough to have anything to lose; and, at this moment of doubt and difficulty, a small flock of turkeys, belonging to our major, presented themselves, most imprudently, grazing opposite the windows of our council-chamber, two of which were instantly committed to the bottom of a sack, as a foundation to go upon. One of our spies, soon after, apprehended a sheep, the property of another officer, which was committed to the same place; and, getting the commissary to advance us a few extra loaves of bread, some ration beef, and a pig-skin full of wine, we placed a servant on a mule, with the whole concern tackled to him, and proceeded on our journey.[71]"

Jonathan takes up the story: "The snow was so deep on the mountains, that we passed them with infinite difficulty; and, but for the honour of the thing, might as well have left our guns behind us, as the only living animal we saw was a wild boar, going at the rate of thirty miles an hour[72], many gunshots distant.

The old don, his wife and daughters, received us kindly and procured billets for us in the village. They beat up for volunteers, and having collected the village belles, and a fiddler or two, we danced with great glee; after

[68] La Atalaya.
[69] Robledillo de Gata.
[70] Kincaid (1981: 48) says this man was the Chief Magistrate of Ciudad Rodrigo, who had taken shelter at Robledillo with his daughter and two other young women.
[71] "So far so good," adds Verner, "the difficulty was to account for the disappearance of the stock on their return. This was however triumphantly overcome, for one of the party getting killed in action soon afterwards, the remainder, devoid of all shame, put the whole blame on his shoulders! It would be difficult to imagine greater cynicism." (Verner, 1919: 299).
[72] Approximately 50 k.p.h.

which, we gave the fair ones a supper at our billets. This was followed by
duets, trios, catches, and glees, and melodies of all sorts and kinds, both
Spanish, Irish, Scotch, and English. Some young padres, with the crowns of
their heads shaved, were amongst the party invited to accompany the ladies
to our fête; and these lads were evidently much annoyed at the preference
which the signoras evinced towards the heretical Englishmen; nor did they
attempt to disguise their feelings. I am free to confess that I never had a
great predilection for any of that idle, vagabond class; and in this I was no
means singular, for I found my comrades quite ready to join in any frolic or
fun which might be proposed as a just punishment for their uncourteous
conduct.

When the amusements of the evening were over, and we had escorted
our partners to their homes, we still found some of those *clericos* hanging
about the streets with lanterns in their hands. We suddenly opened a heavy
fire of snow-balls on them, of the hardest and most terrific kind, which
smashed their lanterns to atoms, and battered them from head to foot, to a
degree beyond a joke. We heard their curses and execrations on Englishmen
and heretics gradually die away as they ran from us and hid themselves in
their respective habitations."

Kincaid admits, "We were, afterwards, afraid that we had carried the
joke rather too far, and entertained some doubts as to the propriety of holding
our quarters for another day; but they set our minds at rest on that point, by
paying us an early visit in the morning, and seemed to enjoy the joke in a
manner that we could not have expected from the gravity of their looks.[73]"

The revellers spent two more days in the same light manner, inventing
their entertainments as they went along. Again Kincaid confessing, "We
were malicious enough, by way of amusement, to introduce a variety of
absurd pastimes, under the pretence of their being English, and which, by
virtue thereof, were implicitly adopted.[74]"

On the plain below, however, more serious matters were unfolding.
Wellington had decided to close in on the fortress of Ciudad Rodrigo and
instigate a serious siege[75]. When the party returned from the mountains they
found their Division had moved and it was late into the night before they
rejoined the battalion at El Bodón.

[73] Kincaid, 1981: 49.
[74] Kincaid, 1981: 49.
[75] Prompted by the transfer of 15,000 French troops to support actions on the Mediterranean coast (Oman, 1986: 56-57).

— 10 —

Storms

> The moment which is the most dangerous to the honour and
> the safety of a British army is that in which they have won
> the place they have assaulted.
>
> John Kincaid[1]

At the limits of civilisation lie the rules for the waging of wars. In the Napoleonic era the rules for the prosecution of war against fortified towns and fortresses were well established. There were three levels of attack: the blockade; the siege; and the storm. Blockading supply routes until lack of provisions forced a surrender without casualties – disease and starvation excepted – might work if the blockading army was vastly superior to any relieving force and could keep it at bay, otherwise, as at Ciudad Rodrigo in 1811, the blockaders would simply be pushed aside. The siege was a much closer encirclement of a town and involved artillery bombardment and sapping (undermining the defences by digging away wall foundations) to create breaches in the outer walls in preparation for an infantry assault; the storming of the town. The siege would begin with the digging of trenches approximately parallel to the walls to protect the attacking infantry. The first line of trenches was called the *first parallel*, the next, closer to the defences, the *second parallel*, and so on. At the same time batteries (cannon emplacements) would be constructed facing the points where the walls were to be breached by the heavy calibre battering artillery.

The storming of fortresses was an action notorious for the appalling loss of life that invariably resulted. Accordingly, when breaches had been created and the assault seemed feasible the governor of the garrison was invited to surrender. Surrendering at this point involved no dishonour as the surrounding force had clearly shown its capability by creating the breaches, and surrender could be viewed as an humanitarian act to avoid needless bloodshed. On such a surrender the garrison, including the civilian population, was to be accorded the respect due to prisoners of war, and the provisions and remaining ammunition in the fortress became the lawful prize of the besiegers. When the commander of the French garrison at Almeida in 1811

[1] Kincaid, 1981: 276.

destroyed supplies before evacuating the town he was severely criticised for breaking the rules by depriving the allies of their due spoils. Wellington had already warned him that if he did this, he and every man caught would receive no quarter. Wellington viewed such destruction as contrary to international law and thought anyone acting in this way had forfeited any right to be treated as a prisoner of war[1].

If the governor of the besieged force refused to surrender and obliged the besiegers to storm the breaches, the code was equally clear: if the fortress fell, the victors claimed their right to plunder[2]. In reality this usually involved an orgy of destruction by the rank and file of the attacking army, eager to grab anything of value for themselves. The civilian population could expect to be caught up in this frenzy of greed and violence, and civilised treatment at the hands of the soldiers was seldom a consequence. In 1810 when it was the French besieging the Spanish in Ciudad Rodrigo, Ney baldly told the governor, General Andrès Herrasti, he had to choose between an honourable capitulation or the terrible vengeance of a victorious army. Herrasti held out for more than a week of further cannonading but surrendered before the infantry made their attack and was therefore promised 'the honours of war'.

When an infantry assault against the breaches was necessary, the chance of survival for those who led it was slim. This was recognised in the names given to these lead parties: by the French, 'Les Enfants Perdus', *the Lost Children*; by the British, 'The Forlorn Hope' (actually a corruption of the Dutch *verloren hoop*, the 'Lost Party'.) This was a job for volunteers, but volunteers were seldom in short supply. In the British army the danger of the task was recognised (for officers at least) by the frequent bestowal of promotions on survivors. Some officers of low seniority who would otherwise expect a long wait before their next promotion therefore saw this as a gamble worth taking, despite the odds[3]. There was also the desire to be seen showing courage. This was important in an army where men were judged on their behaviour under fire and life could be made intolerable for anyone who acquired a suspect reputation[4]. In battles at this time even ducking when you saw the cannonball coming would be viewed by some as an act of cowardice. In the Light Division, such was the self-esteem of the corps that storming parties were viewed by the men as normal duty; there was competition to be included and great pride at being selected. Major George Napier[5] of the 52nd Light Infantry, who led the storming party at Ciudad Rodrigo in 1812, said, "I went to the three Regiments, viz., the 43rd, 52nd and Rifle Corps and said 'Soldiers, I have the honour to be appointed to the command of the storming party which is to lead the Light Division to the assault of the small breach. I want 100 volunteers from each Regiment—those who will go with me come forward.' Instantly there rushed out nearly half the Division and we were obliged to take them by chance.[6]"

[1] Stanhope, 1888: 89. As to the threat of 'no quarter' Wellington later admitted, "Why, if it had come to the point, I dare say I should not have done it." (*loc. cit.*)

[2] This principle had applied since the time of the Roman Empire when the cut off point was the first impact of the battering-ram on the fortress gate. After that moment the Romans would show no quarter and, having forced an entry, would put to death every man, woman, child and domestic animal inside the fortress.

[3] 'Low seniority'– i.e. only recently promoted to their current rank. A promotion for actions in the field, such as leading storming parties, would be a promotion 'by brevet' (a 'brevet promotion'). Such brevet promotions were usually a recognition of service. They ignored seniority and were not obtained by purchase. The officer would be promoted in the army but not in their regiment (a system of simultaneous ranks existed at this time). They would wear the insignia of their army rank and would be addressed using their army title, but they would continue in the duty applicable to their regimental rank (unless seconded as a Staff Officer) and would still receive the pay appropriate for their regimental rank. In cases of brevet promotion the army would not have to promote at the same time officers with greater seniority.

When a breach was to be stormed the order of assault would be: (i) a group (often unarmed) to place ladders against the damaged wall and throw large bags of grass or other padding into deep ditches to break the attackers' fall; (ii) the Forlorn Hope (perhaps several dozen men); (iii) the Storming Party (several hundred men); then (iv) remaining troops, excepting any companies detailed to provide covering fire against the breach's defenders.

The Siege of Ciudad Rodrigo

'On the 8th of January,' writes Jonathan Leach, 'the Light Division marched before break of day, and forded the Agueda above the knees, near the convent of Caredad. The weather being very sharp, the process was not a pleasant one. The necessary dispositions for the investment of the place were soon completed, under the immediate directions of Lord Wellington... On some rising ground stood the redoubt of San Francisco, which it was necessary to take before operations could be commenced against the town. At nine o'clock at night, three hundred men, belonging to the 43d, 52d, 95th, and the 3d Portuguese Caçadores, under the command of Lieutenant-Colonel Colbourne[7], of the 52d, stormed and carried it. Our loss was three officers and about twenty men. We lost a lieutenant of the Rifle corps, a most promising young man. All the French troops in the fort, amounting to about seventy men and three officers, were either made prisoners or bayoneted in the assault. Strong working parties immediately commenced the first parallel on the heights where the redoubt stood; and, as the garrison kept up an extremely heavy fire, both of shot and shells, without intermission, throughout the night, we worked like rabbits, and before daybreak were tolerably well covered in the trenches. Daylight enabled the French to direct their fire with greater accuracy, which was tremendous... Having been relieved by the 1st Division, we went through the freezing operation of fording the Agueda, and returned to our villages late at night, they being some leagues distant from the fortress. No rocking was necessary to send us to sleep, after thirty-six hours spent in the manner I have related.'

Fording the Água in January was not to be envied. Rifleman Ned Costello complained, "It was very annoying to have to cross the Agueda going to the trenches, and returning from them. Pieces of ice were constantly carried down this rapid stream, and they bruised our men so much that the cavalry were ordered to form four deep across the ford, under the lee of whom we crossed comparatively unharmed. Nevertheless, by the time we reached our quarters, our clothes were frozen and icy.[8]" The different divisions of the army now worked 24 hour shifts digging the trenches so each was only engaged in this dangerous and onerous duty every few days.

Leach: "On the 12th the Light Division was again in the trenches. We were employed all day in completing some batteries, and at night in laying the platforms for the battering artillery. The garrison kept up, as usual, an eternal fire of shot, shells, and grape, by which we lost many men. Some

[4] At this time the rank and file categorised their officers as 'come-ons' or 'go-ons'. Those who led from the front and rushed towards the enemy yelling back to their men "Come on!" were 'come-ons'; those who hung back but ordered their men to "Go on!" were 'go-ons'. The latter were not appreciated and one soldier noted "Go on!" was a very unbecoming expression from an officer [Could 'go-on' be the origin of the insulting term 'goon'?].
[5] Major George Thomas Napier (1784-1855). Later General Sir George Napier. Made Governor of the Cape of Good Hope and Major-General 1837. Knighted 1838. Lieutenant-General 1846. Full General 1854. The brother of Major William Napier of the 43rd.
[6] From Napier, 1886: 179 (Quoted in Verner, 1919: 340).
[7] Lieutenant-Colonel John Colborne (1778-1863). Knighted *KCB* 1815. Was Lieutenant-Governor of Guernsey then of Upper Canada. Promoted General 1854. Commanded in Ireland from 1855-1860. Promoted Field-Marshal 1860. Elevated to the peerage as Baron Seaton.
[8] Hathaway, 1997: 139.

Attack on Ciudad Rodrigo.

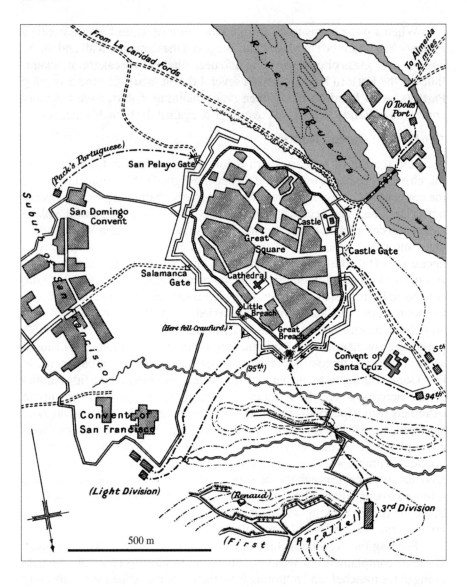

companies of our regiment were sent out of the trenches, after it was dark, to get as near the town as possible, and to fire at the artillery-men through the embrasures. If this operation was a disagreeable one to the enemy, it was far from a delectable one for us: they threw fire-balls among us, which were composed of such combustible matter, that they could not easily be extinguished, and made every thing near them as visible as at broad day. The moment we were perceived, musketry and grape were served out with no sparing hand. When relieved by the 1st Division on the 13th, we went through the same fiery ordeal again, from every piece of ordnance which the garrison could make use of."

The siege went well and by the 15th of January the allies had opened a second parallel less than 140 metres from the battlements. This success, and information that Marmont was about to move in the allies' direction from Salamanca, prompted Wellington to order a full assault. By the 18th two breaches had been knocked in the north wall and the 3rd Division was ordered to storm the larger, the Light Division the smaller, at eight o'clock the following evening.

The Storming of Ciudad Rodrigo

The Light Division began its assault from the cover of the convent of San Francisco, several hundred metres from the town wall. A wide protective ditch had been cut during the night from this point straight to the breach[9]. The Division comprised two Brigades, the 1st Brigade was commanded by Lieutenant-Colonel Andrew Barnard[10], the 2nd by Major-General John Vandeleur[11]. From these brigades the companies of the 95th were allocated various duties. From Vandeleur's Brigade: four companies to provide close covering fire from the glacis[12]; four companies to provide covering fire from the second parallel, 165 metres from the walls; three companies with ladders and axes (but no firearms) to descend into the ditch mid-way between the breaches and destroy any obstacles between themselves and the main breach to their right; some of the remaining companies to move forward with the main assault under Craufurd; Barnard's Brigade (the 43rd Light Infantry, the 1st Caçadores, and the remaining companies of the 95th) was held in reserve at the convent, with orders to advance and support the first wave when it reached the breach[13].

Jonathan Leach presumably led his company in one of these duties. Lieutenant John Kincaid, however, was selected as one of the officers to lead the storming party and his account, given here, commences with the order of attack.

"1st. Four companies of our battalion, under Colonel Cameron[14], to line the crest of the glacis and fire upon the ramparts. 2nd. Some companies of Portuguese carrying bags filled with hay and straw, for throwing into the ditch to facilitate the passage of the storming party. 3rd. The *forlorn hope*, consisting of an officer and 25 volunteers. 4th. The *storming party*, consisting of three officers and one hundred volunteers from each regiment; the officers from ours were Captain Mitchell, Mr. Johnstone, and myself, and the whole under the command of Major Napier, of the fifty-second. 5th. The main body of the division, under General Craufurd, with one brigade, under Major-General Vandeleur, and the other under Colonel Barnard.

At a given signal the different columns advanced to the assault; the night was tolerably clear, and the enemy evidently expected us; for, as soon as we turned the corner of the convent wall, the space between us and the breach became one blaze of light with their fire-balls, which, while they

9 Teague & Teague, 1975: 33.
10   Lieutenant-Colonel Andrew Francis Barnard (1773-1855) Later General Sir Andrew Barnard *KCB*. Exchanged into the 95th in 1809 from the 1st (The Royal) Regiment of Foot.
11   Major-General John Ormsby Vandeleur (1763-1849). Knighted 1816. Promoted full General 1838.
12   'Glacis' – a cleared area sloping down from a line of fortifications.
13 Verner, 1919: 341-342.
14   Major   Alexander Cameron   (1781-1850). Joined the 95th Rifles in 1800 from the 92nd (Highland) Regiment. Promoted to Lieutenant-Colonel, 27 April 1812 and given command of 1/95th until May 1813. Promoted full Colonel 1830. Made Major-General and was knighted (*KCB*) in 1838.

lighted us on to glory, lightened not a few of their lives and limbs; for the whole glacis was in consequence swept by a well-directed fire of grape and musketry, and they are the devil's own brooms; but our gallant fellows walked through it, to the point of attack, with the most determined steadiness, excepting the Portuguese sack-bearers, most of whom lay down behind their bags, to wait the result, while the few that were thrown into the ditch looked so like dead bodies, that, when I leapt into it, I tried to avoid them.[15]"

Rifleman Ned Costello was also one of the lucky few chosen to form the storming party and remembers the order to charge: "The expected signal, a rocket, went up from one of our batteries. "Now lads, for the breach!" General Craufurd called out, and led the way. We started off in double time, and in turning the left corner of the wall, came under fire. As we neared the breach, the shot of the enemy swept our men away fast. Canister, grape, round-shot, and shell, with fire-balls to show our ground, and a regular hailstorm of bullets, came pouring on and around us. General Craufurd fell almost immediately, mortally wounded.[16]"

Craufurd had been hit by a musket ball which, "passed through his arm, broke through his ribs passed through part of his lungs and lodged in or at his spine. The shock was so great that on falling he rolled over down the glacis.[17]" He died five days later[18]. Virtually as Craufurd was falling, Vandeleur was also wounded and command of the assault devolved to Barnard. The troops meanwhile pushed on.

Costello: "Without a pause we dashed onwards to the town, and precipitated ourselves into the ditch before the walls. We did not wait for the ladders for they were carried by the Portuguese, who ran away. The ladders did not make an appearance until their use had been superseded by a series of jumps made by our men into a trench 16´ deep[19]. When one or two ladders were procured, they were instantly placed against the scarp of the trench, and up we mounted to attack the breach. There the fire was constant and most deadly, and for some minutes, small bodies of men were swept away as they appeared. But they persevered, and gradually formed a lodgement. On our right, where the 3rd Division were storming the second breach, we heard a loud cheering. This had a magical effect: regardless of the enemy's fire, and every other impediment, the men dashed in over the breach, carrying everything before them."

In the main assault force, bugler Bill Green was among those reaching the crest of the breach just in time to face the cannon that had caused so many losses to the storming party just minutes before: "Some of us got up to the gun, it was loaded again, and the French gunner was in the act of applying the match, when one of our men knocked him down with the butt of his rifle. If he had been one moment later many of us would have been sent into eternity, as we were close up to the muzzle.[20]"

The conflict at the breaches was severe but of short duration and both were stormed in less than 30 minutes, but with heavy losses. Leading the storming party, Major George Napier lost an arm. Major-General Vandeleur

[15] Kincaid, 1981: 54.
[16] Hathaway, 1997: 142.
[17] Craufurd's Aide de Camp, Shaw Kennedy, quoted in Verner (1919: 344).
[18] After seeking forgiveness from Wellington for his intrigues against him (Pool, 1967: 97).
[19] 16 feet (5m) deep.
[20] Teague & Teague, 1975: 33

had been severely wounded. Royal Engineers Captain George Ross, brother of Major Hew Ross of the Royal Horse Artillery[21], was killed. At the larger breach, less than 200 metres to the west, one of the French magazines exploded at the height of the fighting, killing many combatants of both sides.

Kincaid: 'After carrying the breach, we met with no further opposition, and moved round the ramparts to see that they were perfectly clear of the enemy, previous to entering the town. I was fortunate enough to take the left-hand circuit, by accident, and thereby escaped the fate which befell a great portion of those who went to the right, and who were blown up, along with some of the third division, by the accidental explosion of a magazine... We continued our course round the ramparts until we met the head of the column which had gone by the right, and then descended into the town.[22]'

After the battle

Kincaid: 'A town taken by storm presents a frightful scene of outrage. The soldiers no sooner obtain possession of it, than they think themselves at liberty to do what they please. It is enough for them that there *had* been an enemy on the ramparts; and, without considering that the poor inhabitants may, nevertheless, be friends and allies, they, in the first moment of excitement, all share one common fate; and nothing but the most extraordinary exertions on the part of the officers can bring them back to a sense of their duty...

Finding the current of soldiers setting towards the centre of the town, I followed the stream, which conducted me into the great square, on one side of which the late garrison were drawn up as prisoners, and the rest of it was filled with British and Portuguese intermixed, without any order or regularity. I had been there but a very short time, when they all commenced firing, without any ostensible cause; some fired in at the doors and windows, some at the roofs of houses, and others at the clouds; and, at last, some heads began to be blown from their shoulders in the general hurricane, when the voice of Sir Thomas Picton, with the power of twenty trumpets, began to proclaim damnation to everybody[23], while Colonel Barnard, Colonel Cameron, and some other active officers, were carrying it into effect with a strong hand; for, seizing the broken barrels of muskets, which were lying about in great abundance, they belaboured every fellow, most unmercifully, about the head who attempted either to load or fire, and finally succeeded in reducing them to order[24]. In the midst of the scuffle, however, three of the houses in the square were set on fire; and the confusion was such that nothing could be done to save them; but, by the extraordinary exertions of Colonel Barnard, during the whole of the night, the flames were prevented from communicating to the adjoining buildings.

We succeeded in getting a great portion of our battalion together by one o'clock in the morning, and withdrew with them to the ramparts, where we lay by our arms until daylight.[25]'

[21] Hew Ross had been promoted from Captain to Major for services in the field in December 1811.

[22] Kincaid, 1981: 56-57.

[23] Wellington called Picton, "a rough foul-mouthed devil as ever lived" (Stanhope, 1888: 69).

[24] Kincaid admits to having wielded a musket barrel himself (1981: 276).

[25] Kincaid, 1981: 56-58.

In the harsh light of day Jonathan Leach found his surroundings unwelcoming: "Daylight of the 20th presented a horrid sight, and unfit to be contemplated in cold blood. Many objects, of both parties, lying near the spot where the magazine had exploded, were frightful to a degree. Bodies without limbs, and limbs without bodies, were scorched and scattered about in different directions; and the houses near the breaches were filled with such of the wounded as were able to crawl away from the ramparts, with a view to find shelter from the severe frost, which numbed their wounds."

In the course of the morning, having assembled their men the officers prepared to march them out of the town. Kincaid noted regulation uniforms were not much in evidence: "The fifth division, which had not been employed in the siege, marched in, and took charge of the town, on the morning of the 20th, and we prepared to return to our cantonments[26]. Lord Wellington happened to be riding in at the gate at the time that we were marching out, and had the curiosity to ask the officer of the leading company, what regiment it was, for there was scarcely a vestige of uniform among the men, some of whom were dressed in Frenchmen's coats, some in white breeches, and huge jack-boots, some with cocked hats and queues; most of their swords were fixed on the rifles, and stuck full of hams, tongues, and loaves of bread, and not a few were carrying bird-cages! There never was a better masked corps.[27]" Simmons thought the Division looked like "a moving rag-fair"[28].

Jonathan thought Ciudad Rodrigo had escaped lightly: "When a town is stormed, it is inevitable that excesses will be, as they ever have been, committed by the assailants, more particularly if it takes place at night. It affords a favourable opportunity for the loose and dissolute characters, which are to be found in all armies, to indulge in every diabolical propensity. That this was the case to a certain extent, on the night in question, no one will deny; but, at the same time, I feel convinced that no town taken by assault ever did or ever will suffer less than Rodrigo. It is true that soldiers of all regiments got drunk, plundered, and made great noise and confusion in the streets and houses, in spite of every exertion on the part of the officers to prevent it; but bad and revolting as such scenes are, I never heard that either the French garrison, when it had once surrendered, nor any of the inhabitants, suffered personal indignities or cruelty from the troops."

Marshal Marmont was taken completely by surprise at the speed at which Ciudad Rodrigo fell and he rapidly abandoned his plans to march to its defence. Knowing if he did proceed there he would now have to besiege the fortress himself, his decision was helped by the knowledge that he had left his own battering train of 44 heavy artillery pieces safely secured inside the fortified town of... Ciudad Rodrigo.

On the morning of the 26th of January Robert Craufurd was buried with full military honours in the breach assailed by his men. Kincaid reflected that, "like many a gem of purer ray his value was scarcely known

[26] This exchange was normal practice. Simmons observed, "the men who have stormed a town are seldom fit for anything but vice and irregularity for some time afterwards, if left within its walls." (Verner, 1986: 223).
[27] Kincaid, 1981: 59.
[28] Verner, 1986: 223.

until lost[29]". After the service, as the Light Division marched back to camp their route was crossed by an expanse of deep muddy slush. A low murmur passed down the ranks and, stiffening their backs, the men plunged through[30].

The Light Division remained in the villages near the town for a month then received orders to march the 192 km (as the crow flies) to Badajoz in the south. Having secured the northern route between Portugal and Spain, Wellington – who was elevated to Earl of Wellington when news of the success reached Britain – now intended to secure the southern route. The Light Division marched first to Elvas, confident in the knowledge that as they had participated in the onerous duty of digging the parallels at Ciudad Rodrigo, other Divisions would perform this duty at Badajoz. Their confidence was sadly misplaced.

The Siege of Badajoz

The castle and fortress town of Badajoz sat on a hill surrounded by a formidable wall studded with bastions. The northern stretch of wall lay against the substantial River Guadiana which was crossed only by a long bridge connecting the town to the redoubts and fortification of San Christobal on the northern bank. In the north-east corner the castle connected with the east wall overlooking the slope running down to the Rivillas (a small river running into the Guadiana) on the far bank of which were the redoubts of San Roque and Fort Picurina. The French had dammed the Rivillas and the waters had backed up around the town wall to the south-east. The southern wall was protected by a ditch nearly 3 metres deep. The allied parallels were planned to commence north of Fort Picurina on the opposite side of the Rivillas from the citadel.

'On the 17th of March,' reported Jonathan, 'at break of day, the Light Division marched out of Elvas to the tune of St Patrick's Day[31], in commemoration of that saint; and we joined the 3rd and 4th Divisions before Badajoz, on the left bank of the Guadiana, which divisions had arrived there the day before. Some Portuguese troops invested the town on the opposite bank.

Detachments of the 3d, 4th, and Light Divisions commenced operations as soon as it was dark against a strong redoubt called Fort Piccurina, from which vollies of musketry and shells were fired on the covering and working parties during the night. The rain descended in torrents, and the cold was extremely severe. No sooner had day broke than a heavy fire from the town and the redoubt opened on us. At the expiration of fourteen hours we were relieved by detachments of the three divisions, and returned to our camp, which was a short distance out of range of the guns of Badajoz, situated in a muddy marsh full of water... The siege was prosecuted with the utmost vigour, in spite of the rains, which descended almost without intermission during the first ten days, and filled the trenches with water. So many men were required to carry on the operations that nearly one half of our time was spent in the trenches...

[29] Kincaid, 1981: 193.
[30] Told by Verner (1919: 353-354) and witnessed by Field-Marshal Sir Charles Yorke (1790-1880), then a young officer in the 52nd.
[31] The 17th of March is St Patrick's Day.

171

On the 25th, our batteries opened their fire on the town, which was returned with equal spirit. The same night Fort Piccurina was stormed and carried by detachments from the 3d and Light Divisions, after considerable resistance and with the loss of many men. Immediately on its fall another parallel was commenced. From the ravelin of San Roque and from the walls of the town the covering parties were exceedingly galled by a constant fire of musketry.'

Kincaid said the duties in the trenches were, "like nothing better than serving an apprenticeship to the double calling of grave-digger and gamekeeper, for we found ample employment both for the spade and the rifle.[32]" In reality there was little akin to an apprenticeship. The trenches were extremely dangerous places, as Ned Costello discovered:

'Some days after we had taken one of the forts from the enemy, our battalion was relieved in the trenches and, as was customary with some of us, Brooks, Treacy, and myself jumped out of the trench, exposing ourselves to a fire from the walls of the town, and ran to the next parallel, or trench. A little ahead of my comrades, I heard the rush of a cannon-ball, and felt my jacket splashed by something. I jumped into the next trench, turned round, and beheld the body of Brooks, headless, but quivering with life for a few seconds before it fell... The shot had smashed and carried away the whole of his head. My jacket was bespattered with the brains, and Treacy was materially injured by a splinter of the skull being driven deep through the skin behind his ear.[33]'

Despite the horror – or perhaps because of it – the characteristic black humour of the infantryman also found its way to the surface. Costello again: "The greatest annoyance we experienced during the siege arose from shells thrown at us from the town. Our works screened us from the round-shot; but these dangerous missiles, falling into the trenches where we worked and exploding, frequently did great mischief. Immediately a shell fell, every man threw himself flat upon the ground until it had burst.

Tom Crawley, though tolerably fearless of other shot, had an inveterate dislike of these deadly visitors, and believed that more were thrown where he chanced to be than in any other part of the trenches. At night, in particular, he was always on the look out. As soon as he beheld a shell coming he would call out, "Here's another brute! Look out!" and dive head first into a mud-heap, which he would always manage to have at hand. This did not always protect us, for the head was no sooner in the mud than its presence was again required outside, to watch for falling splinters which, being composed of large portions of metal from the missile, descended with great violence, and were of themselves sometimes sufficient to crush a man into the earth.

Occasionally Lord Wellington would pay us a visit during the work, to make observations and examine the trenches. One day, when Crawley and myself were working near each other, a shell fell inconveniently close to us. Tom was instantly half buried in mud, awaiting the explosion.

32 Kincaid, 1981: 63.
33 Hathaway, 1997: 161-2.

The shell had sunk itself deep into the earth because the fuse was too long, so I decided to play a trick upon Crawley – when the shell exploded, I was going to throw a large lump of clay on his head to make him believe himself wounded. To obtain the clod I sprang at the other side of the trench, and in doing so exposed myself to a grape-shot. It splashed me from head to foot with mud, and I had to throw myself back into the trench upon Crawley who, believing that a shell had fixed itself upon his rear, roared like a bull. In an instant, however, the sunken missile burst, and when the smoke dispersed, I beheld the Duke, crouched down, his head half averted, dryly smiling at us.[34]"

By the beginning of April 1812 the allied siege batteries, hurling 24 pound (11 kg) cannonballs against selected locations on the walls, had battered several breaches at the south-east corner of the fortress. As the weather slowly improved, the engineers declared the breaches practicable and on the 5th of April the storming parties were selected for the following night's assault.

The Storming of Badajoz[35]

One breach had been smashed in the bastion of Santa Maria; one in the bastion of La Trinidad to its right; and one in the curtain wall connecting the two. The Light Division (led by Andrew Barnard since Craufurd's death) and the 4th Division under Major-General Charles Colville[36], were given the task of storming these; Picton would take the 3rd Division and storm the castle by escalade (ladders); the newly arrived 5th Division would make several diversionary attacks against the south and west of the town, to be converted to full attacks if progress was made; and the Portuguese forces on the north bank of the Guadiana would attack Fort San Christobal and the other redoubts protecting the bridge.

Jonathan Leach played a similar role to that at Ciudad Rodrigo[37]. John Kincaid, who for this storm had joined the four companies detailed to provide covering fire, led by Major Cameron, describes how the evening began:

"The enemy seemed aware of our intentions. The fire of artillery and musketry, which, for three weeks before, had been incessant, both from the town and trenches, had now entirely ceased, as if by mutual consent, and a death-like silence, of nearly an hour, preceded the awful scene of carnage.

The signal to advance was made about nine o'clock, and our four companies led the way. Colonel Cameron[38] and myself had reconnoitred the ground so accurately by daylight, that we succeeded in bringing the head of our column to the very spot agreed on, opposite to the left breach, and then formed line to the left, without a word being spoken, each man lying down as he got into line, with the muzzle of his rifle over the edge of the ditch, between the pallisades, all ready to open. It was tolerably clear above, and we distinctly saw *their* heads lining the ramparts; but there was a sort of haze on the ground which, with the colour of our dress, prevented them from seeing us,

[34] Hathaway, 1997: 162. Wellington was an Earl at this time.

[35] See Haythornthwaite (1996b: 165-191) and Hathaway (1997: 159-181) for coverage of this action.

[36] Major-General Charles Colville (1770-1843). Knighted (GCB) 1815. Promoted Lieutenant-General 1819. Commander-in-Chief Bombay 1819. Governor of Mauritius 1828-1834. Promoted full General 1837.

[37] Kincaid (1981: 65) says at Badajoz the Light Division formed in the same manner as for the storming of Ciudad Rodrigo.

[38] Cameron was not promoted to Colonel until later. He was a Major at this time.

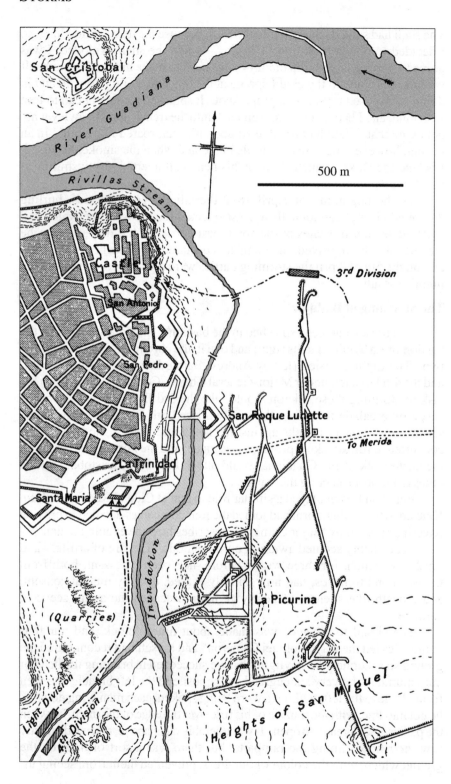

Attack on Badajoz.

although only a few yards asunder. One of their sentries, however, challenged us twice, '*qui vive*,' and, receiving no reply, he fired off his musket, which was followed by their drums beating to arms; but *we* still remained perfectly quiet, and all was silence again for the space of five or ten minutes, when the head of the forlorn hope at length came up, and we took advantage of the first fire, while the enemy's heads were yet visible.

The scene that ensued furnished as respectable a representation of hell itself as fire, and sword, and human sacrifices could make it; for, in one instant, every engine of destruction was in full operation.[39]"

Leach: 'The discharge of grape-shot and musketry, with buck shot in addition to bullets, the hand-grenades, rafters of wood, and various weapons of destruction hurled from the ramparts on the heads of the assailants in the ditch, in their desperate and reiterated attempts to force their way through the breaches, and to mount the ladders for the escalade of the castle and town, was of so dreadful and destructive a nature, as to beggar all description... The enemy had dug deep trenches between the top of the breaches and the town, and had fixed sword-blades and pikes in the trench. From some houses near the top of the breach a terrible fire of musketry was poured on such as contrived to reach its summit. Those obstacles alone were insurmountable, without the addition of a continued and most deadly fire of grape and musketry from the ramparts, and from the summits of the breaches; in the repeated and fruitless attempts to carry which, the assailants were falling in vast numbers every moment.'

On a hilltop facing the breaches Wellington watched anxiously. With him was William Surtees, now Quartermaster[40] of the 3/95th, who saw the events from Wellington's perspective:

"Not long after, it opened out at the breaches and was most awfully severe; indeed it was so heavy and so incessant, that it appeared like one continued sheet of fire along the ramparts near the breaches, and we could distinctly see the faces of the French troops, although the distance was near a mile[41]. All sorts of arms, &c. were playing at once, guns, mortars, musketry, grenades, and shells thrown down from the walls, while every few minutes explosions from mines were taking place. The firing too appeared to have such a strange death-like sound, quite different from all I had ever heard before. This was occasioned by the muzzles being pointed downwards into the ditch, which gave the report an unusual and appalling effect. This continued without a moment's cessation, or without any apparent advantage being gained by our struggling but awfully circumstanced comrades. Lord Wellington had also taken his stand upon this hill, and appeared quite uneasy at the troops seeming to make no progress, and often asked, or rather repeated to himself, "What can be the matter?"[42]"

'The matter' was the competence of the French commander, General Armand Philippon[43]. A master of siege defence he had prepared meticulously for the assault. The French had placed all manner of obstructions in the

[39] Kincaid, 1981: 65-66.
[40] Surtees had been Quartermaster-Sergeant of the 2nd battalion in Denmark. He had now been promoted into the 3rd battalion as Quartermaster, a commissioned officer rank.
[41] 1600 m (From the map opposite, Surtees would appear to be overestimating the distance).
[42] Surtees, 1973: 139.
[43] Général Armand Philippon, Baron (1761-1836). Said to be an uninspiring commander in the field but a master of siegeworks.

ditch in front of the breaches; and in the breaches; and behind the breaches. The base of the ditch was cut with trenches, increasing its depth to five metres, and some had been flooded. Much of the rubble from the smashed walls, forming a slope to the breach opening, had been removed and in its place had been thrown anything the garrison could find to impede the progress of men on foot: overturned carts; smashed boats; old wicker baskets; tangles of rope; doors and beams spiked with nails; and finally, at the breach, a sea of planks, set with iron spikes, that slipped under the attackers' feet, tripping the men onto the skewers and sending them careering back down the slope into those following. The ground was strewn with caltraps[44] and at the breach openings were *chevaux de frise* (heavy beams suspended horizontally from chains at each end and spiked in all directions with razor-sharp sword blades). If the struggling and virtually stationary attackers overcame all this – through a continuous hail of artillery, shells, musket balls, buck-shot, grape-shot, exploding mines, fire-balls and all the rocks, staves and cartwheels hurled from the ramparts nine metres overhead – a second wall of defences of compacted earth and sandbags, protected by further spike-lined trenches, had been raised inside the original stone enclosure. But the attackers were not getting that far.

In the bowels of the ditch all was turmoil. The gulley was filled with dead and wounded, and many of the Light Division, caught up in the delayed advance of the 4th Division and with their guiding engineers shot, were carried to the wrong breach. The central breach, which had only been opened that afternoon as an alternative to the formidable defences in the other two, was virtually ignored in the confusion. At the two side breaches assault after assault was thrown against the slopes, only to meet unspeakable slaughter. Ned Costello was knocked to the ground more than once by men falling around him and onto him. He lost his rifle, then his sword-bayonet, stumbled into water up to his neck, crawled out unarmed, and pressed on:

"I now attempted to get to the breach, which the blaze of musketry from the walls clearly showed me. Without rifle, sword, or any other weapon, I succeeded in clambering up a part of the breach where there was a *chevaux-de-frise*, consisting of a piece of heavy timber studded with sword blades, turning on an axis. Just before I reached it, I received a stroke on the breast. Whether it was from a grenade, or a stone, or the butt-end of a musket, I cannot say, but down I rolled senseless, drenched with water and human gore. I could not have laid long in this plight, and when my senses started to return, I saw our gallant fellows still rushing forward, each seeming to meet a fate more deadly than my own. The fire continued in one horrible and incessant peal, as if the mouth of the infernal regions had opened to vomit forth destruction upon all around us.[45]"

Hour after hour, thirty or forty times, parties of men hurled themselves in futility against the blood-soaked slopes. "I had seen some fighting," said Simmons, "but nothing like this. We remained passively here to be slaughtered, as we could do the besieged little injury from the ditch.[46]"

Caltraps

[44] Small pyramids of spikes usually scattered in front of cavalry to impale horses' hooves and so designed that no matter how they fall a spike is always uppermost.
[45] Hathaway, 1997: 170-1.
[46] Verner, 1986: 229.

At midnight word came that the 3rd Division had succeeded in scaling the ramparts and had entered the castle, but its embracing solidity and reinforcements from the garrison had stalled them there. Wellington repeatedly ordered the Light and 4th Divisions to retire and reform for a renewed assault at daylight, but Barnard was reluctant to obey. The men kept driving forward, and he kept leading them. Between midnight and one o'clock[47], after hours of unimaginable butchery, he finally pulled the survivors back 300 metres and reformed. No sooner was this done than reports arrived that the French were deserting the breaches to reinforce the western defences where the 5th Division's 'diversionary' attacks had succeeded in scaling the wall. Wellington ordered the breaches stormed again—but this time the French had gone. Not a shot was fired.

Kincaid: "We stole down into the ditch with the same silence which marked our first advance – an occasional explosion or a discharge of musketry continued to be heard in distant parts of the works; but in the awful charnel pit we were then traversing to reach the foot of the breach, the only sounds that disturbed the night were the moans of the dying, with an occasional screech[48]".

Having reached the defences, to squirm through in the dark was still a dangerous exercise – "next to impossible" said Surtees – and it was only with great difficulty the divisions threaded their way through and entered the town, leaving behind them in the ditch the bodies of almost 1500 dead and wounded lying two and three deep[49].

After the battle

Jonathan Leach makes no mention of the aftermath of the storming of Badajoz, yet the behaviour of the victorious British troops resounds in infamy even today. Perhaps that is why.

When the Light Division struggled through the unmanned defences the 3rd and 5th Divisions were already rampaging through the streets and discipline was dissolving. With the French under guard, the town's population – the Spanish, pro-ally, civilian population – was subjected to an explosion of frenzied brutality.

"Now comes a scene of horror I would willingly bury in oblivion" says Harry Smith with uncharacteristic reflection, "The atrocities committed by our soldiers on the poor, innocent, and defenceless inhabitants of the city, no words suffice to depict. Civilised man, when let loose, and the bonds of morality relaxed, is a far greater beast than the savage, more refined in his cruelty, more fiendish in every act; and oh, too truly did our heretofore noble soldiers disgrace themselves.[50]"

Those that had not entered the town during the hours of darkness, rushed to enter at first light. Barnard and other officers struggled to prevent men of the Light Division joining them, physically wrestling with them at the gates, but these men were insensible to command or reason. They were victorious; they were entitled. They forced their way past into the beleaguered streets,

[47] Kincaid (1981: 67) says 2 a.m., but most authorities vary between midnight and 1 a.m.
[48] Kincaid, 1981: 282.
[49] One of the dead was Charles MacLeod of the 43rd Light Infantry, who had put Harry Smith on his own horse at the Côa and saved his life. Since the beginning of the siege the Light Division had lost 62 officers and 744 men killed; 251 officers and 2604 men wounded. Jonathan Leach's battalion lost 3 officers, 3 sergeants and 24 riflemen killed; 9 officers, 15 sergeants, 3 buglers and 136 riflemen wounded. During the siege and storming the British as a whole had 4670 men killed (Hathaway, 1997: 178).
[50] Smith, 1999: 67-68.

filled with raging drunken soldiers, and they too were soon senseless to everything. Barnard and others followed them in, "to endeavour to restrain," says Surtees, "as much as lay in his power, the licentiousness of those inside, whose bad passions, it was but too evident, would be let loose on the defenceless inhabitants.[51]" In fact the best the officers could do was post themselves at a handful of houses to dissuade looting – and much worse.

Surtees reported that in the town, "no house, church, or convent, was held sacred by the infuriated and now ungovernable soldiery, but that priests or nuns, and common people, all shared alike, and that any who showed the least resistance were instantly sacrificed to their fury.[52]" Costello, wounded in the leg although he could not remember how, had joined the sacking from the start:

"It was a dark night, and confusion and uproar prevailed in the town. The shouts and oaths of drunken soldiers in quest of liquor, the reports of fire-arms, the crashing in of doors, and the appalling shrieks of hapless women, made you think you were in the regions of the damned." He entered a house, already occupied by several men of the 3rd Division. "I sat at the fire, which was blazing up the chimney, fed by mahogany chairs broken up for the purpose. Then I heard screams for mercy from an adjoining room. I hobbled in and found an old man, the proprietor of the house, on his knees, imploring mercy of a soldier who had levelled his musket at him. With difficulty, I prevented him from being shot. The soldier complained that the Spaniard would not give up his money, so I immediately informed the wretched landlord in Spanish, as well as I was able, that he could only save his life by surrendering his cash. Upon hearing this, and with trembling hands, he brought out from under the mattress of the bed, a large bag of dollars enveloped in a night-cap. The treasure must have amounted to 100-150 dollars. By common consent, it was divided among us. The dollars were piled on the table in small heaps according to the number of men present, and called out the same as messes in a barrack-room. I confess that I participated in the plunder, receiving about 26 dollars for my own share.

As soon as I had resumed my seat at the fire, a number of Portuguese soldiers entered. One of them took me for a Frenchman and snapped his piece at me[53]. Luckily it hung fire. Forgetful of my wound, I rushed at him, and a regular scuffle ensued between our men and the Portuguese, until one of the latter was stabbed by a bayonet, and they retired, dragging the wounded man with them. After ejecting the Portuguese, the victors, who by this time were tolerably drunk, proceeded to ransack the house and, unhappily, discovered the patrone's two daughters concealed upstairs. They were young and very pretty. Shortly afterwards, the mother too was dragged from her hiding place.

Without dwelling on the frightful scene that followed, I will just add that our men, more infuriated by drink than before, again seized upon the

[51] Surtees, 1973: 144.
[52] Surtees, 1973: 147.
[53] Fired his weapon. In this case the powder failed to ignite.

old man and insisted upon a fresh supply of liquor. His protestations that he possessed no more were in vain, as were all attempts to restrain them from ill-using him.[54]"

Across the town hundreds of similar nightmares were unleashed. Costello says the allied troops were prejudiced against the inhabitants of Badajoz because they were perceived to have submitted tamely to the French occupation[55]. It was different at Ciudad Rodrigo, where the soldiers felt the Spanish populace had put up a gallant defence. In reality no excuse is worthy of the name.

Through that infernal night Major Cameron had kept his marksmen together as a defence against any French resistance (but only by threatening to have them shot if they disobeyed and by promising not to detain them any longer than necessary). Between nine and ten o'clock the following morning, having confirmed the French garrison had been marched out towards Elvas, he told his men to fall out and enjoy themselves[56].

As day follows night

Wellington had been appalled by the carnage at the breaches. The following morning, despite every attempt to maintain his composure, he sobbed uncontrollably as Picton arrived to congratulate him[57].

In the town the debauchery, looting, and killing continued all day. Soldiers shot and stabbed each other in drunken squabbles over trinkets. At camp when the evening roll was called, the ranks were empty. Detachments of troops who had played no part in the assault were sent into the town to round up the absentees, but instead they joined the riot, eager for their share. Wellington ordered:

"It is now full time that the plunder of Badajoz should cease, and the Commander of the Forces requests that an officer and 6 steady non-commissioned officers may be sent from each regiment, British and Portuguese, of the 3d, 4th, 5th, and Light divisions, into the town to-morrow morning, at 5 o'clock, in order to bring away any men that may be straggling there."

The Provost Marshal was also ordered into the town with instructions to execute any men caught in the act of plunder[58].

The officers' entry the following morning met with limited success, the mayhem still being in full spate. Wellington, angry that the troops who had been sent into the town the previous day to solve the problem had merely added to it, responded the same morning with additional orders:

"The Commander of Forces is sorry to learn that the Brigade in Badajoz, instead of being a protection to the people, plunder them more than those who stormed the town. The Commander of the Forces calls upon the staff officers of the army, and other officers of regiments to assist him in putting an end to the disgraceful scenes of drunkenness and plunder which are still going on in Badajoz.[59]"

[54] Hathaway, 1997: 174-5.
[55] Green too notes, "Lord Wellington had told the Spanish governor to hold out, and he would send him supplies; but he acted in the most cowardly manner, and gave up that stronghold into the hands of the French! And this was a bad blow for the British and Portuguese army; it caused us a great deal of marching and counter-marching for a long time, when we might have been quiet in our camps in the summer, and snug in our cantonments in the winter!" (Teague & Teague, 1975: 25).
[56] Kincaid, 1981: 283.
[57] Bamford & Wellington (1950) 1: 143. There were those who doubted this was a sign of compassion. Wellington's biographer John Tucker declared during Wellington's lifetime, 'Cruelty is abhorrent to his nature, yet it would be difficult to shew that he has any human sympathies... and if he shed tears, as many have reported, on seeing the mangled bodies of his soldiers after a hard-fought battle, it must either be attributed to physical causes, to the exhaustion of the overwrought mind and body, or else we must set it down for one of the many contradictions which are to be found in the human character.' (1846: 434).
[58] Wellington's Dispatches (1844-1847) 5: 577fn.
[59] Hathaway, 1997: 179.

It was yet another day, the 9th of April, before order was finally restored. A brigade of Portuguese infantry was marched into Badajoz with bayonets fixed and paraded in the square while gallows and flogging triangles were erected by the Provost Marshal.

Costello: "I observed a sort of gallows erected, with three nooses hanging ready for service. Johnny Castles, a man of our company, a quiet, inoffensive little fellow, had a near escape. He was rather fond of a drop, but not that distilled by Jack Ketch & Co.[60] He was brought under the gallows in a cart, and the rope placed round his neck, but his life was spared. Whether this was done to frighten him or not I cannot say, but the circumstances had such an effect on him that he took ill, and was a little deranged for some time after. I am not aware that a single execution took place, notwithstanding the known severity of the Duke in matters of plunder and outrage.[61]"

Official records also suggest no men were actually hung, although Kincaid says differently[62]. Many were publicly lashed. Stragglers were finally marched out of the town and a Spanish garrison marched in.

At Badajoz the British army severely damaged its reputation with the Spanish populace and alienated the people whose land it sought to liberate. A disenchanted inhabitant of the Peninsula had earlier suggested the ideal solution to the problems plaguing her country would be to have the French hung using the entrails of the British[63]. This view now gained currency.

[60] 'Jack Ketch' was a nickname for any executioner. Named after John Ketch (d. 1686) the English public executioner during the reign of King Charles II. He became notorious after several inept executions, such as his beheading of the Duke of Monmouth in 1685 when he made five blows with the axe and still had to finish the job with a knife.

[61] Hathaway, 1997: 176.

[62] "the provost-marshal erected a gallows, and proceeded to suspend a few of the delinquents" (Kincaid, 1981: 69).

[63] Clearly a reworking of Diderot's view 'mankind will not be free until the last king is strangled with the entrails of the last priest.' [Denis Diderot, 1713-1784].

— 11 —

Salamanca

Napoleon's own spectacular defeats were elsewhere, but
this Peninsula War, which he had never really understood
and had always treated too lightly, might be said to be the
creeping cancer of his Empire.

J.B. Priestley[1]

During the siege of Badajoz, Marshal Soult's forces, then in the south of Spain, had advanced from Seville, although Soult made no strenuous effort to engage the besieging army. This was 1812 and Napoleon's eyes and the feet of his armies in the east were turning towards Russia. The dispute in the Peninsula had slipped down the Emperor's list of priorities and could no longer rely on the concerned attentions of Paris. When news of the fall of Badajoz reached Soult he was at Villafranca de los Barros, 65 km to the south-east, and he responded by moving his army away from the allies, harassed by the cavalry that had shadowed his movements.

Marmont, in the north, had attempted a half-hearted blockade of Ciudad Rodrigo while the allies were occupied to the south, but on the day Badajoz fell he abandoned the blockade, pushed his way through Portuguese militia and irregular forces, and crossed the border into Portugal. Wellington responded by marching his now disgraced army back to Ciudad Rodrigo, but on its approach Marmont crossed back into Spain, passed the fortress, and moved off to the north-east. The allies took up their old positions on the Águeda where the regiments reorganised and recruited to restore battalion strengths. Brigadier-General Charles Alten[2] was appointed to the command of the Light Division to replace Robert Craufurd, and Andrew Barnard returned to his normal duties. Wellington sent a force under Sir Rowland Hill[3] to cut the lines of communication between Marmont and Soult, preventing the formation of a united French force. This was achieved by late May and on the 11th of June the rested and restored allied army of more than 48,000 men broke camp, crossed the Águeda, and marched for Salamanca.

[1] Priestley, 1971: 61 [John Boynton Priestley (1894-1984) English novelist, playwright and critic].
[2] Brigadier-General Baron Charles Alten (1764-1840) A Hanoverian officer who transferred to the British service in 1803. Served at Copenhagen, Walcheren and in the Peninsula with the King's German Legion. Promoted Major-General 1816. Later General Sir Charles, Count von Alten, and a Field-Marshal in the Hanoverian Army.
[3] Lieutenant-General Sir Rowland Hill (1772-1842). Known as 'Daddy Hill'. Created Baron in 1814. Promoted full General in 1825 and was Commander-in-Chief in England 1825-1829. Created Viscount Hill in 1842.

Salamanca stood on the far bank of the River Tormes and, with the French controlling the bridge from a now fortified convent, the allies forded the river on the 17th and took up position on some heights to its left, overlooking a wide valley in front of the city. The French were assembled on the plain and opposing hills 2-3 km away. Here the armies faced each other without engaging until the 27th, when the 6th Division captured the convent and its garrison of 800 men by setting fire to it with red-hot cannon balls. At the loss of this and other lesser fortifications Marmont withdrew his army 80 km northwards beyond the River Duero with the allies in pursuit.

Leach: "We followed the French rear-guard on the 28th, 29th, and 30th of June, without coming up with it; and on the 1st of July the Light Division and some cavalry entered Navis del Rey, where we made a few prisoners. In spite of fatigue, we contrived to get up a dance at night, which many of the signoras honoured with their presence. Having snatched a couple of hours' sleep, we were again on the road before day dawned; and, after a burning march, reached Rueda, a decent kind of town, a few miles distant from the Douro[4]. Our cavalry made some prisoners from the French rear-guard."

Here the Light Division bivouacked for two weeks in a vineyard, sheltering from the intense heat of the day in the town (and from the intense proximity of the enemy in the company of the local fair ones). Kincaid said of Rueda: "our usual evening dances began there to be graced by a superior class of females to what they had hitherto been accustomed. I remember that, in passing the house of the sexton, one evening, I saw his daughter baking a loaf of bread; and, falling desperately in love with both her and the loaf, I carried the one to the ball and the other to my quarters. A woman was a woman in those days; and every officer made it a point of duty to marshal as many as he could to the general assembly, no matter whether they were countesses or *sextonesses*; and although we, in consequence, frequently incurred the most indelible disgrace among the better orders of our indiscriminate collection, some of whom would retire in disgust; yet, as a sufficient number generally remained for our evening's amusement, and we were only birds of passage, it was a matter of the most perfect indifference to us what they thought; we followed the same course wherever we went.[5]"

On the other side of the river, Marmont was engaged in more serious pursuits. He had been reinforced with the troops of General Bonet[6] and began to play a game of cat and mouse with the allies, manoeuvring and feinting as he tried to deceive them as to his intentions. This soon put an end to the 95th's fun as the officers were summoned from an evening's fandango by the bugles calling the Division to arms.

Leach: "On the night of the 16th, the Light Division marched from Rueda, and the next day we took up our ground near the village of Castrejon, with the 4th Division, General Pack's brigade, and some cavalry. After marching and counter-marching his army for a day or two, with a view of

[4] This river is called the Duero in Spain and the Douro in Portugal. The allied army spent so much time in its vicinity during various campaigns, the troops gave Wellington the nickname 'Old Douro' (He was also Baron Douro, having been given that title after Talavera when he was elevated directly to the higher Viscountcy).
[5] Kincaid, 1981: 76.
[6] Général Jean Pierre François Bonet (1768-1857).

deceiving Lord Wellington, Marmont passed the Douro at Tordesillas, on the night of the 17th, with the whole or greater part of his army, and on the morning of the 18th bore straight down on the troops at Castrejon. A furious cannonade soon commenced; and as the country was quite open, and every way favourable for cavalry, the infantry were ordered to form close columns or squares of battalions: in this manner we remained stationary for a length of time, under a heavy fire of artillery, whilst the cavalry, and some companies which had been thrown out in front, were engaged in a sharp skirmish."

John Kincaid was with one of those companies thrown out in front: 'I was sent on piquet on the evening of the 17th, to watch a portion of the plain before us; and, soon after sunrise on the following morning, a cannonade commenced behind a hill to my right; and though the combatants were not visible it was evident that they were not dealing in blank cartridge as mine happened to be the pitching post of all the enemy's round shot. While I was attentively watching its progress, there arose all at once, behind the rising ground to my left, a yell of the most terrific import; and, convinced that it would give instantaneous birth to as hideous a body, it made me look with an eye of lightning at the ground around me; and, seeing a broad deep ditch within a hundred yards, I lost not a moment in placing it between my piquet and the extraordinary sound. I had scarcely effected the movement when Lord Wellington, with his staff and a cloud of French and English dragoons and horse artillery intermixed, came over the hill at full cry and all hammering at each others' heads in one confused mass over the very ground I had that instant quitted. It appeared that his Lordship had gone there to reconnoitre, covered by two guns and two squadrons of cavalry, who by some accident were surprised and charged by a superior body of the enemy, and sent tumbling in upon us in the manner described. A piquet of the forty-third had formed on our right and we were obliged to remain passive spectators of such an extraordinary scene going on within a few yards of us as we could not fire without an equal chance of shooting some of our own side. Lord Wellington and his staff, with the two guns, took shelter, for the moment, behind us, while the cavalry went sweeping along our front, where, I suppose, they picked up some reinforcement, for they returned, almost instantly, in the same confused mass; but the French were now the flyers; and I must do them the justice to say that they got off in a manner highly creditable to themselves. I saw one in particular defending himself against two of ours; and he would have made his escape from both but an officer of our dragoons came down the hill and took him in flank, at full speed, sending man and horse rolling headlong on the plain.

I was highly interested, all this time, in observing the distinguished characters which this unlooked-for *turn-up* had assembled around us. Marshal Beresford and the greater part of the staff remained with their swords drawn, and the Duke[7] himself did not look more than half-pleased, while he silently despatched some of them with orders. General Alten and

[7] At this time Wellington was an Earl.

his huge German orderly dragoon, with their swords drawn, cursed the whole time to a very large amount; but as it was in German I had not the full benefit of it. He had an opposition swearer in Captain Jenkinson of the artillery, who commanded the two guns, and whose oaths were chiefly aimed at himself for his folly, as far as I could understand, in putting so much confidence in his covering party, that he had not thought it necessary to unfix the catch which horse-artillerymen, I believe, had to prevent their swords quitting the scabbards when they are not wanted, and which, on this occasion, prevented their jumping forth when they were so unexpectedly called for.[8]'

Despite his close shave Wellington had learned what he needed to know. In the face of the forceful French advance over a flat terrain with little cover, ideal for the French cavalry, he pulled his army back to the south-west, towards Salamanca.

Leach: "Lord Wellington now ordered the infantry to retire in columns, covered by the cavalry and horse artillery. No man who was present can possibly have forgotten that magnificent sight, nor the steadiness and extreme regularity with which the columns fell back over this extensive plain, followed and assailed in flanks and rear by overwhelming numbers of cavalry and artillery.

During this retreat we were exposed to a constant cannonade, and threatened by heavy masses of infantry, ready to close with us if our pace was relaxed for a minute. Nor was the steadiness and gallantry displayed by the cavalry and horse-artillery less worthy of admiration. A halt of two or three minutes would have enabled the French infantry to reach us. Thus we marched some miles over a country as level as a chess-board, in columns of battalions, ready to engage the French infantry if they should overtake us, and equally so to receive their cavalry, in square or close column, if they attempted to charge. The beautiful series of evolutions of the two armies on this day, and on the three following, were such as a man may never witness again if he lives for ages[9].

The heat was suffocating, and there being no water on this sun-burnt plain, numbers of men dropped on the road, and, of course, fell into the hands of the enemy, as we could not stop to bring them along. Many soldiers, particularly of the Portuguese, died on the road, from the heat and want of water. At length we arrived at the edge of this elevated plain, which looks down on the Guarena, a small river in the hot months; and when we reached it, man and horse made a rush to quench their thirst. I have never quite forgiven our pursuers for pounding us with round shot from the heights above, and not allowing us time to swallow a mouthful of the lukewarm, muddy beverage, without the accompaniment of a nine-pound shot."

The retreating forces had marched approximately 12 km with the Light Division as usual bringing up the rear of the infantry. They took up a defensive position on some high ground just across the Guareña and after an abortive French attack on the position's flank, the rest of the day was

[8] Kincaid, 1981: 77-79. We have removed some of Kincaid's commas.
[9] Kincaid (1981: 79) referred to this as, "the most beautiful military spectacle imaginable."

relatively quiet. The next day the two armies faced each other until the afternoon when the French began to move upstream towards Salamanca in an attempt to sever the allies' supply route from Portugal. This manoeuvre continued on the following day and Wellington kept his whole force in motion to maintain his communications. The two armies again marched side by side, and the allies crossed the River Tormes just above Salamanca on the evening of the 21st of July during one of the most violent thunder storms anyone could remember. The veterans of the Peninsula noticed the battles of their Commander-in-Chief were often preceded by violent storms and torrential downpours, and came to call this 'Wellington weather.' This was to be such a storm.

The Battle of Salamanca

On the 22nd the French army of 50,000 men was about 8 km south-east of Salamanca and the allies were holding a north-south line between the French and the city, facing east. The Light Division was at the far left of the allied position, on the south bank of the Tormes, accompanied by the 1st Division. Throughout the morning Marmont manoeuvred trying to gain a strategic advantage, but unknown to him Wellington was also moving his forces into an east-west alignment, hidden on the reverse slopes of his position, out of the French line of sight. Only the Light Division and the 1st Division had been left in their original placement. At mid-day Marmont mistook the dust raised by allied carts leaving the field for a general withdrawal and moved his army rapidly westward to place it between the allies and their communications with Ciudad Rodrigo. Little did he realise he was actually marching his forces along the allies' front line one division at a time, like ducks in a shooting gallery. Wellington was not a General to abuse such an opportunity. He brought the 3rd Division from a position on the left, near the Light Division, across the rear of his line and launched it over the rise on the right wing to take the leading French division broadside. As the shocked French survivors fell back on the second French division, creating confusion, Wellington launched his next division against them, and so on down the French line. Marmont, caught in shell-fire, was badly wounded and replaced by Bonet, who shortly afterwards fell wounded himself. French command now devolved to the already wounded General Clausel[10], who rose to the occasion, rallied the French, and counter-attacked with considerable success, penetrating the allied centre. But Wellington brought in his reserves, including the 1st Division from the left wing, pushed forward, and as dusk fell the French were broken and thrown in full retreat across the river, saved by the fading light. Wellington wrote in one of his dispatches, "I never saw an army receive such a beating.[11]" Even the French General Foy[12], whose force covered the retreat, wrote in his diary, 'This battle is the most cleverly fought, the largest in scale, the most important in results, of any that the British have won in recent times... The catastrophe of the Spanish War has come[13]'.

[10] Général Bertrand Clausel (1772-1842). He was later promoted to Marshal and made a Count. A supporter of Napoleon in 1815, he was exiled in the USA from 1815-1820, then returned to France and took up a political career, interrupted by military command in Algeria where he was Governor General from 1835-1836.

[11] Letter: Wellington to Lieutenant-General Sir Thomas Graham KB, 25th July 1812 (*Wellington's Despatches*).

[12] Général Maximilien Sebastien Foy (1775-1825). Made a Baron in 1810 and later a Count. Wrote a French history of the Peninsula War.

[13] Oman, 1986: 58 [Oman's 'English' has been changed here to 'British'. Almost certainly Foy wrote 'Anglais' but the French, like the Americans, tend to use 'English' ('Anglais') as a synonym of 'British'. Many of the British troops were not English. Foy was apparently ignoring the Portuguese and Spanish troops].

The French had lost 14,000 men to the allies' 5000. The Light Division's first action came after dark when they were sent forward to attack the French right wing, which had been their mirror all day, but the French were already withdrawing and there was only a brief exchange of light arms fire.

After the Battle

The Light Division, the 1st Division and a detachment of cavalry were sent after the French rearguard on the morning of the 23rd. The French, still led by Clausel, moved rapidly to the east then turned north back over the open plains by which the armies had reached Salamanca. For days there was little contact between their rear-guard and their pursuers. The Light Division crossed the Duero on the 30th of July and bivouacked on the northern bank near Valladolid.

Leach: 'In every town and village through which we marched, from the Tormes to the Douro, Marmont's death was reported as certain. He positively died at Peneranda, so he did also at Arevalo; and he was buried in half a dozen different towns[14]...

We halted on the Douro about twenty-four hours, which was a great god-send, as, from the 16th of July to the evening of the 30th, the army had been constantly marching or fighting. A day's rest on the bank of a large river, where we could bathe and get our linen washed, was a luxury which we well knew how to appreciate and to make the most of.

Valladolid was soon filled with officers and soldiers, endeavouring to

purchase bread, wine, and other things—those at least in the army who could muster a few dollars, which were rare articles, there being seven months' pay now due to us. For my own part, I sold some silver spoons and a watch to raise the wind[15], considering a loaf of bread, some chocolate, and a few other things of the kind, far more necessary than plate[16], after the scanty allowance of provisions which we had been on for some weeks.'

The French continued their northward retreat to the fortified city of Burgos but Wellington, elevated to Marquess of Wellington[17] when news of the victory reached Britain, halted the chase at the Duero. He

[14] Marmont recovered long enough to die in 1852.
[15] 'to raise the wind' – to obtain the necessary funds.
[16] Silver-plated ware.
[17] 'Marquess' is the British peerage equivalent of the Continental 'Marquis'.

The Alcazar, Segovia.

Segovia.

left the 6th Division at the river to observe the French and marched the rest south-east towards Madrid, a city which the army was, as Jonathan put it, "on the tiptoe of impatience to behold."

"On the 8th of August we halted, after a long march, on the banks of the Eresma; and being only twelve miles from Segovia, which we thought could not be seen too soon, a small party of us stole away from camp on horseback, and did not relax our pace until we had reached that far-famed city." Kincaid, a Scot, thought Segovia "bears a strong resemblance to the old town of Edinburgh, built on a lofty ridge, that terminates in an abrupt summit, on which stands the fortified tower[18]" but Jonathan Leach was not surveying the geology, geognostically or otherwise:

"We met, on the promenade near the town, one of the most lovely women I ever beheld in any part of the world, attired in the most bewitching manner. Years have not erased from my memory her countless charms, which assertion may appear ridiculous and incredible, as we had not the felicity even of exchanging words with her. Her elegant but simple costume of black silk with slashed sleeves, and the numerous *et cetera* of the Castilian female dress, which are perfection itself, her beautiful figure, sparkling intelligent eyes, her small feet and ancles, her easy and graceful walk, and an infinity of female graces happily blended, formed a whole which I have never seen surpassed."

The following day, having scoured Segovia in vain for this vision of loveliness, the party of love-struck officers rejoined their men, now camped near the ancient palace of the kings of Spain, El Palazio del Rio Frio. Continuing their journey towards the capital, on the 11th they crossed the Sierra de Guadarrama and camped in the park of the Escorial, which prompted another rush of sightseeing.

"We soon mounted our horses, and went off, pell-mell, to the palace of the Escurial, which was a few miles from the camp, counting the moments until we reached it. This, like the Palazio del Rio Frio, had nothing left but

[18] Kincaid. 1981: 85. Presumably the 'fortified tower' is the Alcazar.

El Escorial.

the bare walls; the French having carried away all the paintings and valuables. The building is very extensive, but I was altogether much disappointed. Some paintings on the walls, intended to represent battles between the Moors and Spaniards, were much defaced. The only thing which I remember worth seeing, was the sepulchre in which the royal family of Spain are interred. The whole of the dome, as well as the entrance to it, is composed of the finest marble, highly ornamented with gold. The gardens, which are extensive and full of fountains, were entirely neglected, and overgrown with weeds."

John Kincaid was even less impressed. "I had, from childhood upwards, considered this palace as the eighth wonder of the world, and was, therefore, proportionately disappointed at finding it a huge, gloomy, unmeaning pile of building, looking somewhat less interesting than the wild craggy mountain opposite, and without containing a single room large enough to flog a cat in. The only apartment that I saw worth looking at was the one in which their dead kings live!"

Madrid

The officers approached Madrid with some apprehension on the 12th of August. Joseph Bonaparte and most of the garrison had left the previous month, but the capital had known comparative peace for four years and had been the seat of the Spanish court. There was concern the allies would be seen as intruders. Jonathan discovered to his relief they had no cause to be worried.

"It would be labour in vain to attempt to describe the enthusiasm and delight evinced by all classes of the inhabitants on our arrival. Old and

Entering Madrid.

young, men, women, and children, in tens of thousands, filled the streets, embracing the officers and soldiers, kissing the colours of the regiments[18], and the happy ensigns who carried them. They cried, laughed, sung, and danced with joy, so that it was impossible to doubt their sincerity. Few of us were ever so caressed before, and most undoubtedly never will be again."

The Light Division rested at Madrid for two and a half months, "basking" as Kincaid put it, "in the sunshine of beauty, harmony, and peace." During this time the Division was reorganised again to account for its losses. Two companies, N[os] 3 and 4, were disbanded and their men distributed to others. Ned Costello was transferred to Jonathan's N° 2 Company[19].

Wellington was attending to other general housekeeping matters too. For some time he had been harassed by government bureaucrats in London who had clearly lost sight of who was supposed to be supporting whom. On the 12th of August he sent them a characteristically dry reminder:

'Gentlemen: Whilst marching from Portugal to a position which commands the approach to Madrid and the French forces, my officers have been diligently complying with your request which has been sent by H.M. ship from London to Lisbon and thence by despatch to our headquarters. We have enumerated our saddles, bridles, tents, and tent poles, and all manner of sundry items for which His Majesty's Government holds me accountable. I have despatched reports on the character, wit, and spleen of every officer. Each item and every farthing has been accounted for, with two regrettable exceptions for which I beg your indulgence. Unfortunately, the sum of one shilling and ninepence remains unaccounted for in one infantry battalion's petty cash and there has been a hideous confusion as to the number of jars of raspberry jam issued to one cavalry regiment during a sandstorm in western Spain. This reprehensible carelessness may be related to the pressure of circumstances since we are at war with France, a fact

[18] 'Colours' – the flag, and rallying point in battle, of each regiment, embroidered with its battle honours.
[19] Hathaway, 1997: 196-7.

189

Street of San Bernado, Madrid.

which may come as a bit of a surprise to you gentlemen in Whitehall. This brings me to my present purpose, which is to request elucidation of my instructions from His Majesty's Government, so that I may better understand why I am dragging an army over these barren plains. I construe that perforce it must be one of the alternative duties given below. I shall pursue either one with the best of my ability but I cannot do both. 1. To train an army of uniformed British clerks in Spain for the benefit of the accountants and copy-boys in London, or perchance, 2. To see to it that the forces of Napoleon are driven out of Spain.

Your most obedient Servant
Wellington[20]'

With the army reorganised and no French forces in the immediate vicinity the Light Division could devote themselves to rest and relaxation. Kincaid looked back on the time spent around Madrid as the most pleasing period of his military life, marred only by an acute shortage of cash. The other officers had to follow Jonathan's example and sell anything of value to raise the funds for their everyday means. There were, however, public entertainments, although not to everyone's taste.

Jonathan: "On the 31st of August a grand bull-fight was given, in a large amphitheatre called the Plaza de Toro, which is capable of containing many thousand spectators. Tickets of admission were sent to all the regiments, and in we went, all curiosity, to witness this barbarous and ancient national amusement. The countless numbers of Spanish females, of all ages, belonging to the higher class of society, dressed as if for a grand ball, and taking intense interest in this cruel amusement, did certainly puzzle us Englishmen not a little, and was a convincing proof of what early habit will effect. If an

[20] Quoted in Hamilton-Williams, 1994: 129-130. (Also widely displayed on the world wide web). A farthing was a quarter of a penny, with 960 farthings in one pound sterling.

Burgos.

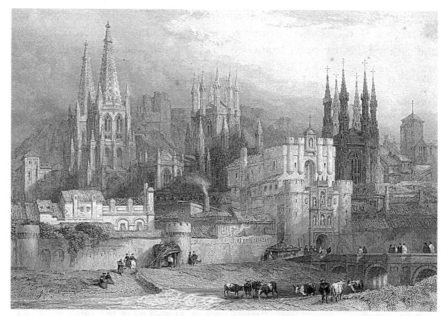

opinion of the general character of Spanish females is to be formed from seeing them once only, and that at a bull-fight, one would naturally conclude them to be utterly devoid of feeling, and a most inhuman set of devils in the garb of angels. But when it is remembered, that from their earliest infancy they are taught to look forward to a bull-fight as the first, the greatest, and most delightful of all amusements, in the same manner as our young misses in England contemplate going to a masked ball or an opera, our wonder will cease in a great measure. I should, nevertheless, be much better satisfied, on account of the admiration which I feel for the fascinating Castilians, if they abhorred the diabolical process of torturing the noble animal to death, and turned from it with the same disgust as the females of other parts of Europe naturally would do."

In September Wellington left Madrid with most of his army and marched to besiege Burgos, leaving only the 3rd, 4th and Light Divisions, with some cavalry, around the capital. The French too were active. In the south of Spain, Soult had been besieging Cadiz[21], but when he heard of Marmont's defeat at Salamanca and the allies' occupation of Madrid he abandoned the siege and headed across the width of Spain towards Valencia. In the north Clausel was reorganising and reinforcing his broken army. By October he was ready and pushed the allied corps of observation back over the Duero as far as Arévalo, half way between Valladolid and Madrid. By late October Soult had rendezvoused at Valencia with the armies of Joseph Bonaparte, Suchet[22] and Decaen and had marched this united force to the River Tagus just south of Madrid. Although this had the benefit of removing French armies of occupation from southern Spain for the first time in many years, the arrival of these now overwhelming forces on the Light Division's doorstep

[21] Cadiz had been under siege at this time for more than 2½ years.
[22] Maréchal Louis Gabriel Suchet, Duc d'Albufera (1770-1826).

was not something they relished. It was time to move. Wellington abandoned the siege at Burgos (which he had never viewed with particular optimism) and ordered the divisions around Madrid to rejoin the army to the north-west. The inhabitants of the capital, who had welcomed their liberators so effusively just ten weeks earlier, were less than happy to see them leave. Jonathan went to say goodbye to his new acquaintances:

'I went into the capital to take a last farewell of it, and of my Spanish friends. There was a gloom and sadness depicted on the countenances of all the inhabitants, and a death-like silence in the streets, which, when contrasted with the unfeigned joy evinced on our entry three months before, was very disheartening...

The moment of our departure had now arrived: the rear-guard of cavalry was gradually falling back towards the heights; and, in a dark, gloomy afternoon, on the 31st of October, we bade farewell to that city, in which I passed some of the happiest days of my life, and which I shall ever look back on with mixed sensations of pleasure and regret. The rains of winter had already commenced; the prospect of a long and dreary retreat, of wet camps and bivouacs, and the long train of privations and vicissitudes which winter campaigning more especially brings with it, stared us in the face.'

After a week of marching, with no sign of the French, the Light Division joined the troops from Burgos, and seven days later they had crossed the Tormes and were on the outskirts of Salamanca, virtually on the same ground on which they had won such a crushing victory four months earlier. The French had now arrived in force. Clausel had united with Soult and their combined army of 100,000 manoeuvred in front of the allied lines.

Retreat

Vastly outnumbered, and with Soult trying to position the French army between the allies and Ciudad Rodrigo, Wellington had no choice but to head west, yet again, for the Águeda and the border with Portugal. For days the army retreated across wooded country in torrential autumn rains; the Light Division as usual bringing up the rear, "ploughing through mud and water to the knees, from before break of day until long after dark, and over as bad roads as are to be found in Christendom.[23]" By a breakdown in communication the commissary waggons had gone on ahead and the army was without food. Conditions quickly deteriorated.

Simmons[24]: 'Numbers of men were left behind, and several died. The road was covered with carcasses of all descriptions, and at every deep slough we found horses, mules, donkeys, and bullocks mingled together, some dead, others dying, all laden with baggage. It is a most disagreeable sight to a soldier to see everything going to rack and ruin without being able to prevent it[25]...

The Light Division, being the rear-guard upon this retreat, were the first under arms in the morning, and the last in bivouac at night, which was generally some time after dark. Our poor fellows lit fires, and then, being

23 Jonathan Leach.
24 An eye-witness account of the dire conditions from a member of the 94th Regt (Scotch Brigade) can be found in Oman (1986: 265-267).
25 Simmons' journal for the 17th November 1812 (Verner, 1986: 257).

nearly starved, went about in search of something to eat. Some lean and half-starved bullocks were here and there lying dead in the mud in the deep parts of the road, yoked to carts laden with baggage. From these, the hungry soldiers sliced off a delightful repast, which was grilled, half-smoked, and half-roasted, and as tough as a shoe sole, but severe hardship and hunger made this an agreeable substitute for better food. Other soldiers would be groping about upon their hands and knees under a bastard description of oak and cork trees for acorns. These trees yield them in abundance, and at this time of year they are to be found in plenty. Although hard and bitter, still such food was found better than none. The country people send their pigs, marked, into the woods to fatten. They are half wild. Some soldiers could not resist shooting them, which caused Lord Wellington to punish with death two men to deter others from such a breach of military discipline.[26]'

(It was always abhorrent to Wellington to have his troops plundering from local inhabitants. He well knew that his army relied on the goodwill of the civilian population. On one occasion, after issuing a string of orders against plundering and failing to achieve the desired result, he hanged 15 culprits in one day. This sent a clear signal to the soldiers, but some of the women accompanying the regiments proved to be worse miscreants than the men, believing they were immune from military discipline. To prove how misguided they were he had more than 12 of them flogged – three dozen lashes each[27]).

On the 17th of November the cavalry of the French advance-guard caught up with the Light Division in open forest. By afternoon Soult had arrived with his leading infantry and artillery units.

Leach: "The enemy had by this time brought forward a large force of infantry and artillery so close to the heels of the Light Division, as enabled them to attack us at the moment we were passing the Huebra, by a deep ford near San Munos. They cannonaded us heavily at this unfavourable moment[28], and at the same instant assailed us with a swarm of light troops, which some companies of ours and of the 52d were thrown out to oppose. No troops at a field-day in England ever manœuvered, or marched with greater steadiness and regularity, than did the Light Division in its retreat from the heights to the river and across it, although exposed to a heavy fire of round shot, which constantly plunged into the columns, and was kept up long after we had reached the opposite bank."

Jonathan's company was one of those held back to slow the French advance while the rest of the Division negotiated the crossing, difficult to master at the best of times with the river chest-high and flowing fast – and this was not the best of times. On the enemy's side of the river Wellington had positioned himself with the covering companies, and as they finally fell back to the ford under artillery and small-arms fire he was passed by Ned Costello:

[26] Simmons' journal for 16th November 1812 (Verner, 1986: 256).
[27] Scott, 1816: 257. These events may not have occurred on this retreat, and did not occur together.
[28] Simmons said the guns "played upon us handsomely, which was fun for them, but death to us." (Verner, 1986: 257).

"Our illustrious chief, who was generally to be found where danger was most apparent, saw us come puffing and blowing up to our column and called out to us in a cheering voice: "Be cool, my lads; don't be in a hurry!" But, in faith, with all possible respect for his Lordship, we were in no greater haste than the occasion demanded, as the French were upon us. We were obliged to dash down the sides of the hill, where we halted for a moment – and his Lordship also – and then ford a river. The stream was much swollen by the late rains, and while we were crossing, a round-shot from the enemy, who were now peppering away at us, took off the head of Sergeant Fotheringham of our battalion, and smashed the thigh of another man. On gaining the other side of the stream we turned to give a salute in return, but owing to the wet, our rifles were unserviceable.[29]"

The French did not pass the river that night. In fact the push to catch the allies, and the inhospitable weather and woods, had exhausted the pursuers as much as the pursued. They gave up their prey and withdrew to Salamanca for the winter. This was good news for the allies, but the road, the frost, and the fact that most of the men's uniforms were in rags and they no longer had serviceable shoes – walking barefoot in the deep, icy, mud – were problems enough. Jonathan wrote in his journal on the 18th, after a day when his only sustenance was some acorns and a glass of rum, "The only enemies we had to encounter were hunger, fatigue, rain, sleet and snow.[30]" There was great relief when the army reached Ciudad Rodrigo the following day.

Discipline

Wellington had not been impressed by the conduct of his men or their officers during this retreat. Lack of discipline was widespread and on one occasion he could not even find his army, his Generals having changed the route of march without informing him[31]. Shortly after arriving at Ciudad Rodrigo he expressed his anger in a long and scolding letter addressed to the Colonels commanding regiments[32]. Amongst other complaints he noted:

"I must draw your attention in a very particular manner to the state of discipline of the troops. The discipline of every army, after a long and   active campaign, becomes, in some degree, relaxed, and requires the utmost attention on the part of the general and other officers to bring it back to the state in which it ought to be for service; but, I am concerned to have to observe that the army under my command has fallen off in this respect in the late campaign to a greater degree than any army with which I have ever served, or of which I have ever read. Yet this army has met with no disasters, it has suffered no privations which but trifling attention on the part of the officers could have prevented, and for which there existed no reason whatever in the nature of the service; nor has it suffered any hardships, excepting those resulting from the necessity of being exposed to the inclemencies of the weather at a moment when they were most severe.

[29] Hathaway, 1997: 204.
[30] Verner, 1919: 429.
[31] Wilson (1927) 1: 78. When asked what he had said to his Generals afterwards Wellington replied, "Oh, by God, it was too serious to say anything."
[32] Letter dated 28th November 1812 and quoted in Tucker (1846: 254-257).

It must be obvious, however, to every officer, that from the moment the troops commenced their retreat from the neighbourhood of Burgos, on the one hand, and from Madrid on the other, the officers lost all command over their men.

Irregularities and outrages of all descriptions were committed with impunity, and losses have been sustained which ought never to have occurred. Yet the necessity for retreat existing, none was ever undertaken in which the troops made such short marches; none in which they made such long and repeated halts, and on which the retreating armies were so little pressed on their rear by the enemy. We must look, therefore, for the existing evils, and for the situation in which we now find the army, to some causes beside those resulting from the operations in which we have been engaged. I have no hesitation in attributing these evils to the habitual inattention of the officers of regiments to their duty as prescribed by the standing regulations of the service, and by the orders of this army. I am far from questioning the zeal, still less the gallantry and spirit of the officers of the army; and I am quite certain that as their minds can be convinced of the necessity of minute and constant attention, to understand, recollect, and carry into execution the orders which have been issued for the performance of their duty (and the strict performance of duty is necessary to enable the army to serve the country as it ought to be served), they will in future give their attention to these points."

Even the domestic arrangements of the rank and file came in for scathing criticism: "In regard to the food of the soldiers, I have frequently observed and lamented in the late campaign, the facility and celerity with which the French soldiers cooked, in comparison to those of our army. The cause of this disadvantage is the same as that of every other description – the want of attention of the officers to the orders of the army, and to the conduct of their men, and their consequent want of authority over their conduct. Certain men of each company should be appointed to cut and bring in wood, others to fetch water, and others to get the meat, &c., to be cooked, and it would soon be found, if this practice were daily enforced, and a particular hour for seeing the dinners, and for the men dining, named as it ought to be, equally as for the parade, that cooking would no longer require the inconvenient length of time it has lately been found to take, and that the soldiers would not be exposed to the privation of their food at the moment at which the army may be engaged in operations with the enemy."

That such criticism of many units was justified is without question. Lack of vigilance by the officers led to the ordered columns of marching men dissolving into a vague red cloud drifting over the countryside. The French found it easy to pounce on isolated groups of stragglers and were capturing several hundred men every day. Three thousand fell into French hands during the retreat[33]. The commissaries failed to distribute bread effectively, although they had it, and disorder in setting up bivouacs left

[33] Bryant, 1975: 44.

men uncomfortable and disaffected. One of the officers wrote afterwards[34]: 'As for fuel for cooking, the men availed themselves of the absolute want of it as an excuse for going in search of it, in the course of which they either fell into the hands of the enemy, or committed the most frightful outrages on the farmers and peasantry... More prisoners were lost in the bivouac, than in the actual engagement with the enemy. The bivouac was hailed by the ill-disposed as the means of escape, plunder, and desertion. The men, perhaps, would disappear for some days, during which they were employed in marauding; they would then return under the pretence of having escaped from the enemy; by whom they stated themselves to have been taken prisoners, on the day they had been missed. The losses of the army in these circumstances became truly alarming.'

However valid Wellington's censure was for the army as a whole, his outburst did not endear him to the officers of the Light Division. "Soon after the army was put into winter quarters," writes Jonathan, "the Commander-in-Chief sent a circular letter to the officers commanding regiments, expressing his highest disapprobation of the conduct of the army at large during the late retreat, which we found as difficult to digest as the acorns in the woods of San Munos. That many regiments were guilty of great irregularities, and did fall to pieces and lose their discipline during this disastrous retreat, was too true; but it was no less so, that many others, which I could name, maintained their order, good spirit, and discipline, throughout the retreat, and left no men behind who were not either too badly wounded on the 17th of November, at San Munos, to be brought on, or were actually expiring from sickness, excessive fatigue, cold, wet, and want of food. The charge was, therefore, thought by many people *too sweeping*."

Kincaid agreed and noted, 'Up to this period Lord Wellington had been adored by the army, in consideration of his brilliant achievements, and for his noble and manly bearing in all things... but as his censure, on this occasion, was not strictly confined to the guilty, it afforded a handle to disappointed persons, and excited a feeling against him, on the part of individuals, which has probably never since been obliterated.

It began by telling us that we had suffered no privations; and, though this was hard to be digested on an empty stomach, yet, taking it in its more liberal meaning, that our privations were not of an extent to justify any irregularities, which I readily admit; still, as many regiments were not guilty of any irregularities, it is not to be wondered if such should have felt, at first, a little sulky to find, in the general reproof, that no loop-hole whatever had been left for them to creep through; for, I believe I am justified in saying that neither our own, nor the two gallant corps associated with us, had a single man absent that we could not satisfactorily account for. But it touched us still more tenderly in not excepting us from his general charge of inexpertness in camp arrangements; for, it was our belief, and in which

[34] Unidentified officer quoted in Tucker (1846: 249-50)

we were in some measure borne out by circumstances, that, had he placed us, at the same moment, in the same field, with an equal number of the best troops in France, that he would not only have seen our fires as quickly lit, but every Frenchman roasting on them to the bargain...

That not only censure, but condign punishment was merited, in many instances, is certain; and, had his lordship dismissed some officers from the service, and caused some of the disorderly soldiers to be shot, it would not only have been an act of justice, but, probably, a necessary example. Had he hanged every commissary, too, who failed to issue the regular rations to the troops dependent on him, unless they proved that they were starved themselves, it would only have been a just sacrifice to the offended stomachs of many thousands of gallant fellows.

In our brigade, I can safely say, that the order in question excited 'more of sorrow than of anger'; we thought that, had it been *particular*, it would have been just; but, as it was *general*, that it was inconsiderate; and we, therefore, regretted that he who had been, and still was, the god of our idolatry, should thereby have laid himself open to the attacks of the ill-natured.'

The retreat itself was seen as a mixed blessing by the troops. They had suffered great hardships and had seen all their gains of territory (and face) neutralised, however in a letter written home to England Guards officer James Stanhope[35] was able to put a positive complexion on their current circumstances, although he was less enthusiastic about the position in which they had left their Spanish allies:

"I think this retreat will give us great advantage next spring. We shall be able to rest the army as long as Lord W. likes, whereas in advance we should have been 'a la disposicion' of the Marshals. We shall be able to reclothe and rediscipline the army, we shall be able to form magazines for our future operations. Had we remained forward the whole of our transport would have been employed in feeding us as from hand to mouth and this important operation without which no army can advance in the spring would have been impossible. Against this we have our great disadvantage that for the third time we have abandoned the Spaniards and we shall never be considered otherwise than as birds of passage and we cannot expect Vivas from the heart whatever the tongue may utter. It really makes one's heart bleed to think of the poor people of Madrid and Salamanca whom we have left to be tenfold worse plundered and more oppressed in proportion to their attachment to us. I cannot blame the Spaniard for being weary of the war, when sacrifices are so recompensed, and when zeal and kindness so repaid, it must be more than human constancy that does not pray for a cessation of such friendship. I well know that the retreat was necessary and though it justifies our conduct, it cannot remove one's feelings for the poor wretches who are paying for their attachment to us.[36]"

35 The Honourable James Hamilton Stanhope (1788-1825). Youngest son of the 3rd Earl of Stanhope. Officer in the 1st Foot Guards. Had arrived in Spain while the army was besieging Burgos and had been Aide-de-Camp to Sir Edward Paget (1775-1849) until Paget's capture by the French at San Muñoz during the retreat (Smith, 1999: 84-85). Stanhope's family was known to Sir Joseph Banks and in his Will Banks left his Lincolnshire estates first to his wife Dorothea for life then to James Hamilton Stanhope and Sir Henry Hawley *Bt* (1745-1826). Stanhope's half-sister was the Near-Eastern traveller Lady Hester Lucy Stanhope (1776-1839), niece of William Pitt the Prime Minister, whose sister Hester was her mother and the 3rd Earl's first wife.

36 Letter: Stanhope (at Mongualde) to Richard Heber (1774-1833, book collector), 10th December 1812 (Cholmondeley, 1950: 250-251).

Winter sports

For the winter the 1/95th was quartered in the village of La Alameda de Gardón, on the Spanish side of the frontier. Here the Division was re-equipped with new shoes and uniforms (long overdue, as Costello noted green had become the least conspicuous colour in the regiment) and the officers turned easily to their usual winter pursuits of dancing, hare-coursing, shooting (a sport which this year was shared by the wolves which scavenged in the villages, and by the vultures drawn to the carcasses of pack-animals left by the retreat), organising races, and walking. Wading up to the waist in the winter waters in the hope of bagging an unsuspecting duck was also an opportunity not to be missed and, needless to say, Jonathan was an enthusiastic participant. A dining club was organised and officers walked to Espeja, 8 km away, to dine with the 3rd battalion, and would think nothing of walking 30 km or more for a good dinner[37].

Eager in the promotion of culture they also commandeered, with the approval of the inhabitants, a disused chapel in nearby Gallegos de Argañán as an amateur theatre, although this sacrilege earned them damnation from the pulpit of the local bishop at Ciudad Rodrigo.

Jonathan: "The Light Division established a theatre during the winter at Gallegos, which might have vied with half the provincial ones in England, if we could but have procured female performers. Lord Wellington and his staff rode over from headquarters one dark night, (twelve miles through execrable roads,) to witness our performance. It is impossible to imagine any thing more truly ludicrous than to see *Lydia Languish* and *Julia* (which characters were performed by two young and good-looking men, dressed uncommonly well, and looking somewhat feminine on the stage,) drinking punch and smoking cigars behind the scenes, at a furious rate, between the acts[38].

There was good coursing and woodcock-shooting in the neighbourhood, which occupied much of our time and attention. Lord Wellington's fox-hounds often met within reach of our cantonments, but such was the miserable state of our horses, that the staff-men only could avail themselves of it[39]. We now, as on former occasions, assembled the village fair ones, and frequently danced half through the long winter nights; nor were our fair partners at all averse to hot punch between the boleros and fandangos. Our nights were spent in the utmost conviviality and harmony, in the old barn where we messed. Here we also perused the English newspapers, which sometimes reached us."

After a number of months spent in this manner, conviviality was tinged with more than a little monotony. George Simmons wrote to his father, "I am heartily tired of this idle life. We have been five months in snug winter quarters without seeing the face of a Frenchman – a thing which has never happened before.[40]" John Kincaid's company commander, Captain Charley Beckwith[41] (who had played the part of *Captain Absolute* during the recent

[37] Surtees, 1973: 187.

[38] Verner (1919: 441) reproduces the text of a theatre programme for a performance of Sheridan's *The Rivals*, performed on Thursday, 4th February 1813 at Gallegos. *Lydia Languish* was played by Lieutenant the Honourable Charles Gore of the 43rd Light Infantry [Charles Gore (1793-1869) Son of the Earl of Arran. Was Andrew Barnard's aide-de-camp at the Battle of Salamanca]; *Julia* was played by Lieutenant Lord Charles Spencer of the 95th. Jonathan Leach was not a player.

[39] Officers assigned to Staff duties (assisting commanding officers to pass orders from senior planners to individual regiments and battalions) were notorious among regimental officers for having the only well-fed horses in the army.

[40] Letter of 30th April 1813 from Alameda (Verner, 1986: 277).

[41] John Charles Beckwith (1772-1862). Nephew of Sidney Beckwith. Others call him 'Charlie' but he spelt it 'Charley' (see Smith, 1901, 2: 210-211).

theatricals), wrote to Major William Napier of the 43rd, recuperating in England from wounds received during the recent campaign:

"We have acted some plays since you left us with various success, we have got drunk with constant success, and I begin to think that the only thing one can be certain of in this life is that you will certainly get drunk if you will but drink enough.

Our mode of life is exactly the same as when you left us. I ride about all the morning in pursuit of nothing. Barnard smokes segars until the very atmosphere between the Coa and Agueda is impregnated with the 'herbiferous herb' as Dr Morgan says, and if you were here again you might draw legs and muscles and Thalia's and Melpomene's until your paint, your paper and your patience were exhausted.

The monotony of the scene is only varied by the reports of Monday which are all found to be lies on Tuesday morning. Sometimes 40,000 Frenchmen march out of the country, sometimes they march in; sometimes the Spaniards have 150,000 men, sometimes 50; sometimes we are to march to France, sometimes to England, sometimes we have plenty to eat and drink, and sometimes we have not. Excepting by this last circumstance, I am altogether unconcerned as to what does or does not occur, very few things give me pleasure, and very few pain.[42]"

1813

By April preparations were underway for the coming season's campaign. Officers were organising new pack-saddles for the baggage horses and mules, and a myriad other details. For the first time tents were issued for all ranks: one for all the officers of each company, and four for the rank and file (about 15-25 riflemen in each)[43]. These were carried by mules. To aid efficient messing the old iron cooking pots, formerly carried by the mules, were replaced by light tin pans that could be carried by the men (something Craufurd had suggested as long ago as 1809). The army's strength was boosted by the arrival of more than 5000 new troops from Britain. For the units already present, company strengths were restored from the reinforcements and by recruiting local Spaniards. These men were virtually press-ganged but quickly became competent and respected soldiers, albeit wantonly vengeful when they got their hands on individual Frenchmen. Jonathan's company received 16 such recruits[44].

With the arrival of so many new men the army was reorganised into eight divisions. The infantry of the Light Division were, as usual, formed as two brigades[45]. The First Brigade under Major-General Sir James Kempt[46] comprised the six companies of the 1/95th (573 men[47]), with the five companies of the 3/95th (347 men), the 1/43rd, and the 17th Portuguese Regiment of the Line. The Second Brigade under Major-General Vandeleur comprised six companies of the 2/95th (411 men), the 1/52nd, and the 1st and 3rd Portuguese Caçadores.

[42] Verner, 1919: 438.
[43] Surtees, 1975: 189. The tents arrived with official instructions to pitch them as far as possible out of sight of enemy reconnaissance, and not to put them in neat rows, to prevent an easy 'tent count' revealing overall troop numbers.
[44] Hathaway, 1997: 270.
[45] For the various changes in the composition of the two brigades during the war see Christopher Thomas Atkinson in Oman (1986: [343]-373).
[46] Major-General James Kempt (1764-1854). Knighted (GCB) 1815. Lieutenant-Governor of Portsmouth 1819. Governor of Nova Scotia 1820-1828. Governor-General of Canada 1828-1830. Privy Councillor 1830. Master General of the Ordnance 1834-1838. Promoted full General 1841.
[47] Battalion 'fighting strengths' as at 20th May 1813, from Verner (1919: 439).

About this time the army's cavalry was reinforced by the arrival from England of a Brigade of Hussars and detachments of horse-guards from the Household Cavalry: the Life Guards and the Royal Horse Guards Blues. Their appearance prompted Jonathan to make some caustic remarks in his journal about Wellington's army having fought five campaigns in the Peninsula while "these gentlemen have been campaigning in London, Brighton, Hampton Court and Weymouth.[48]" Fresh from a London winter he thought they looked, "as fair and beautiful as lilies, when contrasted with the sun-burnt visages and battered appointments of the cavalry regiments which had been many years in the country.[49]" For their part the Household Cavalry mistook the lean, olive-skinned, green-clad riflemen for a Portuguese or Spanish regiment.

As summer began, the army was restored, recovered and reinforced, morale was high and the men were eager to start. On the 21st of May they got their wish; they mobilised and headed again for Salamanca.

Leach: "On the 23d our column encamped, after a tolerably long march, on the left bank of the Huebra, near San Munos; and we found ourselves on the identical spot where we had passed so dreary and miserable a night on the previous 17th of November. What a contrast did our situation now offer! When last there, we had bivouacked without fires, in a deluge of rain and sleet, without provisions for man or horse – cold, wet, half-famished, and nearly in rags. Now, on the contrary, the weather, the country, and every face, looked smiling and gay. A beautiful May morning, the valley abounding with grass for our animals, plenty of provisions in our canteens, the horses and mules quite renovated by rest, men and officers refitted in all the requisites for this their sixth campaign, and having the cheering prospect before them of driving the imperial legions nearer to their own country. We halted on the 24th on the same ground; and having nothing better to do, I went with my subalterns to the Huebra, in which we caught a number of dace, which soon found their way into the frying-pan."

The allied advanced-guard crossed the Tormes on the 28th, the French having fallen back at their approach, and the garrison of Salamanca withdrew towards Toro, on the north bank of the Duero. The French had built considerable fortifications along the line of this river during the winter, but several allied outflanking manoeuvres obliged them to abandon this line almost without a shot being fired. For the new campaign the French commander was Marshal Jourdan[50] – Soult having been recalled, with 50,000 men, and posted to Germany in the wake of Napoleon's disastrous retreat from Moscow. Jourdan had been joined by the army of Joseph Bonaparte, who had abandoned Madrid fearing the allies would drive between his forces and those in the north. Together Jourdan and Bonaparte were now retreating before the allies towards Palencia, on the road north-east from the Duero. The allies followed, marching in the heat through a sea of wheat stubble, but by the time they reached Palencia the French had moved towards Burgos. The allies pressed on, now in heavy cooling rains.

[48] Verner, 1919: 434.
[49] *Rough Sketches.*
[50] Maréchal Jean-Baptiste Jourdan (1762-1833). Had been with Victor at Talavera in 1809 and from 1811 was Governor of Madrid. In 1813 he commanded the *Army of the Centre.*

River Ebro at Miranda

Just after dawn on the 13th of June the earth shuddered and an explosive thunder rolled over the plain towards the allies. The French had mined the castle at Burgos, still 10 km away, and were now in full retreat towards the River Ebro at Miranda. Wellington sent the 4th and Light Divisions and some cavalry to race across-country north of the road being taken by the French, to reach the Ebro at the same time, or before, the enemy. Two infantry divisions and a Spanish corps swung north to do the same, effectively destroying French prospects of drawing up a defensive position behind the river before the allies arrived. The cross-country march to the river, lasting several days, covered the same featureless plain the Division had been crossing since Salamanca. Jonathan thought it, "very ugly, dry scorched, brown, black-guard looking, woodless and waterless.[51]" but the astonishment that overwhelmed the weary troops when they finally reached the river is obvious in numerous accounts, including his:

'After traversing some leagues of the same uninteresting kind of country over which we had been moving for the last fortnight, a scene suddenly burst on our view, when we reached the head of a pass leading down to the Ebro, which it is impossible to forget as long as the powers of recollection remain... From the Tormes to the Ebro our route had lain over one of the most monotonous and uninteresting countries I ever beheld,— without wood, feature, verdure, streams of water, picturesque villages, or any one recommendation whatever to the admirer of fine scenery. Scarcely anything could be purchased as we drew near the Ebro, to help out the homely fare of ship-biscuit, rum, and lean ration beef, which was alive and merry in the morning, and consumed before night. What, then, was our excessive delight on suddenly and unexpectedly beholding an extensive valley at our feet, through which flowed the rapid Ebro; and that valley, as well as the country

[51] Noted in his journal (Verner, 1919: 452).

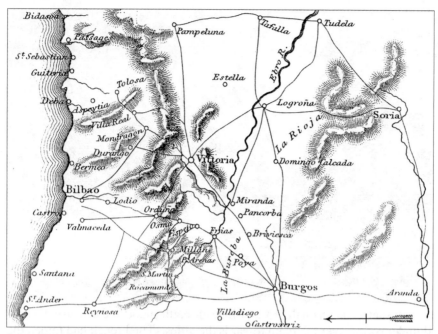

for miles beyond, teeming with fresh woods, fruit-trees, beautiful villages, gardens, and every thing which could delight the sight! For hundreds of miles before, the eyes had dwelt constantly on rocks, brown stubble, and more frequently on uncultivated wilds, where a hare would have been put to its shifts to find sustenance, or a jack-snipe to procure one day's rations. The lofty mountains which overhang the Ebro near the Puente Arena are clothed to the summit with the most luxuriant woods of oak, beech, and birch. Here, also, the box-tree grows to an incredible size. Great numbers of young eagles and vultures were sitting on the ledges of the precipices, whilst the old birds soared far above them.'

The other officers were equally captivated by this startling sensual overload. A spellbound Surtees thought it "appeared like enchantment when we first arrived within sight of it" and Kincaid declared it "one of the richest, loveliest, and most romantic spots" he had ever beheld. The divisions crossed the bridge and settled for the night, Kincaid revealing, contentedly, "I lay down that night in a cottage garden, with my head on a melon, and my eye on a cherry-tree, and resigned myself to a repose which did not require a long courtship.[52]"

Affair near San Millán

The following morning the Divisions marched a short distance along the north bank of the river then turned inland over extremely rugged terrain. This country would have been easily defended if the French had made plans, but Bonaparte and Jourdan had their eyes forward over the river on the force following them up the main road; the back door was wide open. After two

[52] Kincaid, 1981: 103.

days march over tracks too mountainous for the horse-artillery, the Division camped on the night of the 17th of June at Rio de Losa. The next day, Jonathan's company and half a troop of German Hussars formed the advance-guard on the march out of camp.

"As we were feeling our way through an intricate, thickly wooded country, we stumbled on a party of French Hussars, in front of the village of San Millan, with whom our German friends instantly had a brush, and took some prisoners. I know not where Lord Wellington's headquarters had been the night before, nor from whence he came; but in an instant he appeared on the spot, and directed the 1st and 3rd battalions of our corps, supported by the remainder of General Kempt's brigade, to attack a brigade of French infantry, which we had pretty nearly caught napping in San Millan."

The allied advance-guard had actually surprised two brigades of French infantry and a baggage train, passing through San Millán en route to join the main French force assembling around Vitoria, just to the east.

Simmons: "Our 1st and 3rd Battalions were ordered to march over some very steep hills covered with trees to attack them in the rear, at the same time sending two of our companies just to amuse them in the front, and with orders not to press upon the town until we fell upon the rear."

Jonathan led one of the companies holding the French from the front while Barnard took the rest of the 1/95th forward through steeply wooded ground to the left of the town. Coming over the rise, they found the French in column of route and attacked immediately "with loud cries and a bickering fire.[53]"

Leach: "We engaged them briskly in front, whilst some of our companies assailed both their flanks simultaneously. This drove them in confusion from the village with the loss of some baggage. On a rising ground behind it they formed a battalion in line, to cover the retreat of the remainder. A few minutes, however, sufficed to disperse it, and we pursued them closely for some miles, killing and wounding many, and making some prisoners."

Costello: "We found the French rear-guard in possession of a little town called San Millan, in front of which they had drawn themselves up, apparently with the intention of defending it. As we continued to advance in extended order, they changed their minds and turned tail. This day I noticed a novel system many of the retreating enemy adopted, which was to fire their muskets over their shoulders without turning round to face us. This was probably due to excessive fatigue."

Kincaid: "Our battalion dispersing among the brushwood, went down the hill upon them; and, with a destructive fire, broke through their line of march, supported by the rest of the brigade. Those that had passed made no attempt at a stand, but continued their flight, keeping up as good a fire as their circumstances would permit; while we kept hanging on their flank and rear, through a good rifle country, which enabled us to make considerable havoc among them."

[53] According to Major William Napier of the 43rd. Quoted from Napier's *History* by Verner (1919: 455).

Surtees, with the 3rd battalion, recalled a narrow escape in San Millán itself: "During the skirmish in the village, a French hussar chased one of our officers several times round one of the trees growing by the side of the road, and repeatedly cut at him with his sabre, and it is likely would have cut him down at last, had not the officer seen a rifle lying near, belonging to a man just killed; and luckily it was loaded when he picked it up. He waited for the Frenchman, and coolly shot him through the body, and instantly seized his horse as lawful prize; had the rifle missed fire he was gone.[52]"

Simmons: "We chased them through several villages, in which they usually made a stand, to the no small terror of the inhabitants, as it astonished peaceable people to have the balls whistling about their ears."

Barnard led the 1st and 3rd battalions forward with such speed, the remainder of the 1st Brigade saw little action. While Jonathan and his men pursued the leading French brigade throughout the afternoon, the Light Division's 2nd Brigade had captured the French baggage, abandoned as the second French brigade took to the mountains opposite, pursued by a Spanish corps. Throughout the day a cannonade could be heard in the distance where the 5th and 1st Divisions had also contacted the enemy and were driving them south to Espejo. Barnard's men were ordered to assist but by the time they arrived the French had pulled out and were retiring on their army so the Brigade returned to San Millán for the night. The Light Division had lost 300 men in the day's action; the French many more. After this skirmish French prisoners admitted they had had no idea the allies were already across the Ebro. Their rapid forward movement had outflanked the French forces and severed their communications with the Bay of Biscay ports, 50 km to the north. The only French supply routes were now the roads over the Pyrenees from France itself, just 100 km away. Meanwhile the allies' supplies could be brought into the Biscay ports by the Royal Navy, cutting sailing times by days and overland transport by hundreds of kilometres.

The Light Division moved only a short distance the following day, then waited on the 20th for the rest of the allied army to assemble in the surrounding valleys. From the heights in front of their camp they could see the fires of the enemy, drawn up across the River Zadorra in front of Vitoria. The French had stopped running.

[52] Surtees, 1973: 199.

— 12 —

Vittoria[1]

The Light, 3rd and 4th Divisions were the *élite* of my army,
but the Light had this peculiar perfection. No matter what
was the arduous service they were employed on, when I rode
up next day, I still found a *Division*. They never lost one
half the men other Divisions did.

Wellington[2]

At daylight on the 21st of June 1813, on a wet, misty morning, 80,000 allied soldiers threaded their way through the valleys to their positions west of the River Zadorra. On the far bank 70,000 Frenchmen occupied the ground in front of Vitoria. The Zadorra ran forwards along the French right flank then swept left to cover the whole of the front line. Their left flank rested on a mountainous ridge overlooking the field. Within this box the French centre lay on commanding heights in an uneven expanse of low hills, ridges, ditches, woods, enclosures, vineyards and cornfields, broken by the occasional hamlet, which history has termed 'the plain of Vitoria' – but a plain only by comparison with the surrounding highlands.

The Light Division had mobilised long before dawn and was already lying on a wooded rise near the river, facing the French centre just out of musket shot. With the mist lifting, Wellington and his staff arrived to reconnoitre the French positions. As they approached the river, here only 30 metres from bank to bank, the French saw their chance. They threw a body of riflemen across the bridge at Villodas to the right, and from the cover of a village and neighbouring elevated wood they opened fire on the allied officers.

The 3/95th and two companies of the 1st battalion, positioned near the threat, immediately pushed the enemy back across the river before any harm was done, but the French sharpshooters spread out among the rocks on the opposite bank and an exchange of fire began with the two battalions of riflemen, who had pushed forward to the river's edge.

[1] i.e. Gasteiz / Vitoria (As with many locations in the Peninsula War the spelling used by the British does not accord with modern names).
[2] Smith, 1999: 216.

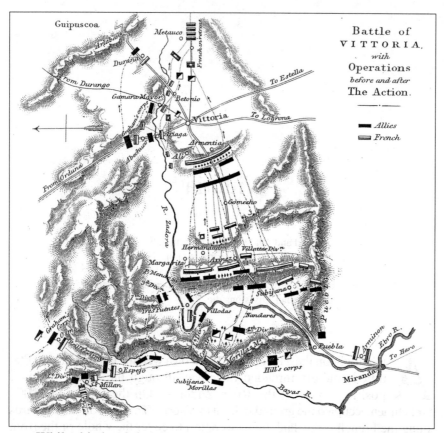

While this local drama was playing in the centre, on the right of the allied line Sir Rowland Hill attacked the French left with his corps, and the crackle of musketry rolled upriver to the Light Division's position. The Battle of Vittoria had begun.

Kincaid: "The affair with Sir Rowland Hill became gradually warmer, but ours had apparently no other object than to amuse those who were opposite to us for the moment; so that, for about two hours longer, it seemed as if there would be nothing but an affair of outposts. About twelve o'clock, however, we were moved rapidly to our left, followed by the rest of the division, till we came to an abrupt turn of the river where we found a bridge unoccupied by the enemy, which we immediately crossed, and took possession of what appeared to me to be an old field-work on the other side."[3]

Having learned from a local resident that one of the bridges to the Division's left was unguarded they had moved quickly under cover of the rough ground, crossed the river, and penetrated several hundred metres into the French lines. Hill's right wing, having forced the river, could be seen fighting their way along the ridge to the French left. Meanwhile the pounding of cannon away on the French right indicated Sir Thomas Graham[4] – whose

[3] Kincaid, 1981: 106-107.
[4] Lieutenant-General Sir Thomas Graham (1748-1843). He was created Baron Lynedoch in 1814 and promoted full General in 1821. James Stanhope was one of his ADCs at Vittoria (He had been an extra-ADC to Graham in 1810).

force had spent the last 24 hours circling behind the hills out of French sight – had launched his attack against the opposite flank.

To the Light Division's left a brigade of the 3rd Division could now be seen approaching another bridge as the French sent a swarm of infantry and cavalry, with artillery support, to oppose them. Seeing the danger, Barnard rushed the riflemen forward between the French cavalry and the river, and attacked the flank of the infantry, driving them back and letting the 3rd Division cross. The 95th now came under heavy artillery fire from the French heights and found the flying splinters from the rocks around them almost as wounding as the accompanying rain of musket balls. To add to their problems the riflemen had advanced so swiftly they were now at close quarters with the French skirmishers, and a British artillery battery on the allied bank mistook their dark uniforms for the enemy and also opened fire, killing several men. This only stopped when the 95th was joined by the more recognisable redcoats. Upstream the 7th Division and another brigade of the 3rd forded the river and also pushed onto French ground.

With his forces now across the river Wellington ordered the 3rd, 4th and Light Divisions to attack the low conical hill in the French centre which protected the village of Ariñez. As the allies moved to attack, the French sent most of the defenders to counter the advance of Hill's corps and, with two companies of the 1/95th leading – one Jonathan Leach's – the 3rd Division soon pushed the remainder off the summit. Pressing ahead down the reverse slope the two rifle companies ran into a blistering fire from a battalion of French infantry positioned behind a wall at the village below and were momentarily checked, losing two officers and thirty men[5]. The 3rd Division deployed into line and delivered a devastating volley which drove the French back, and the two rifle companies pushed into the village and evicted the survivors. In the market square Lieutenant John Fitzmaurice[6] and two riflemen captured the first French ordnance of the day, a howitzer. Two other artillery pieces were also taken in the forward rush. This success was short-lived however. The French counter-attacked with a thunderous cannonade and an infantry assault. Vastly outnumbered the two companies had no choice but to make a running retreat, but with the 3rd Division moving to support them they only retired about a hundred metres before turning and clearing the village again.

Pressing through Ariñez on the line of the main road beyond, it was clear the day was not going Jourdan's way[7]. Pushed in the centre, and by Hill on its left, the French army was being driven back on its reserves on a ridge in front of the city. Seeing the confusion, Wellington and his staff appeared at Jonathan Leach's position. "Send up a few of Ross's guns; here is work for them" Wellington called to one of his aides, then to the riflemen, "That's right my lads; keep up a good fire.[8]" Then he had gone, to urge on others elsewhere.

Kincaid: "The battle now became general along the whole line, and the cannonade was tremendous. At one period, we held one side of a wall,

[5] The casualty returns suggest most must only have been wounded.

[6] John G. Fitzmaurice (died 1865). Was one of the Lieutenants in Jonathan Leach's company in 1815. At that time his name was spelt 'Fitzmorriss' in the Company's manuscript roll (Public Record Office, Kew, London, Ref: W.O. 100/15B 201). Was probably already with Leach at Vitoria. Had been a Lieutenant since the 14th of January 1813.

[7] Technically Joseph Bonaparte was the French commander but the battle was probably fought by the more experienced Jourdan.

[8] Hathaway, 1997: 223.

near the village, while the French were on the other, so that any person who chose to put his head over from either side was sure of getting a sword or a bayonet up his nostrils.[9]"

In the rapid allied advance many wounded Frenchmen were falling into allied hands, not all of whom survived the experience.

Costello: "We had several Spaniards in our regiment and they were generally brave, but Blanco was one of the most skilful and daring skirmishers we had in the battalion[10]. He was always in front, and had been so in every affair since the advance from Portugal. It was a wonder how he managed to escape the enemy's shot, but his singular activity and intelligence frequently saved him. He had great courage, but it was sullied by a love of cruelty towards the French, whom he detested, and never named but with the most ferocious expressions. I believe his hatred of them was occasioned by the murder of his father and brother, who were peasants, by a French foraging party. On this day he gave many awful proofs of this feeling by mercilessly stabbing and mangling the wounded French he came up to. This massacre was stopped by a veteran of our regiment who, although suffering from a severe wound in the face, was so exasperated at the Spaniard's cruelty, that he knocked him down with a blow from the butt of his rifle. It was only by force that we could prevent the Spaniard from stabbing the veteran on the spot.[11]"

In their retreat the French used every defensive position in the uneven ground to stall the advance. Costello noted, "In all my military life, this sight surpassed any thing I ever saw: the two armies, which had been brought beautifully into action, were hammering at each other, yet with all the coolness of a field-day exercise.[12]" The fighting was intense and every position had to be fought for, although Kincaid perceived some lack of enthusiasm on the part of the enemy:

"I could not help being struck with an unusual appearance of unsteadiness and want of confidence among the French troops. I saw a dense mass of many thousands occupying a good defensible post, who gave way in the greatest confusion, before a single line of the third division, almost without feeling them.[13]"

As the allies advanced, the French artillery, unable readily to cross the broken country or use the blocked roads, fell into allied hands at an astonishing rate. They finally made a stand on the ridge west of Vitoria and pounded the 3rd Division with 80 field-guns. At one point the 95th came under such a heavy bombardment they could do nothing but lie face down in a ploughed field for 30 minutes until it had eased. The French stand was well made until the 4th Division turned their flank and forced a continued withdrawal. By late afternoon, as rain fell, the retreat had become a rout.

Kincaid: "The victory, I believe, was never for a moment doubtful. The enemy were so completely out-generalled, and the superiority of our troops was such, that to carry their positions required little more than the time necessary to march to them. After forcing their centre, the fourth

9 Kincaid, 1981: 109.
10 Hathaway (1997: 348, 352) says this was Lazaro Blanco who had joined the Rifles on the 1st June 1812 and was in Costello's (i.e. Leach's) company.
11 Hathaway, 1997: 223.
12 Hathaway, 1997: 223.
13 Kincaid, 1981: 110. Surtees too expressed surprise the French did not defend their withdrawal harder.

The Great Square, Vitoria.

division and our own got on the flank and rather in rear of the enemy's left wing, who were retreating before Sir Rowland Hill, and who, to effect their escape, were now obliged to fly in one confused mass. Had a single regiment of our dragoons been at hand, or even a squadron, to have forced them into shape for a few minutes[14], we must have taken from ten to twenty thousand prisoners. After marching alongside of them for nearly two miles, and as a disorderly body will always move faster than an orderly one, we had the mortification to see them gradually heading us, until they finally made their escape. I have no doubt but that our mounted gentlemen were doing their duty as they ought in another part of the field; yet, it was impossible to deny ourselves the satisfaction of cursing them all, because a portion had not been there at such a critical moment.[15]"

At the front of the advancing allied infantry, Jonathan Leach's company was on the French heels as they withdrew through Vitoria.

Costello: "When we arrived close to the barriers of Vitoria, we found them blocked up by a great portion of the French waggons, bearing the 'materiel' of their army. We passed the gates. Through the town we were engaged in skirmishing with their rear-guard. Despite the street-firing, many of the inhabitants threw open their windows and appeared at their balconies to welcome us with *vivas*. The ladies, according to the established mode, threw flowers into the streets as we passed along.

In following up the enemy, myself and a few others left the company a little in the rear. I went through the square... A few minutes later, some of the 10th Hussars, and a party of the Life Guards, came dashing through the town, swords in hand, shouting as if they had taken it by storm.[16]"

[14] i.e. to force the French to stop and form defensive squares.
[15] Kincaid, 1981: 109-110.
[16] Hathaway, 1997: 224.

The French fell back beyond the city and, cut off from the main road north-east towards France, retreated east towards the French stronghold of Pamplona. Beyond Vitoria the Pamplona road crossed an expanse of boggy marshland where it was elevated between two deep drainage ditches. The only way to join this road was at its end but in their withdrawal across Spain the French had accumulated the plunder of six years occupation. Vast numbers of carts laden with looted art and other treasures joined the jostling supply waggons, quickly clogging the single highway. The French artillery had nowhere to go. Abandoning many of their remaining field guns at the edge of the waterlogged ground they retreated as best they could.

Alongside the road the riflemen broke into a run to overtake the crawling convoy and shot the horses pulling gun-carriages, bringing following traffic to a grinding halt. As the jam of vehicles was overwhelmed by the advancing army, the wives of high-ranking French officers were captured in their carriages and the French military chest (the money carried for making official payments) was taken, as were all French army records. In the chaos and confusion the French lost 151 field guns; 415 ammunition trailers; 56 forage waggons; 44 forge waggons; more than 14,000 rounds of ammunition; nearly 2,000,000 musket ball cartridges; and over 18 tonnes of gunpowder. The entire French artillery escaped with just one field gun and one howitzer. Major William Napier of the 43rd Light Infantry later said, "Never was an army more hardly used by its commander, for the soldiers were not half beaten, and yet never was a victory more complete[17]". By the end of the day the French had lost 7000 men killed, wounded and captured; the allies 5000.

King Joseph himself was very nearly captured by cavalry, having to jump from his carriage and take to his horse to escape, and Jourdan's Marshal's baton fell into British hands. When Wellington sent this to the Prince Regent in London, the Regent returned the compliment by sending Wellington the baton of a British Field-Marshal.

Wellington was not the only officer to benefit in rank from the engagement. Jonathan's company had been at the leading edge of the assault on the French centre for the whole day. For his battlefield services he was promoted to Major[18].

After the battle

The Light Division pursued the French until dark, then halted in a wheatfield several kilometres east of the town.

Leach: "We bivouacked about a league from the city of Vittoria, amidst waggon-loads of captured baggage of all kinds, consisting of boxes of gold and silver belonging to the military chest, clothes, trinkets, horses, mules, ammunition-waggons, guns, commissariat stores, and waggons belonging to French general officers, where we found fresh bread, Swiss cheese, wine, brandy, &c. &c., of which we made good use, having tasted nothing since daybreak."

[17] Napier, 1851: 127.
[18] This promotion was by brevet (see p. 164 note 3). He remained a Captain in the 95th, in command of his company, and stayed on Captain's pay, but wore the insignia of a Major and would have been known by his army rank: Major Leach.

With the victorious army over-running the French baggage train, discipline began to waver and widespread plundering began, especially with the onset of night. All regiments and many officers were involved in the looting and there were plenty of spoils for all of them. Some men walked away with more than a thousand dollars in cash – including Ned Costello, who needed a mule to carry his booty. Everyone seemed to find something to their liking, as Bill Wheeler of the 51st found when he made his way back to his regiment after a less successful foray:

'When I returned to camp, how was I surprised at the great change that had taken place during the short time I had been absent. When I left no fires had been lit, now the place was all in a blaze. I knew of nothing to compare it to but an Arab camp after a successful attack on some rich caravan. Wearing apparal of all sorts and description lying about in heaps or trampled under foot, boxes broken to pieces for fuel. Every one was in motion, some bringing in loads of different descriptions on their shoulders, others leading or driving horses and mules loaded with baggage, provisions and liquors and something of everything that forms the baggage of an army. Dame fortune had distributed her gifts in her usual way, to some money, others bread, hams, cherries, tobacco etc. This of necessity soon established a market. Now the camp represented a great fair and the money and goods soon became more equally distributed. 'Who will give fifty dollars for this pipe.' 'Here is a portrait of Napoleon for one hundred dollars.' Then a General's coat would fetch more dollars than it cost francs. Wine and brandy would fetch a high price. Cognac from forty to fifty dollars per bottle. The market soon changed into a grand maskerade. British soldiers were soon to be seen in French General's and other officer's uniform covered with stars and military orders, others had attired themselves in female dresses, richly embroidered in gold and silver. In the midst of all this hurly burly, frolic and fun, the belley was not forgotten... Twenty four hours before we had not enough in the regiment to bait a mouse trap, this night we could scarce move without trampling on all kinds of provisions.[19]'

The looting on this occasion was unparalleled. Most of the military chest disappeared. The French claimed they had lost a million pounds. Wellington doubted it was that much but admitted official allied coffers only received £100,000; the rest went into the pockets of the soldiers and local Spaniards[20]. On this occasion the British rank and file lived down to the reputation their character (*not* their fighting prowess, but certainly their character) had with their Commander-in-Chief, who later said his army was recruited from, "the scum of the earth—the mere scum of the earth. It is only wonderful that we should be able to make so much out of them afterwards. The English soldiers are fellows who have all enlisted for drink— that is the plain fact—they have all enlisted for drink.[21]" His belief would be reinforced this night.

In an advanced position ahead of the other regiments, the mood in Jonathan's company was less burlesque than in the 51st. The officers'

[19] Liddell Hart, 1994: 118-119.
[20] Stanhope, 1888: 144.
[21] Stanhope, 1888: 14 (see also Stanhope at p. 18 for similar sentiments).

tents were pitched while the riflemen made themselves comfortable among the wreckage of the French baggage train. Costello, back where he belonged, sat at a camp fire with his exhausted comrades:

'At midnight, the wine and brandy went round in horn tots which we generally carried about us. The men mostly lay stretched on the ground, their feet towards the fires, and their elbows resting on their knapsacks. When the grog had roused up their spirits from the effects of the day's fatigue, each one commenced inquiries about absent comrades, for riflemen are always extended in action and seldom know who has fallen until the affray is over.

"Blood 'n 'ounds.[22]" said Dan Kelly, bouncing up from his reclining posture, "don't drink all the wine, boys, until we hear something about our absent messmates. Do any of you know where Jack Connor is?"

"He was shot through the body when we took the first gun in the little village near the main road," was the reply.

"Where is Will John?" asked Bob Roberts, with a sudden glance of suspense.

"A ball passed through his head," said another. "I saw poor Will fall."

"Musha, boys! is there any hope of poor Jemmy Copely getting over his wounds?" said Tom Treacy earnestly, lifting his head from his knapsack.

"Poor Copely!" said another. "Both his legs were knocked off by a round shot."

Treacy laid his head on his kit again. He was silent as each man gave a short account of a fallen comrade, but he was eagerly listening. "Why, by Jasus!" he exclaimed. "By Jasus, they have kilt half our mess. But never mind boys, fill a tot, fill a tot. May I be damned but here's luck." He placed the wine to his mouth, but took it away again untasted and laid it on the ground. "Poor Jemmy Copely! poor Jemmy! They have drilled him well with balls before, damn them, now they have finished him. The best comrade I ever had, or ever will have"...

After recapitulating their different losses, and the good qualities of their fallen comrades (but taking care not to mention any of their bad ones), every man relaxed into a sleep, from which nothing could arouse them save the sound of the bugles, or the hard cracking of the rifle... The crackling of the fires soon ceased for want of fuel, and nothing remained but the embers. The whole camp was as still as the grave, with nothing to disturb the soldiers' repose but the casual braying of the donkeys who answered each other from camp to camp, the sound gradually dying away as an echo in the distant woods.'

Pursuit

It was mid-day on the 22nd of June before the three battalions of the 95th, with some cavalry and artillery, were ordered in pursuit of the French army. They made no contact that day, but on the morning of the 23rd, in

22 'Blood 'n 'ounds' (Blood and zounds – pronounced 'zoondz'). Two oaths. 'Blood' (or the longer 'Bloody') a corruption of the original habit of swearing an oath 'By our Lady' (the Virgin Mary); and 'zounds', swearing an oath 'on God's wounds' (the stigmata of Christ). By 1813 these terms were used solely for conversational emphasis with no religious intention to 'swear' on either. 'Zounds' is now obsolete. 'Bloody' is still a common swear-word used vulgarly for emphasis in Britain and some other English speaking countries. The combination 'Bloody Mary' still occurs in other contexts.

torrential rain, they found the rear-guard and pressed them heavily until the afternoon, taking many prisoners.

Leach: 'The French set fire to several villages in a wanton and cruel manner; and when we reached them, they were half consumed. With great difficulty we were able to get through the streets, as the burning rafters were falling into them every instant. For a moment it was a matter of doubt whether the horse artillery, with their ammunition, should venture to pass; but the ardour of pursuit overcame all other feelings, and they rattled through at a brisk pace, fortunately without any mischief occurring...

On the 24th, the Light Division, with the German Hussars and the 14th Light Dragoons, started again at daybreak, and came up with a rear-guard of several thousand infantry, occupying a formidable position behind a mountain river called the Araquil[23]. The banks being extremely rocky and difficult of approach, and the fords impracticable from the heavy rains, which still descended, they could not be attacked but by a narrow bridge. The only infantry advanced thus far were the 1st and 3d battalions of the 95th Riflemen, with which, however, General Alten immediately set to work, before the remainder of the division arrived. Our 3d battalion climbed a mountain on the left, which enabled them to throw a fire on the enemy's right, whilst the 1st battalion blazed at them in front across the river. This, with the appearance of the remainder of the Light Division approaching, caused the French gradually to melt away and to continue their retreat.

We lost many men in this desultory fight. Coming up with them again soon afterwards, in a more open country, the horse artillery cannonaded them with considerable effect, and the cavalry charged and sabred many men. At this moment there was a strange mixed fight of the three arms, cavalry, infantry, and artillery, all scuffling and pounding their adversaries simultaneously... We stuck close to the heels of the enemy, and captured from them the last piece of artillery but one which remained out of the whole of their immense train before the battle of Vittoria.'

To stall the allies' advance the French rearguard had set up their only remaining guns on the road at a point where it made a sharp turn round a mountainside. Here the track was built up 5 metres above the level surrounds and the sides were raised like a wall. The first French shot tore the arm off one of the Rifles' corporals[24], but Ross's Horse Artillery arrived and returned fire, hitting the horses in one of the gun teams. In the ensuing commotion the French gunners overturned the whole carriage, crushing five soldiers, and had to abandon the weapon – half of their army's artillery – to the riflemen.[25] The 95th had now captured the first and the last gun of the Battle of Vittoria, a fact of which they were very proud. Meanwhile the French rearguard moved off to join the rest of the army under the cover of Pamplona, little more than 30 km from the French border.

"At an early hour on the 25th we advanced towards Pampeluna, and began to think it possible, nay, probable, that ere long we should not only

[23] Río Arakil.
[24] Probably Corporal David Cloudsley of Jonathan Leach's company who was invalided to England (Hathaway, 1997: 231, 349)
[25] Verner (1919: 469) says this weapon was an 8-pounder. Bill Wheeler, following along later with the 51st Regt says they met, "with nothing remarkable on the road only that we passed a howitzer upset in a ditch." This must either be a misidentification or an allied howitzer. Wellington noted in a dispatch to Lord Bathurst of 24th June that the French had lost their last gun and retained only one howitzer (Verner, 1919: 470).

behold from the Pyrenees "the great, the grand, the beautiful France," but tread its soil. Contrasting the present situation and position of our army with what it had been three years before, when shut up in the lines of Torres Vedras it appeared like a dream. Then Marshal Massena threatened to kick us into our ships; whereas now, the "Leopard," having cleared the Peninsula of its invaders, was advancing with rapid strides to threaten in his turn. We threw out strong pickets towards the fortress, and occupied Villa Alba[26], and other small villages near it.[27]"

Pyrenees

During the Battle of Vittoria, General Clausel had been closing from the south with three French divisions. When news of the defeat reached him he had halted his force at Logroño and was now trying to move east to France and safety. On the 26th of June Wellington took the Light, 3rd and 4th Divisions and gave chase. After three forced marches over rugged roads marred by torrential rain it was discovered a Spanish priest had informed Clausel of Wellington's presence and he had dodged the interception and slipped over the Pyrenees. "Bestowing sundry benedictions on the padre[28]" the allies made their way back to Pamplona and took their place in the blockade until the 5th of July when, relieved by a Spanish division, they broke camp and marched east.

"We then commenced penetrating into the Pyrenees, and on the 6th reached Lanz, amidst the most lovely scenery imaginable. The valleys, watered by the clearest streams, are well cultivated with Indian corn, and the mountains clothed to their summits with the most luxuriant woods.[29]"

Leaving the rest of the Division several kilometres to the rear, the Rifles moved forward in subsequent days to Santesteban in the valley of the Bidassoa, where they pushed advanced pickets north towards the French positions at Vera and Etxalar [Echelar] just south of the French-occupied city of San Sebastián on the Biscay coast.

Leach: 'We remained a week in San Estevan; and as it was the first halt of any consequence which we had made since the 21st of May, we enjoyed beyond measure our short sojourn there. We had dances every night, and received the greatest attention from the people of all classes. The tune of one of their provincial dances we converted into a quick march for the band; and I have never since heard it, without being instantly reminded of the few happy days which I passed in that delightful spot. Whilst there, I caught some uncommonly fine trout in the Bidassoa, which abounds with them.

On the 14th July, the Light Division marched towards Vera; and on the 15th approached that town, which the French occupied, as well as some walls and enclosures in its front. A part of the 43d regiment attacked the village, whilst our battalion was ordered to ascend the heights of Santa Barbara, and to drive off their pickets. From its summit we had a distant view of the ocean, which for several years we had not seen. A spontaneous

[26] Villava.
[27] Jonathan Leach.
[28] Jonathan Leach.
[29] Jonathan Leach.

River Bidassoa at Irun, downstream from Vera.

and universal shout was raised by the soldiers, which must have astonished our French neighbours, who were separated from us only by a valley...

A few days after we had encamped near Vera, we saw a gay assemblage of French officers and well-dressed females dancing to the music of a band in front of their tents, on the other side of the valley. The distance across was so trifling, that we distinctly made out the tunes to which they capered away, and, with our telescopes, could see their faces. Here were two large armies so near to each other, that an order for either party to advance would have brought on an engagement in a few minutes. Still, so much were they at their ease, that one party looked on at the other quadrilling! ...

The French held the pass of Vera with a strong force, and had thrown up field-works of different kinds for its defence. The 1st and 5th Divisions were near St. Sebastian; on the left bank of the Bidassoa was the Light Division, fronting the pass of Vera, the 7th Division at the pass of Echelar, and the other four divisions further to the right, occupying Maya, Roncesvalles, and other passes. The greater part of the cavalry were cantoned towards Vittoria and the Ebro, it being impossible either to feed or to employ them in the mountains where the army was now posted, and whence we looked down on, and cast a longing eye at, France.'

Counter-attack

While the adversaries faced each other, the command of the French army passed to Marshal Soult, transferred from northern Europe. Wasting no time, on the 25th of July he launched a major attack through the Pyrenean passes in an attempt to relieve the blockades of Pamplona and San Sebastián. In response, allied forces exposed at Vera, including the 7th and Light Divisions, were pulled back across the mountain tracks.

Leach: "the 7th and Light were ordered, on the 26th of July, to fall back from the passes of Echelar and Vera. But as, in the various intricate mazes and sheep-paths of the Pyrenees, through which we marched day and night, and floundered in the dark amongst precipices, from the 26th to the afternoon of the 30th, a man had quite enough to do to be able to ascertain the route taken by his own division, I shall not venture to detail the movements of the 7th".

Smith: "The Light Division made a terrible night march on this occasion, one of the most fatiguing to the soldiers that I ever witnessed. On the Pyrenees, as on other mountains, the darkness is indescribable. We were on a narrow mountain path, frequently with room only for one or two men, when a soldier of the Rifle Brigade rolled down a hill as nearly perpendicular as may be. We heard him bumping along, pack, rifle, weight of ammunition, etc., when from the bottom he sang out, "Halloa there! Tell the Captain there's not a bit of me alive at all; but the devil a bone have I broken; and faith I'm thinking no soldier ever came to his ground at such a rate before. Have a care, boys, you don't follow. The breach at Badajos was nothing to the bottomless pit I'm now in."[30]"

While the divisions stumbled across the mountains in the dark, using home-made torches and burning straw in an effort to see what little track there was, Soult took his army to the outskirts of Pamplona. Repulsed repeatedly over several days he eventually abandoned his attempts to relieve the city and his defeated army again headed for France. As the French trudged north along the bank of the Bidassoa towards their lines in the passes at Vera and Extalar, the Light Division stumbled back the way they had come to intercept them at the bridge near Igantzi [Yanci].

Leach: "This was effected late in the afternoon of the 1st of August, after some harassing marches over the worst possible roads, impracticable for artillery. Many hundreds of men were left on the road thoroughly exhausted.

On arriving at the top of the mountain, which looks down on the Bidassoa, we found a large body of infantry strongly posted behind walls and rocks, opposite the bridge of Yanci, so as to render the passage of it impracticable. We perceived also a large French column marching, without much order, in great haste, and evidently much jaded, for the passes of Echelar and Vera, by the road which runs close along the bank of the river. Some companies of our regiment were instantly sent down the side of the mountain, with orders to blaze across the river at them. Our fire threw them into great confusion, which was increased by their being aware that the advanced guard of the 4th Division was following their track. Many of the French threw away their arms and knapsacks, and scrambled up the face of the mountain on their right, to get out of the scrape in which they found themselves, and for which there was no other remedy. They lost many men killed and wounded".

[30] Smith, 1999: 114-115.

Kincaid: "the fatigues of the day were forgotten, as our three battalions extended among the brush-wood, and went down to 'knock the dust out of their hairy knapsacks,' as our men were in the habit of expressing themselves[31]; but, in place of knocking the dust out of them, I believe that most of their knapsacks were knocked in the dust; for the greater part of those who were not floored along with their knapsacks, shook them off, by way of enabling the owner to make a smarter scramble across that portion of the road on which our leaden shower was pouring; and, foes as they were, it was impossible not to feel a degree of pity for their situation: pressed by an enemy in the rear, an inaccessible mountain on their right, and a river on their left, lined by an invisible foe, from whom there was no escape, but the desperate one of running the gauntlet.[32]"

At close range, faced with accurate weapons, used from good cover, the dense body of exhausted Frenchmen, with nowhere to run, stood no chance against the 95th's experienced marksmen.

Costello: "to the honour of the British soldiers, many of our men, knowing what the French suffered from what they had themselves endured, declined firing, and called out to the others to spare them, as it was little better than murder.[33]"

The fall of San Sebastián

The following day the Light Division followed the French line of march and returned to their old positions at Vera. In front of the main French lines, a strong French force remained on a mountain peak overlooking the height of Santa Barbara. By late afternoon, as they had shown no signs of withdrawing in the face of the allied arrival, it was decided to remove them. The task was given to the 95th, and the 1st and 3rd battalions under Andrew Barnard were ordered up the near vertical, craggy slope. The 3rd battalion went straight up the face while the 1st battalion spread out in line abreast to their right. Costello noted, "This was a heavy task at the time; but to it we went, and in extended order mounted the hill, on the summit of which the enemy were clustered as thick as bees on a hive.[34]" As the men approached the crest, under French fire, a low cloud enveloped the peak and visibility dropped to about 20 metres. Unable to see anything, the 1st battalion halted while the French fired blindly through the mist. As the cloud passed the battalion pressed on but met stiff resistance and Barnard sent for the 43rd Light Infantry to come forward and support. Although the fighting was fierce and there were a number of casualties in the 95th, the French were driven off the height, which was instantly christened 'Barnard's Hill'. Leaving a Portuguese garrison at the summit, the 95th and 43rd returned to Santa Barbara.

Wellington was unwilling to attack the French in the Pyrenees while they occupied Pamplona and San Sebastián behind the allied lines, so for two months the Light Division camped near Vera while the French continued

[31] French knapsacks were made from unshaved goatskin.
[32] Kincaid, 1981: 120. 'Running the gauntlet' – attempting to overcome danger by racing through it, or running past it, quickly. 'Gauntlet' is a corruption of 'gantelope/gantlet': a former military punishment in which the culprit ran between two lines of sailors or soldiers and received a lash from each as he passed.
[33] Hathaway, 1997: 237.
[34] Hathaway, 1997: 238.

to fortify every defensive position in the pass, and the neighbouring valleys, in anticipation of the inevitable allied advance.

On the 31st of August the town of San Sebastián was stormed by Sir Thomas Graham's corps[35], driving the garrison into the castle (where they eventually surrendered on the 8th of September). On the day the town was stormed, a strong French force[36] appeared on the slopes in front of the Light Division, descended, and – pushing the Spanish corps on the Division's left before them – marched towards the town. Having failed to prevent the storming they returned the same evening, but as the heavy rains had swollen the river the only way they could regain their lines was by forcing their way over the bridge at Vera, held by a 50-strong company of the 2/95th, with a company of the 3rd battalion in support.

Leach: "Some hours before this attack at the bridge took place, General Kempt's brigade was ordered to cross the Bidassoa at the bridge of Lezacca[37], and to operate on the left of the river. I happened to have command of the pickets of his brigade that night, and was ordered to descend from the heights of Santa Barbara as soon as some Spanish troops relieved me, when I was to follow the brigade across the Bidassoa.

I have been out in all kinds of weather, in all seasons; but the thunder, lightning, and rain, the roaring of the Bidassoa and its tributary streams, the utter darkness which succeeded the vivid flashes of lightning, and made our descent down the sides of the mountains, by the narrow rocky paths, so slow and tiresome, rendered that amongst the most dreary nights which I can call to my recollection. In addition to this, we knew the enemy were near us in great force at different points; the two brigades were separated by a rapid river; we knew not what had been the result of the attempt to storm St. Sebastian in the morning, nor of the attack of the French on the Spaniards. In short, all was uncertainty and darkness, which we trusted the morning would do away with; and so it did. St. Sebastian was taken; and the Spaniards had defeated the French, who finally regained their old position in the Pass of Vera, after losing many men in forcing the bridge."

The company of the 2nd battalion also lost many men at the bridge, but, firing from within fortified buildings and making several charges, they inflicted heavy French casualties.

Smith: "Such a scene of mortal strife from the fire of fifty men was never witnessed. The bridge was almost choked with the dead; the enemy's loss was enormous, and many of his men were drowned, and all his guns were left in the river a mile or two below the bridge. The number of dead was so great, the bodies were thrown into the rapid stream in the hope that the current would carry them, but many rocks impeded them, and when the river subsided, we had great cause to lament our precipitancy in hurling the bodies, for the stench soon after was awful.[38]"

Bad weather kept the armies quiet for another month, but the soldiers made distractions and the commissariat made plans.

[35] One storming party comprised volunteers from the Light Division and included riflemen Samuel Royston and Philip Ryan from Leach's company (Hathaway, 1997: 240).
[36] Jonathan Leach says 15,000 men.
[37] Lesaka.
[38] Smith, 1999: 123-124.

Costello: 'While here we used to amuse ourselves bathing. We were soon to cross the river which divides the French and Spanish territories, and it was heart-stirring to see our riflemen unconsciously expose to Spain, the evidence of the dangers they had endured for her liberation, for as they stripped on its banks, and prepared to dash into the clear water, their perforated and wounded exteriors proved what they had seen and suffered. On these occasions, the veterans would generally amuse themselves by remarking and jesting to one another on the peculiar situation of the different bullet holes, and the direction the shot had taken in passing through them...

Here too my old friend, Tom Crawley, got the whole of our regiment out of a precious scrape. Our Division were given linen bags, made exactly to fit across our knapsacks, with three days' biscuit (3 lbs) for each bag[39]. The bags were to be kept well tied, and strapped on the top of each man's knapsack. The brigadier expected us to be on short commons[40] while on the Pyrenees and, as this was to be our last resource in case of scarcity, no man was to taste a morsel of biscuit unless given written orders to that effect.

The bags were examined every morning by officers commanding companies. Seeing them strapped snugly on the knapsacks, they considered them to be all right. However, our fellows were never at a loss for subterfuge, and they planned to evade the officers' vigilance by eating all their biscuits except one whole one, which they kept at the top to be seen. In place of the others, they substituted chips[41]. These did very well for some time, but one day, whilst on private parade, Captain Johnston took it into his head to see his company's biscuit shaken out. The first man on the right of his company was the unfortunate Tom Crawley.

"Untie your bag Crawley," said the Captain. Tom did as he was ordered, and showed the Captain a very good-looking biscuit a-top.

"Shake the whole out. I want to see if they are getting mouldy."

"Faith, there is no fear of that," said Crawley, looking the Captain hard in the face, then casting a woeful eye on his bag. But the Captain was not to be baulked. Taking the bag by both ends, he emptied out its contents, which was no more and no less than a few dry chips. Poor Tom, as upright as a dart, stood scratching his head. His countenance would have made a saint laugh.

"What have you done with your biscuit? Have you eaten it, sir?" Tom, motionless, made no answer.

"Do you know it is against orders?"

"To be sure I do, sir" says Tom; "but, for God's sake, do you take me for a South American jackass, that carries gold and eats straw?"

This answer not only set the Captain, but the whole company, in roars of laughter, and on further inspection, he found that they, and indeed the regiment, had adopted the same plan. Through this our bags were taken away, and we were relieved from carrying chips.'

[39] This would be hard, dry ship's biscuit as used by the Royal Navy. It was dense and stored well for long periods. 3 lbs = 1.4 kg.
[40] 'commons' – rations.
[41] It is not clear what Costello means by 'chips'. The word 'chip' had several meanings: a fragment of wood; a slice of bread; or anything worthless, dried up and lacking nutrition.

The Pass of Vera

At the beginning of October, with winter in prospect, Wellington decided to move his front line forwards. The siege of Pamplona was enforced with a Spanish army and on the 8th of October the allies attacked the passes. The Light Division stormed the Pass of Vera with the Spanish Army of Andalusia and the Spanish guerrillas of General Longa.

Leach: 'The business commenced by our 3d battalion climbing a small mountain, on which the French had a strong advanced post. After a sharp conflict, the enemy were driven from it; and if the evidence of impartial spectators may be credited, the business was done in handsome style. From the summit of this hill we were able to reconnoitre the whole of the French entrenchments in the higher mountains beyond it. Art and nature combined had certainly given it a formidable appearance, particularly that portion allotted to the 2d brigade of the Light Division to assault[42], commanded by Lieutenant-Colonel Colbourne, of the 52d regiment, an officer possessing the most cool and determined courage, coupled with excellent judgment and considerable experience. The Spaniards were already engaged on our right, and General Kempt's brigade was enabled, by a movement to its right and a flank fire on their entrenchment, to dislodge a strong force of French infantry, who must have been made prisoners, if they had not bolted like smoked foxes from their earths.

During these operations, Colonel Colbourne's brigade[43] had a much more arduous task to perform. His opponents could not be taken in flank, and he was therefore obliged to advance straight against them, entrenched up to their chins. The impetuosity of the attack made with the bayonet by this brigade, headed by Colonel Colbourne, and its brilliant success, are like many other conflicts which took place during the Peninsula war, not coming under the head of general actions, but imperfectly known except to those engaged in the operations on the spot. A succession of redoubts and field-works were carried by the bayonet, and those who defended them were either shot, bayoneted, or driven off the mountain. The 52d regiment, the 2d battalion of the 95th, and the 1st Caçadores, which composed this brigade, suffered very severely.

The pass of Vera was now gained; but the French still held the mountain of La Rhune, which overlooked us, out of musket shot. The Spaniards skirmished with them at its base, and attempted to dislodge them; but night closed without their having accomplished it... The following day the French abandoned the mountain of La Rhune, seeing that Lord Wellington was arranging matters to drive them from it. Our division constantly afterwards had a picket of three companies on that mountain, amongst some ruins called the Hermitage'.

John Kincaid found the scenery from the top of the newly acquired strongholds, with their commanding views of France, a refreshing change after spending months staring at fog and mountains.

[42] Jonathan Leach was in the 1st brigade, which was still commanded by Kempt.

[43] Colborne at this time, and until the end of the war, commanded B. Brigade of the Light Division. Kempt commanded A. Brigade (Atkinson *in* Oman, 1986: 370).

St Jean-de-Luz,
looking towards
Font-Arabia in Spain.

"On our left, the Bay of Biscay lay extended as far as the horizon, while several of our ships of war were seen sporting upon her bosom. Beneath us lay the pretty little town of St. Jean de Luz[44], which looked as if it had just been framed out of the Lilliputian scenery of a toyshop. The town of Bayonne, too, was visible in the distance; and the view to the right embraced a beautiful, well-wooded country, thickly studded with towns and villages, as far as the eye could reach.[45]"

Leach: "Pampeluna, although closely blockaded, and the garrison nearly in a state of starvation, still held out; and it was pretty well understood, that we waited only for its surrender to advance into France. A continuation of tremendous gales of wind and rain tormented us for a whole fortnight, which blew down our tents as fast as we pitched them, and almost tore them to pieces; so that we were never dry.

Being on picket at the Hermitage of La Rhune early in November, as furious a gale of wind, with heavy snow, came on, as I ever recollect. To light fires was impracticable; and I believe that troops have but rarely been exposed for twenty-four hours to such weather on so unsheltered a spot. Two Portuguese soldiers belonging to the pickets were carried down to the hospital at Vera next morning in a state of insensibility, and died the following day.

The weather was so inclement during October and the early part of November, that were I to enter into detail, and to describe the actual state of our canvas habitations during the many weeks which we encamped on the pinnacles of the western Pyrenees, I might be accused of colouring matters too highly, except by those who were present. It is enough to say, that day or night we were never dry; springs bubbled up from the ground on which our tents stood, and we began to think it was really time to seek winter quarters in more hospitable regions."

[44] On the Biscay coast of France.
[45] Kincaid, 1981: 126.

The 'more hospitable regions' were the lowlands visible in the distance. Pamplona surrendered at the end of October, the garrison of 4000 having exhausted more than their provisions. Their determined resistance had earned them the respect of many in the army, including Bill Wheeler, now a Corporal, who informed his parents:

"I am inclined to pay a compliment to the brave Garrison of Pampaluna. I am not one who wish to claim all the merit on our side, no, while I endeavour to record the gallantry of the British I cannot in justice to a brave enemy be silent in their praise. Pampaluna held out until the 31st October. A considerable time before they surrendered the Garrison was reduced to the greatest privation, not an animal of any description escaped the butcher save the Governor's horse. Dogs, cats and rats were all devoured, and when they marched out with the honors of war, so gastly were the appearance of the men that one would have supposed they had all risen from their graves. I was told, by some who witnessed the sight that the men could scarcely stand, they had held out until completely starved. What more could be expected from them. They are an honor to the Imperial Army and to their country.[46]"

With Pamplona in allied hands Wellington was free to advance again, but the roads – including new roads his engineers had laid through the passes for his artillery – were in such an execrable state from the recent weather he was obliged to wait another week. Finally he made his decision. The 10th of November 1813 was to see the long awaited invasion of France.

[46] Letter: Wheeler to his parents, 20th November 1813 (Liddell Hart, 1994: 134-135).

— 13 —

The invasion of France

"when we crossed the Pyrenees, there never was an army in
the world in better spirits, better order, or better discipline.
We had mended in discipline every campaign, until at last"
smiling "I hope we were pretty near perfect."

Wellington[1]

In October 1813 Napoleon and his army gave battle for four days at
Leipzig to the combined forces of Prussia, Russia, Austria and Sweden[2].
By the end of this 'Battle of the Nations' the French had put 195,000
men into the field, the allies 365,000. Leipzig was the largest encounter of
the Napoleonic wars. Napoleon's army was badly mauled and the French
lost their foothold beyond the Rhine. The allies were now poised to invade
France from the north-east.

In the south-west Wellington, as yet unaware of the French defeat, had
invasion plans of his own. On the evening of the 9th of November he issued
the order of attack: "To-morrow the army will drive the French upon Bayonne
and behind the river Adour. Light Division will get under arms at 2 o'clock
in the morning and march to the point of attack, where the Division will form
columns of attack and remain until daylight, and the signal to advance will
be a salvo from thirty pieces of cannon.[3]"

Costello: "This night, the company I belonged to was on picket. Our
orders were that, on the first dawn of light, we should attack and drive in the
enemy's picket which was opposed to us. We were preparing for the task
when, to our surprise, about 100 yards in our rear, we beheld the whole of
our Division waiting to support us.[4]"

Leach: "We were ordered to leave our camp early on the night of the
9th, and to approach, in great silence, as near as possible to their advanced
pickets. No horses were to accompany the troops, lest their neighing might
alarm the enemy's pickets, and put them on the *qui vive*. No fires were to be
made, and every thing was to be as silent as the grave. The Light Division
lay down at the back of some rocks, in front of which we were to sally forth
at break of day, and to assault the enemy's advanced position on a detached
mountain, called La petite la Rhune.

[1] Pool, 1967: 99.
[2] 16th-19th October 1813.
[3] Verner, 1986: 325.
[4] Hathaway, 1997: 250.

The signal for the whole army to advance to the attack, was a cannonade on a French redoubt, at Sarr, or Zara[5], opposite the centre of our army. We had been standing to our arms more than an hour before day dawned, straining our eyes towards the French position, and, as the light faintly appeared, momentarily expecting to hear the cannonade, as a signal for a powerful army of British, Portuguese, and Spaniards, to rush forward at the same instant from the different passes of the Pyrenees, and to invade the "sacred territory of France." Whatever fire-eaters and salamanders[6] may say to the contrary, such moments as those which intervened from the time day began faintly to dawn, until it became sufficiently light for the signal of attack to be made, and for the army to be put in motion, are far more trying than the actual strife when once fairly begun."

Costello: "As soon as our attack commenced, we heard the alarm given by at least 100 drums and bugles. As the light dawned more clearly, we could see the French columns all in motion. The remainder of our battalion and Division came up, and we were soon hotly engaged, with only a valley partially separating us from the main body of the enemy.[7]"

Leach: "The fire of artillery in the centre at length opened. The Light Division descended the face of the mountain in columns of battalions, our front covered by skirmishers, and crossing the valley which separated us from the French, instantly attacked La petite la Rhune, on which they had constructed a star redoubt of stone."

Simmons: "We moved forward under a heavy fire from the enemy's works without ever exchanging a shot until we got up to them and scaled the walls. Then the work of death commenced.[8]"

Leach: " The rapidity of the attack was such, that in less than half an hour from its commencement the enemy were driven off the hill, and the redoubt was in our possession. This success was not attained without a heavy loss. Our division reformed columns of attack on La petite la Rhune, whence we could now plainly see the whole train of entrenchments filled with French infantry, the redoubts bristling with cannon, and every thing ready for our reception. The other divisions had also driven in the enemy's advanced posts, and a sharp fire of musketry for some miles to our right and left was kept up."

Kincaid: "Petite La Rhune was more of an outpost than a part of their position, the latter being a chain of stupendous mountains in its rear; so that while our battalion followed their skirmishers into the valley between, the remainder of our division were forming for the attack on the main position, and waiting for the co-operation of the other divisions, the thunder of whose artillery, echoing along the valleys, proclaimed that they were engaged, far and wide, on both sides of us.[9]"

Leach: "It is impossible to conceive a finer sight than the general advance of our army from the Pyrenean passes against the French position. Almost as far as the eye could reach, was seen one sheet of flame and smoke, accompanied with an incessant fire of light troops, and frequent

[5] The modern Sare.
[6] In Classical mythology the salamander was believed to live in fire (The classical writer Pliny once tested this by putting a salamander into a fire but noted it was soon burnt to a crisp.) An old name for Asbestos is 'Salamander's wool'.
[7] Hathaway, 1997: 250.
[8] Verner, 1986: 325.
[9] Kincaid, 1981: 131.

volleys of musketry, as the lines and columns approached the entrenchments. An order now reached the Light Division to advance from La petite la Rhune, to cross the valley in our front, and to storm the enemy's works, in conjunction with the other five divisions, and the Spaniards which were on our right. Long and severe was the struggle; but each division succeeded in forcing the enemy from the numerous entrenchments which were met at every step, and in driving them off their strong position, with the loss of all the heavy artillery mounted in their works. A battalion of the French 88th regiment were made prisoners by the Light Division in a redoubt on the summit of the position."

Costello: 'After we had routed them from their first line, and were getting close to their second, an incident occurred which I, and the greater part of our company, observed. A man of the name of Morely[10], a shoemaker, fell shot through the head. Nearly the whole time we had been in Spain, he had lived with a Spanish woman, who acted in some degree as one of the sutlers to our regiment. She was tenderly attached to him, and during an action would get as near to her lover as possible, generally on a donkey. On this occasion, some of our wounded men who were passing her, informed her Morely was killed. The poor girl was distracted. Leaving her donkey and stores behind, she rushed down to the spot where he had fallen. We were then in the thick of the fight. With the balls coming thick as hail, our only safety was cover, but she, callous to every danger, threw herself on the blood-stained body of her lover, and gave way to the most appalling ebullition of grief, tearing her hair and wringing her hands. I expected every moment to see the poor woman shot.

The gallantry of Blanco, the Spaniard who was so revengeful at Vitoria, was conspicuous. He had been an intimate friend of Morely, and seeing the danger his countrywoman was exposed to, he rushed boldly from his cover, placed himself in front of her, and continued loading and firing at the enemy, swearing loudly all the time in a way only a Spaniard can do justice to. Such were the fierce grimaces and oaths of Blanco, that, notwithstanding the real horror of the scene, it was impossible to resist the impulse to laugh. It was a miracle that he escaped injury...

The enemy, although retreating, did so in an orderly manner, and kept up a tolerably brisk fire. I had no sooner regained the line of skirmishers than I received a severe hit just about the centre of my waist. It nearly knocked me down. For a moment I imagined myself mortally wounded through the body, but on examination I found myself only slightly bruised. A ball had actually stuck in the serpent of my waist belt – the brass clasp or hook that fastens it – from whence it was afterwards taken out with difficulty.[11]'

Kincaid: "Towards the end of the action, Colonel Barnard[12] was struck with a musket-ball, which carried him clean off his horse. The enemy, seeing that they had shot an officer of rank, very maliciously kept up a heavy firing on the spot, while we were carrying him under the brow of the hill.[13]"

[10] John Morely of Leach's company (Hathaway, 1997: 250-251, 351).

[11] Hathaway, 1997: 250-252 [The clasp of the belt was in the form of a horizontal 'S' engraved or moulded in the form of a snake. The bend of the snake's head hooked into a metal eye attached to the other end of the belt (see figures on p. 45). This design of buckle was also in vogue when the author was a child in the 1960s. We called them 'S-belts'].

[12] Andrew Barnard had been knighted (KB) by this time, possibly after Vitoria.

[13] Kincaid, 1981: 132.

Smith: 'Barnard was knocked off his horse by a musket-ball through his lungs. When Johnny Kincaid... his adjutant, got up to him, he was nearly choked by blood in his mouth. They washed it out for him, and he recovered so as to give particular orders about a pocket-book and some papers he wished sent to his brother.[14]'

Simmons: "Just as our gallant Colonel Barnard was reconnoitring how to move to the best advantage, a musket-ball entered his right breast. He fell. I was near him, and got him put into a blanket and taken a few paces to the rear. He began to spit blood, the ball having passed through his lungs. He soon came to himself and said, "Simmons, you know my situation[15]. Am I mortally wounded?" I felt the wound, and answered, "Colonel, it is useless to mince the matter; you are dangerously wounded, but not immediately mortally." "Well Simmons," he replied, "be candid. I am not afraid to die." I answered, "I am candid." He said then, "I am satisfied."[16]"

Costello: "Shots are very strange things. They fly fast, and at this moment, Sergeant Watt of the Rifles received a ball in the head. I was next to him and he laid hold of me with both hands and called out: "Am I dead? Am I dead?" Poor fellow! He was mortally wounded, and it was with difficulty that I extricated myself from his deadly grasp.

The French, after a severe loss, made good their retreat across the river that leads to St Jean-de-Luz. With our usual luck we took up our camp for the night on the side of a bleak and barren hill.[17]"

As Wellington had known, the French did not have sufficient men to occupy all the fortifications they had built. By attacking along the whole line he had prevented them grouping at the points of assault, and no position became strong enough to resist the allied advance. In this *Battle of the Nivelle*, the French had been pushed back into France beyond the River Nivelle, which runs north into the Bay of Biscay at St Jean-de-Luz.

Within a few days the French had pulled further east to an entrenched camp in front of Bayonne, just inland from the mouth of the River Adour where it is joined from the south by its tributary the Nive. The allies followed, on roads awash from heavy rains, and occupied the villages and farmhouses lying in the triangle formed by the coast to the left and the Nive to the right, with Bayonne and the French at its apex. The Light Division occupied the village of Arcangues, with the 1/95th at the chateau, which they strengthened with trenchworks. The French pickets stood just one kilometre to their front.

Now on French soil, Wellington issued the most strict edict against any plundering of civilian property. Not complying, the Spanish army of Lieutenant-General Don Manuel Freyre was ordered back into Spain.

The Battles of the Nive

With the armies so close there was a constant state of readiness and some minor pushes to 'adjust' the other side's pickets. On the 23rd of November the 43rd Light Infantry was given the task of occupying some

[14] Smith, 1999: 146-147.
[15] Simmons was an assistant-surgeon in the militia before joining the 95th.
[16] Letter to parents, 7th December 1813 (Verner, 1986: 326). In fact, the ball had punctured Barnard's lung, but not deeply, and without causing serious damage. It was quickly extracted and he rejoined the battalion three weeks later. Barnard had asked Simmons to nurse him back to health and in return sent to England for a gold watch for him.
[17] Hathaway, 1997: 252.

houses set amongst the French sentry posts. Unfortunately one company of the 43rd pushed forward too far and was exposed in front of the French front line. The 1/95th was sent forward to cover their retreat, but the company was captured, leaving the 95th to take possession of the houses.

Other than these minor skirmishes the armies relaxed into a state of mutual understanding, as on previous occasions when some time was to be spent in each other's company.

Surtees: 'A disposition had for some time been gaining ground with both armies, to mitigate the miseries of warfare, as much as was consistent with each doing their duty to their country; and it had by this time proceeded to such an extent, as to allow us to place that confidence in them that they would not molest us even if we passed their outposts... And this mutual confidence in each other was productive of the most comfortable results to both parties. We could move about at any time, and almost in any place, shooting or otherwise amusing ourselves, without the dread of falling in with an enemy's patrol, or of getting among their sentries. They never molested us from this time, except when we either advanced upon them, or they upon us, in hostile array.[18]'

The officers of both armies conversed regularly and a trade was opened: the French supplied the British with brandy from Bayonne; the British supplied the French officers with tea, for which some had acquired a taste. Some French officers had formerly been prisoners of war in England and passed over letters to be forwarded to their English paramours.

Eventually Wellington put a halt to all such social intercourse, fearing the British officers' poor understanding of the French language – the medium of communication as few French officers spoke English – would lead to their unwitting divulgence of useful military information. It is debatable whether he realised at the time that the rank and file in the picket line had also struck up an accord with their opposite numbers, sometimes posted only 30 metres away. On one occasion some British soldiers advanced money to their French counterparts so they could buy brandy for them. Unfortunately, the mutual trust being less than absolute, the British soldiers took three French muskets as security. An embarrassed French officer had to approach the allies' line the following day to ask if he might have the weapons back. The thirsty soldiers had to be satisfied with a return of their deposit[19].

Costello: "Such a good feeling reigned among the French and our men, that we frequently went into each other's picket houses. These terms of intimacy the French extended to neither the Spanish nor Portuguese troops, for whom they expressed an unmeasured contempt. This state of things at our outposts was too subversive of discipline to be tolerated by those in command, and it was only done on the sly, upon a reliance of mutual honour. Nevertheless, it exhibits a pleasing picture of the absence of all revenge and prejudice on either side among men of opposing interests. This feeling, however, could not stay the effusion of blood that was still to be shed.[20]"

[18] Surtees, 1973: 256-257.
[19] Pool, 1967: 119-120.
[20] Hathaway, 1997: 255.

All conviviality evaporated on the 9th of December. On that day the Light Division and the allies' left wing under Major-General John Hope[21] were sent forward against the French lines as a feint while the right wing under Sir Rowland Hill crossed the Nive and took up a position between the Nive and the Adour to the east of the French. Once Hill's corps was across the river the Light Division and left wing returned to their original positions.

The following day at dawn the French unexpectedly counter-advanced in force. Harry Smith described this as "nearer a surprise than anything we had ever experienced."

Costello: 'the enemy drove in the pickets, which were chiefly furnished by our battalion, and their columns came briskly forward intent on driving us from our position. Our company had been ordered to line some brushwood on the side of a lane that led from the château and, as they came on, we received them with a fierce and deadly fire. They replied with spirit, and endeavoured to outflank our position. Assisting to repel this attempt, we came in for a shower of shot, and Lieutenant Hopwood and Sergeant Brotherwood, with several more of our party, were killed on the spot[22].

By this time they were getting round us, and perceiving how few our numbers were compared to their own, they started to close. We took to our heels down a field and sprang into the lane... Someone made it known that Lord Wellington and his staff were watching our motions through their glasses from the château. Seeing ourselves under the eye of the Commander-in-Chief, we instantly rallied. Our 3rd battalion were hotly engaged on our left.[23]'

Kincaid: We found ourselves "under a heavy skirmishing fire, retiring gradually from hedge to hedge, according as the superior force of the enemy compelled us to give ground, until we finally retired within our home, the chateau, which was the first part of our position that was meant to be defended in earnest. We had previously thrown up a mud rampart around it, and loop-holed the different outhouses, so that we had nothing now to do, but to line the walls and show determined fight. The forty-third occupied the churchyard to our left, which was also partially fortified; and the third Cácadores and our third battalion occupied the space between, behind the hedgerows, while the fourth division was in readiness to support us from the rear. The enemy came up to the opposite ridge, in formidable numbers, and began blazing at our windows and loop-holes, and showing some disposition to attempt it by storm; but they thought better of it and withdrew their columns a short distance to the rear, leaving the nearest hedge lined with their skirmishers. An officer of ours, Mr. Hopewood, and one of our serjeants, had been killed in the field opposite, within twenty yards of where the enemy's skirmishers now were. We were very anxious to get possession of their bodies, but had not force enough to effect it. Several French soldiers came through the hedge, at different times, with the intention, as we thought, of plundering, but our men shot every one who

[21] Major-General John Hope (1765-1836). Promoted Lieutenant-General 1819. Knighted 1821. Had replaced Sir Thomas Graham in command on the left, Graham having been invalided to England.
[22] Simmons notes John Hopwood and William Brotherwood were killed by the same ball, which passed through both their heads as they stood one behind the other.
[23] Hathaway, 1997: 255-6.

attempted to go near them, until towards evening, when a French officer approached, waving a white handkerchief and pointing to some of his men who were following him with shovels. Seeing that his intention was to bury them, we instantly ceased firing, nor did we renew it again that night.[24]"

Costello: "The enemy found themselves unable to make any serious impression and, I dare say, were not sorry when night closed upon their baffled columns. We had little respite from the fatigues of the day, as we were busily employed in fortifying the château for the attack anticipated on the morrow. However the following morning, the enemy retreated within their works, upon which we took possession of our former ground. There we found the bodies of Lt. Hopwood and poor Brotherwood. Both had been stripped, and covered partially with a little loose earth.[25]"

On the 11th and 12th of December there was small arms fire along the lines, but at the Light Division's position there were no major movements. Despite the hostilities and general nervousness, some accord was still possible.

Smith: "Upon the 11th we had some partial skirmishing. The 2nd Battalion Rifle Brigade struck their tents for the purpose of moving their ground. The enemy were most alarmed, and took up their ground to receive us. That night, when our armies were dismissed, rations were served out. In my life I never heard such a row as among the French when preparing to cook. I was posting the night's sentries, when I saw a French officer doing the same. I went towards him, and we civilly greeted each other. I said I wished to speak to him. He came up with the greatest confidence and good humour. I showed him my vedette[26], and then remarked that his was too far in advance and might create an alarm at night when relieving. He said he did not see that, but to please me, if I would point out where I wished he should be, he would immediately move him—which he did. He presented his little flask of excellent French brandy, of which I took a sup, and we parted in perfect amity.[27]"

Leach: "In front of the Light Division, during the 10th, 11th, and 12th, the French constantly employed a swarm of light infantry, with whom we waged a desultory warfare during the whole three days. The enemy constructed a battery for ten guns opposite the Château of Arcanguez, which proved to be precisely what many of us predicted—a mere sham. They had recourse to the same system of humbug at Buzaco and other places, previous to abandoning the position in our front. Soult withdrew, in the course of the night[28], his whole force from our front, and passing with it to the opposite bank of the Nive, made a furious attack on Sir Roland Hill's corps, posted between the Adour and Nive. Nothing could exceed the bravery of the 2d Division, which, though outnumbered beyond all comparison, inflicted a terrible loss on its assailants, defeating them in every attack, and driving them back in confusion under cover of Bayonne, in sight of thousands of

24 Kincaid, 1981: 135-136.
25 Hathaway, 1997: 257.
26 sentry.
27 Smith, 1999: 155-156.
28 The night of the 12th of December.

their countrymen, who witnessed their disastrous defeat from the walls of the fortress. Finding all his attempts fruitless, both on the right and left banks of the Nive, Marshal Soult allowed us to remain pretty quiet for some time afterwards. He withdrew into his entrenched camp, and the allies occupied their original positions."

After these 'Battles of the Nive' the rest of December was spent in another period of featureless waiting.

Costello: "At the outposts, an excellent private feeling was kept up on both sides, although a general order had been promulgated prohibiting all intercourse with the enemy on pain of death. On Christmas night, our company was on picket near a dwelling called Garrett's house[29]. We clubbed half a dollar each, and sent Grindley, our comrade, into the French picket-house to purchase brandy, but when he stayed longer than was usual, we became alarmed and sent two other men in quest of him. From the nearest French sentry, they learned that Grindley was lying drunk in their picket-house. Fearful that the circumstances should come to the knowledge of Lieutenant Gardiner, the officer of our picket, they went to bring him back with them. Grindley was very drunk, and just as they were emerging with him from the French lines, who should ride down to the front post but Sir James Kempt, who commanded our Division at that time. Grindley was instantly ordered to be confined; he was very fortunate to escape with only a slight punishment.[30]"

Leach: "On the last day of the year, we got together some females, French and Spanish, and danced in the new year at the Château of Arcanguez, in spite of our proximity to such queer neighbours as the French advanced posts consisted of.

On the 1st of January 1814, nothing extraordinary occurred. We could not, however, but reflect, that the war, which had commenced on the 1st of August, 1808, in the Peninsula, was still going forward, and that there was no apparent chance of its termination. It was a great consolation to look back to the spring of 1810, when Marshal Massena boasted he would drive us into the sea, and to contrast that period with the present. Four years had now elapsed since that threat was held out; and, instead of finding ourselves performing the part of Newfoundland dogs[31] off the coast of Portugal, the British army had expelled the imperial legions from the Peninsula, and planted its standard in France."

1814

Costello: "About the Beginning of January 1814, the enemy were seen advancing, as we understood, to straighten our lines, which were in a half circle. With three or four others, I was ordered to hold possession of a small farmhouse which communicated with some cross roads, and keep up a brisk fire. If the assemblée sounded, we were to retreat upon the company, which occupied another, larger house, about 200 yards in our rear. On our right was a high stone wall, and on our left, in parallel, was a hedge, which served

[29] According to Simmons the Chateau d'Urdanches near Arcangues was called by the British 'Garat's House' after its owner (Verner 1986: 335).
[30] Hathaway, 1997: 257.
[31] 'Newfoundland dog' – a breed of large dog renowned for their love of, and aptitude for, swimming.

as cover for the French who had possession of it. When we heard the assemblée, we were on the alert to retreat, but this was risky as our only passage was by the open field between the stone wall and the hedge. The moment we showed our noses we were saluted with a hailstorm of bullets. This put us all in a rather moody condition, and it was proposed that we retire by independent files. The first to run the gauntlet was a tall gaunt Irishman. The shower that whizzed about him almost unnerved the rest of us, particularly Johnny Castles, who was at a standstill. Since Castles had figured at Badajoz with a rope round his neck, he had made up his mind to live for ever, on which he had grown fat. Now his corpulence threatened to mark him out.

"Oh, dom your limbs. Ye are the rascals to drink and carouse with as ye did yesterday," he growled in a true Caledonian dialect. He gave an awful grin. "Eh, look at 'em! dom their eyes, they are sure to hit me!" He ducked his head and, with his face half averted and covered by his hands, away he bolted, yelling and screaming all the way. The French peppered away at him in prime style, and the dust rose in every direction from the balls. Being spherical, Johnny puffed and blowed like a whale, but he escaped injury, and rolled over the hedge with a brace of samples through his knapsack and mess-tin. Gilbert[32] and I took advantage of the welcome given to Castles to follow, without allowing them time to reload. As the devil would have it, the pair of us arrived safely. There now remained only one – Jones, a fine, tall, good-looking Welshman. He quickly came after us, but the poor fellow was met half-way by a shot in his hind-quarters, passing from side to side. As soon as they saw him fall, the French ceased firing and he managed to scramble forward over the hedge to join us[33]. After all that, the enemy never took the house, and with a reinforcement from the 52nd, we beat them back again.

I often laugh at the recollection of Johnny Castles, though I must say, I funked dreadfully. Like the frogs in the fable, though death to us, it was sport to the French, who had roared with laughter as we bolted by. After this affair, Castles could never be induced to drink, or hold any acquaintance, with the enemy.[34]"

Leach: "Early in January, Marshal Soult manœuvred on the right and rear of Sir Rowland Hill's corps, crossing the Adour near Dax. The 3d, 4th, and 7th Divisions moved against him, by which he was obliged to retire to his former ground. About this period, the Light Division moved nearer the Nive, and part of Sir John Hope's corps took up our ground. We were for several days called into the field, from cantonments, in dreadful weather, in consequence of some movements of the French beyond the right of the army; but, with the exception of some skirmishing between the light troops, nothing occurred worth noticing. Heavy snow fell about the end of January, which drove the woodcocks in great abundance from the Pyrenees into the low grounds, by which I profited, and had some capital sport."

[32] Private Thomas Gilbert (Hathaway, 1997: 258, 352).
[33] Probably Thomas Jones, although Hathaway notes (1997: 352) that Thomas Jones is not reported as suffering any debilitating wounds at this time.
[34] Hathaway, 1997: 257-8.

In January France was invaded from the east by the northern allies. Wellington was uneasy about the long-term prospects for that invasion and feared pushing his own forces too far into France in case Napoleon turned his attentions to the south-west. The allied plan was therefore to prevent Soult moving north, dragging the allies with him. Staying in southern France would have the added advantage that this region was renowned for its loyalty to the exiled Bourbon King, Louis XVIII[35], and its antipathy to Napoleon. Wellington achieved his aim in February when he pushed his forces across the Adour and Soult abandoned Bayonne and headed east. The allies followed, but the 1/95th, now in the 2nd Brigade of the Light Division (having exchanged with the 2nd battalion[36]) did not accompany them far.

Leach: "About the middle of February the army was put in motion, the divisions following in succession to the right. The Light Division crossed the Nive on the 16th, and encamped near La Bastide, where we remained, in severe frosty weather, for several days. New clothing had arrived from England for the army; and as we were nearly in rags, and our wearing apparel patched with sundry colours, one regiment was sent back at a time, to St. Jean de Luz, to receive its clothing; and as soon as it rejoined the army, another was sent down, and so on in rotation."

On the 19th it was the turn of the 1/95th and the 43rd Light Infantry to march to the coast to be re-equipped. The formalities took two days. On the third they set off to rejoin the Division, now moving after the retreating French, but on the 27th of February the riflemen heard distant cannon fire. Much to their annoyance they were missing the Battle of Orthez, where Soult had taken up a defensive position on a long ridge just over the river.

At Orthez, with the 43rd and the 1/95th absent, the Light Division was held mainly in reserve at Wellington's position, or used to maintain communication between the other divisions. Only the 52nd Light Infantry and 1st Caçadores were much employed, when their brigade stormed the height occupied by the French right wing. A quarter of Barnard's force fell in this severe action but Soult, fearing his retreating centre would separate his wings, withdrew the whole army and continued his retreat. Wellington had had a narrow escape when a musket ball struck his sheathed sword, driving the hilt into his thigh.

Militarily Orthez achieved little for the allies, but yet another defeat for Napoleon's forces not only added to their existing demoralisation – increasingly evident since Vitoria – but also raised pro-Bourbon aspirations in the local population.

The 1st battalion continued their march to rejoin the army, but met a setback at the town of St Palais, where the delighted 79th Regiment (The Cameron Highlanders) handed them a General Order which instructed each regiment to occupy the town until relieved by the next to arrive. The relieved 79th moved out and the frustrated 95th moved in, for a week, none more frustrated than John Kincaid:

[35] Louis Stanislas Xavier, Comte de Provence (1755-1824). Younger brother of Louis XVI who had been on the French throne when the Revolution broke out. King in exile from 1795. In 1814 was living in England.

[36] The battalions exchanged on the 24th of January. The 2nd Brigade was led by Sir Andrew Barnard who, despite his still unhealed wound, had rejoined the Division.

"This was the more vexatious, knowing that there was no other regiment behind to relieve us. It was a nice little town, and we were treated, by the inhabitants, like friends and allies, experiencing much kindness and hospitality from them; but a rifleman, in the rear, is like a fish out of the water; he feels that he is not in his place. Seeing no other mode of obtaining a release, we, at length, began detaining the different detachments who were proceeding to join their regiments, with a view of forming a battalion of them; but, by the time that we had collected a sufficient number for that purpose, we received an order, from headquarters, to join the army; when, after a few days' forced marches, we had, at length, the happiness of overtaking our division a short distance beyond the town of Aire.[37]"

The battalion rejoined the Light Division at Barcelonne-du-Gers, just beyond Aire-sur-l'Adour, on the 11th of March. The French were to the south, towards the town of Tarbes. On the 18th of March Wellington split his force and sent half along each bank of the Adour in pursuit. The Light Division was on the east bank and stopped for the night at Plaisance, where Jonathan's company and two others crossed the small river Arros and billeted themselves in a nearby village. As George Simmons was about to settle down for the night he heard a lone rifle-shot, but thought little about it.

Costello: "On 18 March, at Plaisance, near the town of Tarbes, a French peasant was shot, under circumstances that fixed the crime upon some of the men of our company. The greatest endeavours were made to discover the culprit, and although the company was punished to make them give him up, it was to no avail.

Three months later, I was told who had perpetrated the deed. That evening, Blanco, accompanied by one or two of our men, had gone out in search of wine. They entered the house of a peasant, who resisted the intrusion and struck Blanco, for which the Spaniard shot him on the spot[38]. A very handsome collection was made for the widow and children of the poor peasant[39], for whose distress a very sincere sympathy was entertained by our battalion.[40]"

The action near Tarbes

On the 20th of March a French force of several thousand infantry[41] was seen to have occupied a long wooded height by the left of the road at Orleix, with a windmill at its far end. The Light Division was ordered to attack this position from the front while another division moved to outflank it, but in the ensuing fight only the three battalions of the 95th were employed.

Surtees: "The whole of our 95th people were accordingly ordered forward, to endeavour to drive them from this position. My battalion formed the right, the 2d battalion the centre, and the 1st battalion the left of our line of skirmishers. We found them covered in front with a great number of

[37] Kincaid, 1981: 142.
[38] Is this true? The Spanish conscripts left the army and returned to Spain on the 11th of June, 3 months after this incident. Presumably Blanco, with his reputation for violence, was only identified as the murderer after he had left the regiment and could no longer defend himself. There was a habit in the Rifles of blaming uncomfortable events on men who were no longer present – as in January 1812 when the officers going into the Sierra de Gata stole livestock from fellow officers then later put the entire blame (unfairly) on one of their party who had been killed subsequently (Verner, 1919: 299, and noted above).
[39] The officers of the Light Division contributed 100 guineas (£105).
[40] Hathaway, 1997: 259-260.
[41] Surtees says this was a whole division of 5000-6000 men but Jonathan Leach says this force "belonged to" a division and Kincaid implies only upwards of 2000 men.

light troops, which occupied us some time in driving in, and in which service we suffered considerably, for they occupied the hedges and dikes on the high ground, from which it was necessary we should dislodge them. We had also a considerably sized brushwood to pass through before we could get at them. At length, after much smart skirmishing, we gained the height, but found the whole of their heavy infantry drawn up on a steep acclivity, near the windmill, which allowed them to have line behind line, all of which could fire at the same time over each other's heads, like the tiers of guns in a three-decker. We continued, however, to advance upon them, till we got within a hundred paces of this formidable body, the firing from which was the hottest I had ever been in, except perhaps Barossa[42]. At this moment   I received a shot through my right shoulder, which compelled me for a moment to retire; but meeting the main support of my battalion advancing with Colonel Ross[43] at its head, and finding my wound had not disabled me, I again advanced with him, until we got close under the enemy's line, and took post behind a hillock, which protected us from their fire.

We here found Colonel Norcott[44], who then belonged to the 2d battalion, riding about on his large black mare; but he had not ridden long till he also was wounded through the shoulder, from which he still suffers. While we were in this situation, a shot struck a captain of ours in the side where he had his drinking-horn slung; in fact it struck both the horn and his side; but, from some cause, it did not penetrate the flesh, but bruised it sore, which is generally painful. The captain, and those about him, thought he was shot through the body; they accordingly picked him up, and were carrying him off to the rear, when he cried, "Stop, let me feel," and putting his hand down to the place, and finding no wound, he sprung out of their arms, and, with the most ludicrous appearance possible, returned to his post again. No one present could refrain from laughing at the ridiculousness of this occurrence, although at the moment the men were falling fast around us.[45]"

42 Battle of Barossa, near Cadiz, 5th March 1811.
43 Lieutenant-Colonel John Ross (d. 1835). He joined the Rifles at their formation in 1800 as a Lieutenant from the 72nd Regiment of Foot and was now the Major of the 3/95th. Was later Major-General Sir John Ross *KCB*.
44 Lieutenant-Colonel Amos Godsell R. Norcott (ca 1785-1838). Major of the 2/95th. Later Major-General Sir Amos Norcott *CB, KStA*.
45 Surtees, 1973: 286-288.

The fire was equally intense to the left where the 1st battalion was advancing. Lieutenant George Simmons was struck a glancing blow on the right knee by a ball which fractured his knee-cap and embedded his trousers and underlying long drawers in the wound.

Costello: 'Only at Badajoz were we more warmly engaged. The enemy were in great numbers, our attacking force few, being only our three battalions of Rifles, which their bullets thinned fast as we struggled up the hill: Although under every disadvantage, we, the victors of so many hard fights, were not to be repelled, and the French were obliged to retreat... This day, I stuck a poor Frenchman whom I came up with, and I was sorry for it because I discovered he was badly wounded. I made honourable amends with a sup from my canteen, which he received with grace.[46]'

Leach: "The French being reinforced, tried to retake the ground which they had lost. We inflicted on them, however, a severe loss, and drove them back in great confusion. The vineyards near the scene of action were covered with their killed and wounded in all directions. They then retreated on their reserves, which were formed on another ridge about a mile[47] distant. The contest was not of long duration, but it was extremely hot; and in less than half an hour, our corps lost eleven officers killed and wounded, and an equal proportion of men.

The troops with whom we had been engaged belonged to the division of General Harispe[48], which had recently joined Marshal Soult from Catalonia; and, having been accustomed for many years to oppose imperfectly organised Spaniards, probably did not calculate on so warm a reception as they met with at Tarbes."

In the Caçadores, waiting to support the riflemen if needed, Major John Blakiston[49] watched the Rifles with more than a little appreciation, expressed some years later:

"Nothing could exceed the manner in which the 95th set about this business. Certainly I never saw such skirmishers as the 95th, now the Rifle Brigade. They could do the work much better and with infinitely *less loss* than any other of our best Light troops. They possessed an individual boldness, a mutual understanding, and a quickness of eye in taking advantage of the ground, which, taken altogether, I never saw equalled. They were, in fact, as much superior to the French Voltigeurs as the latter were to our skirmishers in general. As our regiment was often employed in supporting them, I think I am fairly qualified to speak of their merits."

In the action at Orleix the Rifles lost 11 officers and about 100 men killed or wounded. French casualties were estimated at 1000, virtually equalling their attackers' entire strength. Even Harry Smith was surprised: "the loss of the enemy from the fire of our Rifles was so great that one could not believe one's eyes. I certainly had never seen the dead lie so thick, nor ever did, except subsequently at Waterloo. Barnard even asked the Duke[50] to ride over the hill and see the sight, which he consented to do, but added,

[46] Hathaway, 1997: 261.
[47] 1.6 km.
[48] Maréchal Jean-Isidore Harispe.
[49] John Blakiston (1785-1867). Author of *Twelve Years' Military Adventure*, from which the quote, repeated in Verner (1986: xvii), is taken.
[50] Wellington, at this time was still a Marquess.

235

"Well, Barnard, to please you, I will go, but I require no novel proof of the destructive fire of your Rifles."[51]"

Toulouse

Wellington prepared to attack the French in their new positions but the light faded and on a cold, dreary night the Light Division, without its baggage or its supper, bivouacked under cannon fire in front of the French lines. In the darkness Soult's army slipped away east in the direction of Toulouse.

Leach: "The rains continued to fall so heavily and incessantly, that we concluded the long-protracted contest between the French and allied armies would be terminated by a deluge, and our marches and countermarches cease. In spite of all these foretellings and prognostications, we still waded, day after day, through mud and water to the knees, and came up with the French rear-guard on the 26th between Plaisance[52] and Toulouse, where our cavalry lost some men and horses in a skirmish. The next day our 3d battalion had a brush with the French light troops near Tournefuille.

The 29th brought the Light Division within two miles of Toulouse, and we occupied a straggling village called St. Simeon; a long chain of French pickets being near at hand, between our quarters and the city."

For a number of days the army was quiet. Wellington knew Soult was expecting to be reinforced by the army of Suchet, which was en route to join him, and tried to cross the Garonne south of Toulouse to sever French communications. This would also put the allies on the least defended side of the city, where Soult was relying on the speed and breadth of the flooded river and the dire condition of the roads – impassable for artillery. At the first attempt the river proved too wide for Wellington's bridging engineers, but three days later Sir Rowland Hill's corps managed to cross. However, the countryside was so impracticable for the movement of an army they were obliged to return.

Wellington now resolved to cross the river north of Toulouse and attack Soult in his heavily fortified position on that side of the town before Suchet arrived. A pontoon bridge was put in place and on the 4th of April Sir William Beresford took the 3rd, 4th and 6th divisions and a handful of cavalry across. The Light Division and Freyre's Spanish army (allowed back into France after promising to behave) were due to follow, but the French, aware of the pontoon's presence, had begun floating trees downstream from the city to weaken its anchorage. This and the fact the river had become so swollen from the continuing downpour made it necessary to disconnect the pontoon (temporarily) from the far bank.

Beresford's force was now isolated and vulnerable to an expedition in force from the city. To allay his expressed concerns Wellington and several of his staff were ferried across the river in a small boat – their horses swimming alongside – to appraise the situation. They returned having convinced him he was in little immediate danger. Nevertheless, it was to

[51] Smith, 1999: 174-175.
[52] Plaisance-du-Toulouse, on the south western approaches to Toulouse, approximately 12 km from the city centre.

be the 10th of April before the Light Division could cross the Garonne and turn towards Toulouse. They were to attack the same day; Easter Sunday, 1814.

The Battle of Toulouse

Soult was strongly placed to resist an attack. His forces were positioned on fortified heights, Calvinet Ridge, a kilometre to the east of the walled town. The Garonne was to the west. To the north of the town, and turning south between it and the ridge, was the Languedoc canal, crossed by a number of bridges.

In moving forward to their positions the Light Division drove in a considerable number of French light troops occupying houses along the roads running towards the city. They also cleared a fortified convent at one of the bridges over the river.

Leach: "Lord Wellington immediately arranged matters for attacking the enemy, who was in a position on the heights above the city, covered with redoubts and different field fortifications, which had been constructed under the directions of General Cafarelli, an engineer of talent[53]. The different entrances to the town were defended by artillery, and the head of the bridge, opposite to which Sir Rowland Hill's troops were stationed, had been rendered formidable also. The approach to the heights was, in most parts, a *glacis*, which, as it afforded no protection to the assailants, exposed them to a deadly fire.

Sir Thomas Picton's division occupied the ground from the Garonne to the great road leading from Bordeaux into Toulouse[54]. The Light Division covered the ground from the left of General Picton nearly to the base of the French position. On our left again were the Spaniards; and considerably further to their left was Marshal Beresford, with the 4th and 6th Divisions. Sir Rowland Hill threatened the city from the opposite side of the Garonne. The cavalry, I believe, supported Marshal Beresford's column.

The outline of the plan of attack was something like the following. The 3d and Light Divisions were to throw light troops along the canal, and by a constant fire to attract the enemy's attention on that point, and to threaten the entrance by the great road. The Spaniards were to attack the heights in conjunction with the 4th and 6th Divisions; but being nationally and by constitution obstinate and self-opinionated, they thought proper to ascend the heights long before Marshal Beresford's column had made a sufficient *détour* to enable it to attack the French right. The consequence was, that the Spaniards were driven back with great slaughter, and probably would not have halted until this time, if the Light Division had not advanced in line to cover their retreat, and enabled them to form behind it."

To the north of the town, Picton, with questionable judgement, sent the 3rd division to storm the strong fortifications at Pont Jumeaux[55]. The division was repulsed with more than 400 casualties. Beresford, marching

[53] There were two French Generals of that name: Général Louis Marie Joseph Maximilien de Caffarelli du Falga (1756-1799) an engineer who died 15 years before the Battle of Toulouse; and his brother Général Marie François Auguste compte Caffarelli du Falga (1766-1849) who served in Spain from 1809 to early 1813 then in Paris.

[54] This road entered the city from the north.

[55] Wellington had ordered Picton to feign an attack but Picton made a full assault (Wellington, 1956: 7).

the 4th and 6th divisions 3 km under enemy fire around the French flank to attack the heights from the east found the roads too difficult for his artillery. He ordered them to halt and cannonade the north-eastern redoubts while he continued to his point of attack with the infantry and cavalry. When Beresford's artillery opened up, General Freyre's Spaniards assumed the 4th and 6th divisions had reached their post and were engaging the enemy, so they too attacked. This was far too early and they attracted the undivided attention of the French defenders above them.

Smith: "Sir Thomas Picton, as usual, attacked when he ought not, and lost men. The Spaniards made three attacks on a very important part of the enemy's position defended by a strong redoubt. The first was a very courageous though unsuccessful attack; the second, a most gallant, heavy, and persevering one, and had my dear old Light Division been pushed forward on the right of the Spaniards in place of remaining inactive, that attack of the Spaniards would have succeeded. I said so at the moment. The third attempt of the Spaniards was naturally, after two such repulses, a very poor one. At this period, about two o'clock in the afternoon, the Duke's staff began to look grave, and all had some little disaster to report to His Grace, who says, "Ha, by God, this won't do; I must try something else."[56]"

As the Spaniards fell back, the Light Division's left wing had to extend sideways to fill the gap in the allied line and endured some severe fighting as it took the strain.

Costello: "As we proceeded, we heard a heavy firing as if from the left of the town, and soon after beheld a disorganised mass of Spanish soldiers flying towards us. At first some of our fellows took them for the French, and fired among them, by which some lives were lost. They were a part of the Spanish force which attempted to carry a French fort or redoubt, but the enemy had sent them to the right about faster than they had come.

We continued to approach the town, which was protected by a long series of fortifications that appeared to be full of men. When we halted, sheltered by some trees, near to the walls of some houses, they opened up a running fire from some fieldworks, but with little execution. We were not in this quiescent state long, when the thunder of the conflict was heard going on to our left, the salvoes of artillery, the constant cracking of musketry, the rushing sound of shells, and the occasional wild 'hurra', forming a very pretty concert. The scene was still more electrifying when we found it to be the 6th Division engaged in storming the batteries which the Spaniards had just run from. After a hard tug, they carried them in glorious style. General Picton's Division was also conspicuously engaged on our right, close to the river.[57]"

The 6th Division was at first repulsed on the steep, slippery slope, but with their second attempt they dislodged the French who were pushed back, slowly and with great effort. The 6th then moved northwards along the crest of the ridge, clearing the fortifications as it went. The French were

[56] Smith, 1999: 176-177 (Smith's wife was Spanish and he saw more value in the Spanish troops than some of his more jingoistic colleagues).
[57] Hathaway, 1997: 263-4.

driven down towards the city and across the canal. They made this their new defensive line and behind it manned the town walls. Several times they tried to break out and recapture the high ground but on each occasion were beaten back.

This ended the Battle of Toulouse. The allies suffered considerably in this engagement. More than 4600 British and Portuguese troops were killed or wounded. The 6th Division alone lost 1500 men, a quarter of its strength. Freyre's Spanish force lost 2000 men, again a quarter of those in the field. The French, better defended by their fieldworks, lost just over 3250 and had three Generals[58] and 1600 men captured.

After the battle

Within the fortifications of Toulouse Soult's army was now very vulnerable. The captured heights dominated the city and brought it easily within artillery range. After a quiet Easter Monday the French army left Toulouse at night by the only route open to them, to the south, and followed the canal towards Carcassone. The allies entered the city on the 12th. On that day a messenger reached Wellington from Paris. The war was over.

In the north Napoleon had been overpowered by the main allied invasion. Facing overwhelming odds with an ever weaker army, he had fought an inspired but doomed rearguard action. In late March, attempting to cut the communications between the allied forces, he had overstretched his own and left open the route to Paris. The allies marched to the capital unopposed, arriving on the 31st. With his Marshals in revolt Napoleon admitted defeat and signed abdication papers on the 6th of April. Neither Wellington nor Soult had been aware of this as their forces contested Toulouse.

The city itself was a royalist stronghold and the people shed few tears. No sooner had Soult's troops marched out than the city was cloaked in a blizzard of white: the emblem of the Bourbons. White flags were flown; white sheets were hung from windows; white scarves and ribbons and feathers were worn by all and sundry.

Leach: "The allied army entered Toulouse on the 12th (except the 4th and 6th Divisions, which were on the road by which the French had retreated), and was received with the greatest apparent joy. White cockades were in every hat, and white flags displayed from every house.

The same day despatches reached Lord Wellington from Paris, announcing the abdication of Bonaparte, and his being about to repair to Elba[59]. A flag of truce was sent to Marshal Soult from the British headquarters, to apprise him of the fact; but, as no official communication to that effect had reached him direct from the provisional government at Paris, he declined overtures for an armistice. In consequence of this, the allied troops left Toulouse on the 17th[60], and proceeded in the direction of Carcassone, where the French army was concentrated.

[58] Générals Harispe, Baurot and St Hilaire.

[59] After his abdication the allies gave Napoleon sovereignty of the island of Elba, between his native Corsica and the Italian mainland, as a principality. He was also allowed to retain the title *Emperor* and was awarded an annual income of 2,000,000 Francs to be paid by France –although he does not appear to have received this (Hamilton, 2000: 168). He arrived on Elba on the 4th of May 1814.

[60] The Light Division had been cantoned in the suburbs next to the ground where the battle had been fought. The rank and file were under orders not to enter the town but some (Costello for one) disobeyed.

General Count Gazan[61], the chief of Soult's staff, met us with a flag of truce near Baziege; the purport of his mission being to inform Lord Wellington that Bonaparte's abdication had at length been officially notified to Marshal Soult, who was ready to conclude an armistice, and to appoint persons to fix on a line of demarcation between the French and allied armies. Thus we at length witnessed the termination of the war which had so long been waged in Spain, Portugal, and the South of France."

Costello: "We were immediately ordered to the right-about, and marched back to Toulouse. Before we had proceeded many miles, we were overtaken on the road by great numbers of French soldiers who had been disbanded, or had disbanded themselves, and who were returning to their homes. Like ourselves, they were no doubt tired of the war they had been carrying on so long. Generally, these fine-looking Frenchmen had good feelings towards us, and in many instances shared the fatigue in carrying our men's knapsacks.[62]"

Jonathan Leach: "I believe it is common to human nature to forget hardships, privations, and fatigues, of however long continuance, soon after they have ceased, and are succeeded by the common comforts of life. This may account, in some measure, for the assertions which I have heard made by a few zealots and fire-eaters, who, long after the termination of the war in the Peninsula (and not until then), have declared that they were quite inconsolable when the armistice was concluded, and the prospect of no longer being targets for French bullets stared them in the face. But at the moment when hostilities ceased between the armies of France and England, I do maintain that the general and universal feeling was (amongst those, at least, who had been participators in the whole of the war in the Peninsula, from the summer of 1808 to the spring of 1814), that for the present we had had enough of campaigning, and that a little rest and time to refit would be desirable."

[61] Général Honoré Theodore Maxime Gazan, Comte de la Peyrière (1765-1845). Soult's Chief of Staff in the *Army of the Pyrenees* from July 1813 to April 1814.
[62] Hathaway, 1997: 266.

— 14 —

Peace

We had been born in war, reared in war,
and war was our trade; and what soldiers
had to do in peace, was a problem yet to
be solved among us.

John Kincaid[1]

[1] Kincaid, 1981: 147.
[2] Louis de Bourbon, duc de Angoulême (1775-1844). Nephew of Louis XVIII. He landed in France early in 1814 to inspire pro-Bourbon feelings in the population and entered Bordeaux on the 12th of March, the date taken as the beginning of the Bourbon restoration.
[3] This is probably true. Wellington described Soult as, "a very large man—very tall and large, like Marshal Beresford—a harsh voice, and not a very pleasant countenance or manner." (Stanhope, 1888: 19).
[4] As was the cavalry General Sir Stapleton Cotton (1773-1865).

After Napoleon's abdication the armies of Wellington and Soult moved to positions north of Toulouse, separated by the River Tarn. The Light Division was cantoned in villages in the narrow strip of land between that river and the Garonne. The 52nd Light Infantry and the 1/95th were at Castelsarrasin.

"I went from Castel Sarrazin one morning," says Jonathan, "to Montauban, to see the army of Marshal Soult, and a part of Marshal Suchet's, reviewed by the Duke d'Angoulême[2]. The troops were drawn out in several lines, waiting the arrival of the duke; and I had an excellent opportunity of inspecting that very army which we had so often met in the Peninsula. Their general appearance was fine and soldierlike. The Spanish sun had left its mark on their countenances, which were for the most part lively and animated, without the smallest appearance of despondency or disappointment at the late change, or at the loss of their imperial master. Marshal Soult alone appeared sullen and dejected. But this possibly was his natural manner[3]. Marshal Suchet, who sat on horse-back on the duke's left hand, laughed and joked, and had every appearance of being perfectly satisfied."

Another Field-Marshal with more than the appearance of being satisfied was Arthur Wellesley. On the 3rd of May he was elevated yet again in the peerage to become Duke of Wellington. He was also appointed British Ambassador to the Court of France, charged with managing British interests in the new peace. Sir John Hope, Sir Thomas Graham, Sir Rowland Hill and Sir William Beresford were all raised to the peerage[4].

At Castelsarrasin Jonathan's company relaxed as best they could, and some made peace with their erstwhile combatants.

Ned Costello: "Here we came in for delightful quarters, being billeted in the houses. We all had excellent beds. One would have thought these would be most welcome, so it was highly amusing to see our rough, hardy fellows contemptuously spurn this luxury. In the previous five or six years we had been almost constantly exposed. With the earth their rude bed, the sky their canopy, and with generally a stone for a pillow, our men could obtain no sleep on beds of down, and preferred wrapping a blanket round them, and using the hard floor as a place of rest. So much for custom.

At Castelsarrasin we were on our usual excellent terms with the French quartered in the neighbourhood. To while away the time we had constant matches with them in running, jumping, and gymnastic exercises.[5]"

During these athletics meetings Costello struck up a friendship with a Sergeant of the French 43rd Regiment, stationed at Montauban, who invited Costello, Thomas Gilbert – now promoted to Corporal – and another Corporal, to an NCOs' dinner at his mess. With permission from their Colonel, they readily accepted.

"On the day appointed, away we started. I shall never forget it. It was a fine morning, and after crossing the Garonne in open boats[6] – the bridge had been destroyed previous to the battle of Toulouse – we entered Montauban. Our uniforms were almost new, and fitted us well. My two comrades had the advantage of being tall, and exceedingly smart-looking men. I was fat as a butt, and as strong as I looked.

In the square of the town, the 43rd and two other regiments, formed a brigade and were drawn up on parade, with two splendid bands playing in front. As we went in search of our friend, we had to pass down the front of two of the French regiments, which we did, saluting their officers soldier-like. The latter returned our salute in the manner for which they are so justly remarked, and made us feel not a little proud of their courtesy.

We moved along the line until we fell in with the sergeant, who started out of the ranks and gave us a hearty welcome. We waited beside him while the band played some favourite airs, then the regiments were dismissed. As soon as they broke ranks, their officers crowded around us, severally shook us by the hand, and gave us sundry smacks on the shoulders, with '*Bravos les Anglais, soyez les bien venus,*[7]' etc.

The sergeant immediately escorted us to his quarters. The dining-room was a splendid one, and fitted up beautifully; the tables groaned under every delicacy of the season. We did not forget to do justice to the acknowledged merits of John Bull in all matters of this nature, and much good feeling and conviviality followed, with encomiums and compliments being passed on the English. All went on very well until, with the removal of the cloth, singing was introduced. Several famous songs, so far as we could understand, were introduced, and our sergeant gave us an excellent specimen; Gilbert and myself joined in in our own rough manner. It had been agreed among the French that no song should be sung that reflected upon our country,

[5] Hathaway, 1997: 267-268.
[6] Costello must mean the Tarn; Castelsarrasin and Montauban are on the same side of the Garonne.
[7] effectively 'Good for you Englishmen, it was good of you to come.'

but a French corporal, under the influence of wine, commenced a *chanson de guerre*[8], for which, by general consent, and with a very proper feeling, he was kicked down stairs. The guests resumed their seats, and all went on as quietly as before. Here we remained enjoying ourselves till three the next morning when we were accompanied to the boats at the riverside, escorted by a number of their band playing 'Patrick's Day'.[9]"

Others among the British were not on such good terms with their new neighbours, but at Castelsarrasin the officers had time to arrange their own amusements, spending five or six weeks very pleasantly, Jonathan recalled, "receiving the greatest kindness and hospitality from the inhabitants. Dances, fêtes champêtres on the banks of the Garonne, horse-races, and various gaieties, filled up our time; and great regret was expressed when the order arrived which obliged us to leave our new French acquaintance; some of the fair females of whom had ruined the peace of mind (*pro tempore*) of many of our gallant gay Lotharios."

One of these Lotharios, by his own admission ("I was as much in love as anybody"), was John Kincaid:

"Castel-Sarazin is a respectable little town, on the right bank of the Garonne; and its inhabitants received us so kindly that every officer found in his quarters a family home. We there too, found both the time and the opportunity of exercising one of the agreeable professions to which we had long been strangers, that of making love to the pretty little girls with which the place abounded; when, after a three months' residence among them, the fatal order arrived for our march to Bordeaux, for embarkation, the buckets full of salt tears that were shed by men who had almost forgotten the way to weep was quite ridiculous. I have never yet, however, clearly made out whether people are most in love when they are laughing or when they are crying.[10]"

More farewells

The Light Division marched north-west on the 1st of June. In the five years since the 1/95th had landed in Portugal, the 1050 men who were put ashore, and the 100 who subsequently joined them, had been eroded to 500 survivors, virtually all of whom carried the scars of old wounds[11].

On the 11th of June the Light Division reached Bazas. Here the Spanish and Portuguese troops were to take their permanent leave and march to their homes over the Pyrenees.

Costello: "Many deep feelings of regret were felt, particularly by the men of our battalion, on parting with the Spaniards who had been incorporated in our ranks for so long, and who were so distinguished for their gallantry[12]. Sixteen had been drafted into our company, but only five survived to bid us farewell. The poor fellows had grown attached to the battalion and expressed much grief on leaving it: Blanco, the sanguinary Blanco, actually shed tears.[13]"

[8] Song of war.
[9] Hathaway, 1997: 268-269.
[10] Kincaid, 1981: 147-148.
[11] Smith, 1999: 185.
[12] Harry Smith said later of the Spaniards, 'many of them the most daring sharpshooters in our corps... I never saw better, more orderly, perfectly sober soldiers in my life, and as vedettes [sentries] the old German Hussar did not exceed them.' (Smith, 1999: 185).
[13] Hathaway, 1997: 270.

The Portuguese troops, in their own regiments, left with more formality. At 2 o'clock in the afternoon the 1/95th and the 52nd Light Infantry drew up in formation on each side of the market square in Bazas, and as the 1st and 3rd Caçadores[14] and the 17th Portuguese Regiment of the Line marched out between them the British presented arms and gave three almighty cheers for their old comrades in arms[15]. For Jonathan the parting was "altogether affecting."

During the preceding years a number of Portuguese and Spanish women had also become attached to various men in the Rifles and had followed the regiment through thick and thin. An ultimatum was issued: the men could consent to marry their loved ones or those loved ones would have to leave too. Many men did consent, especially, but not exclusively, those who had fathered children during the campaigns. Those women who failed to convince their men, or presumably whose men were already married, were despatched homewards under the care of the Portuguese troops so they could draw rations with the regiments on their journey. "There was much weeping and wailing on the part of the signoras" according to Jonathan[16]. Many British light infantrymen who considered themselves unable or unwilling either to be married or to be separated chose instead to desert, including two from his company[17].

Home

The British contingent of the Light Division reached Bordeaux three days later and camped several kilometres beyond the city on an extensive heath near the village of Blanquefort. They were in the neighbourhood of Bordeaux for several weeks, during which time the Division was "very minutely inspected[18]" by His Grace Field-Marshal the Duke of Wellington. He dressed for the occasion in his best uniform with a full complement of insignia and honours. In all the years the men of the Division had served with him it was the first time any of them had seen him so attired.

Jonathan Leach: "Lord Wellington took a last look, near the suburbs of Bordeaux, at the British regiments of the Light Division, which were about to embark and to be dispersed. He departed amidst loud cheers of men and officers, many of whom had followed him through seven successive, and, I may add, successful campaigns in the Peninsula and the south of France. The cavalry marched from Bordeaux to Boulogne and Calais, where they embarked for England; and the infantry waited at Bordeaux for shipping to take them to England, Ireland, or America, as their destinations happened to be. Bordeaux was thronged with British officers and soldiers, not in gay or flashy costumes, but in remnants of what had once been so."

On about the 12th of July 1814 the 1st and 2nd battalions 95th sailed from Bordeaux aboard the *Ville de Paris*, a man-o'-war of 110 guns, and after ten days they anchored off Portsmouth. Disembarking, they marched for Dover to relax in their native land for the first time in five years. Harry Smith would have to wait longer.

[14] Smith notes, "The 3rd Caçadores at this period were commanded by a fine gallant soldier and a good fellow, but as he rejoiced in a name of unusual length—Senhor Manuel Terçeira Caetano Pinto de Silvuica y Souza— we gave him the much shorter appellation of "Jack Nasty Face," for he was an ugly dog, though a very good officer." (Smith, 1999: 184fn).
[15] Verner, 1986: 350.
[16] Surtees says 800-900 women crossed into Spain with the Portuguese (repeated in Hathaway, 1997: 271).
[17] Hathaway, 1997: 270.
[18] Surtees, 1973: 318.
[19] He had been promoted to Captain between the storms of Ciudad Rodrigo and Badajoz in the Spring of 1812 but had been a Staff officer since March 1811 and had never led his own company in the 1/95th.
[20] Major-General Robert Ross (1766-1814). Lieutenant-Colonel in the 20th (East Devonshire) Regiment in the Coruña campaign. Went to Walcheren then at the end of 1812, to the Peninsula as brevet Colonel. Was promoted Major-General just before Vitoria, where his force was in the 4th Division. Took part in the Battle of the Pyrenees keeping Soult from Pamplona. Was at the Nivelle and Orthez.

Harry Smith

[21] Rear-Admiral George Cockburn [pronounced 'Coe-burn'] (1772-1853) Later Admiral of the Fleet Sir George Cockburn *GCB* and MP for: Portsmouth (1818); Weobley (1820); Plymouth (1826); and Ripon (1841). Succeeded to a baronetcy on the death of his brother James in 1852.

[22] According to the Chancellor of the Exchequer, in a speech to the House of Commons, 14th November 1814.

[23] The 4th (King's Own) Regiment of Foot; 44th (East Sussex) Regiment of Foot; and the 85th Light Infantry (Buckinghamshire Volunteers).

[24] 900 men of the 21st (Royal North British) Fusiliers.

[25] Or Caribbean or American-born? Gleig (1861: 47) does not identify this newly trained unit.

[26] For a first hand account of this campaign and a description of Washington see Gleig (1861 or other editions) who was a British Lieutenant in the 85th Light Infantry with the attacking force.

[27] General Ross later wrote, 'So unexpected was our entry and capture of Washington, and so confident was [President] Madison of the defeat of our troops, that he had prepared a supper for the expected conquerors; and when our advanced party entered the President's house, they found a table laid with forty covers' (*Dictionary of National Biography*, 'Ross').

[28] After the fire the Americans white-washed over the scorch marks on the President's mansion, creating the first 'White-House'.

[29] Smith, 1999: 200-201.

[30] *Dictionary of National Biography*, 'Cockburn'.

Although he was in the 1/95th, and should have gone to Kent, Smith was close to a promotion[19] and some general officers with his interests at heart, fearing peace would slow his progress, arranged that he accompany a brigade being sent from France to the continuing conflict in America. For several years he had served as Brigade-Major (the staff officer attending the brigade commander) for the Light Division's 2nd Brigade, and it was as Brigade-Major to Major-General Robert Ross[20] that he sailed from Bordeaux on the 1st of June. Ross's mission, with the assistance of a naval group under Rear-Admiral George Cockburn[21], was to take an expeditionary force to the eastern seaboard of the United States "to retaliate upon the Americans for the outrages which they had committed upon the frontiers.[22]"

Ross's brigade of three army battalions[23] collected a fourth battalion[24] at Bermuda and Smith was appointed Deputy Adjutant-General. Sailing north to Chesapeake Bay – where the force was increased to 4500 men by the addition of 700 marines and a company of 100 African infantrymen[25] – they travelled up the Patuxent River, and landed at Benedict, south-east of Washington, on the 19th of August. At Bladensburg on the 24th the British defeated the American defenders and marched into Washington virtually unchallenged. Their objective was to execute Cockburn's plan to raze the American capital[26].

Smith: "we entered Washington for the barbarous purpose of destroying the city. Admiral Cockburn would have burnt the whole, but Ross would only consent to the burning of the public buildings. I had no objection to burn arsenals, dockyards, frigates building, stores, barracks, etc., but well do I recollect that, fresh from the Duke's humane warfare in the South of France, we were horrified at the order to burn the elegant Houses of Parliament and the President's house. In the latter, however, we found a supper all ready, which was sufficiently cooked without more fire, and which many of us speedily consumed, unaided by the fiery elements, and drank some very good wine also[27]. I shall never forget the destructive majesty of the flames as the torches were applied to beds, curtains, etc. Our sailors were artists at the work. Thus was fought the Battle of Bladensburg, which wrested from the Americans their capital Washington, and burnt its Capitol and other buildings with the ruthless firebrand of the Red Savages of the woods[28]. Neither our Admirals nor the Government at home were satisfied that we had not allowed the work of destruction to progress, as it was considered the total annihilation of Washington would have removed the seat of government to New York, and the Northern and Federal States were adverse to the war with England.[29]"

Although Ross was given credit in Britain for the raid, he was careful to record in his report, "To Rear-admiral Cockburn, who suggested the attack upon Washington, and who accompanied the army, I confess the greatest obligations for his cordial co-operation and advice.[30]"

Despite Harry Smith's record of government dissatisfaction, publicly the British applauded themselves for their civilised restraint in limiting the destruction[31].

William Surtees

While Harry Smith sailed for the United States and the 1st and 2nd battalions 95th headed for Portsmouth and Kent, the 3rd battalion sailed from France on the 9th of July and disembarked at Plymouth to await orders.

Surtees: "We landed at Plymouth on the 18th, and occupied one of the barracks. We did not exactly know what was to become of us. Kent being our regimental station, we expected to be ordered to march and join the left wing in that county, but were still kept at Plymouth, where we met with great kindness and attention from the inhabitants in general, who are upon the whole, I think, an excellent and a moral people. We also fared sumptuously here, every description of food being both cheap and good. Fish in particular is most abundant and excellent. In short, we were here as comfortably and as well quartered as we could desire, and every thing tended to make us perfectly satisfied with our lot. We relaxed by attending the theatre occasionally, which is one of the best provincial ones in the kingdom, and at this time could boast some very good actors. There were a variety of other amusements, such as fishing, &c., which of course we indulged in occasionally.[32]"

The 3rd battalion was quartered at Plymouth until the 18th of September when, amid great secrecy, it too sailed for the United States to join British units planning to attack the Americans at New Orleans.

[31] Some private property was destroyed, for example a house used by a sniper who narrowly missed Ross, but killed his horse, when firing on a British party advancing under a flag of truce (Gleig, 1861: 69).

[32] Surtees, 1973: 323.

— 15 —

Professionalism

From the standpoint of the early nineteenth century... to seek to earn one's living from something like natural history did not rank as following a profession as that word was generally understood: it was almost tantamount, rather, to running off to sea or joining a circus – a mad gesture by the foolhardy or the desperate.

David Allen[1]

On the 22nd of July 1813, as Jonathan looked out towards the French in the Pass of Vera, Dr George Shaw, the zoologist at the British Museum, died in his museum apartments. He was 61 years old and had worked at the Museum since February 1791, the month Elford Leach was born.

The following week Elford was at Kingsbridge collecting marine crustaceans when Montagu gave him the news. He knew what to do. Without even waiting to return to Woodland, he sat down and wrote to Sir Joseph Banks. Although it was effectively the Archbishop of Canterbury[2] who held the gift of appointing the Museum's officers[3], Banks was the primary scientific trustee, and Elford already knew him. Elford was so enthusiastic to obtain the museum position, he told Banks he would willingly work without a salary.

Elford was taking a social gamble in applying for a professional post as a naturalist. Natural history during the Regency was viewed by many as an honourable pastime but less than honourable employment. Speaking of the move from the self-supported gentleman naturalist to the paid 'jobber', historian of science David Allen notes:

'Natural history was a highly respected leisure pursuit, but to follow it for money was to commit a kind of suicide. Worse, to be seen to have accepted employment, with all its attendant indignities – instead of at least retaining autonomy as a freelance – made the drop in status all the greater and the more painful...

Professions involved expensive training and were exclusive by definition. Once qualified in one of these, a man could expect to be his own master or have other people to order for most of the time at least. But a naturalist? He could expect only to cling to the outermost margins of respectable society

[1] Allen, 1985: 3.
[2] Charles Manners-Sutton (1755-1828). Archbishop of Canterbury 1805-1828.
[3] The 3 Principal Trustees of the British Museum were solely responsible for the appointment of Museum officers (House of Commons, 1835: paras 118-121). These 3 *ex officio* trustees were the Archbishop of Canterbury, the Lord Chancellor and the Speaker of the House of Commons. It was recognised that the Archbishop carried the greatest influence at this time.
[4] Allen, 1985: 3, 9.

and to be sat upon and snubbed. It was anything but a desirable prospect for a person of gentle birth.[4]'

Elford Leach would not be swayed by such concerns for two reasons[5]. First, they probably never crossed his mind. He was engrossed in his science. How having paid employment affected his social standing, and how it appeared to other people, steeped in the attitudes outlined above, would never have occurred to him. He was attracted by the scientific opportunities afforded by the collections and location of the British Museum. Second, however it may have appeared to genteel observers, he was not working for the salary; he was not obliged to earn a living. In his mind's eye he doubtless expected to retain his autonomy. He probably did not even consider the broader responsibilities of the post to museum duties and the constraints of reporting to senior officers. It is also possible the Museum, as a national institution managed by persons of high birth and social rank, was to some extent exempt from the 'jobbing' accusations, despite the impoverished state of the establishment, and of some of its officers, at this time.

[5] This paragraph is an opinion based on reading his manuscripts and published works, as they reveal his character.

Historical note

1812

summer	British harvest is poor. Wheat rises to 16*s* 6*d* per bushel.
September	Riot at Dartmoor Prison.
September	Anti-enclosure disturbances in Wales.
16th September	Napoleon enters Moscow.
October-December	Napoleon retreats from Moscow.

1813

29th January	Jane Austen's book *Pride and Prejudice* is published anonymously (drafted as *First Impressions* c. 1796-1797)
—	Royal College of Surgeons moves into a new building on the site of their existing premises at N° 41 Lincoln's Inn Fields and the neighbouring N° 42[1].
—	Work begins on the new *Regent Street*.
—	The *Philharmonic Society* founded in London.
—	Sir Humphry Davy takes bookbinder Michael Faraday[2] as his assistant at the Royal Institution.
—	Schubert[3] composes his 1st Symphony.
February	Anti-clearance riots in Scotland.
April	Anti-enclosure riots in Wales.
summer	Bumper harvest. Domestic wheat price falls, hitting land-owning producers.
September	Robert Southey becomes Poet Laureate.
—	To celebrate Wellington's victory at Vitoria Beethoven composes the *Battle Symphony* for Johann Maelzel's[4] mechanical 'panharmonicon'.

[1] In 1834 N° 40 on the east side was acquired and another major round of demolition and construction was undertaken.

[2] Michael Faraday (1791-1867). Electrical pioneer and chemist. Discovered Benzene in 1825 (which he called 'Bicarbuet of Hydrogen'). He also discovered electro-magnetic rotations (which led to the electric motor); electro-magnetic induction (which led to generators and transformers); and that light is affected by magnetism (the magneto-optical or 'Faraday' effect). With William Whewell (1794-1866) he coined the terms *ion, electrode, anode, cathode* and *electrolyte*.

[3] Franz Peter Schubert (1797-1828). Composer.

[4] Johann Nepomuk Maelzel (1770-1838). Inventor of the metronome.

Elford was right to move swiftly. Once it was common knowledge Shaw had died, seven other gentlemen were preparing to risk social stigma and apply for the vacancy themselves. One was the Reverend William Bingley[6], who had applied to James Edward Smith for support, but Smith was keeping his powder dry until he knew whether his friend Jamie Sowerby was applying (it seems he was not). Although Smith had been prepared to support an application from Sowerby, he was not optimistic about the prospects for the 'lucky' applicant as his letter to his friend[7] makes clear:

'you may be well assured it will be no *sinecure* to any body, but a place of abject drudgery & dependance. I know the domineering & meddling char[acter] of some of the trustees—but I earnestly beg these last remarks may be a secret between us.'

Not privy to this secret, and in a rush to obtain the appointment, Elford again turned to his old friend MacLeay for a supporting reference, writing in imploring tones from Kingsbridge on the 30th of July:

"May I request your recommendation; my sole object is the good of Science and I have told Sir J.B. that I should be willing to hold the Situation without any Salary, rather than not obtain it.— Should you not think me unworthy, and wish me to hold the Situation, I beg you will lose not time in doing as I request but not any offence can be given by your not doing so, if you think me an improper person, as I wish every one to do what they think correct and proper, and ever respect a man more for doing what he thinks right.[8]" MacLeay agreed to lend his support and Elford's campaign developed. By October he was writing again to MacLeay from Woodland:

"My dear Sir,

From the interest you have taken in promoting my views to the British Museum, I consider any verbal apology, for again troubling you as superfluous, as I can never sufficiently testify the many obligations I am under to you for your extreme kindness.

I yesterday took the liberty of sending two more testimonials, which I requested you to forward to one of the electing Trustees, now as the archbishop has promised his Son in Law[9] to support me, and is undoubtedly willing to oblige his Son-in-Law; I think on mature consideration that the certificates would be produced in a more zealous and determined manner than by either of the other Electors, who might be interested for some other candidate, and therefore not be willing to read or produce them with their full force, and as the certificates are very strong and of course flattering to myself, I am anxious to have them turned to the best account, at the same time Sir I leave every thing to your superior judgement, and I trust the hint given will not give you least offence, as I can assure you I trust implicitly to your zeal and friendship.[10]"

Like any good campaigner Elford pressed home his attack in person. By early November he was in London emphasising his suitability by presenting another paper at the Linnean Society. His second work on

[6] William Bingley (1774-1823).Educated Cambridge. Curate of Christ Church in Hampshire until 1816, then a minister in London. A prolific writer, especially about Wales which he toured in 1798 and 1801. Works included: a handbook to the Leverian Museum (where George Shaw had formerly been curator); *Animal Biography* (1802); *Memoirs of British Quadrupeds* (1809); *Animated Nature* (1814); *Useful Knowledge, an account of the various productions of nature, mineral, vegetable and animal* (1816); *Practical Introduction to Botany* (1817).

[7] Letter: J.E. Smith to J. Sowerby, 27th October 1813 (Loc: Linnean Society, Smith Correspondence).

[8] *fide* letter: W.E. Leach to MacLeay, 30th July 1813 (Loc: Linnean Society, MacLeay Correspondence).

[9] This was originally written "Son" but changed to "Son in Law". The second reference was always Son-in-Law. If son-in-law is correct this will be the husband of one of the Archbishop's 10 daughters.

[10] Letter: W.E. Leach to MacLeay, 20th October 1813 (Loc: Linnean Society of London, Miscellaneous Correspondence).

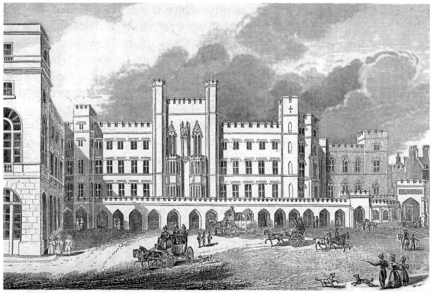

House of Lords and
House of Commons.
(Destroyed by fire in 1834)

oil-beetles, it described more foreign species. On a Sunday evening during this visit, at one of Sir Joseph Banks' regular open house meetings, Charles Abbott – the Speaker of the House of Commons and one of the Museum's three principal (electing) trustees[11] – took Elford to one side and told him his application had been successful; he was to be the new Assistant Librarian at the British Museum.

Librarian?

It was a curious quirk of history that burdened a professional zoologist with the title 'Assistant Librarian', as it similarly burdened the Museum's specialists in Greek sculpture or Roman coins. The British Museum had been founded by Act of Parliament in 1753 when several libraries and the diverse museum of curiosities of Sir Hans Sloane[12] – physician, philanthropist and insatiable collector – had been bought for the nation. The nature of most of these collections led to the adoption of the term 'Librarian' for their custodians in this new national repository. As purchases and (more usually) donations swelled the contents of the new museum, the number of staff also grew. New species of librarian were discovered. The Museum's director was the *Principal Librarian*; the heads of the departments were *Under Librarians* (also known less formally as 'keepers', the term that has survived to the present), each aided by an *Assistant Librarian* ('assistant keeper'). Below this Officer class were the Attendants[13], warders, messengers, porters, housemaids, gardener, and stove-keeper.

The number of departments and their titles changed frequently during the life of the Museum but in Elford Leach's day there were four: *Printed Books* (the library); *Antiquities Coins Drawings & Engravings* (Antiquities); *Natural History and Modern Artificial Curiosities* (Natural History); and

[11] Charles Abbott (1757-1829). Speaker of the House of Commons 1802-17 and a very active Trustee. The *Dictionary of National Biography* says, "The appointment of days for the free admission of the public, the opening of the library for the accommodation of students, and the purchase of almost all the collections that were added to it between the years 1802 and 1817, are due to his suggestions."

[12] Sir Hans Sloane *Bt* (1660-1753). Physician-in-Chief to King George I. President of the Royal Society. Wrote *Natural History of Jamaica*. Cadbury Brothers bought the recipe for drinking chocolate from Sloane. In modern London, Sloane Square; Sloane Street; Hans Place; and other London locations are named after him, as (indirectly) are 'Sloane Rangers' (Barr & York, 1982)

[13] Attendants were technical assistants attached to departments for the everyday manual work. In 1820 Natural History had two. The word 'attendant' was sometimes also used less rigorously for the tour guides (cicerones) who led parties of visitors around the Museum until about 1814.

Charles König in 1831.

[14] British Museum, 1816: xxxii.

[15] How this came about is not known to us but König was the same age as the Queen's 7th son, Adolphus Frederick, Duke of Cambridge (1774-1850) who also studied at Göttingen.

[16] Jonas Dryander (1748-1810). Known as 'Old Dry'.

[17] In the Palaeontology Library of The Natural History Museum, London. König's handwriting is difficult to read. A copy (also at the Natural History Museum) was made in 1942 by Dr G.F. Herbert Smith but needs to be compared to the original. We would dispute several entries Smith thought referred to Elford Leach. Smith's reading of the entry for 30th September 1820 'Sent Dr L a flute' appears to say 'Dr E' in the original and 'flute' is also unlikely, the word appearing to start with 'L' or 'S'. Smith read the entry for 7th August 1818 as, 'spoke to Leach resp. his conduct towards me in the rules (?) of assistance +c. I rather think I have suspected his selfish reasons: at least I might suppose so from his protestation (?)' However, The original appears to say 'her' throughout, not 'his', and the first name is not 'Leach', but may be 'Lucy' (KH *pers. obs.*).

[18] In the early 1820s (Smith, 1969: 254).

[19] Figures from Priestley (1971: 145). 'Upholstery' at that time covered all forms of domestic decoration, not just furniture.

[20] British Museum, 1816: xxxii.

By courtesy of The Natural History Museum, London

Manuscripts[14]. Until his death George Shaw had been the Under Librarian for Natural History. He was a zoologist and former botany lecturer, while his Assistant Librarian Charles König was a mineralogist who had also been a botanist. With Shaw's death König had become the new Natural History Under Librarian with Elford Leach as his assistant. However the title assistant was hardly accurate. Elford would report to König, but would be solely responsible for the zoological collections.

König had been born in Brunswick and educated at the University of Göttingen. His correct name was Karl Dietrich Eberhard König, but in England he adopted the name Charles. An experienced botanist, he first came to Britain in 1800 to arrange the collections of Queen Charlotte, wife of George III[15]. He then assisted Joseph Banks' librarian Jonas Dryander[16] until moving to the British Museum as Shaw's assistant in 1807. As Shaw was a zoologist and the Museum had little interest in botany at that time, König had concentrated on mineralogy.

König was apparently a dapper man and his diary[17] notes his sartorial preferences[18]. He liked blue coats, grey trousers, and waistcoats in various shades of yellow (preferably striped in the summer). He was not an original scientist but was a good organiser and arranger and the mineralogical collections benefited greatly under his care.

Under the usual Museum terms of employment Elford was contracted to work two days in each week, for which, as an Assistant Librarian, he would be paid £120 per year, quarterly, in arrears.

To put this in perspective: at about this time approximately one and a half million agricultural labourers in Britain earned £30 per year, a miner would earn about £40, two million craftsmen earned £55, one million farmers, together with minor clergy, and some schoolmasters, earned £120. Unlike Assistant Librarians, most of these worked full-time (At the other end of the scale, in the year 1814 the Prince Regent spent £49,000 on 'upholstery' and was spending £23,000 each year on jewellery and silverware. That the labouring classes did not take him to their hearts is perhaps understandable)[19].

The duties of British Museum officers were, "to arrange and keep in order the several collections committed to their charge, to correct the old, and when required, to compile new catalogues of their contents, and to pay proper attention to visitors of distinction, either for rank or learning.[20]" These duties are memorable for the absence of the word 'research', as were the careers of the Museum's previous zoologists. Fortunately Elford Leach interpreted his duties liberally rather than literally.

Miscellaneous matters

Since 1789 George Shaw had been producing a monthly journal for anyone interested in natural history called the *Naturalist's Miscellany*. The publishers, Nodder & Son[21], clearly did not want to lose this established market. While Elford was in London he came to an arrangement with them that he would continue Shaw's work. The plan was to describe new and little-known animal species from around the world, which would be illustrated by Richard Nodder, in full colour and life size if possible. However, with the change of authorship this would now be called the *Zoological Miscellany*.

Elford prepared the first issue, for publication in January 1814 (describing animals from the collections of his various friends, including the long-suffering Alexander MacLeay), before he left to spend Christmas in Plymouth and arrange his removal to London.

It is not clear exactly when he planned to arrive at the Museum – he was paid from the beginning of January – but he was late. To be fair it was not his fault. The decade 1810-1820 was one of the coldest in the past thousand years and 1813-1814 was the most severe winter for centuries. A period of intense Arctic conditions began on the 29th of December, heralding what would later be called 'The Great Frost'. In London a freezing fog blanketed the city for eight days, compounded by the smoke from countless coal fires. Even in a normal winter this was a problem, as tourist Louis Simond had discovered in 1811:

"It is difficult to form an idea of the kind of winter days in London; the smoke of fossil coals forms an atmosphere, perceivable for many miles, like a great round cloud attached to the earth. In the town itself, when the weather is cloudy and foggy, which is frequently the case in winter, this smoke increases the general dingy hue, and terminates the length of every street with a fixed grey mist, receding as you advance. But when some rays of sun happen to fall on this artificial atmosphere, its impure mass assumes immediately a pale orange tint, similar to the effect of Claude Lorraine glasses[22],—a mild golden hue, quite beautiful. The air, in the mean time, is loaded with small flakes of soot, in sublimation—a sort of flower[23] of soot, so light as to float without falling. This black snow sticks to your clothes and linen, or lights on your face. You just feel something on your nose, or your cheek,—the finger is applied mechanically, and fixes it into a black patch![24]"

The severe and sustained mists of 1814 magnified this problem, anticipating by nearly a century the notorious London 'pea-souper' fogs.

Just after New Year the snowfall in Devon, the mildest corner of Britain, was so heavy Elford was confined to the house for ten days. Lieutenant-Colonel Hew Ross of the Royal Horse Artillery[25], home for some winter

[21] Shaw's *Miscellany* had been illustrated and published by Frederick Polydore Nodder until his death in about 1800. Polydore's widow Elizabeth had continued the business, in Tavistock Street, London, with their second son Richard Polydore Nodder (b. 1774). Their other children do not appear to have been associated with the business, but they were: Frederick William Nodder (b. 1773); Charles Nodder (born 1776); Elizabeth Penelope Nodder (b. 1777); Banks Robert Nodder (born 1781); and Miria Elizabeth Nodder (b. 1783). Their father had illustrated specimens collected by Joseph Banks aboard the *Endeavour* (Diment *et al.*, 1984: *passim*) and 'Banks Nodder' – born just after Banks was made a Baronet at the beginning of 1781– was almost certainly named after Sir Joseph.

[22] Convex mirrors, usually coloured, used for viewing landscapes. Named after Claude Gelée (1600-1682) a French landscape painter, noted for his subtle depiction of light, who had been born at the Château-de-Chamage in Lorraine and was consequently known as 'Claude le Lorrain' (or 'Claude Lorraine').

[23] Four.

[24] Simond (1817) 1: 47-48.

[25] Like Jonathan Leach, Hew Ross had received a brevet promotion for his actions at Vitoria.

leave, docked in the West Country from the Peninsula on the 7th of January. It took him nine days to reach London[26]. The journey usually took two days from Plymouth. By the middle of the month Devon was in the grip of snowdrifts three to four metres deep and carriages could not even reach Exeter from neighbouring Chudleigh[27].

On the 29th of January, with his plans well in hand, Elford had time to dine with friends at Edmund Lockyer's[28]. Also present were Charles Prideaux and Collier Cookworthy (now back from Edinburgh and practising as a physician in Plymouth). Henry Woollcombe recorded in his diary his impressions of this dinner, where a familiar old chestnut was aired.

"Dined yesterday with Dr Lockyer the party consisted of Drs Leach & Cookworthy, Mr W. Eastlake & Charles Prideaux who is a conchologist. I was, and am surprized, when I recollect the conversation that ensued, it was very superior to any thing we are accustomed here, rather too abstruse, but by no means pedantic. Dr Cookworthy was much pleasanter than he is in public, by no means petulant or opini overbearing. I listened to an argument between him & Eastlake, in which in my mind the latter had completely the advantage, the question was whether Mankind were the more benefitted by the productions of the most eminent Poets or of Men of Science, and this led them to state their respective opinions whether Milton or Homer, were not as great Men as Newton; in answer to Eastlake's question whether Shakespeare was not as great a Man as ever lived, Cookworthy denied it conceiving Sir Isaac to be a much greater".

Elford stayed in Plymouth with his family until his birthday on the 2nd of February then left for London[29]. Several days later he stepped from the coach into an alien landscape[30].

The Great Frost

At the end of January 1814 the River Thames froze solid between London Bridge and Blackfriars Bridge. The ice was so thick Londoners stopped using the now redundant arches and simply walked across the river. A regular concourse was established which the locals jocularly named 'Freezeland Street' – a play on Friesland[31] – and shop-keepers rushed to colonise this virgin territory. Tents and stalls selling bread, cakes, meat, oysters and ginger-bread sprang up along the unmetalled road beside the barbers' shops and the bookstalls, and among the customers wandering pie-men plied their trade. With the weather showing no sign of abating the new street was soon incorporated into the life of the city. A 'Grand Mall' was added, running across Freezeland in mid-river, and a Frost Fair moved onto the site, with all the usual fairground attractions. In these winter quarters a string of printing presses churned out souvenir engravings of this once in a lifetime event[32].

As the month drew on, the freeze eased and the new town melted away. Then the snow returned and fell for six weeks, relentlessly, from Scotland all the way to the English Channel.

[26] *Dictionary of National Biography*, 'Ross'.
[27] Jones, 1852: Appendix, *January 1814 The Great Snowstorm.*
[28] Elford had just proposed Lockyer for membership of the Wernerian Society (proposed 4th December 1813, admitted 8th January 1814. Wernerian Society *Minutes*. Loc: University of Edinburgh Library, Special Collections).
[29] He intended to arrive in London about the 6th of February (Letter: W.E. Leach to MacLeay, postmarked 19 January. Loc: Linnean Society of London, MacLeay Correspondence). Whether by design or coincidence, that would have him in Plymouth for his birthday.
[30] In 1784 the coach between Exeter and London took 32 hours. By 1828, with new roads, the journey had been cut to 19½ hours (Hoskins, 1959: 151). In 1814 it would be closer to the longer time, with the journey between Plymouth and Exeter, over poor roads, to be added. Elford Leach made the journey in bad winter weather.
[31] A region of the modern Netherlands which includes land reclaimed from the sea.
[32] see Priestley, 1971: 113-115.

In this winter wonderland Elford had to find somewhere to live. Many officers had apartments in the British Museum but there was not enough room to accommodate all of them and as the latest arrival Elford was at the bottom of the waiting-list. He chose to live south of the river at 20 Canterbury Place, in the suburb of Lambeth, not far from James Sowerby[33]. This was a curious choice[34], as he would now have to travel across virtually the whole of London twice a day, three and a half kilometres each way, to get to and from the Museum, on the northernmost outskirts of the capital.

[33] James Sowerby was at 2 Mead Place, Lambeth.
[34] Perhaps Sowerby helped him find accommodation.

Palm Squirrel
Sciurus palmarum Linnaeus

(syn. *Sciurus penicillatus* Leach)

Illustration from the *Zoological Miscellany*, January 1814.

— 16 —

The British Museum

In general, every practicable facility is afforded that may render this Institution really useful to science and the arts, for which it is chiefly intended, as well as gratifying to the curiosity of the multitude, who incessantly resort to it in quest of amusement.

Synopsis of the Contents of the British Museum, 1816

[1] Which stood on the site of the modern British Museum, the buildings for which were commenced in the 1820s. The current buildings were constructed as far as possible around Montagu House, which was finally demolished in the 1840s. To this day the keys allocated to staff at the British Museum, and at its adult child, The Natural History Museum in South Kensington, are known as 'House Keys' despite the 150 year absence of 'The House'.

[2] See Edwards (1969) and Miller (1974).

[3] Ralph Montagu (?1638-1709). Scheming politician and womaniser. Marquess of Monthermer, then (1705) 1st Duke of Montagu.

[4] The architect was either Pierre Puget (1622-1694) – also an eminent sculptor and painter – or his relation Gaspard Puget (Christopher Date, British Museum, *pers. comm.* January 2000).

[5] The Gordon Riots. Protestant-led violence in reaction to proposed State concessions for Roman Catholics, who were an official under-class at this time.

As soon as the British Museum was founded in 1753 a search began for a suitable building. One of the first properties considered was Buckingham House near Westminster but at £30,000 the price was too high and the Trustees felt the location was not ideal (the house was later sold to George III and enlarged to form Buckingham Palace). After considering several other possibilities the government finally purchased Montagu House in Great Russell Street, Bloomsbury[1] for the princely sum of £10,250. Unfortunately Montagu House had been empty and neglected for years and the repairs, strengthening and maintenance required between the purchase in 1754 and the Museum's official opening in 1759 took the cost up to £21,000[2].

Montagu House was built in the final years of the seventeenth century by Ralph, 1st Duke of Montagu[3], in the French style. Montagu had been British Ambassador extraordinary at the court of Louis XIV until 1678 and he ensured his new mansion was the very pinnacle of fashionable Baroque by bringing the best French artists of the day from Paris to design and decorate it[4].

Originally a formal garden was planned for the front of the building, but by 1814 this had become a large open quadrangle, the Great Court, screened from the street by a solid brick wall 4-5 metres in height. Midway along this wall the entrance was through a tall protruding arch capped with an octagonal lantern and cupola. This entrance had been guarded by a military sentry since the London riots of 1780[5] which left polite Society (to which the Museum's Trustees certainly considered themselves to belong) with a deep-seated fear of the mob. In 1807 the Trustees were granted a permanent Sergeant's guard (an increase in the number of sentries), to be raised to a Subaltern's guard (with even more men) at times of public tension.

The façade of the British Museum in Great Russell Street.

Through the arch the inside of the front wall was an Ionic colonnade facing north towards the house. The east and west boundaries of the Great Court were the wings containing the officers' residential apartments. Outside these wings on each side were small quadrangles, the 'West Court' and 'East Court'. The West (or 'Back') Court contained more accommodation in the form of small terraced houses across the planted courtyard from the rear of the West wing.

Behind the house were three hectares of gardens and shrubberies. At the indulgence of the Trustees neighbouring residents were permitted to treat the gardens as an informal park for their enjoyment, an indulgence that made proximity to the Museum a significant sales asset for local properties. The gardens had originally looked out over open fields extending northwards all the way to the hills of Hampstead and Highgate 5 km away, but by 1814 the Duke of Bedford, who owned the land around the Museum, had granted building leases, and the London suburb of Bloomsbury was beginning to acquire its modern form of terraced Georgian streets enclosing formal squares. The previous decade had seen the complete encirclement of the Museum and its garden, which were no longer the northern limit of the growing capital. Although attempts had been made to maintain the grounds, with new gravel on the paths and some horticultural housekeeping, the cost was an increasing problem for the Museum. When some trees were lost in 1809, they were not replaced.

The House

Montagu House itself comprised two floors of state apartments containing the Museum's holdings, sandwiched between attic rooms in the roof-space and an extensive subterranean basement. The Trustees saw the

The Great Court with the entrance gate and colonnade on the right, Montagu House on the left.

primary benefit of the Museum's exhibits as their value to "men of letters and artists". Public accessibility was considered "a popular, though far less useful application of the Institution.[6]"

Formerly, anyone wanting to visit the public galleries had had to apply in advance for a ticket then wait several days (or longer) for this to be confirmed, but this inconvenient arrangement was replaced in 1808 by a registration book at the entrance. Having signed in, visitors (all of whom had to be "of decent appearance") remained in the foyer until other individuals or groups arrived and a party of 15 could be assembled. They were then led by a tour guide through the public areas.

The decoration in these areas, dating from the time of Lord Montagu, was unreservedly sumptuous. To the left of the main foyer, the Grand Staircase wafted visitors to the upper floor through a cloud of classical fancy. The painted ceiling, by Charles de la Fosse[7], showed Phæton petitioning Apollo for leave to drive his chariot, attended by the Hours in female form. The walls were adorned with architectural details, classical landscapes, tableaux of the Tiber and the Nile, and panels showing the feasts and sacrifices of Bacchus, all painted by Jacques Rousseau[8]. Throughout, the renowned botanical painter Monnoyer[9], had strewn his flowers. This river of colour surged onwards into the main galleries of the upper floor, flowing across the ceilings and down the walls, around the cloth hangings and the oil paintings, a vision of heaven on earth reflecting in the glass of the display cases.

If we step back in time we can join one of the tour parties in the early years of the Regency[10] as they are led from the top of the Grand Staircase into the first room. The ceiling here is also painted by la Fosse, and represents the fall of Phæton. This gallery is dedicated to modern works of art from all

[6] British Museum, 1816: xxxiii.

[7] Charles de la Fosse (1636-1716). Painter. Also painted the dome of the Hôtel des Invalides at Paris. King Charles II was so impressed with de la Fosse's work at Montagu House he wanted him to decorate Hampton Court, but de la Fosse could not accept the commission.

[8] Jacques Rousseau (1630-1693).

[9] Jean Baptiste Monnoyer (1634-1699). Accompanied Montagu to England in 1678 and lived there for the rest of his life. Also executed commissions for the British royal family.

[10] On a tour described in *The Picture of London for 1811* (Anon., 1811: 139-147) and apparently based on an official Museum synopsis of 1808.

Montagu House.

parts of the globe, arranged in glass cabinets. A printed list of the exhibits can be taken from the pile lying on top of the case in the middle of the room. The case itself contains miniature portraits, including images of King Charles I (beheaded by Parliament after the last English civil war) and Oliver Cromwell (head of state when England was a republic)[11]. Displayed with the miniatures are two curious likenesses of King William III and Queen Mary carved on walnut-shells. The cupboards around the room house a strange assortment, in geographical order, of fine chinaware mixed with weapons from around the world. This room also exhibits a rich collection of curiosities from the South Pacific, collected by Captain Cook, which our guide describes for us as we listen attentively:

"In the left corner is the mourning dress of an Otaheitean lady, in which taste and barbarity are singularly blended; and opposite are the rich cloaks and helmets of feathers from the Sandwich Islands. Among these is one which, in elegance of form, vies even with the Grecian helmets. In another case are the cava bowls, and above them baltoons, and other weapons of war. The next objects of attention are the idols of the different islands, presenting in their hideous rudeness, a singular contrast with many of the works of art formed by the same people; near these are the drums and other instruments of music, and a breast-plate from the Friendly Islands".

The second room is empty at the moment. It did contain classical sculptures but these have recently been moved into a new purpose-built facility in the gardens behind the house, the Townley Gallery[12]. The next four rooms contain the collection of manuscripts, many beautifully bound. The seventh room is also dedicated to manuscripts and on a table in a glazed frame is the original of the *Magna Carta*, the charter signed by King John of England in 1215 recognising the rights of the barons, the church and the freemen[13]. Also displayed are the parchment's seal and the documents drawn up

[11] Charles I of Great Britain and Ireland (1600-1649). King from 1625. His Roman Catholic sympathies caused many Puritans to emigrate, especially to America. In 1642 he went to war with Parliament. He surrendered to the Scots in 1646 and was handed to the English. England was declared a republic (a 'Commonwealth') and Charles was beheaded. Scotland retained the monarchy and declared Charles' son, Charles (1630-1685), King Charles II. In England, the leader of the Parliamentary forces, Oliver Cromwell (1599-1658) became 'Protector'. In 1660 England restored the monarchy and accepted Charles II, who became King of Great Britain and Ireland.

[12] Officially opened on the 3rd of July 1808 by the Queen.

[13] John 'Lackland' (1167-1216). Crowned King of England in 1199 despite not being the lawful heir. He was obliged to sign the charter to avoid war with the barons.

Montagu House foyer (in 1845) with the main entrance to the left and the Grand Staircase in the distance.

preparatory to the signing of this *Great Charter* (the basis of the English constitution, stressing the monarch's subservience to the Law of the land).

Next we are led into the magnificent Saloon in the centre of the building. Its impressive domed ceiling has been painted, as before, by la Fosse and seems to depict the birth of Minerva. Immediately above her is Jupiter surrounded by three female figures surmounted by stars, one pouring nectar or healing ointment on his head. On one side of Minerva is Vulcan with Cupid close by with an axe in his hand; on the other side Mercury. Other classical deities surround this group in admiration. In a lower wall painting opposite the chimney the Vices are being expelled from heaven on the manifestation of Wisdom, and in six circular panels near the corner of the room are some of the principal achievements of Minerva: over the door of the Department of Manuscripts she helps Perseus cut off the head of Medusa; in the second she presides over Harmony with some of the Muses; in the third she kills a lion; in the fourth she helps Jupiter fight the Titans; in the fifth she contends with Neptune over the naming of Athens; and the sixth illustrates the fable of Arachne, metamorphosed by Minerva into a spider. Separating the panels are groups of winged boys, representing the arts, sciences, commerce and war[14].

The rest of the Saloon's walls are adorned with more landscapes and architectural decorations by Rousseau, and flowers by Monnoyer. The paintings are in good condition despite their age, having recently been restored[15]. Over the chimney hangs a full-length portrait of George II, and in the middle of the window stands a table made from a variety of lavas from Mount Vesuvius. The body of the Saloon houses extensive displays of minerals[16].

After the Saloon we enter the Department of Natural History which occupies the western half of the first floor. This begins with *Room VIII*

[14] Sharpe, 1906: 157 (quoting the *Synopsis of the Contents of the British Museum*, 1808).
[15] By F. Rigaud, Esq. R.A. shortly before 1808.
[16] Added from 1812 onwards following the purchase of the extensive Greville Collection in 1810 (Smith, 1969: 243-244).

The Grand Staircase, Montagu House.

© Copyright The British Museum

(the 'Mineral Room') containing mainly minerals and fossils, including displays in two glass-topped tables in the centre of the room and 10 glass cases around the walls. More minerals are in more than 200 closed drawers[17]. Most specimens are arranged according to the Wernerian system, with some fossils following Linnæus. The central displays are very valuable and include minerals from Derbyshire, Germany, Siberia and the South Seas, but among the numerous rock fragments room has been found for some of nature's oddities. One is an egg-shaped piece of chalcedony containing water, which can be seen moving when it is gently shaken. Even more curious is an

[17] Smith, 1969: 241 (quoting the *Synopsis of the Contents of the British Museum*, 1808).

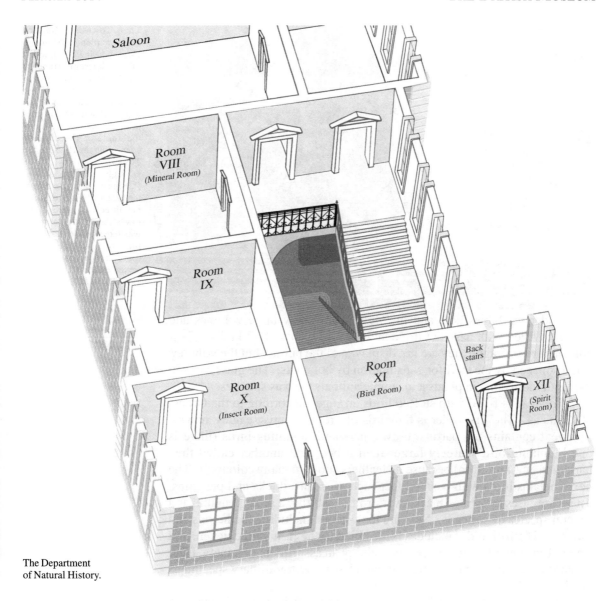

The Department
of Natural History.

Egyptian pebble which has been broken by accident, revealing on both pieces
an image believed to resemble the poet Chaucer[18].

The ninth room is devoted to fossils and shells. In the cases in the
middle of the room is a shell of the species called the Paper Nautilus, or
Argonaut, famous for the delicacy of its parchment-like material, and its
sculptural form. Also displayed are some beautiful bivalve molluscs (molluscs
with two hinged shells, including the scallops, oysters, mussels and clams)
together with fossil shells, sea-urchins, and other species.

[18] Geoffrey Chaucer
(ca 1345-1400). The first
great poet of the English
language. Author of the
(unfinished) *Canterbury
Tales* (1387-).

The Townley Gallery in the garden of Montagu House (during construction of the current Museum buildings). Montagu House is on the left with the windows of Room X of the Natural History Department just under the eaves. Above the angle of the corridor connecting the House to the Townley Gallery is the skylight of the atrium (see image opposite). Note the back of Montagu House has three full storeys, the lowest being the basement with large sash windows. At the front of the house (page 258) the basement is served only by small bulls-eye windows just above ground level.

Under the tables here and in *Room X* are many large volumes and packages filled with pages of dried and pressed plants of all kinds. Their contents are so fragile they are not displayed to the public, but the volumes can be opened by the staff for consultation by botanists. The glass cases in the tenth room contain plants and simple animals such as sponges.

Room XI is filled with stuffed birds arranged according to the Orders of Linnæus. The first order is the birds of prey: vultures, eagles, hawks. The next contains the parrots, crows, jays and humming-birds (there is one humming-bird scarcely larger than a bee; and another called the harlequin humming-bird because its feathers show so many colours[19]). The next contains birds with webbed feet such as swans, ducks and penguins. There are cases housing a black swan from Australia, a great penguin, and several species of pelicans. Next are the waders, including the herons and bitterns. The fifth order includes birds allied to the farmyard chicken, and finally Linnæus's Order *Passeres* containing an assortment of genera, from pigeons to swallows and nightjars, of which some extraordinary specimens are displayed.

Hanging in this 'Bird Room' (as the staff call it) is a painting of a Dodo, produced many years before in Holland. This painting was once the property of Sir Hans Sloane, and afterwards of Sloane's friend and fellow naturalist George Edwards[20], who presented it to the Museum.

The glass-topped table in the middle of the room contains birds' nests – including some of the type used by the Chinese to make soup – and examples of rare feathers. A second table contains more nests and a variety of eggs, including those of the ostrich, the cassowary and the crocodile. Against the wall between the tall windows are glass cases containing rare mammals, of which those attracting the most attention from visitors are two young

[19] The harlequin humming-bird was not a true species, but a composite specimen invented by a taxidermist, and was later destroyed by Elford Leach for that reason (House of Commons, 1836: para. 2953).
[20] George Edwards (1694-1773). An ornithologist.

orang-utans, a monkey, and an 'ermine' (a stoat[21] in its winter colouring). Under the tables are more cases where visitors can find an armadillo, a porcupine, several young sloths and an ant-eater.

The twelfth room is still dedicated to Natural History, but is in startling contrast to the rooms we have just left. This small gallery, unlike the others, displays its specimens pickled in glass jars and the whole chamber is redolent with the overpowering, sweet – though not wholly unpleasant – aroma of spirits of wine. Not all the visitors appreciate having their visual and olfactory senses assailed in this way. Disgust is a common reaction to the ranks of pickled "hobgoblins"[22]. For obvious reasons the staff call this the 'Spirit Room'.

This completes the tour of the upper floor. Ignoring the attic storey above, where the keepers have their offices[23], we are now taken down a secondary staircase (and under a small stuffed crocodile, suspended from the ceiling of the stair-well) to the Townley Gallery, a large free-standing building of simple classical styling (lacking the mansion's riot of colour and ornament) joined to the north-west corner of the main house by a connecting corridor of sculpture galleries. This is the Department of Antiquities. Its 13 rooms house the Museum's collection of classical statuary, marble reliefs and other carvings, most of which originally belonged to the late Charles Townley[24], whose collection was purchased by the government for £20,000. A catalogue describing the exhibits can be bought on the way into the building.

The first room is devoted to reliefs in terracotta, held to be the finest collection in Europe. We next pass into a beautiful circular atrium, lit from a skylight in the dome, which gives a vista up the full length of the building to a sculpture of a Greek discus thrower. This circular room is devoted to Greek and Roman sculptures, among which are some exquisite busts, and beautiful statues, particularly a Venus. The third and fourth rooms are also filled with Greek and Roman sculptures and reliefs. The fifth has a very fine collection of Roman sepulchral works and a beautiful mosaic pavement from London, found while digging the foundations for the new building at the Bank of England. The next

© Copyright The British Museum

[21] *Mustela erminea* Linnæus.
[22] *fide* Sir Joseph Banks (House of Commons, 1836: Appendix 9, p. 574).
[23] Gunther, 1975: 51.
[24] Charles Townley (or 'Towneley') (1737-1805).

View from the atrium into the Townley gallery.

two rooms contain yet more Roman and Greek sculptures of every description, over 100 pieces in all.

The eighth room, which is on the left, contains Egyptian antiquities, among which are two mummies with their coffins (presented by George III), a papyrus taken from a mummy, and an enormous number of smaller articles. The ninth room contains Egyptian sculptures, among which is a famous sarcophagus described in the *Monthly Magazine* for February, 1809, and many other curiosities. The tenth room returns to the theme of Greek and Roman sculpture.

After the tenth room we walk back through the gallery to pass upstairs in this building where the eleventh room is devoted to ancient and modern coins and medals, arranged in geographical order, country by country. This room can only be viewed by a few people at a time, by prior arrangement. Passing on to the twelfth room we find the collection of the late Sir William Hamilton[25], which was formerly housed in the Saloon of the main house. This is an eclectic assortment of Roman and Greek household goods, bronze vessels, utensils, specimens of ancient glass, necklaces, ancient armour, knives, lamps, seals, weights, sculptures in ivory, bracelets, bits, spurs, and ancient paintings from Herculaneum, bricks from Babylon, and his unrivalled collection of Greek vases.

The final room contains an extensive and valuable collection of prints and drawings, but this too can only be seen by appointment.

Here our tour ends. We have not seen the 12 rooms making up the ground floor of the main house. These contain the library of printed books but our guide tells us visitors are not conducted through these apartments as the mere sight of the outside of books conveys neither instruction nor amusement. However there is a reading room where approved visitors may have named books brought to their table by an attendant.

Whether we have derived much benefit from our tour depends to some extent on the personality of our guide. Louis Simond visited the Museum in April 1810 and complained:

'a German cicerone took charge of us, and led us *au pas de charge* through a number of rooms full of stuffed birds and animals;—many of them seemingly in a state of decay... The last and most valuable acquisitions are the Greek and Roman marbles brought from Italy by Mr Townley. The merit, however, of a considerable part of these marbles, consists mostly of their being undoubtedly antique... We had no time allowed to examine any thing; our conductor pushed on without minding questions, or unable to answer them, but treating the company with double *entendres* and witticisms on various subjects of natural history, in a style of vulgarity and impudence which I should not have expected to have met in this place, and in this country.[26]'

By 1815 the system of guided tours had been abolished and visitors were allowed to ponder the collections at their own pace, under the watchful eyes of attendant warders.

[25] Sir William Hamilton (1730-1803). Diplomat and antiquary. Envoy extraordinary to the Court of Naples for more than 30 years. His young second wife, Lady Emma Hamilton (neé Emily Lyon) (ca. 1765-1815) was the mistress of Admiral Lord Nelson and bore him a daughter, named Horatia (1801-1880).
[26] Simond (1817) **1**: 107-8.

The Basement

They seem indeed to dwell in lower gloom
Of mansions, through whose every upper room,
Made wonderful with full and cloudless rays,
My winged soul passed in splendid former days.

Arthur O'Shaughnessy[27]
Zoologist, British Museum 1862-1881

Beneath the two floors of state apartments in the main house was the basement storey. This was closed to visitors and was effectively the storage space and work area of the Museum. It was a semi-subterranean warren of narrow rooms and corridors, with larger chambers, reached by descending winding stairs from the ground floor[28]. Some of this cellar complex was set aside for the house-keeping of the building and used as a coal bunker for supplying the stoves[29], but other chambers were used to store part of the collections and some were used as studies. It was in one of these studies (under Room VIII of the library above) that Elford Leach would spend his early years at the Museum. The basement was ventilated only on the external walls. At the back of the house, looking out onto the gardens, there were full sash windows. Elford's study was probably equipped with these. The basement rooms at the front of the house were deeper underground and would have been much darker, having only small bull's eye windows high in their exterior walls and opening to the outside just above ground level. Moisture soaking into the whole basement from the surrounding earth, and moist air spilling in through the windows, ensured the rooms were permanently damp[30].

Mould was always a problem (in 1800 it was discovered dry rot had caused extensive damage[31]), but into these dank crypts were deposited all those natural history specimens too worn or too damaged by insects to be displayed[32] (although from Simond's comments it appears the damage had to be substantial). Here too were the animal skins awaiting stuffing, and the duplicates. While it was the policy of the Museum to display in the main galleries examples of every species in the collection[33], and sometimes to exhibit ranges of specimens to show variation within one species[34], it was not the policy to fill the galleries with every example of every species held[35]. The duplicates went to the basement[36].

The Trustees were empowered by statute[37] to exchange, sell or dispose of any duplicates[38], but seldom exercised this right, especially when it came to the natural history collections. Needless to say many specimens did not survive the storage, including much of Sloane's original collection. George Shaw had an annual disposal in which he took the worst 'zoological rubbish' into the gardens to be buried and burned. He called these his cremations[39] and on one occasion the residents of the local houses threatened to sue the Museum because they believed moths had been driven into their homes by

[27] Arthur William Edgar O'Shaughnessy (1844-1881) From his poem *Nostalgie des Cieux* (1874).
[28] William Clift (House of Commons, 1836: para. 676).
[29] see Gunther, 1980b: 36.
[30] J.G. Children (House of Commons, 1835: para. 3383).
[31] Miller, 1974: 116.
[32] William Clift (House of Commons, 1836: para. 665).
[33] J.E. Gray (House of Commons, 1835: para. 3277).
[34] J.E. Gray (House of Commons, 1836: para. 3076).
[35] Sir Henry Ellis (House of Commons, 1835: para. 510).
[36] Miller, 1974: 114.
[37] Act 7, Geo. II, c.18.
[38] Miller, 1974: 65.
[39] Edwards (1969: 575-576) tells this story of Elford Leach, apparently confusing him with Shaw.

these bonfires[40]. Elford Leach too would obtain the Trustees' permission to destroy old worthless zoological material[41], as would other officers after him[42]. It was a perennial problem.

In 1805 a special committee of the Trustees investigating the natural history collections reported, "Unfit articles have been, and will from time to time be accidentally admitted, and which ought to be got rid of. Many such are now to be seen in the second room of the collection of artificial curiosities, as well as in the basement story and other parts of the house.[43]"

In 1809 the Trustees finally authorised a partial purge of the basement, selling many old, badly preserved items, and those unsuitable for public display (deformed human foetuses; kidney stones; diseased bones etc.) The purchaser was the Royal College of Surgeons. William Clift[44], the Conservator of the College's Hunterian Museum, examined the basement before the sale and found "chiefly refuse", an "enormous accumulation of trash". He imagined Noah's Ark must have looked something like this, its holds filled with examples of every kind, jumbled one with another. "Chaos" he called it[45].

This sale cleared some space but the basement was soon restored to its former state of dust, decay and neglect. One eye-witness shortly before 1820 would say, "of these subterraneous excavations there are so many, that they resemble the catacombs we have seen at Palermo, where one is opened every day in the year, merely to deposit fresh subjects for decay, and to ascertain how the process has gone on during the last year.[46]"

It was not just the collections in the basement that were decaying. Montagu House itself was now more than a hundred years old and was not ageing well. In 1811 more than half the money granted to the Museum by parliament had been spent fighting the disintegration of the old mansion[47]. In the Great Court the crumbling stone vases decorating the top of the colonnade had long since been removed after one fell onto a visitor's carriage[48]. Repairs to the fabric of the house were continuous[49].

This, then, was the British Museum as Elford Leach knew it, as it was when he arrived in February 1814 to revolutionise British zoology.

[40] Charles König (House of Commons, 1835: paras 2744 & 2755).
[41] e.g. British Museum Trustees' Committee Meeting Minutes, 11th March 1815.
[42] e.g. John Children. British Museum Trustees' Committee Meeting Minutes, 30th June 1827.
[43] Select Committee (House of Commons, 1836: p. 523).
[44] William Clift ('Billy' to his family) (1775-1849). Born in Cornwall, the son of a miller. Was a close friend of John Abernethy. George Macilwain said benevolence had impressed a lifelong smile on Clift's countenance (1856: 175). For biography see Austin (1991: 1-22).
[45] William Clift (House of Commons, 1836: paras 654, 655, 676 & 704).
[46] Swainson, 1840: in 237-240.
[47] Miller, 1974: 96.
[48] Miller, 1974: 116.
[49] When the house was eventually demolished in the 1840s the ceiling and wall decorations were stripped away and bought by the Museum's lodge-keeper, a Mr Sivier (former butler to Lord Lyndhurst). He sold these decorations at a handsome profit (Sharpe, 1906: 81). Bowdler Sharpe does not say to whom the decorations were sold or to where they were transferred.

— 17 —

Elford Leach

If any human being earnestly desire to push on to new discoveries instead of just retaining and using the old; to win victories over Nature as a worker rather than over hostile critics as a disputant; to attain, in fact, clear and demonstrative knowledge instead of attractive and probable theory; we invite him as a true son of Science to join our ranks.

Francis Bacon
Novum Organum (1620)

William Elford Leach strode up the front steps of Montagu House in his heavy winter coat in February 1814. He had just turned 23 years of age and had long passed from adolescence into adulthood. There is no known portrait of him other than one rather comedic and stylised caricature by George Cruikshank[1]. However, we do have several written descriptions[2]. He was lightly built, 'of a slight form and delicate habit[3]', neither noticeably tall nor noticeably short[4]. He was said to be naturally nervous and irritable – today we might say he was highly strung – although he could be very cool and controlled when the situation required[5]. He had 'an intelligent and expressive countenance, which was improved by a pair of most piercing black eyes.[6]' His manner was engaging, animated, sensitive and sometimes rather witty. In fact his humour could be somewhat ribald, as in 1816 when he asks Alexander MacLeay to get him a live Shetland pony (a breed he obviously suspects is a distinct species deserving its own scientific name), "which I will promise on my honor," he swears, "not to disgrace by the title of "horse ass".[7]" He gave no such promise when erecting a new genus for the earwig described by Linnæus as *Forficula minor*[8]. Instead he displayed his anatomical training by creating the genus *Labia*, forcing the uncompromising species name *Labia minor*.

To his friends – and he made friends easily – he was 'warm, frank and generous'. Even Will Bullock, who had every reason to avoid his company, clearly found it possible to forgive him, and the *Zoological Miscellany* for 1814 contains a number of instances where Elford has borrowed specimens or obtained information from him. Elford, for his part, had already donated specimens to Bullock's Museum, possibly as a peace-offering[9].

[1] George Cruikshank (1792-1878). British illustrator specialising in book-plates and political cartoons.
[2] The following description is based on comments by Swainson (1834 and 1840); Reading (1857); the *English Cyclopædia*; and from a reading of his letters.
[3] Swainson, 1840.
[4] Based on Jonathan's implication that he, Jonathan, was 5'7" tall (1.7m). Not short when an infantryman only had to be 5'4" (1.62m).
[5] His facility for handling animals suggests that he appeared calm to them.
[6] *The English Cyclopædia*.
[7] Letter: W.E. Leach to MacLeay, 9th November 1816 (Loc: Linnean Society MacLeay Correspondence). See p. 271 below.
[8] *Edinburgh Encyclopædia*, 9(1): 118 (1815).
[9] Bullock, 1812 (not seen).

Elford Leach by Cruikshank
(enlarged)

Elford Leach was always prepared to devote time to other naturalists, especially young enthusiastic naturalists just developing their interests. He acquired his own disciples, just as he had been a disciple of George Montagu, and they would also become his friends.

We know nothing directly of his political or social attitudes, but we can infer quite a lot from the known attitudes of his brothers. Jonathan leaves us a record of his own views on slavery. Owning slaves within Britain had been held unlawful since at least the previous century but in 1814 owning slaves was still permitted in British dominions and colonies, although trading in slaves had been illegal for the past seven years.

Jonathan Leach on slavery

"I am well aware that different persons look at this question in different points of view; but I am willing, nevertheless, to believe, that the numbers in England who view it with the same degree of indignation, horror, and disgust, which I ever have done, preponderate beyond all comparison; and that the time is not far distant, when the voices of those will be silenced who are not ashamed to declare, that an unfortunate negro, writhing under the lash of the merciless slave-driver, for laying aside his spade for a few minutes in the heat of a tropical sun, or for some offence equally trivial, is infinitely better off, decidedly more happy, and in a more enviable situation, than the labouring peasant in the mother country. Facts are stubborn things; and although many years have rolled over my head since I left the West Indies, I have not yet forgotten what the system of slavery was in 1803, 1804, and 1805. The first exhibition of the kind which met my eye a few days after landing in Antigua, was a huge slave-driver flogging most unmercifully an old decrepit female negro, who appeared bowed down with misery and hard labour. I know not what her offence was, but she was one of a gang, as they are termed, of negroes of different sexes and ages, working with spades under a mid-day tropical sun. A brother officer, who was with me on a shooting excursion, felt as astonished and indignant at this unnatural and inhuman proceeding as myself; and our first impulse was to threaten to shoot the driver if he did not desist. I am not ashamed to say, that, after drawing off to such a distance that our small shot could not seriously injure the vagabond, we peppered his legs pretty handsomely. That we should have adopted so summary a mode of punishment, had we lived twice as long in the world, I will not say; but my conscience has never reproached me for the steps which we took to shew our disapprobation of the diabolical act. I adduce this as only one of the numerous instances of flogging which I had ocular demonstration of. I have too often witnessed the application of the lash to old and young, male and female, and have too frequently heard their cries and lamentations, ever to forget it:—nor shall I ever cease to hold in utter detestation and abhorrence this infernal system. I have several times been on board vessels laden with slaves from the coast of Guinea; and I have no hesitation in saying, that the most highly coloured description of this vile traffic ever given, falls short of the reality of the sufferings of those cargoes of ill-fated human beings. Emancipation of the negroes must necessarily be gradual; but I am one of those who hope most sincerely that it will in due time be effected.[10]"

Jonathan wrote this in 1830 or 1831[11]. At that time slavery was being publicly debated in Britain, where it was finally abolished in 1833[12].

George Leach and liberalism

The early 1830s marked a turbulent period in British political life. In 1832 a *Reform Act* had been passed, broadening the franchise – the right to vote for Members of Parliament – to include a new tier of British men, encompassing much of the growing middle class. In Plymouth Dock[13] three candidates stood in the resulting general election of December 1832, two with strong establishment connections and a third representing the local reformers: solicitor George Leach, Elford's eldest brother. We learn from this that George was actively involved in Liberal politics.

In the early years of the nineteenth century the two shades of political opinion in Britain (it was a little too early to talk about political parties in the modern sense) were Tory and Whig. Liberal politics came into being with the growth of the middle classes, and the Liberal Party was formed from Whig foundations after the 1832 Act. Liberals challenged traditional Tory support for a society dominated by the monarchy, the aristocracy and the church. Liberals wanted: a broader franchise; increased freedom for people to choose their religious and political views without fear of persecution; limited government powers; increased freedom of trade; and a free market economy.

By 1830 the Leach family appears to have supported these objectives, but we would expect them to have sympathised with similar social attitudes much earlier (Jonathan was shooting slave-drivers at the age of 19). Liberal attitudes were strongly rooted in the West Country, which remains today a stronghold of Liberal politics in Britain.

Manner

As is obvious from 'the business of Bullock', Elford Leach was not an artful man. Not for him Machiavellian plots or convoluted scheming. Nor was he one for social subtleties. He was certainly polite, but could be very direct in declaring his views, seldom even aware that a more measured form of expression might be more diplomatic, more effective, or (frankly) more astute. One of his milder examples is in a letter to Robert Jameson of April 1815:

"Cap[n] Laskey[14] wished to have the new appointment of keeper of the reading room and arranger of catalogues for the British Museum; but that department is totally unconnected with mine and one in which Cap[n] Laskey might have been useful (as it would not have been in his power to steal

[10] *Rough Sketches* : 19-22.
[11] *Rough Sketches* was published in 1831.
[12] After *The Abolition of Slavery Act 1833* slavery was finally abolished for the whole British Empire on the 31st of July 1838.
[13] In fact Dock had been renamed *Devonport* in 1824 in recognition of its size and affluence.
[14] Capt. James Laskey *FLS* contributed observations on Devonshire birds to the *Gentleman's Magazine* in 1795 and 1796. He was elected a member of the Wernerian Society on 2nd March 1808 and published a *General Account of the Hunterian Museum, Glasgow* in August 1813.

to which he is very prone) but as one of the old attendants of the Museum, a man of excellent character and equally well fitted for the situation appeared, he was elected by the Trustees. Therefore his statement that he was to be under me; is false, and any use that he may have made of my name was without my permission, and very like the conduct of a man like Cap[n] Laskey who cannot be trusted.[15]" As the son of a lawyer, Elford might have been more circumspect.

Reading his autograph letters, one thing becomes clear: he was always in a hurry. Most correspondence is either scribbled from the outset or starts with several neat lines then deteriorates rapidly into his characteristic untidy scrawl ('1816' opposite). To one correspondent he confesses, "I cannot express to you how very much I detest letter-writing; it anoys and vexes me beyond expression; this must furnish an apology for my hasty mode of scribbling.[16]" It is possible to assess the respect he has for correspondents by the neatness of his hand. When writing to Joseph Banks his deliberate, meticulous script lasts all the way to the very final word.

In company with his penmanship, his punctuation and spelling are also frequently cavalier (although in the early nineteenth century spelling was seldom treated as a high priority, even among the educated classes[17]). It is quite clear, however, that he rarely proof-read his letters.

This perpetual urgency in his writing was symptomatic of a general energy and dynamism. We have already encountered instances where he wishes someone to do something for him. Instead of asking if they will, then waiting for a reply, he invariably asks them then adds, 'and if you are agreeable will you also...' The strain of waiting for several letters to pass when he might put his plan into effect with just one is clearly too great, and the fear that his presumption might offend, while expressed, never actually moderates his actions.

Physically too he was always in a hurry. A friend noted, 'He was so remarkably active... that we have seen him leap up that long flight of steps, constituting the present grand staircase, taking three or four at a bound, and getting to the top, while an ordinary person would have scarcely left the bottom.[18]'

Dr Leach the zoologist

By the time he arrived at the Museum Elford Leach had been trained in most aspects of medicine and had studied under some of the finest anatomists and comparative anatomists in Britain. He had learned the skills of field biology under George Montagu, in our view one of Britain's best field naturalists, and had learned from him the importance of experimenting to answer questions (for example, incubating eggs and watching them hatch and develop, which Elford certainly did with insects and spiders). He had been trained at Edinburgh in field geology and botany. His approach to recording his collecting trips was, on occasion, virtually modern (although not consistently so), especially when collecting insects. He might note the

Opposite:

Examples of Elford Leach's handwriting. All are taken from the collections of the Linnean Society of London.

[15] Letter: W.E. Leach to Jameson, 27th April 1815 (Loc: Edinburgh University Library, Special Collections).
[16] Letter: Leach to Napier, 16th June 1814 (Loc: British Library, ref: BM Add Mss 34,611 ff. 77-78).
[17] Millicent Fawcett says, "Correct spelling was still perhaps considered a more fitting accomplishment for an attorney's clerk than for a gentleman." (1901: 15).
[18] Swainson (1840).

To the Linnean Society, 22nd July 1809.	*Bombyx Pini, which has so long been considered as a doubtful inhabitant of Britain was taken, by Mr Spartial Surgeon, in the Norwich Hospital,*
To Alexander MacLeay, 18th February 1812. (Discussing the term used for the veins in insects' wings.)	*I cannot avoid expressing my regret at the ridiculous terms employed by naturalists in describing what are anatomically speaking bones, which they term nerves or veins;*
To Alexander MacLeay, 2nd July 1812.	*regret argynnis Latthonia F. Ly. Gl. which I find the same as our insect, but from the insects not agreeing with the description, I had always supposed our insect was distinct from the true Latthonia and even now cannot but think the Linnean Insect is distinct or very badly described.—*
To Alexander MacLeay, 9th November 1816 (*in* collection: Ms 237). "I hope that you will get me a Shetland poney (and if possible alive as I do not regard the expence of carriage) which I will promisse on my honor not to disgrace by the title of "horse ass". I remain dear Sir Your sincere obliged W.E. Leach. Will you forward the inclosed."	*I hope that you will get me a Shetland poney (O if possible alive as I do not regard the expence of carriage) which I will promisse on my honor not to disgrace by the title of "horse ass." I remain dear Sir will you forward the inclosed. Your sincere obliged W. E. Leach.*

Autograph manuscript on the Cymothoadæ (ca 1818).
 	
(This is his small neat label and notebook hand.)
	A Posterior ventral appendices with the exterior lamella alone produced.
	    * Thorax with the penultimate joint larger than the last joint. Genera.
	Hinder ventral appendice {*curved elongate* – – – – – – *2. Camptocopée*
	                {*strait moderately long* – – – *3. Nesea.*
	    ** Thorax with the two last joints of equal length.
	Hinder ventral appendice strait moderately long – – – – – *4. Cilicæa*

To Alexander MacLeay, 5th February 1824.	*On looking over my collection of Drawings, I found that the five Figures of Anobella published in Volume XIV of the Transactions of the Society, have not been returned into my hands. They form a part of a copy of all the original Drawings executed by Mrs Dorville for Col. Montague, which by the permission of Mrs Dorville as a artist procured by me by Mr. J. D. Sowerby made*

271

date; the time of day; state of the weather; the type of ground or vegetation on which the insect was found (with an identification of the plant); and say whether the insect was in the sun or shade. He tried to find insects in copulation to be sure of collecting one adult male and one adult female of the same species, and the range of habitats he examined was prodigious. In one entomology trip in 1825 his sample notes[18] record every substratum from the disgusting 'in human excrement' and cadaverous 'in a dead mouse', to the somewhat charming 'on... my sister'.

Before his arrival at the British Museum he had already published Low's work on the animals of Orkney and a monograph on beetles, and had in press: two academic articles on fish; three articles on insects; and six encyclopædia articles (including a massive review of crustaceans, centipedes, millipedes and spiders in which he described 50 new genera and 48 new species). He had also virtually completed a substantial academic paper on these same groups, and was working on a major multi-part work on the larger crustaceans of British waters and on a monthly series detailing new and little known animals of the world. Even if he had not been appointed to the post at the British Museum, these alone would have ensured his place as a major British – and in the case of the Crustacea, world – naturalist of note. In a time of patronage and favour, the Trustees had still found the right person for the job.

To work

As winter passed Elford settled into the Museum, where he had inherited Shaw's Linnæan kingdom. Not surprisingly, his first decision was to rearrange all the collections and displays along modern, natural lines

[18] Loc: Entomology Library, The Natural History Museum, London. Ref: Entomological Memorandums, Samouelle Register, **3**: 229ff.

Historical note

1814	William Wordsworth[1] publishes his poem *The Excursion*.
31st March	Russian and Prussian armies enter Paris.
6th April	Napoleon abdicates.
23rd April	Convention for suspension of hostilities with France.
end of April	12,000 British visitors in Paris[2].
4th May	Jane Austen's *Mansfield Park* published anonymously.
28th May	Military convention between: (1) Britain, Austria, Prussia & Russia, and (2) France.
30th May	Treaty of peace and amity with France.
June	Disturbances among Leicester[3] weavers.
7th July	Walter Scott publishes *Waverley*, the first of his so-called 'Scotch Novels'. It was published anonymously amid much speculation as to the identity of the author.
summer	Poor harvest, leading to large scale imports of wheat.
24th August	British occupy Washington DC and burn public buildings.
29th November	*The Times* newspaper first produced by steam-driven press.

[1] William Wordsworth (1770-1850). English poet.
[2] Priestley, 1971: 116.
[3] Pronounced 'Lester'.

(while continuing his monthly production of the *Zoological Miscellany* and his research). At the beginning of April, as the snow finally cleared and Spring began, Henry Woollcombe visited London and called to see him:

"Dined with D[r] Leach, met Charles Gandy[19] the former seems to be very happy, full of ardour in the pursuit of his Profession as Keeper of the Natural History Department at the Museum[20]. When I am in London I wish for a little more money that I might become a Member of some of the literary & Scientific Societies but Prudence forbids—[21]"

It sounds as though Elford had been trying to recruit again. Woollcombe was at the British Museum a few days later where he was shown one of the Museum's recent acquisitions, a human skeleton embedded in rock, from the Caribbean. Elford mentioned this skeleton in the issue of the *Zoological Miscellany* for April where he implied a distinction between conchology (a study of empty mollusc shells) and the study of molluscs (the shell *and* its occupant). He is usually acerbic about the former, as when he says, 'I think mere conchology a plaything, unworthy of scientific attention, and the study of Mollusca, one of high interest and importance, from its application to physiology and comparative Anatomy[22]', but in the *Miscellany* he admitted conchology had its uses in geology:

"Conchology, when rendered subservient to geognostic investigations, assumes the rank of an useful science, and then becomes a subject of the highest importance. *Bulimulus trifasciatus*, a very common West Indian shell, occurs imbedded in the same limestone which incloses the fossil human skeleton, lately sent to the British Museum, from the *grande terre* of Guadaloupe, by Sir A. Cochrane[23], proving that rock to be of modern date, and contemporaneous with the existing creation of animals.[24]"

His clear acceptance that a modern shell embedded in the rock indicates a modern date for the rock suggests the converse, that a shell not obviously modern would have meant something else.

Fossils

By 1814 extinction was a familiar concept and fossils were already believed to be animals and plants that had lived in earlier ages[25]. Fossils not identifiable as species living today were believed by many to have become extinct as a result of the biblical flood[26] or some preceding catastrophe.

In 1812 the great comparative anatomist Georges Cuvier had studied fossilised bones from different rock strata around Paris and published the results in his *Recherches sur les Ossemens Fossiles des Quadrupèdes*[27]. In this he produced a chronology for the appearance of the different types of animal. He had effectively founded vertebrate palæontology. Cuvier said of this technique:

'It would certainly be exceedingly satisfactory to have the fossil organic productions arranged in chronological order, in the same manner as we now

[19] Possibly a relation of John Gandy, vicar of St Andrew's Church Plymouth from 1769-1824 and/or of Henry Gandy, one of the original movers for the formation of the Plymouth Institution. It is not clear whether Charles Gandy was also dining with Elford and Woollcombe.
[20] Correctly Assistant-Keeper.
[21] Woollcombe's Diary, 3rd April 1814 (Loc: West Devon Record Office, Plymouth).
[22] Letter: W.E. Leach to Jameson, 14th April 1819 (Loc: Edinburgh University Library, Special Collections).
[23] Vice-Admiral Sir Alexander Forrester Inglis Cochrane (1758-1832). Governor of Guadeloupe 1810-1814. In 1814 moved to command the Royal Navy's North American Station and oversaw the British operations against Baltimore and New Orleans. Returned to Britain 1814. Promoted full Admiral 1819. Royal Navy Commander-in-Chief in Plymouth from 1821.
[24] *Zoological Miscellany*, 1: 42.
[25] Philip Rehbock (1985) touches on this when discussing Elford's friend John Fleming (1785-1857).
[26] i.e. extinct because they were not taken aboard Noah's Ark.
[27] *Researches on the fossil bones of quadrupeds.*

have the principal mineral substances. By this the science of organization itself would be improved; the developments of animal life; the succession of its forms; the precise determinations of those which have been first called into existence, the simultaneous production of certain species and their gradual extinction;— all these would perhaps instruct us fully as much in the essence of organization as all the experiments that we shall ever be able to make upon living animals: and man, to whom only a short space of time is allotted upon the earth, would have the glory of restoring the history of thousands of ages which preceded the existence of the race, and of thousands of animals which never were contemporaneous with his species.[28']

Readers at this time were happy to put a biblical interpretation on Cuvier's results – as was Cuvier – as shown by a reviewer of the above work:—'in the relics of a former world, preserved to us in the bosoms of the rocks, we may trace the order and succession of the creation of organic forms, as recorded in [the inspired account of the creation of the world by the great historian of the Jews[29]]. The older classes of secondary rocks contain remnants of vegetable forms alone; a second and a newer division are rich in the remains of all that the waters brought forth abundantly, while the skeletons and impressions of cattle, creeping things, and beasts of the earth, are discovered only in the newest alluvial formations.[30']

[28] Translated by Robert Kerr and published in English in 1813 as *Essay on the Theory of the Earth*, with notes by Robert Jameson.
[29] The first section of the Bible, the Old Testament Book of *Genesis*, held to be written by Moses (see box).
[30] *The British Review and London Critical Journal*, vol. V (issue X): 400-413 (1813).

The Holy Bible
King James ('Authorised') version
AD 1611
The First Book of Moses
called
Genesis
Chapter 1

In the beginning God created the heaven and the earth.
2 And the earth was without form, and void; and darkness *was* upon the face of the deep. And the spirit of God moved upon the face of the waters.
3 And God said, Let there be light: and there was light
9 And God said, Let the waters under the heaven be gathered together unto one place, and let the dry *land* appear: and it was so...
11 And God said, Let the earth bring forth grass, the herb yielding seed, *and* the fruit tree yielding fruit after his kind, whose seed *is* in itself, upon the earth: and it was so...
20 And God said, Let the waters bring forth abundantly the moving creature that hath life, and fowl *that* may fly above the earth in the open firmament of heaven.

21 And God created great whales, and every living creature that moveth, which the waters brought forth abundantly, after their kind, and every winged fowl after his kind: and God saw that *it was* good...
24 And God said, Let the earth bring forth the living creature after his kind, cattle, and creeping thing, and beast of the earth after his kind: and it was so...
26 And God said, Let us make man in our image, after our likeness: and let them have dominion over the fish of the sea, and over the fowl of the air, and over the cattle, and over all the earth, and over every creeping thing that creepeth upon the earth.
27 So God created man in his *own* image, in the image of God created he him; male and female created he them.

Human skeletons at this time had been found only in the most recent geological deposits, hence Elford's confirmation that the shells found with the Guadeloupe skeleton were a modern species "contemporaneous with the existing creation of animals".

At the British Museum fossils were grouped with the rocks in which they were found and were hence the domain of mineralogist Charles König, not Elford. It was König who prepared a paper for the Royal Society on this human skeleton[31].

Peace

In April, with the Russian and Prussian armies in Paris, Napoleon abdicated, signalling peace across Europe. London, having just lost its blanket of snow, was carpeted white again – for the Bourbons and Louis XVIII, who had spent the last seven years of his exile in England.

At the Linnean Society Elford read the first instalment of his analysis of the Crustacea, millipedes, centipedes and spiders. It was such a substantial work it would take him three presentations before he completed the story, the first on the 19th of April, then the 3rd of May and finally on the 1st of June. When this was published in the Society's *Transactions* it occupied 95 quarto pages. During the telling of this story he was elected to the Society's Council where he would serve for the next two years. Appropriately it was also around this time that his extensive descriptive entry on the same subject was finally published in the *Edinburgh Encyclopædia*, but this was not received with universal acclaim.

Elford had created new genera, along modern lines, whenever he felt a new genus was appropriate for one of his new species. Previous authors – especially Linnean authors – had been reluctant to form new genera and had tended to add their new species to Linnæus's existing groups, even when the new species showed clear differences to the species already present. To correct this Elford had also been obliged to divide many established genera. This added even more to the number of his new genera, many of which contained only one species. He was criticised for this, and it would be a number of years before many of his genera were recognised as justified, when similar species were discovered and added to them by other naturalists[32].

In addition to his Museum duties and his publishing, he was, as ever, in contact with local entomologists. In particular he was now friendly with James Francis Stephens[33] and George Samuel. Stephens came from a naval

[31] König, C. 1814. On a fossil human skeleton from Guadaloupe. *Philosophical Transactions of the Royal Society*. [not seen]
[32] Leach, 1852: xii.
[33] James Francis Stephens (1792-1852). Between 1809 and 1812 he compiled a catalogue of British Animals. FLS 1815.

Pied Shrike
Lanius doliatus Linnæus

Illustration from the *Zoological Miscellany* April 1814.

family and for the past seven years had worked as a Victualling Officer at the Admiralty Office in Somerset House, but all his spare time was spent on natural history. He was rapidly building one of the finest entomology collections in the country, which by the time of his death would contain 88,000 specimens, but in 1814 he was about to edit the section on birds in a continuation of George Shaw's unfinished multi-volume work, *General Zoology*.

George Samuel was the drawing master at the Reverend Jephson's boarding school in Camberwell, south London, not far from Elford's new home. It was apparently through him that Elford was put in contact with an 18 year old pupil, then completing his school education before leaving London to study mathematics at Cambridge. His name was John Stevens Henslow[34].

J.S. Henslow

John Henslow was probably the first disciple Elford acquired after arriving at the British Museum. As both were sons of attorneys who had been fascinated by nature since childhood, the two men quickly became friends and Elford took Henslow under his wing. Samuel had taught Henslow the rudiments of entomology but Elford and Stephens now expanded and honed his expertise. The three men explored the highways, by-ways, woods and rivers of Kent for insects and molluscs. Henslow had been examining the more obscure aquatic animals of the Medway estuary since he was a small child but his collecting now acquired a skilled edge under the guidance of his new tutors. It is said, "They at once fixed him down to the pursuits, which he had hitherto taken up as a mere boyish amusement, but which were henceforth to be made regular studies.[35]"

Henslow left for Cambridge in October 1814 but he kept in regular contact with Elford Leach and over the next few years sent him various collections made during excursions around Britain. Inevitably Elford named several species after him: the swimming crab *Polybius henslowi*, found by Henslow off the coast of north Devon, and the bivalve molluscs *Euglesa henslowiana* and *Pera henslowiana*. Henslow maintained his natural history interest after graduating and was soon Professor of Mineralogy at Cambridge (1822-1827) then Professor of Botany (1827-1861), but despite this, for many years his greatest love was still zoology[36].

John Henslow's claim to fame today is his patronage of one of his own students, the apparently ubiquitous Charles Darwin. At Edinburgh Darwin had witnessed several surgical operations – one on a child, and

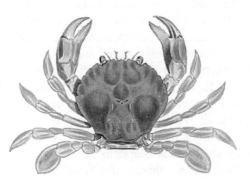

Polybius henslowi Leach

Henslow's swimming crab

Illustration from *Malacostraca Podophthalmata Britanniæ by* Elford Leach.

[34] John Stevens Henslow (1796-1861). His father was originally an attorney, then a wine-merchant/brewer, then returned to legal practice. Both his parents were interested in natural history. Was ordained 1824.
[35] Jenyns, 1862: 8-9.
[36] Jenyns, 1862: 20-23.

all performed without anaesthetic – and had decided medicine was not for him. In 1828 he arrived at Cambridge University to study for the church. Although he shared Jonathan Leach's passion for field-sports, and shooting seemed to be his main preoccupation, he was still interested in natural history, and some beetles he collected were included in a publication by Elford's friend James Stephens. Darwin later said in his autobiography, 'No poet ever felt more delight at seeing his first poem published than I did at seeing in Stephens' *Illustrations of British Insects* the magic words "captured by C. Darwin, Esq."[37]

It was Henslow who was most influential in having Darwin appointed to accompany *HMS Beagle* on her global circumnavigation from 1831-1836 (having considered applying for the post himself), and he took charge of Darwin's natural history collections as they were sent home. Henslow supported his own protégé just as he had been guided by Elford Leach and James Stephens 20 years earlier.

(As an aside, Henslow later became friendly with William Hooker and helped him form a museum of economic botany at Kew Gardens, where William – by then Sir William Hooker – was the Director. Hooker's son Joseph Dalton Hooker[38] (later Sir Joseph Hooker and a close friend of Darwin) married Henslow's daughter Frances. But in 1814 all that was yet to come.)

The British Museum was closed to the public during the months of August and September and it was usual for some officers to take extended leave at that time, having first obtained permission from the Trustees to be absent from London. Elford thought it would be better to work on the collections while the Museum was quiet in September so he applied for "the usual length of absence", but starting in July. The Trustees do not appear to have appreciated this presumption and they made him wait until August to take his break at the normal time. He spent at least part of the summer in Plymouth – while the Rifles' 3rd battalion was at the local barracks awaiting orders – and on the 10th of August he gave a talk on the subject of Cranioscopy. This may have been at the Plymouth Institution. Henry Woollcombe was certainly there:

"Wednesday Even[g]. 10th August— Attended D[r] Leach's Lecture on Cranioscopy, a subject new to me, afforded me much entertainment, but occasioned intense thinking, which I feel the efforts of at this moment. The conversation good Kept up with much spirit—D[r] Cardia of Truro was present, & Mr Butter who asked

[37] de Beer, 1974: 35.
[38] Joseph Dalton Hooker (1817-1911)

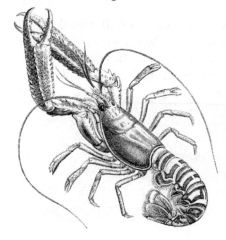

Genus *Nephrops* Leach, 1814

Nephrops norvegicus (Linnæus)

'Scampi'

Illustration from Bell, 1853

pertinent questions & spoke modestly. I was pleased with D^r Ls manner, it was totally free of self sufficiency, candid, open, & liberal.[39]"

Cranioscopy

Elford had written an entry on cranioscopy for the *Edinburgh Encyclopædia* and no doubt based his lecture on his article. There he described this subject as, "a science which teaches us to investigate the eminences produced in the cranium by the brain, and to discover, by such examinations, the particular part of the brain in which the individual organs, influencing our passions or economy, reside." This would later achieve immense popularity in Victorian times – and not a little notoriety as a 'quack' concept – under a different name, Phrenology: 'reading the bumps' on someone's head.

The concept that regions of the brain provided particular attributes, and that the degree of these attributes could be assessed by the size and shape of the bulges in the overlying skull, was first proposed by Franz Gall[40] at the University of Vienna in the 1790s. His public lectures caused so much controversy he was obliged to leave Vienna and eventually settled in Paris. In 1810 he began publishing a four volume work with Johann Spurzheim[41], *Anatomie et Physiologie du Système Nerveaux en général, et du cerveau en particulier*[42]. It was the first volume of this work that Elford had reviewed in the Edinburgh Encyclopædia where, after describing Gall's views, he had offered a critique:

"We cannot conclude, without noticing some of the objections urged against this hypothesis of Gall. He has been accused of describing prominences on those parts under which there is no brain. Thus the root of the nose and eye-brows assume a shape of greater or less prominence, according to the size of the frontal sinuses, which vary greatly in different individuals; yet over these cavities he places the organs of memory and colours; and over the spine of the frons, the organ of aptness to receive an education; and his organ of music, on the external angular process of the same bone."

Although Gall was ridiculed, especially in the years after his death, he has to be recognised as a pioneer of the idea that there are localised centres in the brain which process particular activities. Despite his criticisms Elford was not averse to some of the ideas expressed by Gall and Spurzheim.

[39] Woollcombe's Diary (Loc: West Devon Record Office, Plymouth).
[40] Franz Josef Gall (1758-1828).
[41] Johann Christoph Gaspar (sometimes cited 'Caspar') Spurzheim (1776-1832). Wrote *The Physiognomical System of Drs Gall and Spurzheim* (1815).
[42] *Anatomy and physiology of the nervous system in general, and of the brain in particular.*
[43] Letter: W.E. Leach to Jameson, 27th April 1815 (Loc: Edinburgh University Library, Special Collections).
[44] Letter: W.E. Leach to Jameson, [4th] January 1816 (Loc: Edinburgh University Library, Special Collections. Ref: Gen. 129/141).
[45] John Cranch (1785-1816). Born at Exeter and christened at the Bow (or Georges) Presbyterian Meeting House, Exeter on 4th April 1785. See also biographical information in Monod (1970)
[46] Letter: W.E. Leach to MacLeay, 5th February 1824 (Loc: Linnean Society of London, Miscellaneous Correspondence).
[47] *The Annual Register for 1818* says 10 years old (Anon., 1819: 436).
[48] Jack Cranch should not be confused with the contemporary John Cranch of Kingsbridge (1751-1821), a lawyer, painter and antiquarian.
[49] Fox, 1864: 50-51.

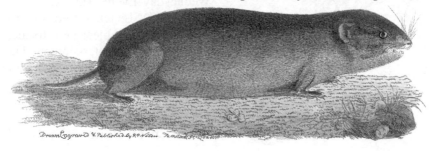

Arvicola xanthognathia Leach
Fulvous-Cheeked Campagnol (vole)

Illustration from the
Zoological Miscellany
June 1814

50 Possibly the Jane Cranch christened 25th June 1786 at the Ebenezer Independent Chapel, Kingsbridge, sister of Roger Denbow Cranch (b. 1783) and daughter of Nathaniel Cranch and his wife Jane (née Beer) who were married at Kingsbridge on 12th August 1782 (*International Genealogical Index*). Sir John Bowring (see later), who provided biographical information about Cranch to the Admiralty, says Jack Cranch married Jane Bowring, Sir John's aunt (Bowring, 1872) but it was Cranch's father Richard who had married Jane Bowring on the 7th of October 1781 at Holy Trinity Church, Exeter. John Cranch married Jane Cranch at Kingsbridge on 29th August 1809. We are indebted for this and other family information to Dr John Lamble of Cambridge whose great-grandmother was Clara Cranch, a relative of the 'other' John Cranch of Kingsbridge.
51 Jane Bowring Cranch (1813 - beyond 1877). Christened 24th October 1813, Ebenezer Independent Chapel, Kingsbridge. A writer. Published *True Greatness* (A poem) (1855); *Whitefield Preaching* (1856); edited *Troublous Times; or, Leaves from the note-book of John Hicks, an ejected Nonconformist Minister, 1670-71* (1862); and a book of poems (1877).

Nebalia herbstii Leach
crustacean

Illustration from the Zoological Miscellany September 1814

He later admitted to Jameson, "You are right in supposing me to be a Spurzheimite, being one of the elect and true believers in the basis of his doctrines, although not convinced of the truth of the whole, Dr S. having as is usual with new Theories, carried it too far.[43]" Elford came to know Spurzheim (perhaps when Spurzheim lectured in Britain) and referred to him as, "my much abused good friend[44]". Spurzheim's ideas acquired quite a following in Edinburgh, and when the first phrenological society in Europe was formed there in 1820 Elford Leach was a member.

In 1814 Elford did not miss the opportunity while in Devon to pursue his zoological interests and it appears to have been during this summer break that he first encountered a self-taught Devon naturalist known to Montagu, John Cranch[45].

John Cranch

John Cranch ('Jack' to his friends[46]) came from an Exeter family of moderately humble origins. His father died when he was eight years old[47], after which he was raised by an uncle in Kingsbridge[48]. Jack was apprenticed to a boot and shoe-maker, to which end he managed a stall at local fairs, but became interested in natural history when he visited Montagu's house and saw his collection[49]. Struggling to learn his trade, he still found time to acquire zoological knowledge from the few books available to him and he taught himself rudimentary Latin and French so he could understand the scientific descriptions and Continental texts. His enthusiasm for collecting was unrestrained and his museum was soon extensive. After completing his apprenticeship he married Jane Cranch (presumably a cousin) in 1809[50], and it appears this marriage brought some financial security. He now turned the laborious aspects of his business over to his journeymen and committed increasing amounts of time to natural history, publishing some short essays on insects, molluscs and crustaceans in the *Weekly Examiner* in 1811. The couple's first child, Jane Bowring Cranch, was born in 1813[51].

Elford visited Cranch for the first time the following year with Montagu and Charles Prideaux and later declared:

"We were all astonished at the magnitude of his collection of shells, crustacea, insects, birds, &c. collected entirely by himself, and still more so with the accuracy of their classification, and with the remarks made by this self-educated and zealous individual. He conversed on all subjects

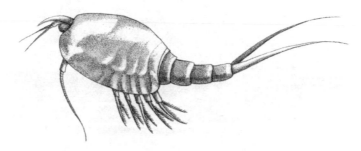

connected with natural history, with modesty, but at the same time with that confidence which is the result of knowledge.[52]"

Elford appreciated enthusiasm wherever it was found and, regardless of their different social backgrounds, he and Cranch became firm friends, even sailing off-shore for days with the commercial fishing fleet, where they dredged the sea-bed for new and exotic species[53]. One of the crustaceans Cranch had written about in the *Weekly Examiner* was the tiny Pea-Crab which lives inside bivalve molluscs. Elford acquired some of Cranch's specimens and included them in the first part of his book on British Crustacea, to be published the following January. He decided they belonged to a new species and named it *Pinnotheres cranchii*, saying, 'This new species was discovered by Mr. J. Cranch (a most assiduous Collector of marine productions)'.

Elford was so impressed with Cranch's ability to find rare species that when the time came for him to return to London he took Cranch into his employment as his collector[54] and promised to try to obtain him a position at the British Museum as soon as a suitable vacancy arose. Cranch was enthusiastic and with this new income was now more than ever determined to become a full-time naturalist. He dismissed his journeymen and converted his shop into a store for his collections. Sampling now took all his time and he travelled extensively around the coasts of Devon and Cornwall, as far as the Scilly Isles, sampling every habitat he could.

Autumn 1814

By October Elford was back in London. Cranch appears to have visited him there shortly afterwards[55], as did his friend from Plymouth and Edinburgh, Frederick Hammick, now a qualified doctor. Hammick was planning to take advantage of the war's end to travel to Paris to extend his medical knowledge. Elford asked him to carry a letter (which would also act for Hammick as a letter of introduction) to Dr Henri Ducrotay de Blainville[56], a French professor of comparative anatomy and zoology. It is obvious from the tone of the

[52] Anon., 1818: 327.
[53] Leach, 1852: 304.
[54] Anon., 1818: 327-328. Leach, 1852: 172.
[55] Letter: W.E. Leach to Montagu, n.d. WM1812 but apparently written about 1814 (Loc: Linnean Society of London, Loose enclosure in a Montagu notebook. Ref: Ms 206).
[56] Henri Ducrotay de Blainville (1777-1850). Began life as a painter but heard Cuvier lecture and became interested in biology.

A 'Hooker' of the Plymouth commercial fishing fleet.

letter[57] that Elford and de Blainville had already made contact and Elford's remark, "Mon[r] Lawrance was much disappointed at not seeing you" (presumably William Lawrence, Elford's old anatomy teacher) suggests de Blainville had recently visited London.

Elford and de Blainville had a reason for keeping in contact. Like James Stephens they had agreed to continue parts of Shaw's *General Zoology*. Elford was going to write the volumes on the Crustacea, de Blainville on the Mollusca[58], and Elford had already set Jack Cranch to work collecting molluscs to be sent to Paris.

It appears neither Elford nor de Blainville had a high regard for their predecessor's efforts; Elford talks of 'the bad plan laid down by Shaw' and appears to be quoting de Blainville when he calls the *General Zoology* a "pitoyable compilation". In fact Shaw had devoted most of his working hours at the Museum to producing populist works of natural history, written mainly to supplement his meagre income[59]. He conducted no original research and consequently earned no credit from the research-minded Elford Leach.

Another person about whom Elford had some reservations (in which respect he was not alone) was Sir Everard Home[60], a comparative anatomist and the Master of the Royal College of Surgeons. Elford confides to de Blainville, ' *"The great Sir Everard Home"* showed me a letter which he received from M. G. Cuvier[61], in which epistle is a most severe and just critique on his opus magnum treating of Anatomie Comparative[62], but I could not assist him in getting out of the ditch into which his hasty mode of writing had caused him to fall.'

An interesting postscript to this letter notes, "Signior Assilini Napoleon's Surgeon is now in London, and from him I learnt some curious anecdotes respecting the Emperor". Infuriatingly he does not say what these curious anecdotes are.

The end of the year was spent re-organising the Museum's galleries. Before his arrival the rooms set aside for natural history had each contained an assortment of natural productions: animals and parts of animals were arranged alongside plants and minerals[63]. He now started to rearrange these so that each room would display fewer branches of the science, and these would be arranged according to natural classifications. This task was to take years.

He started by beginning an arrangement of the shells in the public galleries; examining the shells stored elsewhere in the Museum;

Hippocampus ramulosus Leach

Illustration from the *Zoological Miscellany* October 1814

[57] Letter: W.E. Leach to de Blainville, 24th October 1814 (Loc: Bibliothèque Centrale, Muséum National d'Histoire Naturelle, Paris. Ref: Item 102).

[58] In fact neither was ever published.

[59] Swainson (1840).

[60] Home is reported to have plagiarised the papers of his brother-in-law John Hunter (1728-1793) – the founder of the Hunterian Museum of the Royal College of Surgeons – then burned them to hide the evidence. The *Dictionary of National Biography* says in his later years the Royal Society published 'many insignificant or worthless papers by him'.

[61] i.e. Monsieur G[eorges] Cuvier.

[62] Presumably Home's *Lectures on Comparative Anatomy...* which began publication in 1814.

[63] J.E. Gray (House of Commons, 1836: para. 2456).

and beginning to sort the crustaceans. He then started to move the stuffed birds out of Room XI (the 'Bird Room'), which was to be altered as part of the restoration and repairs taking place continually in the house. He put these into Room X, which contained the insect collections in closed drawers[64] and was hence called the 'Insect Room[65]' although it also contained shells (as did Room IX with the geology) and other invertebrates. He also convinced the Trustees that the collection of fruits and other plant material should be removed from the galleries to create space for displays with more public interest[66]. Like Louis Simond he must have been unhappy with the condition of some of the birds, as the Trustees ordered that "the Bird-Stuffer mentioned in Dr Leach's Report be employed to repair and bake such Specimens of stuffed Birds in the Museum as may require it". Baking (or 'stoving') stuffed specimens was common at this time and was exactly as it sounds. The mounted specimen was put in a hot oven to kill any mites, beetles, moths or their larvae that had infested it and were causing damage or spoiling its appearance. A poorly prepared exhibit could react badly to this draconian treatment and it was a job for a trained taxidermist. The Bird-Stuffer mentioned here was Benjamin Leadbeater. He ran London's leading natural history suppliers at N° 19 Brewer Street, Golden Square[67], where his son later joined him in the business. Whenever the Museum needed expertise in taxidermy, it was to Leadbeater they turned.

With the onset of winter Elford left for Devon to spend time with his family, but all was not well at the Plymouth Institution and when Elford arrived he was obviously in no mood for compromise.

Henry Woollcombe: "Friday Morning 9th Dec[r]. The comfort of our Institution has been much impaired this Winter by the unfortunate dissenssions about Harvey, last night further discussions took place, and another resignation from D[r] Leach, an honorary Member!!! a thing unheard

[64] G. Samouelle (House of Commons, 1835: para. 3819).

[65] In fact we do not know whether it acquired this name before Elford Leach, with his pronounced interest in insects, arrived, or only afterwards as he developed this collection.

[66] J.E. Gray (House of Commons, 1836: para. 2456)

[67] Benjamin Leadbeater (d. 1837). Many sources call him 'Leadbetter', and he presumably pronounced the name 'Ledbetter'. When the father and son died, their business was continued for a while by a nephew (Sharpe, 1906: 411). The son was presumably the John Leadbeater who flourished in the 1820s (Wheeler, 1997: 122) [John may be the John Leadbeater who married Lucy King at Farnborough, Warwick on 10th August 1829. Their 5 children - the eldest Benjamin christened on 2nd January 1831 - were all baptised at St James Church, Westminster. This may also be the same John Leadbeater, son of Benjamin Leadbeater, christened at St Peter Church, Leeds on 30th September 1804].

Historical note

1815	Amedeo Avogadro[1] says molecules could be clusters of atoms.
—	Now 26 miles (41.8 km) of gas mains in London for lighting.
—	With the end of the war, Dartmoor Prison abandoned[2].
—	Schubert composes his 2nd and 3rd Symphonies.
8th February	Declaration by Britain, Austria, France, Portugal, Prussia, Russia, Spain and Sweden, concerning universal abolition of the slave trade.
February	Walter Scott publishes (anonymously) his second 'Scotch Novel' *Guy Mannering*.
March	Disturbances among Tyneside keelmen.
March	Labourers breaking farm machinery in Suffolk.
December	Jane Austen's *Emma* published anonymously.

[1] Amedeo Avogadro. A Piedmontese scientist born at Turin (1776-1856).
[2] It would be empty for at least 3 years (Gill 1983: 206).

of I believe, and which I cannot but highly disapprove. The Meeting went off without any degree of violence, the boisterous having either retired or absented themselves. A becoming dignity was preserved, & though we are shorn of some of our thriving branches, we shall still continue to flourish[68]".

We are given no clues as to the nature of the dissensions about Harvey[69]. There was a George Harvey *FRS, FRSE* in Plymouth at this time who contributed entries to the *Edinburgh Encyclopædia* on: *Plymouth*; *Plymouth Breakwater*[70]; *Shipbuilding*; and *Naval Tactics*. This may be the same person[71]. Whatever the cause of the disagreement a group of members, including Elford, broke away and formed their own group, called by Henry Woollcombe (and possibly by them) 'The Select Society'.

1815

While Elford celebrated the first peaceful New Year's Day Britain had seen since 1803[72], in London the first part of his long-planned book on the British Crustacea was published. Its title was now *Malacostraca Podophthalmata Britanniæ* (literally 'The stalk-eyed thin-shelled shellfish of Britain' or, as Elford called it, 'the pedunculate eyed Crustacea of Britain[73]'). We shall call it *Malacostraca*.

Back in the Museum in February, he arrived just as Charles König was leaving for Munich on Museum business. König would be away until May. In his absence Elford, temporarily responsible for the whole of Natural History, set to work twisting the Trustees' arms. His friend Simon Wilkin had decided to concentrate on British entomology and wanted to sell his collection of Australian, Brazilian and North American insects. At £100 for 2400 specimens Elford desperately wanted the Museum to purchase it but he had a problem. The Trustees viewed insects as perishable items and tended not to buy them[74]. Obliged for once to devise a plan, Elford put a proposal to Sir Joseph Banks: if the Museum purchased Wilkins' collection, he, Elford Leach, would donate to the Museum his own collection of neuropterous insects – to his knowledge the finest collection in existence – *and* three drawers of rare foreign insects (including one beetle that had cost him 5 guineas, and another that had cost him £3) *and* his collection of rare British fishes, collected in Devon, Wales, Ireland and Scotland. Allegedly as an unrelated matter, but nevertheless shrewdly added as a sign of loyalty, if the Trustees would let him send Jack Cranch some old redundant bottles from the Museum, and would pay for transport and preservative, Elford would ask Cranch to collect species for the national collections as part of his duties.

None of this was a problem for Elford as he was already having to curate his own collection as well as the Museum's. Donating his collections brought him no extra work and he still had access to them for his research. He would merely lose their cash value, but he was not concerned about the money. Banks must have convinced the other Trustees they would be getting a good deal, as (unusually) they agreed to everything.

[68] Woollcombe's Diary (Loc: West Devon Records Office, Plymouth).

[69] If indeed this is what the diary says. Woollcombe's writing is not clear here.

[70] To provide calmer water for the naval anchorage, a breakwater was built across the mouth of the estuary, with entry and exit past each end. Work commenced in 1812 but it was not completed until 1848.

[71] In 1831 a "Mr Harvey" in Plymouth wrote to the founders of the newly formed British Association for the Advancement of Science (Howarth, 1931: 23) and in 1836 a J.B. Harvey (d. 26th February 1843) donated "marine productions" from the south coast of Devon to the Zoological Society of London. He was primarily an ornithologist and appears to have emigrated to Australia after 1838 (Wheeler, 1997: 104).

[72] Between the Treaty of Amiens (27th March 1802) which ended the French Revolutionary Wars, and the start of the Napoleonic Wars (May 1803)

[73] Letter: W.E. Leach to de Blainville, 31st March 1815 (Bibliothèque Centrale, Muséum National d'Histoire Naturelle, Paris. Ref: Item 104).

[74] Letter: W.E. Leach to [Sir Joseph Banks], 9th February 1815 (Loc: British Museum, Trustees' Manuscripts. Original Letters and Papers. Vol. III 1810-1816 pp. 1172-3). Elford thought this view mistaken.

Not ignoring his publishing, Elford was busy with a job he had acquired from the Edinburgh publishers several years earlier. He was providing the zoological entries for a supplement to the *Encyclopædia Britannica*. He had planned to write most of these entries himself, starting with *Annulosa* (animals with segmented bodies)[75], but he now contacted de Blainville[76] suggesting he write several entries, including *Mollusca*. The authors were being paid £1 for each printed page and the publishers were paying to produce the plates[77], so this could be an attractive proposition (the *Annulosa* entry was eventually published at 23 pages[78], and another Elford wrote on *Entomology* – effectively an easy rewrite of part of a similar entry he prepared for the *Edinburgh Encyclopædia* – reached 52 pages, almost half his annual salary).

Elford wanted to use this opportunity to introduce the modern Continental system of classification into the work, which may explain why he went to Paris for a contributor for the mollusc entries. He explained this policy in the opening lines of the entry *Annulosa*:

"The Linnean arrangement of the Animal Kingdom has, with some slight emendations, been adopted as the ground-work of the zoological articles contained in the later editions of the *Encyclopædia*. In these Supplemental volumes, we propose to introduce all the recent discoveries in Zoology, and also to avail ourselves of the opportunity thus afforded, of describing the various classes of animals under an arrangement more accordant to the improved views of Science, and to the Order of Nature.[79]"

Elford implores de Blainville to provide his submission in a legible hand and in English, which is explained later when he says, "I beg of you to write to me more plainly; although your writing is very beautiful yet to an indifferent French scholar like to myself it is not very legible.[80]"

An indifferent French scholar he may be but that did not stop him writing in French to Professor Franco Bonelli[81] at Turin, to thank him for sending as a gift his monograph on European beetles. Not one to miss a chance to strengthen his contacts, Elford now assures Bonelli that in return he has asked his friends to collect British insects for him. He also proposed Bonelli and de Blainville as foreign members of the Wernerian Society. With them he proposed another well-known naturalist, famous for being the first to describe many European species: Jules-César Savigny[82] of Paris.

Elford appears to have come into contact with Savigny through his developing interest in the classification of molluscs. Elford had collected molluscs during his trips to Ireland and the Western Isles and it appears he had now started to study his collection. This was to be a major undertaking which would last many years (he had no strong background in this group, which is presumably why he asked de Blainville to write the various mollusc contributions) and he appears to have started his analysis with a small manageable group of species, the sea-squirts. Although sea-squirts (ascidians) are now recognised as an animal group in their own right, at that time they

[75] Cuvier had divided the animal kingdom into 4 basic types, based on body plan: Vertebrosa (vertebrates); Radiata (radiating animals such as star-fish and other echinoderms); Mollusca; and Annulosa (segmented animals)

[76] Letter: W.E. Leach to de Blainville, 8th March 1815 (Loc: Bibliothèque Centrale du Muséum National d'Histoire Naturelle, Paris. Ref: Pièce 103).

[77] Although a different publisher, the *Edinburgh Encyclopædia* may have had a similar arrangement.

[78] Not including the index.

[79] *Encyclopædia Britannica*, Supplement to the 4th Edition, I(II): 401 (June 1816).

[80] 'Like' is smudged here. He probably tried to delete the 'to' following it while the ink was wet and rubbed the wrong word.

[81] Franco Andrea Bonelli (1784-1830). Professor of Natural History at Turin. See D'Entrèves & Gentile (1985).

[82] Marie Jules César Lelorgne de Savigny (1777-1851) At Cuvier's suggestion he accompanied Napoleon to Egypt in 1798 as an invertebrate zoologist. In Paris worked on the Egyptian collections. In 1817 his eyesight began to fail and he had to stop working for several years. He spent some of the time collecting in Italy. He returned to the Paris museum in 1822 but in 1824 became effectively blind.

water enters   water 'squirts' out

Sea-Squirt

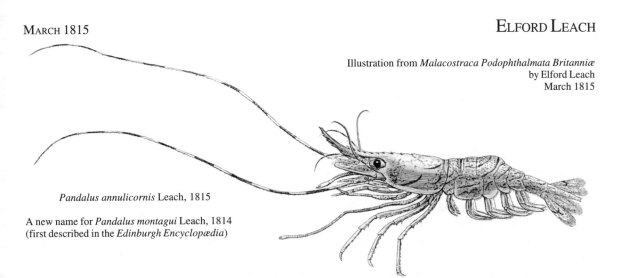

Illustration from *Malacostraca Podophthalmata Britanniæ*
by Elford Leach
March 1815

Pandalus annulicornis Leach, 1815

A new name for *Pandalus montagui* Leach, 1814
(first described in the *Edinburgh Encyclopædia*)

were considered a type of mollusc. Savigny had been studying this group and was examining their internal anatomy, a task for which he was ideally suited as he had a reputation as the most skilled micro-dissector in Europe. When Elford later needed to examine the mouthparts of a particularly small fly he tells us,

"fearing to undertake the dissection, I submitted the specimen to the inspection of Savigny, from whose exact and almost infallible hand and eye, I felt confident of gaining the desired information[83]".

It was to Savigny he turned for assistance with the ascidians and later dedicated part of a book on the molluscs to him.

With the end of the war all Elford's European contacts could now be explored with some enthusiasm. Since armies had stopped rampaging over the continent, there had been a flood of cross-channel travel. De Blainville appears to have been to London, and the English privileged classes *en masse* had been flocking to Europe. There was even a popular song at the time, *All the World's in Paris*. In 1815 Elford decided to join them and in March wrote to Alexander MacLeay:

"My dear Sir,

As I am fully determined to visit the Continent during the summer, I feel a wish to become a member of the royal Society. On a former occasion you and D[r] Maton were kind enough to offer to give me a certificate for that purpose when the business of Bullock should have been forgotten.

I am not aware that I have any enemies or that I have rendered myself obnoxious to the members of that Society by my action. If you have the least objection to give me a certificate, I beg if you will not scruple to say so, and if you have no objection, but think that I have enemies or that I might even make enemies if proposed then I shall be obliged if you will let me know your opinion.

Should no objection be obvious to you I shall then be infinitely obliged if you will write a certificate and obtain the signature of D[r] Maton and of

[83] *Zoological Miscellany*,
3:134.

some other respectable members to whom I may be known, tomorrow eve[g] at the meeting of the Linnean Society, by doing which

you will infinitely oblige
Yrs very truly
W[m] Elford Leach[84]"

To de Blainville he explains: 'I trust to be permitted to visit Paris in the autumn, in the month of August; I hope you will do all in your power to procure for me a passport for that purpose[85]. I have applied to the professors at the Museum d'histoire naturelle and to the president of the Institute[86] for permission to enable me to visit the Jardin de Plantes[87], and as the study of the crustacea will be my only motive, I have some hopes that this indulgence may be given to me.[88]'

This time his ambition to become a fellow of the Royal Society would be fulfilled, but due process had to be observed. It would be February 1816 before he finally acquired the magic letters *FRS*.

As Elford made his plans to visit Paris the streets of London dissolved in chaos around him.

The 1815 Corn Law riots

Riots had been part of British public expression throughout much of the eighteenth century but with a growing population and increasing concentration of the working class the country was becoming a political powder-keg.

After the bumper harvest of 1813 which pushed down the price of domestic wheat, and the poor harvest of 1814 which (coinciding with the end of international hostilities) resulted in a flood of imports, the British cereal farmers were panicking about the threat to their livelihoods. In March 1815, amid widespread protests and petitions, the government introduced a Corn Law which prevented duty-free import of foreign corn unless domestic grain prices rose to £320 per ton[89]. If domestic prices were below this so-called 'famine price' imports were only allowed subject to the payment of import duties which increased if British corn prices fell further.

The intention of the Act was to maintain the market for domestic wheat, but for the consumer the restriction on imports and the maintenance of prices merely served to raise the cost of bread. This was deeply unwelcome at a time of falling wages and rising unemployment as thousands of servicemen were demobilised following the end of the war, but it was not just the working class who opposed the Act. In February, while still in the Bill stage, it had been attacked by London banker David Ricardo[90], today recognised as an influential pioneer of modern economics, in his *Essay on the Influence of a low Price of Corn on the Profits of Stock*, but all protest was in vain. The Bill became law.

The outrage was general and the labouring classes of London marched *en masse* to the affluent residential squares west of the city to vent their

[84] Letter: W.E. Leach to MacLeay, postmarked 20th March 1815 (Loc: Linnean Society, Miscellaneous Correspondence).
[85] At this time a passport was like a modern visa; it was obtained from the country to be visited.
[86] The National Institute of France founded in 1795 by the amalgamation of the Royal Academy of Sciences, the French Academy, the Academy of Inscriptions and Belles Lettres, and the Academy of Painting and Sculpture.
[87] The Jardin comprised not only the botanic garden founded in 1626, but also: the museum of natural history (with its extensive zoological, botanical and mineralogical collections and library); a menagerie; and lecturing facilities for the professors. Elford frequently uses the title of the whole establishment 'Jardin des Plantes' as a euphemism for the museum alone.
[88] Letter: W.E. Leach to de Blainville, 31st March 1815 (Loc: Bibliothèque Centrale, Muséum National d'Histoire Naturelle, Paris. Ref. Item 104)
[89] Expressed as 80 shillings per quarter [i.e. quarter of a hundredweight] with 20 shillings to the pound and 20 hundredweights (cwts) to a ton.
[90] David Ricardo (1772-1823). By 1814 he had made a fortune as a stockbroker. Elected MP for Portarlington in 1819.

St James's Palace, Pall Mall.

anger. Sir Joseph Banks, in Soho Square, had his house stoned and the door and windows smashed, with damage to the furniture, but the rioters did not dare enter the house or they would have been hung as burglars[91]. In the more select St James's Square, home to government ministers and other establishment figures, the violence was even worse, witnessed by a rather snobbish young officer of the 1st Regiment of Foot Guards, Ensign Rees Gronow[92]. Gronow had just completed his duty for the day commanding a guard detail at St James's Palace, and walked around the corner to investigate the disturbance in the square.

'I there beheld, collected together, thousands of the lowest of the London rabble. These ruffians, with loud shouts, and threats of summary vengeance on the Ministers, were at the time I arrived breaking the windows of most of the houses in the square. The Life Guards were patrolling in the neighbouring streets, and, whenever they appeared, were received with volleys of stones mingled with mud, and cries of "Down with the Piccadilly butchers![93]" The mob was evidently bent on more mischief, and I beheld one man exciting the crowd to force the doors of the Bishop of London's residence. As the fellow was making a rush against it, I told him to desist, or I would immediately run my sword through his body. This threat had the effect of calming the gentleman's ardour; he skulked away, and was soon lost in the crowd.

I was afterwards returning towards King Street, when I was accosted by Lord Castlereagh[94] [the Foreign Secretary]. He thanked me for the energy I had displayed, but recommended a little more discretion in future; "for the mob," said he, "is not so dangerous as you think."[95]'

[91] Letter: Banks to Sir James Edward Smith, 18th March 1815 (Dawson, 1958: 767).
[92] Rees Howell Gronow (1794-1865). Welsh officer and dandy.
[93] A reference to an earlier encounter between crowds and the Life-Guards in Piccadilly.
[94] Robert Stewart Castlereagh (1768-1822). Son of the Earl (from 1816 Marquess) of Londonderry.
[95] Gronow, 1964: 163.

What Gronow made of this remark is not known, but it was almost certainly a reference to the fact that at this time the government made extensive use of *agents provocateurs*. Government agents would infiltrate groups which the Establishment feared and would not only keep the authorities informed as to the plans of the Radicals but would sometimes initiate public violence themselves. This somewhat curious approach arose from the government's greatest fear of all, mass *peaceful* protest. Any forceful action taken against a peaceful crowd could stir up an already aggrieved public to a frenzy of resentment. However, if the crowd began throwing stones or produced weapons then a forceful suppression could be justified later. Sometimes those casting the first stones were not without sin.

With hardship increasing across the country and political reform high on the social agenda, the Corn Law riots of March 1815 were only one outburst in what would become a period of growing civil unrest in Regency Britain.

— 18 —

Escape of the Tyger

[In 1815] the lustre with which Napoleon shone, was
not that of a planet duly moving in its regular sphere,
but that of a comet inspiring forebodings of pestilence.

John Tucker[1]

The war with France might be over but in the United States the fighting
went on. By February 1815 the 3/95th had made their way from
Plymouth to the Gulf of Mexico and after a disastrous attempt on
New Orleans[2] were now camped on Dauphin Island, at the mouth of Mobile
Bay, where the British were besieging Fort Boyer[3].

Harry Smith, meanwhile, had returned to England with Ross's report
on the burning of Washington[4], and after giving a personal briefing to the
Prince Regent ("the most gentlemanlike and affable interview I could possibly
imagine") had been sent back to the United States. Sir Edward Pakenham[5]
had taken over as British Commander-in-Chief of land forces, and Smith,
promoted to Major, had been appointed his Assistant Adjutant-General. Like
the 3rd Battalion, Smith had been at New Orleans, where Pakenham and
more than 2000 British troops had been killed. The American defenders,
under Major-General Andrew Jackson[6], had achieved their victory with
minimal losses. What neither side had known was that the war between
Britain and the United States had ended on Christmas Eve with the signing
of the Treaty of Ghent. Still ignorant of this, Smith was now with the
regiments camped on Dauphin Island, where the men had to contend with
more than just Americans:

"I was half asleep one morning, rather later than usual, having been
writing the greater part of the night, when I heard old West say, "Sir, sir."

"What's the matter?"

"Thank the Lord, you're alive."

"What do you mean, you old ass?"

"Why, a navigator has been going round and round your tent all night;
here's a regular road about the tent"."

[1] Tucker, 1846: 347.
[2] Period around, and on, 8th January 1815.
[3] Gleig (1861: 192) calls this Fort Bayo.
[4] After Washington, Ross had taken his force to attack Baltimore. He had been killed on the advance and, with limited naval support, the force had withdrawn.
[5] General Sir Edward Pakenham (1778-1815).
[6] Andrew Jackson (1767-1845) Known as 'Old Hickory'. He was later 7th President of the United States (1829-1837).
[7] Smith, 1999: 253-254.

Of course Harry Smith's servant, West, actually meant an *alligator* had been circling his tent all night. Dauphin Island was alive with alligators and the soldiers caught and ate the young ones, but as the weather warmed, their parents, and the island's other inhabitants, became too bold.

"As summer came on," reported Lieutenant George Gleig[8] of the 85th Light Infantry, "the island sent forth multitudes of snakes from their lurking-places, which infested the camp, making their way in some instances into our very beds. This was bad enough, but it was not the only nuisance to which we were subject. The alligators, which during the winter months lie in a dormant state, now began to awaken, and prowling about the margin of the pool, created no little alarm and agitation. Apparently confounded at our invasion of their territories, these monsters at first confined themselves to the marshy part of the island, but becoming by degrees more familiar, they soon ventured to approach the very precincts of the camp. One of them at length entered a tent, in which only a woman and child chanced to be, and having stared round as if in amazement, walked out again without offering to commit any violence. But the visit was of too serious a nature to be overlooked. Parties were accordingly formed for their destruction, and it was usual on the return of each from an excursion, instead of asking how many birds, to demand how many snakes and alligators they had shot. Of the former indeed, great numbers were killed, and of the latter not a few, the largest of which measured about nine feet from the snout to the tail.[9]"

In a rare show of public spirit one fine specimen, two and a quarter metres in length, was prepared for a trans-Atlantic passage and despatched to the resident zoologist at the British Museum. Elford Leach described this very individual as a new species[10] in the September 1815 issue of the *Zoological Miscellany*, where he named it *Crocodilus cuvieri* after Georges Cuvier. Mistakenly he says it was from South America, rather than the American south, but tells us it was George Gleig's superior officer, Major De Bathe of the 85th Light Infantry, who actually killed the specimen and presented it.[11]

Meanwhile, word finally reached Dauphin Island on the 14th of February that the war with the United States had ended. While both sides waited for ratification by President Madison[12], across the Atlantic – as though Europe could no longer stand the thought of peace – Napoleon Bonaparte sailed from Elba to reinstate his empire.

[8] George Robert Gleig (1796-1888). Later ordained and went on to become Chaplain-General to the Armed Forces.
[9] Gleig, 1861: 195. [9 feet = 3 yards = 2.74 m].
[10] Which, in fact, it was not.
[11] *Zoological Miscellany*, **2**: 115-118, Pl. 102.
[12] James Madison (1751-1836). 4th President of the United States (1809-1817).

Crocodilus cuvieri Leach

Illustration from the
Zoological Miscellany
September 1815

The Hundred Days

It had taken less than a year for Napoleon to decide that after domination of Europe, dominion over Elba was not enough. He sailed from the island on the 28th of February and landed at Fréjus, on the Mediterranean coast of France. As he marched north through the countryside supporters flocked to him; whole army regiments deserted to him. From Paris the French king sent Marshal Ney to imprison the usurper. Ney and Bonaparte met at Auxerre on the 18th of March and in a full about-turn the Marshal and his men rallied behind their old master. Two days later Napoleon entered Paris and the king fled to Brussels.

At the Congress of Vienna the Continental powers had been deciding the future of a post-Napoleonic Europe. They now made one of the most startlingly angry declarations in the history of international diplomacy[13]. Referring to Napoleon's breakout as the latest manifestation of "a criminal and impotent delirium", they declared:

"By thus breaking the convention which established him in the Island of Elba, Buonaparte has destroyed the only legal title on which his existence depended: and by appearing again in France, with projects of confusion and disorder, he has deprived himself of the protection of the law, and has manifested to the universe that there can be neither peace nor truce with him. The powers consequently declare, that Napoleon Buonaparte has placed himself without the pale[14] of civil and social relations; and that, as an enemy and disturber of the tranquility of the world, he has rendered himself liable to public vengeance."

This final phrase was roundly criticised, both by Napoleon and by British politicians, as an invitation to assassinate. In its defence Wellington argued that the original French[15] 'vindicte publique' should have been translated as 'public justice' not 'public vengeance', although Napoleon's claim that the wording 'provokes the crime of assassination, and is almost unparalleled in the history of the world[16]' was presumably based on the original.

Despite the criticisms, the declaration was followed by an alliance of Britain, Austria, Prussia and Russia in which each agreed to put into the field an army of 150,000 men and keep them there until Bonaparte had been 'rendered incapable of disturbing the peace of Europe'. To this end Britain – with some battalions in America and many men already demobilised following the peace of the previous year – united with The Netherlands to produce a joint force. The continent was in conflict again.

English visitors had deserted Paris as Napoleon approached but many felt they were safe as long as they left French soil. Caroline Capel, the sister of Lord Uxbridge[17], had been living in Brussels since the peace of 1814 and wrote reassuringly to her mother in England[18]:

[13] On the 13th of March. Quoted in Kelly (1828: 3).
[14] 'Without the pale' or 'beyond the pale' – Outside the palisade. Beyond the boundary. Exceeding the accepted limits.
[15] French was the universal language of international diplomacy at this time.
[16] Kelly, 1828: 6.
[17] Henry William Paget, 2nd Earl of Uxbridge (1768-1854). His sister Lady Caroline Paget (1773-1847) had married the Honourable John Thomas Capel, a son of the Earl of Essex, in 1792.
[18] Caroline's mother was Jane, Dowager (i.e. widowed) Countess of Uxbridge (1742-1817).

'What annoys and worries me most at the Moment is the Idea that you will feel in a State of Anxiety at the News of the *Tyger* having broke loose; and as distance Sometimes Magnifies Evils will perhaps think there is cause for alarm on our Account, which I assure you there is not—The Numbers of English flocking from Paris will naturally cause consternation in England; but believe me there are as many have flocked here as to a place of Safety, as have gone to England...

with the assistance of our good Troops & the Allies who are pouring in I have no doubt of the Security of this Country — But the Tyger has his hands full, I believe, without thinking of Us, for it is credibly said that there is a Very Strong party against him at Paris as well as in other parts of France...

Of all the Wretches that ever existed what do you think of Ney? There is a Man here who was present when he went on his knees to the King, bathed his hand with tears, & protested that he would never return to him but with *Buonaparte in a Cage*, He immediately marches his 8000 *tried men* (as he told the King), whose fidelity he could depend upon & joins the Tyrant!—Lord Wellington is not yet arrived but is expected every hour & is as much wished for by Foreigners as English.[19]'

No-one wanted to see Wellington more than the British army. In Dutch Belgium[20] the British regiments already present were under the command of the 23 year old Prince of Orange[21], but daily the question was, 'Where is Wellington? Surely we shall not be led to battle by that boy.[22]'

At the beginning of April it was finally announced that Wellington was to command the allied army in Flanders. Bill Wheeler (whose regiment had marched to new positions at Fuentes de Oñoro: "keep step and they cannot hurt us") was now a Sergeant in Belgium and remembered nothing that caused so much joy; the British troops were 'almost frantic'. 'Glorious news,' they reported to anyone who would listen, 'Nosey has got the command, won't we give them a drubbing now.[23]'

London

In London Elford still had hopes he could get to Paris in August. He had just entertained an acquaintance of Robert Jameson, and wrote to Edinburgh at the end of April:

"A thousand thanks for introducing me to your good friend (the *good*) Dr Smith with whom I was indeed much pleased. He did me the honor of dining with me at the Linnæan Club and at my house with Von Buch and Mr Brown. He is now gone to the canary Islands with Von Buch and I expect to see them here in August; indeed it is probable that Dr S. will

Wellington

"We would rather see Wellington's long nose in the fight than a reinforcement of 10,000 men any day."

A British officer

[19] Anglesey, 1955: 93 & 99.
[20] In 1815 Belgium was part of a greater Netherlands ruled by the House of Orange.
[21] Willem Frederik George Lodewijk, Prince of Orange (1792-1849). Nicknamed 'Slender Billy' and 'The Young Frog'. Educated at Oxford. Held a British army commision. Was one of Wellington's ADCs in the Peninsula. In 1815 was a British General (a reflection of his social status rather than his experience). From 1840 he was King Willem II of Holland.
[22] Liddell Hart, 1994: 160.
[23] Liddell Hart, 1994: 161. Wheeler later said, 'If England should require the service of her army again, and I should be with it, let me have 'Old Nosey' to command... There are two things we should be certain of. First, we should always be as well supplied with rations as the nature of the service would admit. The second is we should be sure to give the enemy a damned good thrashing. What can a soldier desire more.' (*op. cit.* p. 196).
[24] Leonard Plukenet M.D. (1642-1706). Botanist.
[25] Letter: Leach to Jameson, 27th April 1815 (Loc: Edinburgh University Library, Special Collections).
[26] Christen Smith (16th October 1785-1816). Born Bragernes, Drammen, Buskerud. Parents: Anders

Gabrielsen Smith and Alhed Smith (née Stillesen). Was a botanist with a particular interest in mosses and lichens. In 1826 von Buch published a biographical memoir of him (*Edinburgh New Philosophical Journal*, **1**: 209-216).

[27] Christian Leopold von Buch (1774-1853) Prussian naturalist and geologist. In 1810 published a record of his travels in Norway and Lapland in 1806-1808, and in 1825 a physical description of the Canary Islands (in German, *Physicalische Beschreibung der Canarischen Inseln*) with a later French edition (1836).

[28] Robert Brown (1773-1858) Scottish botanist. From 1801-1805 accompanied *HMS Investigator* to survey the coast of Australia. In 1810 he published *Prodromus Floræ Novæ Hollandiæ*. FRS 1811. Brown was a lifelong friend of James Mill (1773-1836) the author of *Elements of Political Economy* (1821) which later influenced Karl Marx. James Mill was the father of John Stuart Mill (1806-1873) the social reformer and author of *On Liberty* (1859).

[29] *The Annual Register... for 1818* at p. 435.

[30] In the 'Historical Sketch' added by Darwin to later editions.

[31] König was a botanist of note before becoming a mineralogist, but concentrated on mineralogy at the British Museum. The Museum's Botany department really began in the 1820s when Banks died and his herbarium passed to the Museum, with Brown as its keeper.

Ophiura linckii Leach

Illustration from the *Zoological Miscellany* April 1815

go with me to Paris (if it be not the immediate seat of War) as I have applied to the Institut for pasports for both by his desire and I have received a promise of one for myself which will not be sent alone.

I am sorry that the Herbarium at the British Museum was not worth the examination of D[r] Smith, it is a fine collection for reference as it contains all the plants described by Plucknett[24], Ray &cc.[25]"

Elford's dinner guests were Dr Christen Smith[26], Leopold von Buch[27] and Robert Brown[28]. The Norwegian Smith was Professor of Botany at Christiania (the modern Oslo) and was touring the British Isles to collect live plants for Christiania's new botanic garden. He had met von Buch at Sir Joseph Banks' house the previous autumn and they had agreed to visit the Canaries together[29]. Von Buch was a geologist and naturalist who had travelled extensively in Norway and Lapland some years earlier. Like Jameson, he was a former student of Werner, and like Jameson he subsequently rejected Werner's ideas.

Von Buch and Smith's trip to the Canaries would later feature in *The Origin of Species*, where Darwin notes, "The celebrated geologist and naturalist, Von Buch, in his excellent 'Description physique des Isles Canaries' (1836, p. 147), clearly expresses his belief that varieties slowly become changed into permanent species, which are no longer capable of intercrossing.[30]"

Robert Brown was a Scottish botanist and the 'Clerk, Librarian and Housekeeper' of the Linnean Society. Since 1810 Brown had also been librarian and curator of Joseph Banks' collections, especially his celebrated herbarium. Banks had such a dominant influence on British botany that at this time the British Museum did not even bother to employ a plant specialist[31]; all matters botanical in Britain invariably went directly to Banks, and hence to Brown. In his studies with the microscope Brown would later (1827) discover 'Brownian motion', which is named after him, and would be the first to identify the nucleus of plant cells (1831).

Work, work, work

In May 1815 after more than a year at the Museum Elford Leach offered to work an extra three days every week. This was common practice for Museum officers, although voluntary, and the Trustees agreed. He had already worked some extra days since Christmas 1814, but now this would be his regular routine. For each extra day

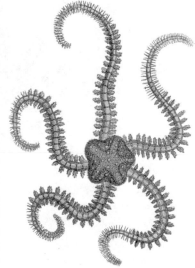

in the week he would receive £75 per year, so his salary now jumped from £120 to £345 a year (which still barely covered his expenditure on specimens and books![32])

He certainly had enough work to fill the extra days. As well as his research on insects, crustaceans and molluscs, and his writing, he had been clearing out the Museum's collection of corals. The condition of some of the soft corals was irretrievable and the Trustees gave him permission to destroy them[33]. They also agreed to auction the duplicate corals[34], presumably to clear space.

In the middle of this increased activity, back in Devon tragedy struck. At Kingsbridge George Montagu was having repairs carried out at Knowle House. Some old timbers lying on the ground and a careless step led to his treading on a rusty nail. To his eternal misfortune infection set in. He contracted blood-poisoning and on the 20th of June he died. June 1815 was to be a bad month for others too.

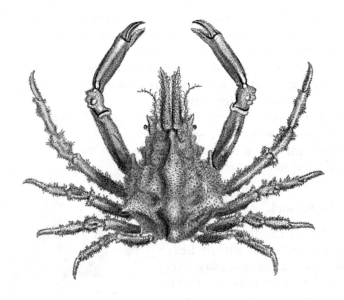

[32] Swainson, 1840. Elford's finances would improve in March 1816 with the abolition of Income Tax (introduced in 1798 to help pay for the war), although many household goods were subjected to increased duties at the same time.
[33] British Museum, Trustees' Committee Meeting Minutes, **9**: 2592-4 (11th March 1815).
[34] British Museum, Trustees' Committee Meeting Minutes, **9**: 2604-6 (10th June 1815).

Pisa gibbsii Leach

Illustration from *Malacostraca Podophthalmata Britanniæ* by Elford Leach, July 1815.

— 19 —

Quatre Bras

> Bonoparte seems like necessity and knows no law.
> Delays are dangerous.
>
> George Eyre[1]

The allied powers were preparing to invade France in July but in Paris Napoleon had his own plans. Throughout April and May he assembled his army, forming 80 infantry and 5 cavalry regiments. Artillery and engineers were added... especially artillery. While he prepared to take the offensive, the fact that war had not formally been declared caused the allies problems[2]. In war they could have reconnoitred the enemy's positions and strengths with free-ranging cavalry. In peace that would have been a territorial violation. Instead, they had to rely on their secret intelligence services, and these clandestine operations were seldom as efficient, or as rapid, as more direct means. Knowing this, Napoleon went to great lengths to obscure his intentions and his troop movements[3]. The allies were left to prepare for a confrontation without knowing where or when or against what force.

In England the 1st battalion of the 95th knew only one thing, they would be needed. On the 25th of April at seven in the evening they sailed from Dover and crossed the Channel in small cargo ships. They had been stationed in the port for some time and the townspeople turned out at the quayside to cheer them off. The battalion embarked five companies, leaving four skeleton companies at camp. Major Jonathan Leach was now the senior company commander. The battalion was led by Colonel Sir Andrew Barnard[4]. Its Major was Lieutenant-Colonel Alexander Cameron[5] and Lieutenant John Kincaid was Adjutant (the commanding officer's personal staff officer, responsible in battle for conveying orders between the battalion commander and other officers).

From Ostend the riflemen travelled inland along the canals in horse-drawn flat-bottomed schuyts to Ghent where the officers paid their respects to the again exiled Louis XVIII. The formalities completed the battalion marched overland to Brussels, arriving shortly before noon on the 12th of May. By now they had collected a sixth company which had been serving in the Netherlands and had rendezvoused with six companies of the 2/95th and two of the 3/95th[6]. At Brussels they were billeted across the city.

[1] Cholmondeley, 1950: 191. Proverb: 'Necessity knows no law.'

[2] The European powers still viewed France as a legitimate monarchy and could therefore not declare war on their ally the King. Napoleon was being treated as an international outlaw.

[3] Anglesey, 1955: 237.

[4] A Lieutenant-Colonel in the 95th; a full Colonel in the army.

[5] A Major in the 95th; a Lieutenant-Colonel in the army.

[6] The remaining companies of the 3rd battalion were on their way home from the United States.

In Paris Napoleon was ready. On the 1st of June he held a grand military pageant of 50,000 men. Regiments were sworn in and eagles (French regimental standards) bestowed.

In Brussels Wellington too was making his preparations. He was to lead the weakest of the allied armies ranged against the new threat. His command comprised a mixture of British, Hanoverian, Brunswick, Nassau and Dutch-Belgian troops totalling 78,000 men, many of whom had never served together, did not recognise each other's uniforms and could not speak each other's languages. Britain had been so eager to disarm and redeploy after the peace of 1814, only 30,000 British troops could be found for immediate use and 80 per cent of these were 2nd battalions[7] and untried recruits. Even Wellington described this motley assemblage as the worst army, with the worst equipment and the worst staff, he had ever commanded[8], an "infamously bad" army[9].

The only other force in the vicinity was the Prussian army of Field-Marshal Blücher[10]. Although this numbered 115,000 it too was poorly equipped and more than half were militiamen or new recruits. Larger armies were being assembled by Russia and Austria but only Wellington and Blücher were close enough to engage Napoleon when he made his move, as they knew he would.

As the preparations were being made, former English MP Thomas Creevey, now living in Brussels[11], met Wellington walking in the park and asked him what he thought of the allies' chances:

" 'He stopt, and said in the most natural manner: 'By God! I think Blücher and myself can do the thing.'

'Do you calculate,' I asked, 'upon any desertion in Buonaparte's army?'

'Not upon a man,' he said, 'from the colonel to the private in a regiment – both inclusive. We may pick up a marshal or two, perhaps, but not worth a damn.'

'Do you reckon,' I asked, 'upon any support from the French King's troops at Alost?'

'Oh!' said he, 'Don't mention such fellows! No: I think Blücher and I can do the business.'

Then, seeing a private soldier of one of our infantry regiments enter the park, gaping about at the statues and images: 'There,' he said, pointing at the soldier, 'it all depends upon that article whether we do the business or not. Give me enough of it, and I am sure.' [12]"

The business

Napoleon's plan was simple. With the European powers arming from the Low Countries in the north to the Apennines in the south, he must pick one point, attack, and win a crushing military victory that would unite France behind him, royalists and all. He had continued to build his strength and gather his old veterans and could now call on approximately 300,000 men.

Blücher

[7] A regiment's 1st battalion was usually the first choice for combat service overseas, second battalions were generally less experienced, having spent much of their time serving in Britain.
[8] Liddell Hart, 1994: 165. In later years Wellington used to say if he had had his old Peninsula army he would have swept Napoleon "off the face of the Earth in two hours." (loc. cit.)
[9] Cotton, 1895: 278. Stanhope, 1888: 221.
[10] Field Marshal Gebhard Leberecht von Blücher (1742-1819). Later Prince of Wahlstadt. Known for his personal courage and deep loyalty to his men and allies. His victories relied more on action and energy than astute tactics. His troops called him 'Papa Blücher' and 'General Vorwärts' ('General Forwards').
[11] Thomas Creevey (1768-1838). Born in Liverpool (apparently the natural son of Lord Molyneux of Croxteth following a liaison of his mother's while her husband, who captained slave ships, was at sea). Lawyer and Whig politician. Member of Parliament for Thetford from 1802-1807 and for Appleby from 1820. Had moved to Brussels with his family in 1814 and would live there for 5 years.
[12] Gore, 1970: 142.

He decided to make his move against Wellington and Blücher before other armies were in place. The force he picked for this assault exceeded 120,000 including nearly 25,000 cavalry and 7500 artillerymen. On the 7th of June he sealed the French frontier, closed all ports and instigated a complete communications black-out. Behind this screen he scattered his forces in great secrecy along the border south-west of Brussels.

Across the River Sambre Blücher had his Prussian corps stretched along the other side of the border, while at Brussels Wellington arranged his army. The 2nd and 3rd battalions of the 95th were put into the 2nd Division. The 1/95th (590 rank and file[13]) was put into the British 8th Brigade commanded by Sir James Kempt. The 8th Brigade was in the 5th Division under the command of Sir Thomas Picton who had not yet landed in Flanders. Picton's Division formed part of the allies' Reserve, held around Wellington's headquarters at Brussels ready to go where the need was greatest.

On the 13th of June Wellington wrote to Lord Lynedoch (who as Sir Thomas Graham had commanded the left wing at Vitoria), "There is nothing new here. We have reports of Buonaparte's joining the army and attacking us; but I have accounts from Paris of the 10th, on which day he was still there; and I judge from his speech to the Legislature that his departure was not likely to be immediate. I think we are now too strong for him here.[14]"

A three day delay in intelligence is three days too long. Napoleon had already left Paris and by the 14th was just across the Sambre, mobilising his army. The allies knew something was afoot, from the commanders down to the battalion Adjutants.

Kincaid: "as the middle of June approached, we began to get a little more on the *qui vive*, for we were aware that Napoleon was about to make a dash at some particular point; and, as he was not the sort of general to give his opponent an idea of the when and the where, the greater part of our army was necessarily disposed along the frontier, to meet him at his own place. They were of course too much extended to offer effectual resistance in their advanced position; but as our division and the Duke of Brunswick's[15] corps were held in reserve, at Brussels, in readiness to be thrust at whatever point might be attacked, they were a sufficient additional force to check the enemy for the time required to concentrate the army.

On the 14th of June it was generally known, among the military circles in Brussels, that Buonaparte was in motion, at the head of his troops; and though his movement was understood to point at the Prussians, yet he was not sufficiently advanced to afford a correct clue to his intentions.[16]"

On the evening of the 15th Wellington issued orders bringing his troops in Brussels to readiness. The 5th Division, reinforced with Colonel Best's 4th Hanoverian Brigade of militia from the 6th Division, was to be ready to march at a moments notice. The rest of his army was mobilised and sent to their assembly points, in marching order, to await further instructions[17].

[13] *Wellington's Supplementary Despatches*, **10**: 734.
[14] *Wellington's Dispatches*.
[15] General Friedrich Wilhelm, Duke of Brunswick (1771-1815). Nephew of King George III and brother of Caroline of Brunswick, estranged wife of his cousin George, Prince Regent [Caroline Amelia Elizabeth of Brunswick-Wolfenbüttel (1768-1821). See Fraser, 1997].
[16] Kincaid, 1981: 152-153 (Written in 1830 with the benefit of hindsight).
[17] Cotton, 1895: 211. *Wellington's Dispatches*, **XII**: 472-473. Wellington added the 2/81st to his Reserve but they were destined to remain in Brussels throughout the coming days (Smith, 1999: 268).

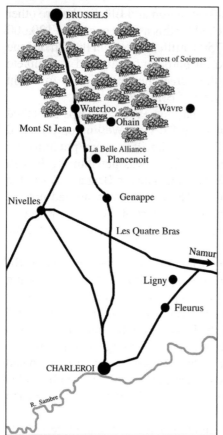

Napoleon had struck. In the early hours of the 15th he had thrown his army across the Sambre, pushed back the Prussian outposts and over-run the town of Charleroi. His objective was to drive between the forces of Wellington and Blücher; beat each separately; and strike for Brussels. While he led the main force north-east to engage Blücher's 84,000 men at Ligny, he sent Ney with the French left wing north up the main road towards the Belgian capital. Ney's orders were to occupy the crossroads of Les Quatre Bras, effectively cutting Blücher's main line of communication with Wellington. Covering the junction and hamlet at Quatre Bras was a small allied force under the Prince of Orange. In Brussels the atmosphere was tense.

Kincaid: "We were, the whole of the 15th, on the most anxious lookout for news from the front; but no report had been received prior to the hour of dinner. I went, about seven in the evening, to take a stroll in the park, and meeting one of the Duke's staff, he asked me, *en passant*, whether my pack-saddles were all ready. I told him that they were nearly so, and added, "I suppose they won't be wanted, at all events, before tomorrow?" to which he replied, in the act of leaving me, "If you have any preparation to make, I would recommend you not to delay so long." I took the hint, and returning to quarters, remained in momentary expectation of an order to move.[18]"

The Duchess of Richmond's Ball

On the evening of the 15th of June the Duchess of Richmond[19] had arranged a ball to which many of the allied officers were invited. It is now legend that this ball was where the Duke of Wellington first heard of Napoleon's advance, and that he was taken completely by surprise at this news. He certainly received several dispatches while attending the dance, and those dispatches prompted activity, but the degree of his surprise has been hotly disputed ever since the occasion itself. This soirée therefore deserves more than a passing mention.

[18] Kincaid, 1981: 153.
[19] Charlotte, Duchess of Richmond (d. 1842). In 1789 married General Sir Charles Lennox, 4th Duke of Richmond (1764-1819). He had no army command position in 1815. From 1818 he was Governor General of Canada.

The ball, with just over 220 guests, was held in the house rented by the Duke and Duchess of Richmond[20]. Their daughter Georgiana[21], 20 years of age and a great favourite of Wellington's, was one of those present and in later life recalled the evening:

'My mother's now famous ball took place in a large room on the ground floor, on the left of the entrance, connected with the rest of the house by an ante-room. It had been used by the coachbuilder, from whom the house was hired, to put carriages in, but it was papered before we came there; and I recollect the paper – a trellis pattern with roses...

When the Duke arrived rather late at the ball, I was dancing but at once went up to him to ask about the rumours. He said very gravely, "Yes, they are true; we are off tomorrow." This terrible news was circulated directly, while some of the officers hurried away, others remained at the ball, and actually had not time to change their clothes, but fought in evening costume[22]. I went with my eldest brother[23] (A.D.C. to the Prince of Orange) to his house, which stood in our garden, to help him to pack up, after which we returned to the ballroom where we found some energetic and heartless young ladies still dancing.[24]'

Also at the ball were Caroline Capel's husband and two of their daughters, Georgiana ('Georgy') and Maria ('Muzzy'). Caroline herself, heavily pregnant, had not attended, but several days later reported to her mother:

"This has indeed come upon us like a Thief in the Night—I am afraid our Great Hero must have been deceived for he has certainly been taken by surprise—There was a general idea that the Army would move forward on the 20th—The Duchess of Richmond gave a sort of Farewell Ball on the 15th—at which all the Military in and about Bruxelles were present—Georgy and Muzzy went to it with Capel—Harriet staid here with me—In the midst of the dancing an express arrived to the Duke with an account of the Prussians having been beat and the French having advanced within 14 Miles[25] of Bruxelles—You may imagine the Electrical Shocks of such intelligence— Most of the Women in Floods of tears and all the Military in an instant collected round their respective leaders and in less than 20 minutes the room was cleared[26]".

Caroline – whose brother Lord Uxbridge was Wellington's cavalry commander – certainly believed Wellington was surprised at the ball. In fact it appears he had heard of the French advance in the afternoon from General Müffling[27] (the Prussian liaison officer attached to his staff) who told him the Prussians were in action. This was confirmed soon after by the Prince of Orange, arriving in Brussels for the dance[28].

Wellington therefore knew the French were moving – if not their direction or level of determination – and had called for a state of readiness before he attended the ball. This accords with Kincaid's experience.

[20] The house was later Nº 9 Rue des Cendres, Boulevard Botanique, near the Cologne Gate.
[21] Lady Georgiana Lennox.
[22] At Quatre Bras.
[23] Charles Gordon Lennox, Earl of March ('Lord March') (1791-1860). A Captain in the 52nd Light Infantry. From 1819, 5th Duke of Richmond. He married Lord Uxbridge's daughter Caroline Paget (1796-1874).
[24] Priestley, 1971: 141-142.
[25] About 22 km (possibly a pessimistic view of the distance which was closer to 28 km, but 6 km multiplied by 120,000 heavily armed Frenchmen tends to produce irrelevant mathematics).
[26] Anglesey, 1955: 111-112.
[27] General Friedrich Karl Ferdinand Müffling (1775-1851). Later Field-Marshal Baron Müffling.
[28] Hamilton-Williams, 1994: 173-179.

Nevertheless, he had been surprised the attack had come so soon. He later said Napoleon's march to Belgium was the finest thing that was ever done, it was so rapid and well combined[29], but its speed was not his only surprise.

When the dispatch arrived at the ball, confirming the full French attack was coming from the south, he asked the Duke of Richmond for a good map and they retired to view it. "Napoleon has humbugged me, by God!" exclaimed Wellington, "He has gained twenty-four hours' march on me." Wellington's intelligence had indicated Napoleon was about to threaten British lines of communication with Ostend so he had moved his forces in such a way as to protect his flank, but this had been a French feint to obscure Napoleon's true intentions. Wellington now had his army positioned too far to the west[30].

When Richmond asked what he intended to do Wellington said he would have to concentrate what forces he could at the crossroads of Les Quatre Bras, "but we shall not stop him there, and if so I must fight him here" indicating a ridge at the hamlet of Mont St Jean 15 km south of the capital, just beyond the village of Waterloo[31].

We shall say no more on this contentious question of surprise, but leave the last word to Jonathan Leach, who obviously had ample opportunity to consider it.

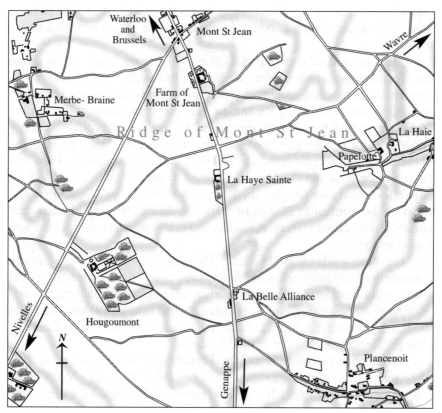

[29] Wilson (1927) **1**: 82.
[30] Scott, 1816: 113. Chandler, 1980: 82.
[31] Holmes, 1996: 68.

"I have often been heartily tired of, and out of all patience with, the one engrossing question, ever uppermost, and ready to be let fly at any one who happened to have served with the Waterloo army, either by non-combatants, or by those who have never given themselves the trouble to investigate the real position of affairs at that period,— "Pray Sir, was not the Duke of Wellington taken quite by surprise, whilst he was at the Duchess of Richmond's ball at Brussels, by the sudden irruption of Bonaparte's army into Flanders?" Now, as every officer stationed in Brussels with Sir T. Picton's division knew, I presume, on the 15th of June, that the French army was in motion on the frontiers of Flanders, and that Prince Blucher's advanced posts had been engaged, it is utterly impossible but that those facts should have been known to the Duke of Wellington long before we could possibly have been informed of them.

I conclude, that those fire-side and feather-bed tacticians would have had the Duke of Wellington, the moment he heard of the affairs which had taken place at the Prussian outposts, mount his horse, draw his sword, and give the word of command himself to the troops in Brussels, to fix bayonets, shoulder arms, and march. I have never, however, distinctly understood to what particular point, or on which of the different roads by which Bonaparte had the option of penetrating into Flanders, these *savans* deemed it judicious that the duke should have ordered a concentration of his army, before he had obtained certain intelligence of the enemy's intentions. A very small share of intellect is necessary to comprehend that the British commander was obliged to canton the different divisions of his army along an extensive frontier, not only with a view of watching the roads by which his adversary might advance, but, moreover, for the purpose of more easily supplying them with provisions, particularly his cavalry and artillery. It would consequently have been a specimen of generalship not very creditable to him, had he directed his army to assemble at any one particular point as long as a doubt existed of the movements of his opponent, or whilst his intentions remained unfathomed[32].

It is doubtless a pleasant and edifying occupation, while sitting by an English fire-side, to criticise and calumniate that commander, who, in spite of his being "taken by surprise," contrived to gain the most splendid and decisive victory ever achieved by the British army or any other. Leaving those critics to rub their shins by a coal fire, and to finish half a dozen of port (on the qualities of which I should infinitely prefer their opinion than on the campaign of 1815 in Flanders), I must return to Quatre Bras."

To Quatre Bras

Leach: "Soon after dark on the evening of the 15th the drums beat to arms[33], and the bugles sounded to assemble the division; but as the soldiers were billeted in every part of the city, the night was drawing to a close and the morning beginning to dawn, by the time the whole of the troops were collected and formed."

[32] *Rough Sketches*, pp. 379-381. Journalist John Scott (see later) heard the same views expressed by many officers in Brussels shortly after the battle (Scott, 1816: 112-113).

[33] The orders to march were issued at 10 p.m. (Cotton, 1895: 13).

Kincaid: 'To the credit of our battalion, be it recorded, that, although the greater part were in bed when the assembly sounded, and billeted over the most distant parts of that extensive city, every man was on his alarm-post before eleven o'clock, in a complete state of marching order: whereas, it was nearly two o'clock in the morning before we were joined by the others...

Waiting for the arrival of the other regiments, we endeavoured to snatch an hour's repose on the pavement; but we were every instant disturbed, by ladies as well as gentlemen; some stumbling over us in the dark—some shaking us out of our sleep, to be told the news—and not a few, conceiving their immediate safety depending upon our standing in place of lying...

The whole of the division having, at length, assembled, we were put in motion about three o'clock on the morning of the 16th[34], and advanced to the village of Waterloo[35]".

Costello: "It was the 16th, and a beautiful summer morning, with the sun slowly rising above the horizon and peeping through the trees[36]. Our men were as merry as crickets, laughing and joking with each other. At times they pondered what all this fuss could be about, for even the old soldiers could not believe the enemy were near. We halted at the verge of the wood, behind the village of Waterloo, where we remained for some hours. The recruits lay down to sleep, while the old soldiers commenced cooking.[37]"

Leach: "No one who has campaigned need be told, that a multiplicity of rumours, reports, speculations, and calculations, most of them vague, contradictory, and unfounded, are the forerunners of the advance of an army. "The enemy is in position at such a point with so many thousand men, his front covered by a deep and impassable river," declares one; "the troops stationed at such a point must inevitably be overpowered and annihilated before assistance can arrive," says a second; "we shall have a brush with their advanced guard in less than an hour," declares a third; and so on: every man conjuring up something wherewith to throw a light, not only on the intended operations and movements of his own army, but, moreover, on those of the enemy. The *on dits* on the present occasion were by no means few; but the heads of the many which had been thus racked and tormented with conjectures, were ere long to be otherwise employed.[38]"

Like the men of Jonathan Leach's Company, Sir Thomas Picton, newly arrived in Brussels, had his mind on his breakfast, but as he sat eating he was ordered to attend Wellington. With Picton as an extra Aide-de-Campe was Ensign Rees Gronow of the 1st Foot Guards, fresh from the Corn Law riots:

'Sir Thomas lost not a moment in obeying the order of his chief, leaving the breakfast-table and proceeding to the park, where Wellington was walking with Fitzroy Somerset[39] and the Duke of Richmond. Picton's manner was always more familiar than the duke liked in his lieutenants, and on this

[34] Their orders were to march at 2 a.m. (Cotton, 1895: 13).
[35] Kincaid, 1981: 153-154.
[36] With less than a week to the longest day of the year the sun probably rose between 3.00 and 4.00 a.m., although this is only an estimate. GMT had not yet been invented and we do not know what the Local Time would have been in Brussels.
[37] Hathaway, 1997: 277-278.
[38] Caldwell & Cooper (1995: 4 & 7) say Jonathan Leach was not on the advance to Quatre Bras, or at the battle (at least in the early stages). They give no authority for this statement. As noted, Jonathan records the mood on the march and later makes it clear he was at Quatre Bras, as does Hart's *Annual Army List* (1848). Caldwell & Cooper also say that in his absence his company was led by Lieutenant Fitzmaurice. Even if he had been absent it is highly unlikely John Fitzmaurice, by far the most junior of his three Lieutenants at that time (promoted 1813), would have commanded the company. It would have fallen to John Cox (1809) or J.R. Gardener (1810 or 1812 – see note below regarding Lieutenant Gardiner) both of whom were with the Company at the time, not on Staff duties.
[39] Fitzroy James Henry Somerset (1788-1855). Youngest son of the Duke of Beaufort. Had been Wellington's aide-de-camp in 1808. Later General Lord Somerset and Baron Raglan.

occasion he approached him in a careless sort of way, just as he might have met an equal. The duke bowed coldly to him, and said, "I am glad you are come, Sir Thomas; the sooner you get on horseback the better: no time is to be lost. You will take the command of the troops in advance. The Prince of Orange knows by this time that you will go to his assistance." Picton appeared not to like the duke's manner; for when he bowed and left, he muttered a few words, which convinced those who were with him that he was not much pleased with his interview...

Sir Thomas Picton was a stern-looking, strong-built man, about the middle height... He generally wore a blue frock-coat, very tightly buttoned up to the throat; a very large black silk neckcloth, shewing little or no shirt-collar; dark trousers, boots, and a round hat[40]: it was in this very dress that he was attired at Quatre Bras, as he had hurried off to the scene of action before his uniform arrived.[41]'

His briefings complete, Wellington and his staff made their own way forward, passing the Rifles on the way. At Waterloo Picton's Division and Best's Hanoverians had been joined by the Duke of Brunswick's 'Black Brunswickers' and his cavalry, who had followed them out of Brussels. The Black Brunswickers were raised in 1809 after the death of the previous duke, and wore black uniforms with a silver skull and crossed bones on the cap[42].

Wellington rode on to Quatre Bras, arriving at about 10 o'clock.[43] All was surprisingly quiet so with one aide[44] and some orderly officers he made his way to Ligny to assess the deployment of the Prussians. He did not much like what he saw. He tended to position his own troops on the reverse slopes of ridges, out of both line of sight and line of fire of the enemy. At Ligny the Prussian army had been deployed in the traditional Continental style, in columns on the forward slope, facing the French like targets on a gunnery range.

'They were upon the declivity of a hill entirely exposed,' Wellington noted later, 'and occupying two points upon a river at the foot of the hill, points much too distant from their main body. I have always held it as a principle, never to occupy seriously points out of gunshot of your force[45], for either the men you place there are cut off from your main body, or by sending continued reinforcements to maintain these points, you are drawn into an action there, and not on the ground you had intended to give battle upon. I said to Gneisenau[46] before the battle, "Had not you better put your men in a less exposed situation than they are on that declivity? They will be without any protection against the enemy's artillery." He answered, "That is true, but our men like to see their enemy."[47]' Wellington replied that everybody knows their own army best, but if he was to fight there with his he would expect to be beaten. To one of his own officers he was more pithy, predicting the Prussians were about to be "damnably mauled"[48]. Riding back the way he came he returned to Quatre Bras.

[40] This would have been a broad 'top hat' which was the fashion at that time.
[41] Gronow, 1964: 66-67.
[42] This was the present Duke's way of mourning the loss of his father in 1806, mortally wounded at the Battle of Auerstädt. In the following century this uniform would be taken as the model for the uniform of a very different German corps.
[43] Chandler, 1980: 90.
[44] Lieutenant-Colonel The Honourable Sir Alexander William Gordon (d. 1815). Wellington apparently called him William Gordon, not Alexander (Stanhope, 1888: 109).
[45] He meant out of range of supporting musket fire (Stanhope, 1888: 109).
[46] August Wilhelm Anton, Count Neithardt von Gneisenau (1760-1831) Blücher's Chief-of-Staff.
[47] Wellington, 1956: 5. This story is also sometimes reported as a conversation with Blücher, not Gneisenau [We have changed Chad's careless punctuation].
[48] Stanhope, 1888: 109. The officer was Henry Hardinge (1785-1856) who was attached to the Prussian staff. He lost a hand later that day in the battle of Ligny. Created Viscount Hardinge in 1846 and was British Commander-in-Chief, 1852-1855.

The Battle of Quatre Bras

Kincaid: 'About twelve o'clock an order arrived for the troops to advance, leaving their baggage behind; and though it sounded warlike, yet we did not expect to come in contact with the enemy, at all events, on *that* day. But, as we moved forward, the symptoms of their immediate presence kept gradually increasing; for we presently met a cart-load of wounded Belgians; and, after passing through Genappe, the distant sound of a solitary gun struck on the listening ear. But all doubt on the subject was quickly removed; for, on ascending the rising ground, where stands the village of Quatre Bras, we saw a considerable plain in our front, flanked on each side by a wood; and on another acclivity beyond, we could perceive the enemy descending towards us, in most imposing numbers...

The village was occupied by some Belgians[49], under the Prince of Orange, who had an advanced post in a large farmhouse, at the foot of the road, which inclined to the right; and a part of his division, also, occupied the wood on the same side.[50]'

The 8000 Dutch-Belgians at the crossroads had been attacked by Ney's leading French corps. He had another corps of 20,000 in reserve. The fierce resistance of the allies coupled with Ney's marked reticence to push forward with any speed (his force was large enough to have rushed the position in the early hours of the engagement) were buying a breathing space for Wellington, who arrived from Ligny in the heat of the action and only just in time, as he later swore:

'By God! If I had come up five minutes later the battle was lost; I found the Prince of Orange just after 20 French had made a spurt at two of our guns and he said, "It is all over, they are driven back."

"Over! But what are those in that wood?"

"They are Belgians."

"No by God, but they are French, and the wood is full of them and they'll come upon you directly—aye and the Emperor is there too" (for I heard them just then shout *Vive l'Empereur!* But I was wrong, he was not there). But I had but just time to save it; they debouched as I expected... The Prince of Orange is a brave young man but that's all.[51]'

As the 1/95th arrived, followed by the rest of Picton's division, with Best's Hanoverians and some of the Brunswickers and Nassau infantry close behind[52], Wellington was surveying the scene with his staff from a field near the Dutch-Belgian advanced post.

Kincaid: "We halted for a moment on the brow of the hill; and as Sir Andrew Barnard galloped forward to the headquarter group; I followed, to be in readiness to convey any orders to the battalion. The moment we approached, Lord Fitzroy Somerset, separating himself from the duke, said, "Barnard, you are wanted instantly; take your battalion and endeavour to get possession of that village," pointing to one on the face of the rising ground, down which the enemy were moving[53]; "but if you cannot do that, secure that

[49] To the British, all local troops were 'Belgian'. In fact Belgium at this time was part of the Netherlands and many local troops were Dutch.
[50] Kincaid, 1981: 155-156. The large farmhouse in advance was Gemioncourt.
[51] Wellington, 1956: 7 [We have changed Chad's careless punctuation].
[52] Cotton, 1895: 15. Picton's column would have extended for several kilometres and would have taken some time to 'arrive'. This may account for the different times of arrival given by different authors, varying between 2.30 p.m. and 3.30 p.m. The 1/95th was the leading battalion.
[53] 'Village' in military circles at this time was used also for a small cluster of farm buildings around a farm-yard. That sense is intended here where the objective was the farm of Gemioncourt (Gomm *in* Siborne, 1993: 24).

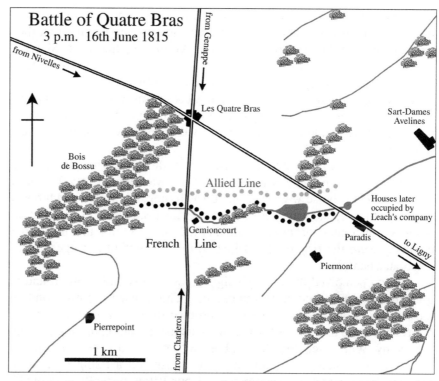

Battle of Quatre Bras
3 p.m. 16th June 1815

from Nivelles

from Genappe

Les Quatre Bras

Sart-Dames
Avelines

Bois
de Bossu

Allied Line

Houses later
occupied by
Leach's company

Gemioncourt

French   Line

Paradis

to Ligny

Piermont

Pierrepoint

from Charleroi

1 km

wood on the left, and keep the road open for communication with the Prussians." We instantly moved in the given direction; but, ere we had got half-way to the village, we had the mortification to see the enemy throw such a force into it, as rendered any attempt to retake it, with our numbers, utterly hopeless; and as another strong body of them were hastening towards the wood, which was the second object pointed out to us, we immediately brought them to action, and secured it.[54]"

Costello: "orders were given by one of the Duke's staff to occupy a clump of trees a little on our left. Our company[55] was ordered to take possession of it. While performing this task I could see the enemy emerging from a wood about a mile[56] on our right. It was on a hill with a clear plain between us.[57]"

Kincaid: "While our battalion-reserve occupied the front of the wood, our skirmishers lined the side of the road, which was the Prussian line of communication. The road itself, however, was crossed by such a shower of balls, that none but a desperate traveller would have undertaken a journey on it. We were presently reinforced by a small battalion of foreign light troops, with whose assistance we were in hopes to have driven the enemy a little further from it; but they were a raw body of men, who had never before been under fire; and, as they could not be prevailed upon to join our skirmishers, we could make no use of them whatever. Their conduct, in fact, was an exact representation of Mathews's[58] ludicrous one of the

[54] Kincaid, 1981: 156-157.
[55] Leach's company.
[56] 1.6 km.
[57] Hathaway, 1997: 278-279.
[58] Charles Mathews (1776-1835). English comedian. Kincaid was probably referring to an anecdote from Mathews' account of his trip to America (see Mathews, 1824)

American militia, for Sir Andrew Barnard repeatedly pointed out to them which was the French and which our side; and, after explaining that they were not to fire a shot until they joined our skirmishers, the word "March!" was given; but *march*, to them, was always the signal to fire, for they stood fast, and began blazing away, chiefly at our skirmishers too; the officers commanding whom were every time sending back to say that we were shooting them; until we were, at last, obliged to be satisfied with whatever advantages their appearance could give, as even that was of some consequence, where troops were so scarce.[59]"

Costello: "We had just taken possession of the wood when, for the first time, I beheld a French cuirassier on vidette. He was immediately fired at by our men, and his horse was shot. As it was falling, he disengaged himself from the stirrups, and waved his sword over his head to put us at defiance, but was immediately dropped by another rifle shot. I think the men in our company were the first of the British army who pulled a trigger at this celebrated battle[60].

I soon perceived the enemy's light troops, in extended order, and in great force, coming down to oppose us. This caused a corresponding movement on our part, and we were ordered to take ground to our left. We passed close to a pond of water, with the main road separating us from the enemy. While executing this the French commenced a very brisk fire on us, until we gained possession of a few houses on a rising ground on the main road, which two companies of our Rifles instantly occupied[61]. The remainder of our Division was now enveloped in one blaze of fire on the plain[62]".

With the remaining companies of the 1/95th was Lieutenant George Simmons: "The enemy commenced a cannonade, and our regiment filed through high corn to the left. Four companies were sent to drive *Johnny* from some fields intersected with thick hedges and also ditches, which we effected.

On this day our cavalry had not arrived, which gave the enemy a decided advantage, and made us keep nearer to each other than otherwise would have been necessary.[63]"

By now Napoleon had engaged Blücher at Ligny, 10 km away[64], and the thunder of artillery was rolling across the countryside to Quatre Bras, but the intervening high ground blinded the allies to the Prussians' fortunes.

With the arrival of the Duke of Brunswick's infantry at about 4 o'clock Wellington made a serious push against the French front line. The Brunswickers were sent up the sides of the Charleroi road in an attempt to recapture the farm buildings of Gemioncourt[65] while Picton's division advanced in line abreast through the head-high crop of rye to their left. Picton's men emerged from the rye into a clover field right in front of the French line and the shock caused by their sudden appearance, followed by an immediate volley and bayonet charge, threw the French back. This,

[59] Kincaid, 1981: 157. Hamilton-Williams (1994: 203-204, 378) claims Kincaid misunderstood what he was seeing. Hamilton-Williams says these were several companies of the 27th Dutch Jägers from the 2nd Netherlands division. They were among the most experienced Dutch troops, having formerly served under Napoleon, and had been holding the allied left wing against Ney's attack until the arrival of Picton's division. Hamilton-Williams argues it was a language barrier that caused the problem and that the Dutch were trying to indicate the overwhelming French superiority in front of the 1/95th. If correct this might explain Kincaid's later complimentry comments re these troops (quoted in the main text below). Costello also says they were 'Belgians' (see below). Conversely, Caldwell & Cooper (1995: 10) identify these troops as a battalion of the Duke of Brunswick's Light Infantry but give no authority for this.

[60] This event was portrayed by William Barnes Wollen (1857-1936) in the painting *The First Shot at the Battle of Waterloo* (this is a rather jingoistic title, the Dutch had been fighting for hours) 'The Battle of Waterloo' is used here in the sense of all actions involving British troops over the period 16th-18th June. Wollen's work is in the Mansell Collection and was illustrated in Chandler (1980: 134) where it was erroneously stated to represent an incident on the 18th of June.

however, did not last. As the British surged forward in pursuit they were brought to a halt by an artillery barrage and a charge of French lancers. The sight of the lancers prompted a rush to form defensive squares but the 42nd (Royal Highland) Regiment was slow to respond. Thinking the lancers were Brunswickers attacking the French in their front, they only began to manoeuvre when warned of their mistake by a German orderly dragoon[66]. In the delay the regiment's outlying skirmishers were overwhelmed and their Lieutenant-Colonel killed. Several lancers managed to penetrate the closing square but were swiftly bayoneted[67].

Wellington's push had failed and he pulled his line back to their original positions along the Namur road.

French attention now swung away from Picton's division towards the Brunswickers to the right and as the Duke of Brunswick rallied his men he was brought down and killed by musket fire. Wellington too was quickly in danger as he fell foul of the French cavalry. After the Duke of Brunswick fell Wellington led the Brunswick hussars forward to cover their infantry, but a combination of French small arms fire and a cavalry charge drove them back. Wellington galloped for the allied lines, enemy lancers in hot pursuit. As he raced towards a ditch and hedge bristling with the bayonets of Picton's 92nd Highlanders he called to them to keep still, set his horse at the obstacle, and jumped to safety clearing everything[68]. With the allied line forming squares the French cavalry withdrew.

Kincaid: "the firing, on both sides, lulled almost to a calm for nearly an hour, while each was busy in renewing their order of battle. The Duke of Brunswick had been killed early in the action, endeavouring to rally his young troops, who were unable to withstand the impetuosity of the French; and, as we had no other cavalry force in the field, the few British infantry regiments present, having to bear the full brunt of the enemy's superior force of both arms, were now considerably reduced in numbers.

The battle, on the side of the Prussians, still continued to rage in an unceasing roar of artillery. About four in the afternoon, a troop of their dragoons came, as a patrol, to inquire how it fared with us, and told us, in passing, that they still maintained their position. Their day, however, was still to be decided, and, indeed, for that matter, so was our own; for, although the firing, for the moment, had nearly ceased, I had not yet clearly made up my mind which side had been the offensive, which the defensive, or which the winning. I had merely the satisfaction of knowing that we had not lost it; for we had met fairly in the middle of a field (or, rather unfairly, considering that they had two to one), and, after the scramble was over, our division still held the ground they fought on. All doubts on the subject, however, began to be removed about five o'clock. The enemy's artillery once more opened; and, on running to the brow of the hill, to ascertain the cause, we perceived our old light-division general, Count Alten[69], at the head of a fresh British division, moving gallantly down the road towards us.[70]"

61 Caldwell & Cooper (1995: 10) identify these two companies as those of Jonathan Leach (with Costello) and Captain Edward Chawner. They give no authority for this.
62 Hathaway, 1997: 279.
63 Verner, 1986: 363.
64 The French attack at Ligny began about 2.30 p.m.
65 Which, as noted in the main text above, had been lost to the French after a fierce Dutch resistance just as Picton's division arrived.
66 Hamilton-Williams, 1994: 207-208, 378.
67 Siborne, 1993: 377. Haythornthwaite, 1979: 9-10.
68 Gore, 1970: 144-145fns. This was a fortunate result. Wellington, like Napoleon, was not a great horseman.
69 Alten was still a Baron at this time.
70 Kincaid, 1981: 159.

After a forced-march from Soignies, Charles Alten's 3rd Division[71] was arriving by the western road from Nivelles. With these reinforcements Wellington sent one of Alten's brigades, under Sir Colin Halkett[72], forward between the Charleroi road and the Bois de Bossu. As they advanced they were caught completely unaware by French cavalry, as cockney private Tom Morris of the 73rd Highlanders[73] admitted:

"The ground, for a considerable distance, being covered with rye, and of an extraordinary height, some of it measuring seven feet[74], prevented us from seeing much of the enemy; but, though we could not see them, they were observing us. We continuing to advance, the glittering of the tops of our bayonets guided towards us a large body of the enemy's cuirassiers, who, coming so unexpectedly upon us, threw us in the utmost confusion. Having no time to form a square, we were compelled to retire, or rather to run, to the wood through which we had advanced; and when we rallied, the 69th unfortunately lost their king's colours.[75]"

Halkett had sent the 69th (The South Lincolnshire) Regiment[76] on ahead of his other battalions to assist Pack's brigade which by now was exhausted and low on ammunition[77]. Having reconnoitred the field himself Halkett passed the 69th on his return and warned them to form square as he had seen the French cavalry massing. They had almost completed this defensive manoeuvre when their Major ordered two companies to form into line to fire on the incoming horsemen[78]. This left the square open and as the cuirassiers swept in the regiment was all but destroyed[79]. Halkett's 33rd Regiment[80] was also driven back into the woodland in some disorder[81].

Behind Halkett the remaining allied regiments had more time to assemble. This was fortunate. The French had mounted a major assault in an attempt to win control of the crossroads before any more allied reinforcements arrived. The cuirassiers, followed by lighter cavalry, swept down the slope with infantry following. This charge took the leading heavy horse brigades past the allied squares and up to the crossroads itself. To the left of the allied line Jonathan Leach's company also came under increasing fire.

Costello: "the French brought up some artillery, and began riddling the house with round shot. Feeling rather thirsty, I asked a young woman in the place for a little water. She was handing it to me, when a ball passed through the building, knocking the dust about our ears. Strange to say, the girl appeared less alarmed than myself.

Fearing that we might be surrounded, we left the building. In doing so, we were fiercely attacked by a number of the French *voltigeurs*, who forced us to extend along a lane from whence we as smartly retaliated. A galling fire was kept up for some time on both sides.

It is remarkable that recruits in action are generally more unfortunate than the old soldiers. Many fine fellows, who had joined us on the eve of our leaving England, were killed here because inexperienced recruits, apparently petrified to the spot by the whizzing balls, unnecessarily expose

[71] In the Prince of Orange's command.

[72] Major-General Sir Colin Halkett (1774-1856). Later a full General and military commander at Bombay. Accounts of the time Halkett's brigade arrived at Quatre Bras conflict. Gronow, extra-ADC to Picton, says Picton arrived [this would have been about 3.00 p.m.] then, "Shortly afterwards, Kempt's and Pack's brigades arrived by the Brussels road, and part of Alten's division by the Nivelles road" (1964: 67). Tom Morris in the 73rd Regiment in Halkett's brigade says Halkett's men arrived about 3 p.m. (Selby, 1998: 67) but he wrote from memory nearly 30 years later. He did say the 73rd charged with Brunswickers and "On our last charge, the Duke of Brunswick was killed". Brunswick was killed shortly before 5 p.m. (Chandler, 98, 102) which would have had Halkett's brigade arriving before then. John Pratt, a Lieutenant in the 30th (Cambridgeshire) Regiment in Halkett's brigade, said in 1835 that the 3rd Division "came into position at Quatre Bras between three and four p.m." (*in* Siborne, 1993: 325). F.H. Pattison, a Lieutenant in the 33rd Regiment in Halkett's brigade, said in 1842 "As far as I remember, I think it must have been between four and five o'clock" [when Halkett's brigade arrived] (*in* Siborne, 1993: 334). Major-General Herbert Siborne (who was not there) deduced from his sources that Halkett's brigade arrived "a little before 5 p.m." (Siborne, 1993: 318) while Lieutenant-Colonel William Gomm, Assistant Quartermaster General to Picton's division, says Alten's 3rd Division arrived "About six o'clock" and Halkett's brigade reinforced the 5th Division

"late in the day" (*in* Siborne, 1993: 25, 28). Cotton (who was not there) says Halkett arrived "Towards six o'clock" (1895: 15). Despite this explicit claim, amid the conflicting reports it is possible Halkett's men arrived before the rest of Alten's division.

[73] 73rd (Highland) Regt.

[74] More than 2 m.

[75] Selby, 1998: 67-68.

[76] 2nd Battalion.

[77] Cotton, 1895: 15. This suggests Pack's men had been fighting for some time before Halkett's arrival, making 3 p.m. too early.

[78] Hamilton-Williams, 1994: 219-220, 379.

[79] Cotton, 1895: 15-16.

[80] 2nd battalion, 33rd (1st Yorkshire West Riding) Regiment of Foot.

[81] Chandler, 1980: 98. Hamilton-Williams, 1994: 220.

[82] Hathaway, 1997: 280-1.

[83] Kincaid, 1981: 158. Picton was wounded in the hip at Quatre Bras, but only his valet knew this (Howarth, 1968: 21).

[84] Hathaway, 1997: 280-1. For the 1/95th the *London Gazette* lists a Lieutenant J.P. Gardiner wounded on the 16th and a Lieutenant John Gardiner wounded on the 18th (Kelly, 1817: 102 & 107). Dalton (1971: 197-200) lists Lieutenant John Gardiner (First-Lieutenant since 30th August 1810) wounded severely on the 18th and a Lieutenant J.P. Gairdner wounded at some time during the three days. According to the published *Army List* for March 1815 this is James Penman Gairdner, promoted to First-Lieutenant 12th May 1812. The only similar name in the manuscript Waterloo Roll of Jonathan Leach's Company (Loc: Public Record Office, Kew, London. Ref: W.O. 100/15 B 201) is Lieutenant J.R. Gardener (*sic*).

themselves to the enemy's fire, whereas an old rifleman will seek shelter, if there be any near his post.[82]"

Kincaid: "The forward movement of the enemy's cavalry gave their infantry time to rally; and, strongly reinforced with fresh troops, they again advanced to the attack. This was a crisis in which, according to Buonaparte's theory, the victory was theirs, by all the rules of war, for they held superior numbers, both before and behind us; but the gallant old Picton, who had been trained in a different school, did not choose to confine himself to rules in those matters; despising the force in his rear, he advanced, charged, and routed those in his front, which created such a panic among the others, that they galloped back through the intervals in his division with no other object in view but their own safety.[83]"

The cuirassiers at the crossroads had been repelled by artillery and musketry from the squares they found there. As the French were driven off the British Foot Guards of the 1st Division began to arrive and Wellington decided it was time to go on the offensive. He ordered his whole line forwards.

Costello: "Being hard pressed by superior numbers, we were at length joined by a number of Belgians. We received orders to advance, and drove the enemy through the skirts of a wood, passing a field of rye, which obstructed them from our view. As soon as we emerged from the wood, a regiment of French infantry on our right received us with a running fire. I was in the act of taking aim at some of our opposing skirmishers, when a ball struck my trigger finger, tearing it off. It also turned the trigger aside. A second shot passed through the mess-tin on my knapsack. Several of our men were killed by this volley, and Lieutenant Gardiner, a worthy little officer of the company, was severely wounded in the lower part of the leg.[84]"

That was the end of the battle for Costello but the rest of the line pressed on. Ney had called for his reserve corps but by a breakdown in French communications it been summoned to Ligny by Napoleon without Ney's knowledge. By the time he called it back it was too late to assist. The failure of the French cavalry charge, and now the boldness of this allied counter-attack, caused a momentary loss of resolve in the French lines:

Our troops appeared intimidated and recoiled with a sort of panic... Marshal Ney... immediately ordered the eighth and eleventh cuirassiers, who happened to be at hand, to charge the first battalions. The charge was executed with the greatest resolution; but these battalions, being supported from behind with the infantry which filled the wood, were enabled to open such a terrible fire upon us, that our cuirassiers, being repelled in their attempt to pierce them, were obliged to make a wheel round; and, as always happens in such cases, retired in much disorder... The retrograde movement which was now sensibly beginning, and the multitude of wounded soldiers who threw themselves into the rear, began to excite an obvious terror amongst their comrades.

The waggoners, the servants, the attendants of the camp of all kinds, saved themselves with precipitation; and, communicating their panic to all they met, soon clogged up the road to Charleroi. The rout, indeed, in this point (Ney's command) was beginning to be complete; everyone was flying in confusion; and the cry of the enemy! the enemy! *was general.*[85']

Although pushed a considerable distance, the confusion in the French lines soon passed. Ney sent forward another division of cuirassiers, at the trot, to support and steady his shaken men, who reassembled on the higher ground.

Our infantry, taking their position upon the heights of Frasnes, were compelled to abandon all thoughts of more forward movement; they confined themselves, therefore, to maintaining their present position, and in this they succeeded.'

Kincaid: "we commenced the offensive, and, driving in the skirmishers opposed to us, succeeded in gaining a considerable portion of the position originally occupied by the enemy, when darkness obliged us to desist. In justice to the foreign battalion, which had been all day attached to us, I must say that, in this last movement, they joined us cordially, and behaved exceedingly well. They had a very gallant young fellow at their head; and their conduct, in the earlier part of the day, can, therefore, only be ascribed to its being their first appearance on such a stage.[86]"

With the loss of the light sometime after 8 o'clock, the fighting all but stopped. The allies still controlled the crossroads. Wellington's report of the action noted, "The troops of the 5th division, and those of the Brunswick corps, were long and severely engaged, and conducted themselves with the utmost gallantry.[87]"

After the battle

Costello: "The dusk of the evening soon set in, and myself and numbers of others who were disabled, took up our quarters for the night in another farmhouse lower down, some distance from the main road. This soon became thronged with the wounded of our Division who were brought in. The outhouses became literally crammed, and all the straw and hay, of which there was plenty, that could be procured was strewed everywhere to lay the men on. To sleep was impossible with the anguish of my shattered hand, and the groans of my fellow sufferers.[88]"

Leach: "The post occupied by our battalion having been given over to General Alten's troops, we were ordered to rejoin our own division, which were lying down by their arms on the ground where they had been engaged throughout the day. Other troops of infantry reached Quatre Bras during the afternoon and evening of the 16th; and in the course of the night the whole, or the greatest part, of the cavalry joined us.

It will easily be credited, that, not having had one moment's sleep on the night of the 15th, and the whole of the 16th having been spent in marching and in engagements with the enemy, very little time was requisite to invoke

[85] A French officer quoted in Kelly (1828: 77-78) and Heath (1991: 6). The identity of this officer is not known to us but he was at Ligny and must be reporting what he heard later about Quatre Bras [Kelly seldom identifies the source of his quotes, possibly because he knows he is breaching the original writer's copyright.]
[86] Kincaid, 1981: 159. See earlier note regarding the identity of these troops.
[87] Letter: Wellington to Earl Bathurst (Britain's Secretary for War and the Colonies), 19th June 1815 (*Wellington's Dispatches*).
[88] Hathaway, 1997: 281.

the sleepy god, as about eleven at night we lay down by our arms for that purpose. But our slumbers were not destined to be of long duration; as we were suddenly broad awake and standing to our arms in consequence of the pickets of both armies blazing away at each other, from some unknown cause, which kept us on the alert until day dawned[89]."

17th of June

Kincaid: "As last night's fighting only ceased with the daylight, the scene, this morning, presented a savage unsettled appearance; the fields were strewed with the bodies of men, horses, torn clothing, and shattered cuirasses; and, though no movements appeared to be going on on either side, yet, as occasional shots continued to be exchanged at different points, it kept every one wide awake. We had the satisfaction of knowing that the whole of our army had assembled on the hill behind in the course of the night.

About nine o'clock, we received the news of Blucher's defeat, and of his retreat to Wavre. Lord Wellington, therefore, immediately began to withdraw his army to the position at Waterloo.[90]"

Leach: "The man of candour will not deny, be he ever so determined a fire-eater, that the news of this disastrous defeat of our allies was calculated to throw a damp[91] on the prospects of the campaign; and notwithstanding I have heard some few individuals since declare that they never entertained the smallest doubt of our success, I never believed them. Nothing is more easy than to prognosticate occurrences which have already taken place. This may be a *bull*[92], but it is nevertheless a system which I have seen adopted by individuals from both sides of the Irish channel."

The Prussian defeat had finally come after dark. As Wellington had foreseen, the Prussian deployment had cost them dear as even the French admitted:

The cannonade, indeed, never relaxed for an instant; and our artillery, as far as I could form a judgment from what I saw, made a most dreadful havoc in the Prussian columns, which, being posted in masses on the opposite ridge of hills, and upon plateaux *just below our batteries and position, afforded us a point-blank aim at less than half-cannon shot.* [93]

The Prussians were driven off as night fell. In an attempt to halt the rout the 72 year old Blücher had led a cavalry charge himself but had been dismounted and trodden under hoof several times. Only just avoiding capture, he finally made his way back with the stragglers, battered and bruised. Gneisenau, not knowing where Blücher was, meanwhile guided the remnants of the Prussian army due north to Wavre (and it was Napoleon's turn to be surprised, he had expected the Prussians to retreat eastwards along the Sambre valley to Namur, their headquarters before the battle). This Prussian decision was crucial: Wavre was only 15 kilometres east of Wellington's chosen position on the ridge at Mont St Jean, south of Waterloo, and the two armies had avoided being separated by the French.

[89] Kincaid (1981: 160) says this appears to have been caused by a patrol of dragoons passing between the pickets in the dark.
[90] Kincaid, 1981: 160.
[91] 'a damp' – a damper; a dejection.
[92] 'a bull' or 'Irish bull', a ludicrous self-contradictory statement.
[93] French officer quoted in Kelly (1828: 78) and (Heath, 1991: 6).

Wellington had arranged with Blücher that he would make a stand at Mont St Jean if Blücher could send reinforcements to his aid. Blücher had promised to send one or more Prussian corps of 30,000 men each. On the morning of the 17th, with the Prussians gone from his flank and the crossroads no longer of significance, Wellington pulled his own army northwards through the village of Genappe. The day had dawned under a dark, lowering sky and the morning had been airless and sultry, as only the pause before a mid-summer storm can be. As the troops withdrew, the heavens opened.

Costello: "Genappe was literally crowded with wounded, and they were conveyed with every possible dispatch to Brussels. Anxious to know the fate of our regiment, I stood on a hedgerow on the skirts of the village as the rain came down in torrents. I descried the Division retreating towards us, and remained until some of the regiments entered the village with many of our wounded, who told me that our regiment, with the cavalry, formed the rearguard.[94]"

In fact the Rifles were not so much a rearguard as a decoy, left on the field to mask Wellington's general withdrawal. Most of the allied infantry had slipped away earlier, leaving their camp fires smoking as they filtered away behind the cover of hedgerows, trying to avoid French observers,[95]. The ruse was well conceived as Napoleon was now leading his victorious army to the crossroads with the intention of crushing Blücher's allies.

It was to realise the hope of exterminating the British that, on the 17th at daybreak, Buonaparte, leaving behind him the third and fourth corps, together with the cavalry of General Pajol[96], under command of Marshal Grouchy[97], to watch the Prussians, marched with his reserve, and the sixth corps, towards Quatre Bras.

The British appeared to occupy the same positions as on the day preceding; and the French army remained until eleven o'clock in the forenoon, observing them, and waiting for the troops from the right, whose arrival was delayed by heavy rains and cross-roads[98] almost impracticable.

Arrangements were made for the attack, and the united corps advanced in front of battle, along the heights of Frasnes, when it was perceived that the British had manoeuvred so as to mask their retreat. The troops we saw on the plain, at the entrance of the wood, and on the road, were only a strong rear-guard to cover the same. Buonaparte set out in pursuit of them with his cavalry, and all the army urged its march to Brussels.[99]

Kincaid: "Sir Andrew Barnard was ordered to remain as long as possible with our battalion, to mask the retreat of the others; and was told, if we were attacked, that the whole of the British cavalry were in readiness to advance to our relief. I had an idea, however, that a single rifle battalion in the midst of ten thousand dragoons, would come but indifferently off in the event of a general crash, and was by no means sorry when, between eleven and twelve o'clock, every regiment had got clear off, and we followed, before the enemy had put anything in motion against us.[100]"

[94] Hathaway, 1997: 282.
[95] Stanhope, 1888: 111.
[96] Général Claude Pierre, Comte Pajol (1772-1844).
[97] Maréchal Emmanuel, Comte de Grouchy (1766-1847).
[98] Cross-country roads. The rough farm tracks cutting across the country perpendicular to the main roads.
[99] French officer quoted in Kelly (1828: 79) and Heath (1991: 7) [We have changed the usual *English* to the more appropriate *British*. Translating 'Anglais' as 'English' is disrespectful to all the non-English Britons who fought and died].
[100] Kincaid, 1981: 161.

Leach: "Tremendous rain commenced falling before we reached Genappe, where we were ordered to take such shelter as the houses on each side of the street at the entrance of the town afforded. Some shots which we heard exchanged between the advanced cavalry of the two armies, obliged us instantly to leave the hovels in which we had taken momentary refuge from the storm; and, as the cavalry very soon afterwards entered Genappe, we retired through the town with them. Our cavalry having formed on the most favourable ground beyond Genappe, became engaged with the lancers and other corps of the French cavalry as they debouched from the town; and notwithstanding some loss was sustained on our side, and the enemy pressed and rather roughly handled the rear-guard, the household brigade, by their resolute and gallant conduct, soon retrieved matters, and drove back the French cavalry in such style, as made them keep at a much more respectable distance during the remainder of the day."

Simmons: "The country being in a high state of cultivation, covered with corn, and the ground remarkably soft, the cavalry could scarcely raise a canter, the animals sank so deep. The 7th Hussars charged, but were sadly mauled. The Life Guards and Oxford Blues made some very fine charges, and literally preserved the 7th from being cut to pieces.[101]"

The army was making its way north as best it could in a broad front, some regiments on the main road, but others spread across the fields. Tom Morris, with the 73rd to the east of the road, also saw the cavalry encounter with the French as his regiment struggled along a muddy track crossing the soaking countryside:

"Having resumed our march, the sky suddenly darkened; and as we were going over a very high hill, we appeared to be enveloped in clouds, densely charged with the electric fluid. The rain descended literally in torrents. At no great distance, we heard the booming of artillery, and we judged the French advanced parties had overtaken our rear. Our journey hitherto had been up hills, and now we had some very steep hills to descend; and the rapidly accumulating water came down with such inconceivable force, that it was with the utmost difficulty we could keep our feet.

On emerging from this obscure road to the main road to Brussels, at the village of Genappe, the scene was grand, but of the most fearful description. On our right was the rear of our troops, on their way to Waterloo. On the hills, to the left, the main body of the French were rapidly advancing; in Genappe, was a body of the enemy's cuirassiers[102], whose advance the 7th British hussars vainly endeavoured to check, when the Earl of Uxbridge

[101] Verner, 1986: 364. For an account of this cavalry exchange see Cotton (1895: 21-24) who was serving with the 7th Hussars.
[102] Actually lancers, not cuirassiers.

French soldiers crossing the countryside. French shakos tapered outwards towards the top, in contrast to the British shakos which tapered inwards.

brought up the Oxford Blues and the Life Guards, and drove the cuirassiers back. I had an opportunity of witnessing the whole of this affair, as our regiment was in the rear, and I was compelled, at this time, to stop, to remove some gravel which had got into my boots.

The French flying artillery were close upon us, and their continual discharges, the cracking of the thunder, the vivid flashes of lightning, and the 'pelting of the pitiless storm', presented, altogether, a spectacle which few who witnessed will ever forget while living.[103]"

French spirits, as they pursued their enemy were very high; too high perhaps to be shared by one of their officers:

During the rapid march, the ardour of the troops was incredible; they saw only in the expert and well regulated retreat of the British, a total rout, which must terminate by their embarkation. Already they were promising themselves that they would no more make a stand, but that, giving up to their own resources, would push on, abandoning Brussels to us, and regain their vessels with all possible expedition.

The artillery, infantry and carriages filed along with great [haste and difficulty[104]] in the high road, covered with a thick mud, while the cavalry marched by the sides, across corn-fields, which were every where very beautiful, and which they reduced to manure.

The horses plunged up to the belly into this black soil, which was softened and extremely adhesive, and could not be detached without great difficulty; which materially retarded the march, and rendered it extremely painful. [105]

Leach: "The march from Genappe to Waterloo was little better than a mud-bath, owing to the deluge of rain which continued to fall.

About two or three hours before dark we reached that position which has been rendered so memorable for the sanguinary contest which took place on it the following day. The French occupied a ridge of heights opposite to us, and kept up an occasional cannonade".

Simmons: "The enemy in parties reconnoitred, and was amused with the music of our cannon till dark. The night was very bad. The field where we were was all mud. I got a bundle of straw to lie upon, and I smeared an old blanket with thick clayey mud, and covered myself with the blanket, which prevented the rain from passing through, and kept me tolerably warm.[106]"

Leach: "The two preceding days and nights having been spent in marching, fighting, and without sleep, the floods of rain that descended the whole night of the 17th, which we passed on the position lying down by our arms, did not disturb our repose. For myself, at least, I can answer, that I never in my whole life slept more soundly, although thoroughly drenched to the skin before I lay down on the ground, which was like a snipe-marsh."

[103] Selby, 1998: 73.
[104] The translation given by Kelly (1828) says "with great embarrassment and precipitation" which we assume is just a poor translation of the French words 'embarras(ser)' and 'précipitation'. Without certainty regarding the French original, we have proposed an alternative, although the French officer may also have meant there was great congestion on the road in the rain.
[105] French officer quoted in Kelly (1828: 79) and Heath (1991: 8) [Kelly's 'English' has again been changed to 'British'].
[106] Verner, 1986: 364.

[1] Wellington to Lord Fitzroy Somerset on the evening of the battle (Chandler, 1980: 172).

[2] There are a thousand published versions of the Battle of Waterloo, giving a thousand different accounts, most written by people who were not there. The broad movements in the battle are known but few authors agree on the details (which company was where; how many men did what; at what time; who said what when). This has always been the case. Hearing the varying accounts even Wellington said, "I shall begin to doubt if I was really there myself" (Stanhope, 1888: 150). This is our route through the confusion, but it can only be a subjective distillation from published sources. We concentrate on Jonathan Leach's position.

[3] Selby, 1998: 75.

[4] Hibbert, 1997: 64.

[5] Waymouth (*in* Siborne, 1993: 45, 53) says this was virtually opposite the farm of La Haye Sainte, but he may have meant behind the farm on the opposite side of the Ohain road.

[6] Kincaid, 1981: 163.

[7] A wide-brimmed hat in which the sides are bent up ('cocked') over the crown.

[8] A large black cockade denoting his rank of Field-Marshal in the British army, and three smaller cockades for his ranks of Marshal-General in the army of Portugal, Generalissimo of the Spanish armies, and Field-Marshal in the army of the Netherlands. The army of the Netherlands was commanded by the Prince of Orange but Wellington (supreme allied commander) passed his orders to the Dutch-Belgian troops through the Prince (Hamilton-Williams, 1994: 177).

— 20 —

Waterloo

I have never fought such a battle, and
I trust I shall never fight such another.

Wellington[1]

Sunday, 18th of June 1815[2]

Soon after dawn the rain eased and the sun climbed into a clear sky[3]. In the morning light the men looked as bad as they felt: stiff, blue with cold, soaked to the skin, covered in mud and sporting several days beard. John Kincaid had a nasty scare when he woke to find his horse had wandered off during the night. He could not function as Adjutant on foot and in a field of 10,000 animals it took him an hour to find his. Slowly the allied line came to life as small groups of men tried to find dry straw or brushwood to light fires and cook breakfast. The air murmured with a thousand speculations. Backwards and forwards flowed the horses of the Brigade Majors and Adjutants carrying instructions from their commanders. At 10 o'clock the order went out to clear the charges that had lain overnight in the weapons[4] and the fields rang to the smoky barking of muskets.

Following the orders, the men of each battalion moved to their allotted positions. The 1/95th were fortunate, they were to stay where they were, by the crossroads at the centre of the ridge. Sir Andrew Barnard had sheltered overnight in a small roofless hovel on the side of the main road[5] and as the sun climbed in the sky the riflemen kindled a fire against its outside wall and boiled a large pan of sweet milky tea. This tempting brew was at the heart of the line and as virtually every commander in the army passed the spot once or more during those early hours few missed the opportunity to dip into it, Wellington included[6].

The allied commander was placing his brigades, and as the clear morning clouded over for a grey day of intermittent rain he drew up alongside the riflemen to survey his handiwork. His only item of uniform was a black cocked hat[7] with four cockades[8]. Other than that he wore his usual field dress of blue frock-coat, covered today by a short blue cloak, a white cravat, white buckskin riding britches and black Hessian boots with tassels. His sword was at his side and his telescope never left his hand. He was mounted on his favourite chestnut stallion, *Copenhagen*, its tail cut short in the English style[9].

The Battlefield[10]

Wellington
(some years after Waterloo)

The field of battle was surprisingly small for a clash of 140,000 men[11]: about 4 km wide with the front lines little more than 1 km apart. The opposing forces occupied low ridges separated by a very shallow valley – little more than a weak depression. This rolling land was planted mainly with cereals but there were patches of beans, peas, potatoes and clover, and the occasional ploughed field[12].

Wellington had taken the northern ridge, with his back to the forest of Soignes. At the centre of his position was an old elm, long past its prime. Standing by this tree, as he did that Sunday morning, and looking south towards the French, the dip between the ridges lay before him.

Along the top of the allied ridge, just behind Wellington's tree, ran a narrow trackway. This joined Braine-l'Alleud, 2 km to his right, with Ohain, 5 km to his left in the forest which extended along the allies' left flank. Beyond Ohain lay Wavre and the Prussians. At right angles to the ridge, a few metres to Wellington's left, lay the main paved road from Genappe, up which the wet and weary soldiers had trudged the previous night[13]. This road came out of the south towards Wellington over the French ridge near the inn of La Belle Alliance then ran down through a cutting in the uneven floor of the intervening dip before rising again and running past him to the farmhouse and hamlet of Mont St Jean to the rear of the allied line. Beyond Mont St Jean it disappeared into the forest towards Waterloo. As it crossed the allied ridge the road ran through another cutting more than five metres deep[14], dug to ease the gradient. On Wellington's side the cutting wall was steep and his tree hung over the edge of the drop, but across the road the ground rose in a gradual, if uneven, slope. Directly behind Wellington the trackway had also been cut down into the ridge to meet the level of the road where they crossed, and for 300-350 metres on this side of the junction – especially the nearest 100 metres – the gulley created was a marked obstacle for cavalry[15]. Across the main road to Wellington's left the trackway climbed slowly back to ground level, flanked by a broken thorn hedge. This hedge, which ran for almost a kilometre[16], was the main allied front line on that side of the road. It ended at a small bulge projecting forwards out of the ridge crest and overlooking the buildings and farm enclosures of Papelotte, La Haie and Smohain.

Straight ahead of Wellington, bordering the road nearly 200 metres away, were the farm buildings and walled farmyard of La Haye Sainte. Wellington was looking down at the back of the house, visible over the low hedge bounding the large square kitchen garden. The side of the garden fronting the main road was walled[17], and the roadside between the end of the

[9] Stanhope, 1888: 108-109. Hamilton, 2000: 6.
[10] For an extensive description of the field and deployment of the armies see Cotton (1895: 26-41, or other editions). Cotton served with the 7th Hussars at Waterloo and later lived on the battlefield for 14 years, working as a guide and managing a museum of the battle at Mont St Jean.
[11] Napoleon's 72,000 to Wellington's 68,000.
[12] Cotton, 1895: 26-27.
[13] In some accounts this is called 'the chaussée', or Genappe causeway, or Charleroi road, or Namur road, or Brussels road.
[14] Kincaid says 20-30 feet.
[15] Cotton, 1895: 283-284. Cathcart and Waymouth *in* Siborne (1993: 32-33, 46-47).
[16] Cotton (1895: 30) says about half a mile.
[17] Cotton, 1895: 32.

Army deployments at noon.

▬▬▬ = infantry.
━━━━ = artillery.

Allied cavalry were on a line between Mont St Jean farm and the infantry, from the Nivelles Road in the west to Papelotte in the east. The French cavalry were south of the French infantry along the whole line. The French Imperial Guard was in reserve near the Genappe road off the map to the south. Lambert's brigade was about to arrive from Waterloo after being detailed to clear the road through the forest, which had been blocked by traffic (Smith, 1999: 267-270).

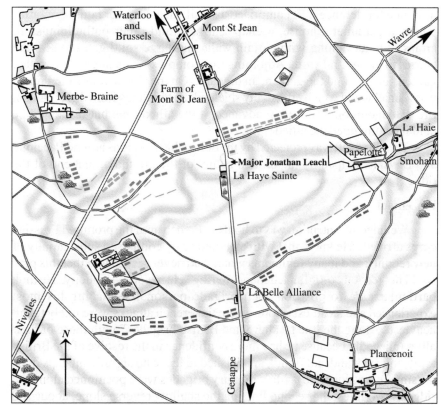

cutting and the start of the wall was marked by an artificially raised mound[18]. On the enemy's side of the buildings, invisible from the ridge, was a narrow orchard.

Across the road from La Haye Sainte, where the allied cutting petered out, a vast expanse of sandy sub-soil had been extracted from the field edge, creating an immense roadside sandpit, lower than the level of the sloping field to its left. Behind this sandpit, and excavated by it, was a pronounced knoll which overlooked both the pit and La Haye Sainte. The top of the knoll was crossed by another short length of hedge, parallel to that in its rear and studded with trees[19]. In front of the knoll the floor of the shallow valley was uneven with undulating ridges and troughs. In front of La Haye Sainte it was flatter.

To Wellington's right his view was less clear. In the distance his ridge ended as the valley swept around its end. Crossing the ridge crest diagonally, 900 metres away in another cutting, was a road joining Mont St Jean behind him to Nivelles in the far south-west. This was a weak spot for the allies. If the French could send troops along the lowest part of the depression to this road they could penetrate or turn the allied right wing. Fortunately for Wellington, where the road dipped towards its lowest point stood the buildings of the Château de Goumont, or, as the allies called it, Hougoumont. Hougoumont had been built more than two centuries earlier and was

[18] Cotton, 1895: 98. Diagram by Hew Ross *in* Siborne (1993: 224).
[19] Cotton, 1895: 33. The hedge was 140 yards (125m) long.

317

designed for defence[20]. It comprised a small vacant manor house[21], a farm-house, a gardener's house, a chapel, a barn and other outbuildings, all arranged in an oblong with curtain walls and large solid gates to seal the entries to the central yard. Adjoining this complex was a large high-walled garden, and beyond the garden, an orchard. On the side towards the French was a small wood which effectively shielded the buildings from direct cannon fire. Hougoumont lay well in advance of the allied line, but if it could be held it commanded the allied right.

The allied left was protected by the defensible positions around Papelotte and La Haie, helped by the broken nature of the ground at that end of the ridge.

Placement

Wellington's intention was to hold the French until the promised Prussian corps arrived. He knew that with an allied army composed substantially of new recruits, and many regiments which had never served together, his plan could not rely on co-ordinated manoeuvring. He needed simplicity. He took particular care to position each brigade personally, placing his most experienced and steadiest troops where the French attacks were likely to fall heaviest. Along the line he alternated British brigades[22] with those of their allies (allegedly because he had more confidence in the resolve of the British army units to stand and fight[23], and wished to leave no significant gaps if his pessimism was justified). Most infantry brigades were positioned along the ridge in two lines; the second line, on the shallow reverse slope, about 100 metres behind the first. The regiments in the second line were in columns or squares, with their light companies thrown forward as a line of skirmishers[24]. Behind these lines was massed the cavalry and behind them the remaining infantry brigades as reserves.

To prevent the French outflanking Hougoumont the Nivelles road was barricaded and covered by the 51st Light Infantry[25] and the light company of the 23rd Fusiliers[26]. Into Hougoumont itself Wellington put a contingent of the British guards with orders to 'hold the post to the last extremity'. It was a key position. A light company of each of the Coldstream Guards and the 3rd (Scots) Foot Guards manned the buildings and garden. A battalion of 600-700 men of the 2nd Nassau Regiment and two companies of Hanoverian riflemen were dispersed in the buildings and woods. Before the day was out Wellington would push 2000 more men forwards at this critical location, including part of the 1st Guards[27].

At the allies' next forward position, La Haye Sainte, the buildings were occupied by 360 sharpshooters of the 2nd (Rifles) Light Infantry Battalion, King's German Legion (KGL), under Major Georg Baring[28]. On the ridge to the rear of the farm, behind the trackway, was the remainder of the 2nd KGL brigade under their Colonel, Baron von Ompteda[29], and the 1st Hanoverian Brigade of Major-General Kielmansegge. This section of the line was under the immediate command of the Prince of Orange.

[20] Cotton, 1895: 28.

[21] The owner, Monsieur de Luneville, was not in residence.

[22] Including the highly regarded King's German Legion, which was part of the British army.

[23] Some of the non-British regiments in his army had formerly served under Napoleon and their loyalty was suspect. Some of the Nassau troops had formed the French rear-guard at Vittoria (Stanhope, 1888: 221).

[24] Cotton, 1895: 30-37. Selby, 1998: 75-76.

[25] The 2nd Yorkshire West Riding. Sergeant Bill Wheeler's regiment

[26] John Ross (Captain in the 51st) in Siborne, 1993: 316. Correctly the 23rd Regiment of Foot (Royal Welch Fusiliers), Captain Frederick Montagu's old regiment.

[27] Two light companies of which had spent the night in the position but had been withdrawn at 10 a.m. (Haythornthwaite, 1996b: 215-218).

[28] Georg Baring (*fl.* 1815). Later Major-General Baron Baring. See *Hannoversches militärischen Journal 1831*, 2: 69-90. [not seen].

[29] Colonel Christian Friedrich Wilhelm Baron von Ompteda (c.1766-1815).

Position of the 1/95th

Contours from Edward Cotton's map of 1846 (Cotton, 1895)

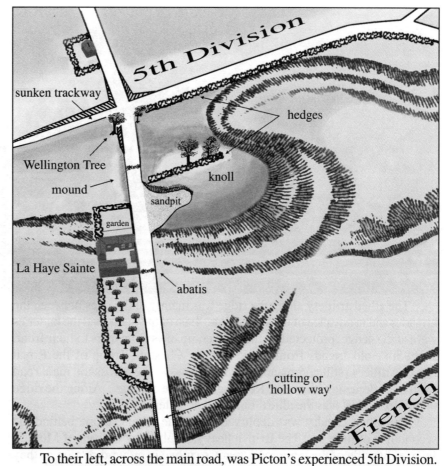

To their left, across the main road, was Picton's experienced 5th Division. Half Picton's regiments were Scottish. His first line comprised the light troops thrown forward as skirmishers. In this line the 1/95th were next to the main Brussels road with a reserve of three companies at the trackway hedge. The other three companies were in advance. One manned the hedge on the knoll, where many of the bushes had been torn out to build a barrier across the main road[30]. Jonathan Leach rode forward with the other two to occupy the sandpit[31]. Ahead of them the Germans in La Haye Sainte had built another barricade across the road.

To the left of the 1/95th, placed along the hedges of the Ohain road and scattered to their front, was the rest of the first line comprising the light companies of Picton's regiments[32]. Well in advance of these skirmishers, on the forward slope, was Major-General Bijlandt's[33] 1st Brigade of the 2nd Netherlands Division. Bijlandt's 2500 men had been in this position since the previous evening but would be dangerously exposed if left where they were.

Picton's second line, the battalion and grenadier companies of his regiments, were in formation on the reverse slope of the ridge, well behind the hedge[34].

[30] Waymouth *in* Siborne (1993: 53) reports Barnard as saying this barrier (abatis) was constructed by the 95th on the evening of the 17th.

[31] Barnard *in* Siborne (1993: 363) says Jonathan Leach occupied the sandpit with one company; Leach says two.

[32] Leslie (a Lieutenant in the 79th Highlanders) *in* Siborne, 1993: 355.

[33] Major-General W.F. Graaf van Bijlandt (or Bylandt) (*fl.* 1815).

[34] Kincaid *in* Siborne (1993: 367) says Kempt's line "seemed to stand about fifty yards from the hedge." Pack's line, further to the left, appears to have been further back – possibly 200m (Siborne, 1993: 371).

The view from the position of the 1/95th at the cross-roads. The hedge and trees on the knoll are directly ahead, with La Haye Sainte and the French ridge beyond.

© Copyright The British Museum

The allied artillery along the ridge was mainly in the gaps between the brigades and in advance of the second line. East of the main road the batteries were at the hedge, protected by the light company skirmishers to their front. The 95th's old friends from the Peninsula, Chestnut Troop of the Royal Horse Artillery (still commanded by Hew Ross) were across the main road from the riflemen, with two of Ross's guns in the cutting[35]. Along the ridge to the Rifles' left was the allies' only rocket battery[36].

The allied cavalry was deployed along the reverse slope behind the second line of infantry. The British heavy cavalry was in front of Mont St Jean, either side of the main road, ready to move in either direction as they were needed. Behind Picton with the cavalry, in reserve and ready to reinforce him, were the three infantry battalions of Sir John Lambert's brigade of the 6th division[37]. Harry Smith, still on detachment as a Staff officer, was Lambert's Brigade Major.

About ten in the morning Wellington spotted Prussians on the edge of the forest to his left[38]. He had been in contact with Blücher, who was trying to evade Marshal Grouchy's French corps and join the allies, but Blücher was not expected this early. This appeared to be a Prussian advance guard waiting for the rest of its corps to arrive. No Prussians were to take the field until much later in the day.

As the army settled in its new positions, to the Rifles' right across the road a young English officer of the King's German Legion, Lieutenant Edmund Wheatley, waited with his men and mused on his surroundings:

'On the opposite heights we could perceive large dark moving masses of something impossible to distinguish individually. Where the edge of the ground bound the horizon, shoals of these gloomy bodies glided down, disjointing then contracting, like fields of animated clods sweeping over the

35 Siborne, 1993: 186. Hew Ross in Siborne, 1993: 223-224.
36 2nd Rocket Troop Royal Artillery under the command of Major (later General Sir) Edward Charles Whinyates (1782-1865). Whinyates troop also managed light 6-pounder cannons and no men were exclusively allocated to rocket duties (Whinyates in Siborne, 1993: 203, 207).
37 Major-General Sir John Lambert (1772-1847). Commanded the 10th British Brigade, in the 6th Division. At Waterloo the brigade comprised the 1st battalions of the 4th (King's Own) Regiment, the 27th (Inniskilling) Regiment, and the 40th (2nd Somersetshire) Regiment. Its other battalion, the 2nd battalion of the 81st Regiment, had remained in Brussels (Smith, 1999: 268).
38 Wellington, 1956: 4 & 7.

The view towards the French from Edmund Wheatley's position, to the right of the crossroads. La Haye Sainte is on the left, La Belle Alliance is on the horizon in the centre, beyond the cutting (or 'hollow way').

plains, like melted lava from a Volcano, boding ruin and destruction to whatever dared impede its course...

It is an awful situation to be in, to stand with a sharp edged instrument at one's side, waiting for the signal to drag it out of its peaceful innocent house to snap the thread of existence of those we never saw, never spoke to, never offended. On the opposite ascent stand hundreds of young men like myself whose feelings are probably more acute, whose principles are more upright, whose acquaintance would delight and conversation improve me, yet with all my soul I wished them dead as the earth they tramped on... When I looked at my own comrades I could not conceive why my animosity was diverted from them in preference to the French who are, by far, more commendable characters than these heavy, selfish Germans.

Here stood a swelled-faced, ignorant booby, raw from England, staring with haggard and pallid cheek on the swarms of foes over against him. One could perceive the torture of his feelings by the hectic quivering of his muscles, as if fear and cold were contending for the natural color of the cheek. And this man is one of the mighty warriors shortly to deal out thunder and confusion to the opposers of the British constitution.[39]'

[39] Hibbert, 1997: 63-64. [Edmund Wheatley (ca 1792-1841). Lieutenant in the 5th Line Battalion, KGL. Married Elizabeth ('Eliza') Brooks/Brookes in London on the 12th February 1820. Hibbert (1997: 88) says they had four daughters, but they also had a son, Edmund, christened 23rd October 1822 at St Ann Blackfriars, London (like the first three daughters). Perhaps this son did not survive infancy.]

The Battle of Waterloo

It was nearly mid-day before the battle began. Wellington, in a defensive position and happy to delay any action, was content to wait for Napoleon. Napoleon, as one of his officers noted, was just happy to find the allies still there at daybreak:

Our first surprise, as the day dawned, was to see that the British, instead of retiring, had resumed their position and seemed resolved to defend it. Buonaparte, who had no apprehension during the night but that they would escape the punishment which he designed for them, was animated

Courtesy of the Director, National Army Museum, London

The French view of the 1/95th's position. Beyond the sandpit on the right two figures stand by a tree on the knoll, while across the main road Wellington's tree hangs over the edge of the cutting behind La Haye Sainte (but see p. 406 below regarding Wellington's tree).

with a most sensible joy at seeing them at their post; he was too fond of the game of war, and thought that he played it so well, to have any pleasure in a game only abandoned to him. He could not retain the expression of his feeling to those around him. "Bravo!" said he, "The British!—Ah! I have them then,—these British!"[40]

Napoleon briefed his staff while he waited for the sodden ground to drain. Eventually, as noon approached, he began his attack.

The first assault was against Hougoumont. The French had two reasons to start their strike here: they might capture it and expose the allies' right wing; or – more importantly – Wellington might move forces to reinforce it, exposing a weakened line to the major central assault Napoleon had already ordered. The fighting at Hougoumont was furious and sustained, and throughout the day became an increasingly crucial battle within a battle[41].

Back at the crossroads the rise of the intervening land hid Hougoumont from the 1/95th, who could only listen. While they did, a lone cannonball came from nowhere and took the head off one of the riflemen. It was an augur of things to come. With the commencement of the French attack Bijlandt's brigade was ordered to withdraw from the forward slope east of La Haye Sainte to a position between the brigades of Kempt and Pack[42]. The 1/95th and the light companies to their left remained where they were.

As the fire raged away to their right, the Rifles noticed activity on the French slope in front of them. Ominously, a battery of more than 80 cannons – half of them the awesome 12-pounders[43] – appeared directly opposite their position. At one o'clock they opened fire[44].

The bombardment was intense and the allied gunners replied in kind. Much of Picton's first line was pulled back to gain the protection of the ridge crest. The French barrage lasted half an hour and would have been more serious if the earth had been less waterlogged. Cannonballs were usually fired to skip along the ground, the bounding ricochets intended to do the

40 French officer quoted in Kelly (1828: 80) and Heath (1991: 8) [Again we have changed the usual 'English' to 'British']. Napoleon seemed more interested in the British than their allies, many of whom he had beaten (or employed) in the past.
41 For an account of the action at Hougoumont see Haythornthwaite (1996b: 212-242 & 249).
42 It has long been held that Bijlandt's brigade remained on the forward slope, with disastrous consequences (Howarth, 1968; Bryant, 1975; Chandler, 1980; Holmes, 1996) but Hamilton-Williams (1994: 26-27, 285-286, 386-387) argues they were pulled back into line before the French attacked and quotes a Dutch account of this movement made in a report to King Willem after the battle. Hamilton-Williams also reproduces the map drawn by W.B. Craan of the armies' deployments at mid-day (1994: rear of dust-jacket and used as the basis for the deployments on p.317 here). According to this map the only battalion in advance of the Ohain road at noon, in that part of the position, was the 1/95th. Conversely, Kempt expressly states the 95th was "in a line with a considerable Corps of Belgian and Nassau Infantry" which remained in that position

The view from the sandpit towards La Haye Sainte.

until the French advanced (*in* Siborne, 1993: 347) but Lieutenant Warde of the Royal Horse Artillery notes (*in* Siborne, 1993: 210) that Whinyates' rocket troop moved at noon to occupy the position vacated by a Dutch brigade of artillery to the left of the Genappe road, suggesting at least some Dutch units had been moved by that time. Jonathan Leach states that before he occupied the sandpit he saw foreign troops in advance to his left but these were "*not numerous*" (he implies two companies) and were only a picket (Letter: Leach to Philippart, 1st October 1840, see p. 528 below).

[43] Firing iron balls weighing 5.4 kg. Hamilton-Williams (1994: 280-281) says there were twenty 12-pounders of the French II and VI Corps; twenty 12-pounders of the Imperial Guard foot artillery; and forty 8-pounders of the I Corps (although he also says 84 guns)

[44] Simmons reports some artillery had been playing on the Rifles' position before then, as noted (Verner, 1986: 365).

[45] A standard artillery technique.

[46] Chandler (1980: 140) estimates about 17,000 men.

[47] Kincaid, 1981: 165-166.

damage[45]. With most of the allies over the ridge, and many of the balls failing to jump, the result was less than Napoleon had hoped, but it was bad enough. While the pounding continued there was more French activity. From his position in the sandpit Jonathan Leach had a clear view:

"Under cover of this cannonade several large columns of infantry, supported by heavy bodies of cavalry, and preceded by a multitude of light infantry, descended at a trot into the plain, with shouts and cries of "Vive l'Empereur!" some of them throwing up their caps in the air, and advancing to the attack with such confidence and impetuosity, as if the bare possibility of our being able to withstand the shock was out of the question, fighting as they were under the immediate eye of their Emperor."

Kincaid: "The column destined as our particular friends, first attracted our notice, and seemed to consist of about ten thousand infantry. A smaller body of infantry and one of cavalry moved on their right; and, on their left, another huge column of infantry and a formidable body of cuirassiers, while beyond them it seemed one moving mass[46].

We saw Buonaparte himself take post on the side of the road, immediately in our front, surrounded by a numerous staff; and each regiment, as they passed him, rent the air with shouts of 'Vive l'Empereur,' nor did they cease after they had passed; but, backed by the thunder of their artillery, and carrying with them the *rubidub* of drums, and the *tantarara* of trumpets, in addition to their increasing shouts, it looked, at first, as if they had some hopes of scaring us off the ground; for it was a singular contrast to the stern silence reigning on our side, where nothing, as yet, but the voices of our great guns, told that we had mouths to open when we chose to use them. Our rifles were, however, in a very few seconds, required to play their parts, and opened such a fire on the advancing skirmishers as quickly brought them to a standstill; but their columns advanced steadily through them, although our incessant *tiralade* was telling in their centre with fearful exactness, and our post was quickly turned in both flanks[47]".

323

Four massive columns had rolled across the valley. The smaller two on the flanks headed for La Haye Sainte and for Papelotte, the two in the centre aimed straight for Picton's Division. What was going through the minds of Napoleon's troops can be gauged from this French officer's account of similar engagements:

As soon as we got about 1,000 metres from the British line, our men would begin to get restless and excited. They exchanged ideas; the march began to get hurried. Meanwhile the British, silent and impassive, arms at the port, looked like a long red wall – most forbidding to our young soldiers. As we get closer shouts of "Vive l'Empereur! En Avant! À la baionette!" break from our ranks. Our march becomes a trot; men fire their muskets into the air. Three hundred metres in front, the scarlet line stands motionless. They do not seem impressed by the storm which threatens to break over them. It is a striking contrast. Some of us begin to think that it will be devastating when, at last, they do fire. Their unshakeable calm is unnerving. Our enthusiasm begins to wane. We try to restore our confidence by redoubled shouting. At last, the British muskets come down – they are making ready. Appalled, many of our men halt and open a scattered fire. Then comes the British volley, precise, deadly, thunderous. Decimated, our column staggers, half turns, tries to regain its balance. The enemy break their long held silence with a cheer. Then a second volley, perhaps a third and, with the third, they are at us[48].

Today the ridge and the hedge hid the main British line. The French saw a hail of iron and lead before they saw the red coats. Corn stalks and mud cocooned and tripped their feet as they ploughed through the wet sticky soil.

As they climbed the slope the nearest column pushed the Rifles aside, coming so close opposing officers fought hand-to-hand.

Kincaid: "a French officer rushed out of their ranks and made a dash at one of ours, but neglecting the prudent precaution of calculating the chances of success before striking the first blow, it cost him his life. The officer he stormed happened to be a gigantic Highlander about six feet and a half[49]— and, like most big men, slow to wrath, but a fury when roused. The Frenchman held that in his hand which was well calculated to bring all sizes upon a level—a good small sword—but as he had forgotten to put on his spectacles, his first (and last) thrust passed by the body and lodged in the Highlander's left arm. Saunders's blood was now up (as well as down)[50], and with our then small regulation half-moon sabre, better calculated to shave a lady's-maid than a Frenchman's head, he made it descend on the pericranium of his unfortunate adversary with a force which snapped it at the hilt. His next dash was with his fist (and the hilt in it) smack in his adversary's face, which sent him to the earth; and though I grieve to record it, yet as the truth must be told, I fear me that the chivalrous Frenchman died an ignominious death, viz. by a kick. But where one's own life is at stake, we must not be too particular.[51]"

[48] From Thomas Robert Bugeaud de la Piconnerie (1784-1849). He was noted for gallantry during the siege of Pamplona. In 1814 he joined the Bourbon cause but rejoined Napoleon in 1815 and commanded a force fighting the Austrians in Savoy. Retired 1815 but recalled 1830. Governor-General of Algeria from 1841. Created Duc d'Isly 1843. He is also noted for saying, "The British infantry is the finest in the world. Fortunately there are not many of them." [The usual 'English' has been changed here to 'British'. This translation was given by Dominic Goh on his excellent Napoleonic Wars website. Oman (1986: 91-92) has an alternative, but much less readable, version]
[49] About 2 metres tall.
[50] We do not understand the reference 'Saunders'. This officer was 2nd-Lieutenant Allen Stewart (or Stuart) of the 1/95th. He was later a Captain in the 3rd (East Kent) Regiment of Foot ('The Buffs') and died in 1847 (Dalton, 1971: 198, 200) in Norwich. He was not in Jonathan Leach's company.
[51] Kincaid, 1981: 252-253.

The columns rolled on. Leach's companies were forced out of the sandpit and fell back on the company on the knoll, behind what was left of the hedge. From there they delivered a withering fire into the French flank[52] supported by a fierce barrage from the Germans in La Haye Sainte. Stung, the head of the nearest column veered perceptibly away from the danger and crowded in on its neighbour, hampering both their deployments[53]. With the French passing their left flank, the rifle companies eventually had to abandon the knoll and fall back on their reserve at the crossroads. Seeing them coming, the officer commanding the reserve thought they were intending to replace his men and started to move his companies back to the second line. Fortunately Kincaid, as Adjutant, saw the mistake and brought them to a halt just to the rear of the road, allowing the incoming skirmishers to form behind them[54]. To their left the other light troops of the first line had been driven back, but as these light companies retired on their battalions Kempt advanced the second line to meet them and all moved up to the cover of the hedge and prepared to charge.

Kincaid: "When the heads of their columns showed over the knoll which we had just quitted, they received such a fire from our first line, that they wavered, and hung behind it a little; but, cheered and encouraged by the gallantry of their officers, who were dancing and flourishing their swords in front, they at last boldly advanced to the opposite side of our hedge, and began to deploy"[55].

To the French, marching over the crest of the rise, the red coats of Kempt's men seemed to rise out of the earth[56]. Then came the volley.

With the French just across the hedge[57] the British forced their way through the tangle of thorns and charged with the bayonet[58].

Lieutenant George Simmons, in front of his men, was caught in the ensuing violence: "hearing the word charge, I looked back at our line, and received a ball, which broke two of my ribs near the backbone, went through my liver, and lodged in my breast. I fell senseless in the mud, and some minutes after found our fellows and the enemy hotly engaged near me.[59]"

Simmons was trampled repeatedly as the fight surged around him. Many other riflemen had fallen and it was some time before he was seen to be alive and carried to the rear[60]. The column, surprised by the sudden appearance of the enemy and staggered by the ferocious hail of musketry, tried to deploy to its right but became confused and started to disintegrate[61]. Picton led Kempt's left wing forward but as he bellowed his orders he slumped lifeless across the neck of his horse, shot in the head.

To the right a new threat loomed. A force of cuirassiers had crossed the ridge onto the reverse slope and were now positioned to the division's rear across the main road[62].

Kincaid: "The command of the division, at that critical moment, devolved upon Sir James Kempt, who was galloping along the line, animating the men to steadiness. He called to me by name where I happened to be standing on the right of our battalion, and desired 'that I would never quit that spot.' I told him that 'he might depend upon it': and in another

[52] Wellington, 1956: 3. Barnard *in* Siborne (1993: 363).
[53] Cotton, 1895: 56. The opposite flank column was also being pushed towards the centre by fire from the Dutch troops among the hedges and enclosures near Papelotte.
[54] Kincaid *in* Siborne (1993: 367-368). Kincaid says Barnard and Cameron had been wounded at this time but this does not accord with Barnard's account (*in* Siborne, 1993: 52, 363). Kincaid appears to have compressed several actions into one.
[55] Kincaid, 1981: 166.
[56] According to Swiss infantryman Lieutenant Martin, author of *Souvenirs d'un Ex-officier*, 1867 (Howarth, 1968: 92 & 236).
[57] Barnard said the French were so close there was barely 2 yards (2 m) between the opposing lines (*in* Siborne, 1993: 363). Kempt said the French were just gaining the road and hedges (*op. cit. p.* 347).
[58] Shelton *in* Siborne (1993: 349).
[59] Verner, 1986: 365. Simmons says he was shot at 4.30 p.m. but he does not describe what happened to the French column or any other events after about 2 p.m. He only states that after being shot, "Their skirmishers were beaten back and the column stopped." We therefore assume he was shot during the charge at that time. Like most timings given by survivors of Waterloo, his should not be read literally.
[60] For his treatment see pages 23 and 24 above.
[61] Shelton *in* Siborne (1993: 349).
[62] Barnard *in* Siborne (1993: 364).

instant I found myself in a fair way of keeping my promise more religiously than I intended; for, glancing my eye to the right, I saw the next field covered with the cuirassiers, some of whom were making directly for the gap in the hedge, where I was standing. I had not hitherto drawn my sword, as it was generally to be had at a moment's warning; but, from its having been exposed to the last night's rain, it had now got rusted in the scabbard, and refused to come forth! I was in a precious scrape.[63]"

Across the cutting the advancing cuirassiers drove towards the King's German Legion and Edmund Wheatley:

"we distinguished by sudden flashes of light from the sun's rays, the iron-cased cavalry of the enemy. Shouts of 'Stand firm!' 'Stand fast!' were heard from the little squares around and very quickly these gigantic fellows were upon us.

No words can convey the sensation we felt on seeing these heavy-armed bodies advancing at full gallop against us, flourishing their sabres in the air, striking their armour with the handles, the sun, gleaming on the steel. The long horse hair, dishevelled by the wind, bore an appearance confounding the senses to an astonishing disorder. But we dashed them back as cooly as the sturdy rock repels the ocean's foam. The sharp-toothed bayonet bit many an adventrous fool, and on all sides we presented our bristly points like the peevish porcupines assailed by clamorous dogs.[64]"

In front of the 95th the French column was collapsing under the bayonet charge and rain of musket balls. Men turned and began flooding down the slope[65] but as Kempt's line followed, the French horsemen hurtled towards them. Kincaid, struggling with his sword, watched them come and contemplated a rapid withdrawal:

"My mind, however, was happily relieved from such an embarrassing consideration, before my decision was required; for the next moment the cuirassiers were charged by our household brigade; and the infantry in our front giving way at the same time, under our terrific shower of musketry, the flying cuirassiers tumbled in among the routed infantry, followed by the life-guards, who were cutting away in all directions. Hundreds of the infantry threw themselves down, and pretended to be dead, while the cavalry galloped over them, and then got up and ran away[66]. I never saw such a scene in all my life.[67]"

At the critical moment, with the French riders thundering towards the division's unprotected flank[68], Uxbridge had launched his heavy cavalry. The 1300 sabres of the Household Brigade[69] hammered into the French horsemen. Some tried to escape by jumping into the sunken trackway behind La Haye Sainte and galloping for freedom through the crossroads[70] but the Life Guards intercepted them at the junction, charging through and carrying everything before them. Cuirassiers trying to escape down the main road encountered the 95th's makeshift barricade. This was easily swept aside but slowed them just enough to allow the Life Guards to cut many down[71]. Others abandoned the road and tried to escape across the knoll but were rammed crossing its crest and somersaulted unceremoniously over the drop into the

63 Kincaid, 1981: 166-167.
64 Hibbert, 1997: 65.
65 Cotton, 1895: 57.
66 Marten (a Lieutenant in the 2nd Life-Guards) says the French infantry threw themselves on the ground until the allied cavalry had passed then rose and fired (in Siborne, 1993: 54).
67 Kincaid, 1981: 167.
68 Tucker, 1846: 386. (Tucker was a Captain in the 27th Regiment in Lambert's brigade, positioned behind Kempt's men).
69 The Life Guards; the Royal Horse (Blues) Guards ['Blues and Royals']; and the 1st (King's) Dragoon Guards.
70 Waymouth in Siborne (1993: 47-48).
71 Barnard in Siborne (1993: 364).

sandpit below, while the Life Guards spurred their mounts and leapt in after them like so many fox-hunters[72]. Any escaping that fate were driven to the left and ridden down among their own infantry as they surged down the slope.

As the cavalry swept the field clear the 95th rushed forwards in their wake, regained the knoll and the pit, and captured hundreds of prisoners[73].

Along the ridge to the left the French were faring better. The second main column had penetrated the hedge and amid a sharp exchange of fire was bearing down on Pack's Brigade and the Dutch infantry drawn up on the reverse slope[74]. They too were rescued by heavy cavalry. The Union Brigade's 900 sabres[75] poured through the line from the rear and bowled the French infantry back down the ridge front. As the attack collapsed along the whole line, the survivors fled, leaving behind them two Eagles[76] and 1700 captives. But the British cavalry's blood was up. On the forward slope they acquired their own momentum. Carried away by their excitement the two brigades raced onwards, officers in full cry trying in vain to turn their men. Life Guards pursued cuirassiers down the main road into the cutting in front of La Haye Sainte. As this became blocked with horses and struggling men the French infantry fired at point blank range from the banks on either side. Many Life Guardsmen died[77]. To the left British squadrons careered across the valley and into the French grand battery. Far beyond the reach of any support they sabred everyone who got in their way until an unseen array of 20 cannons and a counter charge by lancers and cuirassiers bundled them out of the French lines and cut them to pieces. Of the 2200 men who charged, 1000 never returned.

2.30 p.m.

Across the main road Baring's Germans in La Haye Sainte had been driven back into the farmhouse with considerable loss, but after the repulse they swiftly evicted the remaining French from the garden, barn and orchard and received two companies of the KGL's 1st Light Battalion to replace the men they had lost[78]. Across the main road the Rifles were taking stock.

Kincaid: "Some one asking me what had become of my horse's ear was the first intimation I had of his being wounded; and I now found that independent of one ear having been shaved close to his head (I suppose by a cannon shot), a musket-ball had grazed across his forehead, and another gone through one of his legs, but he did not seem much the worse for either of them.[79]"

With the French columns gone from their slope, Kempt's men retraced their steps. Jonathan Leach took his two companies back to the sandpit, the other four occupied the knoll[80]. The riflemen had not long settled before the enemy returned in force. Although their columns had been repulsed they now pushed forward a strong line of infantry to press Kempt's position and La Haye Sainte, which they seemed determined to capture[81].

Leach's riflemen were now only a few tens of metres from the enemy and a face-to-face firefight quickly developed.

[72] Walter Scott *in* Cotton, 1895: 284

[73] Cotton, 1895: 59.

[74] Cotton, 1895: 59. Hamilton-Williams, 1994: 294.

[75] 1st (Royal) Dragoons; 2nd (Royal North British) Dragoons ['Royal Scots Greys']; 6th (Inniskilling) Dragoons. The number of sabres on the field at Waterloo is variously cited by authors. 900 is the figure given by De Lacy Evans, who was an extra-ADC to Major-General Sir William Ponsonby (1772-1815) the commander of the Union Brigade (*in* Siborne, 1993: 64). Clark Kennedy, who was a Captain in the 1st Dragoons, said there were no more than 950-1000 sabres, but there were also many non-combatants in the regiments (*in* Siborne, 1993: 77-78).

[76] Of the 45th and 105th regiments. Two standards were apparently captured from the 105th regiment: a tricolour banner with an eagle on the staff; and a plain dark-blue banner with no eagle (Kennedy *in* Siborne, 1993: 75-76). This may account for the assertions of Kempt (see next chapter) and Harry Smith (1999: 270) that 3 eagles were captured, while other accounts mention 2.

[77] Waymouth *in* Siborne, 1993: 44-45.

[78] Wellington later reported La Haye Sainte fell in this attack, but it did not.

[79] Kincaid, 1981: 168.

[80] Letter: Leach to Siborne, 22nd November 1840 (see p. 532 below).

[81] Barnard (*in* Siborne, 1993: 52) says these were dense bodies of skirmishers but Leach says a strong line of infantry leading a more coordinated attack (see p. 538 below).

As the fire intensified, the French snipers began to find their mark. Barnard was hit and carried wounded from the field[81]. Cameron took his place.

Along the ridge crest the allies were now being subjected to the heaviest artillery barrage anyone could remember. With Kempt's losses mounting, Wellington moved his brigade and led Lambert's forward[82]. The 95th stayed where they were. Among Lambert's men, Wellington consulted his watch, "My God! It is now three o'clock, and no appearance of Blücher. He is sacrificing my army.[83]" In front of him the sacrifice continued. Cameron fell, a musket ball lodged in his throat. Jonathan Leach now commanded the 1st battalion[84].

Across the road the Germans in La Haye Sainte fought on and despite the new assault the French could make no headway. To the right new smoke mingled with the clouds from the ordnance. Hougoumont was ablaze. That engagement was rebounding on the French. Instead of pulling Wellington's troops to its aid, the intractable defence was drawing increasing numbers of French troops to the attack. They filled the wood and pressed up to the walls and gates in their thousands.

Leach: "The roar of cannon and musketry continued without intermission on the right; and although the lesson which the enemy had lately been taught by our division and the heavy cavalry, made them delay a considerable time before they renewed their attack on us in regular form, they kept up a constant and well-directed cannonade, from which we sustained a heavy loss, without the power of immediately retaliating, except from some pieces of artillery which the French batteries vastly outnumbered."

The French may have had more artillery but the allied gunners, including the rocket battery (who fired nearly 300 missiles[85]), were making their mark.

The British artillery made dreadful havoc in our ranks: we were so completely exposed that their rockets passed easily through all the lines and fell in the midst of our equipage, which was placed behind on the road and its environs. A number of shells also burst amongst them and rendered it indispensable for the train to retire to a greater distance. This was not effected without considerable disorder[86].

Any disorder to their rear did not spoil the aim of the French gunners. Their cannons crashed relentlessly hour after hour and the air was filled with the hiss and buzz of high velocity metal. Kincaid noted, "The enemy had, by that time, got the range of our position so accurately that every shot brought a ticket for somebody's head.[87]" Standing near the crossroads surrounded by his staff Wellington was aware of projectiles grazing and splintering his nearby tree. "That's good practice," he observed coolly, "I think they fire better than in Spain.[88]"

[81]Barnard *in* Siborne, 1993: 52).

[82] Calvert (a Major in the 32nd Regiment in Kempt's brigade) *in* Siborne (1993: 353). Drewe (a Lieutenant in Lambert's 27th Regt) *in* Siborne (1993: 396-7).

[83] Tucker *pers. obs.* (1846: 387). Wellington had received word at 4 a.m. that Blücher was on his way with his army and hoped to arrive by 1 p.m. The appalling condition of the roads delayed his arrival (Kelly, 1828: 145-146).

[84] *Wellington's Supplementary Despatches* (**10**: 747)say the battalion was commanded by Cameron then Leach. Therefore Cameron (who carried the musket ball in his neck for the rest of his life) must have been wounded after Barnard, not before. Barnard was wounded (the *Gazette* says 'slightly') at about 3 p.m. during this second attack, which was made about an hour after the first (Barnard *in* Siborne, 1993: 52, 362). Kincaid (1981: 167; and *in* Siborne, 1993: 367-368) says both Barnard and Cameron were wounded by the end of the first attack but he has compounded the attack of the columns with the later French advance. Kincaid implies Cameron was wounded a short time after Barnard. In *Rough Sketches* Leach says Barnard was wounded then Cameron "some time afterwards". In the *Dictionary of National Biography* H.M. Stephens says Cameron was wounded at "the close of day", but this gap would be too great to allow Kincaid to treat Barnard's and Cameron's injuries in the same sentence describing an early French attack. Philippart (1820, **5**: 98) says both Barnard and Cameron were wounded early in the day. For some

Along the line his infantry was pulled back out of sight of the French batteries and ordered to lie down, but enough of the skipping iron balls and exploding shells found targets to lay waste regiments. The attrition from shot, shell and shrapnel was immense. There was no answer but stoicism. "Hard pounding this, gentlemen" said Wellington, outwardly calm as he rode to and fro along the line, "let's see who will pound longest.[89]"

Edmund Wheatley too paced backwards and forwards in front of his men, reassuring the young officers who had never before seen action:

'I took a calm survey of the field around and felt shocked at the sight of broken armour, lifeless bodies, murdered horses, shattered wheels, caps, helmets, swords, muskets, pistols, still and silent. Here and there a frightened horse would rush across the plain trampling on the dying and the dead. Three or four poor wounded animals standing on three legs, the other dangling before. We killed several of these unfortunate beasts and it would have been an equal Charity to have perform'd the same operation on the wriggling, feverish, mortally lacerated soldiers as they rolled on the ground... The carnage was frightful. The balls which missed us mowed down the Dutch behind us, and swept away many of the closely embattled Cavalry behind them.[90]'

4 p.m.

While the guns hammered along the whole front, the point of attack now drove into the ridge between Hougoumont and La Haye Sainte. At 4 o'clock Marshal Ney, commanding the French front line, ordered in wave after wave of cavalry. It was curious to use unsupported cavalry. Usually cavalry charges were accompanied by infantry to exploit the damage. Not here. Here Ney used cavalry alone. The allied horse brigades were detached by Lord Uxbridge to the relative safety of the flanks[91] from where they did what damage they could. The infantry formed squares to brave the storm; two rows, one behind the other, staggered like a chequer board.

Wellington was in the square of the 1st Foot Guards as the enemy rolled towards them[92]. In the square with him was Ensign Rees Gronow[93]:

'Not a man present who survived could have forgotten in after life the awful grandeur of that charge. You perceived at a distance what appeared to be an overwhelming, long moving line, which, ever advancing, glittered like a stormy wave of the sea when it catches the sunlight. On came the mounted host until they got near enough, whilst the very earth seemed to vibrate beneath their thundering tramp. One might suppose that nothing could have resisted the shock of this terrible moving mass. They were the famous cuirassiers, almost all old soldiers, who had distinguished themselves on most of the battlefields of Europe. In an almost incredibly short period they were within twenty yards of us, shouting "Vive l'Empereur!" The word of command, "Prepare to receive cavalry," had been given, every man in the front ranks knelt, and a wall bristling with steel, held together by

battalions (including the 2/95th and 3/95th) the time commanders were wounded is published (*Wellington's Supplementary Despatches*, **10**: 751), but we have not seen this information for the 1st battalion. Caldwell & Cooper (1995: 17) say after Cameron was wounded "command now fell upon the senior Captain, Henry Lee." This is wrong. Jonathan Leach had more than four years seniority over Lee.
[85] Warde *in* Siborne (1993: 210).
[86] French officer quoted in Kelly (1828: 81) and Heath (1991: 10).
[87] Kincaid, 1981: 168.
[88] Kelly, 1828: 51.
[89] Kelly, 1828: 51.
[90] Hibbert, 1997: 66.
[91] Wellington *in* Cotton (1895: 231) quoted from *Wellington's Dispatches*, **12**: 609-610.
[92] In the years that followed the battle many denied Wellington ever sheltered in an infantry square. It is difficult now to see why the question was ever asked. He would never leave the front line, and during such attacks where else would he go? He admitted he sheltered in squares (*Wellington's Supplementary Despatches*, **14**: 618-620).
[93] On the day of the battle he had left Picton and joined his regiment on the field.

steady hands, presented itself... When we received cavalry, the order was to fire low; so that on the first discharge of musketry, the ground was strewed with the fallen horses and their riders, which impeded the advance of those behind them, and broke the shock of the charge... There is nothing perhaps amongst the episodes of a great battle more striking than the *débris* of a cavalry charge, where men and horses are seen scattered and wounded on the ground in every variety of painful attitude.[94]'

The squares withstood the onslaught and the French wave flowed back down the slope to regroup. Again and again they swept in, urged their horses to smash the squares, and ebbed away. Each time they were led by the armoured cuirassiers; behind them the lighter chasseurs and lancers. At least a dozen charges, and before each the shelling stopped; one demon exchanged for another. At each surge the allied artillerymen deserted their guns and sprinted to the safety of the squares, or took cover under their guncarriages. When the horses left they rushed back to duty. Later men wondered why the French had not hauled the guns away, or spiked them[95], but they had not.

Wheatley: "Nothing could equal the splendour and terror of the scene. Charge after charge succeeded in constant succession. The clashing of swords, the clattering of musketry, the hissing of balls, and shouts and clamours produced a sound, jarring and confounding the senses, as if hell and the Devil were in evil contention.

[94] Gronow, 1964: 69.
[95] Hammered a headless metal nail into the touch-hole to prevent firing.

About this time I saw the Duke of Wellington running from a charge of Cavalry towards the Horse-Guards, waving his hat to beckon them to the encounter.

All our artillery in front fell into the french power, the bombardiers skulking under the carriages. But five minutes put them again into our hands and the men creeping out applied the match and sent confusion and dismay into the retreating enemy.

Several times were these charges renewed and as often defeated. Charge met charge and all was pellmell. The rays of the sun glittered on the clashing swords as the two opposing bodies closed in fearful combat and our balls clattered on the shining breastplates like a hail shower.[96]"

On the French ridge Napoleon peered through his telescope and saw his cavalry milling around in the allied lines. "There is Ney" he said, "hazarding the battle which was almost won, but he must be supported now, for that is our only chance" and ordered in another 5300 men[97]. There were so many horses they were getting in each other's way.

Vastly outnumbered the allied cavalry could do little but sit at the edges of the action and pounce on disorganised French groups as and when the opportunity arose. Even then they sometimes pursued their quarry too far down the slope, suffering unnecessary losses and blocking their own artillery's line of fire[98].

At some squares as the French horses turned away the infantry deployed rapidly into line, four men deep, and sent a shower of musket balls after them. The cuirassiers noted this and began to feign retreats, spinning back and trying to catch the squares half-formed. They never succeeded and the infantry openly laughed at the French expressions of disappointment[99].

At other squares a stand-off developed. The allies realised the cuirassiers were reluctant to rush at loaded weapons so they held their fire – and rushing had become increasingly difficult in a muddy field strewn with dead and dying horses and men.

Gronow: 'The enemy's cavalry had to advance over ground which was so heavy that they could not reach us except at a trot... Our men had orders not to fire unless they could do so on a near mass; the object being to economise our ammunition, and not to waste it on scattered soldiers. The result was, that when the cavalry had discharged their carbines, and were still far off, we occasionally stood face to face, looking at each other inactively, not knowing what the next move might be.[100]'

Rivers of scowling cavalrymen circled the bristling walls, sometimes for five, ten, fifteen minutes. Small numbers of brave Frenchmen rode forward and fired into the squares with their pistols in the hope of provoking a discharge of muskets, but the infantry stood firm[101].

Wellington and his staff sheltered in the hollow centres, able only to wait. He later observed, "we had the French cavalry walking about us as if they had been our own. I never saw the British infantry behave so well.[102]"

[96] Hibbert, 1997: 67.
[97] Hamilton-Williams, 1994: 326. This brought Ney's command to about 9000 horsemen against the allies' 5000. Napoleon had planned a major cavalry offensive as the final assault against weakened allied lines but these lines were not yet weak enough, hence his concerns.
[98] Cotton, 1895: 78.
[99] Cotton, 1895: 79.
[100] Gronow, 1964: 70.
[101] Letter: James Stanhope (1st Foot Guards) to Lady Spencer, 3rd July 1815 (Cholmondeley, 1950: 272).
[102] Letter: Wellington to Marshal Beresford, 2 July 1815 (Wellington's Dispatches).

Eventually the French cavalry simply ran out of ideas. Their attacks waned. Wellington moved his squares forward to embrace his own guns and Uxbridge brought the allied cavalry back to the centre[103]. The cuirassiers left, the skirmishers returned and the cannonfire again was constant.

Wheatley: "The field was now thickened with heaps of bodies and shattered instruments. Carcases of men and beasts lay promiscuously entwined. Aid-de-Camps scoured across with inconceivable velocity. All was hurry and indefatigable exertion. The small squares on our right kept up incessant firings and the fight was as obstinate as at the commencement. The Duke of Wellington passed us twice, slowly and cooly.

No advantage as yet was discernible on either side. The French Cavalry were less annoying. Their brave, repeated assaults had cost them very dear.[104]"

La Haye Sainte

While the cavalry had plagued the squares to their right, the 95th had suffered the artillery and the snipers, but now the battle entered a new phase. Opposite the crossroads French infantry began to mass again by the main road.

Leach: "After having endured for a length of time, and with a tolerable degree of patience, this eternal pounding of shot and shells, strong symptoms appeared of a second and equally formidable attack being about to commence on our division and on the farm-house of La Haye Sainte. The second edition of "Vive l'Empereur!" "En avant, mes enfants!" and other stimulating cries, burst forth as their masses of infantry and cavalry again advanced in the most imposing and intrepid style, under cover of a terrible cannonade and of their light troops."

Across the road the French attack concentrated on La Haye Sainte. The orchard was over-run. A fierce bayonet struggle ensued at the wall and the open doorway of the barn[105]. The skirmishers of the German Legion's 5th Line Battalion were sent forward to reinforce the garrison, then 200 Nassauers. Foiled at the doorway, the French set fire to the barn itself. With difficulty it was extinguished, but not without loss of life. An hour of furious assault ensued, but the Germans resisted everything. Eventually the French withdrew. Baring had been calling for rifle ammunition for hours but nothing had reached him[106]. His men now had barely four rounds each. Then the French returned.

Leach: "Nothing could exceed the determined bravery with which the Germans defended the farmhouse of La Haye Sainte; but in the desperate attack which was now made on it, having expended the whole of their ammunition, and there being no means of supplying them with more, they were driven out, and the house was instantly filled with the enemy's infantry."

Against overwhelming odds the Germans were forced from the buildings, the survivors scrambling back up the slope to the sunken trackway. The

[103] Letter: Wellington to unknown recipient, 17th August 1815 (Cotton, 1895: 231).

[104] Hibbert, 1997: 67-68.

[105] One of the doors was missing at this critical location.

[106] Why Baring could not have been supplied from rifle ammunition intended for the neighbouring 95th is not clear. (The story believed by Wellington – that Baring could not be supplied because there was no access via the rear of the farmhouse – is clearly untrue. There was a passage from the garden through to the central farmyard served by a rear door more than a metre wide and there were four windows (Cotton, 1895: 33). Baring was repeatedly reinforced with additional men.)

French filled the rear garden, brought up field guns, and put skirmishers out just 80 metres from the allied front line.

The artillery was initially neutralised by the 95th across the main road, who shot the gunners after one salvo of grapeshot, but matters were very serious. Behind the trackway, Baron Ompteda received orders from Baron Alten to deploy a battalion in line and eject the French.

Ompteda, who earlier in the day had lost the 8th Line Battalion and almost lost the 5th following a similar order, took the unusual step of refusing to advance *in line*, pointing out the serious danger from French cavalry massed in a nearby hollow.

Alten came in person with the Prince of Orange to repeat the order. When Ompteda drew attention to the French cavalry, to everyone's surprise the Prince insisted the horsemen were not French, they were Dutch[107]. Yet again he had misidentified the uniforms of the enemy. The reality and the likely consequence of an advance in open formation were pointed out to him but William, hereditary Prince of Orange, believed ignoring advice was proof of a great mind, and a sign of great character[108]. "I must still repeat my order to attack in line with the bayonet, and I will listen to no further arguments.[109]"

Ompteda saw no way out and resigned himself to a futile sacrifice. He deployed the Legion's 5th Line Battalion and led them himself towards the skirmishers. With him went Edmund Wheatley:

"Colonel Ompteda ordered us instantly into line to charge, with a strong injunction to 'walk' forward, until he gave the word. When within sixty yards he cried 'Charge', we ran forward huzzaing. The trumpet sounded and no one but a soldier can describe the thrill one instantly feels in such an awful moment. At the bugle sound the French stood until we just reached them. I ran by Colonel Ompteda who cried out, 'That's right, Wheatley!'

I found myself in contact with a French officer but ere we could decide, he fell by an unknown hand. I then ran at a drummer, but he leaped over a ditch through a hedge in which he stuck fast. I heard a cry of, 'The Cavalry! The Cavalry!' But so eager was I that I did not mind it at the moment, and when on the eve of dragging the Frenchman back (his iron-bound hat having saved him from a Cut) I recollect no more. On recovering my senses, I look'd up and found myself, bareheaded, in a clay ditch with a violent headache. Close by me lay Colonel Ompteda on his back, his head stretched back with his mouth open, and a hole in his throat.[110]"

The French cavalry had not hesitated. Leaping forward they had swept along the back of the line of helpless infantrymen. It was murder. Kincaid, watching from the knoll, felt, "every man of them was put to death in about five seconds.[111]" But not quite all. Ompteda spurred his horse forward and jumped the hedge into the kitchen garden. French officers tried to spare his life but as he cut at the defenders with his sword he was shot at point-blank range[112]. Behind him allied light dragoons had charged the cuirassiers, but

107 Howarth, 1968: 159.
108 This was the Prince's expressed belief (Anglesey, 1955: 125).
109 Hibbert, 1997: 69.
110 Hibbert, 1997: 70.
111 Kincaid, 1981: 169.
112 *fide* Lieutenant Charles Berger, 5th Line Battalion (Hibbert, 1997: 70).

were too late to save the battalion. Barely 20 survivors made it back to the ridge. Wheatley was captured[113]. The affair was ended by an angry volley from the 95th which sent cavalry of both sides scattering for cover.

Kincaid: "It made me mad to see the cuirassiers, in their retreat, stooping and stabbing at our wounded men, as they lay on the ground. How I wished that I had been blessed with Omnipotent power for a moment, that I might have blighted them![114]"

The French in the farmhouse set to work exploiting their new position. From the loopholes high in the building and the cover of the surrounding walls their sharpshooters now made it impossible for the 95th to hold the sandpit. Leach's companies joined the others on the knoll, but it was not long before they were all driven off that height too and fell back to join Lambert's 4th Regiment behind the hedge on the Ohain road.

A critical point had been reached in the battle. Kempt's command was reduced to a single line of infantry. To the left a determined French attack had captured the farm of Papelotte. To the right across the main road the German troops were thinned almost to nothing. Ney knew one more push would take his men through the crossroads to victory, but he had nothing to push with. His own force was a patchwork of survivors from earlier actions. Urgently he sent back to Napoleon for more troops. The request was received with annoyance. "Troops? Where would you like me to get them? Would you like me to make some?[115]" As he said it Napoleon looked out onto a dozen battalions of the Imperial Guard, as yet unused. In that petulant response, with the battle poised on a knife's edge, he threw away his best chance.

Wellington, as aware of the danger as anyone, led in some Brunswickers to bolster the Prince of Orange's position as best they could. He knew things were critical. "Would to God that night or Blücher were come" he said[116].

To his right, two-thirds of Sir Colin Halkett's men were down. Peering through the smoke Wellington saw what he thought was an infantry square well in advance of the main line and asked Halkett which regiment they were. It was a mass of bodies lying in formation where Halkett had left them as he pulled his men back behind the ridge crest[117]. He urged Wellington to relieve his brigade. "Impossible" was the reply[118]. Beyond Halkett the Guards fared no better.

Gronow: "our squares presented a shocking sight. Inside we were nearly suffocated by the smoke and smell from burning cartridges. It was impossible to move a yard without treading on a wounded comrade, or upon the bodies of the dead; and the loud groans of the wounded and dying were most appalling.[119]"

Around the crossroads the French increased their fire against the now exposed ridge. They forced the allies to abandon their artillery and they advanced to the ridge itself under cover of fire from the farmhouse.

[113] He escaped and rejoined his regiment several days later.
[114] Kincaid, 1981: 169.
[115] "Où voulez-vous que j'en prenne? Voulez-vous que j'en fasse?" (Cotton, 1895: 96).
[116] Kelly, 1828: 51.
[117] Cotton, 1895: 96.
[118] Halkett allegedly said, "Very well my Lord. We'll stand till the last man falls." (Selby, 1998: 79).
[119] Gronow, 1964: 144.

Leach: "For several hours afterwards they kept up a dreadful fire from loop-holes and windows in the upper part of it, whereby they raked the hillock so as to render it untenable by our battalion. They were also enabled to establish on the knoll, and along the crest of the hill, a strong line of infantry, which knelt down, exposing only their heads and shoulders to our fire.

Thus the closest and most protracted contest with musketry perhaps on record, was continued for several hours; during which we were several times supplied with fresh ammunition. The artillerymen were swept from the guns which were within reach of the house and the hillock. The possession of La Haye Sainte by the French occasioned a vast loss to our division, which was so diminished in numbers, that all our reserves of infantry were brought up into our first, and now only, line, as were also the 4th and 40th regiments.

The 27th regiment had its good qualities of steadiness, patience under fire, and valour, put more severely to the test than, perhaps, any corps in the field. It was formed in a hollow square, a short distance in rear of the right of our division, with one of its faces looking into the road, as a protection to it against any attempt which the enemy's cavalry might make by charging up that road. This brave old regiment was almost annihilated in square, by the terrible fire of musketry kept up on it from the knoll, whilst it was impossible for them to pull a trigger during the whole time, as they would thereby have been as likely to kill friends as foes[120].

Every kind of exertion was made by the French officers, during this blaze of musketry, to induce their men to advance from the crest of the ridge and from the hillock, to charge us; and although, by the daring and animating example shewn by many of them, they at times prevailed on a certain portion of their men to advance a few yards, the fire which we sent amongst them was such, that they were glad to get back under cover of the knoll; such of them, at least, as were not disabled. In this manner continued the contest on our part of the line hour after hour, without any appearance of its being decided as long as any one remained alive on either side."

One of his officers suggested a detachment of riflemen should be concentrated on the right of the line to protect against an infantry attack up the main road but he considered the enemy too strong on the ridge for him to spare anyone. The battalion would have to rely on the 27th Regiment to protect its flank[121].

During this prolonged exchange the Rifles directed their fire across the main road towards the French infantry on the ridge behind La Haye Sainte, while the rest of Kempt's and Lambert's divisions tried to counter the threat from the knoll and the ridge to their front[122]. The permanent pall of smoke from so many rifles and muskets was so dense that Kincaid noted all they could see of the enemy were the flashes from their weapons. The allied artillery had virtually been silenced.

[120] The regiment lost 480 men out of 698 (Dalton, 1971: 133). Captain John Tucker was severely wounded (Kelly, 1828: 106).
[121] Leach in Siborne (1993: 366).
[122] Kincaid, reported by Barnard in Siborne (1993: 362).

Kincaid: "A good many of our guns had been disabled, and a great many more rendered unserviceable in consequence of the unprecedented close fighting; for, in several places, where they had been posted but a very few yards in front of the line, it was impossible to work them.

I shall never forget the scene which the field of battle presented about seven in the evening. I felt weary and worn out, less from fatigue than anxiety. Our division, which had stood upwards of five thousand men at the commencement of the battle, had gradually dwindled down into a solitary line of skirmishers. The twenty-seventh regiment were lying literally dead, in square, a few yards behind us. My horse had received another shot through the leg, and one through the flap of the saddle, which lodged in his body, sending him a step beyond the pension-list[123]. The smoke still hung so thick about us that we could see nothing. I walked a little way to each flank, to endeavour to get a glimpse of what was going on; but nothing met my eye except the mangled remains of men and horses, and I was obliged to return to my post as wise as I went.

I had never yet heard of a battle in which everybody was killed; but this seemed likely to be an exception, as all were going by turns.[124]"

Leach: "The arrival of the Prussians had been long expected; but the only intimation we had of their approach was the smoke of a distant cannon occasionally seen far on the left. About seven o'clock in the evening a party of their Lancers arrived on the field to announce the approach of their army. It was about this time that the last and desperate attack was made by Napoleon with his guard, to annihilate us before the Prussians should arrive to our assistance."

Three Prussian corps had been edging closer from the left for some hours[125]. The 4th Corps had engaged the French right wing, especially around the village of Plancenoit in the French rear, where a bitter contest with Napoleon's Young Guard[126] saw the village change hands several times. Eventually von Ziethen[127] led his 1st Corps onto the left of the allied line. Wellington could finally move his own left wing to reinforce his centre. At the same time the Prussian 2nd Corps approached on a line south of Papelotte. Time was running out for Napoleon. He responded by doing two things: he sent word to the front line that the new forces visible to the east were French reinforcements under Marshal Grouchy[128] (which he appears to have believed); and he readied his Imperial Guard.

7.30 p.m.

The last chance for Napoleon lay in breaking the dwindling allied line with one final push of infantry. The Imperial Guard were among his best veteran troops, his 'Immortals'. He assembled a massive column of the Middle Guard[129], put himself at their head, and led them forwards. As they reached the foot of the slope Napoleon turned aside into the opening of the hollow way on the main road and let Ney lead the column to the left, up the

[123] 'a step beyond the pension-list' – dead.
[124] Kincaid, 1981: 169-170.
[125] Cotton (1895: 99) says by 7 p.m. there were about 29,000 Prussians on the field. Most were pressing the far right of the French line.
[126] The Imperial Guard comprised: the Young Guard; the Middle Guard; and The Old Guard.
[127] Lieutenant-General Hans Ernst Karl von Ziethen (1770-1848).
[128] fide Marshal Ney and an unidentified French Officer, both quoted in Kelly (1828: 71-72 & 82).
[129] There are conflicting accounts of the number of battalions and of which units. Cotton (1895: 105) says two battalions of the Old Guard (mainly light infantry 'chasseurs') also participated.

allied rise between La Haye Sainte and Hougoumont. Curiously, but mercifully, the crossroads was to be spared the main blow.

The column marched on, drums beating, two companies wide at its head. Light artillery accompanied it and along the slope more infantry supported its flanks, deployed in parallel columns almost as far as Papelotte. The whole ridge was to be assailed. As the Imperial Guard advanced the allied gunners found their mark. Half way up the muddy slope, pulped to a quagmire by thousands of hooves, Ney's horse was shot from under him. He struggled on on foot. As the river of guardsmen approached its goal it split into two main attack columns, one of light infantry chasseurs a little behind the heavier grenadiers. Now the allied batteries changed to double charges of grapeshot and blasted roads into the 400 metre long trains.

On the rise in front of Ney Wellington quickly rearranged his force and ordered the 1st Foot Guards to lie down behind the crest, invisible to the advancing enemy.

Far along the ridge Jonathan Leach had the 1/95th extended along the battered thorn hedges of the trackway[130]. Mounting the slope in front of them, covered by the fire from the knoll and La Haye Sainte, were small French battalion columns[131]; survivors from the earlier attacks. Their arrival was timed to coincide with the Middle Guard to the west; but the Middle Guard was heading for a severe test[132].

The grenadiers were the first to arrive and as their right wing engaged the remnants of Halkett's depleted brigade[133] Dutch infantry and artillery rushed forward in support. A battery of Dutch horse artillery fired a shocking volley of grapeshot from less than 100 metres. In the column bodies piled onto bodies[134].

The grenadiers forged onwards but as their tall bearskin caps loomed over the ridge's brow in front of Wellington he gave the order: 'Guards, get up and charge![135]' The red coats of the 1st Guards appeared from nowhere and a blaze of musketry destroyed the column's lines. Standing four deep the Guards piled on the pressure, their front row firing independently, each man moving to the back to reload[136]. This deadly conveyor-belt tore the grenadiers apart. Their front ranks were obliterated; those behind dissolved in chaos. In under a minute 300 fell[137]. Then the Foot Guards charged. In the face of this frontal assault and a withering cross-fire from artillery and small-arms[138] the Imperial Guardsmen rallied only briefly then collapsed backwards in disorder.

Moments later the column of chasseurs moved up resolutely. The 1st Guards were recalled to the ridge, in some confusion, where they reformed. The new column pressed on under a fierce artillery barrage and approached the top of the rise. To its right French infantry climbed to attack the remains of Alten's Division and across the main road, in front of Leach's battalion, French columns had reached the ridge crest[139]. The outcome of the battle again hung in the balance.

130 Cotton, 1895: 109.
131 Belonging to the corps of Maréchal Drouet (Comte d'Erlon) (Cotton, 1895: 109, 113).
132 What follows is a very abbreviated interpretation of a complex engagement. Cotton (1895: 104-122) gives a longer version as do various modern authors. Much of the detail is still disputed.
133 By this time Tom Morris's 73rd Highlanders had been reduced from 29 officers and 550 men at Quatre Bras to little more than 2 officers and 70 men and could not hold their ground alone (Selby, 1998: 80).
134 Hamilton-Williams, 1994: 343.
135 Gronow (1964: 71) says these were the exact words he used.
136 Independent file firing (Cotton, 1895: 115. Letter: James Stanhope to Lady Spencer, 3rd July 1815 (Cholmondeley, 1950: 272-273). Stanhope was a Captain and Colonel in the 1st Foot Guards. Only the Guards regiments employed this explicit use of twin ranks.
137 Weyland Powell (Lieutenant and Captain 1st Foot Guards) in Siborne, 1993: 255.
138 The Imperial Guard were attacking the centre of a curved allied line which allowed the flanking allied positions a clear shot at the columns' sides (Cotton, 1895: 115-117).
139 Browne in Siborne (1993: 398-400).

The Imperial Guardsmen fought their way forwards to the crest of the ridge. In front of them the 2nd battalion of the 95th was being pushed slowly backwards. To their right Sir John Colborne, with his Light Division veterans of the 52nd Light Infantry, feared the 95th's backward move would threaten his left flank[140]. On his own initiative he stirred his men into motion. In parade-ground style he wheeled his entire battalion in line four deep until they were parallel with the side of the column then volleyed and marched them in formation straight at the enemy. Sensing the danger the column stalled. Its left files turned and fired. The 52nd returned the fire and pressed forward. Wellington saw Colborne was in a strong position and ordered more battalions to support him. The 2/95th regained their ground and fired straight into the column's head[141].

The French guardsmen were now in an impossible position: unable to advance but unwilling to retire[142]. Many men were unsighted in their dense formations, incapable of bringing their arms to bear. With growing attacks closing from the front and side the column finally crumpled, collapsed and fled with the 52nd in steady pursuit.

For the rest of Napoleon's army the sight of the Imperial Guard in retreat had been unimaginable. 'The Old Guard are fleeing!' was the horrified reaction[143]. As the Guard was driven back down the slope, the whole French attack faltered. Napoleon slapped his hand to his forehead.

140 Dalton, 1971: 171. Hunter Blair (Brigade Major to the brigade of Major-General Adam – see below – which contained the 52nd) says the second column was gaining the ridge and Colborne rotated the leftmost company of the 52nd backwards to protect his flank (*in* Siborne, 1993: 278).
141 Cotton, 1895: 120.
142 Cotton, 1895: 121.
143 'la vieille garde fuyait' (Letter: James Stanhope to Lady Spencer, 3rd July 1815 reported *in* Cholmondeley, 1950: 273).

'There is nothing like the British infantry' he said[144]; but the repulse of his Immortals was not the only shock. Troops were flooding out of the woods to the French right. He saw them coming and asked an aide who they were. Using his telescope the aide announced, "They are the Prussian colours." Napoleon's face turned chalky white. He said nothing; just shook his head once, silently[145].

The French front line still believed the newcomers were Grouchy's reinforcements[146], then the Prussian cannons found their range. In an instant the words 'treason' and 'treachery' echoed through the French lines. Some thought Grouchy had reverted to the King, some that their Generals had deceived them. This further blow was too much. Their resolve evaporated. As more Prussians emerged behind Papelotte and broke through the rear of the French front line Wellington knew his moment had finally come.

'Late in the day,[147]' recalled Harry Smith, 'when the enemy had made his last great effort on our centre, the field was so enveloped in smoke that nothing was discernible. The firing ceased on both sides, and we on the left knew that one party or the other was beaten. This was the most anxious moment of my life...

I saw the Duke, with only one Staff officer remaining, galloping furiously to the left. I rode on to meet him.

"Who commands here?"
"Generals Kempt and Lambert, my lord."
"Desire them to get into a column of companies of Battalions, and move on immediately"...
"In which direction, my lord?"
"Right ahead, to be sure."

I never saw his Grace so animated.[148]'

Kincaid: "Presently a cheer, which we knew to be British, commenced far to the right, and made every one prick up his ears;—it was Lord Wellington's long-wished-for orders to advance; it gradually approached, growing louder as it grew near;—we took it up by instinct, charged through the hedge down upon the old knoll, sending our adversaries flying at the point of the bayonet. Lord Wellington galloped up to us at the instant, and our men began to cheer him; but he called out, 'No cheering, my lads, but forward, and complete your victory!'

This movement had carried us clear of the smoke; and, to people who had been for so many hours enveloped in darkness, in the midst of destruction, and naturally anxious about the result of the day, the scene which now met the eye conveyed a feeling of more exquisite gratification than can be conceived. It was a fine summer's evening, just before sunset. The French were flying in one confused mass. British lines were seen in close pursuit, and in admirable order, as far as the eye could reach to the right, while the plain to the left was filled with Prussians. The enemy made one last attempt at a stand on the rising ground to our right of La Belle Alliance; but a charge

144 "Il n'y a rien comme l'infanterie anglaise." (James Stanhope (*loc. cit.*) Stanhope was an ADC at this time and appears to have heard these reports from a French General he met as a negotiator. He says Napoleon said this to Count Lebon.
145 Kelly, 1828: 144.
146 The blue of French uniforms and grey of Prussian would be easily confused at a distance, with long evening shadows and dense clouds of smoke.
147 It was about 8.15 p.m.
148 Smith, 1999: 272.

from General Adams's brigade[149] again threw them into a state of confusion which was now inextricable, and their ruin was complete. Artillery, baggage, and everything belonging to them, fell into our hands.[150]"

Leach: "The lines moved forward rapidly and in fine order, loudly cheering; and the time only which was required for us to reach the enemy's position, sufficed to complete this most hardly contested, sanguinary, and important of battles."

In the French lines, discipline had collapsed: *The whole army, as if moved by one impulse, abandoned their positions and retired like a torrent; the gunners quitting their pieces, the soldiers of the train cut away the traces of the horses; the infantry, cavalry, all kinds of troops mixed and confounded together, no longer presented the appearance of anything but an unformed mass, which nothing could stop, and which was flying in disorder along the high road and across the fields*[151].

Wellington later said, "I have fought the French as often as any body, and I will say this for them, that I never saw them behave ill, except at the end of the Battle of Waterloo; whole battalions ran away and left their arms piled[152]", but others preferred to judge the French on the day as a whole.

Jonathan Leach: "Those amongst us who had witnessed in the Peninsula many well-contested actions, were agreed on one point, that we had never before seen such determination displayed by the French as on this day. Fighting under the eye of Napoleon, and feeling what a great and important stake they contested for, will account for their extraordinary perseverance and valour, and for the vast efforts which they made for victory.

The loss sustained by the army was such as might have been expected in so long and closely contested a battle. There was a sorry reckoning amongst the officers and soldiers of our battalion, as well as of our 2d and 3d battalions, which were in Sir H. Clinton's division[153].

Marshal Blucher having put his army on the enemy's track, with strict orders that not a moment's respite should be allowed them on their retreat, the Duke of Wellington's army bivouacked for the night on the ground which had been the French position during the battle. Here, amidst heaps of dead and dying, men and horses, captured artillery, ammunition waggons, &c. &c. &c. huddled together in one confused mass, we spent the night."

While the French fled south, Wellington and Blücher met by the inn of La Belle Alliance. Blücher had promised Wellington he would bring one or more Prussian corps, and, ever a man of his word, he had brought three. They agreed the Prussians would pursue the French alone. Although both armies were exhausted, Wellington's was shell-shocked. Besides, there had been enough fatal 'friendly fire' as the Prussians had taken the field. In the smoke and confusion, and the riot of different uniforms and languages, many engagements had taken place between the Prussians and their allies. The darkness would only have made it worse.

[149] Major-General Frederick Adam (1781-1853) commanded the 3rd British Brigade [the 'Light Brigade'] in the allied 2nd Division. His brigade comprised the 2/95th, 3/95th, 52nd and 71st (Highland) Light Infantry.
[150] Kincaid, 1981: 170-171.
[151] French officer quoted in Kelly (1828: 83) and Heath (1991: 13).
[152] Wellington, 1956: 2.
[153] Lieutenant-General Sir Henry Clinton (1771-1829) commanded the 2nd Division which included Adam's 3rd brigade.

— 21 —

Waterloo epilogue

> I could scarcely avoid feeling a contempt for myself when
> I gazed on these maimed soldiers, the relics of the great
> fight at Waterloo,—for how much had they performed, and
> what had I done, but come to stare at them!
>
> John Scott[1]

After the battle Wellington's army slept where it lay, amid the chaos and the carnage. Their commander rode back along the main road through the battlefield, past his tree, and on as far as his headquarters at Waterloo. More than one observer saw him shed tears. At Waterloo he ate and began his report, eyeing the door hopefully every time it opened; waiting for friends who never came. By 11 p.m. he was back in Brussels at his house in the park completing his dispatch when Thomas Creevey called to see him. In response to Creevey's congratulations Wellington declared:

'I have won the greatest battle of modern times, with twelve thousand of my old Peninsular troops'...

'What, sir, with twelve thousand only?'

'Yes Creevey, with twelve thousand of my old Spanish infantry. I knew I could depend upon them. They fought the battle, without flinching, against immense odds; but nearly all my staff, and some of my best friends, are killed.[2]

To Creevey Wellington then gave a brief summary, "in his short, natural, blunt way, but with the greatest gravity all the time, and without the least approach to anything like triumph or joy.— 'It has been a damned serious business,' he said, 'Blücher and I have lost 30,000 men. It has been a damned nice thing—the nearest run thing you ever saw in your life. Blücher lost 14,000 on Friday night, and got so damnably licked I could not find him on Saturday morning; so I was obliged to fall back to keep up my communications with him.'—Then, as he walked about, he praised greatly those Guards who kept the farm (meaning Hougoumont) against the repeated attacks of the French; and then he praised all our troops, uttering repeated expressions of

[1] John Scott (1784-1821). Scottish journalist. Editor of a weekly London journal, *The Champion*, and author of *A Visit to Paris in 1814* (1815). He visited Brussels and the battlefield soon after the battle and spoke to many survivors (Scott, 1816: 201-227).

[2] This paragraph is from Gronow (1964: 157-158) who says he heard it from Creevey. It rings true, if decidedly ungrateful. Wellington certainly called his regiments from the Peninsula 'the old Spanish infantry' (Pool, 1967: 236).

astonishment at our men's courage. He repeated so often its being *so nice a thing—so nearly run a thing*, that I asked him if the French had fought better than he had ever seen them do before.—'No,' he said, 'they have always fought the same since I first saw them at Vimeira.' Then he said: 'By God! I don't think it would have done if I had not been there.[3]'

Monday, 19th of June

Major-General Sir James Kempt to Field Marshal the Duke of Wellington.

REPORT

Bivouac near Genappe, 19th June, 1815

"In consequence of the lamented fall of Lieutenant-General Sir Thomas Picton (who was unfortunately killed early in the battle of yesterday, at a very critical moment, while nobly animating the troops), the command of the 5th Division and the troops that had been placed under his orders devolved upon me, and it is quite impossible for me to convey by words to your Grace the feelings of admiration with which I beheld the invincible spirit displayed by the British troops in repulsing every attack that was made upon the position where I had the honour to command. The troops were formed in two lines, supported by Major-General the Honourable Sir W. Ponsonby's brigade[4] of cavalry. The 1st line was composed of Dutch and Belgian troops, with the 1st battalion of the 95th regiment under Colonel Sir Andrew Barnard posted on a knoll on the right. The 2nd line was composed of the 8th and 9th brigades of infantry under Major-General Sir Denis Pack and myself, and the 4th and 5th Hanoverian brigades of militia commanded by Colonels Vincke and Best. The enemy having concealed his attack to the last moment, advanced rapidly in three immense columns of infantry, covered by 30 pieces of artillery, directing their heads on the right, centre, and left of the position to the left of the Chausée. Our first line, acting as light troops, gave way as the columns approached; but the 8th and 9th brigades of infantry instantly advanced, and charged the heads of the columns just as they had gained the crest of the position: a struggle for a few moments ensued, but the invincible spirit and determination of the British troops were such, that these immense masses directed with the greatest fury were absolutely put to flight by two British brigades, weakened as they had been most materially by the severe action which they had fought two days before. Major-General the Honourable Sir W. Ponsonby instantly availed himself of this, and charged in the most gallant manner at the head of his brigade: many prisoners were taken, and three eagles. Shortly after this, Major-General Sir J. Lambert arrived with his brigade to support the 5th Division; and the enemy having formed fresh columns, renewed the attack with the same impetuosity: they were met and repulsed in a similar manner; part of Sir J. Lambert's brigade charged on this occasion, and behaved nobly.

[3] Gore, 1970: 150-151. This is often cited as, 'I don't think it would have *been* done...' (e.g. Liddell Hart, 1994: 168) or even 'I don't think it *could* have *been* done...' (Bryant, 1975: 246fn). These altered wordings, given by their authors without explanation, would have meant something very different.

[4] The Union Brigade. Ponsonby was killed by lancers while trying to lead his men back to the allied lines after the first charge.

After the failure of these attacks the enemy's efforts were principally directed to the right of the Chausée; and having gained possession of a large farmhouse (La Haye Sainte[5]), and also the adjoining ridge of equal height with the one which we occupied, I requested Sir J. Lambert to cross the great road with the 27th regiment and retake it: but at this period it was found to be impracticable, all the infantry in this part of the position being formed in squares, and the enemy's cavalry around them. A fresh attack was now made by the enemy along the great road, and under cover of the farmhouse which they occupied: the evident intention was to keep down the advance of our line by a superior fire from the farmhouse and ridge, and under cover of it to push on the mass of infantry in its rear along the Chausée. A desperate struggle and fire now took place. I directed all the broken ground that afforded the least cover to be completely lined with troops; but in addition to this I found it absolutely necessary to increase our fire by moving up the greatest part of the 27th regiment, which Major-General Lambert posted in as good a situation as circumstances would admit; but it was unavoidably much exposed. The regiment behaved nobly, and suffered exceedingly. The 95th and 32nd were also near this point, and suffered also great loss. The struggle at this point continued for some hours, but every effort of the enemy proved ineffectual, and he never for one moment gained a footing on the position to the left of the great road[6]."

Wellington's unofficial summary of the whole battle was more succinct: "Never did I see such a pounding match. Both were what the boxers call gluttons. Napoleon did not manœuvre at all. He just moved forward in the old style, in columns, and was driven off in the old style. The only difference was, that he mixed cavalry with his infantry, and supported both with an enormous quantity of artillery."[7]

Back at the battlefield his troops were slowly coming to terms with the fact they had survived.

Kincaid: 'This was the last, the greatest, and the most uncomfortable heap of glory that I ever had a hand in... The field of battle, next morning, presented a frightful scene of carnage; it seemed as if the world had tumbled to pieces, and three-fourths of everything destroyed in the wreck. The ground running parallel to the front of where we had stood was so thickly strewed with fallen men and horses, that it was difficult to step clear of their bodies; many of the former still alive, and imploring assistance, which it was not in our power to bestow.

The usual salutation on meeting an acquaintance of another regiment after an action was to ask who had been hit, but on this occasion it was 'Who's alive?' Meeting one, next morning, a very little fellow, I asked what had happened to them yesterday. 'I'll be hanged,' says he, 'if I know anything at all about the matter, for I was all day trodden in the mud and galloped over by every scoundrel who had a horse'...

[5] French dispatches after the battle referred to La Haye Sainte as 'the village of Mont St Jean' hence French claims at the time that during the battle they had occupied Mont St Jean, which they never did.

[6] *Wellington's Supplementary Despatches*, **10**: 535-537 (1863). The report continues but with less relevance to the 1/95th.

[7] Letter: Wellington to Beresford, 2nd July 1815 (*Wellington's Dispatches*).

We were, take us all in all, a very bad army. Our foreign auxiliaries, who constituted more than half our numerical strength, with some exceptions, were little better than a raw militia—a body without a soul, or like an inflated pillow, that gives to the touch, and resumes its shape again when the pressure ceases—not to mention the many who went clear out of the field, and were only seen while plundering our baggage in their retreat.

Our heavy cavalry made some brilliant charges in the early part of the day; but they never knew when to stop, their ardour in following their advantage carrying them headlong on, until many of them 'burnt their fingers,' and got dispersed or destroyed.

Of that gallant corps, the royal artillery, it is enough to say, that they maintained their former reputation—the first in the world—and it was a serious loss to us, in the latter part of the day, to be deprived of this more powerful co-operation, from the causes already mentioned[8].

The British Infantry and the King's German Legion continued the inflexible supporters of their country's honour throughout, and their unshaken constancy under the most desperate circumstances showed that, though they might be destroyed, they were not to be beaten.

If Lord Wellington had been at the head of his old Peninsula army, I am confident that he would have swept his opponents off the face of the earth immediately after their first attack; but with such a heterogeneous mixture under his command, he was obliged to submit to a longer day.[9]"

That longer day had wrought unimaginable loss. The casualty figures were horrific. 40,000 men and 10,000 horses carpeted the field[10]. Around Hougoumont alone – which was never captured, although it came desperately close – 10,000 men fell, the vast majority French. Bill Wheeler had spent the night amid the shattered and ball-studded trees in the orchard with upwards of 2000 corpses[11]: "I went to the farm house, what a sight. Inside the yard the Guards lay in heaps, many who had been wounded inside or near the building were roasted, some who had endeavoured to crawl out from the fire lay dead with their legs burnt to a cinder.[12]"

The rest of the valley was no different; like the shore after a hurricane[13], the air heavy with an all-pervading, nauseating stench.

Harry Smith: "the *whole* field from right to left was a mass of dead bodies. In one spot, to the right of La Haye Sainte, the French Cuirassiers were literally piled on each other; many soldiers not wounded lying under their horses; others, fearfully wounded, occasionally with their horses struggling upon their wounded bodies. The sight was sickening, and I had no means or power to assist them. Imperative duty compelled me to the field of my comrades, where I had plenty to do to assist many who had been left out all night; some had been believed to be dead, but the spark of life had returned. All over the field you saw officers, and as many soldiers as were permitted to leave the ranks, leaning and weeping over some dead or dying brother or comrade.[14]"

[8] The advance of the French line up to the gunnery positions.
[9] Kincaid, 1981: 171-173.
[10] Plus 7000 Prussians to the east of the main theatre of operations.
[11] Gronow, 1964: 72.
[12] Liddell Hart, 1994: 174.
[13] Tucker, 1846: 394.
[14] Smith, 1999: 275.
[15] Smith, 1999: 279. Two officers of the 32nd Regiment also saw this body (Cotton, 1895: 57).
[16] Cotton, 1895: 57. See also Scott (1816: 150-152) and Haythornthwaite (1979: 152-153) for women killed in battle.
[17] He was not gazetted as wounded but the injury is mentioned by Hart (1848) and in his obituary in *The Times*, 23rd January 1855.
[18] The Order of the Bath is so named from the ceremony of ritual cleansing that preceded the bestowal of knighthood in the 14th century and later. Prior to 1815 there were only Knights of the Bath (KB) but the order was reorganised in 1815 into three classes: Knight Grand Cross (GCB), Knight Commander (KCB) and Companion (CB). A Companion of the order is not a knight.
[19] Captain Lord Arthur Hill. A son of the 2nd Marquess of Downshire. At this time he was not on active service with the army, but on half pay and had attended the battle as an extra-Aide-de-Camp. Later Lieutenant-General. From 1836 he was Baron Sandys (pronounced 'sands').

Harry Smith's brother Charles, a volunteer with the 1/95th, was detailed to remove British wounded from the battalion's position. Among the bodies he found that of a young woman dressed in the uniform of a French officer of hussars[15]. She was not the only woman who fought and died in a French uniform at Waterloo[16].

Among the walking wounded, Jonathan Leach was nursing a shrapnel wound from an artillery shell, but fortunately it was not serious[17]. For his battlefield service as acting battalion commander he was promoted to Lieutenant-Colonel in the army and made a Companion of the Most Honourable Order of the Bath (*CB*)[18]. He too was trying to come to terms with the aftermath.

"Soon after daybreak, the following morning, I mounted my horse for the purpose of glancing my eye over the field of battle. It was not the first of the kind on which I had looked; but the frightful carnage of men and horses lying in so comparatively small a compass, the thousands of the wounded of the two armies which had not yet been removed, together with their groans and lamentations, produced such an impression on the mind, as every writer who has attempted to bring it home to the conception of those who were not eye-witnesses of the bloody scene which this huge charnel-house presented, has failed to effect. I relinquish it, therefore, as a hopeless undertaking; and turn willingly from this scene (which in cold blood will not bear inspection) towards the French metropolis, on the road to which our army was put in motion about nine or ten o'clock on the morning of the 19th."

Tourists

On the 20th Creevey visited the battlefield with one of Wellington's aides-de-camp, Captain Lord Arthur Hill[19]. The French dead and wounded still lay where they had fallen and at the position of the 1/95th Creevey noted, 'just close up to within a yard or two of a small ragged hedge which was our own line, the French lay as if they had been mowed down in a row without any interval. It was a distressing sight... to see every now and then a man alive amongst them, and calling out to Lord Arthur to give them something to drink.[20]'

Nearly six weeks later the First Secretary to the Admiralty, John Croker[21], rode over the field with the Irish Secretary Robert Peel[22]. The whole area was still covered with cartridges and wadding from the host of cannon, the battered remains of hats, caps and helmets, and letters pulled from the pockets of the dead and wounded[23]. The local villagers had collected anything of value left by the vacating armies and were selling assortments of armour, medals, cap badges, buttons, knapsacks and documents to anyone willing to buy them, and there was no shortage of purchasers[24]. The area had by now been given over entirely to the thousands of tourists flocking to Belgium to view the fields where Europe was set free.

[20] Gore, 1970: 152. (Lord Arthur Hill did give the wounded something to drink).

[21] John Wilson Croker (1780-1857). Born Galway, Ireland. Irish barrister. Elected MP for Downpatrick in 1807 under the sponsorship of Sir Arthur Wellesley (then Chief Secretary for Ireland). Croker deputised for Wellesley in Ireland and in parliament when Wellesley took command of the army in the Peninsula. When Wellesley's brother William Wellesley Pole (1763-1845) replaced him as Chief Secretary for Ireland in 1809 (Wellington had just been elevated to the peerage), Croker replaced Wellesley Pole as First Secretary to the Admiralty.

[22] Robert Peel (1788-1850). Secretary for Ireland 1812-1818 where his perceived anti-Catholic attitude earned him the nickname 'Orange Peel'. He was later Home Secretary and Prime Minister. He introduced an organised metropolitan police force for London. The British 'Bobby' (a familiar term for a police officer – now out of fashion) is named after him.

[23] Probably by plunderers looking for money and other valuables. Many wounded from both sides had survived the battle only to be murdered where they lay during the night by stealthy cold-blooded survivors.

[24] Pool, 1967: 30-32. They visited the battlefield on the 27th of July with the Duke and Duchess of Richmond.

Among these was London journalist, John Scott. Standing where Wellington had stood on that fateful Sunday morning, he looked out over the now empty landscape:

'I was struck by the plain of Waterloo. No display, I think, of carnage, violence, and devastation, could have had so pathetic an effect, as the quiet orderly look of its fields, brightened with the sunshine, but thickly strewed with little heaps of up-turned earth, which no sunshine could brighten...

From St. Jean, the road immediately rises up the back of the ridge... The ascent is easy: you reach the top unexpectedly, and the whole field of battle is then at once before the eye. Its sudden burst has the effect of a shock, and few, I believe, are found to put any question for the first five minutes. The point from whence this complete view of the scene, so often pictured in imagination, first presents itself, is one of the most interesting that it includes. It is the summit of the ridge close to the road, over which hangs an old picturesque tree, with a few straggling branches projecting in grotesque shapes from its ragged trunk. The British position extended on the right and left of the road, for the extent of about a mile and three quarters[25], along the top of a continued line of gentle eminences... The tree already mentioned, fixed on the bank above the high road from Brussels to Charleroi, denotes the centre of our position, and the Duke of Wellington having been near it the greater part of the day, it goes by the name of the "Wellington Tree." I found it much shattered with balls, both grape and musket; all of which had been picked out by visitors. Its branches and trunk were terribly splintered. It still retained, however, the vitality of its growth, and will, probably, for many future years, be the first saluting sign to our children and our children's children,... a long survivor of the grand battle in which it was no slight sufferer...

A little way down from this tree, keeping near to the road, is the farm of La Haye Sainte. Here I saw for the first time in my life a specimen of what war does to the habitations of the peaceful. The spectacle was one of horror... The garden was a heap of devastation: hedges were levelled, walls broken down. The door was riddled through and through with all sorts of shot, and furnished a most apalling proof of the fury of the attack, and the determination of the defence... the roofs of the dwelling house and offices were knocked into great holes by bombs and cannon balls: the windows were hideous wrecks,—not a pane of glass remaining in the whole range,—the frames all broken, and the fragments hanging most forlornly[26]...

Turning now again to look back on the English position, the extent of field on the other side of the road from La Haye Sainte, upward to the ridge which is separated from the Wellington tree by the same common track, appeared to have been the theatre of still more terrible combating than any of which we had as yet observed the vestiges. It was here that the Imperial Guard charged upon the hedge where the Highlanders and Scotch Greys were drawn up[27],—and it was here that they were slaughtered... The graves

[25] 2.8 km.

[26] In fact, part of this damage would have been caused when the Nassau infantry sent to reinforce Baring broke holes in the roof to use as firing points, and ripped out the wood of the window frames to build a firing platform (Hamilton-Williams, 1994: 316).

[27] It was not the Imperial Guard, but in the minds of the British public just after the battle, every French attack had been led by the Imperial Guard and every allied repulse had been made by Highlanders (see later).

here lay in large collections,—and pits contained the bodies of hundreds of horses...

neither the battered walls, splintered doors, and torn roofs of the farm houses of La Haye Sainte, astounding as they certainly were,—nor even the miserably scorched relics of what must have been the beautiful Hougoumont,... had, to my mind at least, so direct and irresistible an appeal, as the earthy hillocks which tripped the step on crossing a hedge-row, clearing a fence, or winding along among the grass that overhung a secluded path-way. In some spots they lay in thick clusters and long ranks; in others, one would present itself alone: betwixt these a black scathed circle told that fire had been employed to consume as worthless refuse, what parents cherished, friends esteemed, and women loved. The summer wind that shook the branches of the trees, and waved the clover and the gaudy heads of the thistles, brought along with it a foul stench, still more hideous to the mind than to the offended sense. The foot that startled the small bird from its rest amidst the grass, disturbed at the same time, some poor remnant of a human being[28]'.

Bodies were still being discovered as the reapers harvested those crops that had recovered. Life goes on. The fields were ploughed. Georgiana Capel rode out from Brussels and startled a multitude of crows feasting on the disturbed graves. "Peace which had been scared away, appears almost afraid to return" she thought[29].

France

It fell to Wellington to choose the British name for the battle. That he should choose 'Waterloo' is a little puzzling. Although his headquarters were at Waterloo, the battle was nowhere near the village. The French sensibly called it the Battle of Mont St Jean[30]. To the Prussians, whose main engagement had been in the French lines (and who saw the appropriateness of the name) it was the Battle of La Belle Alliance. It has been suggested Wellington chose a name that had a familiar sound to an English ear. Whatever the reason, the name raises no question today, when *to meet one's Waterloo* speaks for the historical impact of this day of slaughter.

He who met his Waterloo was not captured on the battlefield, although at one time he had to shelter in a square of his Old Guard. His military carriage was found at Genappe and sent to England, where it was purchased and displayed by a certain William Bullock. Napoleon himself made his way to Paris and abdicated (again) on the 22nd of June. After an abortive attempt to obtain a passport for America he left the capital before the allies arrived and travelled to Rochefort, where he surrendered to the British. On the 15th of July he was taken aboard *HMS Bellerophon* – a veteran of Trafalgar known as *Billy Ruffian* to her crew – for transport to Plymouth. Meanwhile the allies had marched into France and on the 24th of June had

[28] Scott, 1816: 201-222 [Scott's narrative has been edited here to change the order of his delivery].

[29] Letter to her grandmother, Lord Uxbridge's mother. Uxbridge had lost a leg but gained an elevation in the peerage. After the battle he was created Marquess of Anglesey (Anglesey, 1955: 138).

[30] French dispatches use this term for La Haye Sainte and the French may have thought they were naming the battle after one of the few positions they captured.

arrived at Cambrai. The town put up some opposition but was soon stormed, the French regular troops retreating to the citadel, the townspeople to their homes. As the allies entered the streets, resistance dissolved. Bill Wheeler wrote home:

'We were as was usual, received by the people with vivas, many of whom had forgot to wash the powder off their lips, caused by biting off the cartridges when they were firing on us from the wall...

The 25th. we halted and His pottle belly Majesty, Louis 18th[31], marched into the loyal town of Cambray. His Majesty was met by a deputation of his beloved subjects who received their father and their king with tears of joy. Louis blubbered over them like a big girl for her bread and butter, called them his children, told them a long rigmerole of nonsense about France, and his family, about his heart, and about their hearts, how he had always remembered them in his prayers, and I don't know what. The presence of their good old fat King had a wonderful effect on their tender consciences, the air rent with their acclamations. The Loyal and faithful soldiers of the Great Napoleon followed their example and surrendered the citadel to their beloved master Old Bungy[32] Louis.

No doubt the papers will inform you how Louis 18th entered the loyal city of Cambray, how his loyal subjects welcomed their beloved king, how the best of monarchs wept over the sufferings of his beloved people, how the Citadel surrendered with acclamations of joy to the best of kings, and how his most Christian Majesty effected all this without being accompanied by a single soldier. But the papers will not inform you that the 4th. Division and a brigade of Hanoverian Huzzars (red) were in readiness within half a mile of this faithful city, and if the loyal citizens had insulted their king, how it was very probable we should have bayoneted every Frenchman in the place. The people well knew this, and this will account for the sudden change in their loyalty or allegiance from their *Idol Napoleon* (properly named) *the Great*, to an old bloated poltroon, the Sir John Falstaff[33] of France.[34]'

Pressing on, the allies pursued the retreating French army to the outskirts of Paris. Jonathan Leach: "we arrived, about the end of June, near St. Denis[35], which town they had barricaded, and appeared determined to defend. Montmartre was in some measure fortified, and looked formidable; but the Prussians having succeeded, after sustaining some loss, in crossing the Seine, and thereby menacing Paris from other points, Marshal Davoust[36], who commanded in the city, sent out a flag of truce; shortly after which the capitulation was agreed on which put the allies in possession of the capital." Paris was entered on the 7th of July. This time the war *was* finally over.

[31] King Louis XVIII was enormously corpulent.

[32] 'Bungy' – a Bedfordshire term for 'intoxicated'; or 'Bungee' – a Somerset term meaning 'short and squat' (Halliwell, 1865).

[33] Sir John Falstaff–an obese character in Shakespeare's play *Henry IV, Parts I-II*.

[34] Liddell Hart, 1994: 176-177.

[35] Then a small town just outside Paris.

[36] Maréchal Louis Nicholas Davout, Duc d'Auerstadt et Prince d'Eckmühl (1770-1823).

— 22 —

Paris

The inhabitants of London would not bear with better grace a
camp of cossacks or imperial guards in Hyde Park, than the
Parisians did the bivouacs of the Tuileries and Champs Eliseés.

Louis Simond (1815)[1]

In London Elford Leach was preoccupied with George Montagu's death
and the conviction that Montagu's extensive museum must not be
dissipated. Beginning to learn the art of subtlety, he engaged the help of
his uncle, Sir William Elford, a former Member of Parliament. In late June
Sir William wrote to Charles Abbott – Speaker of the House of Commons
and one of the British Museum's most active Trustees – extolling the virtues
of Montagu's collection. He offered his services as a negotiator if it were to
be marketed and referred the Trustees to Elford Leach for details[2].

The collection was indeed to be sold, but the Trustees were by no means
sure they wanted it. They responded by deferring consideration to a later
meeting and it would be the following year before the offer was given any
serious thought.

Meanwhile, the annual closure of the Museum for August and September
had arrived. Again Elford applied for leave outside this period, requesting
two months from the beginning of September. The Trustees agreed on
condition his absence did not infringe any of the rules of the House. This
year he would get to France, but during the summer echoes of her recent
conflict were heard in his home town.

Napoleon and Plymouth

HMS Bellerophon arrived off the coast of Devon near Torbay, mid-way
between Plymouth and Exeter, on the 24th of July[3]. After a brief pause she
proceeded to Plymouth Sound where she anchored on the 27th, to the
excitement and jubilation of the townspeople[4]. Napoleon was not allowed
ashore but as he waited aboard for his fate to be decided crowds of tourists
and Plymouth residents flocked to see 'this Fascinating Monster' (as

[1] Simond (1817) **2**: 486.
[2] Letter: Sir William Elford
to The Speaker of the House
of Commons, 26th June 1815
(Loc: British Museum,
Trustees' Manuscripts,
Original Letters and Papers,
3 (1810-1816): 1212).
[3] Newspaper report *in* Kelly
(1828: 263). Tucker, 1846:
419.
[4] Woollcombe's diary (Loc:
West Devon Record Office,
Plymouth. Ref: Catalogue
(701).

HMS Bellerophon (renamed *Captivity*) in her rôle as a prison hulk at Plymouth dockyard in the 1820s (see note 10).

The Western Luminary newspaper called him)[5]. Local boatmen were more than happy to row visitors out to the ship – for a fee – to catch a glimpse of the legend. In response Napoleon, never shy of publicity or public attention, readily made himself visible and hundreds of sightseers made the trip, their boats mobbing the warship. In one of these was Plymouth painter Charles Eastlake.

During the peace Eastlake had travelled to France but when Napoleon arrived from Elba he had returned to Plymouth, and occupied himself painting portraits. As his boat sat alongside the *Bellerophon* the Emperor willingly posed at the entryway and even sent items of clothing ashore to ensure his uniform was portrayed correctly. The result of this informal sitting was Eastlake's first significant painting, *Napoleon at the Gangway of the Bellerophon*. This made a great impression with the public and brought Eastlake to the attention of Regency society. With his new fame and the proceeds from the picture came the freedom to visit the artistic centres of Italy. The following year he moved to Rome[6].

After a week in Plymouth Sound the *Bellerophon* was moved back along the coast to the more secluded Torbay[7]. The allies had reached a consensus regarding the former Emperor's future. His requested asylum in Britain was out of the question. Elba had not contained him; another island within sight of the European mainland was far too close. Instead it was agreed he would be exiled on the most isolated island then under European control, St Helena in the South Atlantic[8]. Even some of his enemies thought this was too harsh[9]. The first Napoleon knew of this decision was when he read about it in the newspapers. He was enraged and swore he would never be taken from the *Bellerophon* alive. Later he calmed down and when given the news officially showed no emotion, but asked if he had a right to appeal. He had not.

[5] Hoskins, 1959: 288-289.
[6] Where he lived until 1830.
[7] On the 4th of August after several people had been killed in the crush of more than 500 small boats.
[8] Orders to the Admiralty dated 30th July 1815 (Kelly, 1828: 265-266). This decision has been credited to John Barrow, Second-Secretary to the Admiralty (mentioned later).
[9] e.g. Letter: Lord Ossulston to Thomas Creevey. "it is difficult not to feel for a man who has played such a part, if he is destined to end his days in such a place as St Helena." (Gore, 1970: 157).

On the 7th of August he was transferred at sea from the *Bellerophon* to *HMS Northumberland* under the command of Admiral Sir George Cockburn, the arsonist of Washington. The next day they began the two month voyage to the South Atlantic[10]. Napoleon Bonaparte would never see Europe again.

Elford Leach had not seen mainland Europe for the first time, but was still determined to do so. With Louis XVIII reinstalled he could finally make his planned trip to Paris, although his anticipated companion, Christen Smith, would be unable to join him. He was still in the Canaries with von Buch.

France

As Elford prepared to travel to Paris the first literary celebrations (and exploitations) of Napoleon's defeat began to appear. Not all lived up to the grandeur of their subject. Georgiana Capel complained to her grandmother from Brussels: 'Has any body read Walter Scott's "Waterloo" to you?[11] I hope, if you have heard it, that you are as much enraged about it as I am, he had better call it "The Towers of Hougoumont" for it is full of *nothing* else—not one word of La Haye Sainte or the Cavalry does he condescend to mention... The fact is Scott came to Brussells with the intention of *writing* a Poem, *par consequence* it is very flat & not altogether correct, for certainly he must have been dreaming when he bestowed *Towers* upon the Farm of Hougoumont[12]'.

Scott's poem was a flop in Britain too and was mercilessly parodied:

> The corse[13] of many a hero slain,
> Lay stiff on the ensanguined plain;
> But none, by sabre or by shot,
> Fell half so flat as Walter Scott[14]

By the time Georgiana vented her spleen, Elford had arrived in the French capital. His visit was well-timed as Jonathan was still in the city with the army of occupation. He too was unhappy with the way the battle was being presented to the public, although inaccurate reporting was perhaps understandable; even those who had fought it were not sure what had happened. Irish Secretary Robert Peel had returned to Dublin where he declared, "I find here plans of the battle from officers who were in the engagement, who have no more notion of it than they have of craniology[15]". Some of the men with Jonathan Leach were finding the journalists equally ignorant:

'In the encampment near St. Denis[16] I one day overheard the following curious dialogue between some soldiers of our division. An Irishman, who was washing his linen under a hedge close to my tent, observed to some of his comrades similarly employed, "I'm tould the newspapers is come out from England, and by J——s[17] thim Highlanders have got all the cridit for

[10] Five weeks later the Royal Navy sold the *Bellerophon* to the Transportation Board. In early 1826 she was fitted out at Sheerness as a convict ship – with the addition of a new under-deck and accommodation for 600 prisoners – and renamed *Captivity*. In June 1826 she was moored at Plymouth dockyard to house convict labourers. She was sold as scrap in 1836 for £4030.

[11] Scott's poem *The Field of Waterloo* was published in October 1815. Georgiana was writing in November.

[12] Anglesey, 1955: 150.

[13] 'Corse' = corpse.

[14] Quoted in Tucker (1846: 395).

[15] Letter: Robert Peel to John Croker, 8th August 1815 (Pool, 1967: 32).

[16] Caldwell & Cooper (1995: 38) say the 1/95th was camped in the village of Clichy (mid-way between St Denis and the Bois de Boulogne) until the 30th of October, then moved to the vicinity of the village of Vaux. They give no authority for this.

[17] Jesus.

the battle." To this, a Highlander, who was on the opposite side of the hedge, and had heard the remark, replied, "And sa they ocht;" meaning thereby, I presume, "so they ought." The Irishman, however, appeared by no means disposed to cede that point, and very naturally proceeded: "Sure, didn't we do our duty as well as any of thim Highland regiments, and lose as miny men?"

I much doubt, nevertheless, whether honest Pat's[18] logic carried with it that conviction to the Highlander which it most indisputably ought to have done. They continued to discuss the point for a considerable length of time, and it terminated, I fancy, in the same manner as all arguments ever do, by each party retaining the same opinions with which they first set out. One cannot but applaud the feeling displayed by the Irishman for the honour of his regiment; and, in good truth, the self-same feeling has manifested itself in hundreds of others, of all ranks and of different regiments, who fought on the bloody fields of Waterloo and Quatre Bras.

No man will deny that the Highlanders displayed invincible courage, and that they nobly upheld the honour of their country and of their respective regiments, in common with their brothers in arms from England and Ireland. The myriads of letters, however, with which the newspapers were constantly inundated for some months after the battle, from Highlanders to their friends in the north, actually had the effect of convincing nine-tenths of the people in England, and nine hundred and ninety-nine out of every thousand in Scotland, that the Scottish regiments were the only people who pulled a trigger on the left of the British position throughout the whole of that protracted struggle, and that they, unaided, defeated the reiterated attacks of the Imperial Legions at that point.

The candid and liberal-minded Scot will neither cavil nor take umbrage at my remarking, that Sir Thomas Picton's division was composed of eight British regiments, three of which were Highland, one (the 1st Royals) Lowland Scotch, and four English or Irish. Whoever has seen that part of the position which our division occupied, need not be informed that every regiment which composed it must necessarily have been exposed in an equal degree to the repeated attacks of the French; and it was therefore utterly impossible that one regiment should have had a smaller or greater degree of pounding than another.

Various panoramic exhibitions have also strongly tended to convince the good people of England, that John Bull and Pat were little better than idle spectators on the left of the British position. In a panorama at Edinburgh, some months after the battle, the Highlanders and Scotch Greys were depicted as giants, and placed in the foremost ranks, cutting, slashing, charging, bayonetting, and sending headlong to the devil, every thing in the shape of a Frenchman; whilst the other poor dear harmless little regiments of the 5th Division were represented as mere pigmies in size and stature, and placed in the background. "Fair play is a jewel, and the devil should have his due".'

[18] 'Pat' (short for 'Patrick') – at that time a general term for any Irishman.

The Occupation of Paris

On their arrival at Paris most of the British troops were put in a tented camp in the Bois de Boulogne – the wood by the village of Boulogne, just outside the city wall. John Croker was in Paris shortly after their arrival and went to sightsee:

"An army encamped does not answer the expectations one entertains of it. It looks more like a fair than anything martial, for you see very few red coats worn. The soldiers had made themselves nice little huts with the boughs and branches of trees, and I think that the mischief they are doing to the wood will in the end improve its beauty, as they break the long formal lines of the rows of trees, and cutting down half-a-dozen leave one or two standing here and there.[19]"

There was less calculated mischief some weeks later when a fierce nocturnal fire destroyed many of these huts, jumping from one to another until an entire row was ablaze. The orange glow reflecting against the sky caused alarm in Paris, but that was nothing compared to the reaction in the camp as a scatter of near-naked soldiers rushed to clear gunpowder out of the flames' path. After that huts were only permitted away from the tented area and at a safe distance from each other[20].

Some Scottish regiments were camped in the Champs Élysées – an open area dotted with houses and muddy paths – where their kilts and bare legs scandalised the local residents. William Surtees was billeted with the owner of the gypsum pits on the side of Montmartre hill, from which the famous Plaster of Paris was obtained[21].

As an echo of the fire, the late summer sky delivered an array of novel amusements. First were the unnaturally colourful, prolonged sunsets (although little did their observers realise the tragic price soon to be paid for these pyrotechnics[22]). As if in concert with the sun's excitement, another technicoloured orb materialised overhead.

"We have nearly had a serious row with the Hanovarian brigade belonging to our division," Bill Wheeler admitted in a letter home, "the following was the cause. A lady having ascended in a balloon at Paris, it came in the direction of our camp. When the Balloon was over the Bois de Bologne the lady detached herself from the Balloon and descended in a parachute in admirable stile[23], the balloon pitched near us and all hands flew to the spot, when a general scramble took place and in a short time it was torn to rags. A battle royal instantly took place between the British and the Hanoverians. Some of the latter ran to their camp and seized their arms, but fortunately the row was stopped without any serious mischief, a few of the belligerents having black eyes and bloody noses.[24]"

This unseemly scramble for aeronautical souvenirs was not the only cause of international friction. The occupation of Paris was diplomatically uncomfortable. The Prussians were determined to seek retribution from the inhabitants for the atrocities committed during the French occupation of

[19] Croker's journal, 15th July 1815 (Pool, 1967: 25).
[20] Selby, 1998: 92.
[21] Surtees arrived from England in July, having taken no part in the Waterloo campaign.
[22] See later.
[23] The first ever parachute jump had been made in 1797 from a balloon at Paris.
[24] Liddell Hart, 1994: 184. The Hanoverians were the 6th Hanoverian Brigade, in the 4th Division.

Place Vendôme, Paris.

Place Vendôme, Paris.

Berlin. Blücher took particular exception to the bridge named to celebrate the Prussian defeat at Jena in 1806, and decided to consign it to the bottom of the Seine. Müffling, who had been appointed Prussian Governor of Paris, disapproved of this, as did Gneisenau, and they conspired with Wellington to have a British sentry posted as a protection, but Blücher was unperturbed. He sent in his demolition teams to blow it up anyway, sentry and all. One charge was exploded but the Prussian engineers were not experienced at bridge demolition and the powder exploded outwards, injuring some of the bombers[25]. The vandals were quickly evicted before more serious structural damage could be done. Blücher, disgusted, then proposed as a consolation to destroy Napoleon's triumphal column in the Place Vendôme. Only the arrival of the King of Prussia put an end to these gunpowder plots[26], but Blücher was still not to be restrained. The Louvre (curiously piebald during a major attempt to clean the dirt from its pale stone[27]) was filled with art treasures plundered from the length and breadth of a subjugated Europe. The peace of 1814 had done nothing to restore these to their countries of origin but the mood was now different and restoration was expected, to the horror of the French. Blücher was in no mood to wait for official negotiations and agreements. He marched his men into the galleries and removed everything that had been looted from Prussia.

This uncompromising attitude of the Prussians to France was reflected daily on the streets. They took from the residents of Paris anything they needed, often with a casual brutality, and were barely less aggressive to the British[28]. Wellington, meanwhile, imposed his usual strict discipline on allied troops, who had to pay for anything obtained.

Despite the tensions, in the fine weather the armies – boosted by the arrival of the Austrians and Russians – gradually relaxed and explored the

25 Stanhope, 1888: 119. Pool, 1967: 25.
26 Wilson (1927) 2: 538-539.
27 Simond (1817) 2: 447.
28 Pool, 1967: 25.

town, playing the tourist in the street cafés and admiring the unfinished Arc de Triomphe; the remaining (and more than impressive) artworks in the Louvre; and the grand pre- and post-revolutionary buildings. Meanwhile the officers sacrificed their income in the shops, cafés and gambling houses of that vast pleasure palace, the Palais Royal.

"It is unnecessary," thought Jonathan, "that I should dwell for an instant on the wonders of Paris: its Louvre, Palais Royal, Boulevards, and a multiplicity of other things of high interest, are too well known to the myriads of my countrymen, who have since seen them, to need description. The swarms of officers and soldiers, British, Hanoverians, Prussians, Russians, Austrians, Dutch, Belgians, Brunswickers, and others, with whom Paris was inundated, and who choked the avenues of the Palais Royal by day and night, were by no means the least interesting objects at that period[29]. Crowds of English families flocked to Paris before we had long occupied it; and there John Bull might be seen, in all his glory, gaping and staring, in every part of the city, at those continental novelties.'

It has to be said, the gaping was mutual. The social seclusion on either side of the Channel during the long period of war had isolated the societies, and fashions of dress had evolved independently. The British tourists may have been gawping at the wonders of France, but to the Parisians it was the British who were the wonders and they drew curious onlookers. The Capels had evoked a similar reaction when they arrived at Dunkirk the previous year: 'we have been walking all over the Town with Papa.' reported Georgiana, 'Crowds of Women & Children follow us with exclamations of wonder, but as they speak low Dutch we can only discover that it is *surprise* which they express... The People are very civil, which however I think they ought to be in gratitude to us for affording them so much amusement.[30]' Although the opportunities for travel during 1814 had removed the primary culture-shock, in 1815 there were still enough differences to maintain an air of curiosity. Across Paris groups of Englishmen in twos and threes could be seen sauntering arm-in-arm (a custom which distinguished them from their French hosts), speaking to no-one but other Englishmen, and criticising everything French[31].

Journalist John Scott arrived from Belgium with an eye for the scene, but also with a thought for its meaning:

[29] Presumably this is a slip of the pen for 'most interesting'. James Stanhope (who was made Assistant Quarter-Master General to the 1st Division just after Waterloo) wrote to book-collector Richard Heber (1774-1833) on the 30th August 1815, "I fear with you our officers will not benefit much by Paris. The houses where play and women are combined attract all, and the former makes large gaps in fortunes: l'autre va sans dire!" [*the other goes without saying*] (Cholmondeley, 1950: 275).
[30] Anglesey, 1955: 42-43.
[31] Simond (1817) 2: 492-495. Simond was in Paris in October 1815, when Elford Leach was there, and had also visited the city in February and March of that year.

Palais Royal, Paris.

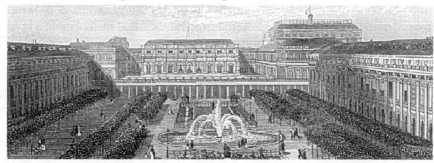

'We saw many of the British privates, sauntering with a lazy air of enjoyment, looking at the print-stalls where they were caricatured, cheapening grapes with the fruit girls, or treating themselves to a glass of lemonade from the portable supplies of that beverage which abound in the streets of Paris. Our officers, too, swarmed about, mounted, some well, and some very badly, for those who could not procure a decent animal, put up with almost any creature that had four legs.

Contrasting themselves remarkably with the heavy cabriolets and clumsy dirty coaches, the awkward calaches and grotesque voitures[32],—English equipages, complete, light, and genteel, glanced rapidly by, spattering, as foreigners, mortification from their wheels on the vehicles of the country. To estimate this exhibition properly, it is necessary to fancy its counterpart displayed by Frenchmen in London: to imagine a French man of fashion, vested with magnificent amplitude of box-coat and commanding longitude of whip, spanking his four blood greys down Bond-street and St. James's-street, or drawing smartly up, in a knowing style of driving, to talk over the topics of the morning with the officer of the French Guards, on duty at the Palace of the King of England![33]'

Parisians did not have to imagine this humiliation, they were living it. French officers in particular were less than enamoured with the hordes of foreign troops treating the French capital as their own and some sought revenge for their discomfort by the only means available – engineering duels with officers of the occupying forces.

In 1815 a demand for 'satisfaction' was still the response of many gentlemen who felt their honour had been slighted, although the practice of duelling had long passed its heyday (Physician George Macilwain thought duelling can be likened to a form of operative surgery. As the insult exists in the mind, having one's brains blown out effectively removes the organ that is causing the problem!)[34]

In occupied Paris one of the favourite methods used by Frenchmen to generate a challenge was to tread deliberately and forcefully on the intended victim's toe. This may have worked with other nations, but John Kincaid noted it did not work with the English:

'As the natural impulse of the Englishman, on having his toe trodden on, is to make a sort of apology to the person who did it, by way of relieving him of a portion of the embarrassment... many thousand insults of the kind passed unnoticed: the Frenchman flattering himself that he had done a bold thing—the Englishman a handsome one[35]'.

Away from the bruising streets, English officers did what English officers always did overseas; they recreated England. Hunting, hare-coursing and horse-racing were their favourite pastimes, and Harry Smith was in the thick of the organisation:

"Our life was now one of continued pleasure and excitement—nothing but parties at night and races by day. At these I was steward. The crowd of

32 These are all styles of horse-drawn carriage.
33 Scott, 1816: 265-266.
34 Macilwain, 1856: 33.
35 Kincaid, 1981: 249-250.

foreign officers being very unruly in riding in after the race-horses, I put some proper fellows of soldiers at the distance-post (who, having resisted many a charge of French cavalry, cared little for an unarmed galloping man), with orders to run the rope across to stop this disorder. My orders were obeyed, as I expected, and that gallant hero, Marshal Blucher, not seeing the rope, rode his horse full speed against it and fell, and in the crash the noble old fellow broke his collar-bone, to my annoyance and distress.[36]"

Sport may have been the pastime of choice, but the British army was also about to receive its ration of culture. On the 23rd of September John Scott made his way to the Louvre and found 150 British riflemen drawn up outside its doors[37]. Months of diplomatic wrangling over restoration of the remaining artworks had finally reached a conclusion and removal of the paintings and sculptures was to begin. Trouble was expected.

Scott joined the crowds of foreign visitors in the galleries – all flocking to Paris to seize the opportunity of finding Europe's greatest treasures in one place before they were again scattered to the winds – but his reverie was soon interrupted.

'I was called from the marbles... by a sudden rushing of feet from without, and, on going to the great stair-case, I saw the English guard hastily tramping up its magnificent ascent: a crowd of astounded French followed in their rear, and, from above, many of the visitors to the Gallery of Pictures were attempting to force their way past the ascending soldiers, catching an alarm from their sudden entrance. We had, in Paris, our daily reports of the probability of convulsions, massacres, insurrections, and what not that was terrible, and the Louvre was by many deemed the spot where the disturbance was most likely to break out, it being there that the highest degree of French exasperation would most probably be kindled...

The alarm, however, was unfounded, but the spectacle that presented itself was very impressive. A British officer dropped his men in files along this magnificent gallery, until they extended, two and two, at small distances, from its entrance to its extremity. All the spectators were breathless, in eagerness to know what was to be done, but the soldiers stopped as machines, having no care beyond obedience to their orders. They proceeded to untie the oil-skins from the locks of their rifles. The bustle, and dust, and buz of the armed men, and of the curious agitated crowds, presented a marked contrast to the tranquil dignity of the Raphaels and Titians on the walls, which nevertheless, were the causes of all this hurley burley...

The work of removal now commenced in good earnest: porters with barrows, and ladders, and tackles of ropes, made their appearance. The collections of the Louvre might from that moment be considered as broken up for ever.[38]'

Most of the removals had been completed by the time the weather finally broke in October, when a sharp frost heralded the approach of winter. With the frost came Elford Leach and his wolf[39].

[36] Smith, 1999: 292-293. After this fall the 72 year old Blücher began to display psychological originality. He informed Wellington that he was now pregnant and was expecting to give birth to an elephant. However, this belief seemed to cause him less distress than his conviction that the father was a French soldier. "Imagine" he said, "that me—me—me ! A *French* soldier !" He never recovered from this belief and was still insisting he was pregnant when he died four years later. (Stanhope, 1888: 119-120, 176). He was quite clearly delusional; the gestation period for an elephant is only 22 months.

[37] Caldwell & Cooper (1995: 38) say these were men of the 2/95th. They give no authority for this.

[38] Scott, 1816: 324-342, 362-366.

[39] He is recorded as having taken his wolf to Paris on at least one of his visits (*English Cyclopædia*). Presumably it was this trip, when he would be able to show the animal to Jonathan.

Jardin des Plantes, Paris.

Elford Leach

Elford had asked to start his vacation at the beginning of September, but was still busy a month later moving birds into Room IX with the shells and fossils[40].

When he did reach this fraught, bustling, cauldron of a city, overflowing with uniforms and uncertainty, he set to work examining the crustacean collections in the natural history museum in the Jardin des Plantes[41]. When the allies first arrived in Paris the Prussians intended to camp some of their troops in the Jardin, but Baron Alexander von Humboldt (an influential Prussian traveller, scientist, and long-standing Paris resident[42]) interceded to avoid the damage this would undoubtedly have caused[43].

Like the Louvre, although without the accompanying public mortification, the natural history museum was under pressure to release

[40] British Museum, Officers' Reports, 1st October 1815.

[41] Different authors call the museum and wider institution by different names at this time as the change from Napoleonic to Royalist régimes caused name alterations. However, old and new names were in vogue simultaneously. By 1818 the museum's headed notepaper was printed with, 'Muséum d'Histoire Naturelle, au Jardin du Roi'. However, contemporary authors still used 'Jardin des Plantes'. By 1823 a history of the museum called it the 'Muséum Royal d'Histoire Naturelle'.

[42] Friedrich Heinrich Alexander, Baron von Humboldt (1769-1859). A student of Werner. His father was Chamberlain to the King of Prussia; his elder brother Karl Wilhelm von Humboldt (1767-1835) was a Prussian government minister; and Alexander was a friend of Prince Friedrich-Wilhelm (1795-1861 – from 1840 Friedrich-Wilhelm IV).

[43] Scott, 1816: 357.

'Georges' Cuvier.

[44] Scott, 1816: 354-357.
[45] This new collection included: 260 quadrupeds; 800 birds; 338 reptiles; 802 fishes; and 300-400 shells (Scott, 1816: 355).
[46] A unified Italy had not yet emerged at this time. Verona was controlled by the Austrian empire.
[47] *English Cyclopædia*.
[48] He spent £41 of his own money buying specimens but was later reimbursed by the Museum.
[49] Letter: W.E. Leach to Speaker of the House of Commons, 6th February 1816 (Loc: British Museum Trustees' Manuscripts. Original Letters and Papers, **3**: 1269-1270).
[50] Antoinette Sophie Laure Duvaucel (1789-1867). For many years was engaged to Londoner Sutton Sharpe (1797-1843) and frequently visited England but they never married. In 1834 she married Contre-Amiral Alexandre Louis Ducrest de Villeneuve (d. 1852). Her brother Alfred (1792-1825), a naturalist, collected in the far east. He travelled to India in 1817 and died there in August 1825. Some of his collections were divided between the Museums of Paris and London.

Sophie Duvaucel.

part of its collections to the allies. Rumours were rife and, not unexpectedly, exaggerated. It was claimed the allies were not only requiring the museum to restore collections taken from other nations, but were also planning to remove from collections originally made by France whatever was needed to complete their own. Fortunately this was quickly shown to be untrue[44]. Some restitution, however, was required.

Twenty years earlier the French had over-run the former Dutch Republic, and Paris had acquired part of that national collection. This should now have been returned but an amicable agreement was reached between the Netherlands and the museum, in which Paris would keep the original Dutch collection and provide Holland with an entirely new collection from its holdings of duplicates[45].

A similar arrangement was reached with Austria, which had lost part of its collection of fish from Verona[46]. Paris would keep the fish and Austria would accept birds in exchange.

As the victorious powers haggled with the Jardin's administrators, Elford Leach explored the museum while his wolf sat outside for hour upon hour, calmly waiting for him[47]. He spent his free time exploring Monsieur Sallée's natural history boutique in the Place Vendôme, buying insects for his own collection. He also bought specimens in Paris for the British Museum (although he does not appear to have had approval for this[48]) but he was not just travelling for his own interests. He had also been asked by the Speaker of the House of Commons to gather information about the administration of the museum, "with a view to improve our own establishment and to render it on an equal footing with that of France[49]".

Contacts

© Le Louvre

His work aside, Elford was finally able to meet the professors whose books he had been reading for so many years, including Cuvier and Lamarck. Even more pleasing, he met Cuvier's 25 year old step-daughter Sophie Duvaucel[50]. Her father had been guillotined in 1794 during The Terror and her mother married Cuvier ten years later. They then had four children of their own in addition to the four children from Madame Cuvier's earlier marriage. Sophie – bright and educated – helped host Cuvier's Saturday evening open house, but received a great deal of attention in her own right[51]. Elford seems to have taken quite a shine to her.

The Chevalier de Lamarck was the Museum's elderly professor of invertebrate zoology. After a lifetime of research he had concluded species were not, in fact, unchanging, but had evolved over time. He called this 'transformism'. His ability to think in this way was perhaps a function of his age. Now 71, his ideas were rooted in the eighteenth century view of the world as a *progressive* arrangement displaying a move towards perfection. Younger thinkers such as Cuvier had been brought up in a later view which stressed divine order – everything in its proper place. Cuvier believed firmly in the fixity of species.

Lamarck proposed that species were descended from other species, which had originally been spontaneously generated. He believed changes occurring in an animal's body during its life could be passed to its offspring (although he could not say how)[52]. An animal reaching up to graze on the branches of trees would stretch its neck and its offspring would then be born with longer necks (he thought). After a number of generations, a giraffe would evolve. This erroneous theory is known as 'the inheritance of acquired characteristics' and Lamarck is remembered today mainly for having proposed it. His views were widely rejected, but by contributing to the discussion and promotion of evolution, he helped pave the way for serious consideration of Natural Selection as an evolutionary mechanism fifty years later.

In 1815 Lamarck was engaged in writing one of his major works, a four volume treatise on animals without backbones (the invertebrates), *Histoire Naturelle des Animaux sans Vertèbres*. This was not to be published until the whole work had been printed[53] but Elford acquired an early copy of the first volume. He also bought 200 crustaceans collected by Lamarck and would later refer to him as "my kind-hearted and excellent friend.[54]"

Petalura gigantea Leach

Illustration from the
Zoological Miscellany
July 1815

Elford was not the only former Edinburgh medical student who travelled to mainland Europe in 1815. His old classmate Robert Grant was also taking advantage of the peace. Grant had graduated MD at Edinburgh the previous year, but from 1815 to 1820 he visited universities in France, Germany, Switzerland and Italy, and spent two years at the museum in Paris studying with Lamarck and some of the other professors. Grant emerged from Paris a

*Epeira giga*s Leach

Illustration from the
Zoological Miscellany
October 1815

51 The writer 'Stendhal' (Marie Henri Beyle, 1785-1842), author of *Le Rouge et le Noir* (1831), was said to be very attached to her. see *Dictionnaire de Biographie Française*, **12**: 1010 ('Duvaucel').
52 These conclusions were published six years earlier in the work *Philosophie zoologique*.
53 Letter: W.E. Leach to Jameson, [4th] January 1816 (Loc: University of Edinburgh Library, Special Collections. Ref: Gen. 129/141).
54 Leach, 1852: 179.

committed believer in evolution along Lamarckian lines and it was this view he would express to his own student and friend Charles Darwin back at Edinburgh. Darwin admitted in his autobiography he may have been induced to think about evolution by hearing Lamarck praised so enthusiastically (In 1827 Grant moved to the new London University where he began promoting evolution[55] in his zoology courses, virtually the only British professor to do so before *The Origin of Species* in 1859[56]).

Elford's friend William Spence was also on the Continent, spending four months after Waterloo visiting entomological contacts and showing them the first volume of the *Introduction to Entomology* which he and Kirby had just produced[57].

Meanwhile, with Elford and other British naturalists making themselves known in Paris, back in London Joseph Banks was involved in the planning for an altogether more formal British overseas initiative.

The Congo

In 1795, at Banks' recommendation, the African Association[58] had employed a young Scottish surgeon, geographer and naturalist, Mungo Park[59], to explore the course of the river Niger. This expedition was followed by a second in 1805 in which Park lost his life, but not before he had explored much of the upper reaches of the river. Europeans, however, still wondered whether the Niger discharged into another great West African waterway, the River Congo (or 'River Zaire'). It was partly to answer this question that a Royal Navy expedition now proposed to sail up the Congo from the sea, this being deemed more likely to succeed than another attempt to pass down the Niger. To navigate the river against the flow the navy was intending to use a small (100 tons) custom-built paddle-steamer with a draught of

[55] Still Lamarck's view of evolution.
[56] Gardiner, 1999: 5-12.
[57] Kirby & Spence, 1859: 602.
[58] Correctly *The Association for Promoting the Discovery of the Interior Parts of Africa.*
[59] Mungo Park (1771-1806). Born near Selkirk, 7th child (of 13) of Mungo Park Snr and his wife Elsbeth (née Hislop). Apprenticed to local surgeon Thomas Anderson then studied medicine at Edinburgh University. His brother-in-law, James Dickson (1738-1822), was one of the founders of the Linnean Society. At Joseph Banks' suggestion Park was employed by the East India Company as ship's surgeon on the *Worcester* for a voyage to Sumatra in 1792-1793, where he collected new species of fish. On the 2nd of August 1799 he married Alison Anderson (b.1780), daughter of Thomas and his wife Elizabeth ('Betty') (née Waugh). Mungo and Alison had four children: Mungo (christened 19th June 1800); Elizabeth (b. 9th September 1801); Thomas (born 29th March 1803); and Archibald (christened 15th January 1805).

An early steamer at Plymouth.

only 1.2 metres, the *Congo*. Paddle steamers were a relatively new invention (the first seen in Plymouth called into the port this year, 1815) and this would have made the *Congo* the Royal Navy's first engine-powered vessel. Unfortunately a breakdown in communications between the naval architects and the steam engineers resulted in a mismatch between plan and reality[60]. With the engine fitted the ship drew too much water and was too slow, so the captain had it removed. Instead, the *Congo* was schooner rigged and entered the navy list as a sloop of 10 guns, but her maximum speed never exceeded 5½ knots and there were many in the navy who believed she would not even survive the voyage across the Bay of Biscay. In fact she proved very sea-worthy. The ship *Dorothy* (350 tons) was to accompany her as a transport as far as the river's mouth[61].

In accordance with Admiralty custom this expedition was to carry naturalists, and as usual Banks had been asked to recommend them. After several abortive attempts to make the appointments, he was waiting for Elford Leach to return from Paris to advise him[62].

When Elford spoke to Banks shortly after his return at the end of November[63] he saw an opportunity. He had promised his collector Jack Cranch that he would use his influence to obtain a position for him at the British Museum. What better way for Cranch to come to the Trustees' notice than as naturalist to a high-profile Admiralty expedition to an unexplored region of Africa? Cranch was duly approached. He too saw the advantage of this appointment but was not exactly overjoyed at the invitation. His wife had recently given birth to their second child[64] and only after some painful soul-searching (apparently occasioned by no small foreboding[65]) did he agree to accept. He would be paid £250, increased to £300 on successful completion, but it would mean not seeing his wife and young family for nearly a year.

In addition to Cranch the expedition would need a botanist. Banks had previously rejected several on the grounds their botanical draughtsmanship was not up to the

[60] Rice, 1986: 42.
[61] Tony Rice (1986: 58), who has explored the archives, calls this vessel *HMS Dorothea*, but as contemporary expedition accounts refer to the *Dorothy* we have preferred this name here.
[62] Letter: Banks to John Barrow (1764-1848) Second Secretary to the Admiralty, 1st December 1815 (Dawson, 1958: 36).
[63] He made a report to the Trustees dated the 23rd of November.
[64] Charlotte Cranch. Christened 16th July 1815 at the Ebenezer Independent Chapel, Kingsbridge.
[65] Anon., 1818: 328.

Pogonius levaillantii Leach

Illustration from the *Zoological Miscellany* December 1815

Ibacus peronii Leach
(crustacean)

Illustration from the
Zoological Miscellany
December 1815

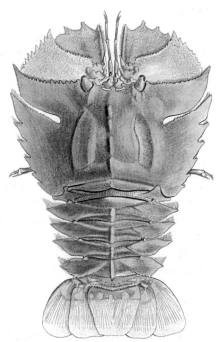

required standard[66]. However, just as the decision was needed, von Buch and Christen Smith returned from the Canaries. Smith readily agreed to join the Congo expedition with responsibility for the plants and was given the assistance of a botanist from the royal gardens at Kew, David Lockhart. Cranch was appointed as 'Collector of Objects of Natural History'. William Tudor, a surgeon and comparative anatomist, was enrolled to collect material for the Royal College of Surgeons and to act as geologist, and all the collecting would be augmented by the efforts of a mineralogist and 'gentleman volunteer', Edward Galwey[67]. The expedition leader would be Commander James Tuckey[68].

With the personnel in place, arrangements were made for a spring departure and Cranch astutely curried favour with Charles König by donating a box of minerals to the British Museum.

Elford now prepared the December issue of the *Zoological Miscellany*, including in it some specimens he had examined at Paris. He appears to have provided the previous months' issues either by preparing them before he left or by sending the text from France. The December issue completed volume 2, but with this the *Miscellany* came to a halt. It is not clear why production ceased but the relationship between Elford and the Nodders cannot have been warmed by the appearance earlier in the year, in the *Edinburgh Encyclopædia*, of Elford's critique of Shaw's *Naturalist's Miscellany*, a work which the Nodders still stocked and were trying to sell, and which had been illustrated by Richard Nodder's late father:

"a work which we scarcely consider as worthy of notice, it is entitled the *Naturalist's Miscellany*, or, as it is also termed, *Vivarum Naturæ*, by G. Shaw; the figures by P. Nodder. It contains a variety of daubed, (or, as they are termed, coloured) figures of the more beautiful and larger exotic insects, as well as other animals, with descriptions extremely suitable to the general class of readers, (children,) for whose purpose, we conjecture, it was designed by its author, who, with greater advantages than any other naturalist in this country, has produced this publication, which, we are sorry to state, reflects the highest disgrace on the class of readers who could give encouragement to so contemptible a performance.[69]" Ouch!

[66] Dawson, 1958: 36.
[67] Or 'Galway' (per Barrow *in* Dawson, 1958: 36). The 2nd son of Edward Galwey, a banker of Mallow, Ireland, Tuckey's home town.
[68] James Kingston Tuckey (1776-1816). Born Mallow, County Cork, Ireland. See biographical notes in Dawson (1969: 67-70).
[69] *Edinburgh Encyclopædia*, 9(1): entry for ENTOMOLOGY at p. 70.

1816

Despite the ending of the monthly *Miscellany* issues, Elford did not have less work for long. He had obviously impressed the scientists at Paris, especially with his knowledge of the Crustacea, and was given the singular honour of being invited to contribute entries for a new edition of a French encyclopaedia being edited by Cuvier's brother, Frédéric Georges Cuvier[70], the *Dictionnaire des Sciences Naturelles*[71]. De Blainville was providing entries on the molluscs.

In Paris Jonathan's relationship with France was being reinforced too. A treaty had been concluded with the allies under which an army of occupation of 150,000 men would remain for five years – at French expense – stationed mainly towards France's borders. The 1st and 2nd battalions of the 95th were to be part of this force[72] and by January it was the turn of the 1/95th to leave Paris. They marched to their new quarters around 'the loyal city' of Cambrai, near the border with Belgium, where Jonathan's company was quartered at Moeuvres. Harry Smith (who, like Jonathan, was now Lieutenant-Colonel Harry Smith *CB*) was appointed Town Major for Cambrai[73], reporting to the town's commandant, Sir Andrew Barnard, now recovered from his Waterloo wound.

Here the officers would spend the next few years living the life of country gentlemen, which certainly suited Jonathan:

[70] Frédéric Georges Cuvier (1773-1838).
[71] His entries were first commissioned in 1816 (Desmarest, 1825: V).
[72] The 3/95th was sent to Ireland.
[73] Hathaway (1997: 290) mistakenly says Smith returned to England.

Historical note

1816	An electric telegraph is built in Britain 8 miles (12.9 km) in length.
—	The new *Regent Street*, being developed from Carlton House in the south, is halted at Piccadilly.
—	Rossini[1] produces *The Barber of Seville* in Rome.
—	With the end of the war the final units of infantry *Volunteers* (part-time soldiers) are disbanded, but the mounted *Yeomanry* volunteers, although reduced in number, are retained.
18th March	Income tax (introduced to pay for the war) ends, but candles, soap, paper, beer, tea and sugar are all taxed heavily.
February	Machine-breaking at Huddersfield.
April to June	Food riots, machine-breaking and arson in Norfolk, Suffolk, Cambridgeshire and Essex.
July to August	Food riots in England.
October	Disturbances among colliers and iron-workers in Wales.
November to December	Food riots in England.

[1] Gioacchino Antonio Rossini (1792-1868). Lived in Naples at this time.

Jonathan Leach's
Waterloo Medal.

© William P.C. Adams

"Those who were fond of field-sports indulged in them to their hearts' content; and I was among the number who did so. Game was very plentiful, and a finer country for coursing is no where to be found. There were several packs of fox-hounds and harriers belonging to different divisions of the army, and greyhounds without number. At Valenciennes we had races frequently, and some decent nags[74] found their way out from England. Champagne, Burgundy, Claret, and other orthodox fluids, were abundant; and the greater part of the army would willingly have protracted their stay a dozen years longer in those quarters."

Shortly after they arrived at Cambrai all those who had fought during the three days of the 16th-18th June were presented with medals sent out by the British government. On one side was the head of the Prince of Wales surrounded by 'GEORGE P. REGENT', on the other an elegant winged Victory holding a palm branch and an olive branch (to indicate that peace resulted from this battle). Victory was surmounted by the word 'WELLINGTON' and seated over 'WATERLOO JUNE 18. 1815'. The edge of Jonathan Leach's was stamped 'Lt. COLONEL J. LEACH 1ST. BATT. 95TH REGT FOOT'. The ribbon was scarlet with royal blue borders[75].

In the British army it was usually only the senior officers commanding regiments at major engagements who were decorated. Waterloo was virtually the first time the rank and file received medals[76]. This was Wellington's idea. He made the recommendation ten days after the battle and proposed all men, regardless of rank, receive the same decoration[77].

[74] 'nags' – Slang: 'horses'.
[75] The medal was designed by the Royal Mint's chief engraver, Thomas Wyon Jnr (1792-1817).
[76] There had been a medal in 1650 for the Battle of Dunbar, but that had been different for different ranks (Liddell Hart, 1994: 185).
[77] Liddell Hart, 1994: 185-186. Cotton, 1895: 232.

Falmouth harbour,
Cornwall.

This was not the only honour bestowed on the riflemen. On the 23rd of February 1816 the 95th Regiment, as a unique distinction for its continuous front-line actions throughout the Peninsula War and at the Battle of Waterloo, was removed from the numbered Regiments of the Line and given its own designation in the British army. It would henceforth be known simply as 'The Rifle Brigade'.

Also on the 23rd of February, in England, the expedition for the Congo set sail from Sheerness and headed out into the English Channel. The intrepid explorers had an inauspicious start. They spent the first month fighting adverse winds within sight of the English coast. It was the 19th of March before they set sail again, this time in earnest, from Jack Cranch's old collecting grounds at Falmouth. It would be another three and a half months before they reached the mouth of the Congo, and as they sailed south Jack may not have realised his wife was now expecting their third child.

Montagu's Collection

Elford decided it was time to make a renewed attack on the Trustees in an effort to convince them to buy Montagu's specimens. He had to report his findings from Paris to Charles Abbott, so he linked to this an observation that he had now received catalogues of Montagu's museum (which he said included the finest collection of British birds ever assembled; nearly all the shells, corals and other zoophytes[78] inhabiting the British coasts; rare fishes; British reptiles and the smaller British quadrupeds; and a good collection of British insects and crustaceans) and he had calculated its value as £1200.

Trying a technique which had worked once before, he said if the Trustees agreed to the purchase, he would add to it his private collection of British

[78] 'Zoophytes' – literally 'animal-plants', simple polyp-like animals whose colonies have a branching plant-like form. Today most are classified as hydroids or bryozoans ('moss animals').

animals. He explained that for years the main aim of his own fieldwork had been to create a complete collection of British animals, and this now comprised:

> '1. British insects consisting of the most extensive series yet brought together, nearly 8000 species all in the best state of preservation;
> 2. British Crustacea, Spiders and Myriapoda, 530 species in perfect state of preservation;
> 3. British shells (nearly all that have been discovered on the British shores) together with their inhabitants (This collection being formed with different views from that of M[r] Montagu will be nearly equally interesting to the Naturalist);
> 4. British corals and coralines dried;
> 5. British Echinodermata, such as Starfishes, Sea-eggs &c, the largest assemblace [sic] yet formed, all in good preservation;
> 6. Intestinal worms; including those inhabiting Man and other British animals[79];
> 7. A few zoophytes in spirits, from Devon and Scotland.[80]'

This collection had cost him £3000 to assemble. Its commercial value was about £600, but the Museum could have it free of charge if they purchased Montagu's. The only condition Elford sought was that the Trustees would waive the regulation prohibiting officers taking museum material off the premises. He wanted permission to take parts of his current collection to his home for study if it became Museum property. Sir Joseph Banks, he said, approved "most thoroughly" of the purchase.

The problem for the Trustees was the cost. As they approached the end of the financial year, their Natural History spending was heading for a deficit. The grant for 1815-1816 was £250 and they had spent nearly £577. The shortfall would have to be made up from the Museum's General Fund[81]. Another £1200 was not available. However, the Trustees accepted the value to the Museum of Montagu's collection, especially with the no-cost bonus of Elford's. They resolved to apply to the government for permission to commit funds anyway and Banks wrote to the Lords of the Treasury recommending approval.

Within weeks the Trustees had changed their mind. They now decided they might have to ask for large sums of money for "more important" objects, and withdrew their request to the Treasury. These more important objects were probably the marble sculptures from the Parthenon in Athens, brought to Britain by Lord Elgin[82] in 1806 ('The Elgin Marbles'). These were on

[79] This wording might suggest he was grouping humans with other animals, not holding them distinct, but this cannot be assumed. It is probable this is simply unfortunate punctuation. The "and other British animals" is presumably intended to be in the list after '6'. Zoophytes, as distinct from animals, are considered in '7' (although today we would recognise that group as true animals – bryozoans, hydroids, etc.)
[80] Letter: W.E. Leach to the Speaker of the House of Commons, 6th February 1816 (Loc: British Museum, Trustees' Manuscripts, Original Letters and Papers, **3** (1810-1816): 1269-70).
[81] House of Commons, 1835: pp. 301-302. The financial year ended on 25th March.
[82] Thomas Bruce, 7th Earl of Elgin (1766-1841). For the history of the British acquisition of the Elgin Marbles see Smith (1916).

Burlington House

(now the home of the
Royal Academy of Arts)

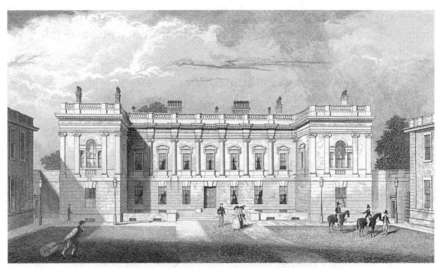

display to artists in side-premises at Burlington House in Piccadilly, but with the pending sale of Burlington House they were to be transferred to the British Museum which had been negotiating for their acquisition since 1810.

By June the Trustees had changed their minds again (possibly because there was now a Bill before Parliament advocating a special grant of funds for the Elgin Marbles, relieving the Museum of the cost). They negotiated a price of £1100 for Montagu's collection, to be paid in instalments over three years with 5% per annum interest to be paid on the outstanding sum until the final payment, this interest to be paid every six months. This plan to spread the financial burden was accepted and Montagu's specimens were finally destined to join the collections in the Museum.

Interestingly it was Eliza Dorville who was to receive the purchase money, despite having no legal relationship with George Montagu. Presumably the collection had become her property under the terms of his Will. She never did receive any instalments of the main sum. The Museum made only the first two interest payments, then nothing. After 16 months her patience understandably wore thin. In November 1818 she wrote a pointed letter from Florence requesting the £1100 for the 'Knowlean Museum' be paid to her London bankers. The Trustees responded by paying the interest they owed her and expressing their hope of being able to transfer the balance by the following summer. She had to wait until July 1819 before they finally approved the payment of the £1100, with more outstanding interest.

— 23 —

The year without a summer

I had a dream, which was not all a dream.
The bright sun was extinguish'd, and the stars
Did wander darkling in the eternal space,
Rayless, and pathless, and the icy earth
Swung blind and blackening in the moonless air;
Morn came and went—and came, and brought no day,
And men forgot their passions in the dread
Of this their desolation; and all hearts
Were chill'd into a selfish prayer for light.

The opening lines of Byron's *Darkness* capture the mood of 1816, 'The year without a summer'. Two months before Waterloo, just south of Borneo, the volcano Tambora had exploded with the force of a hundred hydrogen bombs – the largest volcanic explosion in history[1]. Ten thousand people were killed outright and the blast was heard as far away as Malaya[2]. Ash rained down for more than 1000 km and on surrounding islands it buried everything; 80,000 inhabitants starved to death. Enough land was thrown into the sky to blanket the whole of England to a depth of more than a metre[3] and a finger of fiery cloud reached up and touched the edge of space[4], shrouding the planet in dust and chemical haze. It was this that had caused the brilliant sunsets in Europe in the autumn of 1815. The atmospheric pollution disrupted global weather patterns for years. In the summer of 1816 it snowed in the United States and in Europe, burying the struggling crops. Harvests failed. Despair was rife.

In April 1816 Byron left England for the Continent, driven out by an undercurrent of scandal. By the summer, when he wrote *Darkness*, he was living on the shores of Lake Geneva, with Tambora's influence in full spate. One particularly stormy night in June Percy Shelley and 19 year old Mary Godwin[5] were among his visitors. The weather was so bad the guests were confined to the villa and for amusement Byron suggested they each write a ghost story. Although it took several days for the creative spark to animate Mary Godwin, when it did she penned her gothic tale *Frankenstein*[6]. We owe the existence of this book – one of the most enduring horror-stories in the English language – to a volcanic eruption on the other side of the world (A direct influence of geology on literature. Werner would have been proud).

[1] On the official scale of 0-8 this was a 7, a 'super-colossal' explosion. For details see Stothers (1984).
[2] More than 2000 km away.
[3] About 150 cubic km of ash, 25 cubic km of ignimbrite, and pumice. In 1980 Mount St Helens ejected 1 cubic km.
[4] The material appears to have reached an altitude of 20,000-50,000 m (65,000-165,000 feet).
[5] Mary Godwin (1797-1851). The mother of Shelley's son, William (b. 24 January 1816; died 1819). They married on the 30th December 1816 (Shelley's first wife having committed suicide earlier in the year while pregnant by drowning herself in the Serpentine, a stretch of water in Hyde Park, London)
[6] *Frankenstein, or, The Modern Prometheus* was published anonymously two years later by which time she was Mrs Mary Shelley.

The Capels too were now on the shores of Lake Geneva, having struggled from Brussels through an incessant downpour. The countryside was bleak. A depressed Caroline wrote to her mother in July: "the Oldest Man in the country does not remember the price of Bread so high as it is at this time—The dreadfull & tremendous rains which have now continued so long are the cause of this, the Vineyards are totally spoilt as well as the Corn, & the greatest scarcity is apprehended. The same accounts are received from Italy & your letter mentions the bad Weather in England— Heaven defend us from a Famine! sometimes I have the most gloomy forebodings – I mean on general concerns – The fear of the end of the world has also pervaded this Country"[7].

London

The weather affected the poor far more than the privileged. The end of hostilities had deprived thousands of people of their livelihoods. A national economy rooted for nearly twenty years in war had not yet been reorganised for peace, and the expected export markets for the products of the new manufacturers had failed to materialise. Demobilisation of the army had added 400,000 men to an already depressed labour market. Thrown into unemployment, now they were starving too. On the streets civil unrest and calls for political reform increased, but in the British Museum the work went on.

Elford was arranging the Museum's birds and insects but, despite his boundless energy, was finding the repetitive journey from his room in the basement to the zoological collections on the first floor a strain. In March König had applied to have a new door knocked through from Room XI to the back staircase, to allow the Spirit Room to be converted to a work-area for him, but the Trustees refused.

Room XI now contained some stuffed mammals, with fish in glass cases on the walls, but Elford and König had a better plan for this room. With Montagu's collection, and the addition of Elford's, it would be possible to devote an entire public gallery to a display of British animals. Elford's friend James Stephens obviously approved as he offered to donate from his own collection any species still required, as long as he could obtain leave of absence from the Admiralty Office to sort through his material. It was about this time that Stephens introduced Elford to one of his young contacts, a sixteen year old medical student called John Edward Gray[8].

J.E. Gray

Gray had family connections with the British Museum; his great-uncle Edward[9] had been Under Librarian for Natural History for 19 years until his death in 1806. George Shaw had been his assistant.

John Gray's father trained as a surgeon and apothecary, but had a strong interest in natural history and lectured to medical students in botany, *Materia Medica* and pharmaceutical chemistry. Gray himself was a druggist's

[7] Anglesey, 1955: 168-169.
[8] John Edward Gray (1800-1875). See Gunther, 1975 and 1980a.
[9] Edward Whitaker Gray (1748-1806). Secretary to the Royal Society under Sir Joseph Banks. See Gunther (1976).

[10] In 1821 his father Samuel Frederick Gray (1766-1828) published *A Natural Arrangement of British Plants* with his sons' help.

[11] König thought having unknown persons working in his department was an "enormous irregularity" which should be stopped immediately (Gunther, 1978: 92).

[12] Gray says the attendant was 'Saunder' (Gunther, 1974: 56). König mentions a 'Saunders' in his diary for 18th September 1820. Records show a William Sanders who, with William Church, was one of the attendants in Natural History by 1820-1821 (House of Commons, 1835, Appendix 3(5): 370-377) but allowing for misspelling the name was probably Saunders. John George Children says an attendant Frederick Saunders came to Natural History after 1821 (House of Commons, 1836: para. 2862).

[13] J.E. Gray (House of Commons, 1836: para. 2456).

[14] His handwriting indicates he had difficulty with this word. He may have meant 'Paracelsial'. Paracelsus (the chosen name of Theophrastus Bombastus von Hohenheim: 1493-1541) was a renowned medical practitioner of the 16th century whose work would have been known to Elford. Although Paracelsus had no contact with Paris, the Jardin des Plantes included a garden of medicinal plants and Elford may simply have been using the term 'Paracelcial Garden' to mean the Jardin des Plantes.

[15] Letter: W.E. Leach to Duvaucel, "June 8th". The year is not stated but circumstances suggest 1816 (Loc: Bibliothèque Centrale, Muséum National d'Histoire Naturelle, Paris).

assistant, and studied medicine in his spare time, but he was sufficiently knowledgeable about botany to give lectures to other medical students and to lead field trips at Battersea Fields, on the south bank of the Thames west of Elford's home. At weekends he would head off into the open countryside to collect plants, insects, shells, and anything else that took his fancy, sleeping under a hedge or in a haystack, and returning for work on Monday. It was during one of these excursions he had met James Stephens.

Gray was already familiar with the concept of natural classifications[10] and with the published works of Cuvier, Lamarck and Latreille. Elford warmed to him immediately, inviting him to the Museum to assist with the arrangement of the insect and shell collections (This was almost certainly an informal arrangement; it is doubtful König or the Trustees would have approved[11]). Elford also took Gray with him when he went to Battersea Fields to collect insects with one of the natural history department's attendants[12], which he did frequently at this time.

Through this collaboration Elford encouraged Gray to concentrate on zoology rather than botany, which Gray was more than happy to do despite zoology's reputation in Britain as a poor relation to the other branches of natural history, and one which few people chose to study.

When not tutoring Gray, Elford pressed on with the arrangement of the British animals. The reorganisation of the room to house them would require some structural alterations and the construction of new display cases, but the government's Board of Works, which carried out any alterations to the fabric of the Museum, had its own priorities and the work was slow. The zoological rearrangement also had to take its place among Elford's other duties. Meanwhile these ground to a halt in April when he was turned out of his room in the basement so the builders could shore-up the floor of Room VIII of the library, directly above him.

It would actually be another two and a half years before the British gallery opened to the public[13], but as a first step the collection could be sorted and listed. Meanwhile Elford had not seen his parents since 1814, and wanted to get home to Devon this year, as he explained in a letter to Sophie Duvaucel. He had kept in touch with Cuvier's stepdaughter and had sent her a small gift. His affectionate note is the most personally expressive of the correspondence we currently have by him:

"In future, I will obey the terms agreed on between us to the very letter, but you must say nothing on the subject of the books and pencils, which, I destined as a present. Do employ me as your commissioner and I will execute your orders and even make known the costs. Do therefore give me your orders and they shall duly be executed.

I assure you "giddy creature" that I am going neither to Orkney nor Teneriff. I shall only visit my Father, whom I have not seen for nearly two years. I wish that I could visit the Parasilsial[14] Garden, this year, but as it is impossible to do it in person, I must be contented by doing so in my dreams. Adieu.[15]"

It seems Elford was harbouring a desire, but the Orkneys were not to be on his itinerary this year. In fact vacations this year could be a problem. Montagu's collection was still in Devon and until it was retrieved and sorted Stephens could not make his planned donations. Elford set off at the beginning of July to collect Montagu's material. Meanwhile he asked the Trustees to apply to the Admiralty Office to have the use of Stephens' time in August[16].

Elford obviously did not like the idea of losing his August holiday. He still applied for the usual two months leave, but knowing this would start late and would again have to run into the time when the Museum was open to the public, he reinforced his application.

As the Trustees had resolved to confine their attentions to British zoology (he noted), he wished permission to be absent for two months "to visit the British Isles and such parts of the Coast of Britain as produce peculiar Species of Zoology, for the purpose of collecting them for the Museum". This was a ploy. He would actually go to the West Country as usual, although he did plan to collect animals, and to visit northern Cornwall, a coastline he had not seen before. To help the Trustees make the right decision he also offered to give up all short vacations, single holidays and Saturdays to compensate for the time he would be away.

Perhaps surprisingly, given that he was already in Devon by the time he made the request, the Trustees accepted these terms, but said he had to agree never to absent himself on such excursions without talking to the Principal Librarian first. It sounds as though he had left for Devon without telling anyone.

He returned with Montagu's collection (except the shells, which he left for his next trip) and some additional specimens from Charles Prideaux. By the end of August he had obtained the extra material from Stephens, who was later thanked for donating "several Birds and Shells, and about four Hundred Insects, not before in the Museum[17]". Unfortunately the Board of Works' craftsmen were extremely busy at this time constructing minstrels' galleries (raised walkways) in some of the public rooms[18] and erecting a large temporary building in the garden, west of the Townley Gallery, to house the Elgin Marbles, which had just been transferred to the Museum[19]. There had been no time to make display cases for Room XI and there was still nowhere to display Montagu's specimens. Everything, including his famous bird collection, had to go down into the basement – the Museum's all-devouring sarcophagus[20].

If Elford could not display the specimens, he could at least catalogue some of them. He prepared a list of the Museum's holdings of British quadrupeds and birds, adding the species that were still needed, and had this printed. This 'catalogue' was almost certainly intended primarily as a set of printed labels for the specimens[21]. Each entry includes only a scientific name, common name, collection locality and donor. There is no other text and the labels are in two columns down the page. No publisher is mentioned.

16 British Museum, Officers' Reports, vol. 4, Leach, 2nd July 1816; König's Diary, 13th July 1816.

17 British Museum Trustees' Committee Meeting Minutes, 11th January 1817.

18 Robert Smirke (House of Commons, 1836: para. 5425).

19 On the 8th August 1816. The temporary gallery opened to the public in January 1817.

20 'Sarcophagos' – Greek: 'flesh eater' (Sarcophagos was originally a type of limestone which, like quicklime, consumed corpses encased in it).

21 As noted by Osbert Salvin (1882: [iii]).

The temporary Elgin Marble gallery built during 1816 in the garden of Montagu House.

However, Elford seems to have had extra copies printed (or there may have been a minimum print run) and he circulated this list, which openly solicited additional donations, noting, "Any species, sex, or accidental variety that is not enumerated in this Catalogue will be an acquisition to the collection, and the name of the donor will be constantly registered.[22]" To emphasise this he gave a separate list of some of the donors who had already contributed, which included his brother George and uncle Sir William.

We do not know how many copies of this work were printed, but it seems few people kept it. By 1836 even John Gray had difficulty finding one[23]. However, despite the absence of any accompanying descriptions, Elford's names, especially for the birds, were used by many subsequent authors – much to the disgust of others. When the catalogue was reprinted in 1882 by the Willughby Society the editor, Osbert Salvin, claimed the chief value of the reprint was that it showed "the worthlessness of the Tract, and that far higher consideration has been set upon it by writers on European birds than it at all merits.[24]"

It does not seem to have been well received at the time either[25]. Certainly Alexander MacLeay had some criticisms (which Elford accepted were valid[26]), and complained that scientific names had been included which had never before been published. This Elford disputed, identifying the writers who had used these names, some of whom had published long before Linnæus. He had been drawing on his knowledge of ancient natural history publications, going back to the sixteenth century and beyond, which had been sharpened during his work for the *Edinburgh Encyclopædia*.

[22] In a manuscript catalogue at the Museum.
[23] J.E. Gray (House of Commons, 1836: paras 2614, 2633-2634).
[24] Salvin, 1882: iv.
[25] J.E. Gray (House of Commons, 1836: paras 2614, 2633-2634).
[26] Letter: W.E. Leach to MacLeay, 9th November 1816 (Loc: Linnean Society, MacLeay Correspondence). We do not know what MacLeay's "just strictures" were.

Sterna Dougallii, jun.		*Procellaria pelagica.*	
Roseate Tern, young.		Stormy Petrel.	
FRITH OF CLYDE.	Dr. M'Dougall.	FRITH OF FORTH.	P. Neill, Esq.
Sterna Boysii.		*Uria Troile.*	
Sandwich Tern.		Foolish Guillemot.	
SANDWICH.	H. Boys, Esq.	PEMBROKESHIRE.	G. Montagu, Esq.

Excerpt from Elford Leach's *Catalogue* to show format.

The catalogue had been completed by August[27] but despite Elford's desire to get back to Devon he delayed his departure, receiving a visit during September from one of de Blainville's Italian correspondents[28]. While he worked on, in West Africa catastrophe struck.

Jack Cranch[29]

The *Congo* and the *Dorothy* ("that brute of a transport" as Tuckey called it) had sailed south past Madeira, the Canaries and the Cape Verde Islands. For the first few days on the open ocean the *Dorothy* made the naturalists "most grievously sea-sick[30]", but they soon found their sea legs. Unfortunately Cranch had to cope with more than sea-sickness. He did not have a comfortable voyage. Something in his nature – whether his social background, his non-conformist religious beliefs[31], his personality (he was prone to melancholy), or a mixture of all of these – seems to have irritated his shipmates. Smith confided to his journal, "Cranch, I fear, by his absurd conduct, will diminish the liberality of the Captain towards us. He is like a pointed arrow to the company." (The friction must have been considerable if it threatened the relationship with Tuckey, who is described as, "at all times gentle and kind in his manners, and indulgent to every one placed under his command". He behaved like a father to his men[32].) Nor does the tension seem to have eased. In a later entry Smith adds, "Poor Cranch is almost too much the object of jest. Galwey is the principal banterer.[33]"

Despite his obvious social isolation Cranch set about the business for which he was employed. He spent the voyage hanging over the *Dorothy*'s rail in his blue waistcoat and red cravat[34], trailing his small net behind the ship, collecting animals floating at the ocean's surface. At times he brought up large numbers of Portuguese Men-o-War[35], leading him to note in his diary:

'Some of us were severely punished by making [too] free in examining those animals... the sensation occasioned by the wound is very similar to the sting of the common nettle[36] but continues much longer and is more violent; it produces a considerable inflammation which does not wholly subside for some hours.[37]'

[27] The Preface is dated 30th August.

[28] Letters: W.E. Leach to de Blainville, 30th September and 7th November 1816 (Loc: Bibliothèque Centrale, Muséum National d'Histoire Naturelle, Paris. Ref: Items 108-9). Elford writes the name of his visitor Cherirchi / Cheirichi. Could this be 71 year old Stefano Chiereghini (1745-1820) an Italian abbot who studied marine animals from the Gulf of Venice?

[29] The following is drawn mainly from Monod (1970).

[30] According to Tuckey.

[31] A later commentator says, "Unfortunately, however, he had embraced a very gloomy system of religious belief." (Anon., 1818: 329). He and his wife attended the Ebenezer Independent Chapel, Kingsbridge (John Lamble, *in litt.*, 2000).

[32] Dawson, 1969: 67-70.

[33] Monod (1970: 6) has the word 'barterer' but Louise Gallant (see References) amended this to 'banterer'. The latter is almost certainly correct.

[34] Monod (1970: 10) gives a list of the clothes Cranch took with him.

[35] Stinging jelly-fish with an inflated gas bladder acting like a sail, e.g. *Physalia physalis* (L.)

[36] The stinging herbaceous plant *Urtica dioica* L.

[37] Monod (1970: 19). Cranch writes "to".

The naturalists also caught fish of many types and sizes, including Great White sharks and the less fearsome flying-fish and tuna. This sampling went well apart from some confusion when the cabin steward, not quite understanding why the fish were aboard, served the day's collection for dinner.

When the expedition arrived at the mouth of the Congo in July they suffered a bitter disappointment. The information they had been given in England, and on which their planning relied, was wrong. The river was much smaller than they had been led to believe and was not as navigable. However, leaving the *Dorothy* at its mouth they took the *Congo* as far as Boma, 70 km upstream.

The animals in these lower reaches and on the banks were also a disappointment. Cranch complained:

'It might reasonably be expected from the reports which were currant before we left England relative to the natural production of this River that the collector would here find a golden harvest in every branch of Zoology;... I can declare excepting Birds (and those not numerous in point of species) all other classes of animals are extremely scanty and not easily obtained.[38]'

Leaving the *Congo* at Boma and resorting to the ships' boats, they travelled about another 170 km until halted by the rapids called 'Yellala's Wife', just before the great cataracts proper at Yellala. From here they would have to walk. They scrambled along the line of the riverbank for about another 40 km, but just as the river widened to a broad stream thousands of metres across, sickness began to plague the company. Cranch became feverish on the 23rd of August. It was clear his contribution to the trek was at an end and he was carried in a hammock by local porters back to the river below the rapids. By canoe he was transported downstream to Boma, arriving ten days after he turned back. He was not the only invalid. The sickness produced a general lethargy and exhaustion; at times Cranch appeared delirious. He was in no pain but complained of an uneasy sensation in the abdomen. By the 3rd of September his face had turned a dirty yellow and his pulse was faint and racing. The following day he deteriorated badly. His whole body was now yellow and his pulse was too faint to be measured. That evening, "after uttering a devout prayer for the welfare of his family, and with the name of his wife quivering on his lips[39]" he died. Back in Kingsbridge, as yet unaware of her loss, his wife gave birth to their son, Nathaniel[40].

By permission of the King at Boma, Cranch was interred in the royal burial ground, with military honours. He was laid next to William Tudor, who had been buried in similar style six days earlier. Cranch was followed five days later by his tormentor Edward Galwey.

Up-river the expedition was aborted. It had penetrated inland 450 km, but without answering the Niger question. Back on the *Dorothy* Christen Smith died on the 22nd of September and was given a naval burial in the river he had come to explore. Tuckey died at the beginning of October.

[38] Monod (1970: 49).
[39] Anon., 1818: 328.
[40] Nathaniel Cranch was Christened on the 6th of October 1816 at the Ebenezer Independent Chapel in Kingsbridge.

In accordance with naval custom the belongings of the dead were sold and the ships, with another 10 crewmen dead and 32 on the sick list, fled to sea in an effort to escape the pestilence[41]. Limping across the Atlantic with skeleton crews they anchored on the coast of Brazil at Salvador (Bahia) on the 30th of October. It was the shipping agent of Lloyds Coffee-House[42] at Bahia who sent word of the disaster to London. In all, two thirds of the expedition lost their lives.

Some of the collections eventually found their way back to Britain. Tudor's were never located, despite his sample cases being deeply inscribed *Belonging to the Royal College of Surgeons in London, to the care of Mr Tudor*. William Clift, the Conservator at the College's museum (and an acquaintance of Elford Leach since his first residence in London[43]) tried repeatedly to trace them but to no avail[44]. Elford received some of Cranch's material, but a case of animals in jars was lost and many of the birds were completely destroyed by insect pests, although Leadbeater later provided an estimate for stuffing 33, which must have been in reasonable condition. Most of the insects were destroyed by other insects and by damp[45]. Cranch's land collections were therefore of little use. Nevertheless some of his marine animals, pickled in jars, survived.

In a perverse way the failure of the Congo expedition acted as a springboard for more successful British exploration, and consequently for the enhancement of the collections in the British Museum. After the Congo the Admiralty turned its back on major tropical investigations and focused instead on the Arctic and the search for a short-cut to the Pacific and south-east Asia[46]. To some extent the great British polar explorers of the following decades owe their achievements to a few lonely graves in the royal cemetery at Boma.

As to Jack Cranch's achievements: he deserves to be remembered as one of the first European marine zoologists to collect in the Gulf of Guinea, and his collections during the voyage south make him one of the earliest

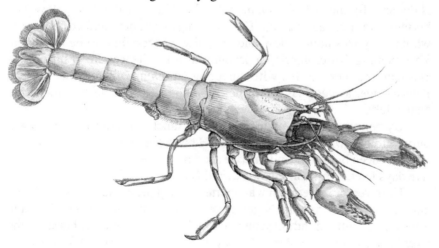

[41] *Naval Chronicle*, **37**: 86 (1817).
[42] Fore-runner of the modern Lloyds of London.
[43] Elford will have met him when he examined crustaceans in the College's museum during 1808-10 (*Edinburgh Encyclopædia*, **7**: 395, 400).
[44] Royal College of Surgeons Donation Register, **3**: memorandum to donation 842.
[45] The destruction of ships' cargoes by insects was a serious problem at this time. A merchant once offered Elford Leach £10,000 – nearly 30 years salary! – if he could solve the problem. He could not. (J.F. Stephens reported in Neave, 1933: 18).
[46] Rice, 1986: 42.

Axius stirynchus Leach

Illustration from *Malacostraca Podophthalmata Britanniæ* by Elford Leach. September 1816

biological oceanographers. His small net was among the fore-runners of thousands of oceanic plankton trawls conducted since[47].

Elford Leach's reaction to Cranch's death was profound. He had always named new species after people he knew, but following the Congo expedition he seems to have experienced intense grief, or guilt. His friend was dead, leaving a wife and young family, and he had orchestrated his demise. In the years that followed he named 17 new species *cranchii*; two *cranchianus*; and a new genus *Cranchia*. In his manuscript notes he coined many other names based on 'Cranch'. One of these was, he explained:

"a slight testimony due for his meritorious exertions in the cause of zoology, and of my gratitude for the eagerness of his pursuits while in my service, and of his zealous perseverance during the whole of the unfortunate voyage to the Congo, by which I lost a true and sincere friend and a faithful servant.[48]"

In October 1818 John Bowring[49], Cranch's cousin, wrote to the Trustees of the British Museum asking them to recommend a grant of money for Cranch's family[50]. The Trustees considered the letter but 'declined making any order upon its contents' (Civil-Servant-speak for "No").

Kent

In September in England – still oblivious to the drama in Africa – Elford had not yet returned to Devon, but that did not stop him getting out of London. He went to the coast of Kent (probably staying at Sandgate[51]) to collect marine animals , and found a new species of colonial sea-squirt. He passed the news to de Blainville[52] and the specimen to Savigny, who published a description of it in December, naming it *Botryllus leachii*. Earlier in the year de Blainville had similarly honoured Elford by naming a new species of sea-slug *Doris elfortiana*. In his letter to de Blainville Elford added that he had seen part of a new natural history work being published in France:

"I have no news, but I have seen the Entomological volume of the "Tableau de la Nature" which give me but a mean opinion of the merits of the work. The first Vol. I saw in Paris and did not much like its plan, which is not founded on any principal. I shall analyse it and that too severely, after having first given an account of your views, which in the Mollusca (the only part I have examined) is far, far superior. The Leviathon of Science in his ardor to grasp all, has completely lost himself.[53]"

The 'Leviathon of Science' is Cuvier. Elford closed his letter to de Blainville – whose knowledge of the Mollusca he clearly admired – with two poetic, if somewhat gushing, lines of advice[54]:

"Go on my friend on Light by genius borne
Regard the crowd of little men with scorn"

These profuse compliments may have verged on toad-eating, but de Blainville had originally been trained by Cuvier and would later succeed

---

[47] Monod, 1970: 6.

[48] Leach, 1852: 172.

[49] John Bowring (1792-1872). Linguist, writer and traveller. MP for Bolton from 1841. Made Governor of Hong Kong and knighted after 1854. His aunt, Jane Bowring, was Cranch's mother.

[50] The request was for the "Widow and Orphan of Mr John Cranch" (An orphan at this time was any child without a father). The singular 'orphan' suggests Charlotte and Nathaniel had not survived early infancy.

[51] Leach (1852) mentions this location several times.

[52] Letter: W.E. Leach (London) to de Blainville, 30th of September 1816 (Loc: Bibliothèque Centrale, Muséum National d'Histoire Naturelle, Paris. Ref: Item 108).

[53] In another letter to de Blainville of 7th November (*loc. cit.* Ref: Item 109). Elford said the Mollusca contribution to the *Tableau de la Nature* "will retard the advancement of science."

[54] Presumably a quote, but from — ?

him as professor of comparative anatomy. His work, especially on the molluscs, did deserve serious consideration.

By October the Board of Works had still not constructed display cases for Room XI and Elford had been unable to move any collections into the room. Giving up any thought of doing so in the near future, he finally took the coach to the West Country just as the Museum reopened to the public.

On this trip he was not heading for *Woodland*. His parents had moved house and were now living at Spitchwick Park, near Ashburton, midway between Plymouth and Exeter. Elford's sister Jenny was still living with them, and his brother George was still an attorney in Plymouth Dock. George had originally practised alone in St Aubyn Street[55], but for several years he had been using that office for his new partnership, *Leach & Lugger* Attorneys[56], while keeping an office for himself in Chapel Street.

Spitchwick

Spitchwick (or Spitchweek or Speechwick – the name means 'Fat Bacon Farm'[57]) was an ancient manor mentioned in the Domesday Book[58]. The late Lord Ashburton[59] had taken a long lease on the land in the 1700s and had built a house in a particularly beautiful location, in wild countryside on the southern edge of Dartmoor. It was this house that George Snr was now renting from Lord Ashburton's family. Henry Woollcombe visited Spitchwick and was captivated:

'I had a delightful ramble in a part of the scenery I did not survey when last here, it was the higher part of the River Dart amongst scenes so vast and savage as to create the most pleasing emotions of terror and surprise... I took to wandering through the river and its stupendous banks. In short I am highly delighted and am more convinced than ever that Dartmoor is well worth exploring... When we quit Spitchweek after tea we were accompanied

[55] Anon., 1812.

[56] Rowe, S. (1814) [a directory of Plymouth and Plymouth Dock mentioned in JES's Mss]. 'Lugger' is possibly John Lloyd Lugger of Stoke Damerel (christened 30th November 1785).

[57] from the Old English 'Spic' = 'fat bacon'; and 'wic' = a dwelling or collection of dwellings with a special purpose; a farm.

[58] An AD 1086 gazetteer and economic description of the English kingdom the Normans had acquired in 1066. It noted especially how much wealth each manor generated and how much passed to the king.

[59] John Dunning (1731-1783). Lawyer. Attorney-General 1767.

North Cornwall coast near Boscastle and Bossiney.

by Miss Leach and George. We walked through the grounds below Buckland by the side of the Dart, nothing I think can surpass some of its scenes. I was delighted to renew my acquaintance with it.[60]'

Elford did not spend much time sightseeing. He had no sooner arrived in Devon than he was off to North Cornwall. He too was "much delighted with the fine bold scenery" but collected few new animals despite scouring shores, woods and hills. He returned to Spitchwick[61] and with the help of Charles Prideaux went to work arranging Montagu's shells. He planned to return to London in late December when this was completed[62].

From Spitchwick he also wrote to Charles König asking if the Museum would send some glass bottles to a Mr Swainson in Liverpool, with whom Elford had been in contact from Cornwall[63]. Swainson was going to Brazil the following year and had agreed to collect fish for the Museum.

William Swainson[64]

William Swainson had been born in Liverpool. His father[65], a Collector of Customs, also collected insects and shells, and as a child William developed a passion for natural history. When the late Sir Ashton Lever's Museum was sold in London in 1806 the teenage Swainson, like Will Bullock, had been one of the buyers[66].

Swainson began his working life at the age of 14, also in the Customs service, but his sense of adventure inspired him to travel. After four years his father arranged a transfer for him to the army commissariat in the Mediterranean, and he was posted to Malta then Sicily (from which he visited Italy and Greece). With the end of the war in 1815 he was put on half-pay[67], and returned to England with his collections of Mediterranean plants, animals and drawings. It was undoubtedly these that brought him into contact with Elford.

Swainson had only been in England a short time when the opportunity arose to accompany Henry Koster[68], author of *Travels in Brazil* (1816), who was returning to South America. Swainson would be away for two years, but on his return he would renew his acquaintance with Elford and the British Museum.

At the end of November the Principal Librarian, Joseph Planta[69], wrote to Elford and invited *him* to renew his acquaintance with the British Museum. Although Elford had not yet completed the two months leave agreed with the Trustees, clearly as far as they were concerned he had taken the wrong two months. Characteristically, his response was to write back and ask for a three week extension to the agreed time. He would return, as planned, in late December.

Winter of discontent

After the dismal European summer the winter set in early. Caroline Capel wrote again to her mother from Switzerland: 'Your account of the cold and scarcity is really distressing. Indeed every English paper we see is

[60] Diary for 5th May 1817. Typescript seen.
[61] On Sunday the 20th of October.
[62] Letters: W.E. Leach to de Blainville 7th November; and to MacLeay on the 9th of November (see earlier notes for locations).
[63] Letter: W. Swainson (Liverpool) to A. MacLeay, 20th October 1816 (Loc: Linnean Society of London, MacLeay Correspondence).
[64] William Swainson (1789-1855). See biographical notes in Farber (1985).
[65] John Timothy Swainson (1757-1824).
[66] Bullock had not been there in person. He had sent an agent (House of Commons, 1836: para. 622).
[67] Retired from military duties but kept on the army's payroll and subject to recall if needed.
[68] Henry Koster (ca 1793-1820).
[69] Joseph Planta (1744-1827). Of Swiss parentage. Keeper of Manuscripts 1776-; Principal Librarian 1799-1827. Also served the government as Paymaster of Exchequer Bills 1788-1811. His son Joseph Planta (1787-1847) worked in the British diplomatic service.

full of unpleasant relations, of discontents & Miseries which I always grieve to see. It is not confined to our Country, The same distresses prevail here & in many parts of the Continent—Bread, potatoes, Wine, in short almost every article of Life, is risen in price, & there are Gens d'armes regularly placed in the Markets to prevent anyone buying more than a certain quantity of Potatoes, which is the chief support of the poor. The Cold is very great but has not yet attained what I hear has been felt in the North of England... What you mention of the tops of the Corn being seen above the snow in Ireland reminds me of the scene under these Windows 3 Weeks Ago—The poor Wretches gathering their grapes, or rather their semblance of Grapes, with the snow up to the middle of their Legs.[70]'

In the east-end of London the poor were now starving in their thousands[71] and those political Radicals who wished to see a rapid overturning of the British system – or even a revolution along French lines – found many to listen to their calls for change. Public meetings could attract tens of thousands and the government was increasingly embattled. While Elford Leach was safely in the West Country a public assembly was called on the 15th of November in Spa Fields, London. The posters calling the meeting trumpeted:

> The present state of Great Britain.
> Four millions in distress ! ! !
> Four millions embarrassed ! ! !
> One million and a half fear distress ! ! !
> Half a million live in splendid luxury ! ! !
> Our brothers in Ireland are in a worse state.
> The climax of misery is complete—it can go no farther.
> Death would now be a relief to millions[72].

The gathering was policed by troops and again it was Guards officer Rees Gronow who saw the crowds through fiercely establishment eyes.

"I was sent with a company of the Guards to occupy the prison of Spafields, and to act, if necessary, in aid and support of the civil powers. On arrival, we found that a troop of horse artillery with their guns, had already taken up their position within the yard. We lost no time in making loopholes in the walls, in the event of an attack from without, and made ready for action. The mob, which was not very numerous on our arrival, had by this time increased to an enormous multitude. Sixty or seventy thousand persons must have been present. Their principal leaders appeared to be Major Cartwright[73], Gale Jones[74], and the notorious Henry Hunt, the blacking-maker[75]. The major was an old gray-headed vulgar-looking man. Hunt was a large, powerfully made fellow, who might have been taken for a butcher: he always wore a white hat; which was, I never knew why, in those days supposed to be an emblem of very advanced liberal, or even republican opinions[76]. These two demagogues, and two or three more of the leaders of

[70] Anglesey, 1955: 182. Letter of 4th December 1816.
[71] Priestley, 1971: 162.
[72] Alington, 1921: 72.
[73] John Cartwright (1740-1824). Formerly in the Royal Navy. From 1775 a Major in the Nottinghamshire Militia. He wrote on politics, advocating a range of liberal policies.
[74] John Gale Jones (1769-1838). An active advocate of reform well-known in his day.
[75] Henry ('Orator') Hunt (1773-1835). Originally a Wiltshire farmer who spent six weeks in prison in 1800 after his hot temper caused conflict with the commander of the Wiltshire Militia. He left prison a committed reformer ('Blacking' was boot polish).
[76] More obviously, at this meeting a 'cap of Liberty' was displayed on a pole and the French tricolor was flown in front of the crowd (Bryant, 1975: 374).

the mob, got into a cart, that had been brought up as a sort of tribune or rostrum, from which they harangued the people. More violent and treasonable discourses it was impossible to make; and the huge multitude rent the air with their shouts of applause.

After a time, a magistrate and some constables appeared, and summoned the people to disperse; and, at the same moment, a messenger arrived from the prison, who whispered in Hunt's ear that if the mob committed any outrage, or made any disturbance, and did not quietly disperse, they would be dealt with by the soldiers; who had orders above all to pick off the ringleaders, should any attack be made upon the prison. This intelligence, conveyed to the gentlemen in the cart by one of their friends, produced a very marked effect. In a very short time they got down, as they seemed to consider themselves in rather an exposed position, declared the meeting at an end, and hurried off, leaving the crowd to follow them; which they shortly afterwards did.[77]"

Whether this happened exactly as Gronow says, it was not the end of the matter. A second meeting was arranged at Spa Fields for the 2nd of December. Again Hunt was a speaker. Although he was an inflammatory orator he did not support the use of violence, but this meeting was hijacked by more extreme radicals (incited by government agents?[78]) who gathered several hundred followers and rampaged into the streets, broke into gunsmiths, and threatened to storm the Tower of London and Bank of England (both of which were too well protected). After some skirmishes, including a scuffle with the Life Guards in Aldgate High Street, the rioters dispersed amid window breaking and street robberies. In their wake one man lay dead.

[77] Gronow, 1964: 198-199.
[78] Priestley (1971: 162) says yes.

Aldgate High Street.

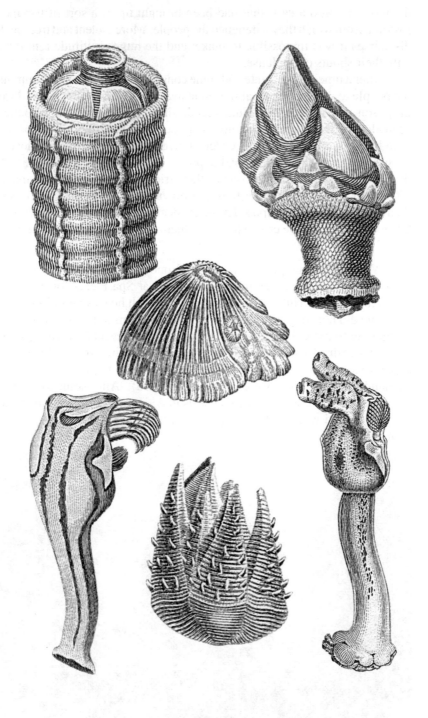

Barnacles

Illustrations from Elford
Leach's article CIRRIPEDES in
*Encyclopædia Britannica,
Supplements to the 4th & 5th
Editions*, volume 3, part 1,
Plate LVII.

— 24 —

On with the new

And o'erthrew them with prophesying
To the old of the new world's worth;
For each age is a dream that is dying,
Or one that is coming to birth.

Arthur O'Shaughnessy[1]
Zoologist, British Museum 1862-1881.

The next twelve months were busy for Elford Leach. He laboured steadily at the Museum to rearrange all the zoological collections into natural genera and tear down the Linnean veil (as he called it) "that has so long darkened true Science[2]". John Gray helped him sort through the drawers and cabinets. Elford paid particular attention to barnacles, writing an entry CIRRIPEDES[3] for the Supplement to the *Encyclopædia Britannica* and preparing a display case containing an arrangement of the species. Such was the meticulous nature of this display it remained in the public galleries virtually unchanged for at least the next two decades[4].

He had returned to the Museum at the end of 1816 laden with his collection of British molluscs and donations from his Devonian contacts: the 'Nest of a Tarantula' from Henry Woollcombe; a snail from William Comyns of Kenton; a mineral and some rare shells from C.W. Loscombe of Exmouth; and from other donors, a Woodchat Shrike[5], six varieties of 'the common squirrel' (which in those days was the red squirrel[6] – anything but common in Britain today), a polecat[7], crustaceans and insects. John Henslow had not forgotten the Museum and had sent a freshwater mussel for the collections, and William Swainson donated his collection of Sicilian fishes[8]. Swainson seems to have given his Sicilian crustaceans to Elford personally[9]. In return Elford arranged another supply of bottles and curation equipment to be sent to Brazil for him.

With the arrival of the shells and Elford's increasing work on molluscs, he made contact with another British naturalist who would become a close personal friend, Thomas Bell[10]. Bell was a surgeon and a British pioneer in the field of dentistry. In 1817 he was appointed lecturer in dentistry and

[1] Lines from *We are the Music Makers* (1874).
[2] Letter: W.E. Leach to Stephens, 7th November 1820 (Loc: Linnean Society of London, Miscellaneous Correspondence).
[3] The scientific name for barnacles (from the Greek: *cirrus* + *pes*, 'curled leg').
[4] Gray (House of Commons, 1836: para. 2457). Did Charles Darwin see this display before commencing his own work on barnacles?
[5] A mainland European bird, *Lanius senator* Linnæus.
[6] *Sciurus vulgaris* Linnæus.
[7] Or 'fitch' or 'fitchet weasel', *Mustela putorius* Linnæus ('fitch' is also the name used for the fur).
[8] Where a species had three specimens, the third was to be passed to the Linnean Society. Presumably the first was for the Museum and the second for Elford. Letter: Leach to Linnean Society Council, 16th June 1818 (Loc: Linnean Society of London, Miscellaneous Correspondence).
[9] Elford noted at this time he had received "an hundred species of crustacea from Sicily and India". Letter: W.E. Leach to de Blainville 18th January 1817 (Loc: Bibliothèque Centrale, Muséum National d'Histoire Naturelle, Paris. Ref: Item 112).
[10] Thomas Bell (1792-1880). Born in Dorset, England. Resigned from Guy's Hospital in 1836 to become Professor of Zoology at King's College London.

comparative anatomy at Guy's Hospital, London, although at this time he approached comparative anatomy from a rather novel perspective. In 1821 he would publish a book *Kalogynomia, or the Laws of Female Beauty*, written (as he tells us in the introduction) to allow readers to use scientific principles to answer the question, "Is she beautiful?" These principles identified three 'species' of woman: 1. the delicate and elegant; 2. the soft and voluptuous; and 3. the graceful intellectual. Nine of the twenty-four plates in this book were stitched separately so they could be safely locked away from the prying eyes of 'Ladies and young persons', and reserved only for the 'higher and more reflecting class of reader'.

Bell had begun his natural history interests as a botanist but by 1817 had developed a particular interest in molluscs (before moving onto other topics later). In 1843 he described the reptiles collected by Darwin on *HMS Beagle* and in 1853 he updated Elford's *Malacostraca* with his own work *A History of the British stalk-eyed Crustacea*, published while he was President of the Linnean Society[11]. Bell was President at the time Darwin and Wallace first outlined the principles of Natural Selection at the Society's meeting on the 1st of July 1858, yet he still managed to say in his presidential address that the year had not been marked "by any of those striking discoveries which at once revolutionise, so to speak, the department of science on which they bear".

In 1815 Bell had been offered the post of naturalist on the Congo expedition, but after discussions with Robert Brown (who had experience of collecting in Australia) Bell had fortunately declined the invitation.

The Congo Expedition

By February news of the disaster in the Congo had reached London and Elford was staking his claim to the collections. He asked Alexander MacLeay to liaise with John Barrow[12], Second Secretary to the Admiralty[13] and the driving force behind this, and other, naval expeditions:

"If you will have the goodness to call on Mr Barrow to speak with him on the subject of the natural history of Congo you will render me a particular favor. I most want to describe the animal of Argonauta which if it gets into Sir E. Home's hands will be superficially examined and as he has committed an erroneous opinion on the subject on paper he will perhaps not adhere to truth in his description.[14]" (We noted earlier Sir Everard Home has come down through history with a rather suspect reputation. Elford was not shy in criticising him to third parties.)

Lobster
Homarus gammarus (L.)

Illustration from Bell's *A History of the British stalk-eyed Crustacea*.

[11] He was described as "one of the most stimulating Presidents the Society has ever had" (Gage, 1938: 48).
[12] John Barrow (1764-1848). Explorer and, from 1804, Second Secretary to the Admiralty. Later knighted.
[13] Where the First Secretary was John Croker, whose correspondence is quoted elsewhere in this work.
[14] Letter: W.E. Leach to MacLeay, 19th February 1817 (Loc: Linnean Society, MacLeay Correspondence).

384

The mystery of the Argonauta, or Paper Nautilus, was one that had been puzzling scientists for a long time. A small octopus was sometimes found floating in open waters encased in a shell composed of a thin parchment-like material. No-one had been able to determine whether this shell belonged to the animal, or whether the animal adopted the shell, much as a hermit-crab lives in a mollusc's shell after the snail has died. Arguments raged on both sides and the shell was given its own name, *Argonauta argo* – a name for a species no-one had seen. We now know this structure is secreted by the female octopus to carry her eggs, which she lays inside it. She secretes the shell around herself using modified tentacles, so the original confusion is perhaps understandable. By April Elford had succeeded in obtaining the specimens he wanted and he read a paper to the Royal Society on the 5th of June. In it he again drew on his knowledge of the ancient authors:

'Pliny, Aldrovandus, Lister, Rumphius, d'Argenville, Bruguiere, Bosc, Cuvier, and Shaw[15], have described a species of this genus, that is often found in the *Argonauta argo* (common paper-nautilus) and which they have regarded as its animal, since no other inhabitant has been observed in it.

Sir Joseph Banks, and some other naturalists, have always entertained a contrary opinion, believing it to be no more than a parasitical inhabitant of the Argonaut's shell, and Rafinesque[16], (whose situation on the shores of the Mediterranean, has afforded him ample opportunities of studying this animal, and of observing its habits) has regarded it as a peculiar genus, allied to the *Polypus* of Aristotle [*Sepia octopodia* Linne], residing parasitically in the above mentioned shell.

Dr. Blainville, ten months since, when speaking of the *Argonauta*, said, "animal unknown," and he has lately informed me, that he has written a long dissertation to prove, that the *Ocythoë* of Rafinesque, does not belong to the shell in which it is found.

[15] Pliny the Elder (Gaius Plinius Secundus) (AD 23-79) who wrote *Historia Naturalis* (AD 77); Ulisse Aldrovandi(-dus) (1522-1605); Martin Lister (1638-1712); Georg(ius) Everhard(us) Rumph(ius) (1628-1702); Antoine-Joseph Dezalliers d'Argenville (1680-1765); Jean Guillaume Bruguière (1750-1799); Louis Augustin Guillaume Bosc (1759-1828); Georges Cuvier and George Shaw.

[16] Constantine Samuel Rafinesque (or Rafinesque-Schmaltz) (1783-1840). Had a French father named Rafinesque and a German mother (née Schmaltz). Spent some time living in Sicily. William Swainson met him here. He usually called himself 'Rafinesque' but during the conflict with France he added his mother's name for security. In 1818 he travelled to America and met wildlife illustrator John James Audubon (1785-1851). Rafinesque tried to catch flying bats by swinging at them with Audubon's favourite violin, which broke. Audubon took revenge by drawing imaginary fish and passing the drawings and descriptions to Rafinesque, who took them in good faith and duly described them as new species (Markle, 1997). Rafinesque advocated natural genera and by 1819 was Professor of Botany and Natural History at the University of Lexington, Kentucky.

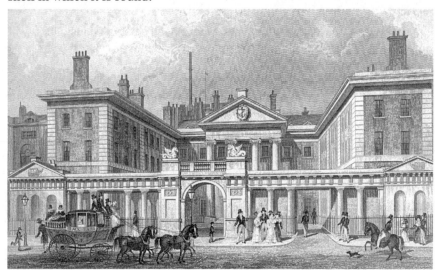

The Admiralty, London.

The observations made by the late Mr. John Cranch, zoologist to the unfortunate Congo expedition, have cleared from my mind any doubts on the subject. In the gulf of Guinea, and afterwards on the voyage, he took by means of a small net, (which was always suspended over the side of the vessel) several specimens of a new species of *Ocythoë*, which were swimming in a small *argonauta*, on the surface of the sea.[17]"

Needless to say, Elford called the new species *Ocythoe cranchii* and in his paper he paraphrased Cranch's observations that when alive they appeared to show no adverse effects when removed from the shell[18]. Although he says 'The observations made... have cleared from my mind any doubts' he never explicitly states his conclusion. In fact he followed Banks and de Blainville in believing (wrongly) the animal inhabits the shell of another species.

Repression

While Elford struggled with these rarefied problems, the British government struggled to maintain control of the streets, which they feared they were in danger of losing. When the deeply unpopular Prince Regent had opened the new session of parliament in January his carriage had been stoned by violent crowds. At least one of its windows was broken and there was some question as to whether a shot had been fired. "The general spirit of the country is worse," thought Robert Peel, "than we understood it to be.[19]" Coming within weeks of the Spa Fields riot, this was too much for the government. It acted swiftly to increase security and in March introduced new legislation: the so-called *Coercion Acts* or *Gagging Acts*[20].

First parliament suspended writs of *habeas corpus*[21] (by which anyone arrested had to be brought before a court and formally charged). Now it was possible for the authorities to arrest someone, even on suspicion of

[17] Leach, W.E. (1817) Observations of the genus *Ocythoë* of Rafinesque, with a description of a new species. *Philosophical Transactions of the Royal Society*, 1817: 293-296 & Pl.12 (which is usually bound in the centre of the subsequent paper).

[18] See Cranch's original text in Monod (1970: 42).

[19] Priestley, 1971: 187. No shot had been heard but an airgun was suspected.

[20] Neither was an official name for this legislation. Previous laws going back to the 18th century had been termed 'gagging acts' when they were perceived to restrict freedoms, especially freedom of expression.

[21] 'Habeas corpus' – Latin: 'You may have the body'.

1817

January	Jane Austen starts a new work *Sanditon* but by March illness will have ended her writing.
February	Food riots in Wales.
March	Food riots in England.
3rd March	John Keats[1] (a friend of Plymouth painter Benjamin Haydon) publishes his first collection of poems, entitled *Poems*.
April	David Ricardo, under encouragement from Robert Brown's friend James Mill, publishes his classic *Principles of political Economy and Taxation*, an expansion of his 1815 attack on the Corn Law.
June	'Risings' in Derbyshire and Huddersfield.
18th July	Jane Austen dies.
December	Jane Austen's *Northanger Abbey* (first drafted as *Susan* c. 1798-1799) and *Persuasion* are published posthumously. Her brother Henry identifies her as the author of these and the earlier books.

[1] John Keats (1795-1821). British poet.

wrongdoing, and hold them in prison without trial. To this they added tougher powers for magistrates, allowing them to arrest anyone they thought likely to commit acts leading to public disorder; they banned all meetings of more than 50 people within a mile[22] of Westminster; they renewed laws against trying to tempt soldiers and sailors away from their duties to the crown; and they extended laws against sedition (a usefully vague concept covering any attempts to disturb the tranquility of the State that fell short of treason).

The imposition of these new restrictions did reduce the number of protests as the year progressed, but this erosion of personal liberty, for people who felt they had very little control over their own lives as it was, was just one more oppression to add to the list. The government was merely tightening the lid on the pressure-cooker.

Burchell's mammals

As parliament rushed through the new measures, Elford pressed on with his work. At the end of March he wrote to de Blainville for his help as a member of the Philomathic Society of Paris, which published a scientific journal, the *Bulletin des Sciences*[23]:

"You will receive with this note a notice from M[r] Burchill, who has penetrated in a North-Eastern direction from the Cape of Good hope and has brought home a superb collection of 120 mammalia, several hundred birds and an infinity of plants &c. The mammifers are deposited in the British Museum[24].

As fate would have it, I most fortunately called on M[r] Burchill as he was on the point of sending the notice to the scientific Napoleon (*our* friend the *crocodile*), but I arrested his hand by informing him, that you were the meteor of the day and that the Leviathan's sun was setting in the west, as yours was leaving the Eastern point.

Pray insert his notice in the Bulletin des Sciences and mention that he was in the interior of Africa for four years.[25]"

These obsequious compliments reflect Elford's obvious idolisation of de Blainville. The "scientific Napoleon (*our* friend the *crocodile*)" is almost certainly Cuvier; 'the crocodile' probably an allusion to Elford's species *Crocodilus cuvieri* from Dauphin Island. In a previous letter[26] Elford had spoken of "the crocodile of science or literary Bonaparte". These Napoleonic labels, the pair's private joke, presumably refer to Cuvier's dominant position in zoology, especially in France.

De Blainville – said to be an extremely hot-tempered individual – had begun his training with Cuvier in 1810, but later fell out with his teacher. Here we may be seeing an admiring Elford Leach pandering to de Blainville's personal prejudices. Elford himself seems to have had a good relationship with Cuvier, despite these barbed comments behind his back.

[22] 1.6 km.
[23] *Bulletin des Sciences de la Société Philomathique de Paris.*
[24] Only 43 of the mammals (mammifers) were donated to the Museum.
[25] Letter: W.E. Leach to de Blainville, 30th March 1817 (Loc: Bibliothèque Centrale, Muséum National d'Histoire Naturelle, Paris. Ref: Pièce 110).
[26] Letter: W.E. Leach to de Blainville, 18th January 1817 (Loc: Bibliothèque Centrale, Muséum National d'Histoire Naturelle, Paris. Ref: Pièce 112).

The 'Mr Burchill' in the letter is William Burchell[27] who had spent the years 1810 to 1815 in southern Africa. He travelled more than 7000 km in the region, amassing a huge collection of more than 63,000 objects, drawn from anthropology, geology, botany and zoology. The notice Elford had passed to de Blainville described a new species which we now know as the White Rhinoceros[28], and was published in the *Bulletin des Sciences* in June.

Elford was under the impression the mammal skins had been donated to the British Museum on condition they were not displayed until Burchell had had an opportunity to describe the species[29]. This was certainly not a problem. Although Elford had talked him into donating 43 skins, there were no facilities to have them all stuffed, and there was certainly no space to display them[30]. Zoology had only three dedicated rooms[31]: the Insect Room (X), the Bird Room (XI) and the small Spirit Room (XII), and the Bird Room had been closed since 1816 (and would not open again to the public until 1818). König had recently obtained the Trustees' permission to arrange a display of British minerals in Room X, to complement the British zoology intended for Room XI[32], and this had also eaten into zoology's space. In response Elford asked that the spirit collection (the hobgoblins) be moved to the basement to create space for other exhibits, but this was refused[33]. There was also another problem: when Burchell had collected the skins they had been badly sun-dried, then the smaller examples had been thrown flat in the back of the waggons, with the larger skins draped across the waggons' covers. The shrinkage from the sun and the chafing on the journey rendered many of them unfit for stuffing[34]. In July the Trustees did order some prepared[35], but it is not clear which specimens, or their sizes.

Burchell's embargo on display may have been the initial arrangement, but he became increasingly annoyed that his donations were not in the galleries. He complained to the Trustees in September 1819, and became even more agitated after the publication of his *Travels in the Interior of Southern Africa* in 1822-1823, by which time many of the stored skins were being damaged by insects. After he made a fuss, and in 1825 made the public aware of his gifts, some larger quadrupeds were finally prepared and by 1826 two giraffes stood on the landing at the top of the Grand Staircase[36], although Gray noted, "the Museum were quite as much abused for showing such bad specimens as it was for not having more stuffed[37]".

Dr Leach and the Elephant

Unlike Burchell, Elford had never travelled to the tropics to see exotic wildlife, but he did see live tropical animals that travelled to him, and on one occasion this gave him an opportunity to draw on the veterinary teachings of his old tutor John Barclay[38]. The incident in question took place at Exeter 'Change, by then owned by Edward Cross. Cross's star attraction was his elephant, 'Chunee', who was famous throughout London,

[27] William John Burchell (1782-1863). See background information in Pickering (1997).
[28] Described as *Rhinoceros simus* Burchell [now called *Ceratotherium simum* (Burchell)]. White is not its colour; it is a corruption of the Africaans for 'wide', this species having a wide, square top lip. The Black Rhinoceros *Diceros bicornis* (Linnæus) has a pointed prehensile top lip.
[29] J.E. Gray (House of Commons, 1836: paras 2918-2922).
[30] Charles König (House of Commons, 1835: paras 2805-2815).
[31] And some shells in Room VIII with Charles König's displays.
[32] November 1816. This was partly to take weight off the floor of the Saloon where the minerals were currently displayed, although it had been König's desire to have a display of British minerals since at least 1810 (Smith, 1969: 247-248).
[33] British Museum, Trustees' Committee Meeting, 14th June 1817.
[34] Gunther, 1980a: 217. Pickering, 1997: 312.
[35] British Museum, Trustees' Committee Meeting, 19th July 1817.
[36] Where they were described as "two enormous giraffes, in the character of stuffed guards, or emblems of English taste." (*English Diary* of Hermann Ludwig Heinrich, Prince of Pückler-Muskau (1785-1871) 15th October 1826. See Butler, 1957). By 1836, seventeen specimens were stuffed and displayed (House of Commons, 1836: para. 2918).
[37] Gunther, 1980a: 217.
[38] It is not known when during Elford Leach's time at the British Museum the following events occurred.

not just for mashing root vegetables or emulating Byron's butler, but for his stage appearances in pantomime (when the jealous props designer from a rival playhouse sourly observed, "I should be very sorry if I couldn't make a better elephant than *that*.[39]")

Visiting the menagerie one day, Elford noted Chunee had developed a serious growth on his trunk, not far from one of his eyes. He pointed this out to Cross, warning if it was left untreated it would probably expand and could well prove fatal. Cross agreed but did not see that anything could be done. Elford, however, was not prepared to give up that easily. His solution was described many years later by Mr J. Reading of Plymouth[40]:

'Dr Leach said that if bound tight round near the roots, circulation would be stopped and the excrescence would die and fall out. "Yes," said Mr Cross; "but who is to tie it?—he might crush the man to pieces." "I will venture it," said Dr Leach; "for, though it will give him pain, I think he may be made to understand that it is for his good to get rid of a sore and troublesome excrescence; so get me some strong silk thread, and let his keeper go in with me, and keep him soothed and occupy his attention." Accordingly, having obtained the thread, he mounted up, he and the keeper both speaking to the elephant, and induced him to submit to the operation. When it was bound round many times and securely tied, he descended to the floor of the menagerie, and observed the animal casting a knowing look upon him. On going to see him next day, he learned that after he was gone the elephant had turned up the finger of his trunk, and felt the binding all round till he found the knot, which he had either untied or broken, and then unwound the silk and threw it down. Dr Leach therefore talked to him in a reasoning manner, and, with the keeper's aid, induced him to submit to the operation a second time; but Dr Leach, observing the same knowing look, talked to him more upon the subject, and fastened the silk, as he thought, securely. However, he was no sooner gone than the animal began to try the fastening, and persevered until he had got it off again. On finding this, the next day Dr Leach brought some annealed brass wire, with which he again bound the excrescence, drawing the ends in under the binding so that they could not be got at. The substantial texture of the wire and its polished surface now baffled the attempts of the elephant, who at last gave it up, and submitted to the temporary annoyance, manifesting no displeasure at Dr Leach on his next visit. The result was, as Dr Leach had foretold, that the excrescence worked out in course of time; and the sore was not difficult to heal. Thus the elephant was saved; and Mr Cross insisted on Dr Leach receiving about twenty (I think) £5 notes for the venturous cure.'

Chunee survived and continued to entertain for many years. Unfortunately in 1826 he developed behavioural problems and became unmanageable. After an attempt to poison him failed an army firing squad was summoned.

[39] Lemon, 1867: 256-258.
[40] Reading (1857). Reading says he originally heard the story from a Mr I. Prideaux (this may be Roger Ilbert Prideaux (1765-1850) a Kingsbridge attorney and cousin of Charles Prideaux). Reading's 'Crosse' has been corrected to 'Cross'.

"Upwards of 260 shots were fired into the animal, who received the attacks of his assailants apparently unmoved. The guns were kept constantly firing at him until one took aim and shot him under one of the ears. The ball penetrated the brain, from which an enormous quantity of blood flowed. The noble brute seated himself on his haunches then folded his fore-legs under him, adjusted his trunk, and ceased to live—the only peaceful one among us cruel wretches.[41]" His skeleton was sent to William Clift at the Royal College of Surgeons.

Zoological Miscellany III

After a gap of 18 months, Elford decided it was time to publish another volume of the *Zoological Miscellany*, but this time James Sowerby was proposed as the publisher[42]. Unlike the earlier volumes this would not be issued in monthly parts, but would appear as a book containing 30 separate articles. These were a collection of the various oddments Elford had been working on, some in the style of the earlier volumes (illustrated descriptions of particular species), others a tabulation of characters for larger groups of animals. He may have decided to write a volume in this way because it allowed him to publish many articles while keeping control of the production, rather than submitting so many items to other journals.

Despite the plan, Sowerby did not publish the book, although he did prepare some of the original drawings[43]. It was produced in the autumn by Richard Nodder, who turned the drawings into coloured plates. This was to be the last volume of the *Miscellany*[44].

While he worked on this Elford had his eyes on the future. He wanted to get back to Paris. In July he asked the Trustees for permission to be absent from the Museum for three months from October to complete his studies at Paris and to attend lectures in zoology and comparative anatomy. He rather cheekily supported this application by saying he had already given up his Saturdays and short vacations for the past year. This is a clear case of double accounting. He had worked the vacations and Saturdays to compensate for his British collecting trip in 1816! Nevertheless, the Trustees granted his request.

Moving House

As the summer passed, Elford's life in the Museum became a little easier. A year earlier another of the Assistant Librarians, William Alexander in the Department of Manuscripts[45], had died. Alexander had lived in one of the officers' houses in the West Court of the Museum, which now became available, and although other officers had applied for the accommodation Elford was next in line for this perk. Unfortunately before he could give up his home in Lambeth, Alexander's house needed some repairs and the Board of Works were no swifter in this than they were with the Bird Room, where the delays were now becoming critical. Montagu's collection, in the basement

[41] Quoted without attribution on British television, 15th April 2000, in a BBC2 documentary (*Kings & Beasts*) about ancient menageries of London.
[42] Letter: W.E. Leach to G.B. Sowerby, n.d. (Loc: Central Library (Sowerby Archive), The Natural History Museum, London).
[43] Letter: W.E. Leach to James de Carle Sowerby, dated "Sept 8 Sat^y Mor^g" (Loc: General Library (Sowerby Archive), The Natural History Museum, London).
[44] John Gray used the name for another publication from 1831-1844.
[45] William Alexander (1767-1816). An artist who worked in the Department of Manuscripts with the title of Keeper of Prints (although not an Under-Librarian).

Great Russell Street, Bloomsbury, looking east along the front of the British Museum. The West Court is over the wooden fence on the left.

for nearly ten months, was beginning to deteriorate and Joseph Planta himself asked the Trustees to apply pressure to the government's Surveyor General to have the work in Room XI completed without delay.

By the middle of 1817 the Board of Works had at least completed Alexander's apartments, and Elford could move to the Museum. His new house adjoined Charles König's and they shared a common front door and staircase. He had seven rooms: on the ground floor a dining-room and a kitchen; above the dining room, a large drawing room leading to a smaller living room; a bedroom; and two garrets[46] (presumably intended for servants, although Elford does not appear to have used them for this). We must hope his new house was no colder than his last. After a warm summer[47] October 1817 began with a severe cold snap, more reminiscent of December. Piercing northerly winds brought the overnight temperatures close to freezing[48], but at least the cold arrived after the harvest, which, to the immense relief of the country after the acute shortages of 1816, had produced a plentiful crop.

After arranging the British crustaceans Elford spent the autumn working on the insects and birds. The Board of Works continued their efforts in Room XI and he kept a close watch on their activities, repeatedly requesting modifications to their plans for the display cases: ordering the addition of dust-excluding seals (as used in Paris); asking for different styles of hinge; and changing the sides of the bird cases from eight small panes of glass to four large panes.

Although he had arranged to leave for Paris in October, as usual he was still in the Museum when November arrived and while he worked and waited the nation was suddenly stunned by the announcement that Princess Charlotte, the only daughter of the Prince Regent and his estranged wife Princess Caroline, had died in childbirth[49].

[46] This is from König's description of his own house (House of Commons, 1835: paragraph 2547) but Elford had the same number of rooms (*op. cit.* Appendix 10(2): 399) and his adjoining house was probably identical, although it may have been a mirror image of König's.

[47] Bryant, 1975: 378.

[48] Kirby & Spence, 1859: 531fn.

[49] Charlotte Augusta (1796-1817). One of the doctors attending her labour was John Sims of the Linnean Society (page 110 above). Charlotte's son was stillborn and her death on the 6th of November diverted the line of succession for the British throne. Her father would now be succeeded by his brother William (William IV) then by William's niece, Victoria.

The West Court of the British Museum, seen from the street with the viewer looking over the fence. Elford Leach's house is on the left and the front door he shared with Charles König is visible between the trees.

(Illustrated in 1845 with the current Museum buildings under construction in the background)

Charlotte was a great favourite with the public. After the peace of 1814 she had been engaged to be married to the 'brave but that is all' William, Prince of Orange. With plans for their marriage well underway, her father had sent a guest list for her approval but when she noticed her mother's name was missing she simply drew a line through her own and sent it back. Two years later she married Prince Leopold of Saxe-Coburg[50] and William married Russian Grand Duchess Anna Pavlovna.

Charlotte's death in 1817 rocked the nation. A foreign observer in London described how she 'met in the streets people of every class in tears, the churches were full at all hours, the shops shut for a fortnight (an eloquent testimony from a shop-keeping community), and everyone from the highest to the lowest in a state of despair.[51]'

In December, as the nation slowly climbed out of mourning, Elford was still working in London as the carpenters put the finishing touches to the old Bird Room. Coincidentally, as 1818 arrived he finally completed his modern arrangement of the Museum's collections, and as nothing more could be done with the British displays until the varnish in the new room had dried, he decided this was a good time to take his leave. He finally set off for Paris at the beginning of February armed with £30 from the Museum to buy specimens, and with copies of his latest *Zoological Miscellany* for Lamarck and de Blainville.

1818

For the previous six months or so de Blainville had been the editor of the *Journal de Physique*[52], a French natural history periodical. Elford used their friendship to publish a number of original papers in this journal, and to have de Blainville publish abstracts of his longer works, but sometimes de Blainville's enthusiasm to fill his pages ran away with him and Elford's letters or pre-printed separates, sent for information to Paris, found

[50] Anglesey (1955: 231 note 7) says it was Prince William's name Charlotte crossed out. She married Leopold of Saxe-Coburg-Saalfeld (1790-1865), later King of the Belgians.
[51] Dorothea, Princess Lieven (1784-1857) (born Dorothea von Benkendorf) wife of Prince Lieven (1774-1857), a Russian diplomat (Robinson, 1902: 34). Henry Woollcombe recorded his own profound sense of shock in his diary.
[52] *Journal de Physique, de Chimie, d'Histoire Naturelle et des Arts.*

themselves in print in French before the publication of Elford's originals. The encyclopaedia article on barnacles was one example. Elford's brief letters discussing these had been turned into an article by de Blainville and published in Elford's name in July 1817, a full seven months before Elford's CIRRIPEDES entry in the *Encyclopædia Britannica*, which appeared just as he left for France. When he arrived at Paris one of Elford's first tasks was to pay a visit to Alexander MacLeay's son William[53], who was then living in the French capital.

William Sharp MacLeay had graduated from Cambridge in 1814 and moved to Paris as attaché at the British embassy. After the occupation of 1815 he became Secretary to the board for the liquidation of British claims in France. Like his father he was interested in natural history and would later know the professors at the Jardin des Plantes, especially Cuvier and Latreille. When Elford arrived in February 1818 MacLeay was working on a manuscript about insects, *Horæ Entomologicæ, or essays on the annulose animals* (published in two parts in 1819 and 1821[54]). Having spoken to him about his classification of beetles, Elford wrote to Alexander noting, "W[ms] general distribution of the Linnean Scarabæi into five families is excellent.[55]"

This division into *five* families was not an accident. William MacLeay was trying to understand how natural classifications reflected the overall pattern of nature, and had come to the conclusion this pattern revolved around the number 5. This led him to develop a classification in which each animal group is composed of five smaller groups, each of which is also composed of five groups, and so on. He represented this graphically as a ring of five 'osculating' (kissing) circles. For example, MacLeay said the animal kingdom was composed of the 5 groups: Vertebrata (animals that have backbones); Annulosa (animals with hard segmented bodies – insects, crustaceans etc.); Radiata (starfish and their allies with radiating bodies); Mollusca; and Acrita (a miscellaneous group of species). Of these, the Vertebrata (for example) comprised the 5 groups Mammals, Birds, Reptiles, Amphibians, and Fish. Within this classification he allowed for intermediates (or *osculating classes*) where

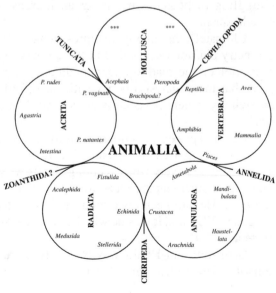

53 William Sharp MacLeay (1792-1865). Lived in Paris 1814-1819 then returned to London. In 1825 moved to Havanna, Cuba, as Commissioner of Arbitration to the British-Spanish court for the abolition of the slave trade. He was a judge in this court 1830-1835 then returned to England. In 1839 he moved to New South Wales, Australia (formerly called New Holland).
54 He named two species, *Areoda leachii* and *Paxillus leachii*, in the part for 1819.
55 Letter: W.E. Leach to A. MacLeay, 16th February 1818 (Loc: Linnean Society, MacLeay Correspondence).

the circles touched, and for affinities between groups in different circles. *Horæ Entomologicæ* introduced this arrangement, which he called the 'Circular System of Affinities'. However, it relied so much on nested sets of 5 that others called it 'The Quinary System'.

This system of classification was given serious consideration during the 1820s, although it was not widely accepted. In December 1821 William Kirby wrote to his friend Alexander MacLeay paying the fulsome compliment:

'I cannot go far in this letter without congratulating you upon the eminence to which your son is fast rising in Entomology. Whatever difference at present there may be in our sentiments as to some points in his system, I shall always be ready to pay the just tribute of applause to the depth, erudition and genius that are so conspicuously displayed in his truly Opus magnum. It has diffused a new and copious flood of Light over the whole science of natural History – and whether his System abide the ordeal trial or not, if not the *very* System of Nature it will lead to the discovery of it and his name will always stand at the head of the Science[56]'.

In the 3rd and 4th volumes of *Introduction to Entomology* (both 1826) Kirby discussed this in print[57] and wrote, "Mr MacLeay's whole system upon paper appears very harmonious and consistent, and bears a most seducing aspect of verisimilitude; but it has not yet been so thoroughly weighed, discussed, and sifted, as to justify our adopting it *in toto* at present[58]" (the Reverend Kirby, steeped in the word of the Bible, also felt the number 7 had a greater claim to be the Creator's yardstick[59]).

When William Swainson returned from Brazil he became a great supporter of the quinary system, and when William MacLeay was posted to Cuba in 1825 Swainson became the system's staunchest advocate in Britain, struggling to promote it among an increasingly sceptical zoological establishment.

Ultimately, this attempt to represent natural classifications by repetitive geometry did not wear well and the quinary system was later seen as an aberration on the road to understanding, owing more to a presumption of order than to an analysis of observations. Elford may have liked the look of the quinary system in its early stages, but he never adopted it in his own work.

Having spoken to William, Elford settled down to work at the Paris museum and reported to Alexander MacLeay, "Cuvier and all the Professors have received me very well excepting Geoffroy, who has not called on me.[60]" This was another significant zoologist of the time, Étienne Geoffroy Saint-Hilaire[61]. He had been appointed Professor of Zoology at the Jardin des Plantes in 1793 and it was he who had attracted Cuvier to the museum two years later.

Geoffroy Saint-Hilaire was especially interested in the physical form of animals. He studied this in part by investigating physical defects and

[56] Letter: Kirby to MacLeay, 27th December 1821 (Loc: Linnean Society of London).
[57] Kirby & Spence (1826) **3**: 12-15, 19-21; **4**: 359-363, 465-470.
[58] Kirby & Spence (1826) **3**: 20.
[59] Kirby & Spence (1826) **3**: 15fn.
[60] Letter: W.E. Leach to A. MacLeay, 16th February 1818 (Loc: Linnean Society, MacLeay Correspondence).
[61] Étienne Geoffroy Saint-Hilaire (1772-1844). In 1798 he had accompanied Napoleon to Egypt. Since 1809 had been Professor of Zoology at the University of Paris.

embryonic deformities across a range of species, being the first to elevate this 'teratology' [study of monsters] to a true science. In 1818 he and Cuvier were in the early stages of an amicable disagreement about the relative importance of form and function which would reach a head in a series of public debates in the spring of 1830.

Essentially, Geoffroy Saint-Hilaire believed all vertebrate animals were based on one body plan[62]. He went further, saying animals were obliged to live in certain ways, dictated by the structure of their body. Cuvier, on the other hand, said the form of the body was dictated by the way of life. He approached comparative anatomy from a functional viewpoint, believing different species displayed similar anatomy because the parts resembling each other performed similar functions – for example the tail of a fish and the tail of a whale (a mammal) resemble each other because both propel animals through water. In modern language, Geoffroy Saint-Hilaire stressed homology, Cuvier stressed analogy. Although today we acknowledge the importance of both, in the early nineteenth century the differences were a matter for strong feelings.

In his search for the relationship between organs and a common pattern, Geoffroy Saint-Hilaire was a pioneer in uncovering the relative relationships of bones and muscles in different species. Darwin later said in *The Origin of Species*:

"This is the most interesting part of natural history, and may be said to be its very soul. What can be more curious than that the hand of a man, formed for grasping, that of a mole for digging, the leg of the horse, the paddle of the porpoise, and the wing of the bat, should all be constructed on the same pattern, and should include the same bones, in the same relative positions? Geoffroy St Hilaire has insisted strongly on the high importance of relative connexion in homologous organs: the parts may change to almost any extent in form and size, and yet they always remain connected together in the same order.[63]"

Geoffroy Saint-Hilaire eventually took his ideas too far, claiming there was only one fundamental body plan for the whole animal kingdom and that the organs of a man could be traced in the same pattern in an octopus or an insect. This was too much for Cuvier, who was able to show otherwise, but both men deserve credit for the advances in understanding they produced.

When Elford arrived in Paris in 1818 the anatomical investigations of the day were less sweeping, as he told Patrick Neill[64], the Secretary of the Wernerian Society, 'The position of the organ of hearing in fishes, and the structure and modifications of the Os linguæ [tongue-bone] and sternum [breast-bone], are the principal, I may say the only points of discussion in the zoologic world in Paris at this moment. Geoffroy St Hilaire and Blainville pursue this object with very different ideas and views. Spurzheim and myself too differ as to the number of soldered vertebræ that form the base of the skull in vertebrose animals, and Blainville has still a different

[62] He expressed this in his book *Philosophie Anatomique* in 1818.
[63] Chapter 13; Section *Morphology* (Darwin, 1859).
[64] Patrick Neill (1776-1851). Secretary since the foundation of the Wernerian Society in January 1808. Was also the Secretary of the Horticultural Society, Edinburgh, and contributed entries to the *Edinburgh Encyclopædia*.

opinion on this difficult subject; yet we carry on our scientific war without volcanic explosions or Wernerian deluges, striving each one to ascertain the truth.[65]'

a chiton

Elford has clearly been collaborating with his friend Spurzheim, who was still working on the anatomy of the skull, and also collaborated with Cuvier in an investigation of the nerve pathways in chitons (marine molluscs that cling tenaciously to intertidal rocks in a manner similar to limpets), part of his ongoing investigation of this group of animals[66].

During this trip a unique honour was bestowed on Elford; he was permitted to present a paper to the Académie Royale des Sciences, the first Englishman to do so. Elford – the self-confessed "indifferent French scholar" – talked to the academicians about the hinge mechanism of bivalve molluscs (much to their amusement according to John Gray[67], who nevertheless assures us, "I need not add, with his vivacity, that he did not disgrace his country[68]"). Another indication of the seriousness with which the French professors took Elford's work was that he was appointed the British Museum's correspondent for the French national museum[69]. The Academy of Natural Sciences of Philadelphia had already elected him a member in January, as had the Academy of Sciences at Turin, and he was by now a member of the Société Philomathique in Paris and the Natural History Society of Berlin. His international reputation was growing.

Dufresne's Collection

Although Elford had not yet displayed Montagu's collection in London, when he discovered another major collection was for sale in Paris he was determined to secure it for Britain. This was the collection of Louis Dufresne[70], the head of the zoological laboratories at the Jardin des Plantes,

who had responsibility for preparing and conserving the zoological collections. Dufresne was in contact with many explorers and his ornithology collection alone amounted to 1500 birds (1400 species and varieties) and 700-800 eggs. He was asking 1600 guineas (40,000 francs) for the birds[71], or £2240 for the zoological collection as a whole, which Elford and other informed observers felt was a bargain[72].

Elford knew there was little hope of the Trustees at the British Museum buying the collection, but there was always Edinburgh. He wrote to Patrick Neill on the

[65] Letter: Leach to Neill, 1st March 1818 (Loc: Edinburgh University Library, Special Collections). His spelling has been corrected and Latin terms explained.

[66] Leach, 1852: 227.

[67] Gray, 1824: 220. Gray was reporting hearsay.

[68] Leach (1852: 246) says he also gave this talk to the Philomathic Society in Paris in 1815. This may be a misprint for 1818, but aspects of the hinge mechanism of bivalves had been indicated to him by John Miller of Bristol by 1814 (Gray, 1824: 213).

[69] Deleuze, 1823: 184.

[70] Louis Dufresne (1752-1832). See Sweet (1970b).

[71] See Note on the collection of Birds from Mr Dufresne's cabinet of Natural History by Royer at Paris (see later) sent on 2nd March 1818 to Patrick Neill (Loc: Edinburgh University Library, Special Collections. Ms 1801/2/1). Elford helped prepare this. Sweet (1970b: 43) says the monetary conversion was "25 francs to the £", but the enclosure says 25 francs / guinea [1 guinea = £1.1s.0d].

[72] Letter: Thomas Brown to Jameson, 29th March 1819 (Loc: Edinburgh University Library, Special Collections. Ref: Ms 1801/2/14). The informed observers were Brown and William Bullock. [Thomas Brown (1785-1862) Born Perth. Captain in the Forfarshire Militia and primarily a conchologist. By 1838 was Curator of Manchester's Natural History Museum].

[73] François Levaillant (1753-1824). French explorer and ornithologist. A friend of Dufresne.

Margarita sinensis Leach (a bivalve mollusc)

Illustration from the *Zoological Miscellany* October 1814

[74] Coenraad Jacob Temminck (1778-1858). Ornithologist and first Director of the Rijks Museum van Natuurlijke Historie at Leiden from 1820-1858.

[75] Letter: W.E. Leach to Neill, 1st March 1818 (Loc: Edinburgh University Library, Special Collections).

[76] George Bellas Greenough (1778-1855). Geologist and M.P. for Borough of Gatton 1807-1812. Founder member and first President of the Geological Society of London (1808). Served on the Geological Society's council from 1810-1855. By the late 1820s he was living in a large detached villa, Grove House, in the newly developed Regent's Park. The villa is described at length and illustrated by Shepherd & Elmes (1829: 30-34 + plate).

[77] Charles Stokes (1783-1853). Member of the Stock Exchange and enthusiastic collector. Elford described molluscs he collected at Lymington, by Southampton (Leach, 1852: 319).

[78] Letter: Leach to Jameson, 14th April 1819 (Loc: Edinburgh University Library Special Collections).

[79] This seems optimistic. There was nowhere to display 1400 birds.

[80] Letter: W.E. Leach to [Jameson], 15th November 1818 (Loc: Edinburgh University Library, Special Collections).

[81] Letter: Thomas Brown to Jameson, 29th March 1819 (Loc: Edinburgh University Library, Special Collections. Ref: Ms 1801/2/14). Brown acted in Paris on behalf of Edinburgh University.

[82] Letter: Brown to Jameson, 22nd May 1819 (Loc: Edinburgh University Library Special Collections. Ref: Ms 1801/2/30).

[83] Letter: Brown to Jameson, 22 May 1819 (loc. cit.)

1st of March urging him to raise money to bring the birds (at least) to Edinburgh University. Neill had obviously been to Paris and was familiar with the collection.

'It is unnecessary for me to point out to you the advantages that would result to Science, were the invaluable collection of Dufresne deposited in your magnificent room in Edinburgh, since you have seen its contents. I wish most sincerely that you may be so fortunate as to obtain from the Government or Town Council the sum demanded for this scientific assemblage of riches, which have been named by actual comparison with the original specimens contained in the National Museum, and in the collections of LeVaillant[73] and other celebrated Ornithologists. Many of the genera and species too are unique and have been determined by Temminck[74] and other writers who have visited them. Had I the cash to spare or could I prevail on our Trustees to purchase it, I can assure you, that many weeks should not elapse, before it should be deposited in our National Establishment.[75]'

In fact the French zoologists were a little reticent at the idea of such a fine collection going to Edinburgh, rather than London. They felt it would be less accessible in Scotland. In response Elford started a subscription among his friends (including Alexander MacLeay, James Stephens, George Greenough[76] and Charles Stokes[77])[78] to attempt to raise the funds to buy the collection for the British Museum[79] or any other appropriate London venue. He warned Robert Jameson of this[80] but told him if he could not raise the money he would do all he could to see the collection went to Edinburgh.

It would be the following year before the fate of Dufresne's collection was decided. Elford and his friends pledged over £800 and he tried to induce the Treasury to provide funds[81], but to no avail. The University of Edinburgh borrowed money from the Edinburgh banks and purchased the whole collection, despite a last minute attempt by Elford to buy the shells separately[82]. Greenough in particular had wanted the shells to go to London and was very annoyed they did not. He claimed he would have increased his subscription to have access to them. Alexander MacLeay would have doubled his[83].

Historical note

1818

28th January	Right to issue writs of *habeas corpus* is restored.
March	Mary Shelley's *Frankenstein* published anonymously.
5th May	Karl Heinrich Marx (1818-1883) born at Trier.
1st June	In parliament a motion for franchise reform is defeated.
July to August	Disturbances during strike of Manchester cotton spinners.
August	Riots at Stockport during strike of power-loom weavers.
August	Squatters riots in Wales.

This attempt to divert the shells reflected Elford's increasing interest in molluscs, and his knowledge of the British species made his trip to Paris very convenient for a French worker with similar interests, the Baron de Férussac[84]. Férussac was Professor of Geography and Statistics at the School of the General Staff in Paris, but with a private interest in molluscs he was trying to bring himself up to date with the activities of British workers during the long war that had restricted Anglo-French communication. In this Elford was ideally suited to help him[85]. In return Férussac gave Elford a collection of insects from southern France[86].

For European Crustacea, Elford's expertise was already becoming widely known through the publication of his *Edinburgh Encyclopædia* article; the regular appearances of *Malacostraca*; and his major paper in the *Transactions of the Linnean Society*. Recognising this, one of Férussac's contacts, a Monsieur d'Orbigny, had given Férussac a small collection of crabs to pass on to him. Elford promised d'Orbigny[87] he would send him some molluscs and crabs in exchange as soon as he returned to England[88].

Elford was planning to be back in London at the beginning of April. True to form, his deadline slipped back to the beginning of May[89] but this may not have been his fault. He was delayed because he would no longer be returning alone. Latreille and Cuvier had decided to visit Britain. Latreille was planning an extended visit to examine insects, especially Linnæus's collection in the Linnean Society, Sir Joseph Banks' collection, and the collection in the British Museum. Cuvier initially intended to stay only three weeks, but he decided to mix business with pleasure and make this a family holiday. He would now be accompanied by his wife and daughters (presumably including Sophie Duvaucel[90]) and by his friend and secretary Charles Laurillard[91]. They would all be staying for six weeks.

England

The party arrived in London in the first week of May and Cuvier began a hectic round of socialising and information gathering, during which Elford was his 'incessant chaperon'[92]. At a meeting with the Prince Regent Cuvier famously noted that if all the private natural history collections in Britain were united they would form the finest national museum of natural history in the world (which could be seen as a clear indictment of the state of Montagu House, when the nation's collections were dispersed in private hands rather than lodged in the existing national museum).

The Cuviers were also lavishly entertained by Sir Joseph Banks at his country house, *Spring Grove*[93], and visited the 80 year old astronomer Sir William Herschel[94] and his sister Caroline[95]. Herschel had discovered the planet Uranus in 1781 (when he originally named it *Georgium Sidus* – the George star) and Caroline, an astronomer in her own right, had discovered no fewer than eight comets. Cuvier also visited Oxford University where he was warmly fêted and presumably where he met geologist and

[84] Baron André Étienne Justin Pascal Joseph François d'Audibert (or d'Audebard) de Férussac (1786-1836). He gave the genus name *Littorina* to the ubiquitous winkles in 1822.
[85] Férussac, 1820: 213-214.
[86] Letter: W.E. Leach to A. MacLeay, 16th February 1818 (Loc: Linnean Society, MacLeay Correspondence).
[87] This person is not fully identified but is almost certainly the physician and naturalist Charles-Marie Dessalines d'Orbigny (1770-1856) who had served as Surgeon-Major to the French expedition to Ireland in 1798. He was now a civilian doctor at Esnandes, north of La Rochelle but had a passion for natural history, especially the biology and commercial culture of mussels, on which he wrote several pioneering works. Less probably this could be his eldest son, the 15 year old Alcide Charles Victor Dessalines d'Orbigny (1802-1857) later a disciple of Cuvier [Alcide was sent to South America by the Paris museum in 1826 and stayed until 1833 studying the geology, natural history and the people of the continent. He is famous today for his interest in microscopic fossils, through which he virtually founded the science of micropalaeontology, an important tool used for determining the sequence in which rock strata were deposited, and a discipline central to oil exploration. Alcide d'Orbigny was one of the most distinguished geological stratigraphers of the 19th century].
[88] Letter: W.E. Leach to Mon[r] D'Orbigny, 27th April 1818 (Loc: Wellcome Institute for the History of Medicine, London. Ref. WMS/ALS:Leach).

palaeontologist William Buckland[96], the university's Reader in Mineralogy and soon to be its first mineralogy Professor. Buckland, a Devonian, later supported Elford's consortium trying to purchase Dufresne's collection for London[97].

Cuvier did not want this visit to be solely scientific, he also wanted to see for himself the British style of constitutional government. His involvement in legislation and public administration in France had already led him to take an interest in the very different political system across the Channel and public figures who met him were astonished at his detailed knowledge of British public affairs, right down to the history and financing of public institutions.

It was while he was pursuing this interest on one of the rare days when Elford could not accompany him (he needed to assist Latreille) that Cuvier had one of his most enjoyable outings. Elford had entrusted him to the care of the 18 year old John Gray (a clear indication of the respect Elford had for Gray's competence and character) and Gray took him to witness an example of British democracy in action.

In June 1818 there was a parliamentary general election in Britain and Gray and Cuvier went to hear the politicians addressing a public gathering at Covent Garden during the contest for the seat of Westminster. The speeches from the open-air platform drew a large crowd, most of whom were doubtless not eligible to vote, few of whom had much interest in what was being said, and the majority of whom saw this as one of the few remaining lawful opportunities to express their innermost feelings. Cuvier's student and biographer Sarah Lee[98] described the scene:

"These orgies of liberty were then unknown in France, and it was a curious spectacle for a man who reflected so deeply on every thing which passed before him, to see and hear our orators crying out at the tops of their voices to the mob, who pelted them with mud, cabbages, eggs, &c.; and Sir Murray Maxwell[99], in his splendid uniform, and decorated with orders, flattering the crowd, who reviled him, and sent at his head all the varieties of the vegetable kingdom.[100]"

The mob grew increasingly boisterous and eventually Cuvier and Gray had to beat a hasty retreat to avoid being caught in the botanical crossfire, much to the great man's amusement. In later life he used to relate the story with a great deal of animation and obvious pleasure.

As the elections continued they became even more unruly. The Clerk to the Privy Council, Charles Greville[101], noted in his diary for the 24th of June:

"The disgraceful scenes which have taken place in Westminster excite universal shame and indignation. The mob seem to have shaken off the feelings and the usual character of Englishmen, and in the brutal attacks which they have made on Captain Maxwell have displayed the savage ferocity which marked the mobs of Paris in the worst times. He has been so

[89] By which he missed one of the wettest Aprils in Britain's history.

[90] Her brother Alfred had sailed to India the previous December with another naturalist, Pierre Médard Diard (1794-1860), to collect specimens for Cuvier.

[91] Charles Laurillard (1783-1853). Became Cuvier's draughtsman and secretary in 1804 and was his friend until Cuvier's death.

[92] Lee, 1833: 39.

[93] At Isleworth, 14 km west of London.

[94] Sir Frederick William Herschel (1738-1822). Born in Hanover. Came to England as a musician and taught music at Bath. Took up astronomy as a hobby.

[95] Caroline Lucretia Herschel (1750-1848).

[96] William Buckland (1784-1856). Ordained 1809. Professor of Mineralogy at Oxford from 1819.

[97] Letter: W.E. Leach to Jameson, 8th February 1819 (Loc: University of Edinburgh Library, Special Collections. Ref: Ms 1801/2/9).

[98] Sarah Lee (née Wallis) (1791-1856). See Beaver (1999).

[99] Sir Murray Maxwell (1775-1831). A Royal Navy Captain knighted only several weeks earlier (27th May 1818). Elected FRS 18th February 1819. He was not elected to parliament.

[100] Lee, 1833: 37-38.

[101] Charles Cavendish Fulke Greville (1794-1865). Clerk to the Privy Council 1821-1859.

much hurt that his life is now in danger"; and six days later, "There was an affray yesterday afternoon in Covent Garden. Sir Murray Maxwell's people paraded about a large boat drawn by six horses. Burdett's[102] mob attacked and demolished the boat, and this action having raised their spirits, the contest continued. The consequence was that a large party of Horse Guards were marched into Covent Garden, and paraded there during the rest of the night. The people expressed their discontent by cries of 'This is what they call freedom of election!'[103]"

Amid the general hubbub, Elford and Latreille toiled quietly over the insects, and while they did Elford was approached by one of his contacts from London's community of amateur entomologists, George Samouelle[104]. Samouelle, a porter at the publishers *Longmans*, was planning to write a simple introduction to the practical aspects of entomology, describing which collecting equipment to use, how to prepare specimens, how to use a microscope, and how to arrange a collection. It was well known in entomological circles that Kirby and Spence were planning to include a section of this nature in their *Introduction to Entomology*, but it had not been incorporated in the first two volumes (the second volume had been published in 1817[105]) and the need for such a work was widely recognised.

Elford immediately saw the potential for expanding Samouelle's plan to include the classification of British insects. Collectors could then have in one volume advice on how to collect insects, when and where to collect them, and how to identify them. They could also be encouraged to arrange them in their cabinets according to Elford's preferred modern, natural system. Samouelle accepted the challenge and Elford handed over his manuscripts and the works he had already published. Samouelle's book appeared in June 1819[106] and the subtitle explained its scope: *The Entomologist's Useful Compendium; or an Introduction to the Knowledge of British Insects comprising the best means of obtaining and preserving them, and a Description of the Apparatus generally used; together with the Genera of Linné, and the modern method of arranging the Classes Crustacea, Myriapoda, Spiders, Mites and Insects, from their Affinities and Structure, according to the Views of Dr Leach.* The dedication was "to Dr W.E. Leach FRS &c. &c." and concluded, '... It is also to be hoped that in England, ere long, Entomology will stand on the same ground with Botany, Chemistry, or Mineralogy; and that your labours will eventually be as duly appreciated in this country as they are now on the Continent'.

Francillon's Sale

When Cuvier and Latreille returned to France Elford could finally start arranging the British zoology displays in the newly refurbished room. This would take six months to complete and would keep him indoors throughout the particularly warm summer. Meanwhile, another sale of natural history specimens was taking place in London, this time of insects. The extensive

[102] Sir Francis Burdett *Bt* (1770-1844). He was one of the two successful candidates.

[103] Wilson (1927) **1**: 324-325.

[104] George Samouelle (d.1846). He lived in Blackfriars Road, London. Elford Leach had known him since at least 1817 (*Zoological Miscellany*, **3**: 83).

[105] In the year 1818 Spence succumbed to intense headaches which forced him to stop working and to withdraw from the collaboration. He handed all his notes to Kirby, who did not publish the final two volumes (volume 4 with collecting advice) until 1826.

[106] Published by *Thomas Boys*. A reprinting in 1824 was published by *Longman, Hurst, Rees, Orme, Brown and Green.*

collection had belonged to John Francillon[107], an enthusiastic collector and dealer who, like Dufresne, had used a wide network of contacts to acquire specimens from exotic far-flung locations.

Francillon had recently died and in early 1817 his executors had offered his collection of insects and drawings to the British Museum for £1450. Elford had tried very hard to induce the Trustees to purchase at least part of this. Even the government had been approached for funds but showed no interest. Elford then suggested the Trustees might purchase only the duplicates. They still declined to take the bait but in July 1817 had given him permission to spend £20 on British insects at the forthcoming sale and up to £300 on drawings of insects from the American state of Georgia[108]. In fact the sale did not take place until June 1818 but in the interim Alexander MacLeay had access to the collection[109] and Elford wanted to buy some specimens ahead of the auction. He had written to MacLeay from Paris in March:

'After you have picked out 100 Insects from Francillon's collection of exotic Insects, I will readily take all the [*lists the groups he wants*] at the rate of 8[d] or 9[d] an insect. If you can secure these for me, I shall feel most deeply obliged and if the dust[110] be wanted before I return, I will send you a draft for the amount as soon as I hear from you again.[111]'

It is not clear whether Elford received any insects through MacLeay because in June 1818 the Trustees allowed him to spend up to £40 (double their offer of the previous year) buying insects belonging to the same orders he had asked MacLeay to obtain for him. The Museum's donation book records a range of specimens from this sale presented by Elford, including spiders (which he certainly had no approval to buy) and it appears he bought some items with his own money then gave them to the Museum.

While Elford struggled on with the British gallery he was distracted by the arrival of another African collection. This came from Thomas Bowdich[112] (at that time Sarah Lee's husband). Although the same age as Elford, he had just made his second trip to the Gold Coast – the modern Ghana – and returned, in poor health, with a collection of works of art and zoology. Elford took receipt of the animals and prepared a description for Bowdich's published account of his travels[113] during which he got to know Bowdich and his wife quite well. The following year the Bowdiches decided to move to Paris for several years to study at the museum, and left for France armed with a letter of introduction to Cuvier from Elford, by now their "mutually cherished friend[114]".

Caroline?

In France in 1818 the *Dictionnaire des Sciences Naturelle* published Elford's first entries on Crustacea[115]. Secreted among these was a tantalising puzzle for posterity. Elford described a number of new genera of isopod crustaceans (carnivorous marine relatives of the humble wood-louse) and

[107] John Francillon (1744-1816).
[108] The drawings were by John Abbot (1751-1840).
[109] As had others. In 1817 Charles Lyell (1797-1875 – later the eminent geologist whose work influenced Charles Darwin but now at the end of his first year as a student at Oxford and interested in entomology-visited London specifically to see Francillon's collection (Gardiner, 1998: 10).
[110] 'dust' – Slang: cash; money.
[111] Letter: W.E. Leach to MacLeay, 15th March 1818 (Loc: Linnean Society, MacLeay Correspondence).
[112] Thomas Edward Bowdich (1791-1824). His uncle was Governor-in-Chief to the settlements of *The African Company*. In 1814 Bowdich obtained a post in the Gold Coast, returning the same year. In 1815 he went to the Gold Coast for three years with his wife and made his collections. On his return he criticised *The African Company*'s administration so severely the government took control of its territories.
[113] Bowdich (1819).
[114] Lee, 1833: 5.
[115] Cuvier (1818) **12**: 347-352.

for nine of these genera he invented names that were anagrams of 'Caroline' (Some of his *scientific* names are actually anagrams of 'Carolina', but in those cases the French common name – which he must also have invented – is the anagram of 'Caroline').

These names, scientific and French, were: *Nelocira* (Nélocire); *Cirolana* (Cirolane); *Conilera* (Conilère); *Rocinela* (Rocinèle); *Canolira* (Canolire); *Anilocra* (Anilocre); *Olencira* (Olencire); *Nerocila* (Nérocile); and *Lironeca* (Lironèce). Unfortunately the printer misread his hand-writing for the last name and it was published as *Livoneca*[116]. In his unpublished manuscripts he had also used the name *Cilonera*[117]. But, who was Caroline?[118]

Niel Bruce, a modern crustacean worker, has suggested this could be a disapproving reference to Caroline of Brunswick, wife of the Prince Regent.

'It would appear that the use of Caroline/Carolina anagrams for blood-sucking parasites was a cunning, repetitive and enduring insult to Caroline, who was the estranged wife of the Prince of Wales and who has been described as an unlovable adulteress... Evidently Leach was sympathetic to the Prince's cause.[119]'

There is no doubt that at various times during the early years of the nineteenth century the British press and popular opinion polarised in their support for George or for Caroline. When William Clift was at Cheltenham with his good friend John Abernethy in 1821 (by which time the prince had become King George IV and Caroline had become Queen) he wrote home to his wife, "All the Cheltenhammers are violent Queenites but we carried *God save the King* through in Triumph last night, in spite of a violent opposition. They would have God save the Queen, but I insisted upon having the Queen's hornpipe if any.[120]" Clift obviously favoured George.

In truth the royal couple were an equally unlovable pair. George, just as unfaithful as Caroline and the architect of their separation, openly loathed his wife. When Napoleon eventually died on St Helena in 1821 an aide took the news to him with the words, "Sire, your greatest enemy is dead." "*Is she by God?*" he replied.

George was a frivolous man obsessed with fashion and little else. Personally he could be very charming (as Harry Smith had discovered) but many members of the public just saw him as a drain on the economy. Leigh Hunt[121], editor of the weekly *Examiner*, had been imprisoned for two years in 1813 for seditious libel after telling his readers George was, "a libertine over head and ears in debt and disgrace, a despiser of domestic ties, the companion of gamblers and demireps, a man who has just closed half a century without one single claim on the gratitude of his country or the respect of posterity" (all of which was probably true) and Wellington once said George was the worst man he fell in with in his whole life, the most selfish, the most false, the most ill-natured, the most entirely without redeeming quality[122]. Others have noted George III mad probably had greater respect from his subjects than George IV sane[123].

[116] In the archives of the Linnean Society in London there is an English version of the French text, written in Elford's hand (Ref: SP 586), in which he has clearly used the form 'Lironeca' (KH *pers. obs.*) and in the reprint he gave Latreille he corrected 'Livoneca' / 'Livonèce' to 'Lironeca' / 'Lironèce' several times (Monod, 1931: 5 footnote). Similarly, in his earlier entry for the *Dictionnaire*, 'CRUSTACÉS', in which a French form appears, this is printed 'Lironecée'. The International Commission on Zoological Nomenclature has nevertheless determined 'Livoneca' must be the name used for this genus (Opinion 1849. *Bulletin of Zoological Nomenclature*, **53**(3): 210-212 (1996)).

[117] White, 1847: 108.

[118] Arguments that there was no Caroline, and that this combination of vowels and consonants simply appealed to Elford (as suggested by Thomas Stebbing in 1893) can be dismissed as too improbable.

[119] Bruce, 1995: 69.

[120] Letter: William Clift to Caroline Clift, 21st August 1821 (General Library (Owen Correspondence), Natural History Museum, London). Queen Caroline had died two weeks earlier.

[121] James Henry Leigh Hunt (1784-1859).

[122] Bamford & Wellington (1950) **2**: 266. At George's death Wellington was more forgiving, saying he had been, "The most extraordinary compound of talent, wit, buffoonery, obstinacy and good feeling — in short a medley of the most opposite qualities with a great preponderance of good—that I ever saw in any character in my life." (Bamford & Wellington (1950) **1**: xv).

[123] Evans, 1989: 3.

On the other hand, it has also been said with some justification that "Caroline was vulgar and indiscreet; her conduct, if not actually criminal, was of a levity and folly which it is impossible to defend; nor would any have been found to champion her cause had she not suffered from the unspeakable misfortune of being the wife of George IV[124]". In 1820, after spying on her for years, parliament finally summoned Caroline and (in all but name) tried her for adultery. During the proceedings an epigram appeared which summed up the attitudes of many:

> Most gracious Queen, we thee implore
> To go away and sin no more;
> But if that effort be too great,
> To go away at any rate[125].

Even those who supported Caroline in these years of regal mud-wrestling did so not because they thought she was innocent, but because they knew George was guilty.

The problem with treating Elford's genus names as a calculated insult is that he named the species after people he clearly respected: *Cirolana cranchii*; *Conilera montagui*; *Olencira lamarckii*; *Nerocila blainvillii*. This might suggest the nature of the animals' blood-sucking life-style was irrelevant and his names were intended to express support for Caroline.

Princess Caroline had been living on the Continent since 1816 and ordinarily would not have been prominent in anyone's mind at the time Elford was preparing his text. Princess Charlotte's death at the end of 1817 did increase sympathy for her mother but it is difficult to see why Elford would choose to name genera after Caroline and not after Charlotte if it was this that had prompted him.

It may be that Caroline of Brunswick is not the right Caroline. Elford could just as easily have been honouring Caroline Herschel for the comets she had discovered. However there is no reason why the Caroline in question must be a Caroline that is visible to us, nearly 200 years later. During the Regency the name Caroline was extremely popular. Virtually every family, especially genteel families, had Carolines. We have already met Caroline Capel. William Clift's wife was a Caroline and so was his daughter.

The search, without further evidence, is too difficult. Perhaps from our distance we shall never know who Elford Leach's Caroline was or why she was so important to him, but clearly something moved him to generate names in this very deliberate way.

Postscript

124 Alington, 1921: 75.
125 Alington, 1920: 76.
'At any rate' – a southern English expression meaning 'anyway'.

Subsequent authors have considered this game too good to ignore, and further anagrams of Caroline and Carolina have been published: *Renocila* Miers, 1880; *Corilana* Kossman, 1880; *Alcirona* Hansen, 1890; *Lanocira* Hansen, 1890; *Nalicora* Moore, 1902; *Orcilana* Nierstrasz, 1931; *Creniola* Bruce, 1987 and *Norileca* Bruce, 1990. There is still potential for more.

PART FIRST,

containing the first six days' sale.

Catalogue

(without which no Person can be admitted to the View or Sale)

of the

ROMAN GALLERY,

of

ANTIQUITIES AND WORKS OF ART,

and the

LONDON MUSEUM OF NATURAL HISTORY:

(unquestionably the most extensive and valuable in Europe)

at the

EGYPTIAN HALL IN PICCADILLY;

WHICH WILL BE SOLD BY AUCTION,

positively without the least reserve,

BY MR. BULLOCK,

on the premises,

on Thursday the 29th of April, 1819,

And continue every Tuesday, Wednesday, Thursday, and Friday, till the whole
is sold.

To commence precisely at ONE o'clock.

The remaining Parts of the Catalogue, about Twenty days, will be published with all possible
speed; the Articles to be viewed THREE DAYS previous to that on which they are respectively
sold.

The wording presented here is believed to be correct but the actual typesetting of the original has not been seen.

— 25 —

Bullock's sale

Duties which, to be performed, would have required the activity of five or six naturalists, were imposed upon one; the task was Herculean.

William Swainson[1]

In September 1818, while the British Museum was closed to the public, Elford Leach worked on, setting out the British zoology. Meanwhile another Assistant Librarian, John Children from the Department of Antiquities[2], took his vacation and travelled to the Continent with his 19 year old daughter Anna[3] and John Gray's older brother Samuel[4]. Children had once spent three years as an officer in the West Kent Militia[5] and a visit to the battlefield at Waterloo was on the party's itinerary.

Like thousands of tourists before them they hired a local guide to show them the key parts of the field; in their case François Brassine from Mont St Jean. Brassine led them to the brow of the ridge behind La Haye Sainte and as he identified the now famous Wellington Tree Anna Children could not resist taking out her sketch-pad to record this icon of a free Europe[6].

As she drew, their guide started to herd the party towards the next point of interest but Children asked if they could wait until Anna had finished. Happy to oblige, Brassine remarked it would be a timely illustration. If they had arrived one day later there would have been nothing to draw. Thousands of tourists carving mementoes from the tree's trunk had achieved something Napoleon's artillery had not, and it could not have survived much longer. The owner of the land[7] was also unamused by these armies of whittlers trampling his crops and had decided it was time the elm was felled. The ground had already been cleared around its base and its main roots cut. The execution was to take place the following day[8].

In the right place at the right time, Children immediately offered to buy the tree. Brassine interceded with the owner, a price was agreed, and in due course it was shipped to England where Children engaged a cabinet-maker to turn the wood into commemorative items of furniture[9]. Three chairs were made: one was presented to the Duke of Wellington[10]; one to the

[1] Speaking of Elford Leach (Swainson, 1834: 335).
[2] John George Children (1777-1852). See biography in Gunther (1978).
[3] Anna Children (1799-1871). Later Mrs Atkins. Anonymous author (1843-1853?) of *Photographs of British Algae*. Cyanotype impressions (8 vols), and as 'Anna Atkins': (1852) *The Perils of Fashion* (3 vols); (1853) *The Colonel. A story of fashionable life.* (3 vols) Hurst & Blackett, London; (1853) *Memoir of J.G. Children Esq. FRS L and E, FSA, MRI etc. including some unpublished poetry by his father and himself.* (privately printed) 313 pp; (1859) *Murder will out. A story of real life*; and (1863) *A Page from the Peerage* (2 vols).
[4] Samuel Forfeit Gray (1798-1872). 'Forfeit' was his mother's maiden name. We do not know how he was known to John Children, but he was only one year older than Anna.
[5] 1802-1805 (Gunther, 1978: 78).
[6] "the first saluting sign to our children and our children's children" ! (Scott, 1816: 210).
[7] The occupier of the farm of Papelotte.
[8] Anon., 1852b.
[9] Gunther (1978: 82) says Children engaged Thomas Chippendale the Younger (1749-1822) to make the furniture but Chippendale the Younger only continued his father's business until 1813. Is this an error or did Chippendale come out of retirement?
[10] He apparently used this chair when sitting for portraits.

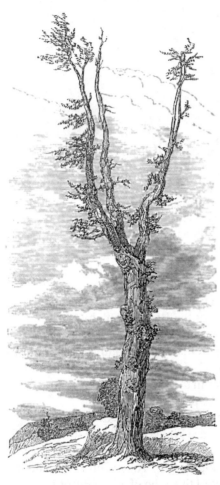

king; and one found its way to the Duke of Rutland at Belvoir Castle[11]. Children had a cabinet made for himself to house his mineral collection[12], and had smaller tokens made for his friends. Samuel Gray later donated a snuff box made from the wood to the Royal Gardens at Kew, and Children gave the British Museum a section of trunk containing an embedded iron chain, which had apparently been wrapped around the tree when it was a sapling.

Jonathan

As Children stood on the battlefield purchasing his share of history, just across the border Jonathan Leach was on the move.

The intention to maintain an army of occupation in France for five years had been reconsidered by the European powers. To the relief of the French, and to the distress of the allied troops, three years was held sufficient and plans were made to bring the army home. At the end of June Jonathan's company had been moved to a camp on open land in front of Cambrai, and towards the end of October they marched to the coast, sailed to Dover, and returned to their barracks at Shorncliffe for the first time since 1815.

Leach: "The beginning of the winter of 1818 witnessed the evacuation of France by our troops, which were immediately afterwards scattered all over the world, like dust before the wind. A few regiments went to England, many to Ireland, and still more to the East and West Indies, Canada, the Cape, the Mediterranean; and, in short, to every creek and corner where we had colonies or garrisons. Thus was dispersed an army, many regiments of which had been together from the year 1808 to 1818; the whole of which time, with the exception of the few months that Napoleon spent at Elba, was passed in the Peninsula and in France. It was the breaking up of a large family".

As the two battalions of the Rifle Brigade arrived in England they were reduced in size. Four NCOs in each company were to be discharged, wounded men to take priority. Ned Costello was one of the first to go. He had been

'The Wellington Tree' ? (see below) in 1818 on the battlefield at Waterloo. Engraved from the sketch by Anna Children.

There are some curious aspects to this story of the purchase. If the Wellington Tree was at the edge of the road by the crossroads behind La Haye Sainte, as Scott describes (and as is shown in the 1846 map of Edward Cotton, who was a guide on the battlefield for 14 years): why were crops being trampled by people visiting it, and why was the surrounding land being cultivated by the occupant of Papelotte not by the occupant of La Haye Sainte? This story would make more sense if John Children had purchased a tree growing on the knoll rather than Scott's 'Wellington Tree'. The three main upright branches in Anna Children's sketch also match the three main uprights of the tree on the knoll in the illustration on p. 322 above. We also note that in the engraving shown here on page 320 (published in May 1816) the small tree in the right foreground, behind the knoll and on the opposite side of the road to Scott's tree, was clearly labelled by the engraver (below the image and not shown here) 'Wellington Tree'. It seems the identification of this famous tree depended very much on which guide was pointing at it.

[11] Pronounced 'beaver' castle.
[12] This cabinet is now in the Mineralogy Department of The Natural History Museum, London.

promoted to Corporal in 1816 and now had a French 'wife' Augustine (although their union was not formally recognised). She was about to give birth to their child and had stayed in France[13], but no sooner had Costello set off for Chatham to await an assessment of his pension entitlement than Augustine arrived unexpectedly at Shorncliffe.

Jonathan put her on a coach to Chatham, paying her fare for her[14], and gave her directions where she could find Ned. She arrived just in time. Their baby was born at Chatham and they moved to London to try to eke out an existence on a paltry army pension of six pence a day.

The rest of the 1st battalion were only briefly at Shorncliffe before being posted to Gosport, Portsmouth, where they would stay until the following autumn.

London

November 1818 was a very busy month for Elford Leach. Monsieur Royer[15], the administrator of the Paris museum, had arrived from France[16] and Elford, as the British Museum's official Correspondent with Paris, had to stop everything he was doing to look after him. While he was distracted a new zoological collection arrived.

During the very warm summer the Arctic seas had become unusually clear of ice. To capitalise on this, the government had offered rewards to anyone finding a north-west passage (north of Canada) to the Pacific and the far east, and to anyone sailing to 89°N (almost to the North Pole). Two Royal Navy vessels, the *Dorothea* under David Buchan[17], and the *Trent* under John Franklin[18], had sailed due north from Spitzbergen. The expedition

was foiled by the permanent ice cap and was not a great geographical success, but the natural history specimens they collected were donated to the museum in November. As Royer left, Elford began sorting the animals and selecting examples for stuffing.

He was still completing the displays of British zoology, and as this meant bringing much of Montagu's collection upstairs from the basement, he decided to continue clearing the space below ground. William Swainson had returned to England during the summer and found him in the subterranean chambers, where Swainson "very frequently assisted him for hours in rummaging out and rescuing some

[13] As their marriage was not legally recognised Augustine would not have been able to travel with the army (Hathaway, 1997: 356 note 8).

[14] Hathaway, 1997: 295.

[15] A.A. Royer (fl. 1793-1833). Was employed in the central administration office of the Paris museum from 1793-1833, where he was the Chief Clerk from 1825 (Sweet, 1970: 44fn). He translated Deleuze's official history of the museum (1823) into English (1823).

[16] Bringing with him for Edinburgh University the Certificate of Value of Dufresne's collection signed by Cuvier, Geoffroy Saint-Hilaire and Lamarck, to which Elford added his signature.

[17] David Buchan (1790-1845). Tony Rice (1986: 58) tells us *HMS Dorothea* is the *Dorothy* which accompanied the *Congo* to West Africa.

[18] John Franklin (1786-1847). Fought at Trafalgar. Explored Arctic waters and Canadian coast. Knighted 1829. Governor of Van Diemen's Land (Tasmania) 1834-1845. Died seeking a north-west passage.

One of the chairs made from Children's Wellington Tree (This example is in the Royal collection).

of the more valuable subjects from that oblivion to which they were fast hastening.[19]" Swainson says Elford, "set to work manfully in cleaning out what was then an Augean stable—a chaos of "confusion worse confounded." But the effects of long years of misrule and of disorder were not to be overcome by a single individual, who, while he was stopping the plague in one quarter, was necessitated to permit its full rage in another.[20]"

Now Swainson had returned from Brazil, he thought he could support himself financially, at least in part, by publishing natural history illustrations. Elford advised him to consider the new printing technique of lithography, which involved drawing directly onto stone and using this as the printing surface rather than having a copper plate or wood block engraved[21]. This technique had been invented in Germany in 1798 and was currently attracting a lot of interest in Europe and America[22]. Swainson took this advice and taught himself the new craft. When he published the first volume of his *Zoological Illustrations* in 1820 it was hailed as a work of brilliance and he became one of the foremost exponents of lithography in Britain.

(The stone used for lithography needed to be particularly fine-grained with an unblemished even texture and a flat bedding plane. In 1861 near Solnhofen in Germany a quarry was producing Jurassic limestone of just this type when the workmen split a slab to reveal one of the most famous and important fossils ever discovered – *Archaeopteryx*. The same fine texture that gave the stone its printing characteristics had preserved the most minute details in the fossil, which was given the full scientific name *Archaeopteryx lithographica*[23]. The fossil was bought by the British Museum and studied by Jameson's old student, and William Clift's son-in-law, Richard Owen.)

For Elford the work involved in: receiving Montagu's collection, and Cranch's collection, and Burchell's collection, and Bowdich's collection, and a polar collection; chasing Dufresne's collection; moving house; going to Paris; chaperoning Cuvier and Latreille; overseeing the alterations to Room XI; arranging a whole gallery of British animals (including all the new display cases); clearing out the basement; writing articles for the French *Dictionnaire*, and for the *Encyclopædia Britannica*, and for the Royal

---

Historical note

1818	Building of Regent Street recommences and proceeds north of Piccadilly.
November	Food riots in the north of England.
1819	
July	Riots in Liverpool.
August	Reform disturbances in central England.
October	Disturbances among seamen on Tyneside.

[19] Swainson, 1840: 237–240. The exact months when Swainson helped in this way are not known.
[20] Swainson, 1834: 335.
[21] That this was Elford's suggestion is noted in the *Dictionary of National Biography*: 'Swainson'.
[22] See Weimerskirch (1985).
[23] *Archaeopteryx lithographica* von Meyer, 1861.

Society, and for the Linnean Society, and for de Blainville's journal, and about the Congo expedition and Bowdich's travels; producing a catalogue of British animals, and several issues of *Malacostraca*[24], and a whole volume of the *Zoological Miscellany*, while still researching the molluscs and insects and rearranging all the zoological collections in the Museum along modern lines—meant he had not seen his parents for more than two years. He had not been able to take a break during the summer so he took the unusual step (although increasingly usual for him) of asking for special leave of absence at the end of the year. The Trustees allowed him a month "immediately after Christmas", but on the 8th of January he was still in Montagu House, although at last was able to report that the British display was ready for inspection. Then another collection arrived.

This was from a second polar expedition looking for a short-cut to the Pacific. While the *Dorothea* and *Trent* had sailed due north, two other naval vessels, the *Isabella* under Commander John Ross[25] (a relative of Hew Ross of the Royal Horse Artillery[26]), and the *Alexander* under Lieutenant William Parry[27], had sailed around the north of Canada, probing for a north-west passage. Scientifically this expedition had been much more successful (spending more time near land), and had taken many biological and geological samples and a range of measurements.

The arrival of these vessels and their cargo created a lot of interest in London, pushing the expedition of the *Dorothea* and *Trent* into the shade. For public consumption cartoonist George Cruikshank illustrated the arrival of the natural history collection at the British Museum, and provided at the same time the only known 'portrait' of Elford Leach[28].

Elford himself did not wait to incorporate the new finds; in mid-January he headed for Devon for a well-earned break, but before he left he had news of yet another natural history sale. The size of this one would swamp all those that had gone before – William Bullock was parting with his collection.

Devon

When Elford arrived in Devon he wrote to Sir Joseph Banks saying rather curiously that he had nothing to communicate, but adding, "Should any thing occur, depend on my writing instantly." Obviously Banks was expecting some news from Devon, but it is not clear what[29].

To fill his letter Elford talks about something that has happened at Spitchwick. From Paris the previous spring he had shipped a young wild boar and sow back to England and they had been put out to forage in the woods with Spitchwick's domestic pigs ('Fat Bacon Farm' was obviously not an obsolete name although the countryside around Spitchwick was primarily given over to sheep, farmed for their coarse Dartmoor wool). The consequence was, as Elford related, "The boar has played the duce here with all the Sows, young and old, and sad complaints have been made to me about the spoiled breed, since he has covered every sow in our stock.[30]"

[24] But no parts were issued between December 1817 and March 1820.

[25] John Ross (1777-1856). Scottish Arctic explorer. Led a second expedition in 1829-1833. Later knighted. See biographical notes in Sweet (1974: 34-46).

[26] John Ross was the uncle of James Clark Ross (1800-1862) who accompanied John Ross and William Parry on this and other Polar explorations. James was also later knighted. Hew Ross was James Clark Ross's cousin (Dalton, 1971: 220).

[27] William Edward Parry (1790-1855). Also led Arctic expeditions in 1819, 1821-1823, 1824-1825 and 1827. Knighted 1829. Promoted to Rear-Admiral 1852.

[28] See Chapter 17. George Cruikshank's full cartoon is reproduced in Rice (1975: 292-293).

[29] Perhaps the arrival of a particular ship at Plymouth.

[30] Letter: W.E. Leach to Banks, 20th January 1819 (Loc: Museum of the History of Science, Oxford).

The Royal Theatre, George Street, Plymouth. The far end of the building, beyond the portico, formed the Royal Hotel. The building was erected between 1811 and 1813 and the foundation stone was laid by Edmund Lockyer during one of his terms as Plymouth's Mayor. Beyond the hotel and built in a matching architectural style is *The Athenæum*, the new home of the Plymouth Institution.

In Plymouth during Elford's absence the Plymouth Institution had been going from strength to strength. Its long-running difficulties had finally been resolved in September 1816[31] and 'The Select Society' had come back into the fold. Henry Woollcombe had regretted "the union was not so cordial as I would have wished but experience will make all parties more cautious in their further conduct[32]". The membership had been increasing steadily and at the time of reunion stood at 26 ordinary and 22 extraordinary members while the increase in subscription income had allowed the purchase of books, an air-pump and other experimental apparatus. Woollcombe had hoped the Institution would go on "swimmingly" and in the years that followed, it had. On Mayday 1818 he had laid the foundation stone of a grand new meeting house to be built next to Plymouth's Royal Theatre in a matching classical style, the *Athenæum*, and the construction was now finished. The building was formally opened on the 4th of February 1819 while Elford was in Devon, two days after his 28th birthday.

Elford was clearly not planning to use his break from London to take a break from work. From Spitchwick he wrote to Robert Jameson saying he hoped the government could be induced to buy Bullock's collection for the nation (he was to be disappointed), adding, 'I am hard at work with those parts of Comparative Anatomy that depend on Zoology and on which also the classification of Animals itself depends. My elementary work is in progress, but as I do not wish to give a superficial popular view, or a compilation, I must see every genus myself and what of its structure is known. We can depend on no observator, not even on the zoologists of the French School.[33]' Here he may have been talking about his mollusc work, which had now grown to become a substantial manuscript.

Jameson had his own eye on Bullock's collection and had been in contact with its owner[34]. Although Edinburgh was buying Dufresne's

[31] Just before his previous visit.
[32] Henry Woollcombe's Diary for 3rd September 1816 (Loc: West Devon Records Office, Plymouth) [Typescript seen].
[33] Letter: W.E. Leach to Jameson, 8th February 1819 (Loc: Edinburgh University Library, Special Collections. Ref: 1801/2/9).
[34] *inter alia*, Letters: Bullock to Jameson, 24th January, 9th February & 8th April 1819 (Loc: Edinburgh University Library, Special Collections. Ref: Mss 1801/1 Bullock Nos 1, 2 & 4).

The lecture room, or Hall, of the Plymouth Institution's new *Athenæum*.

This engraving is taken from a sketch made by George Wightwick, one of the institution's curators. When Britton & Brayley published this they noted, "resemblances of several of the principal members have been introduced as memorials of their praise-worthy exertions in the establishment and support of this valuable institution." (1832: 105). Sadly they do not say when the sketch was made or who these principal members were. The family group in the left foreground is intriguing. Who is this?

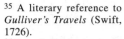

collection, that was not enough to make a significant display in the expansive Edinburgh museum (it would be "a Lillyputian in a Brobdignay Castle" said Bullock[35]). Jameson needed larger animals to exhibit. Bullock told him this and said his own reason for selling was that he had plans to buy an estate in Lancashire and had had an offer for the purchase of his premises "that it is not in my interest to refuse"[36]. While Elford was in the West Country Bullock wrote to Jameson and told him (in his somewhat functional English):

"I have offered my whole Collection of Natural History for Nine Thousand Pounds which I realy think will be deemed a sufficient sacrifice as it has certainly cost me Twenty five thousand many of Birds and Shells are matchless and a few of the Fossils are unique and as fine as they can be The Lizard Serpents and Fishes are good and beautifully put up and I realy believe so generous a collection does not exist there is not a specimen that has been assisted by art except the head of the Boa Constricta which being part destroyed (which is the case in all the largest specimens) has been modelled from life in wood and has always been described as such I mention this as I know a certain little aquiantance of yours has endeavored to injure me much in this particular I pledge myself not a Feachure in my whole ornithological collection will be found spurious I appeal to yourself if a man who has had his Heart in his collection as I have could derive pleasure from looking at a deception but I said to much on this subject but alway wax warm when I speak of it

In fixing the price the lowest pennie that will be taken is named it will be a loss of time to offer less than the sum mentioned am firmly of opinion that it would sell for more by auction but cannot make up my mind to its dispersion[37]".

[35] A literary reference to *Gulliver's Travels* (Swift, 1726).

[36] Nevertheless, he went on to sell his collection but keep Egyptian Hall for holding auctions and new exhibitions.

[37] Letter: Bullock to Jameson, 9th February 1819 (Loc: Edinburgh University Library, Special Collections. Ref: Mss 1801/1 Bullock № 2). "cannot make up my mind to its dispersion" either means he cannot decide how to dispose of it or he cannot bear the thought of it being dispersed.

Bullock had already spoken to Sir Joseph Banks about the possibility of selling his collection to the British Museum, but Banks did not see that as very likely. After due consideration Edinburgh too chose not to buy it and Bullock tried Banks again[38] before arranging an auction at Egyptian Hall to begin at the end of April. The "certain little aquiantance" [sic] is almost certainly Elford Leach who, having now expended his four weeks leave, headed back to London and some good news: the Trustees had finally agreed to let him have Room XII as a private study[39].

Spring 1819

Since 1817 Robert Jameson had been editing the *Edinburgh Philosophical Journal*[40] with David Brewster, but to give it a new lease of life this was about to be re-launched as the *Edinburgh Journal of Science*. Elford wrote to Jameson, "Dr Brewster as well as yourself have mentioned the new Philosophical Journal, to which I will readily contribute. If it be likewise a review; I will give a sketch of the present state of Zoology and Comparative Anatomy; with what I think the great desiderata, in both sciences.[41]" Jameson's response must have touched a raw nerve, as Elford replied with uncharacteristic sharpness:

'Respecting your Journal. I must first remind you that I am not a scribler for money; I am solely actuated from a desire to promote science: and as I am much occupied and when I write, do not wish to be too general and thus render myself liable to be misunderstood, I feel great reluctance in writing any of the proposed articles; the intent of which, you my dear Sir, have totally miscomprehended. The title of Article 28 is totally misworded: I intended to write on the present state of two sciences and not confine their State to Gt Britain. If so the paper would consist of the following line. "These sciences are at their lowest possible ebb in Gt Britain."[42]'

He spent March and April continuing his general arrangement of the Museum's holdings, working on the molluscs and examining the new polar collection. He wanted to have 16 quadrupeds and 56 birds stuffed and asked the Trustees to set money aside, but they were not prepared to do this and asked him merely to ensure the skins were protected from damage. Doubtless they were consigned to the basement.

Bullock's sale

Bullock's sale began on Thursday the 29th of April and ran every afternoon from Tuesday to Friday until June. It attracted buyers from all the major European museums: Professor Lichtenstein from Berlin; Baron Laugier from Paris; and a Mr Fector from Vienna[43]. Temminck bought for Leiden, and with an allowance of £7000-£8000 a year to spend on natural history[44] he was a difficult person to outbid. Private purchasers included William Swainson, Benjamin Leadbeater and Captain James Laskey.

Elford's Italian contact, Franco Bonelli, had travelled from Turin and had taken the opportunity to assess the state of zoological knowledge he

[38] Letter: Bullock to Banks, 31st March 1819 (Dawson, 1958: 185).

[39] J.E. Gray (House of Commons 1836 at para. 2456) says only that Room XII was 'taken for a private room' at this time, but this was presumably for Elford.

[40] Which had formerly been called the *Edinburgh Magazine*.

[41] Letter: W.E. Leach (Spitchwick) to Jameson, 8th February 1819 (Loc: University of Edinburgh Library, Special Collections. Ref: 1801/2/9).

[42] Letter: Leach (London) to Jameson, 14th April 1819 (Loc: University of Edinburgh Library, Special Collections).

[43] Sharpe, 1906: 218. The purchasers were: Martin Heinrich Karl Lichtenstein (1780-1857), Director of the Berlin Museum from 1815; Baron Meiffren Laugier de Chartrouse (often reported in English texts as 'Logier'); and the 'Mr Fector' (should this be 'Fechter'?).

[44] Letter: Adam to Jameson, 18th May 1819 (Loc: University of Edinburgh Library, Special Collections. Ref: 1801/1 Bullock Nº 14).

[45] D'Entrèves & Gentile, 1985: 45. Translated from the Italian by KH.

[46] Letter: W.E. Leach to Jameson, 14th April 1819 (Loc: University of Edinburgh Library, Special Collections).

[47] Letter: William Bullock to Jameson, 23rd April 1819 (Loc: University of Edinburgh Library, Special Collections. Ref: 1801/1 Bullock Nº 7). Wilson is referred to only as 'the Janitor', or 'Janitor Wilson' but as he clearly had natural history knowledge this is presumably Janitor of the museum (Curator?).

found on his journey. He was not impressed with the British, writing home: 'I do not see there is any great thing for entomology here, or even for ornithology. The naturalists advancing zoological science are reduced to Dr Leach and, for some parts of entomology, Mr MacLeay Jnr who is engaged on a monograph of the genus *Scarabaeus* Linn.[45]'.

At the auction Elford was planning to buy mainly British birds for the Museum, to fill remaining gaps in the new gallery, but he also offered to buy exhibits on behalf of Edinburgh if Jameson did not plan to be there[46]. In fact Jameson had intended sending the Edinburgh Museum's Janitor, Wilson, but he was ill and unable to make the trip[47]. His place was taken by Dr Walter Adam who had reported to Jameson two years earlier on the management of collections in Germany[48]. After travelling to London and meeting Elford, Adam told Jameson, 'It is a load off my mind that every thing is cleared up between you and Dr Leach[49]' which may be a reference to the sharp riposte of just over a week earlier regarding the new journal. Elford agreed to advise Adam in selecting the purchases for Edinburgh, but as Adam did not want it known publicly that he was bidding for the university, they agreed not to sit together at the auction. Adam was worried that if it was known he was bidding on behalf of an institution, rather than as an individual, it may push the prices up[50], and he thought being seen with the British Museum's buyer might show his hand. Instead Elford agreed to sit behind him in the hall and whisper advice in his ear[51] (In fact Adam's role was probably one of the worst kept secrets at the sale).

Jameson had sent Adam a list of animals he wanted him to buy on each day – chosen from Bullock's sale catalogues – and at the end of virtually every session Adam wrote giving a report of which he had purchased (or lost) and a general account of the proceedings. He and Elford first attended on the third day, Tuesday the 4th of May. This seems to be when many of the birds made their first appearance. Elford did not restrict himself to British birds and bought 13 lots for the Museum, spending just over £21. He had a bidding tussle with Baron Laugier for one exhibit but eventually had to let it go to Paris for £10.

He must have been saving himself for the next day, 'British Land Birds', when the birds of prey went under the hammer. Now he spent about £100 on 19 lots, including one of Bullock's gothic mounts: a male Golden Eagle preying on a white hare. The ornithologist Bowdler Sharpe, who curated the birds at the British Museum later in the century, said in 1906, "Many of us can still remember this Eagle, with its wings outspread, and the bloodstains (sealing-wax) on the stomach of the Hare which it held under its feet. The group was purchased by Dr Leach, and long held a place of honour in the British Gallery of the old British Museum.[52]" This exhibit was also illustrated in many nineteenth century natural history books.

Elford's greatest outlay was an astonishing 25 guineas on one male Snowy Owl[53] from the Shetlands[54]. Adam was in awe and told Jameson, "Dr Leach bought to a huge amount today[55]", adding that Elford wanted to

Elford calls him "J. Wilson" in a letter and this may be the "Mr John Wilson of the College, Edinburgh" he mentioned in 1815 in the *Edinburgh Encyclopædia*, (9: 141) assuming he did not mean Professor John Wilson, brother of his former classmate James Wilson. James Wilson does not appear to be 'Janitor Wilson', although he also became ill around this time and moved to Italy in 1820 to recover from a pulmonary complaint. Elford had another Natural History classmate 'J. Wilson' in the winter session of 1811-12. This was Joseph Wilson from Newmonkland.

[48] Walter Adam (1792-1857). Son of the Rector of the Royal High School of Edinburgh. Graduated MD at Edinburgh in 1816. He lived at N° 39 George Square, Edinburgh. Jameson lived at N° 45. Adam had first met Elford Leach in London in April 1815.

[49] Letter: Adam to Jameson, 23rd April 1819 (Loc: Edinburgh University Library, Special Collections. Ref: 1801/1 Bullock N° 8).

[50] Letter: Adam to Jameson, 23rd April 1819 (*loc. cit.*).

[51] Letter: Adam to Jameson, 4th May 1819 (Loc: Edinburgh University Library Special Collections. Ref: 1801/1 Bullock N° 10).

[52] Sharpe, 1906: 212.

[53] *Nyctea scandiaca* (Linnæus, 1766).

[54] Yarrell, 1871-4: 187-188. William Yarrell (1784-1856) was at Bullock's sale.

[55] Letter: Adam to Jameson, 5th May 1819 (Loc: Edinburgh University Library, Special Collections. Ref: 1801/1 Bullock N° 11).

buy the Great Auk in the following session, which would begin with 'British Water Birds'.

Auks are sea-birds of the northern hemisphere. Here they occupy the same biological niche as penguins in the south. As they have similar life-styles the two groups of birds bear a strong superficial resemblance – an example of Cuvier's functional morphology. The most obvious difference is that most auks retain the power of flight, although with their short stubby wings this is restricted to energetic bursts skimming the wave tops. Like penguins, the wings are also used to 'fly' underwater when chasing fish. Many auks are common, including the Guillemot[56] and Razorbill[57], and with their gregarious coastal habits they are familiar to today's Europeans as among the first birds to suffer during catastrophic oil spills.

In Elford Leach's day the largest of the auks was the Great Auk, or Garefowl[58], which lived around the cold islands of the north Atlantic. The splash of white on either side of its face led to this species being called 'white head', or, in Welsh, 'pen gwyn'. The penguins of the southern hemisphere were apparently named after the Great Auk when sailors noted their similarity[59].

In earlier centuries the Great Auk lived in huge colonies and its world population numbered tens of millions. Early northern mariners were so sure of seeing these birds they sometimes set sail with little food on board their vessels, filling the hold with eggs and auk meat when they found them. This practice had little impact on the overall numbers, but when the American eiderdown industry collapsed in the mid eighteenth century following overcollecting of feathers and birds, the Great Auk was seen as a ready replacement for the Eider Duck[60]. Unregulated industrial-scale harvesting of the

Golden eagle.
Aquila chrysaetos (L.)

[56] *Uria aalge* (Pontoppidan, 1763)
[57] *Alca torda* Linnæus, 1766.
[58] *Alca impennis* Linnæus, 1758
[59] Welsh derives from the original language spoken in the British Isles before the Roman and Anglo-Saxon periods. Other derivations have been suggested but this one seems most convincing. In Welsh, pen = head, gwyn = white.
[60] *Somateria mollissima* (Linnæus, 1758).
[61] Day, 1989: 42-45.

Snowy Owl

Great Auk

62 Yarrell, 1884-5: 63 (quoting Montagu).

63 Letter: Thomas Brown & Walter Adam to Jameson, 7th May 1819 (Loc: Edinburgh University Library Special Collections. Ref: 1801/1 Bullock N° 12).

64 Michael Walters of *The Natural History Museum* kindly provided this information. [*The Natural History Museum*, London – formerly called the *British Museum (Natural History)* – was opened in West London at South Kensington in 1881 to house the natural history departments of the British Museum. The collection of birds and associated research were later moved to the Museum's facility sited at Tring in Hertfordshire: *The Walter Rothschild Zoological Museum*].

65 Louis Jean Pierre Vieillot (1748-1831) had already described this species in 1817 as *Procellaria leucorhoa*. Its scientific name is now *Oceanodroma leucorhoa* (Vieillot).

66 *Branta ruficollis* (Pallas, 1769).

67 Letter: Thomas Brown & Walter Adam to Jameson, 7th May 1819 (Loc: Edinburgh University Library Special Collections. Ref: 1801/1 Bullock N° 12).

68 See preceding letter.

Leach's Storm Petrel.

birds at their western nesting colonies, and their easy availability to Europeans in the east, brought the population close to extinction within decades. By 1800 the Great Auk was becoming rare and it was the turn of the ornithologists to target it. Its extinction was now assured. The last living individuals ever seen were killed on Eldey Island, off Iceland, on the 3rd of June 1844[61].

In 1812 or 1813 in the Orkneys, Bullock, in a six-oared boat, had chased a male bird for hours without getting close enough to shoot it[62] but in May 1813 the locals caught a bird (possibly the same one) and sent it to him. This was the last Great Auk ever captured in the British Isles and it was a prize Elford Leach wanted. It was also a prize he got, for the sum of £16. 5s. 6d. ("a great bargain" Adam told Jameson[63]). This bird was proudly displayed in the public galleries at the British Museum for the next 50 years and is still in the collection of Britain's Natural History Museum today[64].

Elford had obviously decided to display other sea-birds occasionally found around the far-flung limits of Britain and bought a petrel which had been collected by Bullock the previous year at the island of St Kilda, off the west of Scotland. This bird was believed to be new to science but Elford did not publish a description of it. It was Temminck who described the species in 1820, calling it *Procellaria leachii*. We know it today as 'Leach's Storm Petrel'[65].

Despite his high spending of the day before, Elford managed to beat his most expensive purchase by buying a Red-Breasted Goose[66] for £27. For Edinburgh Adam had bought only one seagull and a 'Tame swan with case'. He told Jameson diffidently, 'The swan is useless enough but it is large and the case and stuffing would cost what I paid[67]' [£3.10s.]. The following day the mammals came up for sale and Adam's only comment was, "Today I have perhaps too many monkeys[68]".

Knowing Edinburgh wanted large exhibits seems to have led Elford to make a somewhat startling invitation. Through the medium of Adam he offered to sell Jameson 30 duplicate skins from Burchell's African collection – mainly antelopes – for £80[69]. It is most unlikely he had authority to do this and even more unlikely the Trustees, or Burchell especially, would have appreciated the act had they known. Elford may have been prompted to make the offer because he knew the skins were at imminent risk in the basement and the Trustees were not able or willing to display them. He would rather see them displayed elsewhere. No more is said about this offer and presumably nothing came of it.

This spirit of co-operation between the British Museum and Edinburgh was extended to the sale but conflicts did occur. Adam warned Jameson, 'I am sorry that Dr Leach wants both the Elephant and the Ostrich. He will get you another Ostrich and it would be a good plan to get our friend Yule to employ a good marksman to shoot a wild Elephant in Ceylon. The skins of tame ones not being worth from the chafing of their harness' but in a postscript he added, '6 o'clock Rejoice Leach gave up the Elephant and   I have got almost all you wanted.[70]' Adam had bought 32 lots, mainly of large quadrupeds. In addition to the adult elephant, he bought a young elephant, a rhinoceros, an antelope, a wolf, two lions with five cubs, a wild boar and a giraffe ('camelopard'), spending over £156.

At the next sale day on Tuesday the 18th of May Elford decided on reflection not to bid for the ostrich – a beautiful adult male 3 metres high. It was bought by Temminck for £38. 6s. 6d. Elford decided instead to concentrate on petrels. He spent £25 on these, paying £10 to secure the Great Petrel (or 'Mother Carey's Goose'[71]), nearly a metre in length. He had seen this exhibit several days before and some of its features led him to believe Bullock's specimen might be a new species.

After the purchase Adam told Jameson, 'It is unfortunate that you and Dr Leach both want petrels. Dr Leach was set on all those in this day's sale because they had been brought home by Sir Joseph Banks[72]... One of the large Petrels Dr Leach bought had a pair of *Duck's* feet and sold for two pounds more on that account.[73]' (Of all people, Elford should have known better. Bullock finally had his revenge).

'The articles not bought at Friday's sale' added Adam, 'were either too dear or bad specimens. The best plan would be to give an order to Leadbetter, the man employed in the British Museum, for what you want, who will furnish them better and cheaper than they have been sold at Bullock's Sale, where bargains have been rather rare. Large specimens are generally lumber to dealers and may be had for the expense of stuffing. They are obliged to buy them with other things. Both the lions I got on Friday are very fine. The Camel Leopard was bid for by Lichtenstein and is of course worth the money [£24]. Dr Leach at first advised strongly against buying it, but altered his opinion. The group of the Boa and Tiger brought 37 Guineas, this only for skins. What is called the Boa is made of the skins of two serpents with a wooden head added.[74]'

[69] Letter: Adam to Jameson, 14th May 1819 (Loc: Edinburgh University Library Special Collections. Ref: 1801/1 Bullock N° 13).
[70] As preceding.
[71] *Macronectes giganteus* (Gmelin, 1788) or the 'Southern Giant Petrel'.
[72] Letter: Adam to Jameson, 18th May 1819 (Loc: Edinburgh University Library Special Collections. Ref: 1801/1 Bullock N° 14).
[73] Letter: Adam to Jameson, 21st May 1819 (Loc: Edinburgh University Library Special Collections. Ref: 1801/1 Bullock N° 16).
[74] Letter: Adam to Jameson, 18th May 1819 (Loc: *loc. cit.*)

Wednesday the 19th was a sale of 'Foreign Birds' and Elford did not attend, but he appeared the next day and bought four lots including a Zone-Tailed Eagle, a female Egyptian Vulture and a white Jer Falcon (Gyrfalcon). On Friday it was the turn of the parrots and Elford bought nine lots for the Museum, again buying many from Cook's voyage brought back by Sir Joseph Banks.

Adam, on the other hand, reassured Jameson, "My Dear Sir, It is well that you are no admirer of Parrots as I have not been able to get one", adding they were all too expensive and Bullock was certainly not making a loss by disposing of his collection in this way[75].

Tuesday the 25th was an assortment of birds ('Herons, Ducks, Woodpeckers, Bee-eaters &c.') and again Elford did not attend. Adam bemoaned his absence and admitted, 'I felt today the cost of being engaged on matters I do not understand. Dr Leach could not attend the sale, neither was Mr Leadbetter there. Dr Leach referred to Mr Temminck for the prices of the articles he did not know. Mr T. was, as he [has] always been, very polite but some of the best things he wanted for himself[76]'.

The next day Elford bought only two lots, one a pigeon from the South Sea voyages. In addition to British birds he clearly wanted to bring into the Museum specimens collected by Banks (Banks had originally given these to Sir Ashton Lever and to Bullock). Adam, who bought nothing, had been talking to Elford and tells Jameson, 'Dr Leach is to give a receipt for the medicine he uses to destroy insects, which he recommends you to wash over all the animals with as soon as they arrive in Edinburgh[77]. Dr L talks sometimes of going northwards. I wish you could persuade him to go and give you his advice about the arrangement of your Zoological department. He seems to undervalue very much the qualifications of the gentleman you would be most likely to be guided by, as having no idea of natural classification...

Dr Leach thinks you ought to lay open the museum to study to such students as choose to pay for it and employ the money so raised in the purchase of such new things as may occur[78]' (Jameson appears to have taken up this last idea and an entrance fee of half a crown[79] was introduced at the Edinburgh museum in 1820[80]).

Elford was not present on Thursday the 27th, but Adam bought three lots. Some birds of paradise and humming birds were offered in advance of their main appearance on the following Tuesday but Adam did not dare "meddle" with any of those in Elford's absence. For the sale this day Baron Laugier had been given money by Cuvier to buy one particular lot on his behalf. According to the sale catalogue this was 'A magnificent species of turkey, from the Bay of Honduras, undescribed; it was sent as a present to Sir Henry Halford[81], and died on its passage: the only one known.[82]' Laugier warned Temminck that he had instructions to buy it at any price but Temminck still opposed him and it eventually cost Cuvier £54. 12s. 0d.[83]

[75] Letter: Adam to Jameson, 21st May 1819 (Loc: Edinburgh University Library Special Collections. Ref: 1801/1 Bullock No 16).
[76] Letter: Adam to Jameson, 25th May 1819 (Loc: Edinburgh University Library Special Collections. Ref: 1801/1 Bullock No 17).
[77] This recipe ['receipt'] is not in the archives at Edinburgh with Adam's letters.
[78] Letter: Adam to Jameson, 26th May 1819 (Loc: Edinburgh University Library Special Collections. Ref: 1801/1 Bullock No 18).
[79] 2 shillings and 6 pence (one eighth of a pound).
[80] Sweet, 1970a: 28 note 32.
[81] Sir Henry Halford *Bt* (1766-1844) Physician extraordinary to King George III in 1793.
[82] Sharpe, 1906: 230-231.
[83] This is the figure from Adam. Sharpe says it was £34. 12s. 0d

On Friday the sale included some birds but was mainly of corals, sponges, shells and fish. Elford bought three lots. He was planning to form a collection of corals for the British Museum but was only interested in pieces the size of a fist (presumably due to the limited display space)[84].

On Tuesday he bought four lots, all birds, including another Great Petrel and two American birds of prey. He did not attend the next day but bought 18 lots on Thursday. The sale was now beginning to draw to a close and like the good businessman he was Bullock had been saving some of his most spectacular pieces until last, both natural history and historical. Many items of armour were sold on the Thursday, much of it bought by Walter Scott, author of *The Field of Waterloo*. Scott had romantic aspirations and in 1811 had bought 1200 acres of land (486 hectares) in southern Scotland together with Cartley Hole farmhouse. He renamed this *Abbotsford* and was furnishing it at huge expense in the style of a medieval baronial hall.

On Friday Bullock sold "The Great Boa Constrictor, thirty-two feet long, in the act of seizing a Deer; most beautifully set up, and considered as the finest subject in the Museum." It was bought by the Marquess of Buckingham for £47. 5s. 0d.

Tuesday the 8th of June began the final week of the sale and the natural history was restricted to many of the smaller animals. William Swainson bought a great many birds. Elford only seems to have attended on the Thursday to buy a 'Cancer' from Tristan da Cunha for his personal collection (presumably a crab or prawn).

Friday the 11th of June, the last day, was Bullock's *pièce de résistance*: Napoleonic relics, including "the Emperor's carriage, taken on the eve of Waterloo, and sent, with the officer who took it, by Marshal Blücher, to the Prince Regent, from whom it was purchased by its present proprietor for the sum of three thousand guineas." This was bought by a Mr Hopkinson, a coach-builder of Holborn, for £168 (although it is estimated Bullock had already made a fortune from this one exhibit alone[85]). Walter Scott acquired two mementoes of Waterloo: a silver helmet and the dark blue standard of the French 105th regiment captured during the attack on Kempt's position[86].

Walter Adam had completed his purchases the previous week and had already wrapped the animals in cloth and put them on the ship for Edinburgh. They arrived before the sale ended but Jameson was not happy. Clearly he thought they were not up to the standard he had been expecting and wrote to Adam expressing his disappointment. Adam penned an uncomfortable reply, rather graciously accepting full responsibility and explaining some incidental damage:

'My Dear Sir

I write immediately that you may make enquiry about the ear of the Rhinoceros. It was knocked off as the cart on which the animals were carried passed under Bullock's archway, but when I saw it at the wharf it still remained attached by the matting. I had another piece of matting put

[84] Letter: Adam to Jameson, 21st May 1819 (Loc: *loc. cit.*).
[85] In 1903 the Cincinnati newspaper *The Enquirer* estimated he had made US$ 130,000 (Shepperson, 1961: 146).
[86] Sharpe (1906). Kennedy *in* Siborne (1993: 75-76).

Leith Harbour, the port for neighbouring Edinburgh.

over the head to protect it where the former had been injured and to keep on the Ear which I thought better than taking it off altogether. The ear was in this state when the animal was put into the hold of the vessel and it must have been roughly handled if it has been removed. With respect to the horn, the one that was stuck on the nose of the rhinoceros did not belong to it. Dr Leach meant to have bought the animal for the British Museum but was induced to give it up to me by my engaging to take off the horn. He is to give me a proper one instead of the old one which he now has. There are besides two smaller horns, bought in the same lot which I shall get from Bullock's and send down with the rest of the articles. I am quite grieved that the purchases do not give you satisfaction. Do not blame Dr Leach in scientific matters. He is a good deal of a citizen of the world no doubt, but I believe he feels a warm interest in the Edinburgh museum and has always advised what he thought best. What has been done wrong is I daresay chiefly owing to me. I made [a] point of getting Dr Leach to look at the articles as often as I could and always, except one day, marked in the prices he thought them worth. Many I should not have bought for myself, they appeared in such conditions, but I saw the foreigners buy worse and you seemed disappointed at losing many things, so that I did not think it right to follow my own taste as I am perfectly unacquainted with the market value of articles of natural history. I was at first amazed at the prices that were given and have all along felt little disposed to spend the money of the college on what seemed not really valuable. I think you will find that those articles you regret my not having bought sold too high. Dr Leach always assured me they might be had for less. Neither he nor I knew the baking many of the quadrupeds, I find, have under-gone. Some he bought himself have fallen to pieces. What you have in a bad state are chiefly vile baboons which I got generally a good deal under Dr Leach's prices. The pygmy antelope is miserable to be sure; I was quite ashamed of it when it came home but I had missed one on a former day because I did not like its appearance. The one you have, though dear, is a good deal cheaper with two musk deer into the bargain. I am sorry the Heron is so little worth. There were many pieces of manufacture in the sale. A bird of paradise I bought for 6 Guineas, after Dr Leach had inspected it, turned out afterwards to be a compound. I am to sell it again. What is entered as *nigricans* is not so but a species you want... D͏ʳ Leach is a man quite regardless of money himself and may have led me not to make the most of yours, but I hope till better specimens occur those from Bullock's will do. I should think the little elephant is real, observe the Ears[87]'

On the day Adam wrote this Elford donated to the British Museum, "Shells from New Holland; Five Varieties of Rhinoceros Horns; and a Collection of Corallines". He had presumably bought these with his own money. From Museum funds he had spent just over £527[88].

Summer 1819

With the completion of Bullock's sale Elford could return to the routine of the Museum, but his long-held desire to visit the far northern islands had re-surfaced, as had his liking for taking extended leave of absence at times other than the Museum's summer closure[89]. This year he applied for three months leave, starting in October, to visit the Orkneys. He gave his usual mitigation: he had worked all short vacations and Saturdays for the last year (this time it was not double accounting) but also adopted a suitably supplicant tone, assuring the Trustees there would be no additional expense and he would only wish them to agree to his request if they were satisfied his absence would not be injurious to the Museum. They must have been getting used to his somewhat idiosyncratic calendar as they granted his request.

During 1819 an artist known to John Gray produced a painting of the interior of the temporary gallery in the Museum's garden housing the Elgin Marbles[90]. In it he portrayed some of the Museum's officers. Joseph Planta, Charles König and John Children were all shown. Even the 19 year old John Gray managed to appear in the background in the guise of an artist at his easel[91], but sadly Elford Leach was not included.

Elford spent the summer adding the purchases from Bullock's sale to the British Gallery, preparing an arrangement of the shells and corals, and continuing his rearrangement of the general collections. At the same time he was developing an interest in fish anatomy and intended to explore this subject in the Orkneys. He was also still working on the comparative anatomy of the skull, and had developed an interest in the classification of bats, which he was pursuing using the extensive collection owned by

[87] Letter: Adam to Jameson, 12th June 1819 (Loc: Edinburgh University Library Special Collections. Ref: 1801/1 Bullock Nº 20). Jameson's letter, to which this is the reply, is not known to exist.
[88] Cowtan, 1835: 418-419.
[89] As so much of his museum work was, and had been, concerned with rearranging the displays in the public galleries, he presumably found this more convenient when the public were not admitted. The Trustees appear to have recognised this – and that allowing him to work in August and September would minimise disruption to visitors – hence their sympathetic attitude to granting him leave at other times.
[90] Gunther, 1975: 29 & 38. The artist was "A. Archer". Was this Archibald Archer of 38 Rathbone Place, London, who exhibited paintings in London (mainly subjects from the scriptures but also natural history) between 1810 and 1845?
[91] See Smith, 1916: 352-354. John Gray later acquired this painting and presented it to the Museum in 1872, having identified many of the people portrayed.

The Lesser Horseshoe Bat
Rhinolophus hipposideros
(Bechstein).

Elford Leach described it as:
"a very cautious animal; very
easily tamed, but fond of
concealing itself."

Illustration from the
Zoological Miscellany
1817.

naturalist Joshua Brookes. These lines of research were not part of his Museum duties so he did the work in his own time at home, where he had two small rooms set aside (presumably the garrets in the roof), one for the skulls and one for the bats. He called these rooms his 'Scullery' and his 'Battery'! (He may have got the idea for dedicating entire rooms to particular topics from Cuvier, who had adopted this approach at Paris). It is clear Elford's extensive homework must have left no living space in his apartments for any domestic staff, and his servant must have lived off the premises[92], although it was probably a relief not to share the house with a wolf.[93]

Temper temper

Elford's uncharacteristically sharp treatment of Robert Jameson in the spring seems to signal a general change in his temper around this time. He had always been forthright, but not rude. His 1815 criticisms of Shaw's *Naturalist's Miscellany* had been severe but – written about someone who was no longer living – they had not been intended as personal. He now published an attack that was both sharp *and* personal.

The matter concerned the auks. At that time British naturalists believed there was one species of guillemot, which they called *Uria troile* ('The Foolish Guillemot'). In 1818 Frederick Franks[94] had sent Elford a guillemot from the north Atlantic[95] which Elford had recognised as a distinct species and had displayed at the Linnean Society in November, giving it the name *Uria francsii* (Franks' Guillemot). A notice of this had been published in January 1819 in the *Annals of Philosophy* .

When the collections from Ross's expedition reached Britain they were found to contain many examples of this species from Greenland, all of which had been labelled as *Uria troile* by the expedition members. After consultation with Elford, the first edition of Ross's account of the

92 We know very little about his servants. In October 1819 William Clift speaks of Elford and mentions "his man" (Letter: William Clift to Caroline Clift, 30th October 1819. Loc: General Library (Owen Correspondence) The Natural History Museum, London), and in 1820 Elford had a servant called Ann at the Museum (König's diary, 20th May 1822).
93 We do not know when the wolf died. In May 1819 Elford donated 'a Pyrenean Wolf' to the Museum, but this was during Bullock's sale and he also donated a Dromedary so that wolf may have been bought.
94 Not traced.
95 "off Ferroë" ['Ferroë' has not been traced. Is this the Færoes?]

The Foolish Guillemot

voyage, published in April 1819, called the species *Uria francsii*. The second edition, to be published in July, would do the same, but in the meantime Captain Edward Sabine – a Royal Artillery officer who had accompanied the expedition as an astronomer but was also interested in natural history[96] – prepared an account of this species for the *Transactions of the Linnean Society* for July[97], giving it his own new name *Uria brunnichii* (Brünnich's Guillemot). Elford was furious.

Sabine's (rather technical) argument for naming the species after Morten Brünnich[98] was based on the history of guillemot names:

In 1758 Linnæus had described a species of guillemot which he named *Alca lomvia*. Several years later he described it again but moved it into the genus *Colymbus* with other diving birds and gave it a new species name. He now called it *Colymbus troille* (which he later amended to *troile*)[99]. *Troile* was still the name used for the common British guillemots in 1819.

In 1764 Brünnich identified the common guillemot of Denmark as Linnæus's species. He moved this into the genus *Uria*[100] but used Linnæus's original species name and called the birds, *Uria lomvia*. Brünnich believed there was a second species of guillemot, but he referred to this as *Uria troille*, despite the fact that both Linnæus's names (*lomvia* and *troille/troile*) had referred to the same species.

Sabine argued that as Brünnich had been the first to recognise there was more than one species of guillemot, the northern species should be named after him. Elford was incensed that the species should be named after someone who (as he saw it) had given the name of the common bird, *Uria troile*, to the rare bird, and had changed the name of the common bird to *Uria lomvia*, but he was even more infuriated that his advice was being ignored. He inserted a response into the second edition of Ross's report, where he was writing his own section on the new species discovered by the expedition[101]:

"It was sent home by all the ships employed in the northern expedition, under the name *Troile*, and it was even received as such, and believed to be no other, by the collectors of birds in this country. I was the first who perceived the distinction, and that too without comparison, and I instantly endeavoured to convince those who entertained doubts on the subject. Notwithstanding this, Captain Sabine who sent it home to his brother E. Sabine, Esq. as the *Troile*, and who first learnt from me that it was a distinct species, has, without any reference whatever to what I had told him, proposed to name it after an ornithologist, who was ignorant enough to describe it under the name of *Troile*, and to give the true *Troile*, (one of the most common and best known of the European birds,) under a new name!"

This is petulance in print. (Before we leave for ever the horrible complexities of species' names, we should mention that everyone was wrong. Brünnich's *Uria troille* is now believed to be the same species as his

[96] Edward Sabine (1788-1883) FRS 1818. Later worked on pendulums and terrestrial magnetism. Was President of the Royal Society 1861-71. Knighted 1869. Promoted General 1870.
[97] *Transactions of the Linnean Society*, **12**(2): 538-539 [published 2nd July 1819].
[98] Morten Thrane Brünnich (1737-1827) of Copenhagen.
[99] Linnæus spelt this 'troille' in 1761 but changed it to 'troile' in 1766.
[100] *Uria* had been created by Mathurin Jacques Brisson (1723-1806) in 1760.
[101] Ross, 1819 2nd edn: Vol. 2: 170-172. The "E. Sabine, Esq." appears to be a typographical error or lapsus calami. Edward sent birds home to his eldest brother Joseph Sabine (1770-1837).

Uria lomvia, and the species Linnæus had seen was not the common guillemot of Britain; it was a northern species that does not live as far south as the British Isles. Linnæus's species was, in fact, *francsii / brunnichii* which is known today by his first choice of species name, *Uria lomvia* (but Elford Leach would be very unhappy to learn that its common name is still 'Brünnich's Guillemot'). Linnæus had not seen the guillemot found around Britain but – unknown to the protagonists in 1819 – that had been described as a distinct species as early as 1763 by the Dane Erik Pontoppidan[102] and is now known by his species name, *Uria aalge*).

While Elford was fuming at Edward Sabine the Trustees received a complaint about his behaviour from another quarter. Devon naturalist William Turton[103] had intended to donate his personal shell collection to the Museum but Elford had refused to receive it, apparently saying he would never accept anything from Turton. Turton was deeply upset. His pride was obviously hurt, but pride seems to be something he had in abundance. In biology it is viewed as utterly unacceptable to name a new species after yourself, but Turton got around this by naming *Turbo turtonis* in honour of his unmarried daughter's family. The Trustees refused to have anything to do with this squabble – presumably because the collection had never belonged to the Museum – and ordered the Secretary to answer the letter in a private capacity.

Violence

In August tensions in the country again reached fever pitch. On the 16th a mass meeting was arranged at St Peter's Fields in Manchester to protest at the Corn Laws and to hear more calls for parliamentary reform. The main speaker would again be Henry Hunt.

Hunt and the other spokesmen arrived behind waving flags and a marching band to be greeted by a crowd of up to 80,000 men, women and children. The meeting was policed by the regular army and by contingents of cavalry from the local volunteer Yeomanry, the sons of local employers and land-owners.

Hunt had barely started speaking when the magistrates, watching from a nearby house, ordered his arrest and sent in the cavalry to clear a way to the speakers' platform. The reasons for what happened next are still unclear. The Yeomanry spurred their horses into the packed crowd and began slashing left and right with their sabres. The unarmed mass was helpless, the centre too tightly packed to move until the outer edges had scattered. When they had, the field cleared within minutes, but they were very long minutes for anyone within reach of the hooves and the swords.

As the horsemen pursued the fleeing crowd into the side streets the devastation they left was shocking. Over 400 people had been wounded, more than a quarter of them women. Nine men and two women were dead. The field was strewn with hats, shawls, shoes and bodies[104].

[102] Erik Pontoppidan (1698-1764). Danish theologian and naturalist. Professor of Theology at Copenhagen (1738); Bishop of Bergen, Norway (1747).

[103] William Turton (1762-1835) Physician and amateur conchologist. Originally lived in Swansea, then Dublin. By 1819 he was living in south Devon.

[104] See Priestley (1971: 233-240) for eye-witness accounts.

The Prince Regent – his finger on the pulse of the nation as ever – sent a letter of congratulations to the magistrates and the military for their "decisive and efficient measures for the preservation of public peace."

Hunt had been snatched from the podium and severely beaten by the constables. At his subsequent trial he was sentenced to three years imprisonment.

The country was electrified. In bitter irony the affair was christened *Peterloo* and across the industrial areas men began sharpening knives and making pikes for the uprising they felt sure was coming. The government sharpened its teeth.

Zoology

If fear of insurrection had pervaded Montagu House, its presence was not obvious. In September Elford wrote to de Blainville hinting at de Blainville's deteriorated relationship with Cuvier: "I have for you some fishes & reptiles in Alkohol. How shall I send them? I fear that you are not on sufficiently good terms with the Jardin, for me to send them through that channel.[105]"

October arrived and the Museum re-opened but Elford had still not made time in his busy schedule for the planned trip to the Orkneys, and his temper was not improving. He wrote again to Paris but now it was de Blainville's turn to suffer his irritation. Elford had earlier sent to France a dog from Baffin's Bay, brought home by Ross and about to give birth. In Ross's account of the voyage Elford had reported that in Baffin Bay dogs "The great toe on the hinder feet is wanting[106]" but de Blainville had subsequently published the news that in a puppy born to this dog shortly after its arrival in Paris (and being raised by zoologist Anselme-Gaetan Desmarest[107]) the toes were present. Elford had a surprise for him:

"If the dog brought up by Mr Desmarets, be the production of the Baffin's Bay Dog, it is a matter of importance to observe that when I sent the dog to the Jardin, it was with young, by a very different race of dogs; by a dog belonging to Captain Sabine. I am astonished my dear Blainville that you did not write to me, for the purpose of acertaining wether the bitch   I sent was impregnated by a dog of its own race, or by that of another when so highly important a statement as that relating to the variation in dogs which is so nearly connected with the variation of the human race was under discussion[108]."

(Apart from his astonishment and annoyance, his wording makes it clear he felt a study of other mammals could shed light on human variation. He is not placing humans far above the other species in God's creation.)

Jumping from one animal group to another, Elford was now diverted to a consideration of tropical birds by the arrival at the Museum of the American naturalist Thomas Horsfield[109], the new Curator of the East India Company's museum in London. Horsfield had just spent 17 years in Java

[105] Letter: W.E. Leach to de Blainville, 28th September 1819 (Loc: Bibliothèque Centrale, Muséum National d'Histoire Naturelle, Paris. Ref: Item 116).

[106] Ross, 1819 2nd edn: 169.

[107] Anselme-Gaetan Desmarest (or Desmarets – both forms were used in publications) (1784-1838). A zoologist particularly interested in Crustacea. By 1825 (at least) he was Professor of Zoology at the Royal Veterinary School at Alfort, just outside Paris.

[108] Letter: W.E. Leach to de Blainville, 10th October 1819 (Loc: Bibliothèque Centrale, Muséum National d'Histoire Naturelle, Paris. Ref: Item 117).

[109] Thomas Horsfield (1773-1859). Born Bethlehem Pennsylvania. Educated University of Pennsylvania (MD 1798). Visited Java in 1800 and returned there in 1801. Stayed when the British took control from the Dutch in 1811 and was encouraged by the new Lieutenant-Governor, Thomas Stamford Raffles, (1781-1826) to examine all branches of art and natural history. Stayed after Dutch restoration in 1816. Travelled to England, arriving 12th July 1819 and remained until his death. For biography see Bastin & Moore (1982: 75-81, 113-115).

East India House, London.

and was preparing a systematic catalogue of Javanese birds. He compiled this at the British Museum under Elford's guidance and later admitted, "from him I received many of those general views in science, which I have found of great advantage in prosecuting my researches subsequently[110]".

Horsfield's studies in the Museum prompted Elford to resurrect some notes he had made in Paris on birds in the French collections. Horsfield's catalogue[111] and Elford's article (describing two new species, one from Java) were later published together in the *Transactions of the Linnean Society*.

By November it must have become clear Elford would not get to the Orkneys this year, and the Trustees allowed him to defer the visit until the following May, at the same time granting him "the usual Vacation for a Month in the present Autumn". This is a rather curious allowance with the Museum open to the public and only seven weeks of the year remaining, and it may have been a strong hint that he should take a break. Apart from his increasing irascibility he was also beginning to show eccentric mannerisms which may have attracted the Trustees' attention[112]. It is clear he did not take the break as his report to the Trustees on the 11th of December informed them he had been arranging the foreign shells.

Jonathan

Elford may not have been going to Scotland in the autumn of 1819, but Jonathan was. On the 9th of September he was promoted in the Rifle Brigade from Captain to Major, giving up his company to become second in command of the 1st battalion. Just over a week later the battalion set sail from Portsmouth for Edinburgh. Their final destination was the other side of Scotland where they were to be used to suppress civil unrest in the aftermath of *Peterloo*. In the textile industries of Glasgow the wages of the handloom weavers had been dropping steadily for decades (while the cost

[110] House of Commons, 1836: para. 2535.
[111] Horsfield, 1821.
[112] Henry Ellis (House of Commons, 1835: para. 1590). Of Elford in 1819 Ellis says, "at that time he showed great eccentricity" but gives no examples.

425

of living rose) and had now reached five shillings a week, half of what they had been three years previously and a fifth of what they had been at the industry's height[113]. As elsewhere, poverty was fuelling discontent and the weavers were organising themselves along military lines, in battalions, street by street[114].

Glasgow and its surrounds were to be the riflemen's uneasy home for the next 12 months. William Surtees, now in the 1st battalion[115], called this 'The Radical War' but it was to avoid war that in December the government unleashed the latest round in its escalation of repression: the *Six Acts*.

The Six Acts

This legislation added new layers to the suppression of free assembly, free speech, and a free press. *The Seditious Meetings Prevention Act* banned public meetings of more than 50 people without official permission; *The Blasphemous and Seditious Libels Act* increased penalties for, and allowed the banning of, publications judged seditious or blasphemous; *The Newspaper Stamp Duties Act* was extended to any periodical containing news, which now included radical pamphlets discussing what was happening in the country and had the effect of increasing the cost of their production; *The Training Prevention Act* allowed the arrest of any unauthorised person attending a gathering for the purpose of drilling or training in arms, with a maximum penalty of transportation for seven years to an overseas penal colony; *The Seizure of Arms Act* gave local magistrates new powers of search over persons and property to seek weapons; and *The Misdemeanours Act* increased the speed of the judicial process following any arrests.

The Acts were received with the enthusiasm to be expected and an unpopular government plumbed new depths. On Sunday the 1st of April 1820 a proclamation appeared on the walls in Glasgow signed by a *Committee of Organisation for forming a Provisional Government*. It called the people to arms and urged them to claim their own country. Britain was slipping closer and closer towards civil war. The Glasgow authorities responded by putting the Rifle Brigade and several other regiments onto the city streets[116] and imposing a 7 p.m. curfew.

Following this incident the ensuing months saw several convictions for High Treason and one of the Radical leaders, hosier James Wilson, was hanged and beheaded in Glasgow on the 30th of August 1820 in front of 20,000 onlookers. He had many sympathisers in the crowd and cries of "*Murder*" and "*He is a murdered man*" rang out as he climbed the scaffold. Policing this huge assembly were the Rifle Brigade, the 33rd Regiment[117] and a contingent of the 3rd Dragoon Guards[118].

Jonathan Leach did not much like this style of soldiering. He referred to the task as one of "over-awing cotton-spinners and colliers" adding it was "by no means a delectable service, for we found them a most nefarious crew."

[113] Bryant, 1975; 383. See also Simond (1817) 2: 279.
[114] Harry Smith reported in Bryant (1975: 385).
[115] Surtees, now the 95th's senior Quartermaster, had been transferred to the 1st battalion in February 1819 when the 3rd battalion had been reduced.
[116] The 80th (Staffordshire Volunteers) and the 83rd Regiment, with some regular army cavalry. The Yeomanry was also mobilised
[117] 33rd (1st Yorkshire West Riding) Regiment of Foot.
[118] *Glasgow Herald*, 1st September 1820.

— 26 —

Vaulting the zebra

Deign on the passing world to turn thine eyes
And pause awhile from letters to be wise.

Samuel Johnson

Although Britain was ripe for revolution at the end of 1819, even anger at Peterloo and the Six Acts was not enough to urge the people over the threshold. At the beginning of 1820 a small group of republicans decided to give them a push. The plan was to explode a bomb under the entire British Cabinet as they assembled at a widely publicised dinner. What the conspirators did not know was that one of their number was a government agent and the authorities had known about them for months. There was no Cabinet dinner. The trap was set. On the 23rd of February, as the would-be assassins assembled at their hideout in a hay loft in Cato Street, London, the police pounced. Five of the plotters were transported to a penal colony. The five leaders were hanged and beheaded on the 1st of May[1].

This murderous plot[2] was a godsend for the government who could now argue their repressions were justified. Liberal political reform suffered a significant setback.

1820 had already been a year marked by death. On the 29th of January, after 60 years on the throne, George III finally died and the Prince Regent became King George IV. Sir Joseph Banks died five months later at the age of 77[3] and was succeeded as President of the Royal Society (and hence as an Official Trustee of the British Museum) by Sir Humphry Davy.

Elford Leach devoted the time covered by all these events to the general arrangement of the collections and to the molluscs, which he studied with increasing fervour. Some of the plates for his immense manuscript on the British species were now being engraved and would soon be printed[4]. Meanwhile he was arranging the Museum's foreign shells and was granted £50 to fill gaps in the collection. His other interests continued unabated.

[1] On the day of public execution one of the heads slipped from the hands of the executioner and rolled away across the scaffold, stimulating a cry from the watching crowd of "Yah! Butterfingers!" (Bryant, 1975: 390fn).
[2] Called 'The Cato Street Conspiracy'.
[3] At his country retreat, *Spring Grove*, on the 19th of June.
[4] Leach (1852) figure imprints dated June and July 1820 and bearing the name of the publishers *Baldwin, Cradock & Joy*. Elford clearly felt this work was approaching a conclusion and on the 1st of March 1821 the *Monthly Magazine* would report, "Dr. LEECH has nearly completed his Synopsis of British Mollusca" (at page 160: Literary and Philosophical Intelligence).

Historical note

1820   John Constable[1] paints *Stratford Mill*.

March   Disturbances among seamen on Tyneside.

March   Anti-clearance disturbances in Scotland.

March to April   Disturbances among wool-croppers and an uprising in Yorkshire.

4th April   'Battle of Bonnymuir' near Glasgow when weavers armed with pikes form square and are overwhelmed by troops of the 7th Hussars.

12th May   Florence Nightingale[2] born in Florence.

27th June   After years of spying on Princess (now Queen) Caroline the government begins investigation of evidence against her personal indiscretions. The public demonstrate in her support.

5th July   Parliament commences the reading of a *Bill of Pains and Penalties* (a trial for adultery in all but name) investigating Caroline's conduct. If adultery is proved George will divorce her and strip her of her title as Queen (At the Foreign Office Joseph Planta's son, Joseph Planta *Jnr*, is involved in arranging foreign witnesses).

8th July   Coronation of George IV postponed.

10th November   After evidence against Caroline is heard, preliminary voting produces only a very narrow margin in favour of Pain and Penalty. The proceedings are adjourned for 6 months (effectively the 'trial' is abandoned). The public sees this as a victory for the Queen. There are widespread demonstrations in her favour, with supporters wearing white buttonholes and cockades. The public generally believe her guilty but support her anyway because of the shabby treatment she has received at the hands of her husband, whom they dislike.

1821   Constable paints *The Hay Wain*.

January   Disturbances in Shropshire during colliers' strike.

March   Anti-clearance disturbance in Scotland.

5th May   Napoleon dies on St Helena.

19th July   Coronation of George IV. Queen Caroline arrives at the doors of Westminster Hall without a formal invitation and is turned (or turns) away.

7th August   Caroline dies after a short illness.

14th August   Riots in London during Caroline's funeral as the crowd prevents the cortège bypassing the centre of London. The Life Guards shoot two men dead.

[1] John Constable (1776-1837). English landscape painter.
[2] Florence Nightingale (1820-1910). English hospital reformer.

The bat *Mormoops blainvillii* Leach.

Illustration from Elford Leach's article published in the *Transactions of the Linnean Society* (1820).

At the beginning of the year he drew together his work on bats and presented two papers to the Linnean Society, announcing, "On a future occasion it is my intention to lay before the Society the details of all such new genera as may be discovered by my friends in different parts of the world, which shall be followed with descriptions of all the species. To further my purpose, I solicit the aid of travelling naturalists, and request them to have the goodness to send me specimens of Bats (preserved if possible in spirits) from every part of the world.[5]" He would need a larger battery.

His crustacean work was ongoing and in March he published the 17th part of his *Malacostraca*, the first issued since 1817. In the same month he presented his paper on tropical birds to the Linnean Society. In May his increasing activity at the Society was reflected in his election, again, to the Linnean's Council. Also in May he bought fossils at *Egyptian Hall*, which Bullock had retained and was now operating as a sale-room. Among other items Bullock was auctioning Colonel Birch's[6] collection of bones from 'The Dorsetshire Fossil Lizard' (a species of ichthyosaur found in rocks on the south coast of England). The sale included a full skeleton but Elford was only authorised by the Museum to spend £25 and the skeleton was bought by the Royal College of Surgeons for four times that amount[7].

Elford had still not arranged his trip to the Orkneys, and was now apparently engrossed in the curation of the Museum's pickled collections. He had been allowed to order nearly 100 bottles the previous April and spend another £14 on glassware in July, but by January 1820 he was asking for more bottles and Spirits of Wine; in May he was allowed to spend £30 on spirit and bottles, then ordered more jars and alcohol in June.

[5] Leach, W.E. 1821. The Characters of seven Genera of Bats with foliaceous Appendages to the Nose. *Transactions of the Linnean Society of London*, **13**(1): 73-82 at p. 73. [paper read 7th March 1820].
[6] Colonel J. Birch (ca 1768-1829).
[7] Sharpe, 1906: 245.

Glareola orientalis Leach (from Java).

Illustration from Elford Leach's article in the *Transactions of the Linnean Society* (1820).

He was also arranging the insect collections and adding the new acquisitions. In the previous year the Museum had received nearly 1300 specimens from various sources, as well as three orders of insects from the collection of Thomas Marsham (one of Elford's proposers at the Linnean Society) who had just died. Elford warned the Trustees the insects must be stored in closed drawers or they would deteriorate, but he was allowed to arrange drawers full of duplicates, to be left open for public inspection.

The squid called *Loligo parva* by Elford Leach in his mollusc manuscript.

Illustration printed July 1820 (published in Leach, 1852).

He was still writing for the French *Dictionnaire*, and the *Encyclopædia Britannica*, and was now translating French texts in the only time left to him, during the night[8]. He was working virtually round the clock by oil-lamp and candle-light and was becoming pale and drawn, while his irritable temper of the previous year was more pronounced. He took a sudden and unexplained dislike to James Stephens and John Gray, whose company was no longer welcome[9]. Swainson still saw him but found him increasingly agitated and prone to irregular and intense bouts of gymnastic exercise, one of which involved vaulting repeatedly over a stuffed zebra in the middle of one of the galleries[10].

As the summer arrived his planned trip north had not materialised and he had not been to Devon for 18 months. By July he was reporting to the Trustees: "Dr Leach, owing to the business of the Museum, could not avail himself of the permission granted to him last year by the Trustees to go into the country and he now requests them to allow him to be absent this year for two months, or such time as may not interfere with the interest of the Museum.[11]"

They agreed to two months leave during the summer closure but, true to character, he worked on regardless. By now Swainson noticed he had become highly nervous and his eyes shone with an "unnatural brightness". In September König made a short trip to Gravesend in Kent. When he returned on the Monday morning he found Elford "in a very bad state[12]". The strain had finally overwhelmed him. He had snapped.

Breakdown

He was in a state of complete mental collapse: rambling, incoherent and quite unable to look after himself. His condition, thought Swainson, "rendered the care of his friends absolutely essential to his welfare[13]". After three days in his house at the Museum it was clear he needed professional help. On the Thursday his Museum keys were taken from him and he was sent to his old teacher John Abernethy. The following day Abernethy put him in the care of his son-in-law, Dr John Warburton[14] whose father, Thomas, had treated George III during his descent into madness[15]. Thomas Warburton managed asylums at Hoxton, a small hamlet on the outskirts of London renowned for centuries for its collection of private madhouses. Shakespeare was allegedly once an inmate, Charles Lamb and his sister Mary certainly were (For the period being considered, the terms 'hospital' and 'patient' are not appropriate. At this time madhouses – the official term for these establishments – were fiercely brutalising environments).

[8] Gunther, 1980a: 210.
[9] Gunther, 1974: 58.
[10] Which Swainson (1840) says he cleared "with the lightness of a harlequin".
[11] Report: W.E. Leach to Trustees of the British Museum, 7th July 1820 (Loc: British Museum, Officers' Reports, **VI**: 1351).
[12] König's Diary: 11th September 1820.
[13] Swainson (1840).
[14] John Warburton (1792-1845) of Nº 5 Clifford Street, Bond Street, London. Educated Cambridge, MB 1815, MD 1820. Married Abernethy's eldest daughter, Anne. A friend of William Clift.
[15] Thomas Warburton (*fl.* 1770-1820). Had no medical qualifications but was still called 'doctor'. He had a reputation for institutionalised cruelty. George III hated him so much he would not look at him, saying "Take away that fellow with the long nose—take him away, away, away." (This and other information from Morris, 1958).

On the following Monday it was discovered Saunders, the natural history attendant, had returned Elford's keys to him and they were now with his servant[16]. Planta reclaimed them and the Trustees imposed the two months leave already arranged.

By the end of September Elford's mental confusion seems to have eased a little. König was able to write to Swainson, now in Liverpool:

"Dear Sir,

I have the pleasure of acquainting you in answer to your enquiries respecting our friend, Dr Leach, that I have received a letter from him written a few days back, in which he states that his health is mending daily by the good air, moderate diet and gentle opening medicines which, he adds, perform all the good effects that Cheltenham water did when he first drank them. He is at present with a friend in the neighbourhood of London; but   I hear to day that, owing to the still better health he is enjoying at this moment, he will perhaps very soon be allowed to go to his friends in Devonshire or to Cheltenham where part of them are[17]. As part of the regimen prescribed to him is to abstain from study and writing, it may perhaps, not be advisable for you to write to him at present; but as soon as I shall again have an opportunity of communicating with him, I shall tell him that you have made enquiries respecting his health.

Believe me

Dear Sir

very faithfully yours

Chas Konig

P.S. I open the letter to add that I have just received another letter from Leach in which he informs me that he is nearly well again; and Saunders tells me that he receives and answers letters. I still would advise you not to write a letter to him that may require an answer.[18]"

By mid-October William Kirby could write to Alexander MacLeay, 'I am rejoiced to hear so good an account of poor Leach, and I hope it will please God to restore him to the full use of his powers of mind, that he may not like poor Spence, be wholly disabled from the use of his pen—but he must be cautious and go on very quietly and remember—non semper arcum tendit Apollo[19]' [*Apollo does not keep his bow forever strung* – a quote from Horace[20]].

Notwithstanding his improvement Elford visited the Museum with John Warburton on the 14th of October to remove personal possessions from his workroom. Three weeks later he wrote a lucid letter to James Stephens in which he asked Stephens to pass some observations from a correspondent in the Orkneys to Alexander MacLeay for reading at that evening's meeting of the Linnean Society. Despite this obvious upturn in his mental state the Trustees were taking no chances with his recovery and gave him another two months leave. This was a wise decision. His lucidity was a deceptive

[16] Presumably Ann.
[17] His friends would be at Cheltenham for the social season. Cheltenham was a spa town and polite Society descended on it for the summer (perhaps staying as late as October) where they would take the waters and attend various social gatherings to dance or to play cards. Elford had visited Cheltenham at least during the summer of 1809. During the winters this social scene moved south to Bath, another spa town. Sir William Elford moved in these social circles where he was renowned as a whist player.
[18] Letter: König to William Swainson, 29th September 1820 (Loc: Linnean Society of London, Swainson Correspondence).
[19] Letter: Kirby to MacLeay, 13th October 1820 (Loc: Linnean Society of London, MacLeay Correspondence).
[20] Quintus Horatius Flaccus Horace (65 BC – 8 BC). Roman poet and satirist.

oasis of calm which did not last. At the end of November John Lees[21] wrote to Swainson, "I suppose you have heard of the most distressing state of health of our friend Doctor Leach. I am sorry to say his medical friends do not think he will recover for a considerable length of time[22]". By the following week Elford's brother George had arrived from Devon and with Joseph Planta, Charles König and James Stephens cleared some of Elford's personal belongings out of his Museum house. On the 9th of December König wrote ominously in his diary, "Leach cut another".

It seems Elford was not being confined and was moving within London under the constant care of an attendant[23]. About the same time as he was wounding someone he visited Will Bullock, who reported, "Poor Leach was here a day or two since attended by a Keeper He look very ill   speaks rationaly except on the subject of museums and snuff manufactories[24]".

In mid-December Warburton decided Elford would be better served by the more peaceful surroundings of the countryside and recommended he be taken to the West Country to recuperate. Being near the Museum seemed to prevent him from relaxing. As Christmas approached[25] he was discharged from Warburton's care and taken home to Devon.

1821

Jonathan, in the far north and fully engaged on government business, had been in no position to help Elford, and was made less so by new orders sending his battalion to Ireland. By January they were in Belfast and in the spring they marched to Armagh before moving on to Naas, then Kilkenny, Fermoy and finally Newcastle in the county of Limerick. They were being sent to suppress another civil disturbance, this time of self-styled Whiteboys.

'Whiteboys' was the name given in 1761 to Irish Levellers in Limerick who tore down the fences that had been erected to enclose and partition common pastureland, formerly available to anyone for grazing their stock. To symbolise their unity the Levellers wore white shirts over their other clothes. In the early years of the nineteenth century the name Whiteboys was still in use in Limerick for groups taking direct action to oppose government policy[26].

While Jonathan settled into his new duties, news of Elford's breakdown had spread far and wide and rumours were beginning to fly. From the Paris museum in January Joseph Pentland[27] (an Irish-born naturalist who had been working in Cuvier's laboratory since 1818 and probably met Elford during a trip to England in the spring of 1820) wrote to William Buckland:

"I am sorry to hear that poor Leach is not better or at least that you are not pleased with the last news you have had of him. We have had a report that he was replaced at the British Museum by a Mr Stevens. This I cannot believe as I am sure that the Trustees would not be guilty of such an injustice, and as we have never heard of Mr Stevens' reputation as a Zoologist, I beg you to let me hear from you on this head.[28]"

[21] Not identified.
[22] Letter: Lees to Swainson (still in Liverpool), 24th November 1820 (Loc: Linnean Society of London, Swainson Correspondence).
[23] Possibly James Beresford, who is later mentioned by George as having had care of Elford (Will of George Leach dated 25th October 1861. Loc: West Devon Record Office, Plymouth). By 1861 James Beresford lived at Nº 11 Harrington Street, Oakley Square, London (probably not built in 1820).
[24] Letter: Bullock to unknown recipient, 15th December 1820 (Loc: Linnean Society of London, Swainson Correspondence [but clearly not to Swainson]). Snuff manufactories? Perhaps Elford had suffered in the past from air-borne pollution from these establishments, possibly at Edinburgh where the last snuff mill was in operation until as late as the Second World War (*Observer Magazine*, 20 July 1986, p. 34).
[25] König (*Diary*) says Leach left London on the 12th of December; Warburton (see later) says the 16th.
[26] The nineteenth century Whiteboys were a rural group. In the north of Ireland were similar groups in the manufacturing centres known by various names such as 'right boys' and 'peep-of-day boys' (Simond (1817) **2**: 427fn).
[27] Joseph Barclay Pentland (1797-1873). The mineral Pentlandite and the fossil *Hippopotamus pentlandi* (Falconer, 1860) are named after him. See Sarjeant & Delair, 1980.
[28] Letter: Pentland to William Buckland, 21st January 1821 (Sarjeant & Delair, 1980: 266).

The Trustees had taken no such action. Elford's leave expired on the 11th of January but it was the 30th before he returned to London and his apartments, where he was allowed to stay, but not to work. Just over a week later his brother George submitted a memorial to the Trustees asking them to extend the sick-leave and requesting that they pay Elford his full salary during his absence. It seems any funds Elford had used before he arrived at the Museum in 1814 had long since been exhausted. He had been living off his salary and the fees received for his numerous encyclopaedia articles.

'The Memorial of George Leach states
that his brother Doctor Leach was appointed to the situation which he now holds in the British Museum in September 1813 with a Salary of 120£ for which he was required to attend at the Museum two days in each week and with an extra allowance of 75£ per Annum for every additional day in each week which he should devote to the Service of the Public at the Museum – That in the Month of September last Doctor Leach was attacked by mental derangement, occasioned solely (as appears by the certificate of Doctor Warburton under whose care he was placed) by his unceasing application to the duties of his Office – That in consequence of this unfortunate malady he has already incurred expences which the whole salary and other emoluments of his office will barely enable him to defray, and which expences, as Doctor Leach has no private fortune whatever, must be sustained by his family if any part of his salary or other Emoluments is withdrawn – That in all cases of sickness hitherto the Officers of the Museum have, during their necessary absence from it, enjoyed the full salary and other emoluments of their situation – That it is the opinion of Doctor Warburton, as expressed in the Certificate, that quiet and retirement are indispensably necessary to the restoration of Doctor Leach's health – It is therefore confidently hoped that the Trustees of the British Museum, taking into consideration the very peculiar circumstances of the present case, will grant to Doctor Leach such an extension of leave of absence as will give him every chance of obtaining a perfect recovery of his health and that they will allow him in the mean time to enjoy the full salary and all the other emoluments of his office – It may be added also that Doctor Leach has an additional claim to every possible indulgence from the circumstance of his having freely and without remuneration given to the Public a most valuable collection of British insects, formed by himself during a space of ten or twelve years, the formation of which, besides an immense sacrifice of time and personal labour, actually cost him at least Eight hundred pounds, and the collection would now sell for that or probably a larger sum, and it should be remembered that such a sum would have been most beneficial to him under his present unfortunate circumstances—[29]'

The accompanying certificate from John Warburton declared:

[29] British Museum Trustees' Manuscripts. Original Letters and Papers, **IV** (1816-1821): 1623–1624.

'I hereby certify that Doctor William Elford Leach was placed under my care on the 16th day of September 1820 and remained so until the 16th December 1820.— During this period he was labouring under mental derangement, evidently produced by too serious an attention to his Scientific pursuits and in my opinion increased by his anxiety about the performance of his duties at the British Museum. At the expiration of the above stated time, I strongly recommended to his friends the necessity of his being placed in the Country where he might enjoy exercise and where his mind might be more at ease than it could be while he remainined in the vicinity of the Museum. I am also of opinion that for the re-establishment of his mental health, it would be proper for him to remain a considerable time in the Country in order that every possible chance may be given for his complete restoration—[30]'

At their meeting on the 10th of February the Trustees took a remarkably sympathetic view of George's request. It was agreed Elford should have another four months leave during which he should return to Devon. In addition to his salary they made him a gift of £100 – the equivalent of 10 months basic pay – under "the peculiar circumstances of his Case" (presumably the fact that his illness had been brought on by overwork in their service).

The extension of his leave does not appear to have been a difficult decision. Although Buckland was reassuring Pentland of Elford's continuing recovery, Pentland replied in late February, "I am very happy to have so good an account from Leach, I have just received a letter from himself which is evidently written by a person in a rather disturbed state of mind.[31]"

On the 17th of February Elford had been removed again from the Museum, this time in the care of a different Hoxton doctor, naval surgeon James Veitch[32]. Since 1792 the Royal Navy had sent officers and seamen suffering from mental complaints to Hoxton House, one of the Hoxton madhouses. Veitch was a staff surgeon with special responsibility for the care of these naval inmates. He had formerly been a surgeon at the Royal Naval Hospital, Plymouth and at the Antigua hospital.

At the Museum, Elford's continuing absence was causing the Trustees problems. It was now six months since anyone had taken any steps to maintain the zoology collection and protect it from pest damage. To rectify this they instructed Joseph Planta and Charles König to find someone to curate the collections until Elford returned. Coincidentally, at about this time William MacLeay happened to meet fellow entomologist George Samouelle for breakfast, where Samouelle expressed concerns about the current neglect of the collections. MacLeay passed these comments on to Charles König, who in turn consulted Robert Brown at the Linnean Society. König had heard good reports from Elford about Samouelle so it was agreed to nominate him as a suitable caretaker. MacLeay promoted the idea with the Marquess of Stafford, one of the Trustees[33], and Planta and König made

[30] British Museum Trustees' Manuscripts. Original Letters and Papers, **IV** (1816-1821): 1625. 'The Country' = the countryside; away from the bustle of towns.

[31] Letter: Pentland to William Buckland, 21st February 1821 (Sarjeant & Delair, 1980: 268).

[32] James Veitch (1769-1856). MD Edinburgh. In 1821 he lived at N° 4 Charlotte Street, Pimlico, London. Later Deputy Inspector of Hospitals and Fleets. Author of *Essays on Insanity* (1829) and *Essay on the Prevention and Cure of Yellow Fever*.

[33] George Granville Leveson-Gower, Marquess of Stafford (1758-1833). His art collection ('The Cleavehouse Gallery') was open each Wednesday afternoon in May, June and July to anyone known to, or recommended by, the Leveson-Gower family (Anon., 1811: 318-319). He married the Countess of Sutherland in 1785 and was made Duke of Sutherland just before his death. He was a notorious landowner in Scotland who (allegedly) saw his highland tenants living in poor conditions and 'for their own benefit' instigated a *Highland clearance* from about 1810, resettling them near the coast (Actually the land was wanted for sheep for the wool trade). His orders were carried out with great brutality and today he bears much of the blame for a misguided policy badly implemented.

a formal application at the Trustees' meeting in March. Samouelle was duly appointed, on a daily wage of 15 shillings, to assist primarily with the insect collections for as long as he would be needed (In fact he would work at the Museum for the next 19 years[34]).

For the remaining collections, König himself took responsibility for the birds in the galleries. Edward Sabine had examined the birds in February and had drawn König's attention to an error Elford had made with regard to a gift from him[35]. König did not approve of Elford's arrangement or the fact that he had applied names that many visitors did not recognise, either because they were new names that Elford had not yet published, or very old pre-Linnæus names of which most workers were ignorant. Elford's labels were also in very small writing that was difficult to read from outside the cases[36]. In Elford's absence König, with Samouelle's help, rearranged the entire bird collection and removed the offending identifications. König then personally wrote new labels restoring the familiar scientific names and adding the common names in English, French and German[37]. Elford would not have approved, but he was in no position to complain. He was currently suffering James Veitch's personal brand of mental health-care.

When Veitch was interviewed in 1815 by a Select Committee of the House of Commons investigating the regulation of English madhouses[38], the committee members were critical of what they saw as his excessive reliance on "the practice of salivating patients by the great use of mercury[39], and by giving them digitalis" (a heart stimulant and potential poison extracted from the Foxglove[40] and related plants). Veitch explained he had no confidence in the prescription of sedatives in cases of mental disturbance, but his use of mercury produced good results (although he admitted the mouths of his patients did suffer). To mitigate the accusations he noted that in addition to mercury he also used purging, bleeding, cupping[41] and blistering and he emphasised no patient had been prescribed a daily dose of more than 60 drops of digitalis. Nevertheless, the Committee heard that in one 20 day period at Hoxton Veitch had prescribed: 5 bleedings, 5 cuppings, 8 setons (pushing a needle through a fold of skin and keeping the wound open with a twist of silk) and 11 blisters, but 425 mercurial pills and 670 powders of calomel (mainly mercurous chloride) and digitalis. Elford Leach was in Veitch's care for three months and later referred to him as "that Devil-incarnate[42]".

Napoleon

On the 5th of May 1821 Napoleon died on St Helena after a long illness and an era finally ended. When it was later decided to return his ashes to Europe a deferential British government asked his old adversary the Duke of Wellington if he objected to the restoration. Wellington replied:

"Field Marshal the Duke of Wellington presents his compliments to His Majesty's Ministers. If they wish to know Field Marshal the Duke of

[34] He was at the Museum until 1840 but his work deteriorated during his later years and he took to drinking heavily. He was eventually dismissed.
[35] König's diary, 7th February 1821. Could the 'error' have concerned the name of a guillemot?
[36] Samouelle (House of Commons, 1835: para. 3865). This may have been a reference to the printed 'labels' cut from the 1816 Catalogue of British animals, which are not in a large font.
[37] König (House of Commons, 1835: para. 2628); Children (*op. cit.* para. 3399); and Gray (House of Commons, 1836: para. 2660).
[38] *Report of a Select Committee of the House of Commons appointed to consider the provision being made for the better regulation of Madhouses in England.* (11th July 1815).
[39] Eminent surgeon Sir Astley Cooper (1768-1841) also complained in 1828 about the excessive prescription of mercury, particularly in London hospitals (Macilwain, 1856: 305).
[40] Genus *Digitalis* Linnæus.
[41] Cupping – applying a suction cup to the skin to draw blood to the surface.
[42] Letter: W.E. Leach to A. MacLeay, 5th February 1824 (Loc: Linnean Society of London, Miscellaneous Correspondence).

Wellington's opinion as on a matter of public policy, he must decline to give one. If, however, they wish only to consult him as a private individual, Field Marshal the Duke of Wellington has no hesitation in saying that he does not care one twopenny damn what becomes of the ashes of Napoleon Buonaparte.[43]"

In the month Napoleon died James Veitch reported to Joseph Planta: 'I have the honor to acquaint you, for the information of the Trustees of the British Museum, that on Sunday the 20 past, Dr Leach was discharged from under my care perfectly cured of every mental aberration likely to interfere with the exercise of sound reason and Judgment, and the most satisfactory intelligence has this day been communicated to me of the continuance of that state of mind; but having advised a prolongation of his stay in the country in order to confirm his mental health, I have therefore to beg that you will have the goodness to obtain him leave of absence until the 10th of July next[44]'.

The Trustees agreed. Conversely, across the Channel the grapevine was in knots. From Paris Pentland wrote again to Buckland: 'I am extremely glad to hear that Leach is so far recovered as to be able to return to the Museum. If you should have any news of him between this and your next letter be so good as to mention it, as everyone here (Cuvier's family) are extremely interested about him.[45]'

Far from being at the Museum, Elford was now at Spitchwick, and Planta wrote to tell him to stay there, at least until after the July meeting of the Trustees. Elford was suitably appreciative:

"Dear Sir I duly received your very kind and friendly Letter of the 22 of June, and return to you my most grateful thanks for your paternal attention to my interest. All my Medical Friends recommend horse exercise in my native, subalpine Air, and I daily find that I gain health and strength, in my present Residence.[46]"

Despite his optimism the Trustees were still not convinced he was close to returning to work. At their meeting in July they ordered that he stay in Devon until after their quarterly General Meeting in September. They must have been receiving intelligence about his condition, and were obviously not heartened by what they heard because in September they extended his leave again until the next General Meeting in the middle of December.

Jonathan

In Ireland Jonathan was finding the Whiteboys more than a handful. He casually dismissed his duties as hunting illicit stills, hunting Whiteboys, and guarding county jails, but this was not the full story. William Surtees was more forthcoming. Noting Newcastle was the cradle of the Whiteboy insurrection, he acknowledged, "Here we were for a time actually shut up

[43] Alington, 1921: 84. 'Twopenny' is pronounced 'tuppenny'. (Alington does not give a date for this letter. Napoleon's remains were eventually returned to France in 1840, by which time Victoria was on the British throne).
[44] Letter: Veitch to Planta, 30th May 1821 (Loc: British Museum Trustees' Manuscripts. Original Letters and Papers, IV (1816-1821): 1659).
[45] Letter: Pentland to Buckland, 21st June 1821 (Sarjeant & Delair, 1980: 272).
[46] Letter: W.E. Leach to Planta, 8th July 1821 (Loc: British Museum Trustees' Manuscripts. Original Letters and Papers, IV (1816-1821): 1670).

as in a besieged town; and no individual belonging to the army durst attempt to move out without a sufficient number being together, to deter the misguided peasantry from attacking us. Innumerable were the murders that were committed about this neighbourhood at this time; and one's blood runs chill to think that these miscreants, when taken and brought to the gallows to atone for their crime, protested their innocence with their last breath, although hundreds around them could attest their guilt. This Rockite war[47] gave us considerable trouble, and it was not for a long time after that it was finally put down.[48]"

Jonathan would not see it put down. He had had enough of domestic soldiering and after 20 years in the army decided it was time to move on.

"I am free to confess" he admitted, "that I feel no particular *penchant* for passing the remainder of my days in marching off guards, going grand rounds and visiting rounds, and performing other dull, monotonous, and uninteresting duties of the kind, on which such great stress is laid, and to which such vast importance is attached, in various stiff-starched garrisons; but, on the contrary, prefer to range, henceforth, free and unfettered by military trammels, wherever my fancy leads."

In September 1821 his battalion moved a short distance to Rathkeale, but a few weeks later, on the 24th of October, Lieutenant-Colonel Jonathan Leach sold his commission and rejoined the civilian world.

London

Four days earlier, Elford – who should have been recuperating quietly in Devon – suddenly appeared in an agitated state at his Museum house. Henry Ellis, the Museum's Secretary, wrote swiftly to his brother George:

'Dear Sir

In Mr Planta's absence I take the liberty of naming to you that your brother has returned to his Apartments in the Museum: and that I understand (for I have not seen him) that he has a considerable degree of hurry upon his Spirits.

The direction of the Trustees at their last General Meeting (when they prolonged your Brothers leave of Absence) that he was not on any Account to return to the Museum till after the Next General Meeting, (which will be on the second Saturday in December), induces me to fear he may have come to Town without the concurrence of his friends.

Be this, however, as it may, under present circumstances I think it would be best for you to get him back, if possible, into the Country.

No one can, I assure you, offer this advice with a kinder intention than his and your

sincere friend and Servant

Henry Ellis[49]'

[47] The leader of one of the Irish groups adopted the name 'Captain Rock', hence 'Rockite'.
[48] Surtees, 1973: 417.
[49] Letter: Ellis to George Leach Jnr, 22nd October 1821 (Loc: British Museum Trustees' Manuscripts. Original Letters and Papers, **IV** (1816-1821): 1684-5.

The clue to what happened next is in Charles König's diary for the 27th of October where he states simply, "Leach did not return from Lady Molesworth". It seems Elford had been taken in by Lady Mary Molesworth[50] at the Molesworth's London house, but how he knew this family is not clear.

Lady Mary was the wife of Sir Arscott Molesworth *Bt*[51] who had donated animals to the British Museum as early as 1817[52]. The Molesworth family had a country house, 'Pencarrow', in Cornwall 30-40 km west of Plymouth, and may have known the Leach family – or more probably the Elford family – in the West Country. However, Lady Mary was the daughter of Captain Patrick Brown of Edinburgh and his wife Elizabeth 'Betsy' Hume (a well

Lady Mary Molesworth.

known Edinburgh beauty of her day), so it is also possible Elford knew the Molesworths from his time in Edinburgh. He had a further connection through his friend, Cornishman William Clift. Clift's brother John[53] had been the general foreman for estate works at Pencarrow for many years until his death at the end of 1819.

It is most likely there was a West Country family connection. Sir Arscott's mother[54] was the daughter of the Commissioner of Plymouth Dockyard and his father, Sir William Molesworth *Bt*[55], had been MP for Cornwall from 1785 to 1790 and Sheriff[56] of Cornwall in 1791[57]. He may well have been known to Elford Leach's uncles, Jonathan Elford[58] (who was Recorder for Tintagel in Cornwall from 1786 to 1810) and Jonathan's brother Sir William Elford (MP for Plymouth from 1796 to 1806).

When Elford Leach appeared unexpectedly at the Museum, Henry Ellis's first reaction had been to call on Lady Molesworth (where he had been upset by the way one of her young daughters had spoken to him![59]). This suggests Mary Molesworth had taken care of Elford during the earlier stages of his illness. Perhaps she was the "friend in the neighbourhood of London" mentioned in König's letter to Swainson just after Elford's initial breakdown. Whatever the connection, a week after he returned to London Elford was with the Molesworths, but presumably only until he could be escorted back to Spitchwick.

His confusion again appears to have eased as the months passed. In December his old friend John Butter was proposed for Fellowship of the Royal Society and Elford signed his certificate of nomination, as did Sir William Elford[60] and Butter's old teacher John Abernethy, among others[61].

[50] Mary Molesworth (d. 1877).
[51] Sir Arscott Ourry Molesworth *Bt* (1789-1823).
[52] He was thanked on 19th July 1817 for donating 'Five British Quadrupeds and Seven varieties of British Falcons', doubtless destined for the British gallery.
[53] John Clift (1759-1819).
[54] Lady Catherine Treby Molesworth (née Ourry) (ca 1761-1842).
[55] Sir William Molesworth, 6th Baronet (1758-1798). Born at Langdon near Plymouth.
[56] 'Sheriff' – from the old title 'Shire Reeve', the monarch's representative in a shire (i.e. a county).
[57] Sir Arscott had been Sheriff of Cornwall in 1816.
[58] Jonathan Elford (1743-1832). Born Bickham, christened Kingsbridge 1748. Attorney, Plymouth Dock. Partner *Elford & Foot* Attorneys, 1797. Deputy Recorder for Tintagel, Cornwall, 1781-1786; Recorder 1786-1810. Town Clerk and Deputy Recorder, Bossiney, 1791-1798 (not an onerous task. Bossiney was a rotten borough of about 20 cottages); Lt-Col., First Devon Local Militia until 1812.
[59] König's diary for 22nd October 1821 says Ellis "did not like the manner in which Miss M. had spoken to him." If 'M' meant 'Molesworth' it could have been any of the daughters: Elizabeth, aged 10 (1811-1836); Caroline, aged 8 (1813-1824); or Mary, aged 5 (1816-1871). Less probably, 'M' could have meant 'Miss Mary'.
[60] Who signed simply 'Will Elford'.
[61] Butter was elected FRS on the 21st March 1822.

By now Elford had been absent from his duties for 15 months and it must have been clear to everyone that his return was increasingly unlikely. John Children braved any charge of insensitivity and applied to the Trustees to be allowed to occupy Elford's Museum house if it became available. In a clear indication of their frame of mind the Trustees accepted this claim, but they had reason to do so, they had just received another formal letter from George Leach:

"As the leave of Absence granted to Doctor Leach in consequence of his unfortunate malady is now expired, and he is not yet sufficiently recovered to be enabled to resume the duties of his Office, his friends must now leave it to the Trustees to adopt such measures respecting him as they shall judge fit – The friends of Doctor Leach, well knowing his zealous attachment to the science of Natural History, are assured that in the event of his recovery (of which his medical attendants still entertain the most confident hopes) it will be the first wish of his heart to resume his situation at the Museum – If the Trustees however feel that they cannot, consistently with their duty to the Publick, grant any further extension of leave of absence to Doctor Leach, it is hoped that they will allow him to retire with such a Salary as will enable him to live with some degree of comfort –

In deciding on the amount of the Salary it is hoped that the Trustees will take into their consideration not only the zealous personal services of Doctor Leach for the last eight years, but also the great pecuniary sacrifices which he has made for the advancement of his Department of science – The list of presents made by Doctor Leach to the Museum, accompanying this memorial, affords a strong proof of his disinterested zeal in the cause of science, as most of those collections were purchased by him out of the savings of his income, which (independent of his income of 330£ from the Museum) at times was very considerable in consequence of his having written much for the Cyclopedias and other public works –

The value of Doctor Leach's service may be fairly estimated by a comparison of the Zoological department of the Museum at the time of his appointment to his situation with its present state —

It is hoped therefore that the Trustees will consider that Doctor Leach has sacrificed his time, his health and his fortune in the service of the Public, and that he is now without any income whatever and suffering under a calamity which precludes him from acquiring one, and that they will grant him every possible indulgence in his present unfortunate circumstances[62]"

It is clear his family no longer considered him likely to return to work. This letter was a transparent invitation to retire him on a pension. The Trustees did not formally commit themselves but they asked one of their members, Sir Charles Long[63], to consult the Prime Minister[64] and the Chancellor of the Exchequer[65] about a suitable financial provision for Elford. They were going to let him go.

[62] Letter: George Leach Jnr to the Trustees of the British Museum, n.d. but considered 8th December 1821 (Loc: British Museum Trustees' Manuscripts. Original Letters and Papers, volume IV).
[63] Sir Charles Long (1768-1838). Politician and art expert. Later 1st Baron Farnborough.
[64] Lord Liverpool.
[65] Nicholas Vansittart (1766-1851). Chancellor of the Exchequer 1812-1823. Created 1st Baron Bexley in 1823. His fellow politicians called him 'Van' (Pool, 1967: 41).

Replacement

It was not the policy of the British Museum's Trustees to advertise vacant positions in newspapers or gazettes[66], but without a formal advertisement, there was no formal start date for any applications. Potential replacements would have to express their interest in the position, and submit supporting documentation, as soon as they felt the timing accorded with common decency, but finding the appropriate moment was a delicate balance. Submitting too early would be to apply for someone's job while they were merely on temporary sick-leave (a terrible social blunder), while waiting until their formal retirement could mean missing the opportunity.

When a vacancy was suspected, or confirmed through knowledgeable contacts, prospective appointees would write to the Archbishop of Canterbury enclosing testimonials from 'persons of rank or learning', or would approach one of the other Trustees in the hope their support could be obtained before an approach to the Archbishop.

Before the Trustees even read George Leach's letter inviting them to retire his brother, across the zoological community would-be replacements were sharpening their quills. Pentland, for one, had been discussing his interest openly since November when he wrote to William Buckland in Yorkshire (where Buckland was excavating Kirkdale Cave, a prehistoric den filled with animal bones[67]), "I am sorry to learn that Leach still   continues so ill. I shall write to you at Oxford respecting my plans with regard to the British Museum.[68]" Two days later he did just that:

"I am extremely sorry to hear of poor Leach. As to the Museum, if the thing is worth having and if I get my parents' consent, my health continuing good, at Mr Cuvier's request, it is my intention to apply for it. I hope that you will exert yourself with your friends, and advise me how to proceed without being obliged to go to England. Lord Granville[69] might be got to assist me with your interest. — I presume I shall run as fair a chance as another, and in case of not proceeding shall be able to console myself without difficulty. — Mr Cuvier will write to Mr Davy on the subject.[70]"

One week later Pentland had obviously had some feedback and wrote again to Buckland:

"Before proceeding farther I request you to give me your advice on the subject. I am sorry you are already so far engaged for Mr Miller, however I fear, poor man, he has a very poor chance, when in competition with Horsfield & Stevens—I have seen his work, it is not held here in great estimation. We have a Mr Orbigny[71], a most assiduous Naturalist, who is working on the same subject, but God knows when he will publish as he is as poor as a Church Mouse.[72]"

Buckland had obviously already promised his support to John Miller[73], Curator at the Bristol Institution, who had recently published his book

[66] *fide* Henry Ellis (House of Commons, 1835: paras 364-369).

[67] In Buckland's 1823 book *Reliquiæ Diluvianæ; or, Observations on the Organic Remains Contained in Caves, Fissures, and Diluvial Gravel, and on other Geological Phenomena, Attesting the Action of an Universal Deluge*, he argued these bones were evidence for Noah's flood.

[68] Letter: Pentland to Buckland, 24th November 1821 (Sarjeant & Delair, 1980: 284).

[69] Granville Leveson-Gower, Viscount Granville (1773-1846). Brother of the Marquess of Stafford. From 1833 1st Earl Granville and Baron Leveson of Stone

[70] Letter: Pentland to Buckland, 26th November 1821 (Sarjeant & Delair, 1980: 285).

[71] Alcide d'Orbigny.

[72] Letter: Pentland to Buckland, 3rd December 1821 (Sarjeant & Delair, 1980: 286).

[73] John Samuel Miller (1779-1830).

A Natural History of the Crinoidea, or lily-shaped animals (living and fossil relatives of the star-fish)[74]. Elford had known Miller since at least 1814[75]. It also seems Thomas Horsfield and James Stephens ("Stevens") were publicly known to be expressing interest[76]. They were not alone. On the 7th of December Pentland contacted Buckland again:

"Any news about the museum? My memorial will be presented shortly to the Archbishop — Davy has written a polite letter to Cuvier on the subject — and as Muller is a German, I have every reason to suppose that an Englishman[77] & a native will be preferred to a foreigner — if his grace does not wish to make the Museum an ~~reception house~~ Asylum for ~~foreigners~~ Germans & such.[78]"

"Muller" was possibly Johannes Müller[79], later Professor of Anatomy and Physiology at Berlin, but the list was still growing. Three days later, on the 10th of December, Pentland wrote yet again. Emphasising his own pedigree in comparative anatomy, schooled by Cuvier, he notes:

"The opening that now exists in London for a comparative Anatomist is now very great, as Sir E. Home is going off.— For a Zoologist the opening is no less advantageous.— As to the Candidates for the situation, I without self-conceit may say that not one of them appears to me adequate for the Task— at the Museum, General Zoology is the object, where a single person is charged with the care of the entire Animal Kingdom.— Swainson is a very poor Ornithologist & Entomologist & does not see beyond specific distribution, and his Brazilian Birds: Dr Horsfield appears exclusively ornithologist & that only of Java, his learning does not seem to extend even to the 3 other classes of Vertebrate Animals.— Stevens is exclusively entomologist. As to Miller I do not know upon what he is strongest.[80]"

Most of these criticisms are inaccurate and unjust, but here we learn William Swainson is showing interest. John Gray had also approached König, who advised him to keep his ambitions quiet[81], and later Pentland mentioned an application from a Mr Harker, a botanist (an application Pentland viewed as "really ridiculous"[82]).

To Pentland, Buckland reiterated he was unable to help as he was committed to supporting Miller. Pentland was "extremely sorry" to hear this and was filled with more than a little pique, clearly expressed in his letter the following week:

'I am confident that Mr Miller, who has never seen what a collection of Zoology is, will find himself embarrassed on entering the Museum.— I am sorry that he is your protégé, not I assure you on my own account, but on your own for having recommended a man so unfit for the situation to all appearances... But I will ask, as a man conversant with science, to which of the Candidates would you give your vote as a Trustee of the Museum? to a person conversant with the subject or to one who is not? With this question

[74] Miller, 1821. Miller also provided information on the fossils of Devon for Lysons & Lysons (1822: cclxx-cclxxi).

[75] Gray, 1824: 213.

[76] Sarjeant & Delair (1980: 311) suggest "Stevens" was Samuel Stevens, entomologist and brother of natural history auctioneer J.C. Stevens. This cannot be. John Crace Stevens was born in 1809; his brother Samuel was born in 1817.

[77] Pentland was born in Ireland and appears to be using 'English' in the sense of anyone from the British Isles.

[78] Letter: Pentland to Buckland, 7th December 1821 (Sarjeant & Delair, 1980: 287-288).

[79] Johannes Peter Müller (1801-1858).

[80] Letter: Pentland to Buckland, 10th December 1821 (Sarjeant & Delair, 1980: 288-289).

[81] Gunther, 1974: 58.

[82] Letter: Pentland to Buckland, 25th February 1822 (Sarjeant & Delair, 1980: 295).

I shall close my letter, and shall for the last time speak to you on the subject— as you can no longer be of any use to me.[83]'

In fact that was neither the end of the letter nor the end of Pentland's friendship with Buckland, and not the last time Pentland spoke to him on the subject, but while the letters passed to-and-fro, the grapevine was still twisting the messages. Pentland (and presumably others in Paris) was now under the impression Elford had died, which he certainly had not although it may have looked like it to dispassionate observers: the applications reaching the Museum were being dropped by circling buzzards.

[83] Letter: Pentland to Buckland, 17th December 1821 (Sarjeant & Delair, 1980: 290-291).

Plate IX from Leach, 1852. (Printed July 1820)

Legend (*per* Leach, 1852: 376)

Fig. 1. *Temesia variabilis.*
Fig. 2. *Trochus Montagui.*
Fig. 3. *Epheria Goodallii.*
Fig. 4. *Assiminia Grayana*
        with its animal.
Fig. 5. The Operculum.
Fig. 6. *Turbo sulcatus.*
Fig. 7. *Margarites diaphana.*
Fig. 8. *Scalaria clathrus*
        with its animal.
Figs. 9 and 10. *Scalaria Turtoniana.*
Fig. 11. *Zippora Drummondiana.*

— 27 —

Retirement

> How happy it would have been if poor Leach had gone mad
> before he did so much mischief! His labours at the Br. Mus.
> are only a monument of his insanity.
>
> Sir James Edward Smith
> President of the Linnean Society

No sooner had the Trustees signalled their intention to retire Elford than Sir Humphry Davy began to turn this to the advantage (as he saw it) of his old friend John Children. Children had been born at Ferox Hall near Tonbridge in Kent, 45 km southeast of London. His father George Children[1] was a wealthy country gentleman and banker with an interest in experimental science, especially electrical research. In 1800 both he and John became Life-Subscribers of the then newly-founded Royal Institution.

In 1805 when John Children's poor health (possibly malaria) caused him to resign his commission in the West Kent Militia, he decided to dedicate his life to science. He was particularly drawn to mineralogy, chemistry and mechanics, and in 1806 he toured England collecting minerals, especially from the rich collecting grounds of Cornwall. His Wellington Tree would later house some of this collection.

At Ferox Hall John helped his father in the laboratory they had built in the grounds, where they investigated the new 'galvanic fluid' using a custom-built voltaic pile (effectively a large acid battery). By October 1808 their success and reputation were such that Humphry Davy stayed at the hall for several days, working with them on the best method of constructing such piles for use in chemical analysis. Davy was at the height of his success at the Royal Institution, and this was about the time he was lecturing to a young medical student called William Elford Leach. Davy and John Children became firm friends and Children presented the results of the investigations to the Royal Society at the end of November 1808[2].

[1] George Children (1742-1818).

[2] Children (1809). John Children had been a Fellow of the Royal Society since March 1807.

443

Davy was clearly impressed with this work and told Children, 'I hope you will not suffer these beautiful and satisfactory experiments of the capacities of metals to remain still... You are pledged to do good and noble things, and you must not disappoint the men of science of this country.[3]'

Davy continued to visit Tonbridge and for a while even entered into partnership with Children and a James Burton with the intention of opening a factory to manufacture gunpowder. This was a dangerous move and Davy was nearly maimed at Ferox Hall in 1812 when a new detonating compound they were developing exploded, injuring his eye and one of his hands. Perhaps it was fortunate this business venture never came to fruition.

John George Children
in the 1830s.

(From Gunther, 1978: 93. Reproduced by courtesy of The Natural History Museum, London)

Meanwhile the electrical research continued and in 1813 the Childrens constructed the largest battery then known, with 20 bimetal plates, each measuring almost one and a half square metres, immersed in a tank containing 4300 litres of acid[4]. However, their work was about to be brought to an untimely halt. The Tonbridge Bank, where George Children was the senior partner, had been failing for some years and in 1812 business had been suspended. The family was now falling into financial difficulty.

When George Shaw died in 1813 John Children wrote to Davy asking if he thought there was any opportunity for employment at the British Museum. Presumably he hoped to replace Charles König as the Museum's mineralogist when König became Under Librarian. Davy discovered the appointment lay within the gift of the Archbishop and wrote back to Children, "I wish it were in my power to serve you more. If the election had been in the Trustees in General I might have been of some use.[5]"

As we know, in 1813 König retained responsibility for mineralogy after his promotion, and Elford Leach was appointed as his assistant. John Children does not appear to have gained employment elsewhere but by 1816 the bank was officially declared insolvent and his father, at the age of 74, was bankrupt. Ferox Hall was sold and George, a broken man, was put under the care of Sir Everard Home in London. John's need for paid employment was now desperate and he wrote again to Davy, and to other influential contacts. Davy did all he could and several possibilities were pursued, but with no success. Finally, in December 1816 through the patronage of Lord Camden[6], a Kent politician and family friend, Children obtained a position as the Assistant Librarian in the British Museum's Department of Antiquities.

Here Children specialised in medals and Roman silver, but he never abandoned his interest in, or practice of, chemical research. He clearly felt science was his true vocation and in 1817, when he became despondent at his position in the Arts, Davy had to reassure him that science was not yet lost to him as a profession:

"You may be assured that whenever a favourable opportunity occurs I will not lose it; but I pray you do not adopt so despairing a tone. You have numerous friends, a fixed station in society, a comfortable income, more than many men of science can command and prospects of better things.[7]"

3 Gunther, 1978: 80.
4 Each copper and zinc plate was 6 feet long and 2 feet 8 inches wide. The tank contained 945 gallons of fuming nitrous acid, sulphuric acid and water in the ratios 3:1:30.
5 30th August [1813] (Gunther, 1978: 82). Gunther assumed the letter related to the appointment of an Assistant Librarian in the Department of Antiquities but the timing, and Children's interests, would suggest Natural History.
6 John Jeffreys Pratt, Marquess Camden (1759-1840).
7 Undated letter of 1817 (Gunther, 1978: 83).

In December 1821 the 'favourable opportunity' arrived at last and Davy did not intend to let it escape. Not only was he now the Museum's main scientific Trustee, but he knew the other Trustees' minds regarding Elford Leach's future. He began to promote the idea of transferring John Children to Natural History as Elford's replacement. Children was barely consulted and with no background in any aspect of biology was not keen to make the move, but Davy had made up his mind. Children had little choice but to follow[8].

1822

On the 12th of January John Children and Dr Georg Noehden[9] (the extra-Assistant Librarian in the Department of Printed Books) called on Charles König to discuss Elford's post, but König too had not been consulted[10] and was not enthusiastic to have Children transferred to his department against both their wishes.

At the Trustees' General Meeting on the 9th of February no decision was taken regarding Elford's retirement, but the pressure was mounting on König. The following day Noehden sent him a note urging him to write to Humphry Davy to say he had no objection to having Children as his assistant[11]. In his diary König observed, "It is obvious that Sir H. + Mr Ellis try if they can make me commit myself." He was not prepared to do so but wrote to Davy anyway – "a sort of protest" he called it[12]. It did no good. At the next Trustees' meeting on the 9th of March it was announced Elford had retired 'in consequence of infirmity' and John Children was formally transferred to Natural History as his replacement.

The outside world was oblivious to these machinations. Pentland had still not submitted his application, and apparently never would[13], but at the end of May Swainson sent copies of his certificates to König – presumably as a courtesy – clearly unaware that the opportunity had long since evaporated.

8 Children (House of Commons, 1835: para. 3070 and 1836: para. 2863).
9 Georg Heinrich Noehden LL.D. (1770-1826). Extra-Assistant Librarian 1819-1822. Author of several German grammars as well as translations and works on art in English and German. Why he was involved in Children's planned transfer is not clear.
10 König (House of Commons, 1835: paras 2555-2557).
11 König's Diary 10th February 1822.
12 König's Diary 11th February 1822.
13 Pentland visited Britain in 1824 and finally left Paris in 1826. He spent 1826 and 1827 in South America where he conducted the first extensive survey of the new nation of Bolivia, covering all social, geographical and biological aspects (Fifer, 1974). He returned to Paris but in 1836 was sent to Peru as British Consul-General, a post he held for three years. His later years were spent travelling between Italy, France and Britain. He died in London in 1873.

Historical note

1822

May	Disturbances in Wales during a colliers' strike.
May	Riots near Bath over introduction of the flying-shuttle in weaving.
July	Disturbances among Norwich weavers over a wage reduction.
8th July	Shelley drowns in the bay of Lerici, Piedmont.
22nd July	'Gregor' Mendel[1], the founder of genetics, born at Heinzendorf (Hyncice) in Austrian Silesia.
October to November	Disturbances on Tyneside, north-east England, during a seamen's strike.

1 Johann Mendel (1822-1884). 'Brother Gregor' of the Augustinian Order of St Thomas.

Elford Leach

While Davy had been engineering Children's future, Elford had returned to London. At the end of January he had even been allowed to come into the Museum for several days to examine shells[14] despite the fact that he was still in the care of an attendant. Whether that attendant was ideally suited, however, was a matter for debate. In April a Mr Capper called on König to report that the attendant was treating Elford very badly, which roused James Veitch to visit the Museum the following week to refute this as "a gross lie"[15].

Meanwhile the trustees had asked Alexander MacLeay to calculate the monetary value of Elford's numerous donations over the years to help them assess how the Museum had benefited from his service. MacLeay reported that £955 9s 6d was a fair and reasonable estimate, and with this information the Trustees turned their attention to the matter of Elford's pension. The Chancellor of the Exchequer and Sir Charles Long had had several conversations on this subject with the Prime Minister, and it had been agreed Elford would receive a pension from the government of £100 a year net[16]. In addition the Trustees personally subscribed £850 for the purchase of a government annuity which would pay him another £58 2s 6d[17]. The first payments began in April and after eight years at the British Museum Elford Leach, still only 31 years old, was once again an independent gentleman.

Home

No sooner was Elford's future secure than another personal tragedy struck. His mother had been ill for some time and like her son had suffered a deterioration in her mental faculties—to the distress of her family who now had two invalids to nurse. On the 14th of May she finally died and was buried in the churchyard at Buckland Monachorum, north of Plymouth.

By November Elford was at Bath with his father and brother George for the beginning of the winter social season[18]. From here his father wrote to George Sowerby in London, whose own father James had just died. Sowerby had contacted Elford's father regarding a letter from Royer in Paris which Sowerby had received for forwarding (?to Elford). Elford's father noted his son George had just left for business in London and could collect the letter from Sowerby while he was there. Regarding Elford he wrote: 'I have the pleasure to inform you that my Son is much better and is going into Devonshire with me. I had once the pleasure of your father's company at my House near Plymouth, and I called on him not long before he died[19]'.

Elford may have been much better, but after more than two years of illness he was still not well. On the 11th of December, from Bath, he wrote a letter of introduction to William Clift for a family who wanted to visit the museum at the Royal College of Surgeons. Elford had known Clift for

[14] König's Diary 28th January 1822.
[15] König's Diary 23rd and 30th April 1822. A note found among JES's Mss identifies the 'Mr Capper' of König's diary as George Robert M. Capell, of Nº 43 King Street, West Bryanston Square, London, a professor of medical botany, but JES gives no authority for this observation.
[16] British Museum, Trustees Committee Meeting Minutes, 13th July 1822 & 9th November 1822.
[17] British Museum, Trustees Committee Meeting Minutes, 13th July 1822 & Trustees General Meeting Minutes, 26th June 1823.
[18] Jenny and Jonathan may also have been at Bath but they are not mentioned in sources.
[19] Letter: George Leach Snr to George Brettingham Sowerby, 21st November 1822 (Loc: Welsh Folk Museum, National Museum of Wales, Cardiff. Ref: Nº 75).

Venereal Disease?

In a series of publications between 1974 and 1980 author Albert Gunther[1] claimed Elford Leach's illness was "reputed to be", "said to be" or "attributed to" venereal disease[2]. Unfortunately Gunther gave no authority and no evidence for these repeated assertions and the only source we have found proposing venereal disease is Albert Gunther. In fact there is no reason to suspect any cause other than mental breakdown due to overwork. Elford Leach was naturally highly strung and his increasing workload and unwillingness to take leave in the years leading to his illness are clear from the Museum records. In an age without penicillin the doctors treating him would have been well aware of venereal disease (In the 1820s London had a hospital dedicated solely to the treatment of 'syphilitic maladies' – the Lock Hospital at Hyde Park Corner). These doctors expressly stated his condition was the result of overwork, and even if his brother George had suspected this was not true he would have been very unlikely, as an Officer of the Court, to lie to the Lord Chancellor[3]. All three professionals, Warburton, Veitch and George Leach, would have destroyed their careers if they had been caught attempting to deceive the Trustees.

The Trustees themselves clearly believed the illness resulted from overwork. It is inconceivable they would have given an unsolicited gift of £100; arranged a state pension; and personally subscribed £850 for Elford Leach's future welfare if they had believed they were being deprived of his services following the acquisition of a self-induced sexual contagion.

[1] Albert Everard Gunther (1903-1998).
[2] Gunther (1974: 59); (1975: 63); (1978: 84); (1980b: 51).
[3] One of the Museum's Trustees.

The Lock Hospital.

more than a decade and was a member of the College but instead of addressing the letter, 'Wm Clift Esqr, Lincoln's Inn Fields' he addressed it, "Wm Cliff Esqr, Leicester Fields". His unsteady blotted writing shows he was still a long way from recovery. The pressures of work that had led to this situation were not unique to Elford. Clift too had sole responsibility for a zoological collection and he also found it increasingly stressful, as he had admitted in a letter to his sister Joanna[20] the previous month:

'My dear Sister

I received your letter of October 17 and would have answered it sooner if I could have found a minute's leisure to do so but every day brings me three days work, and I am almost driven out of my senses by its continual increase. I have really no time to write to any body and hardly any for eating or sleeping; having for a long time past seldom more than four or five hours for sleep. I am sure I have the best possible reason to wish that the labour and the good things of this World were more equally divided, as I know I have more than my share of the first, and not so much as I ought of the last, or I should have more power to assist those who are not able to help themselves. However I ought not to complain, for if I have no opportunity of getting money, having but barely sufficient to carry me on – yet I have that which pleases me better as far as concerns myself – peoples good opinion in regard to my profession – and now the Museum is becoming so well known all over the world I have so many people continually sent to me by those who have been here before that it leaves me hardly a minutes leisure through the day and obliges me to work most of the night to do that which would be otherwise done in the day. and this being of a nature in which no body can assist me I am obliged to do it myself or it must remain undone...

I have been several times inclined to be ill but have really had no time to think seriously about it and so have got well again.[21]'

John Gray too was feeling the strain. Although Elford's illness, and earlier antipathy, had excluded Gray from the Museum, his private studies and worries about his future left him deeply troubled, especially after he failed to obtain the position at Montagu House. He later recalled how he had to seek medical help.

'After suffering much I called on Abernethy to consult him on my case. He said, "You must leave off study, and go into the country. Have you any friend in the country to whom you could go? If you do not go you will go mad like your friend." I said I had a cousin at Hastings who had already been kind to me and I knew she would receive me. "Oh! It is a *she* cousin is it? That's well." he said. "Go into the Waiting Room until I send for you." At length he came in and said, "Your place is booked and paid for to Hastings and the coach goes at 12 today, so go." and he disappeared.[22]'

[20] Joanna Honey (née Clift) (1765-1846).
[21] Letter: William Clift to Joanna Honey, 10th November 1822 (Austin, 1991: 222-224).
[22] Gunther, 1974: 59. Punctuation and italics have been added to Gray's narrative. With regard to mental strain, Gray later noted, "The overworking of the brain on the same subject produces fatigue of the brain more permanently than is generally suspected. During the time I have been Keeper of Zoology 4 Assistants have suffered more or less severely from this dreadful malady." (Gunther, 1980a: 235). It must also be wondered whether the extreme toxicity of the chemicals used to preserve specimens at that time and the way these were applied may have had consequences for the health of zoologists.

Gray did stay with his cousin, Maria Emma Gray[23], and several years later they were married[24]. Maria, 14 years older than John, was a cousin by her former marriage to Francis Gray[25] (the son of Edward Whitaker Gray of the British Museum) who had died in 1814.

1823

After Bath Elford returned with his father to Spitchwick, where it appears he finally began to recover some semblance of his former health. By August 1823 he had taken up the reins of science in earnest and was writing to William Buckland:

"My dear Buckland

You will very much oblige me by examining the Cuttle Fish in the Sipthorp's Collection. I wish to acertain the position of the Suckers on the Arms, whether they are placed in a double or single Series. If in a double Series are they placed ∴ or :: , and the Form of the Expansion on the Extremites of the longest Legs; if you will be so good as to give a slight Scetch of that Part I shall be very thankful. I am making a Monograph on the Cephalopoda. My Work on the british Mollusca will be published in October; I will send to you a Copy as well as for our Friend, Kidd[26].

I employ my Time in examining the Granite of Dartmore and intend to send a Series of the Varieties, to You, to König and to Grenough.

I remain my dear Sir

Yours most sincerely

Wm Elford Leach.[27]"

In fact his work on the British Mollusca would not be published in October but as he returned to his studies, in Plymouth Henry Woollcombe was doing some homework of his own:

"I am reading a very entertaining number of the Edinburgh Review, the article relating to the British Museum has afforded me much information on that subject. I regret to find so much neglect amongst its conductors. I hope this exposure will occasion steps to be taken to remove the stigma which necessarily attaches to those to whom the superintendence is entrusted.[28]"

Woollcombe had been reading an anonymous article in the May issue of the *Edinburgh Review*, heavily critical of the Museum. It is now believed this article was written by Liverpool physician, author and science lecturer Thomas Traill[29], using information supplied by his friend William Swainson (who had been bitterly disappointed not to succeed Elford). This article pulled no punches and its criticisms raised questions in the House of Commons. A Commons Select Committee investigating the management of the Museum in 1835 and 1836 also referred repeatedly to this article, which therefore deserves consideration in some detail. It concentrated particularly on the zoological collections and bemoaned the fact that:

[23] Maria Emma Gray (née Smith) (1786-1876).
[24] On the 29th of July 1826 at Old Church, St Pancras, London.
[25] Francis Edward Gray (1785-1814) had married Maria in 1810.
[26] John Kidd (1775-1851). Professor of Chemistry at Oxford from 1805-1810 then continued his studies privately.
[27] Letter: W.E. Leach to Buckland, 18th August 1823 (Loc: Wellcome Institute for the History of Medicine, London. Ref: WMS/ALS: Leach).
[28] Henry Woollcombe's Diary, 31st August 1823.
[29] Thomas Stewart Traill (1781-1862). Educated in medicine at Edinburgh. Moved to Liverpool in 1803.

'Foreigners inquire with eagerness where this department of the British Museum is to be viewed; and, in spite of politeness, are tempted to laugh outright when they are referred to the half dozen quadrupeds that are exhibited on the staircase, and the few specimens of birds, which add little either to the interest or ornament of one of the saloons of Montague House.

The state of decay and ruin in which the Zoological collections of the Museum in general exhibit, and the very little which can be learnt in a visit to it, from the small number exposed to public view, the want of labels or references to most even of these, and the strange names attached to the most familiar animals in some of the cases, where a second *Adam* appears to have been at work[30], have long excited our surprise and our enquiries; and we are concerned to state, that the result of our investigation reflects no credit on those whose duty it was to have seen that due attention was paid to the preservation of this species of national property...

We may here take the opportunity of stating, that the zoological specimens which have been arranged and named, are of comparatively little utility to the student who visits the Museum for information; for the attached names are generally such as are not to be found in any published system; and the caprice of the nomenclator seems not to have allowed almost any specimen to retain the appellation imposed by his predecessors. The rage for new nomenclature is the epidemic malady of our Continental neighbours. With all due respect for the French naturalists, we cannot admit the propriety or utility of their perpetual endeavours to substitute a nomenclature of their own, for that which has been long received by civilized nations...

We are far from being hostile to *all deviations* from a received nomenclature or arrangement. Where there is an evident impropriety in descriptive language, or where an arrangement is founded on erroneous principles, or may lead to false conclusions, we always wish to meet the correcting hand of the scientific reformer; but we object to all unnecessary deviations from established nomenclature; especially to all changes which have no ostensible motive, but the silly vanity of proposing new names, or the pompous egotism of dabblers in classification. The adoption of such innovation in a private collection, would be ascribed to bad taste; in a new book they would draw down the wholesome castigation of the reviewer; in a public museum they merit the reprobation of every true friend to science.

If called on to state what nomenclature or classification we should prefer in a national collection of organized nature; we have little hesitation in saying, that we should be inclined to recommend a system, which has for its basis the outline of the illustrious Swede[31], corrected, modified, and subdivided, according to modern discoveries; because its language is interwoven with the national science of civilized nations, for more than half a century of most important discoveries in this branch of knowledge, and is the most universally received of any which has ever been given to the world...

[30] A reference to the Bible in which Adam was the first man created by God and God allowed him to name all the animals (*Genesis*, chapter 2, verse 19).
[31] Linnæus.

[Observations] on the neglected state of the Ornithological department of the Museum, do not apply to the British birds, which make a part of the collections lately purchased from the heirs of Colonel Montague for 1000*l*. These are fitted up with taste, and even elegance, in a separate room, and are provided with labels; but here, again, we recognise the rage for new names in its wildest form. Our old acquaintance the yellow wagtail, that has often delighted our boyish eyes, we were surprised to find metamorphosed into the *yellow bradyte*—an appellation not to be found in any published system of ornithology with which we are acquainted...

At no period since the opening of the Museum to the public, has there been sufficient attention paid to the preservation of the zoological specimens: and the almost total disappearance of the animals of Sloane's Collection, and of the immense number of donations of this sort from private individuals, is highly disgraceful to those to whose charge this department was committed. We are not prepared to state at what period the work of destruction began to make rapid strides: but we are certain that, before it came under the superintendance of Dr Leach, much irreparable mischief was done. When that gentleman came into office, in 1813, his zeal and talents prompted him to attempt all that the efforts of one man could perform in this Augean stable; and his generous donation of his own private collections, sufficiently evinced his wish to improve the National Museum. Unfortunately, the ruin of innumerable specimens was already completed; and, latterly, he was infected with the rage for new names. These circumstances rendered his labours less valuable than they would otherwise have been, to the public; and his health has compelled him to resign the situation, while the various contents of the vaults are still very imperfectly explored. It is but justice to this gentleman to state, that, while health permitted, he was assiduously employed in arranging a series of Entomological cabinets, which he left in a good state of preservation; and he had made considerable progress in the classification of the shells in the Museum. The arrangement of the British Zoological Collection is likewise due to him.

It is about four years since Dr Leach was occupied in the Museum[32]: and all that appears to have been done since his retirement from its duties, is the restoration of some of the British birds to their old appellations. With the highest respect for the acquirements of his successor, we cannot approve of his appointment to that department, in which he had certainly little previous experience, and of which, we are told, he has even professed his entire ignorance. No talents and no industry, without long previous study, and practical application, can qualify a man for the charge of the Zoological Collection in the British Museum... To much practical knowledge of zoology, he should unite great zeal for the science, and intensity of application for years to come, before our National Collection can be rendered respectable. In its present state, it is an object of disgust and lamentation to native naturalists, and of ridicule and contempt to foreigners.[33]'

[32] Actually 2½ years at the time of publication.
[33] Traill (1823).

The criticism of Elford for having a 'rage for new names' is in part justified and in part the reaction of a Linnean naturalist, despite Traill's protestations to the contrary.

Much to the discomfort of the Trustees, Traill's article raised to public view the under-investment in, and the parlous state of, the Natural History department. The negative image created was one the Trustees found hard to dispel. It was also a reality they found difficult to change. Fifteen years later, despite many of the Museum's exhibits having moved into a new building in 1829[34], William Jameson, a relative of Robert Jameson, could still write from London to his cousin Thomas Torrie in Edinburgh:

'The British Museum fully bears out the character it has received, it being a complete disgrace to the attendants. The Quadrupeds are huddled together in a wretched manner and to examine an immense number of them is impossible. Imagine to yourself a quantity of decayed specimens thrown in any manner into presses[35], and you have the collection in [the] British Museum.[36]'

Obviously nothing was to change after Elford left and it would take decades, and ultimately a new dedicated museum solely for natural history, to change the ethos of the Trustees. But what about Elford's 'rage for new names'?

Names

In Elford Leach's day there was no *International Code of Zoological Nomenclature* guiding the choice and application of scientific names for animal species. Today's Code developed gradually from a document[37] issued by the British Association for the Advancement of Science[38] in 1842. Also, there was no official 'start date' for zoological nomenclature. Today zoologists do not accept as valid any scientific names used before the 10th edition of Linnæus's *Systema Naturæ* (1758). In Elford's day this was not the case, although the publication of the 12th edition of this work in 1766 – the last edition produced by Linnæus himself – was held by some to be a significant event. When George Shaw threatened to crush any shell not in *Systema Naturæ* he specified the 12th edition.

Without standardisation, there was great variation in the way zoologists approached the practice of naming new species and genera. It was growing confusion that prompted the British Association to issue its proposed code of conduct. There is little doubt that of those whose works generated a need for some guidelines, Elford Leach was towards the guilty end of the spectrum. He came under increasing criticism during his time at the Museum, and later, for the way he introduced new names. However, these attacks came from diverse quarters for diverse reasons and covered everything from the large number of new genera and species he named, his tendency to rename known species, and the nature of the new names he chose. To assess the validity of the complaints the different types of criticism have to be carefully unravelled.

[34] Miller, 1974: 228. The new building was part of the present British Museum complex, which was built, as far as possible, around Montagu House. The transfer of exhibits liberated some space in the main house and Natural History expanded to occupy other rooms. The British Gallery (Room XI) became an office for John Gray who was by that time employed by the Museum (see p. 466).

[35] 'Press' – a cupboard, usually shelved, in which items can be tightly packed.

[36] Letter: William Jameson (b. 14th October 1816) to Thomas Jameson Torrie (christened 12th January 1809) 7th June 1838. Jameson adds, "I was introduced to Darwin at the Geological Society by Grant, who inquired particularly after the Professor and mentioned that he had been a pupil of his ten or twelve years ago." (Loc: Edinburgh University Library, Special Collections. Ref: Gen. 1996/5/39).

[37] *Series of Propositions for rendering the Nomenclature of Zoology uniform and permanent.*

[38] Founded in 1831, with David Brewster as one of the prime movers.

1. Even as a young man, Elford Leach had a prodigious knowledge of the old authors and frequently applied names used during the 16th and 17th centuries and by the ancient classical writers. Not everyone shared his familiarity with these works and some assumed the names he used were new and were being introduced without comment. Alexander MacLeay had believed this of some names in his 1816 catalogue of British animals.

2. He felt all names that were based on an animal's physical characteristics should not only be correct but should also refer to a characteristic shown only by that one species. For example, an animal with a brown head should not have a Latin name that meant 'red head', and if there were several species within one genus with brown heads, no one of them should have a name meaning 'brown head' as the name would not single out that species (In this regard he was confusing the concepts of 'label' and 'description' which Linnæus had been careful to separate. The name is only a label. Elford may have had difficulty with this idea because he spent so much time reading pre-Linnean texts in which the name was also the description).

These views guided his choice of names for new species, but they also affected his treatment of familiar species. If he was publishing an account of a known species in which the existing name did not meet his strict criteria, he gave it a new name. Few workers even in his day would have adopted this approach and we would never do it today. He was particularly prone to this in his later years at the Museum and this may have contributed to the criticism that he was afflicted with 'a rage for new names'. There are a number of examples in his mollusc manuscript[39]:

He changed the name of the European water snail *N. fluviatilis* Linnæus ('fluviatilis' meaning 'of a river') to *N. europaea* saying, 'This is a genus containing a vast number of species, only one of which... inhabits Europe; and as all the species inhabit rivers, I have altered the name to *Europæa*'.

He changed the name of Montagu's species *Bulla plumula* ('plumula' meaning 'a small feather', a reference to the shape of the gill) to *montagui* saying, 'I have named this species after Montagu, by whom it was first discovered, and have rejected the term *Plumula* since it is equally applicable to all the species'.

He changed *Turbo petraeus* (Montagu) to *Turbo petricola* because, 'petræus signifies, according to Pliny, any substance that *grows* upon a rock, such as alum, nitras, &c., which seems to me to be inapplicable to an animal that only *lives* on rocks[40]' ('petricola' means 'inhabitant of rock').

3. He tended to create new species and genera for animals that differed in relatively small ways from known examples. In modern terminology, he was a 'splitter'. Followers of Linnæus tended to be 'lumpers' as they strove to fit newly discovered species into Linnæus's existing plan. Such traditionalists did not approve of Elford's immense number of new genera and species (and hence immense number of new names) and he was criticised when his early crustacean work appeared. Subsequent discoveries tended

[39] Leach, 1852 at pp. 182, 29 and 188 respectively.
[40] Italics added here.

453

to support many of his new genera so he chose not to alter his approach, explaining himself in the introduction to his mollusc work in what was effectively a pre-emptive strike:

"I feel that I shall be accused (as I was when I first submitted my arrangement of the Crustacea, Arachnoidea, Acari and Insecta to the public eye) of having constituted too many genera. It is necessary for my justification to observe, that although I formed families containing but one known genus, and genera with but one species, many of these vacancies have been filled up by Cuvier in his 'Règne Animal;' by Rafinesque, Say[41] and other authors. I shall therefore in this Work follow precisely the same plan which I formerly did in the above-mentioned classes.[42]"

In fact his critics were too harsh, and he was too bold. While many of his new genera were justified, many of his 'new' species were the same as those described by earlier workers, and some were later found to be based on different sexes, ages, or minor variants within the same species (although he was usually alert to the dangers of males and females of the same species having a different appearance – as in many birds – and hence appearing to be different species).

4. Some traditionalists simply disliked the fact that his actions changed the names used by Linnæus and other early workers. They disliked all modern arrangements. When König removed Elford's names from the British birds in the Museum he said he did so because they, "were complained of as new-fangled. He had his own terminology and nomenclature, and great complaints were excited by his introducing that instead of the old nomenclature[43]".

5. Changing the names in any way would certainly have annoyed some ardent Linnæans, but in the Museum's public galleries Elford went further than just applying names resulting from modern classifications. He also applied names resulting from his own research which he had not yet published. This generated labels which only he could understand. This was clearly not acceptable. He was focusing only on the accuracy of the classification, not on the utility of the displays to visitors. He was treating public exhibits as though they were part of his private research collection and was rightly criticised for this.

6. His unpublished manuscripts (of which there appear to have been a significant number[44]) contained new genera and species, and hence many new names. This would not have been a problem if he had been the only person reading these notes, but he made them available to his various correspondents and friends, some of whom later included these names in their own articles without detailed comments. This generated many published names attributed to 'Leach' but accompanied by little supporting information. In this the friends and correspondents must share a portion of the blame. He did not force them to use his manuscript names without adequate descriptions.

41 Thomas Say (1787-1834). American entomologist, carcinologist & malacologist. Worked as an apothecary in his native Philadelphia until he was 25. He was a charter member of the Academy of Natural Sciences of Philadelphia when it was founded in 1812. Collected extensively in the less settled areas of the USA. Married Lucy Sistaire, a zoology illustrator who became the first female member of the Academy. Say corresponded with Elford Leach at the British Museum and sent him type specimens, some of which are still in The Natural History Museum in London.
42 Leach, 1852: xii.
43 Charles König (House of Commons, 1835: para. 2552).
44 For example, in 1815 he mentions a study of the insect parasites of birds to which he has devoted "a considerable portion of time" and an entomological monograph he "is about to publish" entitled *Trichoptera Systematica* (*Edinburgh Encyclopædia*, **9**: 77 and 136). We are not aware either was ever published but manuscripts must have existed. See further examples below.

7. Many later complaints related to his mollusc book, but this is unfair. He was writing this during his decline in mental health, when an obvious eccentricity was becoming evident[45]. When his breakdown finally came the work was still a manuscript with some of the early sections printed to the proof stage. Despite his optimism he never published this work, although several copies were circulated to friends. The manuscript was finally acquired more than 25 years later by John Gray who steered it through the press in 1852, virtually as a form of homage. By this time many of the included names had already been published by those who had seen the proofs, and the work was 30 years out of date. To hold Elford Leach responsible for the inadequacies of this book would be grossly unjust.

8. One of the most publicised attacks against him was the accusation that many of the names he coined were 'nonsense names'. In 1842 the committee of the British Association singled out his names *Azeca* and *Assiminea* (both from his mollusc manuscript[46]) for particular disapproval, saying, 'Some authors, having found difficulty in selecting generic names which have not been used before, have adopted the plan of coining words at random without any derivation or meaning whatever... It is particularly annoying to the etymologist, who, after seeking in vain through the vast storehouses of human language for the parentage of such words, discovers at last that he has been pursuing an *ignis fatuus*.' [a Will-o'-the-wisp][47].

Elford expressed his policy on the creation of new names in the introduction to that same manuscript:

'Respecting the names that I have given to what I consider distinct genera, I have always invariably named the genera, as far as possible, from their essential characters; except only when I have perceived that the names of the parts constituting a generic distinction might probably equally apply to some other genus not yet discovered... Where I have not been enabled to find sufficient and certain essential characters, I have followed the rule laid down by Fabricius, the first naturalist who attempted to form a natural arrangement of Insects,—"Nomina generica nil significantia omnino optima;" [*Generic names signifying nothing are altogether best*] and as far as possible I have selected, according to the rule laid down by the same author, that "Nomina barbara nullo modo sunt toleranda" [*barbarous names by no means are tolerable*][48]'

It has never been clear exactly what Fabricius meant by 'barbarous names'. He may simply have been saying that words taken unchanged from modern languages – *Dog, Chien, Hund* etc. – should never be used as scientific names.

This policy explains to some extent Elford's tendency to name genera after people (*Cranchia, Montagua, Dorvillia*) and his acceptance of anagrams, neither of which signify anything in descriptive terms. In addition to his anagrams of 'Caroline'[49], when he needed a new genus name for a

[45] For some reason, in this manuscript Elford took a dislike to the usual genitive ending '–ii' for species named after men (cranchii, 'of Cranch'; henslowii, 'of Henslow') and changed almost exclusively to the ending '–ianus, –iana', as with his new species *Chiton cranchianus* and *Pera henslowiana*. This appears solely to be a personal whim manifested from this time.

[46] Published in the work of John Fleming (1828) who had presumably seen the proofs.

[47] Knight, 1900: 271.

[48] Leach, 1852: xii.

[49] He included a new species name *Doris rocinela* in his mollusc manuscript (Leach, 1852: 19-20).

kookaburra (a type of kingfisher)[50], he scrambled Linnæus's name for the kingfishers, *Alcedo*, to make *Dacelo*, the name still used today[51].

Although he set out this policy, he did not always practise what he preached. His earlier genus name *Labia* for *Labia minor* did not fit his laudable criteria; it was clearly a calculated frivolity. A similar light-hearted attitude spilled over into his species names when in 1818[52] he described a new fish in the genus *Oxyrhynchus*[53]. Telling the reader "its flesh is of a most exquisite flavour" he named it *O. deliciosus* (In his defence, this type of joke was always popular. In 1781 Franz Schrank[54] named a mite often found among books in libraries, *Acarus eruditus*, 'the educated mite').

Following the British Association's criticisms of Elford's 'nonsense names' it was left to the Reverend Frank Knight in 1900 to point out that many of these were actually derived from biblical and middle-eastern sources. *Azeca* was from Azekah, a town mentioned repeatedly in the Bible[55] and *Assiminea* may have been derived from Assemani, the family name of four famous 18th century oriental scholars[56]. Other names that had irritated workers included *Macoma* (which Knight showed was from the Hebrew 'makom', 'a place'), *Barnea* (again from the Bible[57]) and *Balcis* (from Balkis, the Arabic name for the Queen of Sheba).

Knight revealed many other similar derivations and interpreted this to mean Elford had a deep interest in eastern languages and literature and was steeped in the lesser-read verses of the scriptures. This is doubtful. While Knight must be thanked for setting the record straight, he has taken a rather isolationist view of Elford Leach's life. The British Museum was not just a natural history museum. Indeed, as far as many of the Trustees were concerned Natural History was very much a poor relation by comparison with the other departments. The Museum was primarily a centre for the Arts, especially: literature (the vast library filled the entire ground floor); painting (there was no National Gallery or National Portrait Gallery at this time); and sculpture (Greek and Roman primarily, with some Egyptian beginning to make an appearance). Elford Leach was surrounded by Arts scholars.

When he was preparing his mollusc work he had already created more than 600 new names. It would not be surprising if unused classical names were increasingly difficult to find, but he had the solution close to hand. The Assistant Librarian in the Department of Manuscripts was the Reverend Thomas Maurice[58], acknowledged as one of the finest eastern scholars of his day. Maurice was a prolific author, publishing many works, especially about India, and was one of the first British writers to popularise eastern religion and history. It seems more than probable that Elford drew on Maurice's biblical, eastern and middle-eastern expertise to harvest names from a virgin crop.

In general, it is wise to treat Elford Leach's approach to names under four distinct categories: his generic names; his species names; his formation of names; and the way he made his names public.

[50] *Zoological Miscellany*, **2**: 125-126, pl. 106 (1815).
[51] The Blue-winged Kookaburra, *Dacelo leachii* Vigors & Horsfield, 1827, is also known as 'Leach's Kookaburra' or 'Leach's Kingfisher'.
[52] Leach *in* Tuckey (1818: 410).
[53] A name he adopted from the Greek writer Athenæus (2nd century AD).
[54] Franz de Paula von Schrank (1747-1835).
[55] e.g. *Joshua*, Chapter 10, verse 10.
[56] Although Knight's route to this derivation does not seem probable.
[57] *Numbers*, Ch. 34, verse 4. When Gray published Elford's mollusc work this name was published as 'Barnia' but this was undoubtedly a misreading of Elford's handwriting.
[58] Thomas Maurice (1754-1824). First employed at the Museum in 1798. During Elford's time was employed in the Reading Room of the library for two days every week. He lived in apartments at the Museum.

His profusion of new genera, which sometimes upset his contemporaries, was usually the result of an improved classification. He was restructuring existing genera to create natural groups in which the species were more closely allied to one another, and he was recognising that some new species did not fit into any of the known genera and would need a new genus of their own. He therefore did generate an immense number of new names, but many of his genera have stood the test of time and demonstrate the grasp he had of this aspect of his science.

His approach to describing new species, however, was frequently too enthusiastic and many were subsequently found not to be distinct from species already known. In that sense he generated unnecessary names (although we must be careful not to judge through modern eyes. Our own ability to recognise species – which is not infallible – has been built on the experience of workers from Elford Leach's generation and generations since. He was one of the pioneers struggling to recognise the appropriate characters for distinguishing species. Invariably he made mistakes). Regarding his casual renaming of known species: this was unusual even in his own day and rightly brought him criticism.

In the way he formed his new names he was no worse than other workers of his time and it was a failure to recognise his derivations that generated criticism, rather than the names themselves.

The greatest complaint that can be levelled against him is undoubtedly his approach to the publication of his names. His total absorption in his research led him virtually to ignore the impact of his actions on the wider world. This was especially true in his Museum duties. His relabelling of the Museum's exhibits without reference to names familiar to the visitors was short-sighted, as was his use of ancient and obscure names without explicit reference. Similarly when he renamed known species simply because he felt the existing name was not appropriate he failed to consider the confusion this might cause.

In summary, Elford Leach's approach to names does warrant some criticism but in the past he has been unfairly judged and it is always advisable to look for possible bias in the particular critic. Sir James Smith's outburst at the head of this chapter must be seen both in the context of a Linnean naturalist who did not appreciate Elford's modern Continental approach, and in the context of the annoyance and irritation Smith was showing in the rest of this letter to James de Carle Sowerby[59], where he was discussing some illustrations being prepared for publication:

... 'The accident to the drawing of *Reseda alba* is unfortunate, but it is the first accident of the kind we have had. I hope it will be the last. Water, ink, &c. should always be kept out of the way of the drawings...

Your name engraver is a precious blockhead. I only wish him to use his *eyes* if he has no *brains*, & pray tell him to put the letters of reference where I put them, not above or below at his pleasure. I only wish him to copy what I write.

[59] James de Carle Sowerby (1787-1871). Son of James Sowerby. Brother of George Brettingham Sowerby.

As to capital letters I wish only to be followed accurately, I take care to be right...

I know not what sort of zoologists you are engaged with, but most of them now are doing all they can to corrupt the science, splitting & subdividing without science or learning. How happy it would have been if poor Leach had gone mad before he did so much mischief! His labours at the Br. Mus. are only a monument of his insanity.[60]'

No, they were not.

[60] Letter: J.E. Smith to James de Carle Sowerby, 10th October 1824 (Loc: Linnean Society of London, Smith Correspondence).

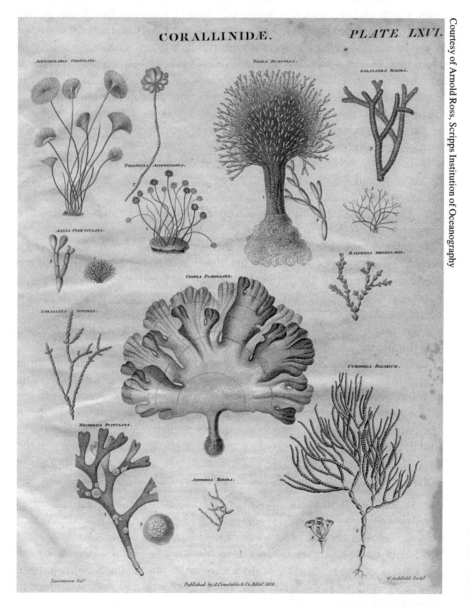

Courtesy of Arnold Ross, Scripps Institution of Oceanography

Plate from Elford Leach's entry CORALLINIADÆ in the *Encyclopædia Britannica*, Supplement to the 4th & 5th Editions, Volume 3 (published in January 1819 and re-issued in 1824).

— 28 —

Travels

Unfortunately Britain now possesses no
naturalist who has a reputation that may
be called European.

Sir Humphry Davy (1824[1])

In 1823, as Traill launched his attack on the Trustees, Elford was recovering well, but his father was beginning to feel the loss of his wife. George Snr's sombre mood was not helped by the recent death of his nephew Jonathan Elford – Sir William's son[2].

In September Henry Woollcombe, whose brother William had died the previous year[3], stayed at Spitchwick and wrote his diary with a heavy heart:

'The scene I am surrounded with here is melancholy & painful, my friend Mr Leach received me with tears and in his conversation painfully alludes to all that has past since we met, the death of his wife, the prior dirangement of her intellects, the state of Dr Leach, the deaths of Elford and my brother. I fear his comforts are now my fear, and he does not seem to me to desire the consolation from Religion which its holy considerations are calculated to inspire.[4]'

The following month George Snr's health deteriorated. In less than a week he was dead. His eldest son, now head of the family, broke the news:

"My Dear Woollcombe,

A most severe and unexpected calamity has fallen on our family since we last met. After an illness of six days my dear and venerable father has been taken from us. He expired at seven o'clock last evening without a struggle. His death was a fit termination of a virtuous and honorable life — Calm, tranquil and devout he resigned his soul to God with hope and confidence. All his children have reason to deplore his loss most severely, for a better, kinder, more beloved father never existed – he lived for his children and made sacrifices for them during his life which are almost

[1] Letter: Davy to William Vernon Harcourt (1789-1871 – 4th son of the Archbishop of York and founder of the Yorkshire Philosophical Society), 21st January 1824 (Thackray & Morrell, 1984: 16).
[2] Died 11th March 1823.
[3] William Woollcombe, a Plymouth physician (d. 27th May 1822).
[4] Henry Woollcombe's Diary 14th September 1823 (Loc: West Devon Record Office, Plymouth).

without parallel — I know that none of his friends more truly estimated his virtues or had a sincerer regard or respect for him than yourself, and I am now about to tax your friendship with a request that you will be directive regarding his funeral which will take place on Friday next at Buckland. My uncle[5] has such an invincible antipathy and repugnance to encountering any painful sensation that I cannot ask him to give the necessary direction. Very little will be necessary as my father wished to be buried in as quick and unostentatious a way as possible. He had left written directions respecting his funeral from which I send you an extract on the other side, and if you will have the goodness to order what he has requested to be done you will confer a great obligation on me. Will you also undertake to inform the different branches of your family of the melancholy event.

Believe me,
My dear Woollcombe,
Yours very sincerely,
Geo. Leach Jnr"

[*overleaf*]

"I desire that I be carried to my grave by six poor men (labourers of Sir William Elford) to whom I desire five shillings each may be given with a pair of gloves.

In the Church of Buckland Monachorum I have built three walled graves each of them sufficiently large to receive two bodies – in one of these graves are the remains of my ever dear and respected wife and in her grave I most earnestly desire to be buried.

I would have a hat band and scarf of one pound given to the Clergyman who performs the funeral service and a hat band to the Clerk and any other fees which may be necessary.

I have been informed on my return from B[*page torn*] that by mistake the remains of my late dear friend Mr Elford were buried in one of the walled graves that were made at my expense – I do not know in which of these graves, but should it be in the same grave in which my late dear wife is interred, I earnestly request that when I am dead Mr Elford's may be removed from my wife's grave into one of the adjoining ones which may be done in five minutes.— By this means there will be room to place my Coffin by the side of her who was most dear to me and I hope no objection will be made to so reasonable a request.[6]"

George Leach Snr was buried in the last week of October, just as the snow started. Woollcombe clearly saw his death as a merciful release and at the end of December went back to the diary entry for his miserable visit and added the postscript, "A few weeks after this it pleased God to remove him from this sad scene. I was truly thankful for its occurrence and I think with undiminished satisfaction of it now".

George Snr had rewritten his Will[7] two months before he died and must have realised his time was near. He left most of his real-estate

[5] Sir William Elford.
[6] Letter: George Leach to Henry Woollcombe, 27th October 1823 (Loc: West Devon Record Office, Plymouth. Ref: 710/599).
[7] Will of George Leach Snr dated 19th August 1823 (Loc: West Devon Record Office, Plymouth).

(a substantial area of agricultural land in various West Country locations) to his eldest son George. Jonathan received 13 acres (5.26 hectares) on the outskirts of Plymouth. Elford was given no land directly – almost certainly because he was not deemed mentally competent when the Will was written – but further land was left jointly to George, Jonathan and Jenny to be held in trust for him. Elford would receive the rents from the tenant farmers as they were paid (which would supplement his pension and annuity). Other land was left to George and Jonathan jointly in trust for Jenny, who likewise received the rents.

Jonathan was left his father's gold watch-chain and letter seals, which had been in the Leach family for more than 120 years. The gold watch went to Jenny as did all her mother's possessions, including the books that had been inherited from Lancelot Elford. Jenny's mother had particularly wanted her to have these.

George Snr's books were divided between George, Jonathan and Jenny and his 'plate' was divided equally between Jenny and Jonathan with the exception of two silver salvers which were bequeathed to George. Their father explained this distribution, saying, "I think it unnecessary to give any other part of my plate to my sons George Leach and William Elford Leach as they have a sufficient quantity of their own and I do not give any of my Books to the said William Elford Leach because he has a large collection of his own[8]".

Everything else was left to George. Elford took over the occupation of Spitchwick and became master of the house under the caring eyes of Jenny, now 44 and like her brothers still unmarried. George was determined to die a bachelor, despite his social popularity[9], and was increasingly occupied with his growing law firm, now called *Leach, Lugger & Little* following the addition of new partner Philip Little[10], another local attorney.

The growth of George's firm went hand-in-hand with the growth of Plymouth Dock itself. Dock had been better populated than its older parent since the last century and now held more than 33,000 people[11]. The inhabitants had been increasingly unhappy at being seen as an adjunct to the smaller Plymouth and petitioned the king in 1823 to have Dock's name changed to something more in keeping with its status. They wanted to be called 'Devonport'. The change was agreed and from 1824 Devonport it was.

1824

As his health continued to improve Elford devoted at least part of his days to zoology. In London a new periodical, the *Zoological Journal*, had been started by Thomas Bell, brothers James and George Sowerby, and John Children, so Elford resurrected one of his manuscripts describing a family of beetles – written in 1815 for the *Zoological Miscellany* but never included – and sent it to Children for publication[12]. Elford's main project,

[8] Elford had at least 182 books (Letter: Leach to Alexander MacLeay, 5th February 1824. Loc: Linnean Society, Miscellaneous Correspondence).
[9] Letter signed 'Philo' ca. March 1862 in the *Plymouth, Devonport and Stonehouse Herald* and *United Services Journal* (cutting in West Devon Records Office, Plymouth. Ref: WDR Acc. 581/1) (See later).
[10] Apparently Philip Moysey Little (b. 1791). A Master Extra in Chancery.
[11] In 1821 (Hoskins, 1971: 120).
[12] Leach, William Elford 1824. Monograph on the Cebrionidæ, a Family of Insects. *Zoological Journal*, 1: 33-46 [and see comments on pp. 282-283].

however, was still his manuscript on the British molluscs, which had now grown to several volumes. In January he contacted George Sowerby regarding its production:

'My dear Sowerby

    I have received at last the Mss of the first Volume of my Mollusca and shall in the course of three or four weeks transmit the Mss into Balwin's Hands[13]; you will very much oblige me by procuring for me a set of the impressions of the uncolored Plates without which I cannot go on. I have no doubt that M[r] Barrow will frank them to me in one or two packets.

    Respecting the 2nd Volume it is in a very imperfect State; however I will give the copyright and the Mss into your Hands and you may get Balwin to publish it on your account if you will give to me 60 coloured Copies.   I have the Plates here of the 2nd Volume which contains the Bivalves, which I fuse into a separate Class, under the title Ginglymochoncha; these I will send to you as soon as the Mss of the first Volume is ready for the Press the Synonyms are what are most wanted to compleat it. . . .

    I am preparing a Monograph on the Cephalopoda; I have coloured figures of the five Species that inhabit the five Species of Argonauta known. and a vast number of new Species and five new Genera.[14] '

Two weeks later the recovery of his mental competence was formally recognised when he travelled the short distance to Widecombe-in-the-Moor to sign a new Will in the parsonage of his local church. He intended to leave to the Linnean Society a number of books, all his own manuscripts and drawings, and the drawings and manuscripts from the Congo expedition (which had been left to him by the Wills of Christen Smith and Jack Cranch)[15]. Explaining this to Alexander MacLeay (still the Society's Secretary) he asked him to send the Devon and Exeter Institution any original drawings or engraved plates from *Malacostraca* that had found their way to the Linnean, then continued:

13   This should read 'Baldwin', of the publishers *Baldwin, Cradock & Joy.*
14 Letter: W.E. Leach to G.B. Sowerby, 13th January 1824 (Loc: Wellcome Institute for the History of Medicine, London. Ref: WMS/ALS: Leach).
15 Curiously, he was believed to have died intestate and none of these bequests was received by the Linnean Society. The Congo manuscripts are now in the Paris museum (Monod, 1970).

Church of St Pancras, Widecombe-in-the-Moor, Dartmoor (known as 'the cathedral of the moor').

'On looking over my Collection of Drawings, I found that the five Figures of Terebella[16] published in Volume xij[17] have not been returned into my hands. They form a part of a Copy of all the original Drawings executed by Mrs Dorville for Col. Montague, which by the permission of Mrs Dorville an Artist procured by me by Mr G.B. Sowerby made facsimile Copies—Mr G.B. Sowerby will vouch for the truth of what I affirm. Should these drawings be found you will very much oblige me by causing them to be put into the Hands of Mr Stephens, who will transmit them into my Hands through the Medium of my Brother Col. Leach now at Hastings, but who has promised to call on Mr Stephens for some other Articles of mine in his hands, on his return to London.

With my kindest Regards to all your Family
and to our Friends in the Working-bee-Club
I remain your sincere and grateful Friend
Wm Elford Leach

Give my most espetial regards to Mrs MacLeay[18], and inform her that I shall by the first opportunity that offers, transmit to her for the ornament of her chimney-piece some Ornaments in the form of Columns made of Yew, Labernum and Holley in a Lathe in which I employ many hours in the day, espetially in bad weather in turning various Articles of use to be sold by Ladies at the Exhibitions of Plymouth and Exeter for charitable services.

I am very sorry to say that the immoderate of Mercury instilled into my Constitution by that Devil-incarnate Dr Veich; keeps up a continuall Salivation, and passes down my Throat as fast as the Chatarracts of Niagara. And my medical Friends assure me that it is not likely to be totally eradicated for five six or even seven years.[19]'

Jonathan, it seems, was living in London (where now, or later, he bought several houses[20]).

As the spring arrived and the insects emerged, entomology came to the fore. Elford began to collect seriously and in June and July sent boxes of Devonian species to the British Museum, both for their own collections and for forwarding to other enthusiasts. He also prepared another paper for the *Zoological Journal* describing a new species of bat he had caught at Spitchwick[21].

While he worked on his scientific articles he also provided background information on geology, ornithology and entomology to accompany the publication of a new poem entitled *Dartmoor* by local author Noel Carrington[22]. The geological note was included but sadly his other observations were so extensive they had to be omitted. The poem's preface claimed so many insects had been discovered on Dartmoor that Dr Leach said their names would fill a separate volume, and hoped "this great naturalist will some day publish a complete list, his residence at Spitchwick being favourable for observing the natural productions of Dartmoor[23]".

[16] Marine tube-worms.
[17] From Montagu (1819).
[18] Elizabeth MacLeay (née Barclay).
[19] Letter: W.E. Leach to MacLeay, 5th February 1824 (Loc: Linnean Society of London, Miscellaneous Correspondence).
[20] Will of Jonathan Leach dated 28th April 1851 (Loc: Public Record Office, Kew, London. Reference: PROB || 2210).
[21] Which he named *Vespertilio pygmaeus*.
[22] Noel Thomas Carrington (1777-1830).
[23] William Burt *in* Carrington (1826: lxv-lxvii, lxxviii, cv).

Spitchwick may have been favourable, but Elford had no intention of restricting his collecting to the wilder edges of Dartmoor. He had something altogether more exotic in mind. As the summer of 1824 faded he and Jenny packed their belongings and said goodbye to Spitchwick for ever.

Touring

By October they were at the Bedford Hotel in London[24] on their way to the Mediterranean. They had decided to have a year abroad visiting one of Elford's marine biology contacts at Nice, Antonio Risso[25].

A number of factors could have prompted this: the tenancy of Spitchwick had been held by their father and they were presumably continuing to live there only under a temporary arrangement; with his passing both their finances improved, while their immediate family ties to Devon diminished (apart from the Elfords, only their brother George remained in the county); the idea of a winter in the sun cannot have been repugnant to them; and the cost of living was generally lower on the Continent, which was important for anyone on a fixed income (When the Capels moved to Brussels in 1814 it was because they were a relatively impoverished family, despite their aristocratic blood. Thomas Creevey too had taken his family there for financial reasons. On the European mainland, as long as British expatriates avoided tourist centres such as Paris they could maintain the same standard of living for significantly less money). Elford and Jenny had not intended to visit the Continent quite so soon[26], but whatever the reason for the acceleration of their plans, the end of 1824 saw them on the move.

From the Bedford Hotel at the beginning of October Elford wrote to James de Carle Sowerby[27] apologising that his busy schedule in London would not give them time to meet, and asking Sowerby to send a copy of the existing parts of *Malacostraca* to Gotthelf Fischer, Professor of Natural History at Moscow[28]. For several years Elford had been a Member of the Imperial Cæsarian Society of Naturalists at Moscow, and was now also a member of the Cæsarian Leopoldine-Caroline Academy of Bonn and of the German natural history societies at Leipzig, Halle and Ehren.

On his way out of the country he donated nearly 400 British insects and a specimen of his new bat to the British Museum. By December he and Jenny were settled at Nice[29].

1825

Nice was renowned for the health of its climate[30] and had been recognised as a coastal resort for centuries, nestling on a small plain between the sea and the towering natural amphitheatre of the maritime Alps. The stone-built town of narrow streets and red-tiled roofs looked out across richly cultivated fields: a vast market-garden planted with citrus fruits, cereals, salad vegetables and flowers (which were cut and transported for sale as far away as London in the cool, preserving air of winter). Scattered

[24] The Bedford Hotel, Southampton Row, Russell Square.
[25] Giovanni Antonio (or Joseph Antoine) Risso (1777-1845). A druggist with interests in botany, zoology and geology.
[26] Letter: W.E. Leach to König, postmarked 20th April 1926 (Loc: British Museum, Add. Mss. 32441 No 7).
[27] Letter: W. E. Leach to James de Carle Sowerby, 7th October 1824 (Loc: General Library (Sowerby Archive), The Natural History Museum, London).
[28] Johann Gotthelf Fischer de Waldheim (1771-1853). A naturalist of German descent.
[29] They would presumably have travelled via Paris but there is no record of them visiting the Jardin des Plantes. It would be unusual if they had not.
[30] See for example Smollett (1981: 187-189).

across this plain were the houses of the labourers, plastered white under the bright Mediterranean sun.

Nice had once been a thriving metropolis of the Roman Empire, *Nicæa*, and the town boasted the ruins of an amphitheatre, aqueducts, baths and other public buildings, but by the 18th century this province was part of the Kingdom of Sardinia (also known as Piedmont), controlled from Savoy to the north. The local people, the Nissards, were proud to call themselves Italian. During the recent wars Napoleon had overrun the whole region from neighbouring France but the Congress of Vienna in 1815 – when the victorious powers fixed the post Napoleonic boundaries of Europe – had restored Savoy's control[31].

Whether Elford travelled to Nice to complete his recuperation or as an unrelated diversion, recuperation appears to have been the result. His extensive collection notes from this trip[32] show he was pursuing insects virtually every day for the first six months, sometimes in the garden of the house he and Jenny rented with their domestic servant, but often further afield in and around the town, including the Roman ruins and surrounding hills. As usual he managed to find helpers, including his sister, their servant, new friends and members of Risso's family. We can imagine the scene when he says for one species[33]: "found on the Sea-shore, where it is extremely common but owing to the Velocity of its Flight it was with the greatest Difficulty, that after chasing many I at last succeeded in capturing one single Specimen." Quite what the locals made of these antics is not recorded.

Although he had not completed his major manuscript on the molluscs, he was now working on another. He was compiling an English edition of Cuvier's work, and in April wrote to its author:

"I am very sure that you and your kind-hearted family as well as my Parisian friends generally, will be glad to hear from myself of my gradual recovery to my former state of health; since my arrival in this city, I have lived out of doors, worked in the garden and with my kind friend Risso made excursions in pursuit of zoological subjects. I have nearly completed

[31] Nice did not become part of France until 1860.
[32] Loc: Entomology Library (*Entomological Memorandums*, Samouelle Register Vol. 3), The Natural History Museum, London.
[33] Nice, 2nd June 1825.

the translation of your work on the anatomy of the Mollusca, to which I have added many observations of my own, as well as from the Mss of the late George Montagu, and I shall illustrate it with nearly three hundred coloured species of the animals of which your work treats.[34]"

In their excursions Elford and Risso were collecting a wide range of animals: insects, millipedes, crustaceans, leeches, sea-anemones, sponges and molluscs, among others. Elford sent a paper describing some new barnacles to London for July's issue of the *Zoological Journal*[35] and took the opportunity to name two new species *Cineras rissoanus* and *Otion rissoanus*.

It is clear from the text of this article that Elford had been reading Risso's unpublished notes[36], which were probably from his major study of the natural history of southern Europe, now nearing completion[37]. Risso in turn had been reading Elford's manuscripts and adopted many of his views on mollusc genera. When Risso's work was published the following year it included these genera and Risso became the first to use many of Elford's new names[38], but he paid his debt by naming a number of his own new species in honour of his friend (*Planaxis elfordiana*, *Portunus leachii*, *Lymnea leachiana*, *Thynnus leachianus*) and by creating a new genus *Leachia*[39].

While Elford worked steadily in Nice, John Gray re-entered his life. However, this time Elford was not making contact with Gray, he was making contact with the Trustees about Gray.

John Gray and the British Museum

After his disappointment at the Museum following the appointments of Samouelle then Children, Gray had thrown himself into his medical studies and his private interests, including the production of his father's botanical work *A natural Arrangement of British Plants* (1821). He had also arranged with James Sowerby Snr that they would publish a work on shells; Gray would produce the text and Sowerby the illustrations. In 1822 Gray visited the Museum to examine the shell collection in preparation for this and met John Children[40], who was trying to ease himself into zoology by translating the sections on molluscs from Lamarck's recent volumes on the natural history of the invertebrates[41]. Children was immediately impressed with Gray's knowledge of the molluscs and his familiarity with the Museum's collections, and asked him to come into Montagu House on a voluntary basis to assist him. Gray was more than happy to be restored to the Museum and, still hoping to obtain employment there, agreed despite the financial difficulties this caused him.

James Sowerby Snr's death in October ended the plan to produce the joint work but Gray continued to help Children until, in 1824, he happened to reveal the hardship he was under. Children did not want to lose his help so he arranged for him to be employed by the Trustees on a casual contract[42],

[34] Letter: W.E. Leach to Cuvier, 19th April 1825 (Loc: Bibliothèque Centrale, Muséum National d'Histoire Naturelle, Paris. Ref: Ms 2753 pièce 49). The mollusc work was presumably Cuvier's 1817 publication, *Mémoires pour servir à l'histoire et à l'anatomie des Mollusques*. We are not aware a translation by Elford Leach was ever published.

[35] Leach, W.E. 1825. A tabular view of the genera composing the class Cirripedes, with descriptions of the species of Otion, Cineras, and Clyptra. *Zoological Journal, London*, **2**: 208-215. We have no evidence the manuscript was sent from Nice but text and context suggest this.

[36] He adopted one of Risso's manuscript names for one of the new species.

[37] Risso, (1826-1827).

[38] *Jaminia, Mangelia, Turbonilla, Gibbula, Cemoria, Abra, Acicula, Truncatella* (the eventual publication of Elford's manuscript by Gray has this name as 'Truncatula' but that was probably a mis-reading of Elford's handwriting) and *Barnea* (spelt correctly. Gray read it as 'Barnia' when he published Elford's Ms).

[39] Elford seems to have convinced Risso to adopt -ianus and -iana as endings. Charles-Alexandre LeSueur (1778-1846) had already named a mollusc genus *Leachia* in the *Journal of the Academy of Natural Sciences of Philadelphia* (1821).

[40] Gunther (1980a: 211). Gunther previously (1978: 86) said they met in the summer of 1823 but it was more likely to be in 1822 prior to Sowerby's death on 25th October. Presumably Gray and Children already knew each other. Children had visited Waterloo with Gray's brother in 1818.

initially for six months. John Gray was to work at the British Museum for the rest of his life.

After Children published his translation of Lamarck's work, with additions of his own and 250 illustrations by his daughter Anna[43], he moved from shells to an interest in insects, becoming the first President of the new Entomological Society of London in 1833[44]. When the Museum's Natural History department was re-organised in 1837 he became the first Keeper of Zoology[45] and on his retirement three years later he was succeeded by Gray[46].

John Gray would be one of the Museum's most influential and active Keepers of Zoology, holding the post for 35 years until his death in 1875, a period that included the impact of Darwin's *Origin of Species* in the years after 1859. However, despite the major contributions to come, in the spring of 1825 Gray had somehow earned the intense disapproval of his former friend and tutor Elford Leach.

Elford had written to Charles Abbott, the former Speaker of the House of Commons. Abbott had retired from the Speakership in 1817 when his health was failing and had been elevated to the peerage as Baron Colchester, but he had been so active and influential as an *ex-officio* Trustee that the permitted number of elected Trustees was deliberately increased to allow him to remain. Elford had contacted him to make certain accusations regarding Gray. König heard about this on Saturday the 7th of May (presumably after the Trustees' committee meeting) and wrote to Abbott two days later regarding the charges. Sadly König does not disclose in his diary, where we learn of this event[47], what the charges were or what the outcome was, but this episode suggests that although Gray appears to have felt a genuine fondness and appreciation for Elford and all he had done for him[48], Elford's break with Gray at the onset of his illness had been severe.

At the beginning of June Elford wrote again to London, but on less odious subjects. He sent William Clift a letter of introduction to be carried by a friend from Nice who wanted to see Clift's museum. Elford entreats Clift, 'every since I have had the pleasure and honour of being introduced you we have, as you will know, loved and esteemed each other cordially, and I feel therefore that you will feel pleasure in paying a little attention to him, who has payed much to me.[49]' He goes on to add that he has sent Charles König some fossil molluscs and a fragment of an animal resembling an ichthyosaur through the Genoese agent of "our worthy friend Mr Hunemann".

Italy

By late June Elford and Jenny had decided it was time to leave Nice. On the 21st they said farewell to Risso and headed north-east into the mountains. The next six days were spent ascending the peaks and heading through the small towns of Roccavione and Demonte to Vinádio[50], a spa resort known for its thermal springs. Along the way Elford collected more insects.

[41] Lamarck, J.B.P.M. de, 1815-1822. *Histoire Naturelle des Animaux sans Vertèbres*. 7 vols.

[42] Paid 15 shillings a day.

[43] Published anonymously in parts from 1822-1824 in the *Quarterly Journal of Science, Literature and the Arts*, **14-16** (later, assembled parts appear to have been bound as a book called *Lamarck's Genera of Shells* but few copies seem to have been produced).

[44] An earlier Entomological Society had been founded in London in 1806. This society met monthly and its President in 1811 was A.H. Hasworth of Little Chelsea (Anon., 1811: 243) who died from cholera in 1833 (Jarvis, 1976: 94). We do not know what became of this earlier organisation.

[45] König became Keeper of Mineralogy, which he always viewed as a demotion.

[46] Whose brother George Robert Gray (1808-1872), an ornithologist, had been recruited by the Museum in 1831.

[47] Charles König's Diary, 7th & 9th May 1825.

[48] Throughout his life he always acknowledged how much he owed Elford Leach, "to whom I am so deeply indebted for the opportunities he afforded me of studying zoology" (Preface in Leach, 1852).

[49] Letter: 5th June 1825 (Loc: General Library (Owen Correspondence), The Natural History Museum, London). The friend was a Dr Skirving. Elford does write "every since".

[50] Then called 'Venai'.

Paradoxically, they may have moved away from the coast to escape the insects. Scotsman Tobias Smollett[51] had lived in Nice in 1764 and had nothing good to say about them:

"In summer, notwithstanding all the care and precautions we can take, we are pestered with incredible swarms of flies, fleas, and bugs; but the gnats, or *couzins*, are more intolerable than all the rest. In the day-time, it is impossible to keep the flies out of your mouth, nostrils, eyes, and ears. They croud into your milk, tea, chocolate, soup, wine, and water: they soil your sugar, contaminate your victuals, and devour your fruit; they cover and defile your furniture, floors, cielings, and indeed your whole body. As soon as candles are lighted, the *couzins* begin to buz about your ears in myriads, and torment you with their stings, so that you have no rest nor respite 'till you get into bed, where you are secured by your musquito-net.[52]"

It is perhaps no coincidence that Elford sent another article to the *Zoological Journal*, this time describing species of mosquitoes and ants from Nice.[53]

After three weeks in the mountains they travelled east to Savona[54], then took the coast road through Genoa to Pisa. Moving inland they had reached Florence by the beginning of August. Elford had done very little collecting since Vinádio[55] but now they rested for a month and his nets came out again. Florence had a good natural history museum[56] and Elford made contact with local naturalists, including Dr Antonio Tozzetti[57], the Professor of Botany, *Materia Medica* and Chemistry at the hospital of Santa Maria Nuova, who had an interest in entomology[58].

After a month in Florence Elford and Jenny started their journey home to England, but instead of returning the way they had come they headed north across the Apennines to Bologna then took the road through Modena, Parma, Piacenza, Alessandria and Asti to Turin, with Elford collecting along the way. They were presumably travelling by coach, and he must have arranged his forays when they stopped to eat or change horses. From Turin they crossed the Alps at Mt Cenis and entered France on the road to Lyons, where they turned north for the English Channel[59]. By mid-October they were in Cheltenham for the end of the social season, and although Elford had amassed a collection of two-and-a-half thousand insects[60], that did not stop him slipping out of town to collect some more in the Forest of Dean[61].

1826

On their return to Devon Elford and Jenny took up residence for five weeks at Compton near Plymouth, where the Leach family owned land, then at Woodside, a small row of houses just outside Plymouth's town boundary[62]. Here Elford wrote two more articles[63]. The first, for the *Zoological Journal*, described more beetles, including some from the recent tour[64]. The other recorded animals collected in Nice and Italy. This second paper was submitted to the proposed new *Transactions of the Plymouth*

[51] Tobias George Smollett (1721-1771). Originally a surgeon. Later a novelist, dramatist, editor, translator, satirist, poet and traveller. He published *Travels in France and Italy* in 1766.
[52] Smollett, 1981: 192 (His account of his travels were generally so critical that Laurence Sterne (1713-1768) who published his own *A sentimental Journey through France and Italy* in 1768, nicknamed him 'Smelfungus').
[53] Leach, W.E. 1825. Descriptions of Thirteen Species of Formica, and Three Species of Culex, found in the Environs of Nice. *Zoological Journal*, **2**: 289-293 (October 1825).
[54] They left Vinadio on the 20th of July. Savona is not mentioned in Elford's notes but Ceva (on the road to Savona) is.
[55] According to his notes.
[56] This was visited in 1820 by William Allen (1770-1843). Allen was a leading Friend (i.e. a Quaker) who lectured at Guy's Hospital London and the Royal Institution. A friend of Humphry Davy, Lewis Dillwyn and other scientists. FLS 1801, FRS 1807. (Hall, 1953: 20 21, 27, 90).
[57] Antonio Targioni Tozzetti (1785-1856) (It is just possible Elford's contact was Ottaviano Targioni Tozzetti (1755-1826) the former Professor of Botany at the hospital, but he had moved to Pisa by this time).
[58] He showed Elford his notes. See Leach, W.E. 1826. On the Stirps and Genera composing the Family Pselaphidæ; with Descriptions of some new Species. *Zoological Journal*, **2**: 445-453 at pages 448 & 453 where 'Tozzetti' is erroneously printed 'Tozzelfi'.

Florence.

---

59 Again they would presumably have passed through Paris.

60 He donated 2469 European insects to the British Museum in 1826. This could include some specimens sent by his contacts after his return, but would not include specimens he kept.

61 His notes record a collection he made on the 13th October in the Forest of Dean (west of Cheltenham).

62 Woodside was only 500m north-east of the formal streets of Plymouth. In 1812 Charles Prideaux's brother William Prideaux (1778-1843) had lived at 'Woodside Cottage' but by 1823 he had a house called 'Green Bank'.

63 These may have been written during the tour, but on his return seems more probable. Both mention Italy.

64 Leach, W.E. 1826. On the Stirps and Genera composing the Family Pselaphidæ; with Descriptions of some new Species. *Zoological Journal*, 2: 445-453 [vol. for January-April 1826]

65 Leach, W.E. 1830. Description of some new species of the Class Myriapoda. *Transactions of the Plymouth Institution*, 1: 158-168. (the paper includes a number of animal groups, not just Myriapoda and the header changes part way through to 'Dr Leach on various zoological genera').

66 The genus *Anemonia* and the species *Anemonia vagans* (sea anemone); *Succinea elegans* (mollusc); and the leech *Sanguisuga meridionalis*.

67 Letter: W.E. Leach to G.B. Sowerby, 22nd January 1826 (Loc: General Library (Sowerby Archive), The Natural History Museum, London). Bell did not publish the work.

Institution[65]. Elford appears to have been submitting articles to this planned volume for some years, certainly since he was at the British Museum, but there had been serious delays in its production. By the time the first part finally appeared in 1830, with the Nice article and three others, Risso had already published descriptions of some of Elford's species[66], although among those he had missed was a new millipede Elford called *Euopus rissonianus*.

Now apparently in much better health and clearly committed to his work Elford threw himself into his studies. He wanted to complete his unfinished *Malacostraca* and in January was in contact with the Sowerbys, asking them to send him any paperwork they had relating to the final parts. He told them he would complete the descriptions as far as he could using specimens in the museum of the Plymouth Institution, but Samouelle would have to provide descriptions of any remaining. He also wrote to Thomas Bell about his manuscript on the British Mollusca, and appears to have asked Bell to oversee the publication, at least of the first volume, although he promised to answer any questions Bell might have by return of post[67].

As soon as the insects appeared in April he resumed his intensive programme of collecting[68], and as usual he scoured his whole local area. Beyond the house he swept Lipson Hill and Lipson Wood, or went into Plymouth to patrol the streets and gardens of the town centre or the allotments of local nurseryman William Pontey[69]. On the far side of Plymouth he found the marsh of *Penny-come-quick* a particularly profitable hunting ground. After three months of this he must have been a familiar sight to local residents.

At the end of June he and Jenny appear to have moved again, a few kilometres north to Bickleigh, and for the next month all Elford's collections were made there. He was prepared to accept insects in any condition if they belonged to a species that interested him, as with one specimen he, 'found dead in the Window of a Farm-house, and glued together as well as I could. It being rather decayed and mouldy rendered this more troublesome.[70]'

Emigration

This nomadic lifestyle, moving from house to house, indicates Elford and Jenny knew their return to England was not permanent. They had already decided to go back to the Continent with the intention of living there for three to five years[71]. The reason may have been the allure of Italy, or it may have been financial – this decision came hard on the heels of a crisis at the bank of their uncle, Sir William Elford.

Like many country banks at that time this was a local concern underwritten by the personal assets of its partners. Sir William's son Jonathan had joined the business in 1801 and on his death in 1823 it had been necessary to examine the bank's books. It was immediately obvious all was not well.

68   Collection   notes: Entomology   Library (*Entomological Memorandums* Samouelle Register Vol. 3), The Natural History Museum, London.
69   William   Pontey of Frankfort Street (Anon., 1812). A nurseryman who published several books on forestry and decorative tree planting between 1800 and 1826. Pontey had four plots of land: one forming the north side of the market square, another just to the west of the town limits and two more by Woodside. By 1841 there was also an Alexander Pontey in Plymouth (*fide* List of persons eligible to receive the published volume of the British Association for the Advancement of Science following its annual meeting at Plymouth).
70 Collection notes: 15th July (his punctuation has been altered here).
71 Note: W. E. Leach to British Museum Trustees, 1826 (Loc: Entomology Library (*Entomological Memorandums*, **2**: 222), The Natural History Museum, London).

Cann slate quarry, Bickleigh Vale, north of Plymouth. Elford Leach collected near the quarry in April 1826. The village of Bickleigh, with its church tower, is on the ridge in the far distance.

Sir William Elford *Bt.*

© William P.C. Adams

The bank was badly mismanaged and the partners had been overdrawing their accounts for more than a decade. Jonathan Elford died owing more than £29,000. To cover this Sir William gave a personal guarantee of £24,000 (using his estate at Bickham as collateral) with an additional loan making up the difference. When a replacement partner was appointed in 1823 the total deficit was still £70,000 but the bank felt it was protected by mortgages from Sir William of £75,000.

Two years later a short-lived British economic boom collapsed in the autumn of 1825. Confidence plummeted and there was a general run on the banks. One by one, country banks across Britain began to fail, unable to satisfy their customers' rush to withdraw their savings. Nationwide 79 went out of business. At the beginning of October Plymouth newspapers printed notices thanking readers for showing confidence, but banks had already closed their doors in Devonport[72] and Kingsbridge[73]. Without warning, on the 25th of November 1825 Sir William's bank, *Elford, Tingcombe & Clarke: The Plymouth Bank*, failed to open and notices appeared in the windows announcing business had been suspended.

[72] *Sheills & Johns Bank.*
[73] *Square, Prideaux & Co.*
[74] December 1825. See Elford (1976: Part II p. 4a). Laura Elford says *Plymouth and Devonshire Weekly Journal* but in 1822 there had been a *Plymouth and Plymouth Dock Weekly Journal* so 'Devonport' seems more likely.
[75] *fide* bank partner John Tingcombe (b. 1782) reported in the diary of Plymouth painter Benjamin Robert Haydon for 2nd August 1826 (Elford, 1976: Part II p. 4). Sir William Elford and John Tingcombe had purchased Haydon's painting *The Judgement of Solomon* for 700 guineas.

"The astonishment and distress which this announcement excited are beyond description." reported the *Plymouth & Devonport Weekly Journal*[74], "Multitudes were collected round the doors during the whole day and their countenances powerfully depicted the various passions with which they were inspired. The pangs of disappointment and the deeper emotions of despair and agony might be traced in almost every face. We never remember witnessing such a strong excitement of public feeling and his heart must be utterly callous who could be insensible to the prevalence of so much misery."

The partners had taken the wise precaution of insuring the life of Sir William for the value of the bank's entire deficit[75], but – somewhat inconveniently – he lived on.

In January 1826 bankruptcy proceedings began, and the first of a series of creditors' meetings was held. Sir William was interviewed by the

Commissioners several times during the next two months but did not acquit himself well and in March bankruptcy was proved. To help meet the Bank's debts the personal assets of the partners were liquidated and at the end of June there was a sale of estates, farm stock and household effects[76] (If the house at Woodside was a property belonging to Sir William[77], that would explain why Elford and Jenny moved to Bickleigh at that time).

Sir William moved out of the area, eventually settling along the coast at Totnes [78], and the Elford family estate at Bickham, where Elford Leach's mother had been born, finally went under the hammer in 1830, all 257 hectares[79].

About the beginning of June Elford had sent his personal collection of 2560 European and Devonian insects to the British Museum and asked in return if he might be allowed to have a few pounds-worth of entomological pins and other collecting apparatus for his excursions in Europe. The Trustees agreed. Their plans made, Elford and Jenny packed their belongings and by the beginning of August were in London again and on their way.

[76] Even then the creditors only received 5 shillings in the pound (25% of what they were owed).
[77] This is speculation.
[78] Pronounced 'Tott-ness'.
[79] 635 acres.

— 29 —

Endings

When you arrive at Rome, you receive cards from all your country-folks
in that city: they expect to have the visit returned next day, when they give
orders not to be at home; and you never speak to one another in the sequel.
This is a refinement in hospitality and politeness which the English have
invented by the strength of their own genius, without any assistance either
from France, Italy or Lapland.

Tobias Smollett[1]

[1] Smollett, 1981: 241.
[2] In fact, his concluding sections of this work were never published. The final parts, with additions, were eventually produced in 1875 by George Sowerby's son, George Brettingham Sowerby THE YOUNGER (1812-1884) who provided text and figures. Elford's Introduction, family characters and systematic indices were not included, but Sowerby did add his own index to the genera and species.
[3] Letter: W.E. Leach (London) to James de Carle Sowerby, 7th August 1826 (Loc: General Library (Sowerby Archive), The Natural History Museum, London). Bell still had these papers in 1836 (House of Commons, 1836: para. 359).
[4] Letter: Clift to Cuvier, 28th September 1826 (Loc: General Library (Owen Correspondence), The Natural History Museum, London).
[5] In the summer/autumn of 1826 both John Gray and John Children were in Paris (Gunther, 1978: 88-89) but it is not known whether Elford and Jenny passed through Paris on this trip. Their journey via Rotterdam suggests they may have travelled through Germany and Switzerland, not France.

In London, as Elford and Jenny prepared to sail to Rotterdam, Elford donated more of his collection to the Museum: over 500 British insects (many new records for the British Isles), spiders from his Nice collection and four bats. He also passed to Samouelle the sections of *Malacostraca* he had been preparing. This included an Introduction to the whole work; the characters of the families; and a systematic index of the families, genera and species. Samouelle was asked to hand these on to the Sowerbys[2]. Many of Elford's manuscripts, and most of his diplomas, were left with his friend Thomas Bell[3].

It seems Elford and Jenny left England in August, just missing Sophie Duvaucel, who visited London in September[4]. This time the Leaches were heading for Rome[5], where Charles Lock Eastlake had been living since 1816 following the success of *Napoleon at the Gangway of the Bellerophon*. In late September Eastlake wrote to Henry Woollcombe:

"Several Devonshire families will be here I understand this winter. Mrs Duckworth and Miss Leach will soon be here. I have taken a place for all the winter for the first and should have been glad to do as much for Miss Leach and her brother but I have not heard of them since they left England. Every year about this time there are the same reports of the number of English visitors who are *sure* to be in Rome, reports which interest many persons as affecting the price of lodgings, but it does appear that several persons of rank are to be here, among whom are the Duke of Hamilton and Lady Westmoreland. People are even beginning to be less frightened of Rome (at least its immediate neighbourhood) as a summer residence. Three or four families, Lord and Lady Compton among them, have passed the summer at Tivoli for the first time. Albano, which has been hitherto a more favorite place has also been the residence of several English all the summer. The ladies complain of the salutary caution of the Italian Physicians not to wander among dewy groves at moonlight for fear of catching the fever and I have heard one of them say in a pet that "every thing agreeable was either unwholesome or wicked". The long intercourse which the English have now had with the Italians has been still insufficient to bring them well acquainted with each other – the higher ranks of society are the same everywhere with some slight modification, but the bulk of the nation – of the Romans particularly, is still shy and particularly jealous of the English. No doubt religion and the influence of its ministers are at the bottom of this, but it is almost impossible for an attentive observer even after many years residence to give an accurate picture of Italian manners – there is so little *above board* with them and so much convention of harmless but contemptible duplicity.[6]"

It appears English émigrés in Italy had relocated their winter social season from Bath to Rome, and descended on the city every year about this time.

A new life

As Elford and Jenny made their home in Italy, so our view of them fades. We catch only brief glimpses during the following years. If they spent their winters at Rome, we do not know where they spent their summers (possibly at Florence, or travelling). Wherever it was, they may have been visited by Jonathan who travelled in the Apennines and Alps and traversed much of Switzerland during the 1820s[7] before returning to England to publish his memoirs, *Rough Sketches of the Life of an Old Soldier*[8].

In the summer of 1827 Elford wrote to König proposing an exchange of duplicate shells with the British Museum. It is not clear whether this was an exchange with himself or with one of his zoological contacts, but the Trustees declined the offer[9].

By the beginning of 1828 the Leaches had returned to Rome for the winter, with Jenny travelling ahead, as before, to make the arrangements. Again Eastlake wrote to Woollcombe:

"Among the visitors here who may be known to you are Mrs Starke, who lives at Exmouth where she tells me she saw my brother. Mr and Mrs Martin (Sir Henry's son and Sir Byam's daughter), Miss and Dr Leach – the first arrived a few days since – and Capt. and Mrs Hillyer (I don't know if I write the name correctly). I met Mrs H. lately and she mentioned Plymouth names enough to lead me to think hers cannot be unknown there. The fashionable diversions of Rome, I mean among the English, generally take a particular turn according to the tastes and talents of the leaders of ton[10] – one winter they had private theatricals, last winter tableaux and

[6] Letter: Charles Eastlake to Henry Woollcombe, 21st September 1826 (Loc: West Devon Record Office, Plymouth. Ref: 710/110). 'A pet' – a fit of petulance.
[7] *Rough Sketches* at p. 310.
[8] *Rough Sketches* appeared in 1831. Jonathan may have been prompted to publish by the appearance in 1830 of John Kincaid's lively *Adventures in the Rifle Brigade*, or the two may have been writing simultaneously.
[9] British Museum, Trustees' Committee Meeting Minutes, 14th July 1827.
[10] 'ton' – style, fashion, distinction (an 18th century French word).

races. This year seems remarkable for splendid entertainments on a larger scale and balls which are footed by legions.[11]"

During the winter the families of Leach and Bonaparte came into contact when Elford socialised with one of Napoleon's nephews, Charles Lucien Bonaparte[12], Prince of Musignano. Several of Elford's letters to him still survive.

Charles' father was Napoleon's brother Lucien[13], a staunch republican who had been influential in the years following the revolution. His disapproval of his brother's imperialist ambitions had led to quarrels and he had distanced himself from Napoleon's activities, living for some time in the Papal States, where the Pope made him Prince of Canino and Musignano. After criticising his brother openly he had been advised to emigrate but *en route* to America in 1810 his ship was intercepted by the British. He was held briefly in Plymouth[14] before being interned on an estate in Worcestershire[15] until the peace of 1814, when he returned to the Continent.

Lucien's brother Joseph Bonaparte – sometime King of Naples and of Spain – had moved to the United States after the war and had settled at Bordentown[16], where he was joined by Lucien's son Charles. In 1822 Charles married Joseph's daughter, Zénaïde[17].

Although still a young man Charles was an accomplished naturalist with a particular interest in ornithology. He soon became a member of the Academy of Natural Sciences of Philadelphia, and began publishing a multi-volume work on American birds[18]. By the late 1820s he had returned to Europe and was living in Italy. Although two of Elford's letters to him are undated, all appear to have been written during this period and are worth repeating in full for the personal information they contain. The first mentions an article by William Swainson which was published in 1827, the year Charles Bonaparte was elected a Foreign Member of the Linnean Society at the age of 24[19]. Among the signatories on his certificate were Charles König, John Children, James Stephens, Thomas Bell, Thomas Horsfield, Benjamin Leadbeater and Everard Home. Elford's letters read[20]:

'My dear Prince

As I had a bilious fever four days since and have a slight cold accompanied with a slight inflamation in the Oethophagus, I do not think that it will be prudent for me to go out to day. The first fine Day, I will not fail to pay you a visit; and if you will permit me to bring my Sister with me to see your Birds, you will much oblige me.

I send you the number of the Philosophical Magazin which contains Swainson's Synopsis of the Birds discovered in Mexico by Mr Bullock and his Son[21].

I met two Ladies in the Pincio after I saw you, who wished to know how they can see the Vases found by your Father in his Estate. When we meet, we will talk over this matter.

[11] Letter: Charles Eastlake to Woollcombe, 1st January 1828 (Loc: West Devon Record Office, ref: 710/79). 'Mr and Mrs Martin' are Admiral-of-the-Fleet Sir (Thomas) Byam Martin's daughter Catherine and her husband Henry Martin, son of Sir Henry Martin *Bt*. Catherine and Henry had married in March 1825.

[12] Charles Lucien Jules Laurent Bonaparte (1803-1857).

[13] Lucien Bonaparte (1775-1840).

[14] He was held under light guard at *The King's Arms*, a coaching inn in Exeter Street. (Gill, 1979: 135).

[15] This is pronounced 'Wooster-shuh'.

[16] Bordentown, New Jersey, north-east of Philadelphia.

[17] Zénaïde Bonaparte (1801-1854).

[18] *American Ornithology*. 4 vols (1825, 1828, 1828 & 1833).

[19] Proposed 19th December 1826, elected 1st May 1827.

[20] The letters printed here are in the Central Library of the Muséum National d'Histoire Naturelle, Paris.

[21] Swainson, W. (1827) *Philosophical Magazine*, New Series, **1** (Part 6, June 1827). Bullock had visited Mexico in 1823 (mounting an exhibition 'Ancient and Modern Mexico' at Egyptian Hall on his return) and again in 1826. His son was William Bullock Jnr.

All my books are at your Service; all the rest of my Library shall be in Rome before next Autumn, and I have commissioned one of my old friends in London, to take the parts of the Transactions of the Royal and Linnean Societies as they are published, which I have authorized him to do.

I remain my dear Prince,
your very sincere friend
William Elford Leach[22]'

*   *   *

'My dear Prince

It gave me great pain to find that you have a bad leg and still more so that you will not remain in the house a few days untill it is cured; and I was very much vexed to find that you were so kind as to pay me a friendly visit, the day I was in Florence. When you return to Rome, I will call on you, and invite you to come and see the collection of Italian Insects that I have collected. Three or four times after I saw you on horseback in the Bourgazie Park, when I promised to call on you at your country Villa, with a friend of mine, an embargo was lagged on me, if I may use such an expression, by a young and an old Scotch Lady, who obliged me nolens, volens[23] to walk with them, what could I do in such a case? But obey the commands of the fair sex, who always require us to lay aside our own pleasures and persuits, to accomodate theirs. Should I meet with another such interruption I will take them with me to see your collection of Birds &c. at your Paulina Palace.

Hoping that when we next meet, that your leg will be quite well, and wishing you every happiness, I remain, my dear Prince

Your very sincere and true friend
William Elford Leach[24]'.

*   *   *

'My dear Prince,

If you be still on friendly terms [with] the last Miss Fiorini[25], who is, as you well know married to the Governor of Ferra Cinna, direct the inclosed to her and receive from her (as I have desired to do in the inclosed) some valuable papers that I intrusted to her care more than two years since. Should you receive them before I leave Rome, which I think will be on Fryday next, send them in inclosed in one packet to me by your Servant, as if they came from you, as my Sister would be made very ill indeed if she knew or thought that I had the least communication with the Fiorinis. By doing this you will very much oblige your very sincere friend

William Elford Leach

If you receive them after my departure keep them in your hands my dear Prince untill I claim them from you.[26]'

22 Not dated. (Bibliothèque Centrale, Muséum National d'Histoire Naturelle, Paris. Ref: Ms 2605 pièce 1870)
23 'nolens, volens' – Latin: 'unwilling, willing'.
24 Letter: W.E. Leach (at 'Badia') to C.L. Bonaparte at Florence. 29th October 1829 (Loc: Bibliothèque Centrale, Muséum National d'Histoire Naturelle, Paris. Ref: Ms 2605 pièce 1869). 'Badia' is almost certainly not the town to the north of Verona. It appears to be an abbey (It. 'Badia') in the vicinity of Florence. Could this be the Badia Fiesolana? In 1753 the Accademia dei Georgofili (the first agricultural institute in Europe) had been founded at this abbey and Elford Leach was a member of this Academy (Ms note by Jenny Leach at the Academy of Sciences of Turin). Church property had been seized in 1778 and the abbey had been abandoned by the monks. We are not sure of its use in the 1820s.
25 In March 1828 Elford Leach was a friend of a Miss Fiorini (Letter: W.E. Leach to Robert Brown, 3rd March 1828.Loc: British Museum, London. Ref: Additional Manuscripts 32441 Nº 51 – original not seen by KH). This is probably Elizabetta Fiorini-Mazzanti (1790-1879) who wrote *Specimen Bryologiæ Romanæ* (1841).
26 Not dated.(Loc: Bibliothèque Centrale, Muséum National d'Histoire Naturelle, Paris. Ref: Ms 2605 pièce 1871).

It is noticeable that in the signatures to these letters he writes William in full, not 'W^m' as is usual. Jenny appears to have called him William, not Elford[27], and he may therefore have been known to others as William while he and Jenny travelled together. With regard to the last letter, it would be interesting to know why Jenny had such a dismal opinion of this family.

In late 1830[28] Elford sent a large collection of insects from the neighbourhood of Rome and Florence to the new Zoological Society of London, who exhibited the collection at their rooms[29]. The society had been founded in 1826 with the objective of bringing live animals from all parts of the world to one institution 'as objects of scientific research, not of vulgar admiration;—and... pointing out the Comparative Anatomy, the habits of life, the improvement and the methods of multiplying those races of animals which are most useful to man[30]'. Elford was a corresponding member.

Upheaval

The 1830s were a turbulent time in Europe with many nations dissolving into bloodshed following changes of monarch, coups d'état and revolutions.

In Portugal King João VI had died in 1826. His heir, Dom Pedro (Pedro IV), was already Emperor of Brazil and handed on the crown of Portugal to his infant daughter Isabel Maria (Maria II), making his younger brother Miguel Regent for the time being. In 1828 Miguel seized the throne and Portugal was plunged into war. It was 1834 before Miguel was defeated.

In France Louis XVIII had died in 1824 and had been succeeded by his brother Charles (Charles X[31]). Charles fought hard to maintain royalist control of the government, introducing increasingly repressive laws until finally, in July 1830, there was a major revolt in Paris. Charles abdicated on the 2nd of August and fled to Britain. He was replaced on the throne by the Duc d'Orléans – from a junior branch of the Bourbon family – who became Louis-Philippe, King of the French[32].

Following this upheaval in France, in August 1830 a revolution erupted in Belgium. The Belgians had long felt they were not fully recognised in the Dutch-Belgian 'Kingdom of the Netherlands' – dominated by Holland and ruled since 1815 by the Dutch House of Orange in the person of King Willem I[33] (father of the Prince of Orange[34]). In October Belgium declared independence and the Dutch bombarded Antwerp. Britain – eager to prevent war and keen to curb French influence in Belgium – brokered talks in London in an attempt to resolve the crisis. In December the Kingdom of the Netherlands was formally dissolved and the following year the Belgians chose Prince Leopold of Saxe-Coburg, the widower of Princess Charlotte, as their King. Terms were proposed for an armistice between Holland and an independent Belgium but were rejected by Willem who invaded. The French responded by sending troops into Belgium, forcing the Dutch to withdraw. It was late in 1832 before the threat of military intervention by France and Britain obliged the Dutch to accept terms.

[27] See later.

[28] When the *Transactions of the Plymouth Institution* finally appeared in 1830 Elford's address was given as 'London' but this may reflect the many years this work was in preparation rather than showing he was in London in 1830. Further research is needed to clarify the movements of Elford and Jenny from 1830-1832.

[29] *Proceedings of the Committee of Science and Correspondence of the Zoological Society of London*, Part 1, p. 24 (11th January 1831). He had planned to send these to the Society in the autumn of 1828 (Letter: W.E. Leach to Robert Brown, 3rd March 1828. Loc: British Museum, Add. Mss 32441 No 51). The Zoological Society's rooms at this time were at No 33 Bruton Street, London. See Wheeler (1997) for a history of the Zoological Society's collections.

[30] *Zoological Journal*, **2**: 288 (1825).

[31] Charles X (1757-1836). Lived in Britain from 1793-1814. In 1830 returned to Britain then went to Prague.

[32] Louis-Philippe (1773-1850). Had lived in Britain from 1800-1814.

[33] Willem Frederik (1772-1844). Abdicated in 1840.

[34] Who was King Willem II of Holland from 1840 to his death in 1849.

WILLIAM ELFORD LEACH:

ELECTION TO LEARNED SOCIETIES

Fellow of the Linnean Society of London[1]

Member of the Wernerian Natural History Society of Edinburgh[2]

Honorary Member of the Plymouth Institution[3]

Fellow of the Royal College of Physicians of Edinburgh[4]

Member of the Royal College of Surgeons, London[5]

Member of the Medico-Chirurgical Society of London[6]

Fellow of the Royal Society of London[7]

Correspondent of the Société Philomathique de Paris[8]

Member of the Society of the Friends of Natural History in Berlin[9]

Honorary Member of the Philosophic Society of London[10]

Fellow of the Accademia delle Scienze di Torino[11]

Corresponding Member, Academy of Natural Sciences, Philadelphia[12]

Correspondent of the Muséum d'Histoire Naturelle, Paris[13]

Member of the Imperial Cæsarian Society of Naturalists of Moscow[14]

Member of the Cæsarian Leopoldine-Caroline Academy of Bonn[15]

Member of the Natural History Society of Leipzig[16]

Member of the Natural History Society of Halle[17]

Member of the Natural History Society of Ehren[18]

Honorary Member of the Philosophical Society of Cambridge[19]

Honorary Member of the Phrenological Society of Edinburgh[20]

Correspondent, Accademia Gioenia di Scienze Naturali di Catania[21]

Correspondent, T.E. Reale Accademia dei Georgofili di Firenze[22]

Corresponding Member of the Zoological Society of London[23]

[1] From 7 March 1809. Minutes, Linnean Society.
[2] From 9 March 1811. *Memoirs of the Wernerian Society*, **1**: xv (1811).
[3] By 1814 (co-founder 1812). Correspondence and *Transactions Plymouth Institution*, **1**: 353 (1830).
[4] By 1814. *Zoological Miscellany*, **1**: T.P. (1814).
[5] By 1814. *Zoological Miscellany*, **1**: T.P. (1814).
[6] By 1814. *Zoological Miscellany*, **1**: T.P. (1814).
[7] From 15 February 1816. *Record of the Royal Society*, 1940: 448.
[8] By 1817. *Zoological Miscellany*, **3**: T.P. (1817).
[9] By 1817. *Zoological Miscellany*, **3**: T.P. (1817).
[10] By 1817. *Zoological Miscellany*, **3**: T.P. (1817).
[11] From 7 January 1818. Minute Book, Academy of Science, Turin.
[12] From 27 January 1818. Academy of Natural Sciences, Philadelphia, *in litt.*
[13] By 1818. He signed the Certificate of Quality for Dufresne's Collection as such ["Correspondent"] dated 8th Nov. 1818 (Loc: Edinburgh University Library, Special Collections Ms Ref: 1801/2/5)
[14] By 1820. Leach, 1852: T.P. (Ms ca 1820).
[15] By 1820. Leach, 1852: T.P. (Ms ca 1820).
[16] By 1820. Leach, 1852: T.P. (Ms ca 1820).
[17] By 1820. Leach, 1852: T.P. (Ms ca 1820).
[18] By 1820. Leach, 1852: T.P. (Ms ca 1820).
[19] By 1820. Leach, 1852: T.P. (Ms ca 1820).
[20] By 1820. Leach, 1852: T.P. (Ms ca 1820).
[21] From 25 September 1834. *Atti dell'Accademia Gioenia*, **10**(1) (1836).
[22] By 1836. Ms of Jenny Leach at the Academy of Sciences, Turin.
[23] By 1836. As note 22.

35 Letter: W.E. Leach (in Malta) to William Clift, 28th October 1832 (Loc: Wellcome Institute for the History of Medicine, London. Ref: WMS/ALS: Leach). An introduction for Captain Richard Lanslowe.
36 Wheeler, 1997: 106.
37 If he had visited N. Africa he would probably have donated more specimens.
38 Joseph Ritchie (1786-1819), friend of John Keats. In 1818 he led an overland team south from Tripoli with Capt. George Francis Lyon (1795-1832) to seek the River Niger. Sent animals from Malta and Tripoli to the British Museum (British Museum, Officers Reports, Ms p.1692—n.d. but 1819). He took insect collecting equipment and probably contacted Elford before leaving England. Mentioned by Elford Leach in Cuvier (1820: 51).
39 The minuted note of his election gives his address as 'Londra' but this may only indicate his strong London connection, not that he was then in London. See Atti dell'Accademia Gionenia di Scienze Naturali di Catania, 10 (1st series) (1836).
40 Cavaliere Giuseppe Gioeni (1747-1822). Geologist who studied Vesuvius.
41 Their address was Nº 22 Via Felice. Letter: Leach to Children, October-December 1835. Loc: Bibliothèque Centrale, Muséum National d'Histoire Naturelle, Paris. Ref: Ms 2313 pièce 140. This letter was originally part of the Ms collection of Ernest-Théodore Hamy, bought by the MNHN in 1959-60. (fide C. Hustache, MNHN Central Library, in litt. to KH 1986).
42 Letter: Leach to Children, October-December 1835. (Loc: loc. cit.).
43 Letter: Leach to Children, October-December 1835.

On the southern coast of Europe the ripples from the revolution in Paris unsettled a still regionalised Italy (not yet united as one nation) and the political situation deteriorated. In March 1831 uprisings in the northern states of Parma and Modena were suppressed by Austria, which operated effective control in these regions. At about the same time a new revolutionary society ('Young Italy') emerged with ideas for unifying the nation along republican lines and ejecting the ruling powers. At the end of 1831 disturbances broke out in the Papal States. In Piedmont a general uprising was planned for June 1832, but the authorities discovered the plans in March and arrests followed. In Paris in June violence again broke out on the streets and Marshal Soult had to take command of the French government.

It was presumably to escape this political and social unrest that in 1832 Elford and Jenny left Italy to live for a while on the island of Malta[35]. Malta lies near the coast of Tunisia and this year Elford gave the Zoological Society of London a North African reptile[36] which he presumably obtained from one of his contacts[37]. More than a decade earlier he had received Maltese animals from Dr Joseph Ritchie, an explorer who had died in the Sahara in 1819 trying to discover the route of the River Niger[38].

On the 25th of September 1834, Elford was elected a corresponding member of the Gioenian Academy of Natural Sciences at Catania in Sicily[39] (named in honour of Giuseppe Gioeni[40], a volcanologist and founder of Catania's natural history museum). The Leaches may have passed through Catania on their way to and from their Maltese haven.

1835

In the spring of 1835 they were back in Rome[41] where Elford was busy arranging the beetle collection of Roman entomologist Sebastiano Rolli. Rolli had a good collection of insects from the Papal States, especially butterflies and moths. Elford, on the other hand, was interested in insects from the whole of Italy. A Swiss national named Morell sent him specimens from Naples, and when he was away from Rome a gardener was employed to collect in the city during his absence[42].

1835 was a bad summer and collecting was poor. On the 11th of July Elford left his collections and library in Rome and he and Jenny made their way north to the bustling port of Genoa. From here in October he began a long letter to John Children in London which he completed, after many additions, in December[43]. In it he discussed the possibility of exchanges of insects between Italy and England and assures Children:

'It gives me pleasure that you have taken up Entomology so warmly... If you will send me a list of the European Insects wanting at the Museum... I will send all that you want that pass through my hands from my Russian and Italian Correspondents which are not found in Italy, and I will exchange with the B.M. in preference to my Italian Correspondents'.

He also says if he has time next winter he will prepare an article on beetles, describing some new genera.

At the time of writing Genoa was not the healthiest of locations. Like many European coastal towns it was suffering the ravages of an epidemic of Asiatic cholera that had been sweeping through the continent since 1830. In October 1831 the disease had reached England, and spread rapidly. In the months that followed Plymouth had the seventh highest mortality rate in Britain with more than 1000 deaths across The Three Towns[44]. By April 1832 there were mass migrations out of Paris where the disease had appeared without warning. In his letter to Children Elford squeezed in just one isolated reference showing he and Jenny were not detached at Genoa from the pestilence: 'Sickness in our house and the colera raging in the city'.

It is not clear how much longer Elford and Jenny stayed in Genoa but eventually one of their domestic servants[45], who was from Frascata, a small village in the hills above Tortona, about 45 km from the coast, suggested they move inland to put some distance between themselves and the epidemic. They agreed and in late July 1836 they headed towards their servant's home town, settling in the neighbouring village of San Sebastiano Curone where they found lodgings at the house of the Ferraris[46]. For the next month Elford indulged in the predictable collecting, mainly butterflies, but on the morning of the 25th of August he was clearly unwell, feverish. It took just nine hours for the cholera to kill him[47]. He was 45 years old.

[44] Gill, 1979: 149-150.
[45] At this time they were employing a woman and a man.
[46] They lodged with the Ferraris from the 25th of July. This and subsequent information is taken from an excellent Italian account of these events by Eduardo Zavattari (1959). An amateur English translation © Keith Harrison is in the library of The Natural History Museum, London (unpublished manuscript).
[47] Death Certificate, transcribed in Zavattari (1959: 41).

— 30 —

Epilogue

I: Family

Elford Leach, who was always so active in life, found it equally difficult to rest in death. As a member of the Church of England, a Protestant, he could not be buried in the local Roman Catholic cemetery so a grave was made for him in a small meadow just beyond its wall, near the new parish church. Jenny, however, was unhappy with this arrangement and made representations to the Ferraris who very graciously agreed to have Elford's ashes removed to a small monument built against the wall in the courtyard of their house, an act of unusual compassion.

The courtyard was open to the highway on one side and a small pedestal of local stone was built against the wall facing the road. On top of this was fashioned a steeply pitched capping stone with a brief inscription, and the whole was enclosed by ornate iron railings. On the wall above the monument Jenny commissioned a large tablet of stone declaring to the world in Italian:

© *Natura*, Museo Civico di Storia Naturale di Milano

Elford Leach's sepulchre in the Ferraris' courtyard.

An artist's reconstruction by Dr Riccardo Giani (see below) of the appearance of the courtyard before later building works.

D.O.M.
GUGLIELMO ELFORD LEACH ESIMIO Dre E FISco
D'ISTORIA NATURALE PROFre EGREGGIO
ACCADEMICO ED AGGREGATO A DIVERSE SOCIETA'
LETTERARIE E SCIENTIFICHE
MEMBRO ONORARIO DELLA SOCIETA' REle DI LONDRA
DI QUELLE DI LINNEO E DEL COLEGGIO REALE
DI CHIRURGIA E DELLA ZEOLOGIA DI LONDRA DEL
COLLEGIO DI FISca E DI QUELLO DI WERNERIAN
D'EDIMBURGO
DELL'UNIVERSITA' DI MOSCOVIA DI BON DI CATANIA & c
EBBE E SUOI NATALI IN PLYMOUTH NEL Gno 2 FEBBo 1791
CONSACRO' DI CONTINUO I SUOI GIORNI ALLE LETTERE
ED A SOLLIEVO DEI SUOI SIMILI
PER LA SUE VIRTU' MORALI E SOCIALI
CARO ALLA PATRIA ALLA SOCIETA' ED ALLI AMICI
COLPITO DA CHOLERA MORBUS ASIATICO TERMINO'
IL CORSO DI SUA CARRIERA MORTALE IN S. SEBASTIANO
NELLA CASA DE FERRARIS LI 25 AGOSTO 1836
L'INFELICE SUA SORELLA CHE PREGA DAL SIGNORE
IL RIPOSO ETERNO AL SUO FRATELLO E CHE L'ETERNA
LUCE RISPLENDA SOPRA DI LUI HA POSTO QUESTA
LAPIDARIA MEMORIA

LE CENERI ESISTONO   QUI SOTTO OUE
VEDESI IL PICCOLO   MONUMENTO[1]

D.O.M.[2]

William Elford Leach eminent doctor and naturalist, Professor of Natural History, distinguished academic and associate of diverse literary and scientific societies, Honorary Fellow of the Royal Society of London and of the Linnean Society and of the Royal College of Surgeons and of the Zoological Society of London, of the College of Physicians and of the Wernerian Society of Edinburgh, of the universities of Moscow, of Bonn, of Catania &c.; having been born in Plymouth on the 2nd day of February 1791; continually dedicating his days to writing and to the relief of his fellow man through his moral and social virtues, beloved by his homeland, by society and by his friends; stricken by an epidemic of Asiatic cholera, ending the course of his mortal career in S. Sebastiano in the house of the Ferraris there[3] on the 25th August 1836; his unfortunate sister who prays to the Lord for eternal rest for her brother and for eternal light resplendent over him has placed this memorial stone.

The ashes exist here beneath the small monument you see before you.[4]

1   Zavattari, 1959: 42.
2   Deo Optimo Maximo ('God best and greatest').
3   Several obituaries and biographies say he died at the "Palazzo St Sebastiano". This should read 'palazzo of the Ferraris in San Sebastiano Curone'.
4   Translated by KH.

Thus passed William Elford Leach, and there he rested – for a while. Years passed until, in the early 1920s, Professor Pietro Giani was researching the history of San Sebastiano Curone and discovered the story behind this unusual sepulchre in the courtyard by the road. He also heard that the Ferraris' house had been sold and the new owner wanted to demolish the wall supporting the monument. With some urgency he tried to interest the British Consul at Genoa in rescuing the mortal remains of this English naturalist, but with no success[5], and his published article drawing attention to the dangers[6] failed to reach an international readership.

Despite Professor Giani's best efforts nothing could be done and the courtyard was roofed-over and turned into a storeroom for the new owner's wine business. Fortunately the whole wall was not demolished, but Elford Leach's monument now disappeared from view into a dark cellar surrounded by barrels and other casks. However, Pietro Giani's clarion call had not been in vain; he had alerted others to the existence of this long forgotten grave. Several years later Dr Riccardo Giani arrived to photograph Elford's last resting place. It took him some time to locate the right building, now so changed in appearance, but eventually he found himself in the wine-merchant's vaults:

'In the darkness, in a corner half concealed by barrels and covered by débris of every kind, Leach's sepulchre was finally discovered, still enclosed by the remains of iron railings, now almost completely destroyed. Freeing the monument from the wreckage and cleaning off the thick layer of dust disclosed, engraved on the stone, the following inscription:[7]'

[5] He also contacted the University of London who, not unsurprisingly, showed no interest. Unfortunately Jenny's dedication does not mention the British Museum and they were not contacted.
[6] Giani (1925).
[7] Dr Riccardo Giani *in* Zavattari (1959: 39). Translated by KH.

© *Natura*, Museo Civico di Storia Naturale di Milano

Elford Leach's sepulchre in the cellar of the wine merchant (Photograph by Riccardo Giani).

```
┌──────────────────────────────────┐
│   D. D. GULIELMI ELFORD LEACH     │
│              HIC                  │
│          IACENT OSSA              │
│      DIE 25 AUGUSTI 1836⁸         │
└──────────────────────────────────┘
```

Of the large stone dedication there was no sign, but a brief search located it on the other side of the cellar, on the ground behind some barrels.

Riccardo Giani published an account of his discoveries[9] and included a plea that the grave be rescued from this unseemly destruction. Noting that the grand entrance to the parish cemetery was about to be restored, he suggested this might provide both an excuse and an opportunity to bring Elford back into the light and set his monument there, against the outside wall. This time the community of San Sebastiano Curone wisely took their own decisions without waiting for the British. Elford Leach was raised from the cellar and laid to rest for the third time, by the cemetery's main gate, back in the sun of his adopted land where the beetles could crawl across his headstone, and the butterflies could flutter overhead.

Jenny

When Elford died Jenny did not return to England, but stayed in Italy for a number of years. She appears to have been unaware that Elford had prepared a Will[10] and as a result the Linnean Society received none of the gifts he had intended. In May 1839 she wrote to Italian entomologist Massimiliano Spinola[11], 'Have the goodness to inform me how I can send from London the work on molluscs of the late Dr Leach, which will soon be published. I have set aside *three copies*, one for you, one for Count Contarini, who did so much for me, if you would be kind enough to present it to him and to give him my most respectful greetings; and the final copy for the Academy of Sciences of Turin, of which W^m my brother was a member for eighteen years. I take the liberty of entrusting you with this because I am going soon to Rome, and from there pass to England[12].'

With this letter are Italian copies of: an obituary which had appeared in Britain in September 1836; an address to the British Association for the Advancement of Science's annual meeting at Edinburgh in 1834, where Leonard Jenyns[13] mentions Elford's work (see below); the list of Elford's publications from Cuvier's work *Règne Animal*; and a list of the societies of which Elford was a member[14]. It is clear Jenny called her brother 'William', despite his own preference, but it is not clear which of his mollusc works was soon to be published: his monograph on the British species, which had not progressed since he set it aside in the 1820s; his translation of Cuvier's work, which had never appeared; or another manuscript.

Jenny did not leave for England when she had planned. The following year she was at Florence writing to an unidentified correspondent at Turin:

---

[8] Dono Dedit ('Given to God') William Elford Leach. Here lie his bones. 25th day of August 1836.

[9] Giani (1928).

[10] Some years later when some of the Leach family lands at Compton, on the outskirts of Plymouth, were being sold, Jenny declared Elford had died intestate. It seems unlikely he had revoked his Will of 1824 and left nothing in its place.

[11] Marchese Massimiliano Spinola (1780-1857).

[12] Letter: Jenny Leach to Spinola, 19th May 1839 (Loc: Academy of Sciences of Turin). This is an English translation by KH from an Italian text which was probably a translation of an English original.

[13] Leonard Jenyns (from 1871 'Leonard Blomefield') (1800-1893). Ordained. A friend and biographer of John Henslow. In 1835 published *Manual of British Vertebrate Animals*, with the ornithology written by Charles Lucien Bonaparte. He assisted Henslow in recommending Darwin for a position on the *Beagle* (after first Henslow then Jenyns had decided not to apply for the position themselves). Jenyns edited a publication on the fish collected by Darwin.

[14] Jenny says Elford was a Fellow of the Royal Society of Edinburgh. He never claimed this himself and the Royal Society of Edinburgh has no Fellowship record for him (Dr Lesley Campbell, Fellowship Officer, *pers. com.*, 2000).

'Most illustrious Sir

Please forgive me if I send to your lordship[15] some papers concerning my late brother Dr Leach, in the knowledge that he had the pleasure of meeting your lordship at the home of Marchese Massimiliano Spinola, just before you were about to leave for Sardinia in 1836. As he was a member of the Academy of Turin for eighteen years, I wish your lordship to see in how much esteem he was held by your fellow academicians.

In a short while one of his works on molluscs will be made public, a copy of which will be delivered to the Academy of Turin by Marchese Massimiliano Spinola. Last year I sent a copy of these papers to the aforementioned Marchese Spinola, that they should be added to the work on molluscs at the time of publication. But since there were a number of errors in the extract published in the journal[16], and the article regarding the works of my late brother was badly translated, I ask your lordship that if you should ever receive this version, not to give it any consideration.[17]'

Despite the optimism regarding the imminent publication of the mollusc work, it appears it was still not forthcoming.

Jenny may have remained in Italy for several more years as the first record we have of her return to Plymouth is a directory entry for 1850 when she was living at N° 3 Brunswick Terrace, Stoke[18]. She lived in this house for the next nine years[19], dying there at the age of 79 on the 1st of December 1859, exactly one week after the publication of *The Origin of Species*.

Jonathan

There is no record Jonathan ever returned to live in Plymouth. He presumably made his home initially in London where – in later life at least – he owned two leasehold houses, N[os] 10 and 35 Gilbert Street, Oxford Street[20]. His memoirs, *Rough Sketches of the Life of an Old Soldier*, were published in 1831. Four years later he followed them with a summary of the knowledge gained by the 95th in its habitual role in the Peninsula, *Recollections and Reflections Relative to the Duties of Troops Composing the Advanced Corps of an Army*, and three years after that he published a *Sketch of the Field Services of the Rifle Brigade, from its Formation to the Battle of Waterloo*. This last work, of 32 pages, was the first attempt to record the wartime services of British rifle units (rather than the activity of individual riflemen)[21].

By November 1840 he seems to have been spending at least part of the year in Worthing, on the English south coast, and may already have retired there. He would maintain his links with this town until his death.

In 1841 the British Association for the Advancement of Science held its 11th Annual Meeting at Plymouth. Jonathan was present as an annual member of the Association and presumably joined in order to attend this conference. He is listed as 'Colonel Leach, Penlee Villas, Stoke, Devonport' but George was also an annual member for that year, when his address is

[15] The Italian phrase used, "V. S. Illma", technically means 'your illustrious person' (Dott. Alessandra Flore, Department of Italian, Leeds University, *pers. com.* 1997) but it is unlikely this was the original English. We have substituted 'your lordship' as a probable original without knowing whether the recipient was titled.

[16] One of the obituaries included with the letter to Spinola was an Italian translation of an obituary dated September 1836, "estratto da una Gazetta Inglese" (*extracted from an English journal*).

[17] Letter: Jenny Leach [to ?] 11th May 1840 (Loc: Academy of Sciences of Turin). Translated from an Italian translation of an English original by Dr Alessandra Flore. The original bears the Italian subscript "Translated from English by Luigi Battilana, Principal Tutor of the Institute of the Deaf and Dumb, Genoa".

[18] White (1850). She was not mentioned in Flintoff (1844).

[19] Her servant during part of this time was a Mary Bassett (mentioned as such in the Will of her brother George dated 25th October 1861. Loc: West Devon Record Office, Plymouth).

[20] Will of Jonathan Leach dated 28th April 1851 (Loc: Public Record Office, Kew, London).

[21] Currently (January 2002) the full text of this work is on the world-wide web site: home.vicnet.net.au/~rifles95/ (Although we appreciate this is unlikely to assist those reading this in 2052).

© William P.C. Adams

Jonathan Leach's campaign chest.

The feet can be unscrewed and the top and bottom separate (see detail below) so they can be placed in a canvas pannier slung across the back of a baggage mule.

given simply as 'Stoke'. By 1844 George lived at Penlee Crescent. If he had moved before 1841 Jonathan may simply have been visiting Plymouth and using his brother's address[22]. Jonathan does not appear as a Plymouth resident in any of the Plymouth directories seen.

In 1847 he published his last book, *Rambles along the Styx: Being Colloquies between Old Soldiers who are Supposed to have met in the Stygian Shades*. This was a series of fictional conversations between old soldiers, woven with his opinions on military policy (and policy-makers). At this time he was still in touch with some of his old Peninsula colleagues and they would meet regularly for dinner in London. Perhaps these social gatherings gave him the idea for the book.

Jonathan died in Worthing on the 14th of January 1855 shortly before his 71st birthday. Like the rest of the family he had never married but he seems to have had a close relationship with a Miss Jane Boxall[23]. He made financial provision for her in his Will, left her money to buy mourning dress, and bequeathed to her his watch and letter seals and all his 'wearing apparel' (this last a strangely personal gift).

George

When Elford and Jenny left for the Continent in 1826, George continued to put his efforts into his Devonport law firm. By 1830 the name had changed to *Leach, Little & Woollcombe* following the retirement of Lugger and the recruitment of new partner Thomas Woollcombe[24], but the offices were still

[22] Penlee Villas may also have been known as Penlee Crescent or the address may have been incorrectly transcribed. On the 1st of October 1840 Jonathan had written to John Philippart from Stoke, but on the 22nd of November that year he wrote to William Siborne from Worthing (see letters in Appendix 5).
[23] She was originally from Canterbury in Kent. We do not know when they first met. It is possible she was his maid.
[24] Presumably a relation of Henry Woollcombe but we have been unable to trace Thomas's dates or family ties. He was Town Clerk for Devonport in 1850 (White, 1850).

St Michael's Terrace, Stoke.

at Nº 53 St Aubyn Street. The firm was obviously thriving and both George Leach and Philip Little had moved to homes in the recently built St Michael's Terrace in Stoke: George to Nº 5 and Little to Nº 4[25]. Stoke was a leafy up-market suburb on rising ground behind Devonport containing a scattering of fruit-gardens and tea-shops, thronged with sightseers during the summer months. St Michael's Terrace dominated the high ground in the village, giving it commanding views over Plymouth Sound and the surrounding countryside.

As the 1830s dawned and tension again mounted in Britain (as elsewhere in Europe), the pressures for political reform increased. More than a decade after Peterloo and under a different government, the reformers began to make some headway. After several attempts in 1832 to pass a Bill in parliament giving the vote to much greater numbers of men, the *Reform Act* was finally passed. This Act redistributed seats in the House of Commons; removed 'rotten boroughs' (virtually fictional communities of a handful of houses that were nevertheless sending MPs to London under the patronage of local landowners); and gave better representation to the growing urban centres. The electorate of Britain was increased by 50%, primarily by giving the vote to men living in houses worth £10 per year in rent. The right to elect MPs was now held by what we would recognise as the men of the new middle class.

To introduce the new system a general election was required and this was held in December 1832. Devonport had been allocated two seats in the restructured House of Commons and the local reformers proposed their own candidate to stand against the establishment's nominees. They chose local lawyer, zealous Liberal and popular man-about-town, George Leach.

Unfortunately for the reformers, the voters of Devonport saw their futures linked inexorably to the town's main employer, the Royal Naval

[25] By 1857 Little was living at Nº 2 (Billing, 1857). It is not clear whether he had moved or the houses had been renumbered.

487

Devonport in the late 1820s.

In the centre is the classical Town Hall, built 1821-1822. Beyond the Town Hall is a column surmounted by a statue of George IV, erected to commemorate the change of name from Plymouth Dock to Devonport in 1824. On the right, in Egyptian style, is the Devonport Library, originally built in 1823 to be the Devonport & Stonehouse Mathematical School (which went out of business). Between the Library and the column can be seen Mount Zion Chapel, built in the Hindu style in 1823-1824.

dockyard, and the other candidates, Sir George Grey[26] and Sir Edward Codrington[27], had strong naval influence. Grey was the nephew of the Prime Minister, Lord Grey[28], and son of a naval Captain who had been superintendent of the Royal Navy's dockyard at Portsmouth[29]. Codrington was an Admiral who had captained *HMS Orion* at Trafalgar, where he also led a squadron, and was a former naval Commander-in-Chief in the Mediterranean. With all three aspirants standing as Liberal candidates, George Leach did not stand much of a chance. The votes cast were[30]:

Sir George Grey *Bt* (Liberal) 1178
Sir Edward Codrington (Liberal) 891
George Leach (Liberal) 575

The campaign on the part of the reformers must have been rather turbulent as after the election Thomas Woollcombe – who appears to have acted as George's political agent – was sued for libel, fined and spent a month in prison[31]. George did not stand for parliament again and Grey and Codrington were re-elected at the general elections of 1835 and 1837.

In 1833 George showed his own interests in ships and sail when he sat on the Council of the *Port of Plymouth Royal Clarence Regatta Club* when it changed its name to *The Royal Western Yacht Club*. Henry Woollcombe was also a Council member.

George also seems to have had some natural history interests and by the late 1830s he owned an extensive collection of birds and mammals, especially from Dartmoor, which he eventually presented to the Devon and Cornwall Natural History Society at Plymouth[32]. It is not clear whether George built this collection himself or inherited Elford's collection following his death, but he was certainly interested in birds as a sportsman[33] and had donated a grebe to the British Museum by 1816[34]). It may have been this interest, and

[26] George Grey (1799-1882). Had inherited a baronetcy from his father in 1828.
[27] Edward Codrington (1770-1851).
[28] Charles, 2nd Earl Grey (1764-1845).
[29] Captain Sir George Grey RN, *Bt* (d. 1828).
[30] Dod, 1852: 81.
[31] Gill, 1979: 115.
[32] Bellamy, 1839: 194-195, 454; D'Urban & Mathew, 1892: lxxxv. D'Urban and Mathew confuse this George Leach of Stoke with his father George Leach (who never lived at Stoke), saying it was the latter who had the natural history collection.
[33] Moore, 1830: 300.
[34] Leach, 1816. *Systematic Catalogue* at p. 35.

his active social enthusiasm, that led to his registering as an annual member of the British Association for its 1841 Plymouth meeting.

It was about this time, or shortly before, that he finally retired from work[35] and his firm became simply *Little & Woollcombe*. Although he was now a man of considerable property and means, and despite the attractions of the impressive St Michael's Terrace, on his retirement he moved a short distance to Nº 6 Penlee Crescent, Stoke. Here he maintained his interests in politics and public life, and his support for Devon's philanthropic causes. He was also by this time a good friend of Liberal politician Sir William Molesworth, the son of Lady Mary Molesworth, until Molesworth's death in 1855[36]. George kept his good health during his retirement and after ten more years in Stoke the lure of the open countryside drew him to a house he had been building in the country at Crapstone, 13 km away at Buckland Monachorum. He had built this new home near the old mansion of Crapstone, which earlier in the century had been the property of the Elfords.

It was shortly after moving to Crapstone that George was contacted by John Gray at the British Museum, now Keeper of Zoology. Gray wanted permission from the family to edit for publication Elford's manuscript on the British molluscs, cared for by Thomas Bell for the last 25 years or more[37]. George and Jenny agreed and the work finally appeared as a single volume in 1852 (although whether Elford would have approved of the manuscript appearing without updating must be questioned).

Some years after Gray's contact, in about 1856, another caller enquired about Elford. This time it was Plymouth dentist Spence Bate[38]. Bate had developed a great interest in the Crustacea and was a Fellow of the Royal Society and of the Linnean Society. At this time he was preparing a two volume work on the smaller British crustaceans with John Westwood[39], Professor of Zoology at Oxford. He was also preparing a talk for the Devonshire Association entitled *William Elford Leach M.D.* and was gathering background information. He gave this talk on the 12th of February 1857 but sadly no text survives. However it was almost certainly Spence Bate who provided the information for the excellent (although not wholly accurate) biography of Elford in *The English Cyclopædia*[40]. When the first volume of Bate and Westwood's crustacean work was published in 1863 they included an engraving of Elford's birthplace at Hoegate[41], which was the first public indication he was born here; information presumably provided by Jenny and George.

George was at Crapstone for more than a decade, during which he lost first Jonathan, then Jenny, and was left the sole surviving member of the family; but he too was growing old. In 1861, at the age of 79, he suffered a 'congestion of the brain and partial paralysis[42]' (presumably a stroke), and even with his domestic servant in residence his lapses in mental clarity meant he could no longer be cared for properly in the country. In October he drew up his Will and the following month moved into town to live at Nº 6 Lansdowne Place, Plymouth, in the care of two male attendants.

[35] *The Plymouth and Devonport Journal*, 6th March 1862 says that by 1862 he had been retired upwards of 20 years.

[36] Sir William Molesworth, 8th Baronet (1810-1855). Was elected MP for East Cornwall in 1832 and 1835; Leeds 1837; and Southwark (in London) 1845, a seat he held until his death. He was appointed Colonial Secretary in 1855 but died several months later.

[37] As late as April 1836 Gray had not seen the manuscript (House of Commons, 1836: para. 2606). Only two or three copies ever existed: one in the possession of Thomas Bell, another with John Curtis (*fide* Gray, J.E. 1840. *Turton's British Shells* page 58).

[38] Charles Spence Bate (1818-1889). Kelly & Co. (1856) say Bate was living (or practising) at Nº 8 Lockyer Street. Billing (1857) says Nº 8 Mulgrave Terrace. Elvin's Directory of 1862 [not seen by KH] says Nº 8 Mulgrave Place.

[39] John Obadiah Westwood (1805-1893). He was Hope Professor of Zoology. The first to hold that position.

[40] Knight, C. (ed.). Elford Leach at Vol. 6, BIOGRAPHY: paras 824-826.

[41] Bate & Westwood, 1863: 12. Reproduced here in Chapter 1.

[42] This information and the following details taken from *The Plymouth and Devonport Journal*, 6th March 1862.

This sudden change in his health and circumstances affected him deeply. He was profoundly depressed and on the 19th of December tried to take his own life. For his own protection he was now kept under close observation – one or other of his carers always with him – but on the evening of the 28th of February 1862 his attendant[43] slipped out of the house for half an hour, leaving George alone in the drawing room. When he returned the house was empty.

George's body was found the next day in a sea cave at the foot of the cliffs beneath Plymouth Hoe. Did he fall? The coroner thought not. The verdict was 'Suicide while of unsound mind by throwing himself into the sea.'

George Leach's character was summarised in the *Plymouth Herald*[44] shortly after his death, in an anonymous letter submitted by an old acquaintance:

'The presence of George Leach, when past his seventieth year, was sunshine to the beholder. Handsomeness of person was still the least of the qualities that marked the presentment of a man justly possessing the attachment of his own sex and equally favoured by the regard of the other; not the less, perhaps, because he had lived with more than Benedick's resolve to 'die a bachelor'...

How often has the writer seen his general manner and fair, radiant countenance beam on all alike, to the occasion of an impulsive wish in the observers that they were like him,—that they could realise in themselves the mild contentment and all-harmonious qualities he exhibited. His ever welcoming presence had its recommendation in a peculiar frankness of easy good humour and in a seeming stability of constitutional vigour that left us to contemplate a fine old age, like a 'lusty winter – frosty but kindly' and the memory ever green. Only remembering these last impressions, the verdict of the coroner's inquest came upon one like an incredible 'fallacy'[45]

43 Robert Clifton.
44 Correctly the *Plymouth, Devonport and Stonehouse Herald*.
45 Undated cutting (but seemingly shortly after the announcement of his death) in the West Devon Record Office, Plymouth. Ref: George Wightwick, Newspaper Cuttings, WDR Acc. 581/1 82. The letter was signed cryptically "PHILO".

Plymouth Hoe (in the left distance) with the Citadel beyond.

490

As the last of the family, George left his considerable real-estate to his two former partners, Philip Little and Thomas Woollcombe. Jonathan's medals were left to his cousin by marriage, Henry Cranstoun Adams, an attorney at Exmouth and Clerk to the Magistrates, whose father General Sir George Pownall Adams[46] had married Sir William Elford's daughter Elizabeth[47]. The Leach family paintings were left to the Reverend George James Adams of Budleigh Salterton, Devon. At the end of the 19th century Henry Cranstoun Adams owned portraits of George and Jenny Leach, parents of the four children, painted by James Northcote, but these cannot now be traced. It is through the extreme kindness and interest of the descendants of the Devonshire Adams, especially William (Bill) Adams in Florida, that we have been able to include here portraits of Jonathan Leach and Sir William Elford, and to show Jonathan's campaign chest and medals. We are extremely grateful for the family's assistance with this and other details.

II: Army

In the years following Waterloo the Duke of Wellington returned to public life in Britain, a greater hero than he had ever been. Among the many honours and positions bestowed on him, from 1819-1826 he was Governor of Plymouth (a non-executive role)[48]. As a staunch Tory politician he served as British Prime Minister from 1828-1830 and again in 1834. He held many other public offices under George IV and William IV and under Queen Victoria when she came to the throne in 1837[49]. Wellington spent his life as a living legend, finally dying in 1852. Other than some occasional public acrimony regarding his political decisions, he was universally respected and revered, but he was not much loved—however this may not have bothered him unduly. The Clerk to the Privy Council, Charles Greville said following his death: "The Duke was a good-natured, but not an amiable man; he had no tenderness in his disposition, and never evinced much affection for any of his relations. His nature was hard, and he does not appear to have had any real affection for anybody, man or woman, during the latter years of his life[50]".

Of those more intimately connected to Jonathan Leach: at least four of his Lieutenants went on to become Generals.

Harry Smith left the Rifle Brigade in 1826 to serve as a 'staff officer (unattached)[51]' in Canada, Jamaica, the Cape of Good Hope (where he was promoted to full Colonel in the army in 1837) and India (where he was given a local rank of Major-General in 1840). He was knighted in 1844 and made a Baronet in 1846. His rank of Major-General was extended to the British Army at large in 1846 and he visited Britain briefly in 1847. On the 20th of May, during that visit, he received the freedom of the city of London and in the evening a dinner was held in his honour at Willis's Rooms.

[46] Died 1856.
[47] Elizabeth Elford (1782-1837).
[48] Major-General Denis Pack was the Lieutenant-Governor from 12th August 1819.
[49] George IV's brother, William Duke of Clarence (1765-1837) acceded to the throne when George died on the 26th of June 1830. When William died on the 20th of June 1837 he was succeeded by Alexandrina 'Victoria' (1819-1901) – who had originally been christened Alexandrina Victorina (Stanhope, 1888: 295) – the daughter of another brother, Edward Duke of Kent (1767-1820). Charles Greville said Queen Victoria's father was, "the greatest rascal that ever went unhung" (Wilson (1927) 1: 400).
[50] Wilson (1927) 1: 173.
[51] i.e. not attached to any regiment.

Present were a hundred soldiers including Sir Andrew Barnard, Sir Hew Ross, the Duke of Richmond, John Kincaid and Jonathan Leach. The same year, former Captain, now Major-General, Charley Beckwith[52], had written to Smith, 'The last enemy has done his worst on very many of our Peninsula companions. Sir Andrew and some Riflemen still remain to dine together sometimes in Albemarle Street[53]... Johnny Kincaid regulates the secrets of a prison-house, Jonathan Leach writes histories; thus each labours in his vocation, and has still a conceit left him in his misery.[54]'

From England Smith was posted back to South Africa as Governor of the Cape and Commander-in-Chief, with the local rank of Lieutenant-General. The South African town *Harrismith* was named after him, and neighbouring *Ladysmith* was named after his Spanish wife Juana[55] (whom he had met in the Peninsula at the storming of Badajoz). He returned to Britain in 1853 and was confirmed as a full Lieutenant-General in the army the following year. He died in 1860.

After the Peninsula War William Cox, who had entered Lisbon after Vimeiro with Jonathan Leach and Benjamin Harris, exchanged into the 1st (Royal) Regiment of Dragoons. A lifelong friend of Jonathan, he went on to become Major-General Sir William Cox. His brother John was Jonathan Leach's senior Lieutenant at Waterloo. John was promoted to Captain in 1819 and, like his brother, was later Major-General Sir John Cox. John Fitzmaurice too, Jonathan's junior Lieutenant at Waterloo, went on to become Major-General Sir John Fitzmaurice.

Scotsman Johnny Kincaid was finally promoted to Captain in 1826 and sold out of the Rifle Brigade on the 21st of June 1831. His book *Adventures in the Rifle Brigade*, an account of his service up to the battle of Waterloo, had been published the previous year. This was followed in 1835 by a collection of anecdotes, *Random Shots from a Rifleman*. His lively humorous narrative has ensured these works remain among the best read of all Peninsula memoirs. In October 1844 he was appointed Exon of the Royal Bodyguard of the Yeomen of the Guard[56], and in 1847 also became government Inspector of Prisons for Scotland. This role was expanded three years later to Inspector of Factories and Prisons for Scotland. In 1852 he became the senior Exon of the Yeoman of the Guard and (as was customary for this position) was knighted. He died in Hastings in 1862 at the age of 75. He had never married.

George Simmons recovered from his Waterloo wound to spend another 30 years in the army, with his back supported by stays. He served in Britain until 1825, when he was sent to Canada. In 1828 he was promoted to Captain and in 1834 he married in Jersey. He retired from the army in 1845 as a Major and died in Jersey in 1858 aged 72. Some years after Waterloo Harry Smith had urged him to publish his journals and correspondence from the Peninsula and Flanders, but it was 1899 before these were edited for publication by Rifle Brigade historian Colonel Willoughby Verner[57] under the title *A British Rifle Man*[58].

52 Beckwith had lost a leg at Waterloo while on staff duties as an Assistant Quartermaster General and had been promoted to Lieutenant-Colonel and awarded a *C.B.* As he was unable to resume active field command, he was put on half pay from 1820. He visited Piedmont in 1828 and settled there for the rest of his life, undertaking educational and missionary work among the poor, for whom he established 120 schools. Promotions above Lieutenant-Colonel in the army at that time were on seniority (length of time in the rank; the longest serving officer at any rank would be next to be promoted) so although on half-pay and not on active army duty he was promoted to Colonel in 1837 and had reached Major-General by 1846. He was knighted by King Charles Albert, of the Kingdom of Sardinia, in 1848. When he died thousands of local people attended his funeral.

53 Albermale (*sic*) in the original. Albemarle Street also hosts the Royal Institution.

54 Smith (1901) **2**: 210-211.

55 Juana Maria de los Dolores de León (born in about 1798).

56 Popularly called 'Beef-eaters'. The Yeoman of the Guard are 80 former soldiers of impeccable character who perform state ceremonial functions wearing the livery of the year of their foundation, 1485. Since the time of William IV their 6 officers (1 Captain, 1 Lieutenant, 1, Ensign, 1 Clerk of the Cheque and 2 Exons) have worn the uniform of the Waterloo period, highly appropriate for John Kincaid.

57 Verner had served in the Rifle Brigade.

William Surtees left the Rifle Brigade in 1826 on medical grounds. His health had begun to suffer at Glasgow, aggravated by winter fogs and smoke from the local factories. He published his memoirs in 1833, *Twenty-five Years in the Rifle Brigade*.

Benjamin Harris had been retired on medical grounds after the Walcheren expedition and returned to civilian life as a shoe-maker. By the early 1830s he had a business in Richmond Street, Soho, London, where he related his adventures with the Rifles to Henry Curling, an officer of the 52nd Light Infantry on half-pay. Curling edited the story for publication and it appeared in 1848 as *Recollections of Rifleman Harris (Old 95th): with anecdotes of his officers and his comrades*. Harris died ten years later in a London workhouse, 'believed insane'[59]. He was 77.

Ned Costello and Augustine found they could not live in London on his meagre pension so they decided she would return to France for a while to live with her family (who had always disapproved of their liaison). Costello tells us that some time later he received news she had died. She had not. In 1822 Augustine married a local man from the vicinity of Moeuvres and had three more children[60]. Costello also married and he and his wife had seven children. By then he was apparently a shoe-maker like Benjamin Harris, but with so many children to feed he was tempted to earn his living another way. During The Carlist War in Spain in 1835, although now 47 years of age, he joined the British Auxiliary Legion, an 'unofficial' British corps[61] then being formed to fight on the side of the infant Queen Isabella against the supporters of Don Carlos, who was claiming the Spanish throne. Costello was recruited as a Lieutenant then promoted to Captain. He served in the vicinity of Vitoria, and in an engagement near San Sebastián was wounded in the knee. The Legion was a brutal and unprofessional environment, not to Costello's taste, and after further service in an administrative role he returned to England and his family. In 1838 he was appointed a Yeoman Warder at the Tower of London and the following year the *United Service Journal* began serialising his memoirs. These were collected as a book, *Adventures of a Soldier*, in 1841, with a second edition in 1852. He died in 1869 having written of the colleagues of his Peninsula days, "Their stubborn spirits and perforated bodies formed keystones for the fame of our immortal Wellington, whose standard might have found a sandy support but for the individual bravery of the soldiers of his invincible divisions.[62]"

Medals

It was many decades before the survivors of those invincible divisions were finally recognised by the nation with the award of a decoration. The introduction of the Waterloo medal may have set a precedent, but it was not until 1846 that Wellington, as Commander-in-Chief of the British Forces, agreed to the issuing of a General Service Medal for the wars of 1793-1815; an award he had always previously opposed and which he only

[58] Simmon's brother Joseph ('Joe') (1792-1882) fought as a volunteer with the 95th from 1812 and was commissioned in the regiment, but he later exchanged into the 41st (Welsh) Regiment, ending his career as a Lieutenant-Colonel and *CB*.
[59] Hathaway, 1996: 191.
[60] Hathaway, 1997: 299.
[61] This was not a British army force but the UK Parliament suspended its *Foreign Enlistment Act* to allow the Legion's formation. In fact the Legion was viewed as little better than a force of mercenaries.
[62] Hathaway, 1997: 319.

approved after Queen Victoria expressed a wish that the medal be struck[63].

For the Peninsula Jonathan Leach received the silver medal and an impressive 12 clasps for[64] 'ROLEIA, VIMIERA, BUSACO, FUENTES D'ONOR, CIUDAD RODRIGO, BADAJOZ, SALAMANCA, VITTORIA, PYRENEES, NIVELLE, NIVE, and TOULOUSE'. The edge bears the legend 'JONATHAN LEACH, CAPT. 95TH RIFLES' and the ribbon is scarlet with gold borders.

Regiments

The British Army has undergone many reorganisations during the last 200 years but the legacy of the old regiments from the war with Napoleon lives on. At the end of the Battle of Waterloo the 1st Foot Guards repelled the attack of grenadiers of the French Imperial Guard. The following month[65] the Prince Regent honoured their action by renaming the regiment the '1st, or Grenadier, Regiment of Foot Guards' and today's 'Grenadier Guards' were born.

Jonathan Leach's General Service Medal.

© William P.C. Adams

The Rifle Brigade served continuously in trouble spots throughout the growing (then shrinking) British Empire. Since 1966, together with the descendants of the 43rd and 52nd Regiments, and the 5th battalion of the 60th, it has formed an integral part of the distinguished British rifle regiment *The Royal Green Jackets*[66].

III: Natural History

it may be well to bear in mind that by the word "creation" the zoologist means "a process he knows not what".

Richard Owen
Address to the British Association (1858)

When Elford Leach began his career British zoologists were wedded to Linnæus's system of cataloguing the natural world and were fiercely resistant to modernisation. Twenty years later he was acknowledged as virtually solely responsible for awakening a sleeping nation to the need for

[63] Wilson (1927) **2**: 330.
[64] These are the spellings on the clasps.
[65] 29th July 1815.
[66] The Regimental Museum of the Royal Green Jackets is at Winchester and the regiment has its own world-wide web site. The section on Riflemen in Chapter 2 was written after consulting this site and the Regiment's assistance is gratefully acknowledged.
Postscript
In 2007 *The Royal Green Jackets* was absorbed into a new British regiment named simply *The Rifles*, and history came full circle.

a new approach. William Swainson certainly had no doubt that it was Elford who had, "contributed more than any other to break down the strongholds of Linnean nomenclature, and introduce the numerous improvements of the Continental nomenclature.[67]"

In 1834 the British Association for the Advancement of Science held its 4th annual meeting at Edinburgh, where the Reverend Leonard Jenyns reported on *The Recent Progress and Present State of Zoology*[68]. Discussing the science in the years before 1817 he noted the advances made on the Continent, then continued:

'England, we fear, has but little to produce as the result of her labours in zoology during the same period. Our countrymen were too much riveted to the principles of the Linnæan school to appreciate the value of the natural system. Although there were some good descriptive works in different departments, and a few excellent observers, amongst whom Montagu will ever hold a distinguished place, there was in general but little attention paid to structure with a view to elucidate the natural affinities of animals. The most remarkable, if not the only exception is undoubtedly to be found in Kirby's *Monographia Apum Angliæ* [Monograph on British Bees], a work which, though exclusively devoted to the illustration of a single Linnæan genus of insects, presents a model for naturalists in all departments, from the profound views of its very illustrious author. There were few, however, who followed up the path which was thus opened to them. There was a general repugnance to everything that appeared like an innovation on the system of Linnæus; and for many years subsequently to the publication of the above work, which appeared as far back as in 1802, zoology, which was making rapid strides in France and other parts of the Continent, remained in this country nearly stationary. It is mainly to Dr. Leach that we are indebted for having opened the eyes of English zoologists to the importance of those principles which had long guided the French naturalists. Whilst he greatly contributed to the advancement of the natural system by his own researches, he gave a turn to those of others, and made the first step towards weaning his countrymen from the school they had so long adhered to. [*He then listed Elford's principal publications, saying they...*] sufficiently testify the obligations conferred by him on zoology. At the same time they form a marked epoch in the history of this science, as connected with our own country.[69]'

We do not know whether Elford Leach ever had the satisfaction of seeing this Report when it was published in 1835.

The following year, the year of his death, the House of Commons completed its two year investigation of the management of the British Museum. During their interviews the Committee received confirmation from Edward Griffiths – translator of Cuvier's *Règne Animal* [The Animal Kingdom] – that Elford was the first to give 'the impulse of improvement'

[67] Swainson, 1840: 237.
[68] British Association, 1835: 143ff.
[69] British Association, 1835: 148-149.

to zoology at the British Museum and beyond. Griffiths noted, "zoology was utterly neglected; 20 years ago it was anything but popular; certainly there were very few amateurs that paid much attention to it."

"In your judgment," the committee proposed, "Dr Leach has the eminent credit of having raised the science of zoology in England?"

"Indeed I think so" replied Griffiths[70].

John Gray too made it clear to the committee it was Elford who "was the first to make the English acquainted, by his works and by his improved manner of arranging the collections of the Museum, with the progress that had been made in natural science on the Continent. Thus a new impetus was given to zoology, which has gradually improved into a popular taste[71]".

Elford's influence had been widely felt, and with the improved approach to studying nature came a change of emphasis, away from the particular towards the general.

"The object in former days" said fellow MP Nicholas Vigors[72] when he was interviewed, "was chiefly to investigate the properties of, and to assign names to, individual species. The present improved state of science leads us to consider these species as united by their affinities and analogies into one grand system; to view them not merely as a collection of detached individuals, but as a series of individuals forming one grand and harmonious plan.[73]"

The 1830s were an exciting time for zoology. Ideas were flowing in all directions, but (mirroring the development of the discipline) they were springing, poorly understood, from unconnected individuals. They had not yet merged into their own 'grand and harmonious plan'. That would come with Darwin.

Darwin had sailed from Devonport aboard *HMS Beagle* on the 27th of December 1831, one year before George Leach stood for parliament in the town. Darwin was on the *Beagle* for nearly five years and was on his way home between Brazil and the Cape Verde Islands when Elford Leach died. He finally disembarked at Falmouth on the 2nd of October 1836.

It was 23 years before Darwin published *The Origin of Species*[74]. He had drafted the work much earlier and laid it aside but in 1858 he received a letter from Indonesia from naturalist Alfred Wallace. Wallace asked Darwin's opinion on an idea he had had regarding the way species might change. Darwin was shocked. Wallace had arrived independently at the same view Darwin had expressed in his own manuscripts.

Doing the honourable thing, Darwin arranged that a paper by himself and one by Wallace should be read (in both their absences) at the Linnean Society that same year. This happened on the 1st of July 1858 at a special meeting prompted by the death of botanist Robert Brown. Meanwhile Darwin resurrected his manuscript and prepared a much shortened abstract, written not for scientific readers but for an educated public. This abstract was *The Origin of Species*[75].

[70] House of Commons, 1836: paras 2108, 2119.
[71] House of Commons, 1836: para. 2463.
[72] Nicholas Aylward Vigors (1785-1840). He studied zoology from 1819 until he entered Parliament in 1832. Became editor of the *Zoological Journal* and was the first Secretary of the Zoological Society of London.
[73] House of Commons, 1836: para. 1296.
[74] On the 24th of November 1859. The 1250 copies of the 1st edition sold out on the first day.
[75] The full work, which would have contained more detailed analysis and full references to other scientists' work, was never published. It was never needed. *Origin* alone achieved the desired result.

In this seminal work Darwin made several critical observations:

- resources in nature (food, space) are limited.
- therefore there is competition for them.
- within each species animals and plants show variation.

He argued that in a competition in which the competitors exhibit different attributes, some attributes would give an advantage and some would not. In a "struggle for life" those attributes lending an advantage could lead to that competitor – and hence the attribute – surviving. In this way some characters would automatically be selected by nature, survive, and be inherited by the next generation. In this process of *natural selection,* with some characters passing from one generation to the next and others being eliminated, the species carrying the characters would change over time: there would be evolution.

The concept of evolution, or 'transformism', was an old idea, and change in the appearance of species over time was increasingly under discussion, but there had been two problems: the length of time evolution would take; and the fact that no-one could see a mechanism by which it might occur.

In the late eighteenth and early nineteenth centuries the Earth was thought to be only several thousand years old, too short a time to allow evolution to have an effect. The acceptance of Hutton's ideas (that the complex geological structure of the world had been produced by the slow relentless action of the same mechanisms of deposition and weathering that we can see in action today) awoke scientists to the fact that the Earth must be significantly older than they thought. With that, evolution could be taken more seriously.

Uncovering an evolutionary mechanism was a different problem. Lamarck had struggled with this but his 'inheritance of acquired characteristics' had convinced few people. Darwin and Wallace's Natural Selection provided the key which finally unlocked the door. Once seen, it was considered by some to be glaringly obvious. When British professor Thomas Huxley[76] first read Darwin's text he announced, "How extremely stupid not to have thought of that!"

In fact several people *had* already thought of that. The writing had been on the wall for some time.

As early as 1818 a posthumous paper by William Wells[77] (based on a presentation to the Royal Society in 1813) gave *An Account of a White female, part of whose skin resembled that of a Negro.* In his discussion Wells considered variation in humans and noted not only that skin colour varied, but that natives of equatorial Africa and natives of Europe differed in their susceptibility to tropical diseases. Looking at other species, he observed all individuals vary to some degree and agriculturalists use this to improve their stock by selective breeding. Crucially, he put these facts together, recognising that what humans do by design...

[76] Thomas Henry Huxley (1825-95). Professor of Natural History at the Royal School of Mines, London. When Darwin avoided publicly promoting his own work, Huxley became his greatest advocate and was known as 'Darwin's Bulldog'.
[77] William Charles Wells (1757-1817).

'seems to be done with equal efficacy, though more slowly, by nature, in the formation of varieties of mankind, fitted for the country which they inhabit. Of the accidental varieties of man, which would occur among the first few and scattered inhabitants of the middle regions of Africa, some one would be better fitted than the others to bear the diseases of the country. This race would consequently multiply, while the others would decrease; not only from their inability to sustain the attacks of disease, but from their incapacity of contending with their more vigorous neighbours. The colour of this vigorous race I take for granted, from what has been already said, would be dark. But the same disposition to form varieties still existing, a darker and a darker race would in the course of time occur: and as the darkest would be the best fitted for the climate, this would at length become the most prevalent, if not the only race, in the particular country in which it had originated.[78]'

Wells said this when Charles Darwin was just four years old. This view of a dynamic selection from ever-present variations was a clear expression of the elements of Natural Selection, but its importance was overlooked until comparison with *The Origin of Species* more than 40 years later.

Similarly, in the year the *Beagle* left Plymouth, a somewhat wordy author named Patrick Matthew was thinking about marine animals in which thousands of eggs and young are produced, but only one or two survive to maturity. He felt that with such low survival rates there must be natural competition:

"The self-regulating adaptive disposition of organized life may, in part, be traced to the extreme fecundity of Nature, who, as before stated, has, in all the varieties of her offspring, a prolific power much beyond (in many cases a thousandfold) what is necessary to fill up the vacancies caused by senile decay. As the field of existence is limited and pre-occupied, it is only the hardier, more robust, better suited to circumstance individuals, who are able to struggle forward to maturity, these inhabiting only the situations to which they have superior adaptation and greater power of occupancy than any other kind; the weaker, less circumstance-suited, being prematurely destroyed.[79]"

This observation was secreted in the appendix to a little-read book on *Naval Timber and Arboriculture*[80] and was completely ignored until Darwin said the same thing (in a more accessible style) 28 years later. It was left to Matthew to draw attention to his own comments in a letter to the *Gardener's Chronicle* in 1860[81]. Darwin freely admitted this was a statement of Natural Selection[82], although Matthew had clearly failed to see the importance of his own observations.

Across the English Channel in France it was not just Lamarck who was hunting for answers. Geoffroy Saint-Hilaire wrote in 1833 that the

[78] Wells' passage was quoted by Darwin in the *Historical Sketch* appended to the later editions of *The Origin of Species*.
[79] Matthew too was quoted by Darwin in his *Historical Sketch*.
[80] Matthew, 1831: 384.
[81] *Gardener's Chronicle*, 7th April 1860.
[82] Which led to Matthew having visiting cards printed describing himself as the 'Discoverer of the Principle of Natural Selection'(Barber, 1980: 214).

external world was all-powerful in altering the form of bodies and that these alterations were inherited, "and they influence all the rest of the organization of the animal, because if these modifications lead to injurious effects, the animals which exhibit them perish and are replaced by others of a somewhat different form, a form changed so as to be adapted to the new environment.[83]"

These early statements may not have set the world alight the way Darwin – with his carefully argued and readable text – did, but they show Natural Selection was in the air (and even in print) during Elford Leach's lifetime. Is it possible then, that if Elford Leach had continued to work, *he* might have discovered Natural Selection?—Almost certainly not.

Returning to Nicholas Vigors' assessment of the development of zoology in Britain: Elford Leach was investigating the properties of, and assigning names to, individual species. He did rearrange higher groups – specifically, he created many new genera and rearranged the existing species in a more realistic manner; he provided a firm basis for separating the centipedes and millipedes from the insects, spiders and crustaceans; and his arrangement of the Crustacea was the best in the world for twenty years until replaced by that of Henri Milne Edwards[84] in 1834 – but Elford Leach was not a synthesiser. In his journey through the animal kingdom he was looking at the ground, not the landscape. It is no coincidence that the two naturalists who finally provided the understanding of Natural Selection, Darwin and Wallace, were both experienced field naturalists. Elford Leach made detailed field notes, but only to assist his classification of the individual species, not to help any broader analysis.

Elford Leach made his contribution earlier in the chain. The revolution in the approach to studying animals in the early years of the nineteenth century led to the natural classifications; the natural classifications led to a more realistic understanding of the patterns in nature; and that understanding led to a recognition of closely related, but biologically distinct, species. It was this that led to the elucidation of Natural Selection and the general acceptance of evolution.

However, Elford Leach was a key advocate and enthuser of the modern approach. His presence in the scientific society of the day, and his wide-ranging contacts, introduced and promoted the new zoology to his backward countrymen. The next generation of British zoologists would stand on firmer ground directly as a result of his efforts, and it was the next generation of British zoologists that included both Charles Darwin and Alfred Russel Wallace.

Today much of William Elford Leach's work has been superseded and he has become virtually invisible, but, for his influence in his own time, bringing his country back to the leading edge of his science, he deserves an honoured place in the history of nineteenth century biology.

[83] Geoffroy Saint-Hilaire. 1833. *Influence du monde ambiant pour modifier les formes animales.*

[84] Henri Milne Edwards (1800-1885). Born at Bruges to an English father, Mr Edwards. The family moved to Paris in 1814. He studied under Cuvier and became a French citizen in 1831. Professor of Natural History at the Collège Royale de Henri IV and at the École Centrale des Arts et Manufactures 1832-41; Professor of Entomology at the Paris Museum 1841-61; Professor of Mammalology at the Paris Museum 1861-. 'Milne' was one of his first names but he always used it to distinguish himself from relatives. His son Alphonse Milne-Edwards (1835-1900) – later Director of the Paris Museum – added a hyphen.

Appendix 1

The name Leach and Leach Arms

The name Leech, and its various derivatives, Leach, Leache, Leche (and probably others) derives from the mediæval slang for a medical practitioner, named after their use of medicinal leeches. Dr Johnson, in his English dictionary of 1755, speaks of: *a leech* – a physician; *to leech* – to treat with medicaments; and *leechcraft* – the art of healing.

Grant of Arms

Members of the Leach family of Plymouth are sometimes designated in old texts as "*arm.*" or "*armiger*", indicating they have the right to bear heraldic arms.

Arms were originally the symbols painted on the shields of knights and noblemen to allow men encased in full armour to be recognised on the battlefield. When displaying arms on paper or in other everyday media, a crest is usually displayed in addition to the shield (see opposite). The crest is the emblem worn by the knight on top of his helm for the same purpose of recognition. The name for the shield and crest together is the *Achievement*. The modern tendency to refer to an achievement as a *Family Crest* is doubly wrong: it is not just a crest and achievements do not denote families.

Grants of arms are made only to individuals (or corporate bodies) and all individuals with a grant of arms have different arms. No two individuals living at the same time may share identical arms. Identical arms would have caused confusion in battle. The eldest son inherits his father's arms, but only on his death. Until then the eldest son would have his own grant of arms, probably similar to his father's but bearing a distinguishing mark.

Members of the same branch of the same family do usually have arms based on a design common to members of that branch, but the arms of each person must be unique. To maintain this system there is no automatic right to use arms. Individuals must inherit, or apply for, the right.

However, this correctness has been disregarded by many individuals for centuries. Elford Leach sealed his letters with an achievement (shown opposite) which included the arms of a member of the Leach family, but he does not appear to have had any entitlement to use the arms on this seal.

Leach Arms

Arms granted to individuals in the various branches of the Leach family are usually based on the following pattern: the lower part of the shield is ermine; the top is a colour (usually red) with three coronets side by side. The crest is usually a bare right forearm emerging from another coronet and grasping a green snake which winds around the arm in a loose 'S' (*Leech* is also an old name for a snake). The origin of these arms dates from the 14th century and is allegedly as follows[1]:

In the time of King Edward III[2], the king's physician was a man named John. John lived in Berkshire[3], not far from the Royal Palace at Windsor, and in about the year 1356 King Edward was being entertained at John's manor-house. With him he had brought two other kings, at that time his prisoners: King David II of Scotland (son of Robert the Bruce)[4]; and King John II of France ('John the Good')[5]. Edward III was so pleased with the hospitality they received from John, his leech, he gave him a grant of arms showing the noble motifs of three gold coronets on a scarlet background, above a layer of ermine.

The basic template for the arms of the West Country Leaches – which is similar to the template for Leach/Leech/Leache/Leche arms elsewhere – is as follows[6] (members of the family applying for grants of arms would usually base their arms on this template):

Leach (Cornwall). *Erm. on a chief indented gu. three ducal coronets or*
i.e. Ermine on a chief indented gules, three ducal coronets or.

The body of the shield is ermine with approximately the top one-third to one-fifth (the 'chief') red ('gules'). The junction between the chief and the ermine is finely serrated (indented). On the red chief are three gold ('or') crowns (in the form of dukes' coronets). Different branches of the Leach/Leech/Leache/Leche family have the chief of different colours and the junction with the ermine may be straight, indented or coarsely jagged ('dancettée') depending on the branch.

Other branches of Leach in Devon and Cornwall were:

Leach (Crediton, Devon) extinct 1708, at the death of Sir Simon Leach KB
The same arms.

Leach (Devonshire)[7]. *Erm. on a chief sa. three crowns or.*
Here the chief is black ('sable') and the border with the ermine is straight.

Leach of Trethewell in St Evall[8]. *Party per fesse engrailed, g. and erm. in chief three ducal coronets or.*

In these arms the shield is divided about half-way down by a line in the form of small waves (as on water). The top half is red with the usual three gold coronets, the bottom half is the usual ermine.

Leach of Stoke Climsland and St Eval[9]. *Erm. on a chief indented gu. three ducal coronets or.*

These are the same arms as for Cornwall and Crediton.

[1] From Burke (1884) and Glover, 1833: 250-251.
[2] Edward III (1312-1377). King of England from 1327.
[3] Pronounced 'Bark-shuh'.
[4] David II was a prisoner of Edward III for 11 years from 1346-1357.
[5] In 1356 Edward III's son Edward 'The Black Prince' captured King John II after the Battle of Poitiers. King John was released in exchange for hostages, but when one of the hostages escaped he honourably volunteered to return to England where he died in 1364.
[6] Burke & Burke (1844).
[7] Burke & Burke (1844).
[8] Lysons & Lysons, 1814: clxviii.
[9] Vivian, 1887: 283.

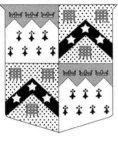

[10] Letter: W.E. Leach to Robert Jameson, 8th February 1819 (Loc: Edinburgh University Library, Special Collections. Ref: 1801/2/9)
[11] Will of George Leach Snr dated 19th August 1823 (Loc: West Devon Record Office, Plymouth). These old seals may have originated in a different branch of the family, possibly that which became extinct in 1708 with the death of Sir Simon Leach (see Appendix 2).
[12] *Journal of the Plymouth Institution*, **9**: 113.
[13] The Elford family had had its arms quartered with Scudamore following a marriage between John Elford (d.1503) and Joan (or Johanne) Scudamore a co-heiress of the Scudamore name (Elford, 1976: figure legend facing p. 1; p. 2; and figure facing p. 16 b).

William Elford Leach's Seal

In the early years of the 19th century there were no envelopes for mail. Letters were simply folded and sealed with a drop of molten sealing-wax into which the writer usually impressed their personal seal. Shown on the left is the seal Elford usually used. The illustration is a reconstruction following examination of numerous impressions in sealing-wax and shows the arms as they should appear (if the reconstruction is correct). The seal itself is too small to show such detail and is much cruder in appearance. The Leach arms are in quarters 1 & 4. In each of these the chief is red (indicated by the pattern of etching on the seal) and its lower margin is dancettée, not indented, although this distinction was not always made in old representations. Quarters 2 & 3 appear to show a variation of the Arms of the Harvey (or Harvy) family from Hale in Cornwall, suggesting an old marriage between a branch of Leach and a branch of Harvey. The published arms for the Harveys of Hale describe a silver background and a plain black chevron separating three harrows. On the seal impressions the background does not appear to be silver (which would be denoted by a smooth surface). It seems to be etched and may indicate gold, as shown here in the formal heraldic code of simple spots, or possibly a fur. In Elford Leach's seal each chevron bears three symbols which in one relatively clear example[10] appear to be 5-pointed stars (in heraldry these are 'mullets' or 'molets' and denote the rotating star found in some spurs). Most seal impressions are difficult to decipher and it cannot be guaranteed that this is indeed the form of these alleged 'Harvey' arms. The author has found no arms identical to those in quarters 2 & 3 for this or any other family in published armouries.

By 1826 Elford was using a second seal showing only the Leach crest over his initials, as shown below. In his father's Will there had been mention of some seals which had been in the family for 120 years[11]. It is possible the quartered seal was one of these, dating from about the year 1700. These old seals passed to Jonathan in 1823 when their father died and any seal among them would have ceased to be available to Elford. If Elford changed seals in 1823 and did not revert to the quartered seal, this might support this interpretation. Unfortunately no record has been kept of which seal was used on each of Elford's letters or how this changed through time.

In the *Journal of the Plymouth Institution* Jewers described[12] what he claimed were the arms of Elford Leach but did not identify his authority (according to the copy seen). These arms were quartered, with quarters 1 & 4 containing Leach (with the red chief indented); 2 containing arms of Elford (the left half of the shield silver, the right blue, meeting at a wavy junction, and overall a red lion rampant); and 3 showing arms of Scudamore (three leathered gold stirrups on a red background)[13]. These arms have never been encountered during the present research and there is no indication Elford Leach ever had a seal of this design – which is curious if these arms were his personal grant. Jewers' view needs confirmation.

Appendix 2

The Leach family of Plymouth

This family could trace its roots to John Leach of Crediton (buried 30 June 1569 at Crediton) who had at least three sons: John, Simon and another. John (from his name, probably the eldest) became a clergyman, while Simon became a blacksmith. Most published pedigrees follow the line of Simon, for reasons which shall become obvious. Thus:

Simon Leach (blacksmith of Crediton, Devon) married Elizabeth (daughter of John Rowe of Crediton) and they had a son Simon (see following); another son John; and four daughters who all married: Margaret (married Nicholas Turbeville), Kate (?short for Katherine) and two others (not named in the texts seen). A grandson of Simon was a tanner in Crediton.

Simon's eldest son and heir was Sir Simon Leach *Kt* (possibly a lawyer) who died in the Spring of 1637. He was High Sheriff of Devonshire in 1625 when King Charles I came to the throne and was knighted by the King at Ford Abbey on 26th September in that year after a royal visit to Plymouth. He was married twice, first to Elizabeth (daughter of Walter Burrough of Exeter) by whom he had two sons, Walter (later Sir Walter) and another who died while young. Sir Simon's second wife was Katherine (daughter of Nicholas Turbeville Esq. of Crediton) by whom he had three more sons, Simon (who died without issue), George and Nicholas, and four daughters all of whom married, Katherine, Elizabeth, Rebecca and Anne. One daughter (texts are vague) married the Rector of Cadleigh; another married twice, firstly to Robert Burrington of Sandford (presumably related to the son-in-law of John Leach, the blacksmith's brother – see later), then to Thomas Gifford of Halsbury. A tomb to Sir Simon Leach and Katherine (*syn.* Catherine) Turbeville is at Cadleigh Church near Tiverton, Devon. Sir Simon and subsequent family members in this line took Cadleigh as their seat after Sir Simon bought Cadleigh in about 1600 from Sir John Horton.

Sir Simon's son Sir Walter Leach (born 1599, knighted 3rd December 1626) had predeceased his father but not before marrying Sara, daughter of Sir Robert Napper *Bt* [= Napier] and producing his own son and heir, Simon, and three daughters.

Walter's son Simon Leach (born 1632, died 25 June 1660) was a zealous supporter of King Charles II when the King was in exile during England's flirtation with republicanism. This Simon Leach married Bridget (third daughter of Sir Bevil Grenvile, a famous Royalist). Bridget died on the 7th March 1691 after remarrying Sir Thomas Higgons *Kt* by whom she had several sons. Simon Leach and Bridget had two children, Simon and Bridget.

Simon's son Simon Leach was knighted on 23rd April 1661 while very young, possibly as a token of his late father's loyalty to the royalist cause. His father had never been knighted, having spent his adult life in the period between 1649, when King Charles I was executed, and 1660, when the monarchy was restored in England. This Sir Simon Leach *KB* married Mary Theresa (daughter of the first Lord Clifford of Chudleigh in Devon) and moved from Cadleigh to Chudleigh. He died without producing children and this Leach line extinguished. He was buried on 30th June 1708. His widow died in 1715.

Returning to Crediton in the mid 16th century:

John, the blacksmith's brother (died May 1613) was Rector of Talaton (Vivian says Rector of Arlington/Allington; Jewers says Rector of Talland), then (1582) Canon of Exeter Cathedral (the 'Cathedral Church of St Peter') and Archdeacon of Totnes; and (1587) Chancellor of Exeter Cathedral. He married Elizabeth (daughter of Sir Alexander Napper/Napier of Exeter and his second wife Grace Taylor; and sister of Baronet Napper). They had at least two children, Margaret and Nicholas.

Margaret married Robert Buryngton of Sandford, a Counsellor at Lincoln's Inn (i.e. a barrister) and they had five children. Tuckett gives ages after the names of the children, which may suggest times of death. In order these were, Margaret (aged 10), Elizabeth (aged 9), Robert (aged 18), John (aged 15), Humphrey (aged 2).

Nicholas Leach (*syn.* Leache) lived at Stoke Climsland in Cornwall at the time of Vivian's visitation in 1620. He married Jenophah (daughter of Edward Hearle of Trenouthe) in March 1616 at Luxulyan. They had at least two sons and a daughter: John (baptised 1617 at Luxulyan), Nicholas and Martha.

Jewers says one of the Rev. John Leach's grandsons was Walter Leach who married Margaret (née Reade). Walter does not appear in the other sources as a grandson. Later in this male line (Jewers implies descended from Walter) is George Leach (born ?ca. 1720; died ?1790), grandfather of William Elford Leach and Jonathan, George and Jenny.

Information from:
Devon Notes and Queries, **2** (1903) : 29-37, 58, 92-95, 204-206 &
Devon Notes and Queries, **5** (1909): 279 (Traces some Devon Leaches from the 17th century)
Jewers, A.J. in *Annual Report and Transactions of the Plymouth Institution*, **9**: 76-139.
Tuckett, J. (1859-61) *Devonshire Pedigrees*. London; John Russell Smith.
Vivian's Visitations of the County of Cornwall (1887) p. 283.
Vivian's Visitations to the County of Devon (1895) p. 526.

The pedigree of the Elford family from the late 15th century down to Sir William Elford can be found in Worthy (1887) **1**: 33-43.

Appendix 3

WILLIAM ELFORD LEACH ITINERARY

dates	place	authority
Born 2 February 1791	Hoegate, Plymouth.	Grave + Bate & Westwood
? to ?	Plympton Grammar School then Chudleigh.	*The English Cyclopaedia*
1803	Apprenticed Devon & Exeter Hospital (WEL says* served 5 yrs then went to London. This would have him start at Exeter in 1803, aged 12). *The English Cyclopaedia* says 1807 but is unlikely.	
5 years	Exeter (Devon & Exeter Hospital).	* MD application 9.i.1812
1808	To St Bartholomew's Hospital, London.	*The English Cyclopaedia*
20 December 1808	20 Southampton Buildings, London.	Application for FLS
"during three winters"	St Bartholomew's, London.	MD application 9.i.1812
2–4 July 1809	Swansea.	Dillwyn to ?J.F. Stephens
28 July 1809	Millstreet, Ireland.	letter to G.B. Sowerby
2–4 August 1809	Swansea.	Dillwyn to ?J.F. Stephens
"Summer 1809"	Cheltenham.	WEL to JE Smith 5.xi.1810
"Summer 1809" (?August)	Carlisle.	WEL to JE Smith 5.xi.1810
"Summer 1809" (?August)	Scotland (after 28 July per letter to GB Sowerby).	WEL to JE Smith 5.xi.1810
Summer 1810	Carlisle (and presumably Scotland).	WEL to JE Smith 5.xi.1810
2 November 1810	20 Southampton Buildings, London	letter to George Anderson
30 November 1810	Edinburgh	WEL to JE Smith 30.xi.1810
Summer 1811	W. of Scotland on fieldwork.	WEL to A MacLeay 14.ix.1811
16 September 1811	51 Merry's Lodgings, Prince's St, Edin.	WEL to A MacLeay.
8 March 1812	Edinburgh.	Wernerian ("Mr Leach read").
2 July 1812	*Woodland*, near Plymouth Dock.	WEL to A MacLeay.
Plan— Jan 1813: London several days; Edin. several weeks; London for winter.		WEL to A MacLeay 12.xii.1812
late June 1813	*Woodland*, near Plymouth Dock.	WEL to ?A MacLeay 24.vii.1813
20 October 1813	*Woodland*.	WEL to ?A MacLeay
1 Dec 1813 WEL appointment known.		Brown to JE Smith
?December 1813 [WEL says appointed]	?London (context suggests this)	WEL to A MacLeay (no date)
9 January 1814 (from context)	(postmarked) Plymouth.	WEL to A MacLeay (no date)
29 January 1814	Plymouth.	Woollcombe diary
9 February 1814	London.	BM Officers' Reports
3 April 1814	London.	Woollcombe diary
8 July 1814	London.	BM Officers' Reports
10 August 1814	Plymouth.	Woollcombe diary
24 October 1814	London.	WEL to Blainville
9 December 1814	Plymouth.	Woollcombe diary

13 January 1815	London.	BM Officers' Reports
WEL to have two months leave		Trustees' Committee 8.vii.1815
Plan— August 1815 until ?	Paris.	WEL to Blainville 31/3/1815
1 October 1815	London (still).	BM Officers' Reports
4 November 1815	Paris.	WEL to Blainville
23 November 1815	London (*cf.* following)	BM Officers' Reports
1 December 1815	"Paris" (but probably not so).	Banks to Barrow
9 December 1815	London.	Trustees' Committee 9.xii.1815
4 January 1816	London.	WEL to Jameson 4.i.1816
Plan— To go to Edinburgh in winter (no indication he did).		WEL to Jameson 4.i.1816
10 February 1816	London (still).	WEL to Speaker of the Commons
March or April 1816	London.	BM Officers' Reports
10 May 1816	London.	BM Officers' Reports
14 June 1816	London.	BM Officers' Reports
Plan— WEL to collect in Britain for 2 months.		König's diary 13.vii.1816
August	London (?with Stephens in Museum).	Trustees' Committee 13.vii.1816
early September	Kent (probably at Sandgate).	WEL to Blainville 30.ix.1816
14 September 1816	London.	WEL to Blainville
30 September 1816	London.	WEL to Blainville
Plan— To move into Museum apartments in June 1817.		WEL to Blainville 30.ix.1816
October 1816 (pre 20th)	North coast of Cornwall.	WEL to A MacLeay 20.x.1816
20 October 1816	Spitchwick Park, Devon.	WEL to A MacLeay
Plan— To return to London ca 11 December 1816.		WEL to Blainville 7.xi.1816
Planta asks WEL to return to London.		König's diary 26.xi.1816
WEL asks Planta and König for 3 weeks extension.		König's diary 2.xii.1816
5 January 1817	London.	König's diary
8 March 1817	London.	BM Officers' Reports
13 June 1817	London.	BM Officers' Reports
28 June 1817 (a short trip?)	Darent Wood, Kent.	WEL to Blainville
Plan— To spend 3 months in Paris after the summer (but did not go until 1818).		Trustees' Committe 19.vii.1817
11 December 1817	London.	BM Officers' Reports
3 January 1818	London.	BM Officers' Reports
16 February 1818	Paris.	WEL to A MacLeay
27 April 1818	Paris.	WEL to Monsieur D'Orbigny
Plan— Return to London 3-4 May 1818		WEL to A MacLeay 22.iv.1818
May 1818	Arrived London.	*Preface* in Samouelle 1819
9 May 1818	London.	BM Officers' Reports
May 1818 speaks of his "appartments"	(not clear when he moved to BM).	WEL to A MacLeay 22.iv.1818
15 June 1818	London (Cuvier and Latreille still there).	WEL to Acad. Nat. Sci. Philadel.
Plan— About to go to Paris (December 1818). Did not do so.		WEL to AcNatSciPhil 1.xii.1818
Permitted 1 months leave after Christmas		Trustees' Comm 19.xii.1818
20 January 1819	Spitchwick Park, Devon.	WEL to Sir Joseph Banks
8 February 1819	Spitchwick Park, Devon.	WEL to Jameson
13 February 1819	(absent from London).	Trustees' Committee 13.ii.1819
26 February 1819	London (presumably. Brown in London).	Brown to Jameson
2 March 1819	London.	WEL to Acad. Nat. Sci. Philadel.
April-June 1819	London.	Attended Bullock's Sale
Plan— To visit Orkneys for 3 months from October 1819.		Trustees' Committee 10.vii.1819
10 October 1819	London.	WEL to Blainville
Plan— Orkneys deferred to May 1820		Trustees' Committee 13.xi.1819

15 May 1820	London (at sale of Birch's fossils).	*History of Collections*, **2**: 245
Plan— To have 2 months leave this year (did not take).		BM Officers' Reports 7.vii.1820
11 September 1820	London (ill, this is the first reference).	König's diary
14 September 1820	London (moved to Abernethy's).	König's diary
Few days before 29 September 1820	Neighbourhood of London.	König to Swainson 29.ix.1820
Plan— Soon after 29 September 1820 to go to friends in Devon or Cheltenham.		König to Swainson 29.ix.1820
16 September 1820	Put in care of John Warburton.	Warburton certificate to Trustees
14 October 1820	London with Warburton.	König's diary
7 November 1820	Apparently London (no postmark).	WEL to Stephens
Few days before 15 December (pre 12th)	London (at Bullock's).	Bullock to [unknown].
12 December 1820	To Exeter from London.	König's diary
16 December 1820	Left care of Warburton.	Warburton certificate to Trustees
30 January 1821	London (returned on this day).	König's diary
Plan— 4 months leave to go to country.		Trustees' Committee 10.ii.1821
17 February 1821	'removed from Town' in care of Veitch.	König's diary
1 May 1821	Spitchwick.	Woollcombe's diary
20 May 1821	Discharged from care of Veitch.	Veitch to Planta 30.v.1821
Leave granted until 10 July 1821	'in the Country'.	Trustees' Comm 9.vi.1821
Leave granted until after September General Meeting		Trustees' Committee 14.vii.1821
Leave granted until after December General Meeting		Ellis to G. Leach Jnr 22.x.1821
20 October 1821	Arrived in London (BM apartments).	König's diary
27 October 1821	"did not return from Lady Molesworth".	König's diary
28 January 1822	At BM examining shells.	König's diary
9 March 1822	Formal retirement.	Trustees' General Meeting
5 April 1822	Commences BM annuity of £100 net.	Trustees' Committee 13.vii.1822
30 April 1822	In care of Veitch (and appears had been).	König's diary
Plan— To go to Devon with father		GL^Snr to GB Sowerby 21.xi.1822
11 December 1822	Bath.	WEL to William Clift
18 August 1823	Spitchwick.	WEL to William Buckland
5 February 1824	Spitchwick.	WEL to A MacLeay
4 October 1824 (on his way abroad)	Bedford Hotel, London.	WEL to J. Sowerby
1 January 1825	Nice.	WEL collection notes at BM
18 February 1825	Nice.	WEL collection notes at BM
19 April 1825	Nice.	WEL to Cuvier
5 June 1825	Nice.	WEL to Clift
20 June 1825	Nice.	WEL collection notes at BM
21 June 1825	Leaving Nice over Mont Braous.	WEL collection notes at BM
23 June 1825	Near Sevorgia.	WEL collection notes at BM
25 June 1825	Between Roccavione and Demonte.	WEL collection notes at BM
26 June 1825	Between Demonte and Venai (Vinadio).	WEL collection notes at BM
27 June 1825	Venai.	WEL collection notes at BM
19 July 1825	Venai.	WEL collection notes at BM
20 July 1825	Between Venai and Demonte.	WEL collection notes at BM
late July 1825	Near Pisa.	WEL collection notes at BM
late July 1825	between Pisa and Empoli.	WEL collection notes at BM
2 August 1825	Florence.	WEL collection notes at BM
29 August 1825	(apparently still) Florence.	WEL collection notes at BM
30 August 1825	Maseara (a village).	WEL collection notes at BM

1-13 September 1825	{ Bologna. Modena. Parma. Plaisance (Piacenza). Alessandria. Asti. Turin. Mt Cenis. }	WEL collection notes at BM
14 September 1825	Between Verpillière and Lyons.	WEL collection notes at BM
15 September 1825	Between Le Maison blanche and Mâcon.	WEL collection notes at BM
16 September 1825	Between Saint Albain and Tournus.	WEL collection notes at BM
17 September 1825	Near "Roche Pont" [= La Rochepot].	WEL collection notes at BM
18 September 1825	Between "Rochepoint" and Saulieu.	WEL collection notes at BM
19 September 1825	Near Saulieu and at Rouvray.	WEL collection notes at BM
October 1825	Forest of Dean (west of Cheltenham).	WEL collection notes at BM
22 January 1826	Plymouth.	WEL to GB Sowerby
April–June 1826	Plymouth (and neighbourhood).	WEL collection notes at BM
Plan— To Leave Britain in June 1826 to spend 3-5 years on the Continent.		*Entom. Memorandums* (BM mss)
21 June–29 July 1826	Bickleigh (immediate environs).	WEL collection notes at BM
7 August 1826	London.	WEL to J. deC. Sowerby
September 1826	Arriving at Rome.	Charles Eastlake to Woollcombe
1827 ?	(No record)	
January 1828	Arriving at Rome.	Charles Eastlake to Woollcombe
29 October 1829	Badia [?Florence], Italy	WEL to CL Bonaparte

1830 ?— Plymouth Institution says "London" in 1830 but may be 'old news.'

1831 ?

28 October 1832	Malta (resided here for some time)	WEL to Clift
1833 ?	(No record)	

1834 ?— September election to Gioenian Academy of Natural Sciences, Catania says "Londra" but may be 'old news'.

1835	22 Via Felice, Rome.	WEL to Children Oct.-Dec. 1835
until 11 July 1835	Rome.	Death Certificate
October–December 1835	Genoa.	WEL to Children
Plan— To return to Rome from Genoa		WEL to Children Oct. -Dec. 1835
25 July 1836-25 August 1836	San Sebastiano Curone, Piedmont.	Death Certificate
25 August 1836	Death at San Sebastiano Curone.	Death Certificate

Appendix 4

Jonathan Leach's Military Service

(i)	70th (Surry) Regiment of Foot	Oct. 1801–May 1806
(ii)	Nº 3 or Nº 4 Company, 2nd Battalion, 95th (Rifles) Regiment of Foot	May 1806–May 1809
(iii)	Nº 2 Company, 1st battalion, 95th (Rifles) Regiment of Foot	May 1809–Feb. 1816
renamed	1st battalion, The Rifle Brigade	Feb. 1816–Sep. 1819
(iv) Major	1st battalion, The Rifle Brigade	Sep. 1819–Oct. 1821

date	event/location
August 1801	Purchased a commission as an **Ensign** (= Second Lieutenant) in 70th Regiment.
October 1801	To Jersey to join regiment having purchased a **Lieutenancy**.
late October 1802	Sailed with regiment to Deal, Kent. Marched to Dover Castle.
November 1802	At Dover Castle for 3 weeks.
late November 1802	To Chatham for Winter.
June–Autumn 1803	Camped on heights of Shorncliffe, Kent when Napoleon threatened invasion. Brigade included 95th Regiment.
end Oct./early Nov. 1803	70th Regiment marched to Portsmouth to sail for West Indies.
mid November 1803	Embarked Portsmouth on *Pandour* (44 gun "old Dutch built tub")
25 December 1803	Anchored in Carlisle Bay, Barbados.
28/29 December 1803	Sailed from Barbados.
31 December 1803	Arrived English Harbour, Antigua (JL had his baggage stolen)
December 1803–	In Antigua.
7 April 1804	**Purchased a Captaincy in the army**
June–Oct. 1804	Yellow Fever raging in Antigua; many deaths. JL briefly ill.
Autumn 1805	JL with slow and debilitating fever. 6 months leave, to include a medical transfer to Europe. 13 week voyage to Tortola then Dublin.
Winter 1805	Dublin Bay (quarantine of several days) then sailed to Holyhead.
Winter 1805	Devon for the remainder of the 6 months leave.
early Spring 1806	**Transfer to 2nd battalion 95th (Rifles) Regiment of Foot** [2/95th] in Kent by exchanging with a Captain of that regiment.
1 May 1806	Holds rank of Captain in 95th from this date.
Spring 1806–	In Kent with battalion at Brabourne Lees Barracks.
26 July 1807	Battalion sails from Deal for Denmark (Army to seize Danish fleet).
early August 1807	Anchored between Helsingør and Copenhagen.
16 August 1807	Landed at Vedbæk, in Zealand, in a force led by Maj.-Gen. Sir Arthur Wellesley.
19 August 1807	2/95th moved further to right, and closer to Copenhagen.
24 August 1807	Fierce fighting from just after 2 a.m. in outskirts of Copenhagen.
26 August	Skirmished behind Køge. Many militia prisoners taken.
29–30 August 1807	Scoured woods from Køge to Herfølge.

2 September 1807	2/95th approached walls of Copenhagen to fire on town while it was cannonaded.
5 September 1807	*Copenhagen capitulated. Truce with some parts of Denmark.*
mid September 1807	JL in Copenhagen hotel for 5 days after truce.
Sep.– 15 Oct. 1807	Occupying villages in the countryside to prevent forces of local militia and other groups organising resistance.
17 October 1807	On board *Princess Caroline*, a Danish prize vessel of 74 guns, for return.
20 October 1807	*Napoleon declared war on Portugal for refusing to end trade with Britain.*
21 Oct.–16 Nov. 1807	Sailed to Deal, Kent. Marched to Hythe Barracks for the Winter.
19 June 1808	Four companies of 2/95th (including Nº 4 Company, commanded by JL) sail from Dover to Cork. Based aboard ship at Cork for 4–5 weeks. Expecting to be sent to South America.
June-July 1808	*Portugal and Spain seek assistance from Britain to oppose French.*
12 July 1808	Sailing from Cork to Mondego Bay, Figueira da Foz, Portugal.
1 August 1808	Disembarked. Part of 15,500 men led by Sir Arthur Wellesley. Marched to a point near the village of Lavos.
9/10–12 August 1808	Marched with army to Leiria then bivouacked.
13? August 1808	Marched towards Lisbon.
15 August 1808	Long march then serious skirmish with French near Obidos. Light Division too enthusiastic and followed retreating French too far. French support arrived and allies suffered unnecessary losses. French withdrew.
16 August 1808	Halted at Obidos.
17 August 1808	**Battle of Roliça** ['Roleia']. 2/95th drove French from succession of mountainous hilltops in thick heath and great heat. (JL recorded as wounded but actually cut his mouth when a musket ball hit the canteen from which he was drinking.) French army withdrew. After battle, 2/95th bivouacked on plains beyond battlefield.
18 August 1808	Bivouacked near Lourinhã.
19 August 1808	Marched to Vimeiro to cover landing of additional 4000 British troops.
20 August 1808	Near village of Vimeiro. JL's company on picket duty that night in a large pine wood on the right and front of the Brigade.
21 August 1808	**Battle of Vimeiro**. JL's company in the wood resisted large column of French infantry but had to withdraw to British lines (which also allowed allied artillery to engage) and joined rest of 2/95th in the front line. French attacked in columns about 9.30 a.m. 95th were deployed as skirmishers in front of the line at the bottom of Vimeiro Hill and were driven back several times. By noon French withdrew.
22 August 1808	*Truce then Convention of Cintra. French agree to withdraw from Portugal.*
23 August 1808	2/95th marched from Vimeiro to Torres Vedras.
31 August 1808	2/95th marched to Sobral.
2–10 September 1808	2/95th marched to Bucellos.
10 September 1808	Bivouacked in the suburbs of Lisbon at a pleasure park, the Campo Grande. French army was camped in the city squares waiting for transport to France.
13 September 1808	Tents provided at the Campo Grande. JL visited city with two men of his company. Were perhaps the first allied troops to enter Lisbon. French troops not friendly.
late September 1808	Now fraternisation between allied and French troops. JL ill in Lisbon "for many weeks" [missed all following actions until rejoined 95th Regiment in Kent]
late October 1808	*Leaving a garrison in Lisbon, allied army leaves to engage French armies in Spain. Marches to attack a French force near Salamanca.*

26 October 1808	*With other reinforcements, 4 more companies of 2nd Battalion reached port of Corunna from Kent.*
20 December 1808	*The new companies joined existing 4 companies at Monastery of Trianis, several kilometres from Sahagún. Received news that Napoleon with a large new French force has entered Spain and is advancing to attack.*
25 Dec.1808–21 Jan.1809	*Disastrous 'Retreat to Corunna' during which 2/95th was in rearguard for a corps retreating more than 300 km to Vigo, in harsh winter conditions, for evacuation. [Rest of army travelled an equal distance to Corunna for evacuation]*
ca April/May 1809	JL recovered and, having rejoined regiment in England, was **promoted to 1st battalion** (promotion of status, not rank).
25 May–3 June 1809	1/95th left Dover for Portugal. Delayed off Kent coast by bad weather.
3–18 June 1809	Ships held in the Solent (JL visiting local towns while delayed).
18–28 June 1809	Sailing to the River Tagus, Lisbon.
2–3 July 1809	From midnight, 24 hours in a boat being towed upriver to Valada.
4 July 1809	Marched to Santarém.
4–7 July 1809	Waited at Santarém for animals, baggage, ammunition etc.
7/8 July 1809	Marched (from midnight until 8–9 a.m.) to Golegã.
8/9 July 1809	Marched (from midnight to 8–9 a.m.) to Tancos.
9/10 July 1809	Marched to Abrantes (night march; midnight to 8–9 a.m.)
10/11 July 1809	Marched to Gavião (13 hours march).
12 July 1809	Marched to Nisa.
13 July 1809	Marched to Pass of Vila Velha de Ródão.
14 July 1809	Marched to Castelo Branco.
16–17 July 1809	At Castelo Branco.
17/18 July 1809	Night march to oak/cork woods near Ladoeiro.
19 July 1809	Marched to vicinity of village of Zebreira.
20 July 1809	Crossed R. Erges into Spain. Camped near Zarza la Mayor.
20–22 July 1809	Marched to Coria.
23 July 1809	At Coria.
24–27 July 1809	Marched to Navalmoral de la Mata.
28 July 1809	Marched to Oropesa (arrived at noon). Then on toward Talavera de la Reina. Could hear battle in distance [Battle of Talavera. Wellesley became Lord Wellington after this battle].
29 July 1809	Arrived Talavera the morning after the battle and took charge of the outposts and a wood in front. Some skirmishing.
29 July–3 August 1809	On the battlefield at Talavera. Very little food. Saddle-horse stolen.
3 August 1809	Marched towards Oropesa (12 hours marching with JL now on foot).
4 August 1809	1/95th and cavalry formed rearguard to cover army's crossing of the R. Tagus at El Puente del Arzobispo.
4/5 August 1809	Marched (15 hrs from midnight) in direction of bridge at Almaraz. Halted for the night in a ravine.
6 August 1809	Marched to Almaraz (another 15 hrs).
6–20 August 1809	Defended crossing near Almaraz at site of (destroyed) bridge. During day occupied hill. At night moved to bivouac near crossing. Very little food.
20/21 August 1809	Marched (from midnight) to allied army HQ at Deleitosa.
21 August 1809	Marched (evening to midnight) ?towards Trujillo.

22 August 1809	After 4 hrs sleep, marched towards Cáceres.
23 August 1809	Arrived Cáceres.
24–26 August 1809	Marched half night and several hours of day towards Portugal.
26 August 1809	Arrived Valencia de Alcántara.
27–28 August 1809	Near Valencia de Alcántara.
28/29 August 1809	Night march into Portugal. Camped near Castelo de Vide.
29 Aug.–7 Sep. 1809	At Castelo de Vide.
1 September 1809	JL shooting red-legged partridges, hares and quails.
7 September 1809	Marched from Castelo de Vide to Portalegre.
8–9 September 1809	At Portalegre.
10 September 1809	Marched to Arronches.
11 September 1809	Marched to Campo Maior.
11 Sep.–12 Dec. 1809	Allied army rested for 3 months near R. Guadiana; an unhealthy region at this season. One third of army ill. Light Division at Campo Maior. Some officers shooting game and hare-coursing. JL presumably got a new horse.
12–22 December 1809	Marched: Arronches, Portalegre, Crato, Ponte de Sor, Abrantes, to Punheite [the modern Constância]
23 December 1809	Marched to Tomar.
24–25 December 1809	Marched to Leiria.
26–27 December 1809	Marched to Pombal.
28 December 1809	Marched to Condeixa.
29 December 1809	Marched to Coimbra.
30 December 1809	At Coimbra.
31 December 1809	Marched to Ponte de Murcella [near modern S. Miguel de Poiares].
1–3 January 1810	Marched to Celorico da Beira.
4 January 1810	Marched to Pinhel (in vicinity of main British army).
5 January 1810	At Pinhel.
6 January 1810	1/95th + some of 1st German Hussars crossed R. Côa to observe French outposts on R. Águeda. Marched to Vilar Torpim.
January–March 1810	Manoeuvring in countryside in response to rumours of French movement.
early March 1810	JL's company marched to Escarigo.
"next day" March 1810	Occupied Barba del Puerco (just vacated by French).
early March 1810	Based at Almofala to watch the fords on the River Águeda.
April 1810	Light Brigade joined by 1st & 3rd Portuguese Caçadores and renamed the Light *Division*. Also more light cavalry and horse artillery.
early March–24 July 1810	Patrolling River Águeda. East of river in late May, French began to assemble army to invade Portugal and laid siege to Ciudad Rodrigo.
4 July 1810	Skirmish with superior French force east of Almeida on Spanish border while rearguard for Light Division withdrawal across R. Dos Casas. Camped near Vale da Mula.
10 July 1810	Ciudad Rodrigo surrendered. 1/95th made night march from Vale da Mula to Barquilla in Spain. Cavalry attacked a French advance post of several hundred men. Infantry not deployed.
16 July 1810	Marched to Junça.
21 July 1810	Advanced towards R. Tourões/Turones to support withdrawal of cavalry being pursued by French.

22 July 1810	Fell back to vicinity of Almeida.
23/24 July 1810	On picket in front of Junça during night. Violent thunder storm.
	24 July 1810 **Action at the Côa**. In early morning French advanced. Light Division with 3 regiments of cavalry and a brigade of horse artillery held French from bridge over R. Côa west of Almeida as rearguard for allied withdrawal. Very severe fighting from Almeida back to river. 95th lost 10 officers and 140 men; 43rd Regiment lost 17 officers and 150 men. JL wounded when a musket ball grazed the side of his head. When allies had crossed bridge French made several attempts to follow. More heavy fighting. Allies withdrew overnight to vicinity of Vale Verde.
25 July 1810	Marched from midnight to vicinity of Freixedas.
26 July 1810	Entered Freixedas.
28 July 1810	Marched to Celorico da Beira (Wellington's HQ).
5 August 1810	Marched to "the front" (French besieging Almeida).
6–20 August 1810	Manoeuvred in response to reports of French movements.
28 August 1810	Long night march in heavy rain to Celorico da Beira.
early September 1810	Rearguard for slow withdrawal towards Coimbra.
23 September 1810	Withdrawal continued; French close by.
25 September 1810	Reached Sierra de Buçaco, north of Coimbra after extended skirmishing with French vanguard. Whole allied army on mountain.
26 September 1810	Occupied position in village of Sula on mountainside. Subjected to cannon fire in morning then light-arms fire exchanged all day.
	27 September 1810 **Battle of Buçaco**. French attacked in column just after dawn. 1/95th pushed back. Light Division counter-attacked and charged. 1/95th supplied flanking fire and column broke. French retreated through Sula. Other French columns attacking elsewhere. All columns repulsed. Small arms fire continued all day until short truce in evening to remove wounded. During this JL conversed with French officers. After truce French effected to remain in Sula and were driven out by 1/95th.
28 September 1810	Light sniping all day.
29 September 1810	Moved several miles to a wood.
3 October 1810	Bivouacked for the night near Pombal.
5 October 1810	Marched to Batalha.
6–8 October 1810	Retreated towards Torres Vedras.
9 October 1810	Marched into Alenquer.
10 October 1810	Expelled from Alenquer by French. Marched to Arruda dos Vinhos then to a tented camp in the Lines of Torres Vedras.
10 Oct.–15 Nov. 1810	In camp in the Lines of Torres Vedras.
15 November 1810	Light Division pursued (to observe) French army, which had left in direction of Santarém. Bivouacked for evening near Alenquer.
16 November 1810	Marched through Vila Nova da Rainha and Azambuja.
17 November 1810	Marched and found French near Cartaxo. French force in Santarém and holding the bridge at Santarém. 1/95th spent night in Cartaxo.
18 November 1810	Skirmish with French rearguard near "the Rio Maior" [R. Asseca].
19 November 1810	Near bridge below stronghold of Santarém.
20 November 1810	Probed French outposts with small-arms fire in heavy rain all day.
December 1810	French in Santarém. Allied army surrounding.

January 1811	French still in Santarém. Allies surrounding. About this time JL and a fellow officer took 5 days leave in Lisbon.
early February 1811	JL at the rear ill with fever. "reduced to a skeleton" [appears to have rejoined his company in mid-late April].
Feb-mid/late April 1811	Sick 'in the rear' (probably Lisbon). [meanwhile French abandoned Santarém and withdrew into Spain, leaving a garrison at Almeida. Light Division followed].
mid/late April 1811	JL rejoined Light Division and occupied same outposts, to R. Azarba, as during Summer of 1810.
2 May 1811	Withdrew to position between Espeja and R. Dos Casas as French advanced across R. Azaba.
3 May 1811	Crossed R. Dos Casas before dawn. Joined rest of allied army in position on heights above Fuentes de Oñoro ['Fuentes d'Onoro'].
4 May 1811	Light Division moved from left of army disposition to centre.
5 May 1811	**Battle of Fuentes de Oñoro.** Light Division occupied a wood in front of and to the right of the 1st Division. French attacked wood while allied army was rearranging its deployment. Extended exchange of fire in wood. French elsewhere advanced on allies' right flank and Light Division retreated from wood, formed squares, and withdrew to 1st Division across a plain in close formation while under cannon fire and pursued by cavalry. French now launched attacks against Fuentes de Oñoro but were repeatedly driven out. In evening, a truce to remove French wounded from village. JL's Brigade was then in Fuentes de Oñoro and some of JL's company guarded bridge over R. Dos Casas. JL and other officers took snuff and conversed with French Officers. Overnight the sentries of the two armies were within talking distance of one another.
6–9 May 1811	No activity. French withdrew behind R. Águeda during night of 9th.
10 May 1811	Advanced to Espeja and Gallegos de Argañán.
10 May–4 June 1811	In position around Espeja.
4 June 1811	Night march from Espeja (after JL left unfinished party in town).
7 June 1811	Bivouacked near Sabugal.
8–23 June 1811	Marched to Arronches via Meimoa, Penamacor, São Miguel de Acha, Castelo Branco, Vila Velha de Ródão, Nisa, Alpalhão and Portalegre.
23 June 1811	Bivouacked with entire allied army on left bank of R. Caia between Arronches and Campo Maior.
24 June–20 July 1811	Remained in position on R. Caia. Disease prevalent among troops.
20 July–10 August 1811	Retraced steps via Portalegre, Nisa, Vila Velha to R. Águeda.
10 August 1811	Forded R. Águeda at Vado de Carros, occupied Martiago.
11 August 1811	Accompanied Wellington to reconnoitre French garrison at Ciudad Rodrigo, now blockaded by allied army.
12 August–9 Sept. 1811	Positioned in and around Martiago and surrounding villages.
9 September 1811	JL's company and a company of Portuguese caçadores sent south to occupy mountain villages of Erias and Aldehuela.
after a fortnight	Returned to Martiago.
22–25 September 1811	In outposts on R. Vadillo [across R. Águeda and "some leagues" from El Bodón]. A French army coming to relieve Ciudad Rodrigo had its advance guard near the R. Vadillo (a tributary of the R. Águeda).
26 September 1811	Crossed R. Águeda by mountain ford. Marched to Fuenteguinaldo.

26/27 September 1811	Marched at midnight as allied rearguard. Marched all day (skirmish at midday with French cavalry) to Aldeia da Ponte.
27/28 September 1811	Marched midnight–8 a.m. to allied army position at "Soita" [?Souto].
end September 1811	Returned to positions by R. Águeda. French army had withdrawn.
10 October 1811	Hare-coursing on the plains near Fuenteguinaldo.
8 November 1811	Deer-hunting in mountains near "Serradilia" [Serradilla del Arroyo or S. del Llano at the western end of the Sierra de la Peña de Francia].
10–11 December 1811	JL shooting Woodcock in mountains while his company was based at La Atalaya, near the Serradillas.
3 January 1812	JL on leave. Visited local Don in mountains at Robledillo de Gata.
?7 January 1812	Back across snow covered mountains to join battalion at El Bodón.
8 January 1812	Forded R. Águeda near convent of Carredad. Advanced on Ciudad Rodrigo. From 9 p.m. attacked and took redoubt of San Francisco.
9 January 1812	Relieved by 1st Division (Divisions were rotating 24 hr shifts in trenches in front of Ciudad Rodrigo). Returned across R. Águeda to rest.
10–11 January 1812	Light Division resting in villages behind the R. Águeda.
12 January 1812	Returned to trenches.
13–15 January 1812	In villages behind the R. Águeda.
16 January 1812	Returned to trenches.
17–18 January 1812	In villages behind the R. Águeda.
19 January 1812	In front of city preparing to storm two breaches in defences. From 8 p.m., **Storming of Ciudad Rodrigo**. Breaches fell after less than 30 minutes severe fighting. French garrison captured. JL's involvement not clear.
20 January 1812	In Ciudad Rodrigo, then back to villages beyond R. Águeda.
21 Jan.–24 Feb. 1812	In villages behind the R. Águeda.
25 Feb.–7 March 1812	Marched south to besiege Badajos. Halted at Castelo de Vide.
7–13 March 1812	At Castelo de Vide.
14–16 March 1812	Marched to Elvas.
17 March 1812	Marched to position in front of Badajoz. After dark, commenced operations against redoubt called Fort Piccurina.
18 March 1812	Relieved 14 hours after fighting began. Withdrew to camp in a marsh.
19–25 March 1812	Spending half the time in rain-filled trenches in front of Badajoz.
25 March 1812	Fort Piccurina stormed at night by part of 3rd and Light Divisions.
26 March–6 April 1812	Artillery pounding city.
6 April 1812	After nightfall, **Storming of Badajoz**. Light Division stormed one breach but defence was well planned and vigorous. Enormous losses and breach only taken after French fell back when 3rd and 5th Divisions stormed other parts of the defences. French surrendered. JL's involvement not clear.
a few days later	Marched north to camp by R. Águeda. French army at Salamanca.
June 1812	Advanced to Salamanca. Armies faced each other in front of city. Skirmishing. French had fortified a convent to guard a bridge.
27 June 1812	Convent fell after attack by 6th Division. French withdrew north.
28–30 June 1812	Light Division acted as advance guard, following French north.
1 July 1812	Entered Nava del Rey. Took prisoners. Held dance. 2 hours sleep.
2 July 1812	Marched out before dawn to Rueda.
2–15 July 1812	In Rueda with HQ of allied army. French to north behind R. Duero.

15 July 1812	French manoeuvring, feinting to move south across R. Duero.
16/17 July 1812	Night march to Castrejón on open plain. French crossed R. Duero.
18 July 1812	French arrived at Castrejón. Allied infantry retired in columns across wide plain under constant cannon fire and threatened by French cavalry. Men died from dehydration and heat. Allied cavalry and artillery defended the columns. Allies halted on raised ground near R. Guareña.
19 July 1812	Armies quiet: faced each other. In evening French moved south to threaten allies' link with Salamanca. Light and 1st Divisions and cavalry shadowed.
20 July 1812	March continued into night. Armies within minutes of each other.
21 July 1812	Halted by R. Tormes in morning. Forded river in evening and bivouacked on its bank.
22 July 1812	**Battle of Salamanca**. Light Division, on far left of allied position, took little part in battle; just a light skirmish before nightfall. French defeated, most withdrew after dark.
23–30 July 1812	Pursued French via Peñaranda de Bracamonte, Flores de Ávila, Aldeaseca, Arévalo, Olmedo.
30 July 1812	Crossed R. Duero. Halted on bank a few miles from Valladolid.
31 July 1812	Halted by river. French heading for Burgos.
1–8 August 1812	Marched to banks of R. Eresma, 19 km from Segovia.
8–9 August 1812	JL in Segovia with other officers, sightseeing.
9 August 1812	JL rejoined Division, camped near El Palazio del Riofrio.
11 August 1812	Crossed the Sierra de Guadarrama. Camped in Park of the Escorial.
12 August 1812	Entered Madrid. French had occupied the city for 4 years. Allies welcomed as heroes.
12 Aug.–25 Oct. 1812	In Madrid. Wellington and most of army besieging Burgos. 3rd and Light Divisions, German Hussars and 14th Dragoons at and near Madrid. 4th Division NW of Madrid. In October French army at Cadiz lifted siege and marched towards Madrid. Allied garrison left Cadiz and marched to Aranjuez. French army arrived at Aranjuez and threatened to cross the River Tagus towards the capital.
25 October 1812	Light Division marched to Alcalá de Henares.
26 October 1812	Marched to Arganda then back to Alcalá de Henares as French manoeuvred.
30 October 1812	Light Division marched back to Madrid: camped on heights nearby.
31 October 1812	JL said goodbye to Spanish friends. Division left Madrid.
2 November 1812	Camped at foot of Sierra de Guadarrama.
3 November 1812	Crossed Sierra de Guadarrama.
4–7 November 1812	Marched to Alba de Tormes. French followed. Heavy winter rains.
8–14 November 1812	Bivouacked in woods by heights of San Cristobal, near Salamanca.
14 November 1812	In similar position to battle of 22 July 1812. Facing French army.
15 November 1812	French army (approx. 80,000 men) tried to outflank allies. Allies withdrew towards R. Águeda. Light Division as rearguard. Rain.
16 November 1812	Retreated through thick mud in gloomy forests in torrential rain.
17 November 1812	Retreated through forests in rain. Skirmished with French cavalry in open areas of woodland. In afternoon attacked by infantry and artillery while fording R. Huebra near San Muñoz. Only this narrow watercourse separated the armies that night.
18 November 1812	Marched through forest in sleet, snow and rain. French did not follow. Bivouacked near Sanctispiritus.
19 November 1812	Marched to Ciudad Rodrigo.

by end of November 1812	Allied army in winter quarters near Ciudad Rodrigo. Light Division in villages near R. Águeda. 1/95th at La Alameda de Gardón on Spanish side of the border with Portugal.
early May 1813	Wellington reviewed Light Division and 1st German Hussars on plains of Espeja.
21 May 1813	Broke winter camp, crossed R. Águeda heading for Salamanca. Wellington and army HQ with Light Division. Camped near Saelices el Chico. 95th (1st & 3rd battalions) now in 1st Brigade of Light Division, under General James Kempt, with 43rd (Monmouthshire) Light Infantry and 17th Portuguese Regiment.
22 May 1813	Marched to Martin del Rey, near R. Yeltes.
23 May 1813	Long march to bank of R. Huebra (at ford of 17 November 1812).
24 May 1813	Rested on bank of river.
25 May 1813	Marched to Robliza de Cojos.
26 May 1813	Marched to El Canto on R. Tormes, 10 km below Salamanca. French left Salamanca in direction of Toro.
27 May 1813	Halted. Wellington and some cavalry entered Salamanca. Was a light skirmish with French cavalry.
28 May 1813	Forded R. Tormes. Camped near Aldeanueva de Figueroa. Wellington and HQ left Light Division.
28 May–2 June 1813	No movement.
2 June 1813	Marched to Toro. French had damaged bridge over R. Duero.
3 June 1813	Division crossed bridge on planks. Marched to "Terra Buena". French headed for Palencia.
4 June 1813	Marched to convent of Espinar.
5 June 1813	Marched to La Mudarra.
6 June 1813	Marched to Ampudia.
7 June 1813	Marched to Palencia and camped by R. Carrion. French had moved towards Burgos.
8 June 1813	Marched to Támara. Weather changed from hot to wet and cool.
9 June 1813	Marched to "La Peña" [?Piña de Campos]
10 June 1813	Marched to bank of R. Pisuerga near Lantadilla.
11 June 1813	Marched to vicinity of Landrino.
12 June 1813	Allied advance guard of cavalry and Light Division found French in force at Isar and "Ornelio" [?Hornillos del Camino]. Halted on high ground. French withdrew into Burgos.
13 June 1813	French blew up castle of Burgos and withdrew to Miranda. Light Division and some cavalry marched, on road to Puente Arena, to Tobar.
14 June 1813	Marched to vicinity of "Quintana Juan"/"Quintanajar" [?Quintanaloma].
15 June 1813	Entered valley of the R. Ebro and camped for the night near "Puente Arena".
16 June 1813	Mountainous march by R. Ebro then to valley by Medina de Pomar.
17 June 1813	Difficult march (too mountainous for artillery) to Rio de Losa.
18 June 1813	Encountered French advance troops at village of San Millán. Cavalry engaged French cavalry then a large number of French riflemen were engaged by the 95th, with the 1st Battalion leading, who pressed the French back so hard the whole leading French brigade was engaged. Wellington arrived during the action then left for Espejo to cut off a French retreat with the 4th Division. 4th Division engaged French. 1st Brigade of Light Division sent to help but French retired towards Vitoria before they arrived.

19 June 1813	Advanced to Salinas de Añana then camped, near Póbes.
20 June 1813	Holding position to allow rest of army to catch up.
21 June 1813	Moved forward. **Battle of Vittoria**. Light Division attacked French centre and were engaged virtually all day. French defeated and lost most artillery (more than 250 pieces of ordnance – all but one cannon and one howitzer), baggage, stores, etc. French made orderly withdrawal towards Pamplona with light troops of both sides in continual action. Light Division pursued for about 6 km then halted. For battlefield action JL **promoted by brevet to rank of Major in the army**.
22 June 1813	Marched to near Salvatierra as vanguard of allied pursuit of French.
23 June 1813	Caught French rearguard early in day. Attacked until afternoon in heavy rain. Running battle through Lakuntza.
24 June 1813	95th (1st & 3rd battalions) attacked several thousand French infantry in positions across the R. Arakil. French pulled back as rest of Division arrived leaving their one remaining cannon. Skirmished again until French reached Pamplona. 95th spent night in Aldaba and other nearby villages.
25 June 1813	Advanced on Pamplona. Put out strong pickets towards fortress. Occupied Villava and other small villages near city. Camped on Pamplona side of Villava.
26 June 1813	A French force which had been at Logroño, not Vitoria, moved east towards France over the Pyrenees. Wellington pursued with Light and 3rd Divisions, and some cavalry. Marched south from Pamplona to intercept. Halted at village of "Muro" [?Muruarte de Reta].
27 June 1813	Marched through Tafalla, camped near Olite.
28 June 1813	Marched to Murillo el Fruto then for 10 hours along the bank of the R. Aragón to Gallipienzo. Roads very rugged. At midnight bivouacked in heavy rain on ploughed land near Cáseda.
29 June 1813	Stayed in bivouac. French had learned of pursuit and changed route.
30 June 1813	French having escaped to France, allies began return march to Pamplona.
31 June–3 July 1813	Returning to Pamplona via Sangüesa and Monreal.
3 July 1813	Arrived in vicinity of Villava, a short distance from Pamplona.
3–4 July 1813	Assisted in blockade of remaining French troops in Pamplona.
5–6 July 1813	Marched into Pyrenees to engage French there. Camped at Lantz.
7 July 1813	Marched to Gaztelu and bivouacked, then moved to Doneztebe/Santesteban to put pickets on roads to Bera/Vera-de Bidasoa and Etxalar.
7–14 July 1813	In Santesteban. Officers had dances every night. JL trout-fishing.
14 July 1813	Light Division marched towards Vera (occupied by French).
15 July 1813	Approached town of Vera. 1/95th drove French advanced posts from heights of Santa Barbara. French in fortified Pass of Vera.
16–25 July 1813	Light Division on bank of R. Bidasoa and top of Santa Barbara, facing Pass of Vera. French army attacked allied positions in border passes to the east and the four allied Divisions there fell back towards Pamplona.
26 July 1813	Light Division ordered to fall back across mountain paths to the west. Crossed R. Bidasoa near Lesaka and marched through Lesaka parallel to river. Camped on height opposite Sunbilla.
27/28 July 1813	At dusk of 27th marched towards Zubieta. Precipitous road. Arrived next morning.
28/29 July 1813	In evening marched towards Saldias. Arrived next morning.
29 July 1813	Stayed at Saldias.

30 July 1813	Marched to "Lecumbra"/"Lecumberg" [?Lekunberri]. In afternoon heard firing from Pamplona. Towards evening news reached Light Division that French army had been beaten near Pamplona and driven back towards the border.
31 July–1 August 1813	Light Division made "harassing" forced marches via Zubieta to bridge of Igantzi on the R. Bidasoa. Many exhausted men left on route.
1 August 1813	Arrived at mountain overlooking Igantzi in afternoon. French held bridge and their army was on other side of river heading for Passes of Vera and Etxalar. Some companies of 95th set up harassing fire on French until French rearguard withdrew into passes after dark.
2 August 1813	Crossed bridge of Igantzi at dawn and advanced to Vera. 95th (1st & 3rd battalions), supported by 43rd Regiment, cleared several French battalions from heights of Santa Barbara in thick fog. 3rd battalion attacked ahead; 1st battalion extended to right. French attacked 1st battalion. A company of 43rd Regiment assisted and French withdrew.
3–30 August 1813	French garrison in S. Sebastián to the north blockaded by British. French garrison in Pamplona blockaded by Spanish. In Pyrenees, no movement of either army. French constructing defences. On 25th August the 73 officers of the 95th Regiment held a dinner and musical entertainment in camp to celebrate the anniversary of the formation of the Rifle Corps. The French outposts watched.
31 August 1813	Storming of S. Sebastián began in the morning by 5th Division with detachments from others. 10-15,000 French forded R. Bidasoa below Vera and headed for S. Sebastián. S. Sebastián fell. French attacked Spanish and were repulsed. JL commanded pickets on heights of Santa Barbara in evening. Ordered to descend and join battalion over bridge at Lesaka. At midnight returning French forced their way over the bridge at Vera. Whole 1st Brigade turned out to fire on them.
September 1813	"tolerably quiet". No movements from either army.
7 October 1813	Allies attacked French in force at various points along R. Bidasoa. 1st Brigade, as part of attack on heavily defended Pass of Vera, drove French from heights above town of Vera.
8 Oct.–early Nov. 1813	Waited for Pamplona to fall before advancing into France. Severe rain and wind blowing down tents made conditions uncomfortable. JL on picket duty in early November in ruins of hermitage on mountain of La Rhune when exposure killed several men. French garrison at Pamplona surrendered on 31 October or thereabouts.
9 November 1813	Light Division left their position on La Rhune soon after nightfall to creep silently across the border into France to get as close as possible to French advanced positions. No horses were taken in case their neighing alerted the French.
10 November 1813	**Battle of the Nivelle**. Allies attacked French along the whole front of approximately 50 km. Light Division, in centre, descended in columns, crossed valley, and stormed redoubt on hill of La Petite La Rhune. Then crossed second valley to storm main French defences. Captured a French battalion. French army withdrew across R. Nivelle towards Bayonne. Allies bivouacked in former French fortifications.
11 November 1813	Followed French towards Bayonne on "execrable" flooded roads.
by 17 November 1813	French in front of Bayonne. Allies between R. Nive and coast at St Jean-de-Luz. 1/95th at chateau at Arcangues. French pickets at Bassussarry, 1 km away.
18 November 1813	French reconnoitred and skirmished with Light Division pickets.

23 November 1813	43rd Regiment sent to push back French pickets from some houses and occupy their positions. One company of 43rd went too far. 1/95th sent to cover their retreat. 43rd company was captured but 1/95th held the houses.
23 Nov.–9 Dec. 1813	No movement. Good relations developed between the front lines. The pickets would not molest men if they were obviously not in hostile formation. British officers shot game and even wandered behind the French outposts without trouble. Conversations were common. French officers obtained brandy for British officers from Bayonne, and British officers gave French officers tea and posted letters from them to correspondents in England via the military mail. Wellington stopped this discourse fearing the French would use English officers' poor knowledge of the French language to obtain military intelligence.
9 December 1813	Light Division and others pushed back advanced French positions while an allied corps crossed R. Nive and moved to new positions to the east of the French, cutting their communication route up the R. Adour. In evening Light Division fell back to original position.
10 December 1813	French attacked in force, pushing back Light Division pickets. 1/95th held fence and ditch in front of chateau at Arcangues, and building itself. Skirmishing continued until dark.
10–12 December 1813	Light Division waged "a desultory warfare" for three days with a swarm of French light infantry sent against them.
12 December 1813	French withdrew across R. Nive and attacked the corps to their east. French were driven back to their entrenchments around Bayonne. This last 5 days called the **Battles of the Nive**.
12–31 December 1813	No movement. On 31st December officers held a new year dance at chateau at Arcangues with French and Spanish "females".
3 January 1814	Light Division moved closer to the R. Nive near Arrauntz and Ustaritz. Light skirmishing over several days when sent into the field to counter French manoeuvres.
late January 1814	No movement of armies. Roads impassable. JL shooting woodcock driven out of the mountains by heavy snow: "had some capital sport."
16 February 1814	Allied army mobilised, divisions moved to the east. Light Division crossed R. Nive and moved towards La Bastide-Clairence. Camped on a heath.
17 February 1814	Reached La Bastide about noon. Camped on hill beyond.
20–23 February 1814	1/95th marched to St Jean-de-Luz for new uniforms (which had arrived by sea). Regiments leaving field in turn for this.
24 February 1814	1st Battalion marched to rejoin army which was advancing east to the R. Gave d'Oloron, where main French force was now massing.
25 February 1814	Marched through Ustaritz.
26 February 1814	Marched through La Bastide-Clairence.
27 February 1814	Marched through Garris.
28 February 1814	Marched to St Palais.
28 Feb.–7 March 1814	Halted in St Palais until ordered to continue.
7 March 1814	Marched to Sauveterre-de-Béarn.
8 March 1814	Marched to Orthez. (1/95th had missed Battle of Orthes on 27th February. 2nd & 3rd battalions had taken part.)
11 March 1814	1/95th rejoined Light Division at Barcelonne-du-Gers on north bank of R. Adour.
12 March 1814	Light Division advanced towards Tarbes. French appeared ahead in force.

13 March 1814	Light Division withdrew through Tarsac and took position in wood half-way between Tarsac and Aire-s-l'Adour. French withdrew leaving only a body of cavalry ahead of Tarsac.
18 March 1814	Light Division marched towards Tarbes. Crossed R. Adour. Spent night at Plaisance. French far ahead on left bank falling back on Tarbes.
19 March 1814	Marched along ridge to Haget for night. Heard fighting near Vic-en-Bigorre.
20 March 1814	Marched south through Rabastens-de-Bigorre. Encountered French on wooded hills [near Orléac-Debat] in front of a windmill just north of Tarbes. Three battalions of 95th (16 companies totalling 1000-1100 men) attacked a French Division of 5000-6000. French were dislodged but counter-attacked before being driven back. In less than 30 minutes of furious fire 95th lost 11 officers (out of about 70) and approximately 100 men killed and wounded. The French lost more than 1000. French withdrew several miles to another range of hills. 95th followed and settled opposite under cannon fire. French withdrew during night and headed towards Toulouse.
21 March 1814	Followed French. Rains and knee deep mud. Halted at Lannemezan for night.
22 March 1814	Marched to Castelnau-Magnoac.
23 March 1814	Marched to L'Isle en Dodon.
25 March 1814	Reached Monferran-Savès west of Toulouse.
26 March 1814	Encountered French rearguard between Plaisance-du-Toulouse (12 km sw of city centre) and Toulouse. Cavalry skirmish.
27 March 1814	3/95th skirmished with French near Tournefeuille.
29 March 1814	Marched to St Simon, within 2 miles of Toulouse. French pickets between village and city.
31 March 1814	3/95th crossed R. Garonne. Rest of Light Division moved up R. Ariège to cross but swollen by rains and recalled.
by 2 April 1814	3/95th had recrossed R. Garonne and moved into new positions further down river. French were dug in on fortified heights above city.
6 April 1814	Light Division moved downriver to vicinity of Grenade, about 20 km north of Toulouse, to cross river by pontoon bridges but bridges damaged by trees deliberately added to the floodwater by the French in the city.
7–10 April 1814	Near Grenade while pontoon bridges repaired.
10 April 1814	Pontoon bridges restored in the morning and Light Division, with 4th and 6th Divisions and a Spanish army crossed the river and advanced south on Toulouse. **Battle of Toulouse**. Light Division positioned to the north of the city, east of the main road to Bordeaux. There was hard fighting on the left of the Light Division's line. They drove in French outposts in houses around city and put troops along the canal that curved around the north of the city to engage the French and divert them from the main assault to the east. That assault drove the French from the heights into the city below. Allies spent night on field of battle.
11/12 April 1814	No activity. French withdrew towards Carcassonne during night/early morning without being molested.
12 April 1814	4th & 6th Divisions of allied army followed French. Rest entered Toulouse. Populace welcomed them and openly displayed their royalist rather than republican tendencies by wearing white ribbons and feathers and hanging many white flags (emblems of the Bourbon Kings of France). News reached Wellington from Paris that Napoleon had abdicated.

After news received.	Offer of truce sent to French army. Marshal Soult declined saying he had not heard officially from Paris of the abdication.
17 April 1814	In absence of truce, allies marched out of Toulouse towards French army. At Baziège met by Soult's chief of staff General Count Gazan. Abdication had been confirmed. Allies returned to Toulouse. **End of Peninsula War**.
late April 1814	Allied and French armies quartered on opposite sides of R. Tarn, N. of Toulouse. 1/95th at Castelsarrasin. Many dances, horse-races, fêtes etc. for 5–6 weeks.
1 June 1814	Marched out of Castelsarrasin bound for Bordeaux.
2 June–10 June 1814	Marched via Grenade, Cadours, Lectoure, Condom, Nérac and Casteljaloux.
11 June 1814	Arrived at Bazas. Portuguese troops left after 4 years with Light Division. Portuguese and Spanish followers also parted from army.
12–13 June 1814	Marched via Langon, Barsac (where a ball was given for the officers of the Brigade) and Castres-Gironde.
14 June 1814	Reached Bordeaux. Camped a few miles from city (3/95th at Blanquefort). On the road, Wellington, in full regalia, inspected British regiments of Light Division.
14 June – ~12 July 1814	At Bordeaux.
~ 12 July 1814	1/95th & 2/95th sailed on *Ville de Paris* (110-120 guns) for Portsmouth. [3/95th sailed from Pauillac to Plymouth then United States, for New Orleans campaign]
22 July 1814	1/95th & 2/95th arrived at Spithead [off Portsmouth].
late July 1814	Marched from Portsmouth to Kent to overwinter at Dover.
July 1814–April 1815	At Dover.
Spring 1815	*Expected to go to America, but Napoleon left Elba and entered Paris 20 March.*
by late April 1815	95th Regiment in Flanders. Ostend to Ghent by boat on canal. Ten days in Ghent then to Brussels. In Brussels army formed into Divisions. JL with 6 companies of 1/95th in the 8th Brigade of the 5th Division. Other units in 8th Brigade were 1st Battalions of: the 28th (The North Gloucestershire) Regiment, 32nd (The Cornwall) Regiment and 79th Regiment (Highland-Cameronian Volunteers). [2/95th & 3/95th in the 3rd Brigade of the 2nd Division].
15 June 1815	In Brussels. Army Reserve called to arms soon after dark.
16 June 1815	Dawn: army Reserve finally assembled. 1/95th marched south through Forest of Soignes to vicinity of village of Waterloo. Halted for 1-2 hours. Joined by Duke of Brunswick with his troops. Advanced. Reached crossroads of Quatre Bras about 2-3 p.m. where French attacking Dutch-Belgians led by Prince of Orange. **Battle of Quatre Bras**. Wellington ordered 1/95th to occupy a wood to left of position. French tried to take wood all day. Attacks and counter-attacks. Fighting until dark. Could hear French and Prussians fighting at Ligny several miles away. At 11 p.m. battalion rejoined Division, on their right, to rest. Only a very short sleep on battlefield. Disturbed by allied and French pickets exchanging fire.
17 June 1815	About 9 a.m. learned of Prussian defeat and withdrawal to north east. At 10 a.m. army began to pull back to position south of Waterloo, about 12-13 km to the north. 1/95th were last infantry to leave Quatre Bras, between 11 a.m. and noon, with cavalry who covered retreat. Torrential rain before battalion reached Genappe (5 km into a march "little better than a mud-bath"). Arrived at position 2-3 hours before dark. French took up position on ridge to south and fired occasional cannon shot. Ground like a marsh and was torrential rain all night. Troops slept on ground next to weapons. JL soaked to skin. Slept soundly.

18 June 1814	**Battle of Waterloo.** Allies in two lines occupying ridge crossing main Brussels road. 1/95th at centre of allied line on left (east) of main road and thrown forward down the slope towards the French. JL led two companies occupying a sand-pit on the forward side of a knoll by the road in an advanced position. About midday massive columns of French infantry attacked along a line east of the road. 1/95th were pushed sideways into the road but their fire pushed the column head away from them. While the French began to fan out to attack in earnest, the troops on the ridge fired into the head of the column and charged while the 1/95th fired into the flank. The French attack was repulsed and finally driven back down the slope by a cavalry charge. French continued to attack and 1/95th lost 3 officers killed and 6 or 7 wounded. Sir Andrew Barnard, commanding, the battalion, was wounded about 3 p.m. Shortly after the next in command, Lieutenant-Colonel Alexander Cameron, was wounded in the throat. Command of the 1st Battalion now devolved to JL who held it for the rest of the day. The French infantry advanced in force. 1/95th abandoned sandpit, knoll and ridge crest. French occupied those positions and for many hours 1st battalion was engaged in exchanging fire at close range while under cannon bombardment. About 7 p.m. the French infantry attacked to west of road and were repulsed. Prussians were arriving from east. Wellington ordered general advance just before sunset. 1/95th pursued French across the battlefield as part of advance until after nightfall, then army halted and bivouacked on what had been the French positions while Prussians continued pursuit. JL had been wounded by shrapnel from a shell during the battle. **Promoted by brevet to Lieutenant Colonel in the army**.
19 June 1815	Marched in the morning to follow the French army towards Paris.
22 June 1815	JL **Made a Companion of the Most Honourable Order of the Bath (C.B.)** Napoleon abdicated.
end of June 1815	Arrived near St Denis, north of Paris, which the French army had entered and barricaded. Montmartre was fortified. Prussians, after some losses, had crossed the R. Seine and were threatening the city.
3 July 1815	Hostilities formally suspended. 1/95th camped near St Denis.
July–late December 1815	Positioned around Paris.
end of December 1815	1/95th & 2/95th marched to northern France to take up placements as part of allied army of occupation in that region.
1816	95th Regiment of Foot redesignated 'The Rifle Brigade.'
1816–late 1818	1st battalion Rifle Brigade occupied region around Cambrai, Valenciennes and other towns in that region. JL enjoying many field-sports (fox-hunting; hare-coursing; falconry) and horse-races.
beginning of Winter 1818	Army of occupation left France.
February–September 1819	1st battalion Rifle Brigade at Gosport, Portsmouth.
9 September 1819	JL **promoted to rank of Major in the Rifle Brigade**.
18–28 September 1819	1st battalion sailing to Leith, Edinburgh on frigate 'Liffy' and a corvette to control radical elements causing unrest around Glasgow.
28 September 1819	Arrived Leith and marched to Glasgow to suppress civil unrest.
Oct. 1819– late 1820	In neighbourhood of Glasgow and Paisley. JL described duties as "over-awing cotton-spinners and colliers in Caledonia".

late 1820	1st battalion sent to Ireland.
January 1821	In Belfast.
Spring 1821	Battalion marched to Armagh. Later marched to Naas then to Kilkenny. Soon moved to Fermoy then to Newcastle West in the county of Limerick where there was unrest.
Summer–September 1821	In Newcastle West. JL described duties as "still-hunting; white boy hunting, and guarding county jails." William Surtees of the Rifle Brigade said, "Here we were for a time actually shut up as in a besieged town; and no individual belonging to the army durst attempt to move out without a sufficient number being together, to deter the misguided peasantry from attacking us. Innumerable were the murders that were committed about this neighbourhood at this time"..."This Rockite war gave us considerable trouble".
September 1821	Battalion left Newcastle West and moved to Rathkeale, Limerick.
24 October 1821	After 20 years service, JL **retired from the Army**. He later received the Silver General Service Medal with 12 clasps.

Appendix 5

Jonathan Leach's Waterloo letters

[*In 1844 Captain William Siborne (1797-1849) published his* History of the War in France and Belgium in 1815. *He also produced two topographic models: one of the entire battlefield at Waterloo; the other of the area around the crossroads of La Haye Sainte. The larger was on display at Egyptian Hall, Piccadilly from 1838; the smaller joined it in 1845. As preparation for these works Siborne corresponded with many officers who had fought at Waterloo. The letters that follow were Jonathan Leach's contribution to this information-gathering exercise. They deal primarily with Siborne's attempt to ascertain whether riflemen of the 1st Light Battalion of the King's German Legion had crossed the Genappe road from their position behind La Haye Sainte to assist the 1/95th, as two KGL officers (Heise and Leonhardt) had claimed. The letters discuss whether this could have occurred during the first attack of the French columns, although Sir Andrew Barnard's view was that, while the Germans may have crossed the road, this could have been later during the second push of the French infantry. He recalled seeing their commanding officer, Lt-Col. Bussche, on the British side of the road at that time* (Siborne, 1993: 52-53).

Mention in the following letters to a 'hollow way' is a reference to the sunken Ohain/Wavre road north of La Haye Sainte, not to the cutting south of La Haye Sainte.]

from : **Lt Col. Jonathan Leach** *C.B.*, **Stoke near Devonport.**
to   : **Sir John Philippart.**
date : **25th September 1840.**
loc. : **British Library (Ref. BM Add. Mss 34,707 ff. 197-200)**

Sir

On my return from the country this Morning, after an absence of some days, I found yours of the 22^d Septr on the table, ^to which I lose no time in replying; first to thank you for your promise of continuing in next Saturdays N: & M: Gazette my suggestions and observations, and secondly to assure you that I shall be most happy to give your friend Capt Siborn every information in my power on the subject so interesting to all Soldiers.— Be so kind as to tell Capt Siborn that I write by this days post to an old Rifleman (Capt Kincaid) who was *Adjutant* of the 1st Batt^n Rifle Brigade at Waterloo, to ascertain from him whether *he* has any recollection of one of the Light battalions of the German Legion having *crossed* the Genappe road to assail the flank of the attacking column of the French.— *I* certainly have no recollection of any such movement, yet I will not *positively* declare that it was not the case.—

One ^light battalion of the German legion held the farm house of La Haye Sainte *previous* to, and *at* and *after* the first grand attack on Pictons Division, nor was it driven out of that building until a very considerable time after ~~the defe~~ that attack was defeated.— The other batt^n of Riflemen (or light Infantry) of the German legion if posted, as stated, on the *British right of the Genappe road*, ^was very probably, moved forward to throw its *fire across the road* on the *left flank* of the French column either during its

526

advance or (what to me appears more probable) during its confused retreat.—
The moment I hear from Capt Kincaid (who, if not gone up the Rhine, as he
occasionally does at this season, will write to me without delay) I will transmit
the content of his letter to you for Capt Siborn.—

The 79th (one of Kempts reg^{ts}) I conclude *did* charge on the *left* of the
32nd; but the *last named reg^t*, aided by the Riflemen, which had been forced
back on Kempts *line*, *must* have come in ∧^{more} immediate contact with that
portion of the French which advanced by the *British left* of the Sandpit than
any other Corps in Pictons Division.

My own impression is and ever has been, that Packs regim^{ts} were *all
formed in line*, not in columns or squares, at the period of the battle alluded
to. Yet I may possibly err, and for the reasons assigned in my former
communication with Capt Siborn on this subject.—

Pray assure Capt Siborn that I regret my inability to furnish him with
more solid information; and I beg him to have no scruple in asking me any
questions; all of which I shall be too happy to answer to the best of my
ability.—

Believe me
Yours very faithfully
J Leach

---

from : Lt Col. Jonathan Leach *C.B.*, Stoke - near Devonport.
to : Sir John Philippart.
date : Thursday 1st October 1840
loc. : British Library (Ref. BM Add. Mss 34,707 ff. 201-202)

Sir

By last nights post I received an answer from my old friend and
comrade Capt Kincaid to whom I wrote last week on the subject of the
attack on Pictons Division at Waterloo. He says— "With regard to your
queries about Waterloo, it requires no great cudgelling of brains to reply to
that relating to the German Legion, for [*deletion*] the same question was
put to me some months ago, and I answered precisely as you have done,
that assuredly no German Legion men came across the road to us in the
course of the day.— They might have fired from the *bank* behind La Haye
Sainte across to *our* side but I do not think they did, for I saw the French
behind La Haye Sainte and in rear of the right of our Battalion before we
abandoned the knoll, and consequently if the Germans fired at all from
their side, it must have been at *us*. The question however coming a
second time from the same quarter and on the evidence (as Capt Siborn
wrote me) of a German Officer who was one of the party, has made a new
light dawn upon me, and makes me doubt whether a company (there might
have been *two*) of foreigners who stood on the *left* of our battalion on the
knoll at the beginning of the battle were not the very folks alluded to,
although we have all along believed that they were Belgians. ⊕ [*unclear
word*] How they came there, the Lord only knows.— If they came from
the *right* they must in the first instance have crossed to our Divisional

position behind the hedge, and advanced to us from thence, for assuredly they came not across the road to us direct; but my impression has always been that they must have been a picquet stationed there before we took possession of the knoll.— *You* were in front of the knoll, and may not have seen them at all.— I observed that they had *great coats on.*— But as I have already said if *they* were not Germans, then were there no Germans with us on that day.—"

This is precisely my ∧own idea of the thing; nor did I *ever* until I lately ∧saw Capt Sibborns queries on the point, hear any one state that Pictons Division received any support whatever throughout the battle from ∧the *Infantry* on the right of the Genappe road.—

⊕ I have a tolerably clear recollection that a short time *before* I was detached with two companies of the 95th Riflemen to the Sandpit in front of the knoll, there were some foreign troops (*not numerous*) on [*deletion*] the *left* of the 95th and advanced (as I thought) some little distance in *front* as a Picket.— Those troops must have been soon driven back; and I conclude ∧they are the two companies which Capt Kincaid states as being ∧subsequently formed on the *left* of the 95th.— J Leach

Kincaid proceeds.— "With regard to the formation of Packs brigade I must profess utter ignorance, for I have no recollection of having once seen them.— Like yourself, I found that I had quite enough to do to look at home."

Hoping that the contents of this letter may be useful to Capt Sibborn, believe me very faithfully

Yours

J Leach

from : Lt Col. Jonathan Leach *C.B.*, Worthing, Sussex.
to   : Captain William Siborne.
date : Wednesday 21st October 1840
loc.   : British Library (Ref. BM Add. Mss 34,707 ff. 205-206)

Sir

I beg to acknowledge the receipt of your polite letter of the 7th Octr which Sir J. Philippart forwarded to me; and I am exceedingly sorry that I have ~~not~~ ∧not been able to furnish you with more copious information on the subject of Waterloo.—

I saw my friend Capt Kincaid very lately and he has also read your letter to me.— We particularly discussed those points relative to that period of the battle wherein one of the light battalions of the German legion is stated by some of their Officers to have *crossed the Genappe road* and to have aided Pictons Division.— Both Capt Kincaid and Myself are very well aware that in researching many conflicting statements, yours is no ordinary task.— We are however strongly impressed with the belief that no part of Baron Altens Division nor infantry of any sort or kind was sent across the road to support Pictons troops in the whole course of the day; but that (as we concluded from the first moment the question was mooted) a part or the whole of one of Baron Altens light battalions very probably threw its fire ᴧ across the road on the left flank of the Enemy.— We think the question might very quickly be set at rest if your informants of the German Legion could state *on what spot the light battalions stood at the moment* when, as stated by them, "It advanced against the left flank of the French column, killed many men, and produced much confusion in its ranks; and that at this moment an English regiment of Cavalry came rushing down the road upon the tail of the column &c &c."—

It is clear that they could not have been *in* the Chaussée for it was never occupied except by two guns— they could not have been on *our* side the road because the Enemy had crowned the *knoll* before we (the 95th) left it; and our reserve kept up a very hot fire on it from the moment we had cleared their front. The only possible position they could have held to do us ᴧ the service they claim would have been by *firing* from the *height* on the *right* of the road (in the short space between the rear of the farm house of La Haye Sainte and the crest of the position) and a glance at the ground will show that they could only have done this whilst the Enemy had *passed* the knoll and were advancing upon our first line.— It would be difficult for them to show that they were *there* (that is on the height on the *right* of the road) for in fact the *front* of that part of the position was attacked at the same moment ᴧ that *we* were; and it is impossible to suppose that *one* of their battalions should have been standing with its *flank* to *their own Enemy*, and firing across the road at those opposed to *us* (the 95th)

And farther to say "That at this moment an English regiment of Cavalry came rushing down &c &c" is furnishing (we conceive) direct Evidence against themselves; for it shows that the French *horsemen* had already advanced over the very ground that the Germans would claim to have been then standing on, and farther that the French were *again* retreating *over that very ground* at the particular moment alluded to.— If those Officers of the German Legion can state *their exact position at the period in question*, some farther light may be thrown on [*deletion*] the business.— At present I cannot but think that my friend Kincaid & myself are not far wrong.— No one holds the German Legion in higher estimation than we do, and very justly; for better Soldiers never took the field; and we put forth these remarks merely with a view of eliciting the real state of things at that interesting period of the battle.

I have the honor to be
Sir
Your most Obᵗ Servᵗ
J Leach

from : Lt Col. Jonathan Leach *C.B.*, Worthing, Sussex.
to   : [Captain William Siborne].
date : Friday 6th November 1840
loc. : British Library (Ref. BM Add. Mss 34,707 ff. 210-211)

Sir

I beg to acknowledge the receipt of your letter of the 28th Oct[r] and to assure you that if I can throw any additional light on the subject of the grand attack on the left and left centre of our Army at Waterloo, it will give me much pleasure.—

I can readily understand that had not the French Cavalry attacked Baron Altens Infantry to our right of La Haye Sainte simultaneously with those columns which crossed the knoll in front of the 95th Riflemen, the 1st light batt[n] of the German Legion would have had such a favourable opportunity for throwing in their fire on the ~~L~~ left flank of the French Infantry as rarely occurs in war; but as we must conclude that the German Riflemen *were* aware of ₐa strong body of Cavalry being actually in progress towards their rear, it appears more than probable that they would lose not one instant in forming *square*; and as self preservation is the first principle of life, it is scarcely possible to doubt that they would place themselves in such a posture as would ensure their safety against those horsemen, and allow *Pictons* Infantry to manage matters as well as they were able with the Enemy in their immediate front.—   But even allowing that the Germans did *not* permit their offensive operations ~~on~~ against the left flank of the column of Infantry on *our* side of the chausee to be interrupted by the hostile cavalry on their *right* and *rear*, it is highly improbable that they would have *advanced across* the chausée (as asserted by some of their Officers) at so critical a moment. That they may have *aided us* by a flanking fire across the road I think highly probable, and I thought so from the first moment the question was mooted; but it could not have been of long duration, for the cause I have stated above.— I can take upon myself to speak confidently also on another point, which is that if the Germans did cross to our side of the road during any part of the day, some of my old regiment must necessarily have seen them; and neither Kincaid nor myself did see one of them, nor have I ever heard any of our Men or Officers state that they saw them either.—

But when you hear farther from your German correspondents, if you will be so kind as to let me know the purport of their communication on this point, I will do my best, with the assistance of Cap[t] Kincaid, to unravel the mystery.—

I am truly sorry that you have not been so successful in collecting information as to the operations of the *Infantry* on the *left* of the road as you have been of that on the *right*.—   Thus much I think I can assert with confidence, which is, that *after* the *second* great attack on Pictons Division (in which the French succeeded in possessing themselves of La Haye Sainte) the contest on *our* part of the position consisted of an uninterrupted fire of musquetry on both sides; The French *kneeling* down behind the crest of the knoll and exposing only their heads & shoulders to *our* fire, and Kempts brigade, ranged along the thorn hedge ⁱⁿ(^{line} together with part of *Lamberts* Division) keeping up as hot a fire [*deletion*] on them as they were able.— Thus matters remained with *us* until Napoleons last grand attack with his guard ~~to~~ _∧^{on} *our right,* _∧(the right of the *Army*) which attack was nevertheless aided by a *general forward movement* of various other troops _∧^{along} ~~towards~~ *our whole position*; which, I conclude, was a diversion in favor of the _∧~~Imperial Guard~~ main attack _∧^{made} by the Imperial Guard.—

For some hours previous to this last attack *none* of *Kempts* reg^{ts} were in square, nor do I think they were in square during the day.— The 27th in Lamberts Division *was almost destroyed in square*, immediately in *rear* of the right of *my own Battalion.* Sir D. Packs brigade towards the after part of the contest was in *reserve* to Kempts brigade & Lamberts people _∧^{who were} posted along the hedge (as above stated) but they were in *columns* of *battalions.*— Such I believe firmly to have been the [*deletion*] disposition and formation of Pictons Division *after* La Haye Sainte was taken. There could indeed have been no necessity, that I am aware of, for forming [*deletion*] *squares*; because Kempts & Lamberts troops, being hotly engaged with *Infantry* some distance in front of Packs reserve, it was quite as probable that the latter might have been called on to *deploy* and to act in *line* against the Swarms of Infantry in our front as that they would be ridden in upon by Cavalry.— The front line must have been first beaten or destroyed _∧^{either} [*deletion*] by the fire of the French Infantry or _∧^{by} charges of their Cavalry.— Neither one or the other took place; and my opinion is that Packs brigade was in columns_∧^{at} ~~of~~ quarter distance or in *close* order.

I must now apologize for the numerous blots and erasures, and beg you will excuse them.

Believe me Yours very faithfully

J Leach

---

from : **Lt Col. Jonathan Leach *C.B.*, Worthing, Sussex.**
to   : **Captain William Siborne.**
date : **Sunday 22nd November 1840**
loc.   : **British Library (Ref. BM Add. Mss 34,707 ff. 215-216)**

Sir

I am very glad to hear by your letter of the 16th which reached me yesterday, that you are in a fair way of getting at the real history of the German light battalion at Waterloo.

I am gratified also to find that my statement as to the distribution of Pictons and Lamberts Divisions towards the latter part of the contest coincides with the information afforded you by Staff and regimental Officers of those two Divisions.—

I cannot speak confidently as to the *first Royals*; they might have been in *line* at the period to which you allude; but if so they must necessarily have been posted on the *left* of Kempts brigade; and as the first Battalion of the 95th Riflemen was on the *extreme right* of the Division, it would have been [*deletion*] impossible for *us* to have seen or, at all events, to have distinguished them in the midst of the smoke.—

That several regiments of Packs brigade were in close column or in column at quarter distance in rear of Kempts brigade, I am very certain.—

Previous to the second grand attack on our Division, I was detached with two companies of the 95th Riflemen as before, to occupy the excavation near the road, from where gravel had been dug, the remaining four companies of our battalion occupying the knoll above it.—

The great effort of the French appeared to be to carry the farm house of La Haye Sainte; and this they were enabled to do (in spite of the obstinate and gallant defence of the occupants) in consequence of the ammunition of the Germans being expended, and there being no mode of supplying them with more.—

This, however unavoidable, was highly disastrous to the troops of Picton and Lambert, for the French instantly filled the house with swarms of Sharpshooters whose deadly fire precluded the possibility of our holding the knoll and the ground immediately about it, and they established also a strong and numerous line of Infantry, [*deletion*] extending along the front of Kempts brigade.—

Those Frenchmen however *knelt down*, and exposed only their heads and shoulders to *our* fire; and in this manner the contest was carried on between them and us until the general advance of the whole of the D. of Wellingtons Army against the French position immediately after the total defeat of the Imperial Guards.—

From the time that La Haye Sainte fell into the hands of the French, until the moment of the general advance of our Army, the mode of attack and defence was remarkable for its *sameness*.—   But I speak merely of what took place immediately about *our* part of the position.

It consisted of one uninterrupted fire of Musquetry (the distance between the hostile lines I imagine to have been rather more than one hundred yards) between Kempts and some of Lamberts reg^{ts} posted along the thorn hedge and the French Infantry lining the knoll and the crest of the hill near it.—   Several times the French officers made desperate efforts to induce their men to charge Kempts line; and I saw more than once portions of the French in our front spring up from their *kneeling position* and advance some yards towards the thorn hedge, headed by their Officers [*deletion*] with vehement gestures; but our fire was so very hot and deadly that they almost instantly ran back behind the crest of the hill; always leaving a great many killed or disabled behind them.

During this Musquetry contest, which I firmly believe was the closest and most protracted almost ever witnessed, some apprehension was entertained that the French would endeavour to force their way along the Chaussée and attack the *rear* of the troops lining the thorn hedge; and on a report of the kind being made to me by one of our Officers, coupled with a suggestion that a part of the 95th Riflemen should be *concentrated* on the *extreme right*, so as to fire into the road, my reply was – "The 27th regiment is in square in our rear, having one of its faces looking directly into the sroad, and that regiment must protect our rear; for the French are gathering so fast and thick in *our front*, that we cannot spare a single man to detach to the *right*."

I merely mention this to show in what manner we were employed at this period of the day.

I concluded also that the regts of Infantry, which were in reserve behind us, and (I believe) some of Cavalry not far off [*deletion*], would have instantly attacked any French force which might ‸have menaced the rear of Kempts brigade by the Chaussée.— A very short time (a few minutes only I think) *before* Pictons Division joined ‸in the general advance against the French position, the French suddenly evacuated the farm house of La Haye Sainte and the ground near it, and retreated in haste; and this I conclude was in consequence of the total repulse of the Imperial Guards, and [*deletion*] the forward movement of a part of the D. of Wellingtons right wing.— Should this imperfect account of what happened in *our* neighbourhood on that momentous occasion prove of any use to you, I shall be extremely happy; and I have only to add that any question which I am able to answer I shall always be happy to do to the best of my ability.

Believe me very faithfully yours

J *Leach*

---

from : Lt Col. Jonathan Leach C.B.
to   : [to, or for, Captain William Siborne].
date : not known.
loc. : British Library (Ref. BM Add. Mss 34,707 ff. 222-223).

In endeavouring to reply to Capt Siborns questions, it is necessary for me to observe that although the 1st or Royals Regiment was in the same Division with the 1st Battalion of the 95th Rifle Corps, it was not in the same *brigade*; the Royals being in Sir D. Packs and the Rifle Corps in Sir J. Kempts.—

The 95th was posted on the extreme right of Pictons Division with its right flank resting on the road leading to Genappe and it was therefore at a considerable distance from the Royals during the first attack on the 5th Division, in which Sir T. Picton was killed.— The 95th Riflemen were so closely and warmly engaged at the moment the heavy cavalry were moved up to support the 5th Division, that I cannot pretend to say in *what manner* those horsemen passed through the intervals of the Royal regiment, nor am I able positively to declare whether they did or did not pass through *that* battalion in particular.

It will not be difficult for me to explain *why* any doubts on this point exist in my mind.

Previous to the attack on the 5th Division, I was sent in command of two companies of Riflemen to occupy an excavation ([*deletion*] from which sand had been dug) *close* to the Genappe road and on its *left*.— This was at the base of the hillock, on the summit of which the remainder of the 95th Rifle Corps was posted to support the two advanced companies.—

The fierce onset of the French with overwhelming numbers forced back my two companies on the main body of the 95th Reg^t; and this hillock was also instantly assailed in such a manner as to render it impossible for one weak battalion, consisting of only six companies, to stem the torrent for any length of time.— We were consequently constrained to fall back on the 32nd reg^t which was in line, near the thorn hedge ∧^which ~~ranning~~ from the Genappe road to [*deletion*] ∧^the left, and along the front of Pictons Division. We were closely pressed and hotly engaged during this retrograde movement; and very soon after reaching the spot where the 32nd was in position, a volley and a charge of bayonets caused the French to recoil in disorder and with a heavy loss; and it was at this moment of fire, smoke, cheering and excitement that the heavy cavalry of the Army suddenly appeared amongst us, and instantly charged that Infantry which the fire and charge of bayonets of Pictons Division had previously shattered and broken.

Capt S. will readily understand that whilst posted *in advance* at the base of the hill, previous to the French attack, as likewise during our retrograde movement |223 movement from thence to the hillock above, and subsequently from thence to the thorn hedge, various changes in the disposition of the troops of the 5th Division might have been made, which I could neither *see* nor attend to if I did see; for no breathing time was allowed us skirmishers by our immediate opponents; to arrest whose impetuous advance was our grand object.—

I am extremely sorry therefore that I cannot give a distinct and satisfactory answer to Capt Siborns questions, which it would have afforded me very great pleasure to have done.—

At a later period of the battle, Sir D. Packs Brigade was formed in squares or close columns in rear of Sir J. Kempts; which latter brigade, together with some of Sir John Lamberts reg^ts fought in *line* up to the termination of the contest on our position. – I must beg Capt Siborn will excuse this long detail.—

---

from : Lt Col. Jonathan Leach *C.B.*, Worthing, Sussex.
to   : [Captain William Siborne].
date : Wednesday 30th December 1840
loc. : British Library (Ref. BM Add. Mss 34,707 ff. 236-237)

Sir

I yesterday received the enclosed letter from Capt Kincaid to you (which I have taken the liberty of perusing) as also a note from you to him of the 22nd Decr and statements likewise of several Officers of the late German Legion.

In my former letter to you on the subject of the cooperation of the German light battalion with Sir J. Kempts brigade, I believe I stated that I was *positive* that not a single *foot* soldier *crossed* the chaussée to assist in repelling the French column— that indeed I never knew of *any* cooperation *whatever* having been made by the troops on the Allied *right* of the chaussée throughout the battle.— With a thorough conviction of the accuracy and correctness of my assertion on this point I should most undoubtedly have gone to my grave.—

Neither Capt Kincaid nor myself *saw*, or (until very recently) ever heard of such cooperation as that claimed by our old and gallant comrades of the legion, nor did I ever hear an individual of my old Corps mention having seen a single Infantry Soldier arrive from the *right* of the road to succour Pictons division during the whole [*deletion*] of the battle.— I scarcely need add that the particular occurrences of that eventful day, I have heard discussed again and again year after year.

Cap[t] Kincaid justly observes that it is impossible to doubt after reading the different statements of the German Officers that some of their companies *did* cross over to the left of the road; and I now no longer entertain doubts on that point.

I am, however, fully borne out in my original opinion and belief *that not an individual of the 95th Reg[t] saw* those companies of Germans which were sent to the *left* of the road; and Colonel [*?Wryken*]s statement, although erroneous in part, explains *why* we (the 95th) did not see them.— Colonel W. says "The 95th (in the first attack of the French) was forced to fall back, and in making this retrograde movement *must have inclined more to the left*, for the road with the hedge opposite the hollow way *was unoccupied* for an extent of about 100 paces; and Colonel Bussche ordered the two companies (Germans) to occupy it."

This ground was, as a matter of course, unoccupied during the time the 95th reg[t] was hotly engaged on the knoll in front of it, but it would appear that if the 95th Riflemen had looked *behind* them at this trying moment instead of attending to matters of far greater importance in their *front* they might have seen the two former companies *temporarily occupying* the ground which the 95th was destined to defend and which it did defend successfully throughout the day.—

When the 95th was forced back to the hedge, on the right of the ground held by the 32nd reg[t], most positive I am that no Germans were then there; and I therefore conclude that they had been [*deletion*] withdrawn by orders from the other side of the chaussée.— The *reason* that Colonel W. saw nothing of the 95th is therefore fully accounted for; although he might have done so had he cast his eyes on the knoll in front.— I should have not the slightest hesitation if necessary, in making an affidavit ^that when my old Corps (95th) was forced back to the hedge, behind which were Kempts reg[ts] in line, it *did not incline to its left*, but that it fell back to its own proper place in the position, which was with its right immediately on the Genappe road.— If it had (as stated by Colonel W.) *inclined more to its left*, it must necessarily have placed itself in *front* of the 32nd or of *some* of Kempts reg[ts], and consequently prevented their firing on the advancing Enemy;

whereas it is most certain that it, on the contrary, *retired slowly* and in the proper direction, and that it occupied the ground between the *right* of the 32nd and the Genappe road.— I can further most unhesitatingly declare that the *sole* and *only* ground held by the 95th Reg[t] from the *commencement* of the battle to its *termination* was -   the *knoll*, with two companies advanced into the Sand pit, and subsequently the ground from the Genappe road (its *right* resting immediately thereon) towards the other reg[ts] of Kempts brigade, behind the thorn hedge.— We might easily therefore have been *seen* from *daybreak* of the 18th June until the general advance of the whole Army after the defeat of Napoleons guards, [*deletion*] at *one* of those points of defence.—

I feel that it would be superfluous, especially after Cap[t] Kincaids statement to you, for me to dwell on the *particular points* at which one or more companies of the Legion *did* file across to the left of the road.— That some of their companies were sent across appears beyond ˄a doubt.— Why we of the 95th did not see them, I have endeavoured to explain; and I hope satisfactorily.

As to the charges of cavalry mentioned by some of the Officers of the Legion, I conclude they must have been very partial and made in an isolated manner, if I may so express myself.— In the first attack on Pictons Division *I* know of but *one great charge* ˄of cavalry and that took place immediately on Kempts brigade having driven back the attacking column by its fire and charge with the bayonet.

Most heartily & cordially do I agree with Cap[t] Kincaid in declaring that all Old Soldiers who have ever served with the late K German legion, hold them in the highest possible estimation, and no one more so than myself.—

Far be it from any of my old Corps (I undertake to answer for the *remnant* of those who were at Waterloo) to wish to detract from their well earned renown.—

Indeed I know not ~~how~~ ˄why any particular *credit* is to be especially awarded to a Soldier on that memorable day for having fought on *this* or on *that* side of any particular road within the allied position.— To get at correct statements of what happened is all you desire, and I very much hope you will fully *succeed in ~~your~~* obtaining such! — believe me very faithfully yours

J Leach

---

from : Lt Col. Jonathan Leach *C.B.*, Worthing, Sussex.
to   : Captain William Siborne.
date : Wednesday 24th February 1841
loc. : British Library (Ref. BM Add. Mss 34,707 ff. 243-244).

Dear Sir

Cap[t] Kincaid has sent me your letter to him of the 16th February and the further remarks of the two German Officers.

With respect to the question of the ground occupied by the right of the 32nd reg[t] during the first attack, I fear I ~~have~~ can add nothing to what I stated in my last letter; but as Cap[t] Kincaid resides in London, he will perhaps be able to collect some further information on that point from Sir J. Kempt and those Officers of the 32nd named in your letter to him; and I shall be very happy if he succeeds in so doing.

I have long ceased (as I mentioned to you in a former letter) to doubt that some companies of the Light Battn K.G. Legion did, at some period of the first attack, move out of the hollow way and cross over to our side of the Chausée; and Major Heise declaring that he is ready to make affidavit that he was wounded on that side of it, can leave no doubt on the mind of any one.

I repeat however that *I* never *saw* a man of the light Bn on our side, nor have I ever heard an individual of the 95th say that he saw them either.

Touching the question of the Lt Battn of the legion crossing the chausée, I beg to remind you that in the first letter I did myself the pleasure of writing to you on the subject of Waterloo, I expressed some surprize that the Battalion in question was not formed in *Square* at the moment the French Cuirassiers advanced against the troops of Count Altens Division in the vicinity of La Haye Sainte, and at the moment when the *right* and *rear* of the said Battalion was thus seriously threatened.

It is *possible* therefore that they deemed their post (formed as they then were) a perilous one; and that crossing rapidly to the *left* of the great road would render them secure from the attack of the Cuirassiers.

On ~~Of~~ the policy or propriety of such a movement [*deletion*] it is unnecessary that I should offer an opinion.

The scattered Cuirassiers, who skirted along the front of our regt, after they had been repulsed on the opposite side of the road by the brigade of household cavalry and ^were followed by some of them out of the hollow way, were (I have ever considered) *retreating towards their own Infantry*, and did not approach our people so very near with a view of attacking us, but did so in their hasty retreat.—

I recollect there were *many ~~of~~ gaps* in the hedges of the *Wavres road.*— The Royal Dragoons passed through some of them, as did (I conclude) the remainder of Ponsonbys brigade farther to the left.

I wish I could send you any information which would tend to render you any assistance in the laborious and meritorious task you have undertaken.

You will however I hope take the hill for the dead.— Begging you will excuse blots and erasures. I am   Dear Sir
Very faithfully yours
J Leach

---

from : Lt Col. Jonathan Leach *C.B.*, Stoke – near Devonport.
to : [Captain William Siborne].
date : Monday 15th August 1842
loc. : British Library (Ref. BM Add. Mss 34,707 ff. 388-390)

Dear Sir
I last Evening received your letter, and shall be extremely happy to give you all the information in my power.—

I have always considered that there but *two French attacks* on Pictons Division; and as in my former letters I detailed as fully as I was able every particular respecting the *first*, which was undoubtedly the most serious of them, it is unnecessary for me again to revert to it.

A considerable time ˬ^elapsed (an hour or more, to the best of my recollection) before the French commenced their *second* attack; during which interval I was again sent with two companies of the 95th to occupy my old post in front of the knoll.

As the French advanced, my companies were as a matter of course, forced back to the knoll, and subsequently still further, as was the case in the *first* attack.—

Sir A. Barnard is perfectly correct in saying that there ~~were~~ was a second attack on Kempts brigade; but the "French skirmishers" which he describes as "coming up in considerable bodies," were in fact a strong line of Infantry, pushed forward in a somewhat desultory manner in front of La Haye Sainte at the moment that post was taken from the Germans.—   This body of the Enemy lined the crest of the position in the immediate front of Kempts brigade; on which, as well as on the 27th regt [*deletion*] formed in square a short distance in rear of the 95th, they kept up an unceasing fire; and to this fire also the other regts of Lamberts brigade were exposed until the moment the whole Army *advanced* after the defeat of the Imperial Guard.—

Your first Model describes most accurately the relative situation of Kempts & Lamberts brigades and that of the French opposed to them from the ~~moment~~ ˬ^time La Haye Sainte fell into their hands up to the moment of the general advance of our Army.

As to the question whether the German light Battalion did or did not cross the Chausée and assist in defeating the Enemy, I really am unable to add one atom of information to that contained in my former letters, which I fear is unsatisfactory enough.

In this *second* attack it was that the French succeeded in possessing themselves of La Haye Sainte; and any *other* attacks on that part of the position held by Kempt and Lambert (Sir J. Kempts letter, you say, mentions *three* attempts) consisted of men rushing suddenly and impetuously forward from behind the *crest* of the position towards our line, without much reference to a regular formation and but imperfectly supported.—   They essayed this kind of thing *several times* in the immediate front of my own regiment and the 4th, which extended its line to our left; but those *spurts*, if I may so term them, were defeated by the fire which we sent amongst them.

You are aware that the 95th was on the extreme right of the Division; and as the [*deletion*] *left* of Kempts line was at a considerable distance from us it is possible that some of the attacks to which I have alluded might have been repulsed by a forward rush of our skirmishers; but I am not aware that such was the case.

That any charge was made down the slope by the main body of the brigade *after* the French had possession of La Haye Sainte and were consequently in great force *in* and *about* and behind the buildings, [*deletion*] must be erroneous; and every one who reflects for a moment must be aware that even if such a charge *had* been well supported by Infantry & Cavalry, and [*deletion*] the Officer in command on the spot had resolved to *retake* and to *keep possession* of the crest of the position, it would have been a rash and unwise measure.— Our brigade, with its ranks greatly diminished, would not only have been opposed to very superior numbers the moment it |390 it topped the crest of the position, and ᵂᵒᵘˡᵈ have been exposed to a most destructive fire from swarms of infantry in and near La Haye Sainte, but to a powerful Artillery also ₐ ᵃⁿᵈ at so short a distance as would have destroyed its remnants by grape shot.— I ought perhaps to observe [*deletion*] that in the *second* attack (the grand ₐ ᵃⁿᵈ ᵖʳⁱᵐᵃʳʸ object of which was to take La Haye Sainte) the French did not advance farther than the *crest* of our position, but contented themselves with keeping up a hot fire from it; making subsequently *several* forward ~~movements~~ ₐ ʳᵘˢʰᵉˢ as I have described.

I have said that I was driven back from my advanced post on the *second* attack; and this will be, I hope, a satisfactory reply to your questions on that point.

The exact *time* at which the French made their first and second attacks on our Division, I conceive is very immaterial; but I have always believed the *first* commenced about *twelve*, and that La Haye Sainte fell into their hands soon after *three*.— I shall feel much obliged by your sending me   a prospectus of your forthcoming history of that memorable campaign.— I must beg you to excuse so many erasures, and I hope you will be able to decipher a hand writing which is none of the most legible.— I assure you I shall at all times feel happy in answering any question you may have occasion to ask on this interesting subject, and beg therefore you will have no scruple in writing to me when you feel at all disposed to do so.—

Believe me very faithfully yours

J Leach

---

from : Lt Col. Jonathan Leach *C.B.*, Blagdon – near Launceston, Cornwall.
to   : [Captain William Siborne].
date : Saturday 3rd September 1842
loc. : British Library (Ref. BM Add. Mss 34,707 ff. 402-403).

Dear Sir

Your letter of the 31ˢᵗ August was forwarded to me from Stoke, to which place I shall return in about ten days.—

As I fear I have been misunderstood in what I stated relative to the *second* attack, a few words in explanation may be necessary.—

The correctness of your information gathered from my old friend Barings narrative, that La Haie Sainte experienced *four* most serious attacks before it was taken, I cannot for an instant doubt; but there were nevertheless but *two grand attacks on Pictons Division*.— In the *second* the French, after driving the 95ᵗʰ from the sand pit and knoll back on their own brigade, established a strong line of Infantry on the crest of our position, and from thence kept up an incessant fire until the general advance of the whole Army after the defeat of the Imperial Guards.

You are well aware that from the ground *at that time held by Kempts and Lamberts brigades*, not an individual belonging to either of them could possibly *see* or *know* at what *precise moment* the French *did* possess themselves of La Haie Sainte.

Having in their *second* attack established themselves in force along the crest of our position, it is well known that large Masses of troops instantly clustered round La H. Sainte, and, as was the case with Hougomont, made repeated attempts to force an entrance by the doors and windows; each of which seperate attacks Genl Baring has, without doubt, very properly designated as most serious.

This farm house *might*, for aught *we* (Kempts people) knew at that time, have been taken at the moment the French established themselves on the crest of our position, or at a considerably later period.

And as all those assaults on the house were made by the troops employed in the *second* attack on Pictons Division, and by those sent to support them, I am not in error in stating that La H. Sainte fell into their hands during the second attack on our Division.

Opinions and accounts of the battle differ as to the exact time the first and second attacks commenced.

My firm conviction has always been that *about three oclock* the *second* was made; but it is possible that La Haye Sainte was not taken until a later hour, as I have already endeavoured to explain.

Both Sir J. Kempt and the field Officer of the 32nd are correct in saying that the Rifle Corps covered the front of the brigade; but this was previous to the first and second attacks, in both of which they were, as a matter of course, driven back on their own brigade as the French Masses advanced.

If the 32nd rested its right on the Chausée it is clear that some of the companies of ~~its~~ ^the right wing could not have delivered their fire without endangering the 95th who were falling back on them; and most certain it is that after the French had, in their *second* attack, succeeded in crowning the crest of our position and from thence keeping up an incessant fire of Musquetry, the 95th rested *its right* on the Chausée, and there fought until the general advance of our whole Army.

It may perhaps be deemed presumptuous to differ from Sir J. Kempt in what he has styled in his letter "*the crest of the position*".—

The *crest*, correctly speaking, I conceive to have been the *knoll* (immediately above the sand pit) and the *ridge* running from the knoll along the front of Kempts brigade.— I may add also (entre nous) that when Sir A. Barnard directed me to occupy the sand pit with two companies I said, "If I am driven from this post I shall fall back on the remainder of our battalion, on the knoll, to which ground, I conclude, Sir J. Kempt will bring up his brigade".— Sir A. Barnards reply was, "I have urged Kempt to do so, but he has decided on awaiting the attack a considerable distance to the rear." and so he did; calling the *crest* of the position ∧the ground almost close to the road, and thorn hedge.— I feel much obliged for your kind offer of sending me Genl Barings narration; but I regret to say that I am not acquainted with the German language.— I shall however endeavour to get Beamish's history of the K.G. Legion.— I regret being unable to add any information to that contained in my former letters on the subject of the ground occupied by the 32nd previous to the charge of Kempts Brigade, and shall conclude by wishing your work every success.— Believe me very faithfully yours

J Leach

---

from : Lt Col. Jonathan Leach *C.B.*, Blagdon near Launceston – Cornwall.
to   : Captain William Siborne.
date : Tuesday 6th September 1842
loc. : British Library (Ref. BM Add. Mss 34,707 ff. 405-406).

Dear Sir

To your letter of the 31st August, which was forwarded from Stoke, I replied some days since; and I have to acknowledge by this days post yours also of the 2nd Sep^tr.—

The only remark I have to make on the letter of the field Officer of the 32nd reg^t is that on the Rifle Corps being driven from the sand pit and knoll in the first grand attack, *many* of the skirmishers *might* and I doubt not *did* retreat through intervals made for them in the line of the 32^d reg^t but you will readily conceive that at such a moment when a battalion consisting of six companies was engaged in such a desultory conflict, it must have been utterly impossible for any officer to ascertain positively the exact point to which *many* of the skirmishers might have fallen back.

I perfectly well remember that the greater portion of the men under my command kept their *right* well towards the Chausée in our retrograde movement; and that at the moment we were approaching the thorn hedge, Kempts line advanced with cheers to the charge and that we (the 95th) rushed forward with them, or rather perhaps, in advance of their *right wing*.—

In my last letter I stated that after the 95th had been driven in on the *second* attack, and the French had established themselves in force on the crest of the position, the *right* of our reg^t *rested on the Chausée*, and there fought until the general advance of the whole line; and on that spot they are correctly represented in your Model.

Hoping [*deletion*] you will find no difficulty in representing and describing matters as they really were at that interesting moment, and that your work will meet with every success, I remain

Dear Sir
Yours very faithfully
J Leach

P.S. I must beg you to excuse erasures &c —

---

from : **Lt Col. Jonathan Leach** *C.B.*, **Worthing – Sussex.**
to   : **Captain William Siborne.**
date : **Thursday 3rd November 1842**
loc. : **British Library (Ref. BM Add. Mss 34,707 ff. 458-459).**

Dear Sir

I do not recollect having seen any French Cavalry at the period of the action alluded to in your letter of the 31st October, dressed in *white coats* and with *brass cuirasses*.— Those who were near us were dressed in *blue coats* and had *steel cuirasses*. I think they wore also red Epaulettes.—

Many thanks for the prospectus of your work.— I saw it announced in last weeks N. & Military Gazette, and instantly wrote to Messrs Boone to have my name put down as a subscriber.—

I look forward with great interest to its appearance.—

Wishing you every possible success, believe me very truly yours
                                        J Leach

---

from : **Lt Col. Jonathan Leach** *C.B.*, **Worthing.**
to   : **[Captain William Siborne].**
date : **Sunday 22nd January 1843**
loc. : **British Library (Ref. BM Add. Mss 34,708 ff. 18-19)**

My dear Sir

I recollect that some rockets *were* thrown; and, to the best of my belief, after Pictons Division had repulsed the French in their first attack.—

I will not be too positive; but my impression is that they were discharged from *near* the spot where ~~the~~ the Abattis had been constructed.

I am very sorry that the publication of your interesting work will unavoidably be delayed for some little time longer.—

Believe me very truly yours
                    J Leach
P.S.

The precise *time* at which the rockets were first discharged, I really cannot now say.—

---

from : **Lt Col. Jonathan Leach** *C.B.*, **Worthing.**
to   : **Captain William Siborne.**
date : **Tuesday 28th February 1843**
loc. : **British Library (Ref. BM Add. Mss 34,708 ff. 60-61)**

Dear Sir

You are aware, I conclude, that the 1st Battalion 95th Rifle Corps had only *six* companies in Belgium in the campaign of 1815; two of which were stationed under my command in the Gravel pit before the battle of the 18th commenced.

On being obliged to fall back from that post to the knoll, I recollect that one of the first people I spoke to on the knoll was Captain Johnstone; whose company therefore must have been one of those stationed there —

I *think* (but am *not certain*) Captain Chawners company was there likewise.— Both these Officers are now dead; so that I am unable to gather any thing *positive* ^as to the *latter*.

Brevet Lt Colonel (now, Major General Sir A.) Cameron was on the knoll, and I think Sir A. Barnard also.

I am not aware that I can give you any further information touching that point.

Believe me very faithfully yours

J Leach

---

from : **Lt Col. Jonathan Leach** *C.B.*, **Worthing, Sussex.**
to : **Captain William Siborne.**
date : **Monday 6th March 1843**
loc. : **British Library (Ref. BM Add. Mss 34,708 ff. 62-63)**

Dear Sir

The following companies of the 1st Batt^n 95th Rifle Corps embarked on the 25th of April 1815 at Dover for Ostend.—

Brevet Major Leach's.—

Brevet Major C. Beckwiths.

Capt Charles Smyths.

Capt Chawners —

Capt Johnstones.—

and on arriving at Brussels, we were joined by Capt Glasses company, which had been in Flanders for some Months under the command of Lord Lynedock.

Major Beckwith and Capt Charles Smyth were both appointed to the *Staff* many weeks before the campaign opened.— Beckwith lost a leg at Waterloo, and C. Smyth was killed at Quatre Bras.—

Captains, Chawner and Johnstone were *both wounded* on the *18th*; Of this I am as *certain* as I am of my existence.—

Lieu^t Johnson (or John*stone*) was ~~also~~ killed on the 18th.—

Capt Johnstone joined us at *Paris* not long after our arrival there; and he *remained* with the Army of Occupation until it left France.—

I certainly *spoke* to him on the knoll; and I conclude therefore that *his company* must have been there also —

Believe me very truly yours

J Leach

turn over

P.S.

The "d" affixed to his name in the Army lists of June & July I can only account for by his being *absent* during the latter *part* of *June* and the month of *July* at Brussels, where he was in Hospital; recovering from his wound in the Shoulder.

J L

Picture credits

All images not displaying a copyright (©) notice are the original copyright creation of Keith Harrison (KH). The sources of some images are given in the figure legends and are not repeated here. Most images in the *Zoological Miscellany* are hand-coloured and have been converted to monochrome. All images from: the *Zoological Miscellany*; W.E. Leach's articles CIRRIPEDES and ANNULOSA; Leach, 1852; and volumes 3 & 4 of Kirby & Spence (1826) have been reproduced from works in the collections of the Linnean Society of London and the Society's assistance is gratefully acknowledged. The sources of the remaining images are as follows, preceded in bold type by the number of the page on which they occur.

Page: **8**, **365**, **471** (painted by James Northcote. This is a detail of a larger image), **486**, **494**: William P.C. Adams, Florida. **13**: British Museum (BM Imperial Box 2, 1862-6-14, 633). Drawn by George Scharf (1788-1860). **14**, **15**, **20**(upper), **21**, **28**, **29**, **32**, **62**, **96**, **123**, **131**, **176**, **261** (this is an artist's impression only, not to scale, and there may have been 8 windows across the west end of Montagu House, not 5 as shown. Also, the far wall of the Bird Room, on which is written 'Room XI' in the figure, probably housed windows to capture light from the main staircase), **284**, **298**, **300**, **305**, **317**, **319**, **465**, **480**, **500**, **503** (both): Original artwork, KH. **16**, **17**(upper), **20**(lower), **22**, **95**, **138**, **350**, **361**, **366**, **378**, **410**, **411**, **470**, **487**, **488**, **490**: Britton & Brayley, 1832. **17**(lower), **31**, **98**, **280**: Bate & Westwood, 1863. **18**, **159**: Hugh Thomson *in* Mitford, 1893. **19**: Foster, 1895. **43**, **45**: Verner, 1919. **50**: Verner, 1912. **57**: Smith, 1901. **59**: Yarrell, 1882-1884. **81**, **234**, **313**, **338**: Tucker, 1846. **85**, **414**(both): Yarrell, 1871-1874. **86**: Yarrell, 1876-1882. **88**, **91**, **93**, **100**, **101**, **256**, **287**, **368**, **381**, **385**, **425**, **447**: Shepherd, 1829. **89**: Herbert Railton *in* Martin, 1891 (amended by KH). **92**: Macilwain, 1856. **94**: Anon., 1870, Pl. 20. **97**: W.E. Leach. 1813. *Transactions of the Linnean Society*, 11(1): Pl. 6. **103**: Ashton, 1906. **106**: Shepherd & Elmes, 1829. **113**, **114**, **115**, **116**, **117**, **118**, **119**(upper), **128**, **129**, **132**(upper), **133**, **135**, **419**: Grant, 1880-1883. **119**(lower): Kirby & Spence, 1826 (vol. 3). **120**, **157**: Kirby & Spence, 1818 (vol. 2). **134**: *Edinburgh Encyclopaedia*, 8(1): Pl. 218. **140**: Kirby & Spence, 1826 (vol. 4). **141**(upper): Victoria & Albert Museum (Ref: E.1113-1927. Neg. N°. HB2350). Drawn by John Sell Cotman (1782-1842). Reproduced by permission of the Board of Trustees of the Victoria and Albert Museum, London. **166**, **174**: Verner, 1919 (amended by KH). **186**, **187**, **188**, **189**, **190**, **191**, **201**, **209**, **215**, **221**: Roscoe, 1837. **202**, **206**: Napier, 1851 (map on p.202 amended by KH). **250**: Lemon, 1867. **251**: *Bulletin of the British Museum (Natural History), Historical Series*, 3(8): Frontispiece (1969). **257**: British Museum (BM Book 3, p.8, 644). By George Scharf. **258**: British Museum. **259**: British Museum (BM Box 17 b, 1862-6-14, 628). By George Scharf. **260**: British Museum (extracted from Ackermann, *The Microcosm of London*). **262**: British Museum (BM Book 3, p.1, 626). By George Scharf. **263**: British Museum (BM Box 17 b, 1862-6-14, 632). By George Scharf. **267**: From the print *Landing the Treasures, or Results of the Polar Expedition!!!* by George Cruikshank, January 1819. Scott Polar Research Institute Cambridge. **292**: Redrawn from Pool, 1967. **296**, **330**: Kelly, 1828. **316**: Pasted as a frontispiece in KH's copy of Tucker, 1846. It is not clear whether this portrait was originally issued with Tucker's work or was added by a later owner. **320**, **321**: British Museum. Engraved by C. Turner after George Jones. **322**: National Army Museum, London. (Neg. N°. 7102-33-513). **323**: National Army Museum, London. (Neg. N°. 29570). Aquatint by J. Rouse after G. Cruikshank. **354**, **355**, **358**: Anon., 1878. **359**(upper): Lee, 1833. **359**(lower): The Louvre, Paris (N° ATLAS 14299). Drawn by Sir Thomas Lawrence (1769-1830). This is a detail from an upper body portrait in crayon. **373**: Smith, 1916. **374**: Salvin, 1882. **391**: British Museum (BM Box 17 b, 1943-5-8, 5). By George Scharf. **392**: British Museum. By George Scharf. **393**: Redrawn from Kirby & Spence, 1826 (vol. 4). **396**(upper): Leach, 1852. **406**: Anon., 1852b. **407**: Anon., 1852a. **415**(both), **421**(lower): Yarrell, 1884-1885. **438**: Fawcett, 1901 (amended by KH). **462**: Carrington, 1826. **469**: Oliphant, 1888. **480**: Northcote, 1828 (amended by KH). **483**, **484**: Zavatarri, 1959.

References

Alington, C. 1921. *Twenty Years, Being a Study in the Development of the Party System between 1815 & 1835*. Oxford; Clarendon Press. Frontispiece, T.P., [1]-207, 11 pls.

Allen, D.E. 1985. The early professionals in British Natural History. pp. 1-12 *in* Wheeler & Price *q.v.*

Anglesey, Marquess of (ed.) 1955. *The Capel Letters: Being the Correspondence of Lady Caroline Capel and her daughters with the Dowager Countess of Uxbridge from Brussels and Switzerland, 1814-1817*. London; Jonathan Cape. 248pp., 8 pls.

Anon. [1806] *The New Picture of Edinburgh, being an accurate Guide to the City and Environs with historical descriptive Accounts of the public Buildings, Offices, Institutions, Curiosties, Amusements, &c., embellished with six views on copper, two large Plans, & upwards of forty Vignettes on Wood*. Edinburgh; William Hunter. [i]-vi, [i]-viii, [1]-360, 2 maps.

Anon. 1811. *The Picture of London for 1811*. (12th edition) London; Richard Phillips. frontis., i-xii, map, 1-444.

Anon. 1812. *The Picture of Plymouth*. Plymouth; Rees and Curtis.

Anon. 1818. Biographical Memoir of Prof. Smith and Mr. Cranch. *Annals of Philosophy*, **11**(5): 321-329. [This memoir is often attributed to W.E. Leach, but internal evidence makes it clear he is not the author]

Anon. 1819. *The Annual Register, or a view of the History, Politics, and Literature, for the Year 1818*. London; Baldwin, Cradock & Joy.

Anon. 1852a. The Wellington Chair. *The Illustrated London News*, **Sept. 25**: 261.

Anon. 1852b. The Wellington Tree on the Field of Waterloo. *The Illustrated London News*, **Nov. 27**: 469.

Anon. 1870. *Beeton's Dictionary of Universal Biography*. 2nd Edition. London; Ward, Lock & Tyler. [i]-iv, 1-[1117], Addenda & Erratum, Pls 41, 1-7, 2, 9-40, 42-46, 12, 48-50, 13, 52-55, 14, 57-58, 15, 60-68.

Anon. 1878. *Galignani's New Paris Guide for 1878*. Paris; The Galignani Library.

Ashton, J. 1906. *The Dawn of the XIXth Century in England, A Social Sketch of the Times*. (5th edition). London; T. Fisher Unwin. i-xx, 1-476.

Austin, F. 1991. *The Clift Family Correspondence 1792-1846*. Sheffield; University of Sheffield. i-xxi, 1-265. (pb)

Bamford, F. & Wellington, Duke of (eds) 1950. *The Journal of Mrs Arbuthnot 1820-1832*. London; MacMillan & Co. Ltd. 2 vols. Volume 1, *February 1820 to December 1825*. Frontis., i-[xx], 1-434, 7 pls. Volume 2, *January 1826 to January 1832*. Frontis., i-viii, 1-490, 7 pls.

Barber, L. 1980. *The Heyday of Natural History 1820-1870*. New York; Doubleday & Co. Inc. 320pp. [First published 1980 in London by Jonathan Cape]

Barr, A. & York, P. 1982. *The Official Sloane Ranger Handbook: the first guide to what really matters in life*. London; Ebury.

Bastin, J. & Moore, D.T. 1982. The Geological Researches of Dr Thomas Horsfield in Indonesia 1801-1819. *Bulletin of the British Museum (Natural History)*, Historical Series, **10**(3): 75-115.

Bate, C.S. & Westwood, J.O. 1863. *A History of the British Sessile-Eyed Crustacea*. Volume 1. London; John Van Voorst. 1-507.

Bate, C.S. & Westwood, J.O. 1868. *A History of the British Sessile-Eyed Crustacea*. Volume 2. London; John Van Voorst. [i]-lvi, 1-536.

Bather, F.A. 1931. The Museums of London, pp. 271-300 *in* British Association for the Advancement of Science. 1931. *q.v.*

Beaver, D. deB. 1999. Writing natural history for survival—1820-1856: the case of Sarah Bowdich, later Sarah Lee. *Archives of Natural History*, **26**(1): 19-31.

Bell, F.J. 1893. *Catalogue of the British Echinoderms in the British Museum (Natural History)*. London; Trustees of the British Museum (Natural History). [not seen]

Bell, T. 1853. *A History of the British Stalk-Eyed Crustacea*. London; John Van Voorst. i-lxv, 1-386.

Bellamy, J.C. 1839. *The Natural History of South Devon*. Plymouth; J. Thomas.

Billing, M. 1857. *M. Billing's Directory and Gazetteer of the County of Devon, &c.* Birmingham; M. Billing's Steam-Press Offices.

Blainville, H.D. de 1816. Sur une nouvelle distribution des Classes des Crustacés, des Myriapodes et des Arachnides; par le docteur Williams Elford Leach. *Bulletin des Sciences*, **1816**: 31-41 [Issue for March 1816, reporting Leach's *Trans. Linn. Soc.* article of January 1816. Article subscribed "B.V." for de Blainville]

Blainville, H.D. de 1818. Sur plusieurs espèces nouvelles d'animaux de différentes classes; par M. le Dr Leach. *Bulletin des Sciences*, **1818**: 49-52 [Issue for April 1818, reporting Leach's Appendix 4 in Tuckey's Congo expedition, published March 1818. Article subscribed "B.V." for de Blainville — **no new taxa**]

[Blainville, H.D. de] 1818. Sur plusieurs espèces nouvelles de la classe des Céphalopodes, et sur une nouvelle distribution systématique des ordres, familles et genres de cette classe; par M. le Dr Leach. *Journal de Physique, de Chimie, d'Histoire Naturelle et des Arts*. **LXXXVI** : 393-396 [May 1818]; 456 [Plate Legend – June 1818]; Plate (not numbered, but dated *Juin 1818*) Figs 1-6 [June 1818]. [**no new taxa** — for these *vide* Leach: *Phil. Trans. Roy. Soc.*, 1817; and *Zool. Miscellany* III]

[Blainville, H.D. de.] 1818. The Zoological Miscellany, etc., C'est-a-dire Mélanges de Zoologie, Ou Description d'espèces nouvelles et intéressantes d'Animaux; par M. William Elford Leach, ... *Journal de Physique, de Chimie, d'Histoire Naturelle et des Arts*. **LXXXVII** : 297-303 [October 1818] [**no new taxa** — for these *vide* Leach: *Zool. Miscellany* III]

[Blainville, H.D. de.] 1818. Zoological Miscellany, etc., ou Mélanges de Zoologie; par M. le Docteur Leach...Extrait (suite). *Journal de Physique, de Chimie, d'Histoire Naturelle et des Arts*. **LXXXVII** : 377-381 [November 1818] [**no new taxa** — for these *vide* Leach: *Zool. Miscellany* III]

[Blainville, H.D. de] 1819. Descriptions par M. le Dr W.E. Leach, de quelques nouveaux genres et espèces d'animaux découverts en Afrique, par M. T.E. Bowdich. *Journal de Physique, de Chimie, d'Histoire Naturelle et des Arts*. **LXXXVIII**: 258-260. [March 1819] [**no new taxa** — for these *vide* Leach: *Bowdich's Mission to Ashantee*].

Blakiston, J. 1929. *Twelve years' military adventure in three quarters of the globe; or, Memoirs of an officer who served in the armies of His Majesty and of the East India Company, between the years 1802 and 1814, in which are contained the campaigns of the Duke of Wellington in India, and his last in Spain and the south of France.* London; H. Colburn. [not seen]

Boase, F. 1965. *Modern English Biography, containing... memoirs of persons who have died since... 1850 (during the years 1851-1900), with an index of the most interesting matter (2nd Impression).* 6 volumes. London; Frank Cass & Co. [First published 1892-1921 by Netherton & Worth, Truro (Cornwall). Jonathan Leach at p. 338 in Volume 2 (I-Q)]

Bowdich, T.E. 1819. *Mission from Cape Coast Castle to Ashantee: with... geographical notices of other parts of the interior of Africa.* London. 512pp., 13 pls, 1 map.

Bowring, J. 1872. Ancient Exeter and its Trade. *Report and Transactions of the Devonshire Association for the Advancement of Science*, **5**: 90-106.

Brewer, E.C. 1988. *The Dictionary of Phrase and Fable*. Leicester; Galley Press. [There are numerous other editions of this classic reference text]

British Association for the Advancement of Science. 1931. *London and the Advancement of Science*. London; British Association for the Advancement of Science. T.P., Preface, Contents, [1]-321.

British Association for the Advancement of Science. 1835. *Report of the Fourth Meeting of the British Association for the Advancement of Science held at Edinburgh in 1834*. London; John Murray.

British Museum. 1816. *Synopsis of the Contents of the British Museum*. 10th edition. London; [?Trustees of the British Museum].

British Museum (Natural History). 1906. *History of the Collections contained in the Natural History Departments of the British Museum*, Volume 2. London; Trustees of the British Museum (Natural History).

Britton, J. & Brayley, E.W. 1832. *Devonshire & Cornwall Illustrated, from original Drawings by Thomas Allom, W.H. Bartlett, &c...* London; H. Fisher, R. Fisher & P. Jackson. A unified volume including—*Devonshire*: illustrated map (imprinted 1831), illustrated T.P., pp. [3]-106 & 47 pls (2 engravings per plate); *Cornwall*: illustrated map (imprinted 1832), illustrated T.P., pp. [3]-48 & 22 pls (2 engravings per plate) [Title pages suggest first published as: (1829) *Devonshire Illustrated in a Series of Views, of Cities, Towns, Public Buildings, Streets, Docks, Churches, Antiquities, Abbeys, Picturesque Scenery, Castles, Seats of the Nobility, &c. &c.* London; Fisher, Son & Co.; and (1831) *Cornwall Illustrated in a Series of Views, of Castles, Seats of the Nobility, Mines, Picturesque Scenery, Towns, Public Buildings, Churches, Antiquities, &c.* London; Fisher, Son & Co.]

Bruce, N.L. 1995. Comments on the proposed conservation of *Lironeca* Leach, 1818 (Crustacea, Isopoda) as the correct original spelling. *Bulletin of Zoological Nomenclature*, **52**(1): 67-69.

Bryant, A. 1975. *The Age of Elegance 1812-1822*. London; Book Club Associates. i-ix, 1-[450]. [First published 1950 by Wm Collins Sons & Co Ltd, Glasgow]

Bullock, W. 1812. *Companion to Mr Bullock's London Museum and Pantherion* (12th edition). London. [not seen]

Bullock, W. 1818. *Preserving Objects of Natural History*. London; W. Bullock. [not seen]

Burke, J. & Burke, J.B. 1844. *Encyclopædia of Heraldry, or General Armory of England, Scotland, and Ireland... Third edition, with a supplement*. London; H.G. Bohn.

Burke, J.B. 1884. *The General Armory of England, Scotland, Ireland and Wales; comprising a registry of armorial bearings from the earliest to the present time*. London; Harrison.

Butler, E.M. (ed.) 1957. *Visitor. The English tour of Prince Pückler-Muskau described in his letters, 1826-1828. From the original translation by Sarah Austin*. London; Collins. 384 pp. [Not seen. First published in English in 1832]

Caldwell, G.J. & Cooper, R.B.E. 1995. *Rifles at Waterloo*. [UK, but no place of publication cited]; Bugle Horn Publications. 47pp. (pb)

Carrington, N.T. 1826. *Dartmoor: a Descriptive Poem*. London; Hatchard & Son / Devonport; R. Williams. [Preface written by William Burt]

[Chambers, R.] 1844. *Vestiges of the Natural History of Creation*. London; J. Churchill. i-vi, 1-390.

Chambers, R. 1869. *Traditions of Edinburgh* (New edition). London & Edinburgh; W. & R. Chambers. [First published in parts from 1824].

Chandler, D.G. 1979. *Dictionary of the Napoleonic Wars*. London; Arms & Armour Press. Frontis., i-[xxxvii], 1-570.

Chandler, D. 1980. *Waterloo: The Hundred Days*. London; Osprey Publishing Ltd. [1]-224, Endpapers (map).

Children, J.G. 1809. An Account of some Experiments performed with a view to ascertain the most advantageous Method of constructing a Voltaic Apparatus for the purpose of chemical Research. *Philosophical Transactions of the Royal Society*, **99**: 32-38. [not seen]

Cholmondeley, R.H. 1950. *The Heber Letters 1783-1832*. London; The Batchworth Press. [1]-355, 9 pages of Plates, 1 pedigree.

Cleevely, R.J. 1978. Some background to the life and publications of Colonel George Montagu (1753-1815). *Journal of the Society for the Bibliography of Natural History*, **8**(4): 445-480.

Cook, C. & Stevenson, J. 1980. *British Historical Facts 1760-1830*. London; Macmillan.

[Copleston, E.] 1810. *A Reply to the Calumnies of the Edinburgh Review against Oxford, containing an account of studies pursued in that University*. (2nd edition). [not seen]

Cotton, E. 1895. *A Voice from Waterloo. A History of the Battle fought on the 18th June 1815. With a Selection from the Wellington Dispatches, General Orders and Letters relating to the Battle. Illustrated with Engravings, Portraits and Plans*. 8th Edition, Revised and Enlarged. Printed for the Proprietor, Hotel du Musée, Braine-l'Alleud [Brussels; Kiessling and Co's Library (*P. Imbreghts, Successor*)]. [i]-xxiv (including 2 plates), Errata slip, pp.1-297 (with 11 pls inserted among text pages), Memorial to Cotton (1 page), "Sergeant-Major Cotton's Waterloo Cabinet" (1 page), "Catalogue of the late Sergeant-Major Cotton's Waterloo Library & Museum" (pp. [1]-15), Advertisement for the *Hotel du Musée*, Fold-out map (= Plate 14). [First published circa 1846]

Cowtan, M. 1835. *Bill for Articles purchased by Dr Leach, for the British Museum, at the Sale of Mr Bullock's Collections*. Appendix 17 (pp. 418-419) *in* House of Commons, 1835 *q.v.*

Cummings, B.F. 1914-15. Colonel Montagu, Naturalist. *Proceedings of the Linnean Society of London*, Session 127: 42-48.

[Cuvier, F.G. (ed.)] 1818. *Dictionnaire des Sciences Naturelles... par Plusieurs Professeurs du Jardin du Roi, et des principales Écoles de Paris*. Volume 12. Paris; F.G. Levrault.

[Cuvier, F.G. (ed.)] 1820. *Dictionnaire des Sciences Naturelles... par Plusieurs Professeurs du Jardin du Roi, et des principales Écoles de Paris*. Volume 18. Paris; F.G. Levrault.

Cuvier, 'G'L.C.F.D. 1812. *Recherches sur les Ossemens Fossiles des Quadrupèdes, ou l'on rétablit les Caractères de plusieurs Espèces d'Animaux que les Révolutions du Globe paroissent avoir détruites, &c*. Paris; Deterville. 4 volumes. [not seen]

Dalton, C. 1971. *The Waterloo Roll Call*. London; Arms & Armour Press. [i]-[xvi], [1]-296. [First published 1890 by William Clowes & Sons, London. 2nd Edition, revised and enlarged (of which this is a facsimile) published 1904 by Eyre & Spottiswoode: London]

Darwin, B. 1943. *British Clubs*. London; William Collins. 48pp.

Darwin, C. 1859. *On the Origin of Species by Means of Natural Selection, or the Preservation of favoured Races in the Struggle for Life*. London; John Murray.

Dawson, L.S. 1969. *Memoirs of Hydrography, including brief biographies of the principal officers who have served in H. M. Naval Surveying Service, between the years 1750 and 1885. Part I. 1750-1830*. 2 volumes in one. London; Cornmarket Press [First published 1883-1885 by Henry W. Keay; Eastbourne]

Dawson, W.R. (ed.) 1958. *The Banks Letters, A calendar of the manuscript correspondence of Sir Joseph Banks preserved in the British Museum (Natural History) and other collections in Great Britain*. London; Trustees of the British Museum (Natural History). [i]-xlii, [1]-965.

Dawson, W.R. (ed.) 1962. Supplementary Letters of Sir Joseph Banks. *Bulletin of the British Museum (Natural History)*, Historical Series, **3**(2): 41-70.

Dawson, W.R. (ed.) 1965. Supplementary Letters of Sir Joseph Banks. Second Series. *Bulletin of the British Museum (Natural History)*, Historical Series, **3**(3): 71-93.

Day, D. 1989. *The Encyclopedia of Vanished Species*. Hong Kong; Mclaren Publishing (Hong Kong) Ltd. 288pp.

de Beer, G. (ed.) 1974. *Autobiographies: Charles Darwin, Thomas Henry Huxley, edited with an introduction by Gavin de Beer*. Oxford; Oxford University Press. [not seen]

Deleuze, J.P.F. 1823. *Histoire et description du Muséum Royal d'Histoire Naturelle*. Paris. [see also Royer below] [not seen]

D'Entrèves, P.P. & Gentile, G.S. 1985. Franco Andrea Bonelli, Zoologo Trasformista. *Studi Piemontesi*, **14**(1): 34-48, 2 pls. [in Italian]

Desmarest, A-G. 1825. *Considérations Générales sur la Classe des Crustacés*. Strasbourg; Levrault.

Devonshire Association, The. 1884-1892. *The Devonshire Domesday and geld inquest: Extensions, Translations and Indices*. 2 volumes. Plymouth; W. Brendon & Son. 1236 pp.

Dictionary of National Biography. 1885-1913. London; Smith, Elder & Co. [Volumes 1-63 (1885-1900) + *Supplement* vols 1-3 (1901) + *Errata* vol. (1904) + *Index & Epitome* vol. (1906)[1] + *2nd Supplement* vols 1-3 (1912) + *2nd Supplement Index & Epitome* vol. (1913). The editors for the work were: Leslie Stephen (vols 1-21); Leslie Stephen & Sidney Lee (vols 22-26); Sidney Lee (vols 26-63, *Supplement, Errata, Index & Epitome, 2nd Supplement, 2nd Supplement Index & Epitome*)]

Dictionnaire de Biographie Française... 1933 –. Paris; Letouzey et Ané. [Ongoing multi-volume work. Volume 18 was published in 1994]

Diment, J.A., Humphries, C.J., Newington, L. & Shaughnessy, E. 1984. Catalogue of the natural history drawings commissioned by Joseph Banks on the *Endeavour* voyage 1768-1771 held in the British Museum (Natural History). Part I: Botany: Australia. *Bulletin of the British Museum (Natural History)*, Historical Series, **11**: 1-183.

Dod, C.R. 1852. *Electoral Facts, from 1832 to 1852...* London; Whittaker & Co. 374pp.

D'Urban, W.S.M. & Mathew, M.A. 1892. *The Birds of Devon*. London; R.H. Porter.

Edmondson, J. 1988. The Regency Exhibitionists: a fresh look at the Bullocks. *The Linnean*, **5**(1): 17-26.

Edwards, E. 1969. *Lives of the Founders of the British Museum; with Notices of its Chief Augmentors and other Benefactors 1570-1870*. New York; Burt Franklin. Frontispiece, [i]-x, List of Illustrations, 1-780. [First published 1870 by Trübner & Co., London]

Edwards, H.M. *see* Milne Edwards, H.

Elford, L. 1976. *The Elford's, the story of an ancient English family*. [sic] Unpublished MS of 93 mimeographed pages (foolscap). Privately produced. Sold locally in Devon.

English Cyclopædia see Knight, C.

Evans, E.J. 1989. *Britain Before the Reform Act: Politics and Society, 1815-1832*. London; Longman. [i]-[vi], 1-138. (pb)

Farber, P.L. 1985. Aspiring Naturalists and their Frustrations: the Case of William Swainson. pp. 51-59 *in* Wheeler & Price *q.v.*

Fawcett, M. 1901. *Life of the Right Hon. Sir William Molesworth Bart, MP, FRS*. London; MacMillan & Co.

Férussac, Baron de. 1820. Concordance Systématique pour les Mollusques terrestres et fluviatiles de la Grande-Bretagne; avec un aperçu des travaux modernes des savans anglais sur les Mollusques. *Journal de Physique, de Chimie et d'Histoire Naturelle*, **90**: 212-217. [Issue for March 1820]

Fifer, J.V. (ed.) 1974. Report on Bolivia, 1827, by Joseph Barclay Pentland. *Camden Miscellany*, **25** (Camden Fourth Series Volume 13): 169-267.

[1] In the copy seen the T.P. of the *Index & Epitome* is marked as the second edition and dated 1906, but also includes the Index and Epitome to the 2nd Supplement dated 1913 in the same volume. An included slip dated 1913 and bound into the work notes this volume covers dates up to 1912. This later date is supported by the citation of the editor as *Sir* Sidney Lee, unlike all other volumes.

Fleming, J. 1828. *A History of British Animals, exhibiting the descriptive Characters and systematical Arrangement of the Genera and Species of Quadrupeds, Birds, Reptiles, Fishes, Mollusca, and Radiata of the United Kingdom, &c.* Edinburgh. i-xxiii, 1-565. [not seen – Published March 1828]

Flintoff, G. 1844. *Flintoff's Directory and Guide Book to Plymouth, Devonport, Stonehouse and their Vicinities.* Plymouth; G. Flintoff.

Foster, B. 1895. *Pictures of Rustic Landscape.* London; Longmans, Green & Co. [i]-xiv, [1]-238.

Fox, S.P. 1864. *Kingsbridge Estuary with Rambles in the Neighbourhood.* Kingsbridge; G.P. Friend.

Fraser, F. 1997. *The Unruly Queen, the life of Queen Caroline.* London; Papermac. [i]-[xxii], [1]-537. (pb) [First published 1996 by Macmillan]

Gage, A.T. 1938. *A History of the Linnean Society of London.* London; Linnean Society.

Gallant, L. [?date] From South Devon to the Congo. John Cranch, Zoologist of the Expedition to the Congo, 1816. *Transactions and Proceedings of the Torquay Natural History Society,* [?volume]: 195-201. [A copy of this English translation of part of Monod, 1970 (see below) was found among the notes of the late Sir Eric Smith. KH has not discovered the year of publication or volume number. The paper was probably produced during the 1970s]

Gardiner, B.G. 1998. Charles Lyell and the importance of fossils. *The Linnean,* **14**(2): 10-19.

Gardiner, B.G. 1999. Picture Quiz. *The Linnean,* **15**(1): 5-12 [portrait of Grant in vol. **14**(3): 19 (1998)]

Gardiner, B.G. 2001. Linnaeus's species concept and his views on evolution. *The Linnean,* **17**(1): 24-36.

Giani, P. 1925. Cronistoria del Borgo di S. Sebastiano Curone. *Rivista di Storia, Arte, Archeologia per la Provincia di Alessandria.* [not seen – Volume and pp. not known]

Giani, R. 1928. Curiosità della Val Curone: uno scienziato inglese sepolto... in cantina. *Il Bianco-verde. Eco della Val Curone,* **4**(1). [not seen – pagination not known to us]

Gill, C. 1979. *Plymouth: A New History. Volume Two: 1603 to the Present Day.* Newton Abbot; David & Charles. 239pp.

Gill, C. (ed.) 1983. *Dartmoor: A new study.* Newton Abbot; David & Charles. 314 pp. (pb) [First published 1970. Third impression 1983]

Gleig, G.R. 1861. *The Campaigns of the British Army at Washington and New Orleans, 1814-1815.* (New edition) London; John Murray. T.P., Advertisement, Contents, 1-208. [First Published 1821 by John Murray]

Glover, S. 1833. *The History of the County of Derby.* Volume 2.

Gore, J. (ed.) 1970. *The Creevey Papers.* London; The Folio Society. Frontis., i-xvi, 1-334, 16 pls. [This edition first published 1963 by B.T. Batsford Ltd]

Grant, J. [1880-1883] *Cassell's Old and New Edinburgh: Its History, its People, and its Places.* London; Cassell, Petter, Galpin & Co. 3 volumes: **1** [1880]; **2**, 1882; **3** [1883].

Gray, J.E. 1824. Conchological Observations, being an attempt to fix the study of Conchology on a firm basis. *Zoological Journal,* **1**: 204-223.

Gray, J.E. 1847. The Classification of the British Mollusca by W.E. Leach. *Annals and Magazine of Natural History,* **XX**: 267-273. [October 1847 – the arrangement of mollusc genera and species used by W.E. Leach in his unfinished mollusc studies from 1818 onwards]

Great Britain. Royal Commission of Inquiry into the State of the Universities of Scotland. 1837. *Evidence oral and Documentary, taken and received by the Commissioners appointed by His Majesty George IV. July 23d, 1826; and re-appointed by His Majesty William IV., October 12th, 1830; for visiting the Universities of Scotland. Volume 1. University of Edinburgh.* London: HMSO.

Gronow, R.H. 1964. *The Reminiscences and Recollections of Captain Gronow: Being Anecdotes of the Camp, Court, Clubs & Society 1810-1860*. London; The Bodley Head. Frontis., 1-384. [Abridgement by John Raymond of work first published 1862-1892]

Gunther, A.E. 1974. A note on the autobiographical manuscripts of John Edward Gray (1800-1875). *Journal of the Society for the Bibliography of Natural History*, **7**(1): 35-76.

Gunther, A.E. 1975. *A Century of Zoology at the British Museum Through the Lives of Two Keepers 1815-1914*. Folkstone; Wm Dawson & Sons Ltd.

Gunther, A.E. 1976. Edward Whitaker Gray (1748-1806), Keeper of Natural Curiosities at the British Museum. *Bulletin of the British Museum (Natural History)*, Historical Series **5**(2): 191-210, pls 1-5.

Gunther, A.E. 1978. John George Children, F.R.S. (1777-1852) of the British Museum. Mineralogist and reluctant Keeper of Zoology. *Bulletin of the British Museum (Natural History)*, Historical Series, **6**(4): 75-108.

Gunther, A.E. 1980a. The miscellaneous autobiographical manuscripts of John Edward Gray (1800-1875). *Bulletin of the British Museum (Natural History)*, Historical Series, **6**(6): 199-244.

Gunther, A.E. 1980b. *The Founders of Science at the British Museum 1753-1900*. Halesworth (Suffolk); The Halesworth Press. [I]-[X], 1-219.

Gurwood, [J.] 1837-1838. *The Dispatches of Field Marshal The Duke of Wellington during his various campaigns in India, Denmark, Portugal, Spain, The Low Countries and France from 1799 to 1815*. A new edition. 12 volumes + General Orders. London; John Murray. [First published 1834-1837]

Gurwood, [J.] 1844-1847. *The Dispatches of Field Marshal The Duke of Wellington during his various campaigns in India, Denmark, Portugal, Spain, The Low Countries and France*. An enlarged edition, in eight volumes. London; John Murray.

Gurwood, [J.] 1852. *Selections from the Dispatches of Field Marshal The Duke of Wellington during his various campaigns in India, Denmark, Portugal, Spain, The Low Countries and France*. New and enlarged edition. In eight volumes. London; John Murray. [This edition is mainly of notes by Wellington, with few to him]

Halévy, E. 1987. *A History of the English People in 1815*. London; Ark Paperbacks. [i]-[xxii], [1]-576. (pb)

Hall, H. 1953. *William Allen 1770-1843, Member of the Society of Friends*. Haywards Heath; Charles Clarke (Haywards Heath) Ltd.

Halliwell, J.O. 1865. *A Dictionary of Archaic and Provincial Words, Obsolete Phrases, Proverbs, and Ancient Customs, from the Fourteenth Century*. 5th edition. 2 volumes. London; John Russell Smith.

Hamilton, Jill, Duchess of. 2000. *Marengo: The Myth of Napoleon's Horse*. London; Fourth Estate. (10 unnumbered pages then) 1-246.

Hamilton-Williams, D. 1994. *Waterloo: New Perspectives. The Great Battle Reappraised*. London; BCA. [1]-416, 16 unnumbered pages of maps after p. 64, 16 unnumbered pages of plates after p. 128, ditto after p. 224, ditto after p. 320 and map of troop deployments at noon 18th June 1815 (drawn by W.B. Craan) on rear of dust-jacket.

Hart, H.G. 1848. *Hart's Annual Army List*. London.

Harvey, A.D. 1978. *Britain in the Early Nineteenth Century*. London; B.T. Batsford Ltd. T.P., Acknowledgements, Contents, [1]-395.

Hathaway, E. 1996. *A Dorset Rifleman: The Recollections of Benjamin Harris*. Swanage; Shinglepicker Publications. 203pp., 16 pls. (pb) [First published 1995]

Hathaway, E. 1997. *Costello: The True Story of a Peninsula War Rifleman (including Adventures of a Soldier)*. Swanage; Shinglepicker Publications. 378pp.

Haythornthwaite, P.J. 1979. *Weapons & Equipment of the Napoleonic Wars*. Poole; Blandford Press. T.P., Acknowledgements, Contents, Figure 1, 1-190.

Haythornthwaite, P.J. 1996a. *British Infantry of the Napoleonic Wars*. London; Arms and Armour Press. 104pp. (pb) [First published 1987]

Haythornthwaite, P.J. 1996b. *Die Hard! Dramatic Actions from the Napoleonic Wars*. London; Arms and Armour Press. pp. [1]-256 & 16pp of pls.

Heath, P.P.H. 1991. *A Voice from Waterloo: Being a French Officer's account of the 1815 Campaign in Belgium*. Marsham; Anschluss Publishing. Introduction, 1-19. (pb) [extracted from Kelly, 1828: 73-88. Not to be confused with Cotton's work of the same name (above)]

Hibbert, C. (ed.) 1997. *The Wheatley Diary: A Journal and Sketch-book kept during the Peninsular War and the Waterloo Campaign*. Moreton-in-Marsh; The Windrush Press. i-xviii, 1-97, 18pls (on 9pp) (pb) [First published 1964 by Longman, Green & Co. Ltd]

Holmes, R. 1997. *War Walks: From Agincourt to Normandy*. London; BBC Books. 224pp.

Home, E. 1814–. *Lectures on Comparative Anatomy in which are examined the preparations in the Hunterian collection. Illustrated by engravings*. London; G. & W. Nicol. [not seen]

Horsfield, T. 1821. Systematic Arrangement and Description of Birds from the Island of Java. *Transactions of the Linnean Society of London*, **13**(1): 133-200.

Hoskins, W.G. 1959. *A New Survey of England: Devon*. London; Collins. Frontispiece, [i]-[xxii], [1]-600, 58 pls. [First published 1954]

Hoskins, W.G. 1971. *Old Devon*. London; Pan Books Ltd. [i]-xiv, [1]-223. (pb) [First published 1966 by David & Charles (Publishers) Ltd]

House of Commons *see* Parliamentary Papers.

Howarth, D. 1968. *A Near Run Thing*. London; Collins. i-[x], 1-239.

Howarth, O.J.R. 1931. *The British Association for the Advancement of Science: A Retrospect 1831-1931*. London; British Association for the Advancement of Science.

International Genealogical Index ™
[This is a database of records for births, baptisms, marriages, deaths etc. assembled from community sources world-wide by members of the Church of Jesus Christ of Latter-Day Saints. This phenomenal genealogical resource became searchable on-line on the world-wide web at the end of the last century. It is difficult to see how we ever managed without it]

Jackson, P. 1987. *George Scharf's London. Sketches and Watercolours of a Changing City, 1820-50*. London; John Murray. T.P., Contents, Acknowledgements, 1-154.

Jarvis, C.M. 1976. A History of the British Coleoptera. *Proceedings of the British Entomological and Natural History Society*, 1976: 91-112, pls V-VIII.

Jenyns, L. 1862. *Memoir of the Rev. John Stevens Henslow*. London; John van Voorst.

Johnson, S. 1755. *A Dictionary of the English Language: in which the Words are deduced from their Originals, and illustrated in their different Significations by Examples from the best Writers. To which are prefixed a History of the Language, and an English Grammar*. 2 Volumes. London; J. & P. Knapton, T. & T. Longman, C. Hitch & L. Hawes, A. Millar, and R. & J. Dodsley.

Jones, M. 1852. *The History of Chudleigh, in the County of Devon, and the surrounding scenery, seats, families, &c*. London. 210pp.

Kelly, C. 1828. *A full and circumstantial Account of the memorable Battle of Waterloo: the second Restoration of Louis XVIII; and the Deportation of Napoleon Buonaparte to the Island of St. Helena, and every recent Particular relative to his Conduct and Mode of Life in his Exile together with an interesting Account of the Affairs of France, and biographical Sketches of the most distinguished Waterloo Heroes. Embellished with Engravings*. London; Thomas Kelly. Frontispiece, Illustrated T.P. [April 26, 1817], T.P. [1828], [1]-509, 18 pls, map. [First published 1817].

Kelly & Co. 1856. *Post Office Directory of Devonshire and Cornwall, &c.* London; Kelly & Co.

Kincaid, J. 1981. *Adventures in the Rifle Brigade, and Random Shots from a Rifleman (abridged).* Glasgow; Richard Drew Publishing. Introduction (5pp. by Lt-Gen. Sir Peter Hudson *KCB, CBE*), Contents (2pp.) + 302pp. [*Adventures in the Rifle Brigade* first published 1830; *Random Shots from a Rifleman* first published 1835; first united abridged edition 1909, of which this is a facsimile. Citations after p. 174 are from *Random Shots.*]

Kirby, W. & Spence, W. 1818. *An Introduction to Entomology: or Elements of the Natural History of Insects: with Plates.* 3rd edition, Volume I. London; Longman, Hurst, Rees, Orme & Brown. [i]-xxiii, Contents, [1]-519, Explanation of plates, pls I-III. [First published 1815].

Kirby, W. & Spence, W. 1818. *An Introduction to Entomology: or Elements of the Natural History of Insects: with Plates.* 2nd edition, Volume II. London; Longman, Hurst, Rees, Orme & Brown. T.P., Contents, Errata, [1]-530, Explanation of plates, pls IV-V. [First Published 1817].

Kirby, W. & Spence, W. 1826. *An Introduction to Entomology: or Elements of the Natural History of Insects: with Plates.* Volume III. London; Longman, Rees, Orme, Brown & Green. Frontispiece, [i]-v, Errata, Contents, Notice respecting Vol. I and II., [1]-354, Fold-out synoptical table, 355-732, pls VI-XX.

Kirby, W. & Spence, W. 1826. *An Introduction to Entomology: or Elements of the Natural History of Insects: with Plates.* Volume IV. London; Longman, Rees, Orme, Brown & Green. Frontispiece, [i]-iv, [1]-602, pls XXI-XXX, [603]-634.

Kirby, W. & Spence, W. 1859. *An Introduction to Entomology...* (7th edition). London; Longman, Green, Longman & Roberts. [i]-xxviii, [1]-607.

Knight, C. (ed.) 1854-1872. *The English Cyclopædia, A Dictionary of Universal Information.* [William Elford Leach in VOL. 6. BIOGRAPHY (GAA.-QVI.) columns 824-826. London; Bradbury, Agnew & Co. The 7 volumes of BIOGRAPHY were reportedly issued from 1856-1872 and there may have been a re-issue in 1875]

Knight, G.A.F. 1900. The Etymology of the Names Azeca and Assiminea of Leach. *Journal of Conchology*, **9**: 271-276.

[Lamb. M. &] Lamb, C. 1807. *Tales from Shakespear. Designed for the Use of Young Persons.* 2 volumes. London. [Although the author is given as Charles, more than half the tales are known to have been written by his sister Mary]

Leach, J. 1831. *Rough Sketches of the Life of an Old Soldier...* London; Longman, Rees, Orme, Brown & Green. i-xxix, 1-411.

Leach, J. 1835. *Recollections and Reflections Relative to the Duties of Troops Composing the Advanced Corps of an Army.* London; T. & W. Boone. i-xii, 1-81. [not seen]

Leach, J. 1838. *Sketch of the Field Services of the Rifle Brigade, from its Formation to the Battle of Waterloo.* London. 32pp. [not seen]

Leach, J. 1847. *Rambles along the Styx*: Being Colloquies between Old Soldiers who are Supposed to have met in the Stygian Shades. London.

Leach, J[2]. 1851. Sketch of the Field Services of the Rifle Brigade, from its Formation to the Battle of Waterloo (6 pp.) *in* Smith, H. Stooks. 1851. *An Alphabetical List of the Officers of the Rifle Brigade from 1800 to 1850.* London; Simpkin, Marshall & Co.

Leach, W.E. 1813. III. An Essay on the British Species of the Genus Meloë, with Descriptions of two exotic Species. *Transactions of the Linnean Society of London*, **11**(1): 35-49, Tabs 6 & 7. [Paper read 19 June 1809[3]; Published May 1813[4]]

Leach, W.E. (ed.) 1813. *Fauna Orcadensis; or, the Natural History of the Quadrupeds, Birds, Reptiles, and Fishes, of Orkney and Shetland* by the Reverend George Low, Minister of Birsay and Haray. From a MS. in the possession of William Elford Leach, M.D., F.L.S. &c. 230 pp. Constable & Co., Edinburgh; Longman & Co. and White & Co., London.

[2] [not seen by us] Colonel Willoughby Verner in his *Memoir of Lieutenant-Colonel Jonathan Leach C.B.* published in *The Rifle Brigade Chronicle* (copy with pages numbered 2-7 seen, but year and volume not known to us) states, "Another book of Leach's, "Thoughts on Various Military Subjects," I have so far never come across. Hence I cannot say when it was written. It is mentioned on the title page of his book "Rambles along the Styx" ". The current authors have found no other reference to a book of this title and it may simply be a reference to Jonathan Leach's previous publishing experience, rather than to a book title. Jonathan Leach may also have published articles in military chronicles but these have not been sought here.

[3] Not 1810 as stated in the *Transactions*. Leach's autograph copy of the opening section of his talk is in the archives of the Linnean Society marked "Read June 19. 1809"

[4] *fide* Raphael, 1970.

Leach, W.E. 1813. Entry: CRANIOLOGY, pp. 318-319 *in The Edinburgh Encyclopædia conducted by David Brewster LLD*. Vol. **VII**(1). Edinburgh.

Leach, W.E. 1813. Entry: CRANIOMETRY, pp. 319-320 & Plate CCXVIII *in The Edinburgh Encyclopædia conducted by David Brewster LLD*. Vol. **VII**(1). Edinburgh. [Plate CCXVIII was issued with Vol. **VIII**(1)]

Leach, W.E. 1813. Entry: CRANIOSCOPY, pp. 320-324 *in The Edinburgh Encyclopædia conducted by David Brewster LLD*. Vol. **VII**(1). Edinburgh.

Leach, W.E. 1813. Entry: CRANIUM, pp. 324-325 *in The Edinburgh Encyclopædia conducted by David Brewster LLD*. Vol. **VII**(1). Edinburgh.

Leach, W.E. 1813. Entry: CRUSTACEOLOGY, pp. 383-384 *in The Edinburgh Encyclopædia conducted by David Brewster LLD*. Vol. **VII**(1). Edinburgh.

Leach, W.E. 1814. Entry: CRUSTACEOLOGY, pp. 385-437, 765-766 (Plate Legend) & Plate CCXXI, Figs 1-12. *in The Edinburgh Encyclopædia conducted by David Brewster LLD*. Vol. **VII**(2). Edinburgh. [Plate CCXXI was issued with Vol. **IX**(1) in 1815[5]]

Leach, W.E. 1814. *The Zoological Miscellany; being descriptions of new or interesting animals...Illustrated with coloured figures drawn from nature by R.P. Nodder &c*. Vol. **I** (Part 1), pp. 1[TP]-18[blank], Pls 1-5. [1st February 1814]

Leach, W.E. 1814. *The Zoological Miscellany; being descriptions of new or interesting animals...Illustrated with coloured figures drawn from nature by R.P. Nodder &c*. Vol. **I** (Part 2), pp. 19-28, Pls 6-10. [February 1814]

Leach, W.E. 1814. *The Zoological Miscellany; being descriptions of new or interesting animals...Illustrated with coloured figures drawn from nature by R.P. Nodder &c*. Vol. **I** (Part 3), pp. 29-38, Pls 11-15. [March 1814]

Leach, W.E. 1814. *The Zoological Miscellany; being descriptions of new or interesting animals...Illustrated with coloured figures drawn from nature by R.P. Nodder &c*. Vol. **I** (Part 4), pp. 39-48, Pls 16-20. [April 1814]

Leach, W.E. 1814. *The Zoological Miscellany; being descriptions of new or interesting animals...Illustrated with coloured figures drawn from nature by R.P. Nodder &c*. Vol. **I** (Part 5), pp. 49-58[blank], Pls 21-25. [May 1814]

Leach, W.E. 1814. Description of a Swordfish found in the Frith of Forth in June 1811. *Memoirs of the Wernerian Natural History Society*, **2**(1): 58-60. Pl. II (Fig. 1). [Paper read 27 July 1811; Published May 1814[6]]

Leach, W.E. 1814. Some Observations on the Genus *Squalus* of Linné, with Descriptions and Outline Figures of two British Species. *Memoirs of the Wernerian Natural History Society*, **2**(1): 61-66. Pl. II (Figs 2 & 3). [Read 18 January 1812; Published May 1814]

Leach, W.E. 1814. *The Zoological Miscellany; being descriptions of new or interesting animals...Illustrated with coloured figures drawn from nature by R.P. Nodder &c*. Vol. **I** (Part 6), pp. 59-70, Pls 26-30. [June 1814]

W.E. LEACH

W.E. Leach's writings are scattered throughout diverse publications, especially encyclopaedias. It is therefore difficult to locate all his output and to our knowledge a full listing has never been attempted. The compilation presented here includes all articles known to us but is unlikely to be comprehensive. We have not included reprintings (such as the 1824 re-issue of the *Supplements to the Encyclopaedia Britannica*) where there is no indication changes were made to the original.

Some of Leach's work was précised by de Blainville for inclusion in the *Journal de Physique*, which de Blainville edited. This can be found above under 'Blainville'.

Please note the monthly contents of vols 1 & 2 of the *Zoological Miscellany* have been deduced by examining the volumes and are not based on definitive evidence.

[5] Sherborn, C.D. (1931) *Index Animalium*, Part XXVI (pp. 6359-6582) at p. 6433 under *Monotoma terebrans* Leach, states Vol. **IX**(1) was published in 1815.

[6] Volume 2 Part 1 (pp. 1-260) was published in May 1814 *fide* an autograph note in the copy belonging to the Natural History Museum, London. Part 2 (pp. 261-700) is said to have been published in 1818, which is the date on the unified title page. Leach's new taxa in this and his *Squalus* paper (following) are dated May 1814 in Sherborn, *Index Animalium*.

Leach, W.E. 1814. *The Zoological Miscellany; being descriptions of new or interesting animals...Illustrated with coloured figures drawn from nature by R.P. Nodder &c.* Vol. **I** (Part 7), pp. 71-80, Pls 31-35. [July 1814]

Leach, W.E. 1814. *The Zoological Miscellany; being descriptions of new or interesting animals...Illustrated with coloured figures drawn from nature by R.P. Nodder &c.* Vol. **I** (Part 8), pp. 81-92, Pls 36-40. [August 1814]

Leach, W.E. 1814. *The Zoological Miscellany; being descriptions of new or interesting animals...Illustrated with coloured figures drawn from nature by R.P. Nodder &c.* Vol. **I** (Part 9), pp. 93-102, Pls 41-45. [September 1814]

Leach, W.E. 1814. *The Zoological Miscellany; being descriptions of new or interesting animals...Illustrated with coloured figures drawn from nature by R.P. Nodder &c.* Vol. **I** (Part 10), pp. 103-114[blank], Pls 47-50. [October 1814]

Leach, W.E. 1814. *The Zoological Miscellany; being descriptions of new or interesting animals...Illustrated with coloured figures drawn from nature by R.P. Nodder &c.* Vol. **I** (Part 11), pp. 115-126, Pls 46, 51-55. [November 1814]

Leach, W.E. 1814. *The Zoological Miscellany; being descriptions of new or interesting animals...Illustrated with coloured figures drawn from nature by R.P. Nodder &c.* Vol. **I** (Part 12), pp. 127-144, Pls 56-60. [December 1814]

Leach, W.E. 1815. No. I. *Malacostraca Podophthalmata Britanniæ*; or descriptions of the British species of Crabs, Lobsters, Prawns, and of other Malacostraca with pedunculated eyes...Illustrated with figures of all the species by James Sowerby, F.L.S. G.S. W.S. &c. Printed by B. Meredith. Published by James Sowerby. London. Jan. 1, 1815. [Pls. VIII, XIV, XXII][7]

Leach, W.E. 1815. Entry: ENTOMOLOGY, pp. 57-172 *in The Edinburgh Encyclopædia conducted by David Brewster LLD*. Vol. **IX**(1). Edinburgh. [month not known but in *Zoo. Misc.* **II**(6):87, probably written in/by May 1815, Leach implies this work has already been published]

Leach, W.E. 1815. *The Zoological Miscellany; being descriptions of new or interesting animals...Illustrated with coloured figures drawn from nature by R.P. Nodder &c.* Vol. **II** (Part 1), pp. 1[TP]-12, Pls 61-65. [January 1815]

Leach, W.E. 1815. *The Zoological Miscellany; being descriptions of new or interesting animals...Illustrated with coloured figures drawn from nature by R.P. Nodder &c.* Vol. **II** (Part 2), pp. 13-28, Pls 66-70. [February 1815]

Leach, W.E. 1815. *The Zoological Miscellany; being descriptions of new or interesting animals...Illustrated with coloured figures drawn from nature by R.P. Nodder &c.* Vol. **II** (Part 3), pp. 29-44, Pls 71-75. [March 1815]

Leach, W.E. 1815. No. II. *Malacostraca Podophthalmata Britanniæ*; or descriptions of the British species of Crabs, Lobsters, Prawns, and of other Malacostraca with pedunculated eyes...Illustrated with figures of all the species by James Sowerby, F.L.S. G.S. W.S. &c. Printed by B. Meredith. Published by James Sowerby. London. March 1, 1815. [Pls. IV, XV, XL]

Leach, W.E. 1815. On the Petrifactions in Plymouth Limestone. *Annals of Philosophy*, **5**: 232. [A letter to the editor, published March 1815]

Leach, W.E. 1815. *The Zoological Miscellany; being descriptions of new or interesting animals...Illustrated with coloured figures drawn from nature by R.P. Nodder &c.* Vol. **II** (Part 4), pp. 45-59, Pls 76-80. [April 1815]

Leach, W.E. 1815. No. III. *Malacostraca Podophthalma Britanniæ*; or descriptions of the British species of Crabs, Lobsters, Prawns, and of other Malacostraca with pedunculated eyes...Illustrated with colored figures of all the species by James Sowerby, F.L.S. G.S. W.S. &c. Printed by B. Meredith. Published by James Sowerby. London. May 1, 1815. [Pls. XVII, XXVIII.A, XXVIII.B]

[7] See also 22B and 22C later.

Leach, W.E. 1815. *The Zoological Miscellany; being descriptions of new or interesting animals...Illustrated with coloured figures drawn from nature by R.P. Nodder &c.* Vol. **II** (Part 5), pp. 61-76[blank], Pls 81-85. [May 1815]

Leach, W.E. 1815. *The Zoological Miscellany; being descriptions of new or interesting animals...Illustrated with coloured figures drawn from nature by R.P. Nodder &c.* Vol. **II** (Part 6), pp. 77-88, Pls 86-90. [June 1815]

Leach, W.E. 1815. No. IV. *Malacostraca Podophthalma Britanniæ*; or descriptions of the British species of Crabs, Lobsters, Prawns, and of other Malacostraca with pedunculated eyes...Illustrated with colored figures of all the species by James Sowerby, F.L.S. G.S. W.S. &c. Printed by B. Meredith. Published by James Sowerby. London. July 1, 1815. [Pls. XIX, XXIX, XLI]

Leach, W.E. 1815. *The Zoological Miscellany; being descriptions of new or interesting animals...Illustrated with coloured figures drawn from nature by R.P. Nodder &c.* Vol. **II** (Part 7), pp. 89-100[blank], Pls 91-95. [July 1815]

Leach, W.E. 1815. *The Zoological Miscellany; being descriptions of new or interesting animals...Illustrated with coloured figures drawn from nature by R.P. Nodder &c.* Vol. **II** (Part 8), pp. 101-112, Pls 96-100. [August 1815]

Leach, W.E. 1815. No. V. *Malacostraca Podophthalma Britanniæ*; or descriptions of the British species of Crabs, Lobsters, Prawns, and of other Malacostraca with pedunculated eyes...Illustrated with colored figures of all the species by James Sowerby, F.L.S. G.S. W.S. &c. Printed by B. Meredith. Published by James Sowerby. London. September 1, 1815. [Pls. XXIII, XXX]

Leach, W.E. 1815. *The Zoological Miscellany; being descriptions of new or interesting animals...Illustrated with coloured figures drawn from nature by R.P. Nodder &c.* Vol. **II** (Part 9), pp. 113-124, Pls 101-105. [September 1815]

Leach, W.E. 1815. *The Zoological Miscellany; being descriptions of new or interesting animals...Illustrated with coloured figures drawn from nature by R.P. Nodder &c.* Vol. **II** (Part 10), pp. 125-134, Pls 106-110. [October 1815]

Leach, W.E. 1815. No. VI. *Malacostraca Podophthalma Britanniæ*; or descriptions of the British species of Crabs, Lobsters, Prawns, and of other Malacostraca with pedunculated eyes...Illustrated with colored figures of all the species by James Sowerby, F.L.S. G.S. W.S. &c. Printed by B. Meredith. Published by James Sowerby. London. November 1, 1815. [Pls. I, II, XXVI]

Leach, W.E. 1815. *The Zoological Miscellany; being descriptions of new or interesting animals...Illustrated with coloured figures drawn from nature by R.P. Nodder &c.* Vol. **II** (Part 11), pp. 135-144, Pls 111-115. [November 1815]

Leach, W.E. 1816. *The Zoological Miscellany; being descriptions of new or interesting animals...Illustrated with coloured figures drawn from nature by R.P. Nodder &c.* Vol. **II** (Part 12), pp. 145-154 + 6pp of Index, Pls 116-120. [December 1815]

Leach, W.E. 1816. No. VII. *Malacostraca Podophthalma Britanniæ*; or descriptions of the British species of Crabs, Lobsters, Prawns, and of other Malacostraca with pedunculated eyes...Illustrated with colored figures of all the species by James Sowerby, F.L.S. G.S. W.S. &c. Printed by W. Arding. Published by James Sowerby. London. January 1, 1816. [Pls. XXIV, XXXVI]

Leach, W.E. 1816. XXIII. Further Observations on the Genus Melöe, with Descriptions of Six Exotic Species. *Transactions of the Linnean Society of London*, **11**(2): 242-251, Tab. 18. [Paper read 2 November 1813; Published 24 January 1816]

Leach, W.E. 1816. XXXI. A tabular View of the external Characters of Four Classes of Animals, which Linné arranged under INSECTA, with the Distribution of the Genera composing Three of these Classes into Orders &c. and Descriptions of several New Genera and Species. *Transactions of the Linnean Society of London*, **11**(2): 306-400 & 'ERRATA'. [Paper read 19 April, 3 May & 1 June 1814; Published 24 January 1816]

Leach, W.E. 1816. No. VIII. *Malacostraca Podophthalma Britanniæ*; or descriptions of the British species of Crabs, Lobsters, Prawns, and of other Malacostraca with pedunculated eyes...Illustrated with colored figures of all the species by James Sowerby, F.L.S. G.S. W.S. &c. Printed by W. Arding. Published by James Sowerby. London. March 1, 1816. [Pls. III, XII, XIII]

Leach, W.E. 1816. No. IX. *Malacostraca Podophthalma Britanniæ*; or descriptions of the British species of Crabs, Lobsters, Prawns, and of other Malacostraca with pedunculated eyes...Illustrated with colored figures of all the species by James Sowerby, F.L.S. G.S. W.S. &c. Printed by W. Arding. Published by James Sowerby. London. May 1, 1816. [Pls. VII, XLII, XLIII]

Leach, W.E. 1816. Entry: ANNULOSA, pp. 401-453, Pls XX-XXVI in *Encyclopædia Britannica*, Supplement to the 4th Edition Vol. I(II). A. Constable. Edinburgh. [Published June 1816]

Leach, W.E. 1816. No. X. *Malacostraca Podophthalma Britanniæ*; or descriptions of the British species of Crabs, Lobsters, Prawns, and of other Malacostraca with pedunculated eyes...Illustrated with colored figures of all the species by James Sowerby, F.L.S. G.S. W.S. &c. Printed by W. Arding. Published by James Sowerby. London. July 1, 1816. [Pls. VI, XXXI, XXXII]

Leach, W.E. 1816. No. XI. *Malacostraca Podophthalma Britanniæ*; or descriptions of the British species of Crabs, Lobsters, Prawns, and of other Malacostraca with pedunculated eyes...Illustrated with colored figures of all the species by James Sowerby, F.L.S. G.S. W.S. &c. Printed by W. Arding. Published by James Sowerby. London. Sept. 1, 1816. [Pls. IX, XI, XXXIII] [8]

[Leach, W.E.] 1816. pp. 51-60 [ZOOLOGY] in *Synopsis of the British Museum* (10th Edn). [not attributed, but as the only zoologist in the Museum Leach must have drafted this and the zoology sections in other synopses during his time in the museum]

Leach, W.E. 1816. *Systematic Catalogue of the Specimens of the Indigenous Mammalia and Birds that are Preserved in the British Museum*, with their localities and authorities to which is added a list of the described species that are wanting to complete the collection of British mammals and birds. London. 8° [Preface dated 30 August 1816; A. MacLeay had a copy before 9th November 1816]

Leach, W.E. 1816. No. XII. *Malacostraca Podophthalma Britanniæ*; or descriptions of the British species of Crabs, Lobsters, Prawns, and of other Malacostraca with pedunculated eyes...Illustrated with colored figures of all the species by James Sowerby, F.L.S. G.S. W.S. &c. Printed by W. Arding. Published by James Sowerby. London. Nov. 1, 1816. [Pls. V, XXI.A, XXI.B]

Leach, W.E. 1816. Note sur les pédoncules des yeux dans quelques crustacés. *Bulletin des Sciences*, **1816**: 14.

Leach, W.E. 1817. No. XIII. *Malacostraca Podophthalma Britanniæ*; or descriptions of the British species of Crabs, Lobsters, Prawns, and of other Malacostraca with pedunculated eyes...Illustrated with colored figures of all the species by James Sowerby, F.L.S. G.S. W.S. &c. Printed by W. Arding. Published by James Sowerby. London. Jan. 1, 1817. [Pls. XVIII, XX]

Leach, W.E. 1817. No. XIV. *Malacostraca Podophthalma Britanniæ*; or descriptions of the British species of Crabs, Lobsters, Prawns, and of other Malacostraca with pedunculated eyes...Illustrated with colored figures of all the species by James Sowerby, F.L.S. G.S. W.S. &c. Printed by W. Arding. Published by James Sowerby. London. April 1, 1817. [Pls. XVI, XXV, XLIV]

Leach, W.E. 1817. No. XV. *Malacostraca Podophthalma Britanniæ*; or descriptions of the British species of Crabs, Lobsters, Prawns, and of other Malacostraca with pedunculated eyes...Illustrated with colored figures of all the species by James Sowerby, F.L.S. G.S. W.S. &c. Printed by Arding and Merrett. Published by James Sowerby. London. July 1, 1817. [Pls. XXII.B, XXXVII.A, XXXVII.B]

[8] See also 9B and (curiously) 9A later.

Leach, W.E. 1817. Notice sur le Cerf Wapiti. *Journal de Physique, de Chimie, d'Histoire Naturelle et des Arts.* **LXXXV**: 66-67. [July 1817]

Leach, W.E. 1817. Distribution systématique de la classe des Cirripèdes. *Journal de Physique, de Chimie, d'Histoire Naturelle et des Arts.* **LXXXV**: 67-69. [July 1817]

Leach, W.E. 1817. Observations on the genus *Ocythoë* of Rafinesque, with a description of a new species. *Philosophical Transactions of the Royal Society of London,* **1817**: 293-296, Pl. XII. [Paper read 5 June 1817]

Leach, W.E. 1817. *The Zoological Miscellany; being descriptions of new or interesting animals...Illustrated with coloured figures engraved from original drawings by R.P. Nodder &c.* Vol. **III**. pp. i[TP]-vi, 1-152, Pls 121-135, 135B-149. R.P. Nodder, London. 8° [published *circa* November 1817 comprising the following 30 articles]

Leach, W.E. 1817. I. On the Characters of the European Species of the Genus *Rhinolophus,* commonly named Horse-shoe Bats. pp.1-3, Pl. 121, in *The Zoological Miscellany; being descriptions of new or interesting animals...Illustrated with coloured figures engraved from original drawings by R.P. Nodder &c.* Vol. **III**. pp. i[TP]-vi, 1-152, Pls 121-135, 135B-149. R.P. Nodder, London. 8°

Leach, W.E. 1817. II. Generic Character of *Elanus,* a Genus of Birds, with a Description of a Species. pp. 4-5, Pl.122, in *The Zoological Miscellany; being descriptions of new or interesting animals...Illustrated with coloured figures engraved from original drawings by R.P. Nodder &c.* Vol. **III**. pp. i[TP]-vi, 1-152, Pls 121-135, 135B-149. R.P. Nodder, London. 8°

Leach, W.E. 1817. III. Notice of a Variety in the common Corvorant. p. 6, Pl. 123, in *The Zoological Miscellany; being descriptions of new or interesting animals...Illustrated with coloured figures engraved from original drawings by R.P. Nodder &c.* Vol. **III**. pp. i[TP]-vi, 1-152, Pls 121-135, 135B-149. R.P. Nodder, London. 8°

Leach, W.E. 1817. IV. On the Characters of the Common Viper. pp. 7-8, Pl. 124, in *The Zoological Miscellany; being descriptions of new or interesting animals...Illustrated with coloured figures engraved from original drawings by R.P. Nodder &c.* Vol. **III**. pp. i[TP]-vi, 1-152, Pls 121-135, 135B-149. R.P. Nodder, London. 8°

Leach, W.E. 1817. V. A Notice concerning the Gigantic or Great Frog of Pennant. p. 9, Pl. 125, in *The Zoological Miscellany; being descriptions of new or interesting animals...Illustrated with coloured figures engraved from original drawings by R.P. Nodder &c.* Vol. **III**. pp. i[TP]-vi, 1-152, Pls 121-135, 135B-149. R.P. Nodder, London. 8°

Leach, W.E. 1817. VI. *Leptocephalus,* its Generic Characters, with a Description of one Species. pp. 10-11, Pl. 126, in *The Zoological Miscellany; being descriptions of new or interesting animals...Illustrated with coloured figures engraved from original drawings by R.P. Nodder &c.* Vol. **III**. pp. i[TP]-vi, 1-152, Pls 121-135, 135B-149. R.P. Nodder, London. 8°

Leach, W.E. 1817. VII. On the Characters of *Matuta,* with Descriptions of the Species. pp. 12-14, Pl. 127, in *The Zoological Miscellany; being descriptions of new or interesting animals...Illustrated with coloured figures engraved from original drawings by R.P. Nodder &c.* Vol. **III**. pp. i[TP]-vi, 1-152, Pls 121-135, 135B-149. R.P. Nodder, London. 8°

Leach, W.E. 1817. VIII. Characters of *Micippa,* a new Genus of Brachyurous Malacostraca, with Descriptions of two Species. pp. 15-16, Pl. 128, in *The Zoological Miscellany; being descriptions of new or interesting animals...Illustrated with coloured figures engraved from original drawings by R.P. Nodder &c.* Vol. **III**. pp. i[TP]-vi, 1-152, Pls 121-135, 135B-149. R.P. Nodder, London. 8°

Leach, W.E. 1817. IX. Monograph on the Genera and Species of the Malacostracous Family Leucosidea. pp. 17-26 & 'Errata et Corrigenda', Pl. 129, in *The Zoological Miscellany; being descriptions of new or interesting animals...Illustrated with coloured figures engraved from original drawings by R.P. Nodder &c.* Vol. **III**. pp. i[TP]-vi, 1-152, Pls 121-135, 135B-149. R.P. Nodder, London. 8°

Leach, W.E. 1817. X. On the Characters of the Genus *Thalassina* of Latreille, with a Description of one Species. pp. 27-28, Pl. 130, in *The Zoological Miscellany; being descriptions of new or interesting animals...Illustrated with coloured figures engraved from original drawings by R.P. Nodder &c.* Vol. **III**. pp. i[TP]-vi, 1-152, Pls 121-135, 135B-149. R.P. Nodder, London. 8°

Leach, W.E. 1817. XI. On the Characters of the Genus *Atya* of Leach, with a Description of one Species. pp. 29-30, Pl. 131, in *The Zoological Miscellany; being descriptions of new or interesting animals...Illustrated with coloured figures engraved from original drawings by R.P. Nodder &c.* Vol. **III**. pp. i[TP]-vi, 1-152, Pls 121-135, 135B-149. R.P. Nodder, London. 8°

Leach, W.E. 1817. XII. The Characters of the Genera of the Class Myriapoda, with Descriptions of some Species. pp. 31-45, Pls 132-140, in *The Zoological Miscellany; being descriptions of new or interesting animals...Illustrated with coloured figures engraved from original drawings by R.P. Nodder &c.* Vol. **III**. pp. i[TP]-vi, 1-152, Pls 121-135, 135B-149. R.P. Nodder, London. 8°

Leach, W.E. 1817. XIII. On the Characters of the Class Arachnides and of its Families. pp. 46-47, in *The Zoological Miscellany; being descriptions of new or interesting animals...Illustrated with coloured figures engraved from original drawings by R.P. Nodder &c.* Vol. **III**. pp. i[TP]-vi, 1-152, Pls 121-135, 135B-149. R.P. Nodder, London. 8°

Leach, W.E. 1817. XIV. On the Characters of the Genera of the Family Scorpionidea, with Descriptions of the British Species of *Chelifer* and *Obisium*. pp. 48-53, Pls 141-143, in *The Zoological Miscellany; being descriptions of new or interesting animals...Illustrated with coloured figures engraved from original drawings by R.P. Nodder &c.* Vol. **III**. pp. i[TP]-vi, 1-152, Pls 121-135, 135B-149. R.P. Nodder, London. 8°

Leach, W.E. 1817. XV. Descriptions of three Species of the Genus *Phthiridium* of Hermann. pp. 54-56, Pl. 144, in *The Zoological Miscellany; being descriptions of new or interesting animals...Illustrated with coloured figures engraved from original drawings by R.P. Nodder &c.* Vol. **III**. pp. i[TP]-vi, 1-152, Pls 121-135, 135B-149. R.P. Nodder, London. 8°

Leach, W.E. 1817. XVI. On the Charactersof the Class Insecta, and of the Orders composing it. pp. 57-60, in *The Zoological Miscellany; being descriptions of new or interesting animals...Illustrated with coloured figures engraved from original drawings by R.P. Nodder &c.* Vol. **III**. pp. i[TP]-vi, 1-152, Pls 121-135, 135B-149. R.P. Nodder, London. 8°

Leach, W.E. 1817. XVII. On the Families, Stirpes, and Genera of the Order Thysanura. pp. 61-63, Pl. 145, in *The Zoological Miscellany; being descriptions of new or interesting animals...Illustrated with coloured figures engraved from original drawings by R.P. Nodder &c.* Vol. **III**. pp. i[TP]-vi, 1-152, Pls 121-135, 135B-149. R.P. Nodder, London. 8°

Leach, W.E. 1817. XVIII. On the Families, Stirpes, and Genera of the Order Anoplura. pp. 64-67, Pl. 145, in *The Zoological Miscellany; being descriptions of new or interesting animals...Illustrated with coloured figures engraved from original drawings by R.P. Nodder &c.* Vol. **III**. pp. i[TP]-vi, 1-152, Pls 121-135, 135B-149. R.P. Nodder, London. 8°

Leach, W.E. 1817. XIX. Synopsis of the Stirpes and Genera of the Family Dyticidea. pp. 68-73, in *The Zoological Miscellany; being descriptions of new or interesting animals...Illustrated with coloured figures engraved from original drawings by R.P. Nodder &c.* Vol. **III**. pp. i[TP]-vi, 1-152, Pls 121-135, 135B-149. R.P. Nodder, London. 8°

Leach, W.E. 1817. XX. On the Natural Characters of Four Genera, which have been confounded under the Name *Silpha*. pp. 74-75, in *The Zoological Miscellany; being descriptions of new or interesting animals...Illustrated with coloured figures engraved from original drawings by R.P. Nodder &c.* Vol. **III**. pp. i[TP]-vi, 1-152, Pls 121-135, 135B-149. R.P. Nodder, London. 8°

Leach, W.E. 1817. XXI. A Sketch of the Characters of the Stirpes and Genera of the Family Histeridea. pp. 76-79, in *The Zoological Miscellany; being descriptions of new or interesting animals...Illustrated with coloured figures engraved from original drawings by R.P. Nodder &c.* Vol. **III**. pp. i[TP]-vi, 1-152, Pls 121-135, 135B-149. R.P. Nodder, London. 8°

Leach, W.E. 1817. XXII. On the Stirpes and Genera composing the Family Pselaphidea; with the Names of the British Species. pp. 80-87 & 'Errata et Corrigenda', in *The Zoological Miscellany; being descriptions of new or interesting animals...Illustrated with coloured figures engraved from original drawings by R.P. Nodder &c.* Vol. **III**. pp. i[TP]-vi, 1-152, Pls 121-135, 135B-149. R.P. Nodder, London. 8°

Leach, W.E. 1817. XXIII. Sketch of the Characters of the Genera of Parnidea, a Family of Coleoptera. pp. 88-89, in *The Zoological Miscellany; being descriptions of new or interesting animals...Illustrated with coloured figures engraved from original drawings by R.P. Nodder &c.* Vol. **III**. pp. i[TP]-vi, 1-152, Pls 121-135, 135B-149. R.P. Nodder, London. 8°

Leach, W.E. 1817. XXIV. On the distinguishing Characters of two Families of Coleopterous Insects named Hydrophilii by Latreille, with a Synopsis of the Genera composing them. pp. 90-94, in *The Zoological Miscellany; being descriptions of new or interesting animals...Illustrated with coloured figures engraved from original drawings by R.P. Nodder &c.* Vol. **III**. pp. i[TP]-vi, 1-152, Pls 121-135, 135B-149. R.P. Nodder, London. 8°

Leach, W.E. 1817. XXV. Synopsis of the Genera composing the Family Sphærididea. p. 95, in *The Zoological Miscellany; being descriptions of new or interesting animals... Illustrated with coloured figures engraved from original drawings by R.P. Nodder &c.* Vol. **III**. pp. i[TP]-vi, 1-152, Pls 121-135, 135B-149. R.P. Nodder, London. 8°

Leach, W.E. 1817. XXVI. On the distinctive Characters of two Species of the Fabrician Genus *Geotrupes*, which have been confounded under the name of *Actæon*. pp. 96-98, Pl. 147, in *The Zoological Miscellany; being descriptions of new or interesting animals...Illustrated with coloured figures engraved from original drawings by R.P. Nodder &c.* Vol. **III**. pp. i[TP]-vi, 1-152, Pls 121-135, 135B-149. R.P. Nodder, London. 8°

Leach, W.E. 1817. XXVII. Synopsis of three of the Genera of the Order Dermaptera. p. 99, in *The Zoological Miscellany; being descriptions of new or interesting animals... Illustrated with coloured figures engraved from original drawings by R.P. Nodder &c.* Vol. **III**. pp. i[TP]-vi, 1-152, Pls 121-135, 135B-149. R.P. Nodder, London. 8°

Leach, W.E. 1817. XXVIII. On the external Characters of the Stirpes and Genera of the Family Tenthredinidea, with Descriptions of several new Species. pp. 100-132 & 'Errata et Corrigenda', Pl. 148, in *The Zoological Miscellany; being descriptions of new or interesting animals...Illustrated with coloured figures engraved from original drawings by R.P. Nodder &c.* Vol. **III**. pp. i[TP]-vi, 1-152, Pls 121-135, 135B-149. R.P. Nodder, London. 8°

Leach, W.E. 1817. XXIX. On the Rhipiptera of Latreille, an Order of Insects named by Kirby Strepsiptera. pp. 133-136, Pl. 149, in *The Zoological Miscellany; being descriptions of new or interesting animals...Illustrated with coloured figures engraved from original drawings by R.P. Nodder &c.* Vol. **III**. pp. i[TP]-vi, 1-152, Pls 121-135, 135B-149. R.P. Nodder, London. 8°

Leach, W.E. 1817. XXX. Synopsis of the Orders, Families, and Genera of the Class Cephalopoda. pp. 137-141 *The Zoological Miscellany; being descriptions of new or interesting animals...Illustrated with coloured figures engraved from original drawings by R.P. Nodder &c.* Vol. **III**. pp. i[TP]-vi, 1-152, Pls 121-135, 135B-149. R.P. Nodder, London. 8°

Leach, W.E. 1817. No. XVI. *Malacostraca Podophthalma Britanniæ*; or descriptions of the British species of Crabs, Lobsters, Prawns, and of other Malacostraca with pedunculated eyes...Illustrated with colored figures of all the species by James Sowerby, F.L.S. G.S. W.S. &c. Printed by Arding and Merrett. Published by James Sowerby. London. December 1, 1817. [Pls. XXII.c, XXXVIII, XXXIX]

Leach, W.E. 1818. III. On the Classification of the Natural Tribe of Insects, *Notonectides* with Descriptions of the British Species. *Transactions of the Linnean Society of London*, **12**(1): 10-18. [Paper read 4 April 1815; Published 25 February 1818]

Leach, W.E. 1818. Entry: CIRRIPEDES, pp. 168-171, Pl. LVII in *Encyclopædia Britannica*, Supplements to the 4th & 5th Editions Vol. **III**(I). A. Constable. Edinburgh. [Published February 1818]

Leach, W.E. 1818. Observations on the Genus Ocythoë of Rafinesque, with a Description of a New Species. pp. 400, 401, 402, 401 (*sic*) & Plate XII, Appendix II *in* Tuckey, J.K., *Narrative of an Expedition to Explore the River Zaire, usually called the Congo, in South Africa, in 1816, under the direction of Captain J.K. Tuckey, R.N.* pp. i-lxxxii, 1-"498⁹", 13 Plates, 1 map. John Murray. London. 4°. [March 1818 – the British Museum received its copy on 14th March *fide* Monod, 1970. This is a reprinting of Leach's *Phil. Trans. Roy. Soc.* article of 1817]

[Leach, W.E][10]. 1818. Appendix IV: A general Notice of the Animals taken by Mr. JOHN CRANCH, during the Expedition to explore the Source of the River Zaire. pp. 407-419 & one coloured plate [not numbered but imprinted 'Published Nov[r].1st.1817. by John Murray.London.'] *in* Tuckey, J.K., *Narrative of an Expedition to Explore the River Zaire, usually called the Congo, in South Africa, in 1816, under the direction of Captain J.K. Tuckey, R.N.* pp. i-lxxxii, 1-"498", 13 Plates, 1 map. John Murray. London. 4°. [March 1818 – the British Museum received its copy on 14th March *fide* Monod, 1970]

Leach, W.E. 1818. Sur Quelques Genres Nouveaux de Crustacés. *Journal de Physique, de Chimie, d'Histoire Naturelle et des Arts.* **LXXXVI**: 304-307, Plate (not numbered) Figs 4-11. [April 1818]

Leach, W.E. 1818. On the Genera and Species of Eproboscideous Insects. *Memoirs of the Wernerian Natural History Society*, **2**(2): 547-566. Pls XXV-XXVII. [Paper read 6 April 1811[11]]

Leach, W.E. 1818. On the Arrangement of Œstrideous Insects. *Memoirs of the Wernerian Natural History Society*, **2**(2): 567-568. [Paper read 6 April 1811[12]]

Leach, W.E. 1818. Entry: CRUSTACÉS, pp. 69-75, *in* Cuvier, F.G. (ed.) *Dictionnaire des Sciences Naturelles* &c. &c. Vol. **12**. Paris. [also a Separate in circulation]

Leach, W.E. 1818. Entry: CYMOTHOADÉES, pp. 338-354 & Plate[13], *in* Cuvier, F.G. (ed.) *Dictionnaire des Sciences Naturelles* &c. &c. Vol. **12**. Paris. [also a Separate in circulation]

Leach, W.E. 1818. Entry: INSECTA, pp. 155-164 *in The Edinburgh Encyclopædia conducted by David Brewster LLD.* Vol. **XII**(1). Edinburgh.

Leach, W.E. 1819. Entry: CORALLINIADÆ, pp. 338-339, Pl. LXVI in *Encyclopædia Britannica*, Supplements to the 4th & 5th Editions Vol. **III**. A. Constable. Edinburgh. [Published January 1819]

[9] Monod (1970: 75) notes a repeat numbering of pages 401 and 402 thus: 401, 402, 401, 402, 403... making 500 pages numbered up to 498.

[10] This work is attributed to Leach in the *Transactions of the Linnean Society*, **12**, at p.591, and he donated a Separate of the work to the Society, having written on it "by W.E. Leach".

[11] Not 10 April 1810 as printed on p. 547 of the original (see Wernerian Society Minute Books).

[12] There is no mention of this paper in the Wernerian Society Minute Books.

[13] This plate may not have been issued at the same time as the text and is not assumed here to be part of the type descriptions of the species.

Leach, W.E. 1819. Notice of some Animals from the Arctic Regions. *Annals of Philosophy*, **XIII**: 60-61. [January 1819]

Leach, W.E. 1819. Sur les Rhipiptères de Latreille, Ordre d'Insectes nommé *Strepsiptera* par Kirby. *Journal de Physique, de Chimie, d'Histoire Naturelle et des Arts.* **LXXXVIII**: 176-177. [February 1819]

Leach, W.E. 1819. Description de deux nouvelles espèces de *Thynnus* (Fabr.) découvertes dans la Nouvelle-Hollande par M. Rob. Brown. *Journal de Physique, de Chimie, d'Histoire Naturelle et des Arts.* **LXXXVIII**: 178. [February 1819]

Leach, W.E. 1819. A List of Invertebrate Animals, Discovered by His Majesty's Ship *Isabella*, in a Voyage to the Arctic Regions, pp. [lxi]-lxiv *in* Appendix II of: Ross, J., *A Voyage of Discovery made under the Orders of the Admiralty in His Majesty's Ships* Isabella *and* Alexander *for the Purpose of Exploring Baffin's Bay, and Enquiring into the Probability of a North West Passage* (**1st Edn**, April 1819, 4°). 252 pp. & Appendices. John Murray. London.

Leach, W.E. 1819. Dr. Leach's Notice of Reptiles, Insects, &c. Appendix 4 (pp. viii, 493-496) *in* Bowdich, T.E., *Mission from Cape Coast Castle to Ashantee, with a Statistical Account of that Kingdom, and Geographical Notices of other Parts of the Interior of Africa.* John Murray. London. 4°. [Printed by 2nd March - Leach gave a copy to the Academy of Natural Sciences of Philadelphia with a letter of that date.]

Leach, W.E. 1819. Descriptions des nouvelles espèces d'Animaux découvertes par le vaisseau *Isabelle* dans un voyage au pôle boréal. *Journal de Physique, de Chimie, d'Histoire Naturelle et des Arts.* **LXXXVIII**: 462-467 [June 1819]. See also correction in Vol. **LXXXIX** at p.160 [August 1819]

Leach, W.E. 1819. Descriptions of the New Species of Animals, discovered by His Majesty's Ship *Isabella*, in a Voyage to the Arctic Regions, pp. 169-179 in Appendix IV *in* Vol. II of: Ross, J., *A Voyage of Discovery made under the Orders of the Admiralty in His Majesty's Ships* Isabella *and* Alexander *for the Purpose of Exploring Baffin's Bay, and Enquiring into the Probability of a North West Passage* (**2nd Edn**, July 1819, 8°). 2 Vols. Vol. I, lxix, 228 pp.; Vol. II, 247 pp. & 13 Appendices. Longman, Hurst, Rees, Orme & Brown. London. [On the printed cover of a Separate in the library of the Linnean Society of London Leach has written, "June 12th 1819"]

Leach, W.E. 1819. Sur l'Orang-Outang et le Chimpanzé. *Journal de Physique, de Chimie, d'Histoire Naturelle et des Arts.* **LXXXIX**: 155-156 [August 1819]

Leach, W.E. 1819. Entry: ENTOMOSTRACÉS, pp. 524-543 *in* Cuvier, F.G. (ed.) *Dictionnaire des Sciences Naturelles* &c. &c. Vol. **14**. Paris. [also a Separate in circulation]

Leach, W.E. 1819. Entry: ENTOMOLOGY, pp. 150-175 in *Encyclopædia Britannica*, Supplements to the 4th & 5th Editions, Vol. **IV**(I). A. Constable. Edinburgh. [Vol. IV part 1 (pages 1-304) published December 1819]

Leach, W.E. 1820. No. XVII. *Malacostraca Podophthalma Britanniæ*; or descriptions of the British species of Crabs, Lobsters, Prawns, and of other Malacostraca with pedunculated eyes...Illustrated with colored figures of all the species by James Sowerby, F.L.S. G.S. W.S. &c. Printed by W. Arding. Published by James Sowerby. London. March 1, 1820. [Pls. IX.B, X]

Leach, W.E. 1820. Entry: GALATÉADÉES, pp. 49-56 *in* Cuvier, F.G. (ed.) *Dictionnaire des Sciences Naturelles* &c. &c. Vol. **18**. Paris.

Leach, W.E. 1820. Entry: GALATÉE, *Galatea* (Crust.), p. 56 *in* Cuvier, F.G. (ed.) *Dictionnaire des Sciences Naturelles* &c. &c. Vol. **18**. Paris.

[Leach, W.E.] 1820. Historical Sketch of Improvements in... II. Comparative Anatomy and Zoology [during the year 1819]. *Annals of Philosophy*, **XVI**: 102-111. [By-lined only, "By a Friend of the Editor". The editor was Thomas Thomson. Both he and Leach were members of the Wernerian Society. Content and style indicate Leach as author]

Leach, W.E. 1821. V. Characters of a new Genus of Coleopterous Insects of the Family Byrrhidae. *Transactions of the Linnean Society of London*, **13**(1): 41. [Paper read 4 May 1819; Published May 1821]

Leach, W.E. 1821. VIII. The Characters of three new Genera of Bats without foliaceous Appendages to the Nose. *Transactions of the Linnean Society of London*, **13**(1): 69-72. [Paper read 22 February 1820; Published May 1821]

Leach, W.E. 1821. IX. The Characters of seven Genera of Bats with foliaceous Appendages to the Nose. *Transactions of the Linnean Society of London*, **13**(1): 73-82, Tab. VII [Paper read 7 March 1820; Published May 1821]

Leach, W.E. 1821. XIII. Descriptions of three Species of the Genus *Glareola*. *Transactions of the Linnean Society of London*, **13**(1): 131-132, Tabs XII-XIV. [Paper read 2 May 1820; Published May/June 1821]

Leach, W.E. 1821. Entry: INSECTA, pp. 41-56, Pl. LXXXV in *Encyclopædia Britannica*, Supplements to the 4th & 5th Editions Vol. **V**(I). A. Constable. Edinburgh. [Part 1 of vol. V (pp. 1-162) published July 1821]

Leach, W.E. 1824. Art. II. Monograph on the Cebrionidae, a Family of Insects. *Zoological Journal, London*, Part 1, Vol. **1**: 33-46. [Part 1 dated March 1824] [see also correspondence re this paper on pp. 282 and 283 of Volume 1]

Leach, W.E. 1825. Art. LXVIII. Description of the Vespertilio Pygmaeus, a new species recently discovered in Devonshire by Dr Leach. *Zoological Journal, London*, Part 4, Vol. **1**: 559-561, Pl. XXII + un-numbered plate legend[14]. [Part 4 dated January 1825]

Leach, W.E. 1825. Art. XXIII. A Tabular view of the Genera composing the Class Cirripedes, with Descriptions of the Species of Otion, Cineras, and Clyptra. *Zoological Journal, London*, Part 6, Vol. **2**: 208-215. [Part 6 dated July 1825]

Leach, W.E. 1825. Art. XXXI. Descriptions of Thirteen Species of Formica, and Three Species of Culex, found in the Environs of Nice. *Zoological Journal, London*, Part 7, Vol. **2**: 289-293. [Part 7 dated October 1825]

Leach, W.E. 1826. Art. XLVIII. On the Stirpes and Genera composing the family Pselaphidæ; with Descriptions of some new Species. *Zoological Journal, London*, Part 8, Vol. **2**: 445-453. [Part 8 dated January-April 1826]

Leach, W.E. 1826. [Observations on the Geology of Dartmoor[15]], pp. lxv-lxvii, *in* Carrington, N.T. *Dartmoor: A Descriptive Poem*. Hatchard & Son. London.

Leach, W.E. 1830. On the Characters of *Abbotia*, a New Genus Belonging to the Family Histeridæ, with Descriptions of Two Species. *Transactions of the Plymouth Institution*, **1**: 155-157.

Leach, W.E. 1830. Description of Some New Species of the Class Myriapoda. *Transactions of the Plymouth Institution*, **1**: 158-168.

Leach, W.E. 1830. On Two New Genera of Crustaceous Animals, Discovered by Mr John Cranch in the Expedition to Congo. *Transactions of the Plymouth Institution*, **1**: 169-171.

Leach, W.E. 1830. On Three New Genera of the Malacostraceous Crustacea, Belonging to the Family Squillidæ. *Transactions of the Plymouth Institution*, **1**: 172-175.

Leach, W.E. 1830. On the Genus *Megalophthalmus*, a New and Very Interesting Genus, Completely Proving the Theory of Jules-Cæsar Savigny to be Correct. *Transactions of the Plymouth Institution*, **1**: 176-178.

Leach, W.E. 1852. *Molluscorum Britanniæ Synopsis. A Synopsis of the Mollusca of Great Britain arranged according to their Natural Affinities and Anatomical Structure.* pp. iii(TP)-xvi, 1-376, Pls II-IV, V*, V**, VI-XIII. John van Voorst. London. [This work was edited for the press by J.E. Gray and was the publication of Leach's mollusc work which was at proof stage when he retired from the British Museum. The plates are dated 1820. See also Gray, J.E., 1847]

[14] Legend for Pls 17-22, bound facing page 1 of Volume 1 in the copy seen.
[15] These observations are quoted in the Preface to the book but are not given a separate title.

Leach, W.E. 1875. Nos. XVIII. & XIX. *Malacostraca Podophthalma Britanniæ*; or descriptions of the British species of Crabs, Lobsters, Prawns, and of other Malacostraca with pedunculated eyes...Illustrated with colored figures of all the species by James Sowerby, F.L.S. G.S. W.S. &c. continued and completed, with a new generic and specific index to the whole, and seven new plates, by George Brettingham Sowerby, F.L.S. Published by Bernard Quaritch. London. November, 1875. [Pls. IX.a, XXIV.a, XXVII, XXXIV, XXXV, XXXVII.c, XLV] These Numbers of this work were produced by G.B. Sowerby THE YOUNGER and differ from Leach's original plan. They are perhaps better attributed as 'Sowerby *in* Leach'.

Lee, Mrs R. 1833. *Memoirs of Baron Cuvier*. London; Longman, Rees, Orme, Brown, Green & Longman. [Author: Sarah Lee]

Lemon, M. 1867. *Up and Down the London Streets*. London; Chapman & Hall. [i]-[viii], [1]-348.

Liddell Hart, B.H. 1994. *The Letters of Private Wheeler 1809-1828*. Moreton-in-Marsh; The Windrush Press. 286pp. (pb) [First Published 1951 by Michael Joseph Ltd]

Low, G. *see* Leach, W.E. (ed.) 1813.

Lyell, C. 1830-1833. *Principles of Geology, being an Attempt to explain the former Changes of the Earth's Surface by Reference to Causes now in Operation*. 3 volumes. London. [not seen]

Lysons, D. & Lysons, S. 1814. *Magna Britannia... Volume the Third... Cornwall*. London; Thomas Cadell.

Lysons, D. & Lysons, S. 1822 ? *Magna Britannia; being a concise topographical account of the several counties of Great Britain. Volume the Sixth, containing Devonshire*. London; Thomas Cadell. Preliminaries, i–ccclv, 1–682, Pls 1–34. [The Title Page and Advertisement in this volume are dated 1822, but in the author's copy a number of plates are watermarked 1825]

Macilwain, G. 1856. *Memoirs of John Abernethy, with a view of his Lectures, his Writings, and Character...* (3rd edition). London; Hatchard & Co. [i]-[xviii], [1]-396, Plate facing p. 217.

Marchand, L.A. (ed.) 1974. *Alas! The love of Women! Byron's Letters and Journals. Volume 3 (1813-1814)*. London; John Murray.

Markle, D.F. 1997. Audubon's hoax: Ohio River fishes described by Rafinesque. *Archives of Natural History*, **24**(3): 439-447.

Martin, B.E. 1891. *In the Footprints of Charles Lamb*. London; Richard Bentley & Son. Frontispiece, T.P., [Preface], List of Illustrations, [1]-193, 13 pls.

Mathews, C. 1824. *Mathews in America; or, The theatrical wanderer: a cargo of new characters, original songs, and concluding piece of The wild goose chase, or The Inn at Baltimore, etc. (Entirely new entertainment)*. London: Hodgson & Co. 36pp., 1 plate; portraits. [not seen. Published in the United States as the following]

Mathews, C. 1824. *The London Mathews; containing an account of this celebrated comedian's trip to America: being an annual lecture on peculiarities, characters & manners, founded on his own observations and adventures. To which are prefixed, several original comic songs*. Baltimore; J. Robinson. 35 pp. [not seen]

Matthew, P. 1831. *On Naval Timber and Arboriculture; with critical Notes on Authors who have recently treated the Subject of Planting*. London; Longman, Rees, Orme, Brown & Green. 1 pl, [v]-xvi, 1-391. [not seen]

Matthews, C. (ed.) 1919. *Chronicles of the Royal Western Yacht Club of England 1827-1900*. Plymouth; [Privately published].

Maurice, J.F. (ed) 1904. *The Diary of Sir John Moore*. 2 volumes. London; Edward Arnold. [not seen]

Miller, E. 1974. *That Noble Cabinet, a History of the British Museum*. Athens [Ohio, USA]; Ohio University Press. 400pp.

Miller, J.S. 1821. *A Natural History of the Crinoidea, or lily-shaped animals; with observations on the genera, Asterias, Euryale, Comatula, and Marsupites.* Bristol; Published for the author by C. Frost, Broad Street. [not seen]

Milne Edwards, H. 1834. *Histoire Naturelle des Crustacés, comprenant l'Anatomie, la Physiologie et la Classification de ces Animaux.* Paris; Librairie Encyclopédique de Roret.

Mitford, M.R. 1824-1832. *Our Village, sketches of rural character and scenery.* 5 volumes. London.

Mitford, M.R. 1893. *Our Village.* London; MacMillan & Co. [i]-lx, [1]-256.

Monod, T. 1931. Sur quelques crustacés aquatiques d'Afrique (Cameroun et Congo). *Revue de Zoologie et de Botanique Africaines,* **21**(1): 1-36.

Monod, T. 1970. John Cranch, Zoologiste de l'Expédition du Congo (1816). *Bulletin of the British Museum (Natural History),* Historical Series, **4**(1): 3-75, pls 1-3. [See also 'Gallant' above]

Montagu, G. 1819. Descriptions of five British Species of the Genus Terebella of Linné. By the late George Montagu, Esq. F.L.S. Communicated by William Elford Leach, M.D. F.R.S. and L.S. *Transactions of the Linnean Society,* **12**(2): 340-344 & pls.

Moore, E. 1830. On the Ornithology of the South of Devon. *Transactions of the Plymouth Institution,* **1**: 289-352.

Morris, A.D. 1958. *The Hoxton Madhouses.* March [Cambridgeshire]; Goodwin Brothers.

Napier, W.C.E. (ed.) 1886. *Passages in the Early Military Life of General Sir G.T. Napier... written by himself.* 2nd edition. London; John Murray. [not seen]

Napier, W.F.P. 1828-1840. *History of the War in the Peninsula and in the South of France from the Year 1807 to the Year 1814.* London. 6 vols.

Napier, W.F.P. 1851. *History of the War in the Peninsula and in the South of France from the Year 1807 to the Year 1814. New Edition, Revised by the Author.* Volume 5. London; Thomas & William Boone. [Vitoria maps here amended from Plate 3]

Neave, S.A. 1933. *The History of the Entomological Society of London, 1833-1933.* London.

Northcote, J. 1828. *One Hundred Fables, original and selected by James Northcote, R.A. &c. &c. embellished with two hundred and eighty Engravings on Wood.* London; George Lawford. T.P., Dedication to George IV, [i]-[iv], [1]-272. (+ 8 pages of advertisements for other works published by Lawford).

Oliphant, Mrs 1888. *The Makers of Florence. Dante, Giotto, Savonarola and their city.* London; MacMillan & Co. [i]-xx, [1]-422.

Oman, C. 1986. *Wellington's Army, 1809-1814.* London; Greenhill Books. [i]-viii, List of Illustrations, Errata, [1]-395, 8 pls. [First published 1813 by Edward Arnold, London]

Oswald, N.C. 1989. Some Devon Postmarks. *Report and Transactions of the Devonshire Association for the Advancement of Science, Literature and the Arts,* **121**: 173-193.

Parliamentary Papers, House of Commons. 1835. *Report from the Select Committee on the Condition, Management and Affairs of the British Museum; together with the Minutes of Evidence, Appendix and Index.* Ordered, by The House of Commons, to be Printed, 6 August 1835. pp. i–iv, 1–623.

Parliamentary Papers, House of Commons. 1836. *Report from the Select Committee appointed to inquire into the Condition, Management and Affairs of the British Museum; to whom was referred the Report of the Select Committee of 1835; with Minutes of Evidence, Appendix and Index.* Ordered, by The House of Commons, to be Printed, 14 July 1836. pp. i–viii, 1–577, Appendix 10 (separate pagination 1–173), 578–606, Index (separate pagination 1–145).

Philippart, J. (ed.) 1820. *The Royal Military Calendar, or Army Service and Commission Book...with details of the principal military Events of the last Century.* (5 vols). London; T. Egerton. [Jonathan Leach in vol. 5, p. 98, entry 1574].

Pickering, J. 1997. William J. Burchell's South African mammal collection, 1810-1815. *Archives of Natural History*, **24**(3): 311-326.

Pool, B. (ed.) 1967. *The Croker Papers 1808-1857*. London; B.T. Batsford Ltd. i-viii, 1-277.

Prideaux, R.M. 1989. *Prideaux: A West Country Clan*. Chichester; Phillimore & Co. Ltd. [i]-[xvi], 1-288, endpaper maps.

Priestley, J.B. 1971. *The Prince of Pleasure and his Regency 1811-1820*. London; Sphere Books. [1]-304 (pb). This biography of George IV carries the somewhat alarming notice, "Any similarity or apparent connection between the characters in this story and actual persons, whether alive or dead is purely coincidental"! We cannot believe this was intended. [First published 1969 by William Heinemann Ltd]

Raphael, S. 1970. Publication dates of the Transactions of the Linnean Society of London, Series 1: 1791-1875. *Biological Journal of the Linnean Society*, **2**: 61-76.

Reading, J.J. 1857. Dr Leach and the Elephant. *The Zoologist*, **15**: 5662-5663.

Rehbock, P.F. 1985. John Fleming (1785-1857) and the Economy of Nature. pp. 129-140 *in* Wheeler & Price *q.v.*

Rice, A.L. 1975. The oceanography of John Ross's Arctic Expedition of 1818; a re-appraisal. *Journal of the Society for the Bibliography of Natural History*, **7**(3): 291-319.

Rice, A.L. 1986. *British Oceanographic Vessels 1800-1950*. London; The Ray Society. Frontispiece, T.P., Frontispiece, Contents, 1-193.

Risso, A. 1826-1827. *Histoire naturelle des principales productions de l'Europe méridionale et particulièrement de celles des environs de Nice et des Alpes Maritimes*. 5 vols. [Vols **1** & **4**, Nov. 1826; **3** & **5**, Sep. 1827; **2**, Nov. 1827] [not seen]

Robinson, L.G. (ed.) 1902. *Letters of Dorothea, Princess Lieven, during her Residence in London, 1812-1834*. London; Longmans & Co. i-xx, 1-414. [not seen]

Roscoe, T. 1837. *Jennings' Landscape Annual, or The Tourist in Spain for 1837. Biscay and the Castiles. Illustrated from Drawings by David Roberts*. London; Robert Jennings & Co. Frontis., Illustrated T.P., [i]-[viii], [1]-294, 19 plates.

Rough Sketches *see* Leach, J. 1831.

Royer, A. 1823. *History and description of the Royal Museum of Natural History, published by order of the administration of that establishment. Translated from the French of M. Deleuze. With three plans and fourteen views of the galleries, gardens, and menagerie*. Paris. [see also Deleuze above] [not seen]

Salvin, O. (ed.) 1882. *Leach's Systematic Catalogue of the Specimens of the Indigenous Mammalia and Birds in the British Museum*. London; The Willughby Society. i-iv, 1-44.

Samouelle, G. 1824. *The Entomologist's Useful Compendium; or an Introduction to the Knowledge of British Insects,...* London; Longman, Hurst, Rees, Orme, Brown & Green. [1]-496, pls 1-12. [First published 1819 by Thomas Boys].

Sarjeant, W.A.S. & Delair, J.B. 1980. An Irish naturalist in Cuvier's laboratory. The letters of Joseph Pentland 1820-1832. *Bulletin of the British Museum (Natural History)*, **6**(7): 245-319.

Scott, J. 1816. *Paris Revisited, in 1815, by way of Brussels: including a Walk over the Field of Battle at Waterloo* (3rd edition). London; Longman, Hurst, Rees, Orme & Brown. [i]-viii, [1]-405. [1st and 2nd editions also published 1816]

Selby, J. 1998. *The Recollections of Sergeant Morris*. Moreton-in-Marsh; The Windrush Press. i-xiii, 1-137 (pb) [First published 1967 by Longman, Green & Co. Ltd]

Sharpe, R.B. 1906. Birds. pp. 83 ff. *in* British Museum (Natural History) 1906. *q.v.*

Shepherd, T.H. 1829. *London and its Environs in the Nineteenth Century, illustrated by a Series of Views from original Drawings...* London; Jones & Co. Illustrated T.P., [i]-iii, [1]-160 & 77 pages of engravings [First published 1827]

Shepherd, T.H. & Elmes, J. 1829. *Metropolitan Improvements; or London in the Nineteenth Century: being a Series of Views, of the new and most interesting Objects, in the British Metropolis & its Vicinity...* London; Jones & Co. Illustrated T.P., [i]-vi, [1]-172 & 79 pages of engravings and one map [First published 1827].

Shepperson, W.S. 1961. William Bullock – An American Failure. *Bulletin of the Historical and Philosophical Society of Ohio*, **19**(2): 144-152.

Sherer, [J].M. 1996. *Recollections of The Peninsula.* Staplehurst; Spellmount Ltd. T.P., Preface, Introduction, 1-262. [First published 1823]

Siborne, H.T. 1993. *Waterloo Letters.* London; Greenhill Books. [i]-[xxvi], [1]-415, 6 maps on 4 foldout sheets. [First published 1891 by Cassell as *Waterloo Letters: a Selection from original and hitherto unpublished Letters bearing on the Operations of the 16th, 17th and 18th June, 1815, by Officers who served in the campaign.*]

Simond, L. 1817. *Journal of a Tour and Residence in Great Britain during the years 1810 and 1811... Second Edition, corrected and enlarged...* Edinburgh; Archibald Constable & Co. 2 volumes, pp. i-xiv, 1-508 [+ 2 fold-out tables after pp 212 and 222] & pp. 1-530. [First edition 1815. See also abridged edition: Hibbert, C. (ed.) 1968. *An American in Regency England: The Journal of a Tour in 1810-1811.* London; Robert Maxwell. 176 pp.]

Smith, A.H. 1916. Lord Elgin and his collection. *Journal of Hellenic Studies*, **36**(2): 163-372

Smith, G.C.M. (ed.) 1901. *The Autobiography of Lieutenant-General Sir Harry Smith Baronet of Aliwal on the Sutlej G.C.B.* 2 volumes. London; John Murray.

Smith, H. 1999. *The Autobiography of Sir Harry Smith 1787-1819.* London; Constable & Co. Ltd. i-xviii, 1-333. [First published as single volume 1910]

Smith, W.C. 1969. A history of the first hundred years of the mineral collection in the British Museum, with particular reference to the work of Charles Konig. *Bulletin of the British Museum (Natural History)*, Historical Series, **3**(8): Frontispiece, 235-259.

Smollett, T. 1981. *Travels through France and Italy.* Oxford; Oxford University Press. 425 pp. (pb) [First published 1766]

Spence Bate, C. *see* Bate, C.S.

Stanhope, P.H. (5th Earl). 1888. *Notes of Conversations with the Duke of Wellington, 1831-1851.* 2nd Edition. London; John Murray. [i]-xvi, [1]-[342] [The 5th Earl Stanhope died in 1875. This work was edited by the 6th Earl and first printed privately for limited circulation, apparently in 1886 (see p. vi)]

Stothers, R.B. 1984. The Great Tambora Eruption in 1815 and its aftermath. *Science*, **224**: 1191-1198.

Surtees, W. 1973. *Twenty-Five Years in the Rifle Brigade.* London; Frederick Muller Ltd. [First published 1833 edited by J. Surtees]

Swainson, W. 1834. *A Preliminary Discourse on the Study of Natural History.* pp. i-viii, 1-462. [W.E. Leach at p. 335][A volume of: Lardner, D. (ed.) *The Cabinet Cyclopædia*]

Swainson, W. 1840. *Taxidermy, with the Biography of Zoologists, and Notices of their Works.* London; Longman, Brown, Green & Longmans. 392pp. [W.E. Leach at pp. 237-240]

Swift, J. 1726. *Gulliver's Travels.*

Sweet, J.M. 1970a. William Bullock's Collection and the University of Edinburgh, 1819. *Annals of Science*, **26**(1): 23-32.

Sweet, J.M. 1970b. The Collection of Louis Dufresne (1752-1832). *Annals of Science*, **26**(1): 33-71, pls V & VI.

Sweet, J.M. 1974. Robert Jameson and the explorers: the search for the north-west passage. Part I. *Annals of Science*, **31**(1): 21-47.

Teague, S.J. & Teague, D.E. 1975. *Where Duty Calls Me: the Experiences of William Green of Lutterworth in the Napoleonic Wars.* Petts Wood (Kent); Synjon Books. Map, Foreward, Introduction, 1-65 (pb).

Thackray, A. & Morrell, J. 1984. Gentlemen of Science. Early Correspondence of the British Association for the Advancement of Science. *Camden 4th Series*, **30**: 1-382.

[Traill, T.S] 1823. Annual Reports of the Trustees of the British Museum, 1822... *The Edinburgh Review, or Critical Journal for FEB 1823.....MAY 1823*, **38**: 379–398.

Tucker, J.M. 1846. *The Life of Field-Marshal the Duke of Wellington...* London; Willoughby & Co. i-viii, 2 maps, 1-446.

Tuckey, J.K. 1818. *Narrative of an Expedition to Explore the River Zaire, usually called the Congo, in South Africa, in 1816, under the direction of Captain J.K. Tuckey, R.N.* London; John Murray. i-lxxxii, 1-"498", 13 plates, 1 map.

Uexküll, D. von. (ed.) 1966. *Arms and the Woman. The Diaries of Baron Boris Uxkull 1812-1819.* London; Secker & Warburg. [1]-319, 5 pages of Plates [English translation by Joel Carmichael]

Verner, W. 1912. *History & Campaigns of the Rifle Brigade. Part I. 1800-1809.* London; John Bale, Sons & Danielsson Ltd.

Verner, W. 1919. *History & Campaigns of the Rifle Brigade. Part II. 1809-1813.* London; John Bale, Sons & Danielsson Ltd.

Verner, W. (ed.) 1986. *Major George Simmons; a British Rifleman. Journals and Correspondence during the Peninsular War and the Campaign of Wellington.* London; Greenhill Books. [First published as Verner, W. 1899. *A British Rifle Man: the Journals and Correspondence of Major George Simmons, Rifle Brigade, during the Peninsular War and the Campaign of Waterloo.* London; A. & C. Black.]

Vivian, J.L. 1887. *The visitations of Cornwall, comprising the Heralds' visitations of 1530, 1573 & 1620.* Exeter; W. Pollard & Co.

Wakefield, P. 1802. *The Juvenile Travellers; containing the Remarks of a Family during a Tour through the principal States and Kingdoms of Europe: with an Account of their Inhabitants, natural Productions, and Curiosities.* London; Darton & Harvey. Map, i-x, 1-417, Notes (14 pp. unnumbered), Route (7 pp. unnumbered).

Walker, M. 1997. Thomas Marsham (d. 1819) – An unfortunate Fellow. *The Linnean*, **12**(4): 16-18.

Weimerskirch, P.J. 1985. Naturalists and the beginnings of lithography in America. pp. 167-177 *in* Wheeler & Price *q.v.*

Wellington, Duke of, 1858-1872. *Supplementary Despatches, Correspondence, and Memoranda of Field Marshal Arthur Duke of Wellington, K.G. edited by his son, The Duke of Wellington.* 14 volumes. London; John Murray.

Wellington, Duke of (ed.) 1956. *The Conversations of the First Duke of Wellington with George William Chad.* Cambridge; The Saint Nicholas Press. Frontis., T.P., Introduction, Editor's note, pp. 1-25, Index.

Wellington's Dispatches *see* Gurwood.

Wellington's Supplementary Despatches *see* Wellington, Duke of, 1858-1872.

Wheeler, A. 1997. Zoological collections in the early British Museum: the Zoological Society's Museum. *Archives of Natural History*, **24**(1): 89-126.

Wheeler, A. & Price, J.H. (eds) 1985. *From Linnaeus to Darwin: Commentaries of the History of Biology and Geology.* London; Society for the History of Natural History (Special Publication Number 3). 214pp (pb).

White, A. 1847. *List of the Specimens of Crustacea in the Collections of the British Museum.* London. i-iv, 1-143.

White, W. 1850. *History, Gazetteer, and Directory of Devonshire, and of the City and County of the City of Exeter; comprising a general survey of the County of Devon, and the Diocese of Exeter, &c.* Sheffield; W. White.

Whitfeld, H.F. 1900. *History of Plymouth and Devonport in Times of War and Peace.* Plymouth.

Wilson, P.W. (ed.) 1927. *The Greville Diary: Including Passages Hitherto Withheld from Publication*. London; William Heinemann Ltd. 2 vols. Frontis., i-[xv], 1-568 & Frontis., i-[xv], 1-602.

Worthy, C. 1887-1889. *Devonshire Parishes, or the Antiquities, Heraldry and Family History of twenty-eight Parishes in the Archdeaconry of Totnes*. Exeter; W. Pollard & Co. 2 vols.

Yarrell, W. 1871-1874. *A History of British Birds. Fourth edition, in four volumes. Illustrated by 564 wood-engravings. Volume I, revised and enlarged by Alfred Newton*. London; John van Voorst. [i]-xii, [1]-646.

Yarrell, W. 1876-1882. *A History of British Birds. Fourth edition, in four volumes. Illustrated by 564 wood-engravings. Volume II, revised and enlarged by Alfred Newton*. London; John van Voorst. [i]-[viii], [1]-494.

Yarrell, W. 1882-1884. *A History of British Birds. Fourth edition, in four volumes. Illustrated by 564 wood-engravings. Volume III, revised and enlarged by Howard Saunders*. London; John van Voorst. [i]-xvii, errata slip, [1]-684.

Yarrell, W. 1884-1885. *A History of British Birds. Fourth edition, in four volumes. Illustrated by 564 wood-engravings. Volume IV, revised and enlarged by Howard Saunders*. London; John van Voorst. [i]-viii, [1]-531.

Zavattari, E. 1959. La Tomba di William Elford Leach in S. Sebastiano Curone (Alessandria). *Natura*, Milano, **50**(2): 33-42

Acknowledgements

Thanks must go first and foremost to Gina Douglas at the Linnean Society of London, whose expertise, encouragement and generosity have kept this project alive for more than 20 years. We must also thank Bill Adams, Vero Beach, Florida for sharing his knowledge and allowing us to publish photographs of the paintings and artefacts now owned by his family. Thanks are also due to: Giles Adams, Northamptonshire; Albert Gunther, London; Sue Goodman of the General Library, British Museum (Natural History), since renamed The Natural History Museum, London; Ann Datta, Zoology Library, The Natural History Museum, London; Eileen Brunton, Palaeontology Library, The Natural History Museum, London; Paul Clark, Joan Ellis, Keith Banister, Gordon Paterson, Ray Ingle, Tony Fincham, Alwynne ('Wyn') Wheeler, Roger Lincoln, Geoff Boxshall and Paul Cornelius, Department of Zoology, The Natural History Museum, London; Vicki Veness, Entomology Library, The Natural History Museum, London; Pam Gilbert, Department of Entomology, The Natural History Museum, London; Michael Walters, The Walter Rothschild Zoological Museum, Tring, Hertfordshire, a branch of The Natural History Museum, London; John Hall and Jo Currie, Special Collections, Edinburgh University Library; Robert Smart, Keeper of the Muniments, University of St Andrews; the library staff of the Royal Society, London; Lesley Campbell, Royal Society of Edinburgh; Janet Wallace and Christopher Date, British Museum; Claire Jackson, Royal College of Surgeons of England; Martin Durrant, Victoria & Albert Museum, London; Victoria Holtby, King's College, University of London; Ian Mortimer, Royal Commission on Historical Manuscripts, London; Lesley Price, Royal Botanic Gardens, Kew, Surrey; the staff of the Public Record Office, Kew; the staff of Harrogate Public Library; the staff of the British Library (London and Boston Spa); the staff of the West Devon Record Office, Plymouth; the staff of the Devon Record Office, Exeter; Mr C.A. ('Ben') Lewis, Exeter; Françoise Serre, Pascale Heurtel, and especially C. Hustache, Bibliothèque Centrale, Muséum National d'Histoire Naturelle, Paris; Isabelle Lhoir, The Louvre, Paris; Mme G. Andersen, Centre de Recherche, Maison d'Auguste Comte, Paris; Pietro Passerin d'Entrèves, Museo ed Istituto di Zoologia Sistematica, University of Turin; Guido Donini, Accademia delle Scienze, Turin; Anna Alessandrello, Museo Civico di Storia Naturale di Milano; Concetta Lombardo, Dipartimento di Biologia Animale, University of Catania; Leonardo Selvaggi, Biblioteca Nazionale Universitaria, Turin; Ugo Rozzo, Biblioteca Civica, Tortona; Hans Hansson, Tjärnö Marine Biological Laboratory (author and manager of the excellent BEMON website—*Biographical Etymology of Marine Organism Names*); Dominic Goh, author and manager of a first class website on the Napoleonic wars; Adrian Roads and David Sadler, 2/95th living history re-enactment unit (Australia); David Damkaer, Washington State; Carol Spawn, The Academy of Natural Sciences of Philadelphia; Ann Upton, Haverford College, Pennsylvania; Patricia Tyson Stroud, Pennsylvania; Anne Larsen, Princeton University; Lady Thelma Smith; Mrs Margaret Goodhart, London; Jane Foxcroft and Paul Jackson, Hong Kong; Zoë Moncrieff, Winchester; Trish Turner, Cambridge; Beth Cooper, Harpenden; Cynthia Stone, London; Richard Axe and

Carol Arthur, Richard Axe Books, Harrogate; Guardsman Mick Vince, Grenadier Guards; Julie Davidson and Daniel Millum, Special Collections, Brotherton Library, University of Leeds; Pippa Jones, Edward Boyle Library, University of Leeds; Sue Bowler, Earth Sciences, University of Leeds; Alessandra Flore, Department of Italian, University of Leeds; Photographic Section, Department of Media Studies, University of Leeds; Bernard Nurse, Senior Librarian, Society of Antiquaries, London; Caroline Hoyle, Royal Geographical Society, London; Christopher Hilton, Wellcome Institute for the History of Medicine, London; William Parry, Oriel College, Oxford; Tony Simcock, Museum of the History of Science, University of Oxford; Jane Baker, Curator of Fine Art, Royal Albert Memorial Museum, Exeter; Win Scutt, City of Plymouth Museums & Art Gallery; The Honorary Curator of the Ashburton Museum, Devon, in November 1985; Jill, Duchess of Hamilton, London and Australia; the peripatetic Niel Bruce who, during more than 15 years, corresponded from Australia, the USA, Denmark and again from Australia; Arnold Ross, Scripps Institution of Oceanography who very kindly made a gift to the author of an original copy of Elford Leach's Corallinidae article; David Heppell, The Royal Scottish Museum, Edinburgh; Mary Lloyd, London; John Lamble, Cambridge; Anne Jarvis, Cambridge; Edwin Ernest Coad III, Florida; Charles MacKechnie Jarvis; Richard Hunter; Elsie Barrow, London; Norman Holmes, Exmouth; Rosemary and Marguerite Nind, Exmouth; Malcolm Spooner, Yelverton; Mr J.H.G. Woollcombe, Plympton; Colonel C.R. Spencer, Elford Town House, Yelverton; the occupants of Spitchwick Manor in the 1980s; and last, but far from least, Zaffar Iqbal of the University of Leeds whose selfless charity to a stranger rescued this manuscript from the inescapable grave of technological obsolescence into which it was about to topple— with sincere apologies to anyone we have missed, especially those people who assisted Sir Eric Smith and about whom Keith Harrison knows nothing.

INDEX

butterfingers 427
butterfly, caterpillar to 124
buzzards, circling 442
'By our Lady' 212
Bylandt. *See Bijlandt*
Byron, George Gordon Noel, Lord 3, 103,
    139, 369
Byron's butler 389

C

C.B. *See Companion*
Cabinet, British government 427
cabinet-maker 405
cabriolets 356
Cáceres 513
Cadbury Brothers 250
Cádiz 32, 157, 191, 234, 517
Cadleigh 505
Cadours 523
Cæsarian Leopoldine Caroline Academy of
    Bonn 464, 478
Caffarelli du Falga 237
cage, Buonaparte in a 292
Caia, River 60, 156, 157, 515
calaches 356
Calais 91, 244
Calcium 95
Caledonia 524
Caledonian Horticulture Society 132
calomel, powders of 435
caltraps 176
Calvert, Major, 32nd Regiment 328
Calvinet Ridge 237
Camberwell 276
Camborne 87
Cambrai 348, 364, 365, 406, 524
Cambrian Pottery 98
Cambridge
    Duke of 251
    University 6, 276, 277, 393
Cambridgeshire 364
Camden, Marquess 444
camel 103
Camel Leopard (camelopard) 416
Cameron, Alexander 167, 169, 173, 179,
    295, 325, 524
    shot in throat 328
camp, Arab 211
Campagnol, Fulvous-Cheeked 278
campaign chest (Jonathan Leach's) 486, 491
Campo Grande 42, 511
Campo Maior 59, 60, 513, 515
Camptocopea (for *Campocopea*) 271
Canada 167, 199, 298, 406, 409, 491,
    492
Canadian 407
Canary Islands 292, 293, 351, 363, 374
'Cancer' (crustacean) 418
cancer, creeping 181
candles, tax on 364
Canino, Prince of 475
canister shot 69
cannonballs
    fired along ground 323
    red-hot 182

Canolira (Canolire) 402
canteen 35, 36, 55, 200, 235, 511
Canterbury 486
Canterbury Place 254
Canterbury Tales (book) 261
cantharidin 98
canyons, natural 114
Cap of Liberty 380
Cape
    Horn 101
    of Good Hope 3, 84, 165, 387, 406,
        491
    Verde Islands 374, 496
Capel
    family at Dunkirk 355
    family to Brussels 464
    family to Lake Geneva 370
    Caroline 291, 299, 370, 379, 403
    Georgiana ('Georgy') 299, 347, 351,
        355
    Harriet 299
    John Thomas 291, 299
    Maria ('Muzzy') 299
Capell, George Robert M. 446
Capitol, the (Washington DC) 245
capitulation, honourable 164
Capper, Mr 446
caps
    bearskin 337
    forage 45, 60
Captain Absolute (dramatic character) 198
Captain, senior 329
Captivity, the (ship) 350, 351
carbine 28, 147, 331
Carcassonne 239, 522
carcinologist 454
Cardia, Dr 277
caressed, never so 189
cargoes
    insect pests of 376
    of slaves 269
Caribbean 25, 120, 130, 245, 273
    flotsam 19
Caridad, convent of 165, 516
Carisbrook Castle 48
Carl Linné. *See Linnæus*
Carlisle 14, 104, 110, 506
    Bishop of 105
Carlisle Bay, Barbados 510
Carlist War (Spain) 493
Carlton House 130, 364
Carlton House Terrace 130
Carolina, North 83
Caroline
    anagrams 402, 455
    of Brunswick
        Princess of Wales 297
        death of daughter 391
        loathed by husband 402
        vulgar and indiscreet 403
        death and funeral 428
Caroline, the Princess (ship) 31
carpet, Turkey 160
carriage, Napoleon's 347, 418
Carrington, Noel Thomas 463
Carrion, River 518

cart, dung 116
Cartaxo 145, 514
Cartley Hole farmhouse 418
Cartwright, Major John 380
Casal Novo 151
case shot 69
Cáseda 519
cash, shortage of 190
cassowary 262
Casteljaloux 523
Castelnau-Magnoac 522
Castelo Branco 52, 55, 512, 515
Castelo de Vide 58, 59, 513, 516
Castelsarrasin 241, 242, 243, 523
Castilian female dress 187
Castilians 191
Castillejo de Dos Casas 68
castle
    a Brobdignay 411
    Belvoir 406
    Burgos, mined 201
Castlereagh, Robert Stewart 287
Castles, Johnny 180, 231
Castrejón 182, 183, 517
Castres-Gironde 523
Castro 202
Castroxeriz 202
cat
    eaten 147
    wild 161
catacombs 266
catalogue
    British Museum 251
    Bullock's sale 404
    of British animals 372-374, 409, 435,
        488
Catalonia 235
Catania 465, 479, 482
catastrophe
    fossils from 273
    of Spanish War 185
'Catch me who can' 96
catch, scabbard 184
caterpillar 124
Catherine Street 108
cathode 248
Cato Street Conspiracy 427
Cattewater, the 20
cattle, shooting 152
cauldron of a city 358
causeway
    Genappe 316
    over R. Asseca 146
cava bowls 258
cavalry. *See also Regiments*
    Household 200
    infantry's square defence against 34
    no British at Quatre Bras 306
    usually followed by infantry 329
cavalry at Waterloo
    allies'
        under Uxbridge 299
        positioned 317, 320
        outnumbered 331
    British
        attack of heavy 326

578

fluviatilis, N. 453
flying-fish 375
foetuses, human 266
Font-Arabia 221
Foolish Guillemot 374, 421
Foot, Elford & (Attorneys) 438
football 65
forage caps 45
  exchanged 79
Ford Abbey 504
Foreign
  Enlistment Act 493
  Office 428
  Secretary 102, 287
forest
  of Dean 468
  of Soignes 298
forestry 470
Forfarshire 134
  Militia 396
Forficula minor 267
Forlorn Hope, the 164, 165, 167, 175
form and function 395
Formica 468
Fort
  Bayo 289
  Boyer 289
  Conception 68, 70
  Picurina 171, 172, 174, 516
Forth, Firth (Frith) of. *See Firth: of Forth*
fortifications on River Duero (Douro) 200
fortified
  tower 187
  towns 163
fortune
  no private 433
  soldiers of (university lecturers as) 128
Fortune, the (ship) 48
'forward, and complete your victory!' 339
Fosse, Charles de la 257
fossil
  Archaeopteryx 408
  bones of quadrupeds 273
  coals 252
  crinoids 441
  dinosaurs 117
  Hippopotamus pentlandi 432
  human skeleton 273, 275
  lizard (Dorsetshire) 429
  molluscs 467
  reptiles 117
  strata around Paris 273
fossils
  at British Museum 260, 261, 275
  belief regarding 273
  Birch's 429, 508
  Bullock's 411
  microscopic 398
  of Devon 441
Fotheringham, Sergeant 194
fox 60
  hounds 198, 365
  hunters, like 326
  hunting 18, 524
Fox, Francis 139
Foxglove 435

Foy, Maximilien Sebastien 185
foyer, British Museum's 257
France. *passim including...*
  Emperor of 84
  invasion of from east 232
  invasion of from west 222
franchise, the 269, 397
Francillon
  John 120, 401
  collection 400, 401
francsii, Uria 421, 422
frank (postage exemption) 110, 462
frank, Elford Leach was by nature 267
Frankenstein (book) 3, 369, 397
Frankfort Place 133
Frankfort Street 470
Franklin, John 407
Franks entry into Lisbon 149
Franks Flight 149
Franks, Frederick 421
Franks' Guillemot 421
Frascata 480
Frasnes 310, 312
Frederick II 98
Frederick the Great of Prussia 97
free
  assembly 426
  market economy 269
  press 426
  speech 426
freedom
  of expression 386
  of the city 20, 491
  of trade 269
freelance 247
'Freezeland Street' 253
Freiberg 121
Freixedas 514
Fréjus 291
French
  Academy 286
  army records 210
  language, was medium of diplomacy 291
  Revolutionary Wars 283
  scholar, indifferent 284
  School, the 124, 134, 410
  tricolor 380
  troops
    'fire better than in Spain' 328
    gallantry of officers 325
    lay as if mowed down 345
    more commendable than German 321
Freyre, Don Manuel 226, 236, 238, 239
Frias 202, 206
Friedrich Wilhelm, Duke of Brunswick 297
Friedrich-Wilhelm IV 358
Friedrich-Wilhelm, Prince 358
Friend (Quaker) 87, 98, 468
'friend in neighbourhood of London' 438
friendly fire 54, 340
Friendly Islands 258
Friends, Society of 87, 98,
Friesland 253
Frith. *See Firth*
frog 124
'Frog, The Young' (Prince of Orange) 292

frons, the 278
Frost Fair 253
Frost, the Great 253
FRS (Fellow of the Royal Society)
  Elford Leach 286
  William Elford 18
  John Butter 438
  Sir Eric Smith 6
Fuenteguinaldo 62, 158, 159, 515, 516
Fuentes de Oñoro 32, 62, 152, 153-155,
    292, 494, 515
Fulton, Robert 12
function, form and 395
functional morphology 414
Fund, General (British Museum's) 367
fundraising 138
'funked dreadfully' 231
fur 383, 503
furniture 91, 405

G

'gagging acts' 386
Gairdner, James Penman 309
Gaius Plinius Secundus 385
Gall, Franz Josef 278
Gallant, Louise 374
Gallegos, Affair at 68
Gallegos de Argañán 62, 65, 67, 68, 198,
    515
Gallery
  Bullock's Roman 404
  The Cleavehouse 434
gallery, public. *See British Museum*
Gallipienzo 519
gallows
  at Badajoz 180
  at Newcastle West 437
galvanic fluid 95, 443
Galway 345
Galwey
  Edward 363, 374, 375
  Edward Snr, Banker of Mallow 363
Gamara Mayor 206
gamekeeper, grave-digger and 172
gammarus, Homarus 384
Gandy
  Charles 273
  Henry 139, 273
  John 273
gang, so termed 268
gantelope 217
gantlet 217
Garat's House 230
Gardener, J.R. 302, 309
Gardener's Chronicle (periodical) 498
Gardiner
  J.P. 309
  John 309
  Lieutenant 230, 302, 309
'gardy loo' 115
Garefowl 414
Garonne, River 32, 236, 237, 241-243,
    522
garrets 391, 421
Garrett's house 230

Loch
Katrine 104, 131
Lomond 131
Ranza 131, 132
Loch, the North 114
Lock Hospital 447
Lockhart, David 363
Lockyer, Edmund 139, 140, 253, 410
Lockyer Street 489
locusts, like 147
lodge-keeper, British Museum's 266
lodgings, furnished (Edinburgh) 115
Lodio 202
Logier. *See Laugier*
Logroño 214, 519
as 'Logrona' 206
as 'Logroña' 202
Loison, Louis Henri 34, 37, 65, 77
Loligo parva 430
Lombardy 95, 465
Lomond, Loch 131
lomvia
Alca 422
Uria 422
London. *passim, including...*
bishop of 287
description 88
London Bridge 253
London Gazette, the (periodical) 309
London Museum and Institute of Natural
History 83, 108
London Museum and Pantherion 106
London Museum of Natural History 108,
404 *cf.* Natural History Museum, London
London University 6, 84, 129, 361, 483
Londonderry, Earl of 287
'Londra' 479
Long, Charles 439, 446
Long Island 85
long nose, fellow with the 430
Longa, General 220
Longford, Lord 33
Longman, Hurst, Rees, Orme, Brown & Green
400
Longmans, publishers 400
looking glass 144
looting 178, 179, 211
Lord Chancellor 13, 247, 447
Lord Justice-Clerk Tinwald 114
Lord March 299
Lord President Craigie 114
Lords, House of 250
Lords of the Treasury 367
Lorraine 252
Lorraine, Claude 252
Loscombe, C.W. 383
loss of life, unnecessary 78
Lost Children, the 164
Lost Party, the 164
Lota 363
Lotharios 243
Lough Leane 99
Louis de Bourbon, duc de Angoulême 241
Louis Stanislas Xavier, Comte de Provence
232 *See also Louis XVIII*
Louis XIV 255

Louis XVI 12, 232
Louis XVIII
south west France loyal to 232
uncle of Duc d' Angoulême 241
exiled in England 275
exiled in Belgium 295
'pottle bellied' 348
reinstalled in 1815 351
died 1824 477
Louis-Philippe, King of the French 477
Louisiana 12
Lourinhã 511
Louvre, the 355, 357, 359
curiously piebald 354
riflemen at 357
love, in 243
loveliness, vision of 187
Low Countries, the 296
Low, George 134
Orkney manuscript 101, 135
Elford Leach
purchasing 135
editing 137
published 272
Orkney pigs 137
Ludd, Ned 130
Luddite 3, 130, 139
Lugger, John Lloyd 378, 486
'lumpers', taxonomic 453
Lundby 29, 30
Luneville, Monsieur de 318
Luscombe
at Devon & Exeter hospital 23, 136
Nicholas 86
Lutterworth 44
Luxulyan 505
Lydia Languish (dramatic character) 198
Lyell, Charles 121, 401
Lymington 397
Lymnea leachiana 466
Lyndhurst, Lord 266
Lynedoch, Baron 206, 297
Lyon
Emily 264
George Francis 479
Lyons 468, 509
Lysons & Lysons 441
Lytta vesicatoria 98

M

M.B. (degree) 137
M.D. (degree) 137
Macartney, James 93, 136
Machiavellian plots 269
Macilwain, George 92, 93, 266, 356
Mackenzie, Charles 140
MacLeay
Alexander
his life 96
Linnean Society Secretary 97
his correspondence (Ms 237) 11
his son William Sharp 393
his wife Elizabeth 463
Dufresne's collection 397
Francillon's collection 401

and Elford Leach
in 1812 141
in 1813 142
and Royal Society 137, 285
letters from 271
'horse ass' request 267, 271
Catalogue 373, 453
Will 462
supports Elford Leach 111, 112, 249
Zoological Miscellany 252
specimens from Leach 119, 132
forwarding gift to Latreille 134
gems and coins from Leach 135
valuing Leach's donations to British
Museum 446
and John Barrow 384
and William Hooker 140
and William Kirby 394, 431
selling duplicates 132
Elizabeth (née Barclay) 463
William Sharp
living in Paris 393
and Elford Leach 393
and George Samouelle 434
and Marquess of Stafford 434
his Quinary System 393
Horæ Entomologicæ (book) 393
living in Cuba 393
Bonelli's view of 413
Kirby's view of 394
MacLeod, Charles 73, 177
Macoma 456
Mâcon 509
Macronectes giganteus 416
Madeira 156, 374
madhouses 430, 435
Hoxton 434
Madison, James 245, 290
Madrid 32, 53, 55
rises against French 31
French vacate (July 1812) 188
"tiptoe of impatience" 187
allies enter (August 1812) 188-191, 517
bullfight 189
allies vacate (October 1812) 192
allies retreat from 195
sorrow for inhabitants 197
French vacate (June 1813) 200
Maelzel, Johann Nepomuk 248
magazine, gunpowder 133, 169
Magazine, Illiger's (periodical) 271
magistrate (JP) 20, 22, 87, 98, 381, 387,
423, 424, 426, 491
Magna Carta 258
Magnesium 95
magnetism 134, 248
terrestrial 422
magneto-optical or 'Faraday' effect 248
Mahomed, Sake Dean 104
Mainwaring, Colonel 154
Maior, River. *See Asseca, River*
Maison blanche, Le 509
majority, age of 135
makom 456
Malabar 48
malacologist 454

Index

604